D1308807

IMMIGRATION
in America Today

AN ENCYCLOPEDIA

Edited by James Loucky,
Jeanne Armstrong, and
Larry J. Estrada

GREENWOOD PRESS
Westport, Connecticut • London

Library of Congress Cataloging-in-Publication Data

Immigration in America today : an encyclopedia / edited by James Loucky,
Jeanne Armstrong, and Larry J. Estrada.
    p. cm.
  Includes bibliographical references and index.
  ISBN 0–313–31214–1 (alk. paper)
    1. United States—Emigration and immigration—Encyclopedias. I. Loucky, James.
II. Armstrong, Jeanne, 1946– III. Estrada, Lawrence J.
JV6465.I4754 2006
  304.8'73003—dc22   2006009760

British Library Cataloguing in Publication Data is available.

Copyright © 2006 by James Loucky, Jeanne Armstrong, and Larry J. Estrada

All rights reserved. No portion of this book may be
reproduced, by any process or technique, without the
express written consent of the publisher.

This book is included in the *African American Experience* database from Greenwood Electronic
Media. For more information, visit www.africanamericanexperience.com.

Library of Congress Catalog Card Number: 2006009760
ISBN: 0–313–31214–1

First published in 2006

Greenwood Press, 88 Post Road West, Westport, CT 06881
An imprint of Greenwood Publishing Group, Inc.
www.greenwood.com

Printed in the United States of America

The paper used in this book complies with the
Permanent Paper Standard issued by the National
Information Standards Organization (Z39.48–1984).

10 9 8 7 6 5 4 3 2 1

Contents

List of Entries

LIST OF ENTRIES

Guide to Related Topics

Advocacy

Agencies
Asylum
Labor organization and activism
Political participation
Rights

Control and enforcement

Border control
Employer sanctions
Expedited entry and removal
National security
Unauthorized immigration
U.S.-Canada border
U.S.-Mexico border

Culture and identity

Assimilation
Ethnicity
Food
Literature and film
Music
Religion
Transnationalism

Discrimination and exploitation

Enslavement
Human smuggling

Racism
Stereotypes
Sweatshops

Education and language

Achievement
Bilingual education
Bilingualism
Immigrant education
Migrant education

Family and community

Adoption
Children
Families
Family reunification
Interethnic relations
Marriage
Social networks

Health

Biological responses
Demography
Fertility
Growth and development
Health
Mental health problems
Posttraumatic Stress Disorder

GUIDE TO RELATED TOPICS

International aspects

Adoption
Borderlands
Diasporas
Dual citizenship
Emigration
Global origins: Asia, Africa, and
  Europe
Global origins: Latin America and
  the Caribbean
International accords
Mexico-U.S. migration
Ports of entry
Temporary Protected Status
U.S.-Canada border
U.S.-Mexico border

Labor and employment

Agricultural workers
Domestic work
Effects of unauthorized immigration
Food processing
Guestworkers
Informal economy
Labor organization and activism
Skilled migrants
Sweatshops
Work

Migration and settlement patterns

Assimilation
Diasporas
Emigration
Migration processes
Remittances
Residential patterns
Return migration

Social networks
Transnationalism

Policy

Agencies
Asylum
Border control
Citizenship
Documentation
Dual citizenship
Expedited entry and removal
Family reunification
Guestworkers
Immigration system
Jus soli
Legalization
Legislation
National security
Refugee law and policy
Temporary Protected Status

Social issues

Crime
Effects of unauthorized immigration
Gangs
Gender
Public charge
Social benefits
Social mobility

Specific populations

Agricultural workers
Children
Older persons
Sexual orientation
Unauthorized immigration
Women

Preface and Acknowledgments

As the twenty-first century unfolds, the United States looks very little like the country that entered the twentieth century, except for one remarkable recurrence: it remains a magnet for people from around the world. The dramatic increase in the numbers and origins of immigrants in the last 30 years has prompted mounting public concerns and policy dilemmas. Contemporary immigration issues are as complex as they are contentious. They range from restrictions to rights, from impacts to integration. Many concerns are being addressed in a growing body of research that includes case studies, comparative analyses, policy proposals, and films and literature. This burgeoning knowledge, and the complexities it encompasses, calls for an integrative resource that summarizes the key themes, trends, and terms relating to recent American immigration.

This encyclopedia is designed to meet the need for a comprehensive thematic guide that provides an overview of major contemporary immigration topics along with points of access for further inquiry. Fifty-two contributors from a variety of backgrounds have authored 81 entries that cover a range of migration concepts and processes, policy, legislation, social issues, and aspects of cultural integration. The interdisciplinary nature of the volume reflects the multiple linkages and tensions between immigration and the economy, ethnicity, social patterns, foreign policy, health, and education.

Immigration has virtually mushroomed as a public concern and governmental priority within the United States. In part this is because it touches on so many social and economic concerns, in part because it challenges the very nature of American society and values. Immigration, to the United States and worldwide, is also being fueled by growing links between immigrant-dependent economies and transnational labor networks, widening wage gaps, and new technologies that facilitate human movement. Furthermore, just as the post-1965 immigration environment accelerated the transformation of the United States as a multicultural nation, the security climate since September 2001 has been one where immigration management and border control have become central concerns. For these reasons, we anticipate that this reference resource will be of wide value for students, academics, policymakers, and the public alike.

Together the topics represented in this encyclopedia encompass the essential, intersecting arenas of immigration today. Entries dealing with motives and patterns of movement and settlement reveal that immigration is as much a temporal phenomenon as a spatial one, and is shaped by social and cultural considerations as well as structural and environmental factors. A number of entries address work and economic issues, which tend to be of great concern to both immigrants and U.S. citizens and residents. Conditions of receptivity and adaptation, and experiences of integration, emerge within topics relating to health, education, language, and community relations. The implications of international borders in integral cultural and environmental regions, new security concerns, and migration pressures in an age of globalization are considered in entries that relate to Mexico, Canada, and international considerations. Finally, a number of entries consider the vexing yet persistent questions relating to appropriate measures for control and enforcement, responding to refugee and humanitarian considerations, and determining citizenship and political rights.

Each entry presents the term or concept and identifies key issues and future trends, providing historical background and information about international context when appropriate. A bibliography of both cited references and recommended readings, as well as cross-referencing to related terms, are provided at the end of each entry. Entries are arranged in alphabetical order, but the "Guide to Related Topics" groups each entry under one or more broad topics for ease of locating relevant entries. The encyclopedia also includes an index, a chronology of U.S. immigration legislation, and an annotated bibliography including books, organizations and electronic sources, and documentary and feature films.

No single volume can deal with every aspect and controversy relating to immigration. What this volume does provide is substantial evidence that the United States continues to be enriched and invigorated in innumerable ways through the many immigrants that have been received, sometimes generously and sometimes not, throughout its history. Setting limits, both formal and informal, has also been a constant in U.S. immigration policy. The multicultural metamorphosis of the last 40 years, coupled with the deep security unease that opened this century, puts immigration front and center of both partisan and philosophical discourse. While predicting future practices or attitudes is risky, immigration policy will continue to be the center of considerable attention. Hopefully, deeper understanding of the issues and reasoned resolution of the debates that are evident in this book will be forthcoming. Discourse must be based on information rather than being driven by emotion. What is at stake, among other things, is the level of divisiveness or societal well-being that will emerge.

ACKNOWLEDGMENTS

We gratefully acknowledge the invaluable assistance of Viva Barnes throughout this project, as well as support provided by the Bureau for Faculty Research at Western Washington University. Yueh-Ting Lee, Joe Heyman, and Joan

Stevenson were instrumental in helping us conceptualize various entries. A number of students and research assistants also contributed to the research, including: Bree Herndon, Kelly Alleen, Lee Lawrence, Jaime Loucky, Ellen Kendell, Katy Kerl, Mary Haycox, Cassie Howe, Tracy Nishimura, Deja Engels, Melissa Mabee, Tawny Townsend, Alison Hill, Hiley Butler, and Jean Webster.

A

ACHIEVEMENT. The successful incorporation of immigrants into American society has always hinged on the potential for personal improvement through educational and economic achievement. Understanding how today's immigrants integrate into society and how their achievement is affected by everyday patterns of social interaction can help ameliorate present and future inequalities and conflicts among ethnic groups. Since the immigrant experience is shared by both parents and children, and since there are so many specific influences that may determine achievement on an individual level, understanding the factors that determine achievement across generations is critical, as is identifying sociohistorical circumstances that continue to determine the ultimate level of achievement attained by immigrants groups.

Immigrants are most influenced by where they settle and by pre-established relationships they have when they arrive (Suárez-Orozco and Suárez-Orozco 2001; Zhou 2001a). Such patterns of integration provide immigrants with the social capital (i.e., access to social networks and resources determined by family relationships) to effectively settle into the community (Portes and Mac-Leod 1999). While many settle in large urban centers, others live in more racially integrated suburban neighborhoods; newly arrived Latino immigrants, for example, tend to live in more segregated neighborhoods and Asian immigrants in more integrated neighborhoods. The different relationships and access to resources associated with these living conditions directly affect the educational opportunities of immigrant children (Suárez-Orozco and Suárez-Orozco 2001).

Children of immigrants have long been expected to assimilate into American society through their school experience. However, different levels of access and exposure to social contexts directly affect the psychological well-being, school performance, and academic aspiration of children, which in turn have a significant bearing on career prospects and life chances (Zhou 2001b). Students who are not from the dominant culture are commonly subjected to pejorative stereotypes and derogatory messages about their intellectual capabilities, causing them to negotiate multiple, and often competing, identities in the schools (Ogbu 1978; Olsen 1997).

Looking at how first- and second-generation immigrant children integrate into the American school system reveals some of the primary influences shaping students' future success or failure. On average, one in five children nationwide is either an immigrant or the child of immigrants; in California, half of the children are immigrants or children of immigrants (Olsen et al. 2005). Such pronounced numbers demand a closer look at the educational achievement patterns of immigrant children and how they are related to different school contexts.

The No Child Left Behind (NCLB) Act of 2002, which mandates that all students be proficient in English and math by 2014 (www.ed.gov/nclb), has pushed states and school districts to implement a battery of standardized tests to gauge performance in order to ensure that this goal is met. One problem confronting immigrant students is that current standardized tests are designed around culturally specific content and normed to mainstream cultural groups. School districts and communities are facing increased pressures to prepare all students, but lack adequate resources to close achievement gaps. Such top-down pressure further limits immigrant students' ability to apply their own culturally appropriate knowledge to bridge the educational gap (Olsen et al. 2005).

Next to families, schools are the most important institutional context for the young and critical for determining the eventual level of economic success of a child (Portes and MacLeod 1999). Establishing a school environment that empowers students and recognizes diverse cultures as part of the mainstream can help create a balance between students' own ways of communicating, learning, and behaving and the need for them to be educated (Schwartz 2001). Common characteristics of an effective school include positive staff members, demanding academic expectations for all students, a sincere interest in the students' cultures and language, and a safe school environment (Suárez-Orozco and Suárez-Orozco 2001).

Even when educators strive to create this type of school context, they often fail to see the negative results inherent in the process of exclusion and sorting by color, class, or English fluency, that relegate students to positions of unequal access to resources and opportunities. Students are often placed in "compensatory" programs designed to help them overcome cultural differences. Even though many of these programs have been initiated with good intentions, their inherent goal is to compensate for deficits which are supposed to result from inadequate training at home or cultural deprivation (Ogbu 1978). Consequently, tracking and compensatory programs are endemic in schools with large minority and immigrant populations.

As the lowest achieving group among all immigrants, Mexican students are likely to attend schools that are primarily minority; by contrast, the highest achieving immigrant students, Asians, attend schools where 75 percent or more of their peers are white (Portes and MacLeod 1999). Perpetual low academic achievement by immigrant students may cause educators to see them as unteachable, even though such sentiments may stem more from a lack of identification with the students' home contexts than with their actual academic performance (Suárez-Orozco and Suárez-Orozco 2001). Among Latino immigrants, students from Mexico, Central America, and Puerto Rico demonstrate the lowest levels of achievement; conversely, Cuban students commonly demonstrate rather high levels of academic achievement (Perez 2001). In general, the Latino group comprises such a large proportion of Mexican students that the overall trends do not accurately represent the experience of most Cuban immigrant students. It is also useful to look at the ethnic composition of the teachers that interact with minority students on a daily basis. Whereas Latino students make up 15 percent of the national student population, only about 4 percent of public school teachers are Latinos (ERIC Digest 2001).

Compared to the Latino experience, Asian immigrant students tend to demonstrate a better record of academic achievement (Portes and MacLeod 1999; Waldinger 2001a; Zhou 2001a, 2001b). The reality, however, is that some follow what is expected of a "model minority" while others have considerable difficulties in school and perform at levels similar to other ethnic and racial minority students (Suárez-Orozco and Suárez-Orozco 2001:135). The erroneous stereotype of the model minority becomes even more significant as increasing numbers of Asian immigrants find themselves in poor and segregated schools, facing the same limited opportunities as other immigrants of color.

Achievement trends also vary across different educational levels. High schools dealing with problems of underachievement may blame results on middle schools, who in turn may press elementary schools to do a better job of preparing students, and they in turn put the blame on elementary schools (Olsen et al. 2005:6). With everyone looking elsewhere for accountability, eventually parents are charged with the responsibility of educating their children before they even start school, a formidable task when one is not familiar with the academic standards and literacy patterns in American schools (Brice Heath 1998). Although children 3 to 5 years old might enter school better prepared to learn if they are read to on a daily basis, one study found that only 70.7 percent of Latino children are read to as compared to 89.4 percent of white children (NCES 2003). While federally funded programs like Head Start provide early education services to economically disenfranchised families, in order to remedy the effects of poverty on educational achievement, young Latino children are less likely to be enrolled in early childhood education programs than other groups (ERIC Digest 2001).

The ultimate results of this educational foundation often surface as students reach high school. Latino students are less likely than white students to complete advanced placement courses in mathematics, science, and English, though they are more likely to complete advanced foreign language classes (NCES 2003). The dropout rate for Latinos is significantly higher than for other groups; in 1998, 30 percent of all Latinos 16 through 24 years old dropped out, whereas the dropout rate was 14 percent for African Americans and 8 percent for whites (ERIC Digest 2001). High school completion rate (via high school diploma or GED) for Latinos is 63 percent, as compared to 90 percent for whites (ERIC Digest 2001). Attrition rates also vary according to the students' foreign- and native-born status; Fry (2003) argues that immigrant Latino youth are no more likely to drop out of high schools in the United States than native-born Latino youth. However lack of achievement is measured, the alarming dropout and completion rates across generations are serious enough to warrant alternative educational approaches.

Beyond high school, while immigrants fall behind natives in educational attainment nationwide, there is an upward trend for college attendance among immigrants, with varying patterns evident (Ellis 2001). Latino immigrants who have completed high school are just as likely as second-generation and third-generation Latino youth to immediately enter postsecondary education. Even though Latinos lag behind every other immigrant group in attaining college degrees (Fry 2003), they have doubled their overall undergraduate degree attainment since 1976; in 1996, Latino students earned 5 percent of all bachelor's degrees and 7 percent of all associate's degrees (ERIC Digest 2001).

Compared with the trends evident among Latino immigrants, the Asian advance into higher education appears remarkable (Zhou 2001a). In Los Angeles, for example, 18- to 24-year-olds in every Asian group attend college at a rate that exceeds that of native-born whites (Waldinger 2001a). Latino undergraduates tend to follow educational paths associated with lower chances in attaining a bachelor's degree, including prolonging study in community colleges beyond their mid-twenties (Fry 2003). Nonetheless, even though a large segment of the Latino population in the 1980s averaged fewer years of formal education than in previous decades, more are completing university degrees (Velez-Ibanez and Sampaio 2002:12–13). Moreover, there is a positive correlation between college attendance and the attainment of professional occupations for both Asian and Latino immigrants, with increasing achievement from the first to second generation (Zhou 2001a).

In addition to educational resources offered to children of immigrants, there are programs for newly arrived adults. Services that help improve the lives and opportunities of immigrant parents and other family members include adult English as a Second Language (ESL) classes, GED programs, and community college courses. These services are even more significant given that the academic achievement of immigrant children has been linked to the overall educational attainment of their parents (NCES 2003:48). There is also a strong correlation between educational achievement and projected occupational salary levels (Velez-Ibanez and Sampaio 2002).

Perhaps the most significant underlying determiner of immigrant achievement in school is the socioeconomic status of parents (Waldinger 2001b; Olsen et al. 2005). When poverty is combined with racial segregation, outcomes may be dismaying. Despite personal traits or characteristics, people who grow up amid poverty and racial isolation are more likely to reach lower levels of education and earn lower adult incomes (Suárez-Orozco and Suárez-Orozco 2001:131).

Other areas of conflict and misunderstanding stem from fundamental differences in cultural expectations and views on schooling. Teachers often ask parents to take part in activities like Parent Teacher Association meetings or volunteer for a variety of fund raisers and extracurricular events. For newly arrived immigrant parents, this experience can be disorienting and overwhelming. Not only may immigrant parents arrive with very different cultural expectations than those found among mainstream American parents, they are often under financial pressures that preclude time to participate in such activities.

The concept of achievement itself may vary across cultural groups. Many non-Western cultures have been described as having a strong orientation to family and community. Motivation for achievement may be associated with wanting to maintain peer ties rather than a desire to attain personal or individual goals (Yeh and Drost 2002:3). The influence of family cohesion not only is important for the overall well being of immigrant communities, but also is a key component of educational success (Zhou 2001b).

Similarly the social environment of the countries from which immigrants come can affect educational opportunities and achievement of immigrant children. Refugee children and those who were marginalized in their home country may maintain feelings of oppression (Zhou 2001b), and children of undocumented parents may live in fear of immigration authorities.

Finally, integration in a society that expects immigrants to immediately learn English can provoke both educational failure and problems within the home setting. While learning English is often seen as a precondition for educational and future occupational success, loss of language fluency in parents (as can result from following an "English Only" ideology) may undermine immigrant families and reduce parental guidance at a crucial time in the lives of adolescents (Rumbaut and Portes 2001:301).

If cultural differences in socialization and development are not understood and incorporated into education programs, children can easily become viewed as deficient. In turn, children's sense of identity may be damaged and early negative labeling and tracking can occur, causing immigrant students to develop adverse perceptions of and responses to discrimination by others in the school. Improving immigrants' opportunities for educational and economic success must begin with erasing this deficit orientation and providing them with the resources necessary to succeed. *See also*: **Assimilation; Children; Families; Immigrant education; Social networks; Stereotypes.**

References

Brice Heath, Shirley. 1998. What No Bedtime Story Means: Narrative Skills at Home and School. In *The Matrix of Language: Contemporary Linguistic Anthropology*. D. Brenneis and R.K.S. Macaulay, eds. Pp. 12–38. Boulder, CO: Westview Press.

Ellis, Mark. 2001. A Tale of Five Cities? Trends in Immigrant and Native-Born Wages. In *Strangers at the Gates: New Immigrants in Urban America*. R. Waldinger, ed. Pp. 117–158. Berkeley: University of California Press.

ERIC Digest Number 162. 2001. *Latinos in School: Some Fact and Findings*. ERIC Clearinghouse on Urban Education, ID # ED449288.

Fry, Richard. 2003. *Hispanics in College: Participation and Degree Attainment*. ERIC Clearinghouse on Urban Education, Institute for Urban and Minority Education, ID # ED480917.

National Center for Education Statistics (NCES). 2003. *Status and Trends in the Education of Hispanics*. Pp. 45–62. Washington, DC: U.S. Department of Education.

Ogbu, John. 1978. *Minority Education and Caste: The American System in Cross-Cultural Perspective*. New York: Academic Press.

Olsen, Laurie. 1997. *Made in America*. New York: The New Press.

Olsen, Laurie, Jhumpa Bhattacharya, and Amy Scharf. 2005. Ready or Not? A California Tomorrow Think Piece on School Readiness and Immigrant Communities. California Tomorrow, http://www.californiatomorrow.org.

Perez, Lisandro. 2001. Growing Up in Cuban Miami: Immigration, the Enclave, and New Generations. In *Ethnicities: Children of Immigrants in America*. R.G. Rumbaut and A. Portes, eds. Pp. 91–126. Berkeley: University of California Press.

Portes, Alejandro, and Dag MacLeod. 1999. Educating the Second Generation: Determinants of Academic Achievement among Children of Immigrants in the United States. *Journal of Ethnic and Migration Studies* 25(3): 373–396.

Rumbaut, Ruben G., and Alejandro Portes. 2001. Conclusion: The Forging of a New America: Lessons for Theory and Policy. In *Ethnicities: Children of Immigrants in America*. R.G. Rumbaut and A. Portes, eds. Pp. 301–317. Berkeley: University of California Press.

Schwartz, Wendy. 2001. *Closing the Achievement Gap: Principles for Improving the Educational Success of All Students*. ERIC Clearinghouse on Urban Education, ID # ED460191.

Suárez-Orozco, Carola, and Marcelo M. Suárez-Orozco. 2001. *Children of Immigration*. Cambridge, MA: Harvard University Press.

Velez-Ibanez, Carlos G., and Anna Sampaio. 2002. Introduction: Processes, New Prospects, and Approaches. In *Transnational Latina/o Communities: Politics, Processes, and Cultures*. C.G. Velez-Ibanez and A. Sampaio, eds. Pp. 1–38. New York: Rowman and Littlefield.

Waldinger, Roger. 2001a. Strangers at the Gates. In *Strangers at the Gates: New Immigrants in Urban America*. R. Waldinger, ed. Pp. 1–29. Berkeley: University of California Press.

———. 2001b. Up from Poverty? "Race," Immigration, and the Fate of Low-Skilled Workers. In *Strangers at the Gates: New Immigrants in Urban America*. R. Waldinger, ed. Pp. 80–116. Berkeley: University of California Press.

Yeh, Christine, and Christopher Drost. 2002. *Bridging Identities among Ethnic Minority Youth in Schools*. ERIC Digest, ID # ED462511.

Zhou, Min. 2001a. Progress, Decline, Stagnation? The New Second Generation Comes of Age. In *Strangers at the Gates: New Immigrants in Urban America*. R. Waldinger, ed. Pp. 272–307. Berkeley: University of California Press.

———. 2001b. Straddling Different Worlds: The Acculturation of Vietnamese Refugee Children. In *Ethnicities: Children of Immigrants in America*. R.G. Rumbaut and A. Portes, eds. Pp. 187–228. Berkeley: University of California Press.

ERIC JOHNSON

ADOPTION. Adoption, referring to formally taking-on a child of other parents as one's own, often involves children from a country different from that of the adoptive parents. International or intercountry adoption (also commonly referred to as "foreign") has become increasingly common in the United States, associated with postponement of age of building a family, difficulties that prospective parents experience in having their own biological children, and limited options for arranging to adopt within the United States. The Census Bureau's first profile of adopted children revealed that in 2000, 13 percent of adoptees under 18 were from outside the United States (NAIC 2001; Peterson 2003). Half of those (49 percent) came from Asia, with South Korea leading the list. In addition to a growing proportion of international adoptions, recent years have also seen an "internationalization" of source countries. In 2005, foreign-born children adopted by U.S. citizens numbered 22,728, twice that of 1996, with China being the greatest source of intercountry adoptions, followed in descending order by Russia, Guatemala, South Korea, Ukraine, and Kazakhstan. For most countries, disparity in genders of children adopted internationally is nonexistent, but in the case of China, up to 96 percent (in 2001) of children adopted are girls (Bureau of Consular Affairs 2006).

International adoption has also grown as the number of children surrendered or abandoned by birth parents within the United States has been limited in recent decades by contraception and the increased tendency of single parents to keep their children, as this has become more socially acceptable (Bartholet 1993). In particular, there are relatively few younger children available for adoption inside the country, while there are many babies and children worldwide in need of homes, including many orphans. So those wanting younger children make arrangements with international adoption agencies or head overseas personally, and adopt children who are typically 1 to 3 years old. International adoption also increases the range of parenting choices for potential adopters, who may rank lower on adoption agency "fitness" scales. Screening processes and criteria vary tremendously in other countries, but single persons or older couples find more legitimate chances to adopt through intercountry arrangements. For parentless children, in turn, intercountry adoption may represent one of the few realistic opportunities to have a permanent family of their own.

While providing a viable alternative to domestic adoption for many families, the intercountry adoption process can be complex, expensive, and fraught with uncertainty. Costs, obligation to travel to the country, and waiting time differ significantly, depending on the country and the child (or children, in the case of sibling groups) chosen. Foreign adoption laws also vary widely and do not always conform to equivalent procedures in U.S. courts. Children adopted by U.S. citizens do not automatically become citizens, nor does a parent's naturalization automatically confer citizenship on their adopted child. Because of the widespread interest of U.S. citizens in adopting overseas orphans, Congress expanded the definition of "child" in 1957 to include a child adopted while under the age of 14. Currently, the amended law states that the child must be adopted while under the age of 16, and the child must have been in the legal custody of, and resided with, either or both of the adopting parents for at least two years. Also, the adoption must be legally valid in the country where it took place in order for the child to be granted citizenship in the United States (Chesser 2000).

International adoption became especially prominent during the global conflicts of the twentieth century. The great number of orphans left by World War I induced many Western countries to pass or revive adoption laws. However, before 1940, there were no special statutory provisions for the naturalization of adopted children, and children adopted abroad by U.S. citizens remained "aliens" until they could apply for citizenship on their own behalf. The absence of such provisions reflected a fear among legislators that special dispensations for internationally adopted children might encourage adoption fraud. With the rising prevalence of intercountry adoption, elected officials recognized the need to promote the unity of bona fide family relationships. This led to the inauguration of provisions in the Nationality Act of 1940, which authorized the naturalization of adopted children, with special safeguards designed to ensure bona fide adoptions.

Following World War II, the movement to rescue the children of devastated countries grew even stronger (Benet 1976). Initially, most countries focused on rehabilitating their own, rather than losing yet another generation. But in countries occupied for long periods of time by foreign armies, adoption became one solution to the unnaturally high population of parentless children. Children from Germany, Italy, and Greece, in particular, were adopted into American families.

The Korean War brought intercountry adoption fully into the American national consciousness. The half-Korean children of American soldiers became the responsibility of the occupying army since many mothers were unwilling or unable to raise them (Benet 1976). As war relief merged into a relief of underdevelopment itself, intercountry adoption from South Korea persisted, resulting in over 50,000 Korean children having been adopted within the United States (Cox 1996). Similarly, as a result of the Vietnam War, "Operation Babylift" succeeded in bringing about 3,000 young children to the United States, beyond those who subsequently entered in association with war-bride arrangements.

A widening of the rationale of intercountry adoption as a form of humanitarian assistance is evident in the post-Soviet era. With the collapse of the Eastern Bloc, rates of international adoption soared in countries which previously had virtually no adoptions outside their borders. Romania, which had only 30 international adoptions in 1989, reached over 10,000 soon after, while Russia has recently provided the first or second highest annual adoption total going to the United States (Kapstein 2003). The 1990s also saw a great increase in adoptions from Latin America. Today nearly all of the top countries from which U.S. citizens are conducting intercountry adoption face significant economic problems.

To better serve the interests of adoptive children, the United States, along with 31 other countries, signed The Hague Convention on the Protection of Children and Cooperation in Respect of Intercountry Adoption on March 31, 1994. This convention is designed to protect the rights of, and prevent abuses against, children, birth families, and adoptive parents involved in real and prospective adoptions, in order to ensure that such adoptions are in the children's best interests. The U.S. delegation to the negotiations, which included adoptive parents, law professors, adoption service providers, public welfare representatives, and government officials, was active in helping to establish mechanisms for cooperation of signatory countries in the areas of intercountry adoption.

The Intercountry Adoption Act of 2000 was enacted to approve the provisions of The Hague Convention. It designates the Department of State as the central authority to oversee the implementation of this Act, coordinate matters between countries of origin for potential adoptive children and the United States, and accredit adoption agencies (AILA 2001). The law also added two new sections to the Immigration and Nationality Act (INA). Section 101 (b)(1)(G) expands the definition of "orphan," stating that a child may be adopted if the child's two living natural parents are incapable of providing proper care and freely consent to terminate their legal relationship; that child is then eligible for adoption and emigration. Also new is Section 204(d)(2), which requires an adoption or custody certificate to be issued by the central authority when the child to be adopted resides in a Hague country.

Apart from the legal complexities, intercountry adoption entails a variety of cultural, social, and psychological issues as new families are created through adoption of children from foreign countries. The decision to adopt presents participants with strong, even unexpected feelings, which may be compounded when international and cross-cultural considerations are involved. Even in the United States, where adoption is accepted more readily than in many other countries, adoption is nonetheless sometimes still viewed as "second-best," suggesting that biological parents failed to care for a child while adoptive parents failed to have their own (Benet 1976). Because adoption challenges basic attitudes about kinship and inheritance, intercountry adoptions introduce even greater dilemmas. Is the adopted child to have a sense of identity with his or her native culture? What motivates this kind of adoption? Do parents have the capacity to identify with the child and see the world from his or her point of view? How do relatives feel about and participate in an interethnic family? One big difference from in-country, same-"race" adoption is that children usually do not grow up thinking or being told that the adoptive parents are biological.

A variety of programs, alliances, and agencies have been initiated in recent years to respond to these challenges. In addition to after-school and Saturday programs, "heritage camps" now exist across the country, including some that are offered for families with adoptive children from Peru, India, Guatemala, Korea, and other countries. Advanced communications and transportation options, which have facilitated international adoption in general, provide opportunities to strengthen information-sharing and advocacy. Families with internationally born children may raise funds for schools or health projects in their child's home country. Many adoptive parents also endeavor to make trips to the child's (children's) country of origin in order to help them feel connected to their roots. Adoptive families' networks have also joined in efforts to curtail corrupt and illegal practices, particularly as concerns about commodification of adoption and media reports of adoption irregularities and baby trafficking have grown (Kapstein 2003).

There are also many support organizations and a wealth of resources intended for adopted children or their parents, including guides and anthologies (Klatzkin 1999), retrospectives (Trout 1997), and children's literature, such as Pearl Buck's 1960 picture book about a Korean orphan girl, "Welcome Child." Oftentimes such information begins as parents or their children search for answers, and meaning, including about how to incorporate birth culture and custom into new lives in the United States. Sometimes the result is much deeper appreciation for the psychological issues involved, which may emanate from prior institutionalization, racial prejudice and discrimination, and other aspects of identity formation (Rojewski and Rojewski 2001). Gatherings of families that include adopted children or first-generation adults become venues for sharing knowledge and perceptions of the process, and its problems as well as rewards.

As demand for adoptive children remains high, and in the face of persistent poverty worldwide, international child adoption will continue to be significant. As the needs of so many children for placement persist, intercountry adoption generally represents the finest of altruism, though cases of child trafficking reveal that it can also sometimes become a new form of exploitation. Furthermore, the growing openness to and incidence of international adoption is increasingly requiring new sensitivities to issues such as "over-availability" of certain kinds of children as well as rights of children to know their heritage or "roots" and to have connection to their communities of origin. How the various nations of the world shape the rules governing international adoption, such as those set forth by The Hague Convention, will to a great degree define the future role of adoption as a family building alternative (Jaffe 1995). *See also*: **Children; Citizenship; Families; Interethnic relations; International accords.**

References

American Immigration Lawyers Association (AILA). 2001. INS on Intercountry Adoptions. http://www.zulkie.com/news/insonintercountryadoptions.htm.

Bartholet, Elizabeth. 1993. *Family Bonds: Adoption and the Politics of Parenting.* Boston: Houghton Mifflin.

Benet, Mary Kathleen. 1976. *The Politics of Adoption.* New York: The Free Press.

Bureau of Consular Affairs. 2006. International Adoption. U.S. Department of State, http://travel.state.gov/family/adoption/adoption_485.html.

Chesser, Lori T. 2000. Family Sponsored Immigration. In *Immigration and Nationality Handbook,* vol. 1. Randy P. Auerbach, ed. Pp. 402–455. Waldorf, MD: American Immigration Lawyers Association.

Cox, Susan Soon-Keum. 1996. The Birth of Intercountry Adoptions. http://www.holtintl.org/cox.shtml.

Jaffe, Elizer D., ed. 1995. *Intercountry Adoptions: Laws and Perspectives of "Sending" Countries.* Boston: Martinus Nijhoff.

Kapstein, Ethan B. 2003. The Baby Trade. *Foreign Affairs* 82(6):115–125.

Klatzkin, Amy, ed. 1999. *A Passage to the Heart: Writings from Families with Children from China.* St. Paul, MN: Yeong and Yeong.

National Adoption Information Clearinghouse (NAIC). 2001. Intercountry Adoption. http://naic.acf.hhs.gov/pubs/f_inter/f_inter.cfm.

Peterson, Karen S. 2003. Census Counts Adoptees: 1.6M Kids; First Such Tally Shows 87% Were Born in USA. *USA Today,* August 22, A1.

Rojewski, Jay W., and Jacy L. Rojewski. 2001. *Intercountry Adoption from China: Examining Cultural Heritage and Other Postadoption Issues.* Westport, CT: Bergin and Garvey.

Trout, Paula J. 1997. The Reality of My Journey as a Transracial Adoptee. In *Korean American Women Living in Two Cultures.* Young In Song and Ailee Moon, eds. Los Angeles: Academia Koreana, Keimyung University Press.

JAMES LOUCKY

AGENCIES. Immigration, the arrival and settling in a country or region to which one is not native, is both a global phenomenon and a complex subject involving such areas as law, sociology, demography, international relations, economics, and community development (Lee and Ottati 2002; Lin 2002; Lee et al. 2004). As a result of this complexity, a number of agencies and organizations influence American immigration policy. Although immigration has primarily been managed by the former Immigration and Naturalization Service (INS) of the Department of Justice, many other agencies and organizations continue to play their own unique part in immigration policy. This entry will provide an overview of a variety of immigration agencies and organizations that each have their own functions and duties to perform concerning immigration. It will be shown that the complexity of the issue of immigration has required the creation of a diverse assortment of agencies and organizations in order to meet the needs of immigrants and refugees from around the world.

Immigration Agencies and Organizations

According to the typology created by Lin (2002:122–123) and used within this entry, there are three basic categories of agencies and organizations that have an influence on immigration policy: governmental agencies, non-governmental organizations, and international organizations.

Governmental agencies maintain the greatest influence on immigration policy. These agencies are responsible for a range of specialized duties and functions that include the enforcement of laws regarding illegal immigration (CBP Web Site; ICE Web Site), assistance for asylees and refugees (ORR Web Site), the creation of policies that affect ethnic and cultural relations within American society as well as affecting all workers (ILAB Web Site; Lee et al. 2003), and many others. These agencies and organizations maintain a series of checks and balances on each other as they work to provide a fair and just immigration policy (Lin 2002:122–128).

Non-governmental organizations have a variety of functions that divide them into the five areas of advocacy, research, refugee resettlement, ethnic advocacy, and business and labor (Lin 2002:128–149). Advocacy organizations tend to concentrate on immigration and refugee policy, although the beliefs of these organizations may be on opposite ends of the spectrum in desiring to increase or restrict immigration (FAIR Web Site; Lin 2002:128–133; NNIRR Web Site). Research centers investigate the people and policies involved within immigration (Lin 2002:128, 133–135; MPI Web Site). Refugee resettlement organizations assist refugees in adjusting to a new life in the United States (CWS Web Site; IRC Web Site; Lin 2002:128, 135–138). Ethnic advocacy organizations, created by specific ethnic groups to generate cultural and economic solidarity, also take a stance on immigration and refugee law and policy (Lin 2002:128, 140–145; MALDEF Web Site). Lastly, many business and labor organizations have taken specific positions concerning immigrant workers within the employment arena (Lin 2002:129, 145–149; UFW Web Site).

A final categorization of immigration agencies and organizations is international organizations (Lin 2002:122, 149–150). These organizations use their global status to "manage migration trends resulting from economic and natural disasters, armed conflict, and human rights abuses" within other countries around the world (Lin 2002:122).

Notable examples of each of these organizations follow. The examples given are not explicitly representative of all organizations within each category and should only be used as a guide to the broad functions and duties of the organizations within that category.

Governmental Agencies

U.S. Department of Health and Human Services, Office of Refugee Resettlement (ORR). ORR provides a vast array of assistance to asylees and refugees so that they may obtain "economic self-sufficiency and social adjustment" within a brief time after their arrival in the United States (Lin 2002:125). This assistance is provided through the forms of "cash and medical assistance, employment preparation and job placement, skills training, English language training, social adjustment and aid for victims of torture" (Lin 2002:125; ORR Web Site).

U.S. Department of Homeland Security, U.S. Citizenship and Immigration Services (USCIS), U.S. Customs and Border Protection (CBP), and U.S. Immigration and Customs Enforcement (ICE). In March 2003, the Immigration and Naturalization Service (INS) of the U.S. Department of Justice was transferred to the Department of Homeland Security (DHS) (USCIS Web Site). At the same time, the functions of the former INS were separated between two agencies within the DHS: the U.S. Citizenship and Immigration Services agency (USCIS) and the Directorate of Border and Transportation Security (USCIS Web Site). By this separation, the USCIS is responsible for providing immigration and citizenship services, while two agencies within the Directorate of Border and Transportation Security provide varying forms of immigration enforcement. The two agencies, U.S. Customs and Border Protection (CBP) and U.S. Immigration and Customs Enforcement (ICE), work to promote the public safety of Americans by enforcing the laws of the United States concerning issues of immigration, terrorism, counterfeiting, and bioterrorism (CBP Web Site; ICE Web Site).

U.S. Department of Justice, Executive Office for Immigration Review (EOIR). EOIR is responsible for the interpretation and administration of federal immigration laws within "immigration court proceedings, appellate reviews, and administrative hearings" (EOIR Web Site).

U.S. Department of Labor, Bureau of International Labor Affairs, Division of Immigration Policy and Research (ILAB). ILAB researches and formulates "international economic, trade, immigration and labor policies" to create an economic system that is stable and beneficial for all workers and a work environment that is safer, healthier, and more respectful of workers' basic rights (ILAB Web Site; Lin 2002:125).

U.S. Department of State, Bureau of Population, Refugees, and Migration (PRM). PRM maintains the responsibility for creating policies concerning "refugee assistance and international migration" (Lin 2002:124; PRM Web Site). PRM has an international migration policy that focuses on "the human rights of migrants, protection for asylum-seekers, oppositions to uncontrolled and illegal migration, support for anti-trafficking efforts, and encouragement of the rapid integration of legal immigrants" (PRM Web Site).

Non-governmental Organizations

Advocacy

Federation for American Immigration Reform (FAIR). FAIR is an organization that calls for immigration reform by putting an end to illegal immigration and placing a reduction of legal immigration to its "lowest feasible levels" (FAIR Web Site; Lin 2002:130).

National Network for Immigrant and Refugee Rights (NNIRR). NNIRR works to promote "full labor, environmental, civil and human rights for all immigrants and refugees" regardless of their status as illegal, temporary, or permanent immigrants (Lin 2002:132; NNIRR Web Site).

Research

Cato Institute. The Cato Institute conducts public policy research of immigration policies. The organization maintains that immigrants are a benefit to the U.S. economy because of their "motivation, risk-taking, and work ethic" (Lin 2002:133).

Migration Policy Institute (MPI). MPI studies the "movement of people worldwide" through its research focuses of migration management, refugee protection and international humanitarian response, North American borders and migration agenda, and immigrant settlement and integration (Lin 2002:134; MPI Web Site).

Refugee Assistance and Resettlement

Church World Service (CWS). CWS is a religious-affiliated organization that works to empower people to move beyond their "poverty and powerlessness" through its programs of "social and economic development, emergency response, refugee assistance, mission relationship and witness, and education and advocacy" (CWS Web Site).

International Rescue Committee (IRC). IRC works to provide those people "fleeing racial, religious and ethnic persecution, as well as those uprooted by war and violence" with humanitarian assistance, protection of basic human rights, and rehabilitation in creating new lives (IRC Web Site; Lin 2002:138).

Ethnic Advocacy

Mexican American Legal Defense and Education Fund (MALDEF). MALDEF works to protect the civil rights of Latinos and to empower the Latinos of the United States in the areas of education, immigration and citizenship, employment economic development, fair share and equal access to public resources, political access, and language (Lin 2002:142; MALDEF Web Site).

Business and Labor Advocacy

United Farm Workers (UFW). UFW was founded by Cesar Chavez in 1966 in order to improve the working and living conditions of agricultural workers (Lin 2002:149). The organization continues to fight for workers' rights, environmental justice, and immigration reform through the use of legislation, litigation, and youth activism (UFW Web Site).

International Organizations

American Refugee Committee (ARC). ARC works to ensure a better life for "refugees, displaced people, and those at risk" through its principles of ethics, dignity, optimism, service, self-sufficiency, advocacy, and stewardship (ARC Web Site).

International Organization for Migration (IOM). IOM works with migrants, governments, and other organizations to "responsibly and humanely address migration issues" (IOM Web Site; Lin 2002:151). This group works to address these issues through its four main programs of humanitarian migration;

migration for development; technical cooperation; and migration, debate, research, and information (Lin 2002:151).

United Nations High Commissioner for Refugees (UNHCR). Founded in 1950, in the aftermath of the suffering of more than a million individuals displaced by World War II, the UNHCR works worldwide to guarantee the basic human rights of refugees to seek and find asylum and to make the decision to either freely return to their homeland, rebuild their life in their country of asylum, or resettle in a completely different country (UNHCR Web Site).

Throughout history, a vast number of agencies and organizations have influenced U.S. immigration policy. Government agencies have played the largest role overall, but advocacy organizations, research centers, refugee and resettlement organizations, ethnic advocacy organizations, labor and business organizations, and international organizations have also significantly influenced the processes and policies of immigration. *See also*: **Asylum; Citizenship; Legalization; Refugee law and policy.**

References

Lee, Y-T., C. McCauley, F. Moghaddam, and S. Worchel. 2004. *Psychology of Ethnic and Cultural Conflict: Looking through American and Global Chaos or Harmony.* Westport, CT: Greenwood Press.

Lee, Y-T., and V. Ottati. 2002. Attitudes toward American Immigration Policy: The Role of Ingroup-Outgroup Bias, Economic Concern, and Obedience to Law. *Journal of Social Psychology* 142(5):617–634.

Lee, Y-T., J. Quinones-Perdomo, and E. Perdomo. 2003. An Integrative Model of Ethnic Contact, Identity and Conflict (CIC): Application to U.S. Immigration and Naturalization. *Ethnic Studies Review* 26(2):57–80.

Lin, A.C., ed. 2002. *Immigration.* Washington, DC: CQ Press.

Web Sites

ARC (American Refugee Committee). http://www.arcrelief.org.

CBP (U.S. Department of Homeland Security, U.S. Customs and Border Protection). http://cbp.gov.

CWS (Church World Service, Immigration and Refugee Program). http://www.church worldservice.org.

EOIR (U.S. Department of Justice, Executive Office for Immigration Review). http://www.usdoj.gov/eoir.

FAIR (Federation for American Immigration Reform). http://www.fairus.org.

ICE (U.S. Department of Homeland Security, U.S. Immigration and Customs Enforcement). http://www.ice.gov.

ILAB (U.S. Department of Labor, Bureau of International Labor Affairs, Division of Immigration Policy and Research). http://www.dol.gov/ILAB.

IOM (International Organization for Migration). http://www.iom.int.

IRC (International Rescue Committee). http://www.theirc.org.

MALDEF (Mexican American Legal Defense and Education Fund). http://www.maldef.org.

MPI (Migration Policy Institute). http://www.migrationpolicy.org.

NNIRR (National Network for Immigrant and Refugee Rights). http://www.nnirr.org.

ORR (U.S. Department of Health and Human Services, Office of Refugee Resettlement). http://www.acf.hhs.gov/programs/orr.

PRM (U.S. Department of State, Bureau of Population, Refugees, and Migration). http://www.state.gov/g/prm.

UFW (United Farm Workers). http://www.ufw.org.
UNHCR (United Nations High Commissioner for Refugees). http://www.unhcr.org.
USCIS (U.S. Department of Homeland Security, U.S. Citizenship and Immigration Services). http://www.uscis.gov.

AMBER L.E. WISCHER AND YUEH-TING LEE

AGRICULTURAL WORKERS. Farm work is seasonal, with its peak periods of work during planting, tending, and harvesting of crops highly variable. Because agriculture is organized as a for-profit industry, particularly larger operations, its workforce has been transitory, forced to travel from site to site and regionally. In 1997, 700,000 temporary farm workers were employed, accompanied by 300,000 children and 100,000 dependents (Rothenberg 1998). Seasonality, low valuation of farm work, and lack of grower incentive to provide quality housing and costly medical and other benefits have produced a transient, primarily minority and foreign, group of workers. Ethnicity or nationality, gender, and citizenship status have been central organizing principles in this process. Yearly, immigrants, primarily from Mexico, as well as Mexican Americans and African Americans, radiate out from impoverished home bases. They primarily travel three routes: (1) Southern California (Central, Imperial, and Salinas Valleys) along the West Coast to Washington and Oregon; (2) South Texas to the Great Plains and the Midwest; and (3) South Florida to other southern states or up the East Coast to New York (Smith and Lindroth 1999). The marginalized character of farm work has left this population chronically impoverished and with few attaining social mobility.

Carey McWilliams, author of *Factories in the Fields: The Story of Migratory Labor in California* (1939), first brought attention to the plight of farm workers prior to World War II. As a wartime measure, however, contract laborers from Mexico, known as "braceros," were brought in to harvest crops, a program that was extended until 1964 (Galarza 1964). In the 1960s, the living conditions of migrant farm workers on the road and at work became a social problem. Migrant farm workers were unprotected by the New Deal legislation of the 1930s; indeed, they were deliberately exempted from the federal minimum wage, social security, overtime provisions, child labor protection, and provisions for labor organizing (Rothenberg 1998). Edward R. Murrow's documentary *Harvest of Shame* (1961) pointed out the lack of a living wage and sanitary living conditions. Lack of tap water, refrigerators, and flush toilets were a major issue. In addition, low wages often resulted in family recruitment of children to work in the fields while the disruption of schooling connected with nomadic movement often resulted in attrition from school and intergenerational poverty. In the 1960s, the social image of the migrant problem was one of impoverished families.

In 1963, the Farm Labor Contractor Registration Act was passed. This required all contractors to register with the federal government, keep wage records, disclose working conditions, and protect workers. Later, the Migrant and Seasonal Agricultural Worker's Protection Act provided further protections and extended liability for failure to meet standards to growers as well as contractors. Most important, the federal government began assistance programs in the areas of healthcare, legal aid, job training, and education, many of which are still operational today. Unfortunately, aside from assistance programs, which have helped U.S.-born migrants to leave farm labor, there has been very limited enforcement of this protective labor legislation to this day (Rothenberg 1998).

As federal recognition occurred in the 1960s, grassroots unionization efforts began in California. The United Farm Workers (originally the National Farm Worker's Association), under the leadership of Cesar Chavez and Dolores Huerta in California, used strikes and consumer boycotts as a means of forcing growers to improve wages and living and working conditions (Ferris and Sandoval 1997). From 1962 through 1975, minority and foreign farm workers fought for the right to organize, which was finally granted by the 1975 Agricultural Labor Relations Act in California. Nationally, however, farm workers are excluded from the National Labor Relations Act, and their right to organize is not protected (Rothenberg 1998).

The public attention to farm workers due to the United Farm Worker's movement prompted federal legislation that established programs to assist and educate migrant families in order to economically integrate them and eliminate poverty. To a degree, these programs have been successful in realizing social mobility for a portion of these families. These programs have allowed some native-born minority workers to become upwardly mobile out of farm labor, yet the citizens and substantial number of foreign workers who remain are still impoverished, as no change in the basic structure of seasonal farm labor recruitment and provisions was actually effected. As a result, the nation has again developed an undocumented or impoverished minority seasonal farm labor force.

Three times a year, the U.S. Department of Labor (1997) conducts the National Agricultural Workers Survey (NAWS). Recent data indicate that farm work has become less of a family activity and more the province of single or married unaccompanied male Mexican immigrants. From 1988 to 1995, the American farm worker population has become increasingly foreign-born, with a greater number of undocumented workers. The NAWS survey revealed that over 80 percent of crop workers are male and 70 percent are foreign-born (Mines et al. 1997). Over two-thirds of agricultural workers are under 35 and about one-fifth are doing agricultural work in the United States for the first time; over three-fifths of migrant farm workers are poor, and there is a trend toward increasing poverty in this group.

The U.S. migrant agricultural labor force has become internationalized. Sixty-nine percent of American farm workers are foreign-born and 94 percent are from Mexico (Mines et al. 1997). Intensified legal presence of Mexicans occurred because of the legalization provision of the 1986 Immigration Reform and Control Act (IRCA), which granted resident alien status to undocumented immigrants living in the United States prior to 1982, and its Special Agricultural Worker (SAW) and Replenishment Agricultural Worker (RAW) programs. These provided documentation and eligibility for citizenship for unauthorized individuals who had worked in perishable agriculture for 90 days under one of the following two conditions: (1) each year for a three-year period ending May 1, 1986, or (2) in the one-year period prior to May 1, 1986. IRCA also contributed to gender asymmetry in the farm labor force. From 68 percent to 61 percent of SAW applicants in the states of California, Arizona, and Texas were male, so although presented as gender neutral legislation, IRCA had covert bias against women immigrants (Arp et al. 1994). The SAW legalization provision was primarily applicable to men who worked in the fields while women, who tend to work in non-field support positions, were not eligible.

Since the extremely low wages are unattractive to native-born U.S. workers, contemporary migrant agricultural workers are most frequently from Mexico, with Mexicans comprising 94 percent of the foreign-born and 65 percent of the total farm labor force (Mines et al. 1997). By 1995, as U.S. citizens continued to leave farm work, undocumented workers increased from 7 percent (in 1989) to 37 percent of farm workers (Mines et al. 1997). The trend toward employing Mexican nationals has effectively resulted in a Latinization of the migrant labor force.

Growers have largely succeeded in their battle against unionization and continue to be reluctant to improve working and living conditions. Farm worker income is often poverty-level, between $2,500 and $5,000 annually for individuals, and three-fifths of farm worker households live below the poverty line of $7,500 to $10,000 for households (Mines et al. 1997). Foreign-born workers had a slightly higher median income than U.S.-born, with green card holders and legal permanent residents earning from $7,500 to $10,000 per year while citizens and amnesty recipients earned between $5,000 and $7,500. By comparison, undocumented workers earned from $2,500 to $5,000. Despite efforts to effect social change, the majority of migrant farm workers live below the poverty line and the overall rate of poverty today, 61 percent, is higher than that in 1990, when approximately one-half lived in poverty. Migrant farm workers are unlikely to utilize social services, but Medicaid is used by a third of authorized workers and Food Stamps by 29 percent. It is ironic that those who grow and harvest the nation's food, especially U.S.-born Hispanic citizens, often resort to Food Stamps.

The efforts to educate and retrain agricultural migrants who are citizens, combined with a movement out of farm work by legalized foreign nationals, is drawing a new and primarily Mexican segment of undocumented workers as replacement. The entrance of unauthorized workers is presumably underestimated by the National Agricultural Worker's Survey due to concerns that illegal immigrants may have about government surveys, yet the presence of undocumented foreign nationals is strongly depicted statistically. Although IRCA was supposed to reduce use of undocumented workers and stabilize the U.S. working population, low wages and lack of worker benefits in agriculture appear to have undermined this strategy of the law. In turn, agricultural labor selection is extensively gendered as unaccompanied Mexican males are the worker of choice for many growers.

The persistence of a poorly paid, seasonal migrant labor force in the United States is primarily caused by circumvention of labor laws through the grower practice of subcontracting. Contractors often make false promises, provide substandard housing, transport crews in poorly maintained cars and vans, maintain false wage records, tamper with workers' wages, and even intimidate workers with threats of violence. The most common tactic of contractors is to pocket the workers' state and federal wage deductions.

The contemporary migrant farm labor structure varies throughout the United States depending on the availability of labor, type of labor, and crop tasks.

Specialized agricultural tasks, or work requiring experience, are conducive to labor stabilization, as loss of such workers can threaten profits. Growers attempt to stabilize labor by raising wages and/or providing inexpensive housing for family groups pooling income. Unless inexpensive housing is available, however, the "ideal" agricultural worker has most often been a male traveling without a family. The degree to which these workers can reunite with spouses and children or form families then depends on whether they can find a niche to support a larger group.

The California strawberry industry provides an example of how undocumented status and labor surplus promote political disempowerment and transnationalize migrant family formation. In the Salinas Valley, Wells (1996) found that transnational family arrangements were more likely when wages did not sustain more than an individual worker, with limited ability to send remittances to Mexico. Yet growers' preference for undocumented labor is not absolute. Some California strawberry growers with more resources shifted from individual to family recruitment as Mexican migrant networks consolidated, and where growers had moderate to high resources and Mexican workers were influenced by unionization and availability of other work, a wage plus bonus structure was offered and U.S. family formation occurred. A key element in stabilization of labor, regardless of crop, is family housing or barracks-style housing, which is critical in peak demand seasonal harvest areas (Griffith and Kissam 1995). Stabilization of family agricultural labor only occurs in locations where housing is very cheap, as in the Lower Rio Grande valley of South Texas, where individuals share homes and incomes.

An inadvertent effect of federal labor legislation is that increased housing standards resulted in many growers closing their labor camps (Rothenberg 1998). As a result, many migrants now live in illegal labor camps, and many growers evade legal responsibility for their living conditions. Migrant workers employ many strategies for finding shelter. Labor camps are usually operated by growers or farm contractors on condition that the unaccompanied "tenants" work for them. Privately arranged housing is more likely to be occupied by families and rents are steep, especially given the periods of unemployment in seasonal agricultural labor. In Immokalee, Florida, lone male or female migrants spend the least income on housing, while working couples and extended families expend moderately greater amounts and extended families expend the most (Griffith and Kissam 1995).

Low wages provided by labor contractors and grower reluctance to assume responsibility for providing adequate support for stable farm employment have ensured that migrant agricultural workers remain a major issue in the twenty-first century. Without wages to support adequate housing and a measure of stability in family support and in the absence of adequate enforcement of existing labor legislation, increased social activism and pressure on the federal government will be necessary to address this problem. *See also*: **Gender**; **Migrant education**; **Unauthorized immigration**.

References

Arp, William, III. 1990. The Exclusion of Illegal Hispanics in Agenda Setting: The Immigration Reform and Control Act of 1986. *Policy Studies Review* 9(2):327–338.

Arp, William, III, Marilyn K. Dantico, and Marjorie S. Zatz. 1994. The Immigration Reform and Control Act of 1986: Differential Impacts on Women? *Social Justice* 17(2):23–39.

Donato, Katherine M. 1993. Current Trends and Patterns of Female Migration: Evidence from Mexico. *International Migration Review* 27(4):748–771.

Ferris, Susan, and Ricardo Sandoval. 1997. *The Fight in the Fields: Cesar Chavez and the Farm Worker's Movement.* New York: Harcourt, Brace, Jovanovich.

Galarza, Ernest. 1964. *Merchants of Labor: The Mexican Bracero History.* Santa Barbara, CA: McNally and Loftin.

Griffith, David, and Ed Kissam. 1995. *Working Poor: Farm Workers in the United States.* Philadelphia: Temple University Press.

Mines, Richard, Susan Gabard, and Anne Stierman. 1997. A Profile of U.S. Farm Workers. Washington, DC: U.S. Government Printing Office. http://www.dol.gov/; http://www .dol.gov/dol/asp/public/programs/agworker/report/main.htm.

Rothenberg, Daniel. 1998. *With These Hands: The Hidden World of Migrant Farm Workers Today.* New York: Harcourt, Brace, Jovanovich.

Smith, Carter, III, and David Lindroth. 1999. *Hispanic American Experience on File.* New York: Facts on File.

Wells, Miriam J. 1996. *Strawberry Fields: Politics, Class, and Work in California Agriculture.* Ithaca, NY: Cornell University Press.

JUDITH WARNER

ASSIMILATION. "Assimilation" is a word that is so integrated with immigration, its significance is felt in immigrant communities today as well as throughout the history of the United States. Initially, the assimilation process referred to a biological function undergone by the body to convert food into an absorbable substance for digestion (Cordasco 1990). This physiological use of the term is rare today, as the term "assimilation" has taken on a great deal of social significance. Many different definitions are applied to this term, exposing its broad use. The *International Encyclopedia of Social Sciences* defines assimilation as a "process in which persons of diverse ethnic and racial backgrounds come to interact, free of constraints, in the life of a larger community." Looked upon as a strictly socially adaptive phenomenon, assimilation can be defined first, as the modification of the individual and collective activity of the immigrants as they adjust to the new cultural environment, and second, as the degree of immigrants' relative change, conformity, and absorption into the host culture or society.

This last part of assimilation is seen as a process, starting with contact, and then continuing with tolerance, accommodation, and finally acculturation. Taken from the 1914 book *Immigration*, the term "assimilation" refers to the "act or process of making or becoming like or identical; the act or process of bringing into harmony" (Alba and Nee 1999).

The debate over the definition of assimilation can be grouped into two arguments. One argument reasons that assimilation is synonymous to the "melting pot" theory and Anglo-conformity, where the immigrant group is seen as moving toward the dominant ethnic status group (Cordasco 1990). Initially taken from the play *The Melting Pot*, written by Israel Zangwill at the beginning of the twentieth century, this term more than any other has come to define the American proposition of complete absorption and envelopment of varied immigrant and ethnic groups into the mainstream of American society. This argument puts assimilation as the opposite of cultural pluralism and declares that the two are mutually exclusive.

The other argument is that assimilation involves first a cultural integration and then a structural integration that is more mutual from both host and immigrant groups. In this construct the immigrant subordinates change to fit into the dominant society while the dominant or majority society incorporates certain values, attitudes, and cultural aspects from the respective immigrant groups that later modify and redefine the host society. Within this model a certain symbiotic relationship occurs between the majority society and the newly infused immigrant group that allows for adaptation and conformity while still preserving certain elements of the immigrant culture such as food, language, and social mores.

Most often, immigrants and members of a minority group, ethnic or cultural, are faced with multiple challenges when making a new home in a foreign land. Migration, whether forced or voluntary, pushes or pulls people into new and different cultural areas. Each respective group is thus faced with the challenge of retaining and celebrating its own culture, assimilating or integrating into the cultural identity of the larger group, or the possibility of blending the old and the new into something entirely different. This decision can be overwhelming to both the individual and the family involved. Long-term implications involving education, employment opportunities, and social and political identity can be based on the initial choice. Assimilation, then, can have both negative and positive implications (Motyl 2001).

Acceptance from members of the dominant sociocultural group and access to societal privileges and benefits are often the greatest inducements behind the decision of immigrants to modify or to let go of a previous cultural identity. Pressure to fit in and not stand out in the crowd can be a very common survival instinct when faced with the situation of navigating a new cultural environment. Children want to fit in at school and in the neighborhoods, particularly since acceptance of peers is crucial for self-esteem and success throughout childhood, adolescence, and leading into adulthood. Adults will oftentimes have similar feelings, and the acceptance issues will carry over into work, social, and even religious areas of life (Castles and Miller 2003).

Assimilation is more commonly recognized among second- and third-generation families whose parents or grandparents originally migrated to the new country. Their children or grandchildren usually gain citizenship in the birth country and have the tendency to subordinate the culture of the parents while adapting to the culture of their birth nation. Many immigrants attempt to teach their children about their ethnicity and home country through language, music, foods, and stories. Stories about relatives and loved ones are a common way for parents to describe their heritage and to retain pride in their own identity within the cultural group (Portes and Rumbaut 1996).

Immigration to the United States greatly accelerated in the late 1960s. A large proportion of America's immigrants are young people who form families after arrival, so there is now a large and rapidly growing second generation, many of them now young adults who recently completed school and started their careers. Much speculation has been projected onto this group in terms of their propensity to assimilate into the economic and cultural mainstream. Individuals of the second generation encompass great diversity depending upon country of origin, but in nearly all comparisons, today's second generation exceeds their first-generation parents in educational attainment, occupational achievement, and economic status. In many comparisons, second-generation groups have educational attainments exceeding those of third and higher generation majority and African American group populations (Farley and Alba 2002).

The assimilation conundrum continues to pose complex issues all over the world, inclusive of the United States (Motyl 2001). These issues range from the needs for increased infrastructure and agencies to assist in the relocation and resettlement of immigrant groups to the growing political trends that warn of the unassimilable nature of particular groups that in turn threaten the cultural fabric of the host society (Huntington 2004). Some theorists observe a difference between earlier and recent immigrants. They fear that "multiculturalists" are rejecting the melting pot concept, wanting to preserve immigrant culture and languages rather than absorb American culture, which could potentially lead to political fragmentation and then chaos (Duignan 2004).

Recent propositions and initiatives sponsored in various states have endeavored to curtail the propagation of bilingual or bicultural measures in education, social services, and the workplace while ensuring the dominance of the English language within the national discourse. Adherents to more restrictive measures placed on immigration policy and language often come into conflict with those who espouse a more pluralistic or multiculturalist paradigm that allows for the retention of distinct cultural attributes and values among immigrant groups (Daniels 2004).

The 1965 Immigration Reform Act not only opened the door to a sharp increase in total immigration to the United States, it was also followed by a dramatic shift in the sources of immigration. By the 1990s, only one out of seven newcomers hailed from a European country (Jacoby 2004). A major question now being posed by contemporary immigration theorists is whether the post-1965 immigrants will melt into American society as successfully as their European predecessors did. Many who doubted that the melting pot really functioned a century ago remain skeptical about the assimilation of recent Asian and Latino immigrants. Some concede that earlier European immigrants were successfully absorbed into mainstream American society while new groups will face greater barriers and posed obstacles because they are non-white. It remains to be seen whether new immigrant groups will tend to remain separate and unassimilated because of their inevitable bitter experience of racial and institutional discrimination (Jacoby 2004).

Projections for the twenty-first century, with little equivocation, indicate that the future tide of American immigrants will largely come from Asian and Latin American nations (Daniels 2002). Between 1980 and 2000, 15.6 million legal immigrants came to the United States, and another 5.5 million immigrants entered the country illegally (Jacoby 2004). The vast majority of these people, 85 percent of documented migrants and 95 percent of those without documents, were non-Europeans, mainly from Asia, Latin America, and the Caribbean.

The author Amitai Etzioni (2004) would contend that there is no such thing as a set of "minority" beliefs, opinions, or political positions. Still more important, groups that are thought of as monolithic, such as "Hispanics" and "Asians," do not share a single, uniform set of beliefs. Significant cultural, social, and regional differences within these groups will allow for a diverse and multifaceted adaptation to the American landscape. Assimilation, therefore, should not be thought of as a static absorption process but more akin to a constantly changing filter that redefines the homeostatic environment. *See also*: **Bilingualism; Children; Immigrant education; Political participation; Social mobility.**

References

Alba, R., and V. Nee. 1999. Rethinking Assimilation Theory for a New Era of Immigration. In *The Handbook of International Migration: The American Experience.* C. Hirschman and P. Kasinitz, eds. Pp. 621–658. New York: Russell Sage.

Castles, S., and Mark J. Miller. 2003. *The Age of Migration: International Population Movements in the Modern World*, 3rd ed. New York: Guilford Press.

Cordasco, F., ed. 1990. *Dictionary of American Immigration History.* Metuchen, NJ: Scarecrow Press.

Daniels, R. 2002. *Coming to America: A History of Immigration and Ethnicity in American Life*, 2nd ed. Princeton, NJ: HarperCollins.

———. 2004. *Guarding the Golden Door: American Policy and Immigrants Since 1882.* New York: Hill and Wang.

Duignan, P. 2004. Do Immigrants Benefit America? *The World and I* 19:20–26.

Etzioni, Amitai. 2004. Assimilation to the American Creed. In *Reinventing the Melting Pot: The New Immigrants and What It Means to Be American.* T. Jacoby, ed. Pp. 211–220. New York: Basic Books.

Farley, R. 1999. *Heaven's Door: Immigration Policy and the American Economy.* Princeton, NJ: Princeton University Press.

Farley, R., and R. Alba. 2002. The New Second Generation in the United States. *International Migration Review* 36(3):669–702.

Huntington, S. 2004. The Hispanic Challenge. *Foreign Policy* (March–April):1–12.

Jacoby, T., ed. 2004. *Reinventing the Melting Pot: The New Immigrants and What It Means to Be American.* New York: Basic Books.

Kraver, J.R. 1999. Restocking the Melting Pot: Americanization as Cultural Imperialism. *Race, Gender and Class* 6(4):61–70.

Moytl, A.J., ed. 2001. *Encyclopedia of Nationalism.* San Diego: Academic Press.

Portes, A., and R. Rumbaut. 1996. *Immigrant America: A Portrait*, 2nd ed. Berkeley: University of California Press.

Simpson, G., ed. 1968. *International Encyclopedia of the Social Sciences.* New York: Collier and Macmillan.

LARRY J. ESTRADA

ASYLUM. Each year, thousands of people flee their native lands to the United States with little else but the hope of finding refuge from persecution, torture, and even death. In U.S. immigration law, asylum is an immigration status afforded to persons who have been persecuted or who fear persecution in their home country because of their race, religion, nationality, membership in a particular social group, or political opinion.

U.S. asylum law is rooted in both international and domestic law. In 1968, the United States acceded to the 1967 United Nations Protocol Relating to the Status of Refugees (1967 Protocol), which incorporated the substantive provisions of the 1951 United Nations Convention Relating to the Status of Refugees. These instruments defined the term "refugee" as a person who "owing to a well-founded fear of being persecuted for reasons of race, religion, nationality, membership of a particular social group, or political opinion, is outside the country of his nationality and is unable or, owing to such fear, unwilling to avail himself of the protection of that country." The Refugee Convention and 1967 Protocol also established the concept of non-refoulement, which prohibits state parties from returning refugees to countries where they would face persecution on account of the grounds contained in the refugee definition.

Between 1968 and 1980, the United States passed a series of ad hoc laws and executive branch policies that provided varying levels of refuge to persons fleeing persecution from a limited number of countries. The selection of these countries was largely determined by U.S. foreign policy priorities. It was not until the United States enacted the Refugee Act of 1980 that there was a comprehensive domestic legislative scheme to bring the United States formally into compliance with its international legal obligations by providing a uniform asylum application procedure for asylum seekers from all over the world. The Refugee Act included a "refugee definition" that was based on the Refugee Convention and 1967 Protocol definition, but was expanded to also include persons who have been persecuted in the past in addition to those with a well-founded fear of future persecution.

The "refugee definition" under U.S. law is as follows: "any person who is outside of any country of such person's nationality or, in the case of a person having no nationality, is outside any country in which such person last habitually resided, and who is unable or unwilling to return to, and is unable or unwilling to avail himself or herself of the protection of, that country because of persecution or a well-founded fear of persecution on account of race, religion, nationality, membership in a particular social group, or political opinion" (Immigration and Nationality Act §101(a)(42)). The definition also includes certain family members of asylum seekers, even if those family members are still within their country of nationality, or, if stateless, within their country of habitual residence. This definition excluded anyone who "ordered, incited, or otherwise participated in the persecution of any person on account of race, religion, nationality, membership in a particular social group, or political opinion." The Refugee Act included other bars to asylum, including when an asylum applicant had "firmly resettled" in another country prior to entering the United States.

The Refugee Act also made a distinction between "refugee status" and "asylum status" under U.S. law and required both refugees and asylum seekers to meet the "refugee definition" in order to receive protection in the United States. The difference between a person granted asylum status in the United States (an asylum seeker) and a person granted refugee status (a refugee) is that an asylum seeker applies for and is granted protective immigration status while physically present in the United States or at a U.S. port of entry, while a refugee applies for and is granted protective immigration status prior to arriving in the United States. Both asylum seekers and refugees are granted permission to live and work in the United States and both provide potential avenues to permanent residency and U.S. citizenship. The Refugee Act enabled refugees to apply for permanent residence after having one year of physical presence in the United States. Asylum seekers could apply for permanent residence one year after receiving a grant of asylum. However, due to bureaucratic delays and a congressionally created limitation of only 10,000 asylum seekers per year that can be granted permanent residence, today many asylum seekers must wait as long as 12 years for their applications for permanent residency to be processed.

The regulations detailing the specific implementation of the Refugee Act were not published in final form until 1990. Before the regulations were issued, asylum applications were adjudicated by immigration officers and judges who were not given training in human rights, international country conditions, or working with traumatized persons. Lawsuits such as *Thornberg v. American Baptist Church* were brought against the Immigration and Naturalization Service, alleging national origin discrimination in the processing of asylum applications. The courts found these allegations to be warranted and, as a result, new forms of immigration relief such as the Nicaraguan and Central American Adjustment Act (NACARA) were created to remedy the bias. When the Refugee Act regulations were finalized in 1990, they provided for the establishment of an Asylum Officer Corps, which is a group of specially trained asylum officers to adjudicate asylum claims. They also provided for the Resource Information Center (RIC), which is a documentation center that researches and generates reports regarding conditions in countries from where asylum applicants come.

In the early and mid-1990s, the executive branch created procedures and reforms in the asylum process to minimize fraud and to reduce accumulating backlogs. Among the reforms was a new requirement that asylum applicants wait to apply for work authorization until their asylum application was approved or until 150 days from the day that immigration officials received their asylum application. This made it very difficult for asylum applicants, who are not eligible to receive most public benefits, to find a way to support themselves. Other reforms created certain crime-related bars to asylum.

In 1996, through the Antiterrorism and Effective Death Penalty Act (AEDPA) and the Illegal Immigration and Immigrant Responsibility Act (IIRIRA), more restrictions were applied to asylum eligibility. One of the harshest reforms was the creation of a new one-year deadline. Under this new requirement, asylum applicants must apply for asylum within one year of their entry into the United States. If one does not file a timely application, the applicant forfeits his or her ability to receive asylum. Limited exceptions apply to the one-year deadline. This rule has been particularly problematic for asylum seekers who often are unaware of this rule. Other obstacles that prevent asylum seekers from applying within one year include lack of knowledge that asylum protection is available to them, language barriers, difficulty in accessing the legal system, challenges associated with integrating into a new culture, and the need to find a way to support themselves while not being work-authorized.

The 1996 legislation also created the "expedited removal process," which permits the U.S. government to expeditiously remove non-citizens who arrive at ports of entry without valid immigration documents. If a non-citizen in this situation expresses a fear of returning to his or her home country, he or she is subject to mandatory detention and referred to an asylum officer for a "credible fear" interview. If the officer does not find that the non-citizen has "credible fear" of persecution, the non-citizen is ordered removed from the United States and does not get the opportunity to apply for asylum. The non-citizen can challenge the asylum officer's credible fear decision before an immigration judge.

If either the asylum officer or immigration judge finds that the non-citizen does have a "credible fear" of returning to his or her home country, the non-citizen is allowed to apply for asylum in immigration court proceedings. Although the non-citizen who establishes a "credible fear" is eligible to apply for release from immigration detention, release is seldom granted in most jurisdictions. This means that detained asylum seekers are often detained at government expense for many months and even years during the duration of their asylum case, regardless of whether they have ever committed a crime. Detention centers are high security facilities similar to jails. In fact, due to limited capacity in U.S. immigration-owned detention facilities, many asylum seekers are held in private and government prisons, where they are sometimes commingled with criminal inmates.

Other restrictions from the 1996 legislation included barring asylum for persons who have been denied asylum in the past and cannot demonstrate changed circumstances that affect their eligibility for asylum. Persons who could be returned to a "safe country" with which the United States has a bilateral or multilateral agreement are also barred, as are persons involved with what the U.S. government designates as a "foreign terrorist organization."

There are two different ways of applying for asylum in the United States. One is an affirmative process, which enables a person who has not been apprehended by immigration authorities to present herself or himself to immigration authorities with the intent to seek asylum protection. In this instance, a person must complete an asylum application (immigration form I-589), provide supporting documentation, and be interviewed by an asylum officer. The applicant may bring an interpreter to the interview if needed. However, the government will not provide an interpreter. The affirmative process is supposed to be a non-adversarial process designed to allow an applicant to present evidence in the form of testimony and supporting evidence such as reports on country conditions, identity documents, affidavits, and other evidence that could corroborate the applicant's claim. After the interview, the asylum officer can choose to grant the asylum application, deny the application (if the person already has some other non-asylum legal immigration status), or refer the applicant into immigration court proceedings, where the applicant can re-apply for asylum in front of an immigration judge.

The other way to apply for asylum is a defensive process in immigration court proceedings. Applicants must apply for asylum with the immigration court if their case is referred by the asylum office, if they are apprehended by immigration authorities and placed in proceedings, or if they are subject to the expedited removal process. This is an adversarial process in which the Department of Homeland Security (DHS) attempts to remove the asylum seeker from the United States. DHS is represented by a trial attorney who plays a prosecutorial role. The asylum seeker is called a "respondent" in this process. An Immigration Judge (IJ) from the Department of Justice's Executive Office of Immigration Review (EOIR) presides over the proceedings. The Immigration Court will provide an interpreter if needed. The respondent has the right to be represented by an attorney but is not entitled to legal representation at the government's expense. Therefore, the great majority of asylum seekers appear in court without the benefit of an attorney because they cannot afford one. According to one study, asylum applicants who are represented by an attorney are up to six times more likely to be granted asylum than those who are not represented by an attorney (Martin and Schoenholtz 2000).

Testimony by individuals stipulated to be experts (including academics) can be very useful and convincing, particularly for providing tangible information about conditions in locations, many times remote and unknown, where human rights abuses may occur (Alvarez and Loucky 1992). However useful, presence of expert witnesses is relatively rare because of a general lack of awareness of this option by applicants and potential experts alike, in addition to preparation time and costs that might be involved.

Either party may appeal the Immigration Court decision to the Board of Immigration Appeals (BIA), which is also part of EOIR. Due to recent streamlining reforms and staffing cuts at the BIA, the BIA is increasingly affirming IJ decisions, often without issuing a separate decision. If the BIA affirms the IJ's decision, the case may be appealed to the federal circuit appeals court with jurisdiction over the state in which the immigration court proceeding took place.

Since 1980, asylum in the United States has become a complex area of law that has provided for the protection of millions of persons seeking refuge within our borders. The system has been increasingly plagued, however, with anti-immigrant sentiments and restrictive government policies aimed at increasing efficiency and eliminating fraud, both real and perceived. Government policies toward asylum seekers have only become stricter since the tragic events of September 11, 2001. Since that time there has been a dramatic increase in detention of asylum seekers and a reluctance to release them even after they are identified as having a credible fear of persecution. In the midst of these policies, the legal community and human rights advocates continue to challenge the U.S. government to ensure that it meets international legal and moral obligations toward those who seek refuge within its borders. *See also*: **Expedited entry and removal; Refugee law and policy.**

References

Alvarez, Darline, and James A. Loucky. 1992. Inquiry and Advocacy: Attorney-Expert Collaboration in the Political Asylum Process. In *Double Vision: Anthropologists at Law*. Randy Kandel, ed. Pp. 43–52. NAPA Bulletin 11. Washington, DC: American Anthropological Association.

Anker, Deborah E. 1999. *Law of Asylum in the United States*. Cambridge, MA: Harvard Refugee Law Center. Chasing Freedom Campaign.

———. 2003. Action Guide. http://www.activevoice.net/pdf/cf_action_guide.pdf.

Fitzpatrick, Joan. 1997. The International Dimension of U.S. Refugee Law. *Berkeley Journal of International Law* 15(1):1–26.

Germain, Regina. 2003. *AILA's Asylum Primer: A Practical Guide to U.S. Asylum Law and Procedure*, 3rd ed. Washington, DC: American Immigration Lawyers Association.

INS Asylum Program—HQASY. 1999. History of the United States Asylum Officer Corps and Sources of Authority for Asylum Adjudication. http://www.uscis.gov/graphics/services/asylum/History.pdf.

Martin, Susan F., and Andrew I. Schoenholtz. 2000. Asylum in Practice: Successes, Failures, and the Challenges Ahead. *Georgetown Immigration Law Journal* 14:589–617.

Plaut, W. Gunther. 1995. *Asylum: A Moral Dilemma*. Westport, CT: Praeger.

U.S. Citizenship and Immigration Services. 2003. *Yearbook of Immigration Statistics.*
http://www.uscis.gov/graphics/shared/aboutus/statistics/RA2003yrbk/2003RA.pdf.

U.S. Committee for Refugees. 2000. Five Years After Asylum Reform: The INS Regains
Control; Practitioners Say Reform Still Needed. http://www.refugees.org/world/articles/
reform_rr00_2.htm.

BINA HANCHINAMANI ELLEFSEN

B

BILINGUAL EDUCATION. Bilingual education has been a subject of national debate since the 1960s, although in the past schools were frequently involved in ethnic issues as successive immigrant communities attempted to use the classroom to maintain their respective linguistic and cultural heritages. For instance, Germans, during the nineteenth century, sometimes went to extraordinary lengths to use public schools, churches, gymnastic associations (*Turnvereine*), and even glee clubs (*Liedertafeln*) for the purpose of strengthening *Deutschtum*, or "Germanness," on American soil, an issue of bitter controversy at the time (O'Connor 1968; Rippley 1976). Similarly, when between 1870 and 1929 about 1 million French-speaking immigrants made their way from Quebec to New England, they created their own schools, newspapers, trade unions, and religious congregations, permanently entrenching French civilization in New England.

Despite beliefs that bilingual education is a new phenomenon, however, issues surrounding bilingual education have long existed in the United States. Early waves of immigrants often enrolled their children in bilingual or non-English-language schools. In the mid-1920s, the U.S. Supreme Court upheld the rights of parents to provide private alternatives in education of their native languages, and the "incompatibility of militant educational Americanization with the founders' ideal of unity in diversity was formally recognized in constitutional law" (Bull et al. 1992).

During the 1960s and 1970s the nationwide debate over bilingual education revolved around whether instruction in the child's native tongue and in English should be transitional. The child's home language, some educators argued, should be used for teaching purposes, so that students would acquire cognitive skills and avoid academic delay. English should be taught as a second language only until the student becomes proficient in English, at which time native-language instruction should end. In theory, attention would continue to be paid to the child's heritage and culture. The basic purpose, at least of federal legislation, was to get students to transfer into all-English classrooms as quickly as possible without falling behind in other subjects.

The English-speaking public generally insisted that English should remain the sole language of instruction in schools. The use of native languages was resented by the descendants of earlier immigrants, whose forebears had learned English by total immersion methods. Anglo-Americans feared it would usher in multilingual and artificial attempts to preserve ethnic cultures. By contrast, for some Hispanics in particular, bilingual education became a civil rights issue and also a means of obtaining heightened respect for their culture, an instrument for fighting discrimination against non-English-speaking groups, and a device for obtaining jobs and increasing political leverage (Guerra 1980:121–132).

Spanish-speaking Americans, in fact, were slow to emulate their European predecessors' demands for bilingual education. Organizations such as the League of United Latin American Citizens (LULAC), the Mexican-American Political Association, and the American GI Forum, while not unmindful of their Hispanic heritage, stressed political, social, and economic equality for Mexican Americans and attempted to integrate Mexican Americans fully into American life. LULAC thus placed special stress on ending de facto segregation in school and job discrimination, not on bilingual education.

But from the 1960s onward, the emphasis shifted from socioeconomic to broader and often diverse objectives set by some Latino leaders as well as certain educational reformers. The demand for bilingual education came from many sources. The first Cuban refugees from Cuba, many of them highly educated, called for quality schooling for their children, an education that would preserve the Cubans' Spanish culture. Bilingual education also was said to be essential for the purpose of gaining a new sense of self-pride for the Hispanic poor. More radical attacks on the existing system came in the 1960s, when student unrest was at its zenith throughout the country, when members of *La Raza Unida* advocated biculturalism as a method of gaining political power in predominantly Chicano regions (Duignan 1998:1–6).

Bilingual education also came to be considered essential because of the relatively poor performance of many Puerto Rican and Chicano students and because of their high dropout rate from schools and low admission rates into colleges. Spanish-speaking educators stated that there were several reasons why Hispanics dropped out. Many Spanish speakers fell behind early in their education because they did not know much English; by the time they reached high school, they were discouraged. Many complained of bad teacher attitudes toward Hispanic students because of the students' color, accent, and poor English skills. Students did not hear enough English spoken at home or in the barrios and received little help in reading and writing English in the home. Failing to see the relevance or economic benefits of further education, they left school to find a job as soon as they could.

Hispanics, though better off than blacks, suffered more severely from unemployment than members of the so-called majority because of their poor English skills and high dropout rates. Overall, Hispanic college graduates did best in the job market, followed by high school graduates; high school dropouts were at the bottom (U.S. Commission on Civil Rights 1982:5, 43). Clearly, argued the advocates of bilingual education, more suitable courses of instruction would help to improve the Hispanics' economic as well as educational position. This view gained additional support in the 1970s with a permanent cabinet committee formed to serve as a forum for Spanish speakers and as growing numbers of Hispanics obtained employment and appointments in various federal agencies.

These changes were accompanied by determined attempts to desegregate schools. In 1964, Congress passed the Civil Rights Act and a year later, the Elementary and Secondary Schools Education Act (ESEA). Studies indicating that limited English proficiency students in English-only classrooms had lower rates of academic success and increased dropout rates led to the Bilingual Education Act of 1968, which provided for bilingual programs in the public schools. Designed as a means of facilitating the learning of English by children with a different mother tongue, it stipulates that a child should be instructed in his or her native tongue for a transitional year, while he or she learned English, but was to transfer to an all-English classroom as soon as possible (Duignan 1998:6–12).

The scope of bilingual education was increased by the Supreme Court decision in *Lau v. Nichols* (1974), which held that students who did not speak English were entitled to instruction in their native language. The *Lau* decision did not establish separate curricula and staff in languages other than English. Congress had set up the Office for Civil Rights (OCR) in the department of Education as part of the federal effort to desegregate southern schools and enforce Title VI of the Civil Rights Act of 1964. OCR staff energetically renewed their enforcement efforts and said that *Lau v. Nichols* required bilingual education at the elementary and middle school levels for national origin minority students who were dominant speakers of languages other than English. The *Lau v. Nichols* decision, therefore, stands out as a landmark on the road to bilingual education for those who are unable to speak English: bilingual education moved away from a transitional year to a multiyear plan to teach children first in their home language, if it was not English, before teaching them in English.

Educational and legal theory then advanced the facilitation theory to support bilingual education, stating that children could not learn English until they had first mastered their native language and culture. Generally this language is Spanish, since about 75 percent of the 3 million K–12 students with limited English proficiency are Hispanic. The psychological cost of abandoning one's native language was also questioned (Nieto 2003). Academic knowledge and English skills have been found to be enhanced through the use of the native language to give a firm foundation in literacy, particularly in the early years (Ovando 2003).

In a typical model of a transitional bilingual education program, students' language skills are assessed upon entry into the school, and students whose proficiency in English is limited are placed in bilingual classrooms. In the early grades, bilingual classes provide instruction in reading and other subjects in Spanish along with instruction in oral and written English. In grades three and four, children learn to read English and are instructed in other subjects in a mixture of Spanish and English. By the fifth grade, reading in Spanish has been phased out, and most instruction in other subjects is conducted in English (Bull 1992). This model seems to have been successful in Arizona, where English language learners in bilingual programs consistently scored higher in English language reading tests than their peers enrolled in English-only programs.

By 1978 the Bilingual Education Act was funding over 500 bilingual, bicultural projects in 68 languages ranging from Spanish (about 80 percent of the total) to

Crioulo, Chinese, and Vietnamese. Separately, the Office of Civil Rights identified over 500 school systems as needing bilingual education programs. OCR became compliance; it was not until 1985 that Education Secretary William Bennett ruled that the 500 bilingual plans OCR had negotiated did not have to follow the so-called Lau Remedies and could use any methods or programs that had proven successful.

Some, including the Center for Equal Opportunity, have claimed that bilingual education programs failed and have undermined the future of the Latino children they were meant to help (Amselle 1997). There is some evidence that Latinos taught in bilingual programs continue to test behind peers taught in English-only classrooms, drop out of school at a high rate, and remain trapped in low-skilled, low-paying jobs. Some studies show that Latino students, even after more than 35 years of bilingual education, have the highest dropout rate of any minority students. In 2000, for example, 27.8 percent of Hispanics aged 16–24 did not complete high school compared to 13 percent of blacks and 6.9 percent of whites (NCES 2001).

Bilingual education was on the California ballot in 1998 in a much-debated "English for the Children" ballot initiative (Prop. 227) calling for cessation of teaching non-English-speaking children in their mother tongue unless their parents requested it. Supporters of the ballot, who included many Latino parents, claimed that most students in bilingual programs never really learn to read or write English well and fail generally to become assimilated into U.S. society. The solution, according to proponents of the proposition, was one year of sheltered English immersion, followed by instruction in regular classrooms (Duignan 1998: 40–41, 47).

There is some evidence that because California adopted a one-year English immersion program, test scores improved. Encouraged by the rise in test scores in California, Arizona similarly voted in November 2000 (Prop. 203) to scrap bilingual education programs and to teach only in English. The Arizona proposition is stricter than the California law in that parents have to fill out a long application and write a 250-word essay on the benefits for their child in a bilingual program, while also providing that an administrator who willfully violates the immersion law may be sued. In New York, then-Mayor Rudolph W. Giuliani responded to criticisms of bilingual education by forming a task force on bilingual education that has proposed giving parents and students a choice between bilingual education and classes in English as a second language for a maximum of three years. The mayor's task force reported that thousands of bilingual education students do not learn English because many of their teachers are not qualified to teach English and are not themselves bilingual (the report noted that New York's 4,000 bilingual teachers were inadequately trained and skilled). The students' stay in the bilingual program would be limited to two to three years.

With bilingual education now scaled back by such states, proponents began to advocate dual-language training by which every child should leave school fluent in two languages: English and, most commonly, Spanish. Students, therefore, are supposed to receive ongoing training in both languages to practice, think, speak, and write in two languages.

Dual-language instruction was tried in Florida in the early 1960s as a way of teaching English to newly arrived Cuban children while enabling them to maintain Spanish. Dual-language instruction got a big push in March 2000, when Education Secretary Richard Riley called for doubling the number of dual-language schools in public school districts. Supporters of dual-language programs cite a long-term comparative study of 40,000 language minority students in dual-language programs, which suggested that such programs produced better test scores than did bilingual education programs (Rossell 1998).

The debate about bilingual education versus English-only immersion continues. Claims of failure are countered by evidence of success, such as in Calexico, California, which implemented bilingual education programs and now has dropout rates that are less than half the state average and college acceptance rates well over 90 percent. Even the dismantling of bilingual education in California has not been the disaster predicted: "Advocates of the immersion method say its role cannot be denied. Pupils in the program have shown stronger gains in both reading and math than have their non-immersion classmates" (Gorov 2001).

Debates about English-only immersion versions of bilingual education will no doubt continue, even as studies show that most U.S.-born Latinos and Asians consider English to be their primary language. In reality, it takes time to learn English, the process of assimilation is often multigenerational, and bilingual education will continue to have a significant if varied and contested role (Parrillo 2001). *See also*: **Achievement; Bilingualism; Immigrant education.**

References

Amselle, Jorge, ed. 1997. *The Failure of Bilingual Education, 1996*. Washington, DC: Center for Equal Opportunity.

Bull, Barry L., Royal T. Frueliling, and Virgie Chatterzy. 1992. *The Ethics of Multicultural and Bilingual Education*. New York: Teachers College Press.

Cortines, Ramon C. 1995. New Beginnings: Ensuring Quality Bilingual/ESL Instruction. In *Report of the Chancellor's Bilingual/ESL Education Practitioners' Workgroup and Policy/Research Panels*. New York: New York City Public Schools.

Duignan, Peter. 1998. *Bilingual Education: A Critique*. Stanford, CA: Hoover Institution Press.

Gorov, Lynda. 2001. Scores Rise as California Schools Immerse: Gains Follow Halt to Bilingual Ed. *Boston Globe*, September 10, A4.

Guerra, Manuel H. 1980. Bilingualism and Biculturalism: Assets for Chicanos. In *The Chicanos: As We See Ourselves*. Arnulfo D. Trejo, ed. Pp. 121–132. Tucson: University of Arizona Press.

Lazear, Edward P. 1996. *Culture Wars in America*. Stanford, CA: Hoover Institution Press.

National Center for Education Statistics (NCES). 2001. *Dropout Rates in the United States: 2000*, NCES 2002-114, by Phillip Kaufman, Martha Naomi Alt, and Christopher D. Chapman. Washington, DC: NCES.

Nieto, Sonia. 2003. *Affirming Diversity: The Sociopolitical Context of Multicultural Education*, 3rd ed. New York: Longman.

O'Connor, Richard. 1968. *The German-Americans*. New York: Little, Brown.

Ovando, Carlos J. 2003. Education in the United States: Historical Development and Current Issues. *Bilingual Research Journal* 17:1–24.

Parrillo, Vincent N. 2001. A Challenge for Educators: Dealing with Demographic Changes in the School System. *Vital Speeches of the Day* 68(1):19–26.

Pompa, Delia. 2000. Bilingual Success: Why Two-Language Education Is Critical for Latinos. *Hispanic Magazine*, November. http://www.hispaniconline.com/magazine/2000/nov/Forum.

Rippley, LaVern J. 1976. *The German-Americans*. Boston: Twayne Publishers.
Rossell, Christine H. 1998. Mystery on the Bilingual Express: A Critique of the Thomas and Collier Study. The READ Institute, http://www.ceousa.org/hml/collier.html.
U.S. Commission on Civil Rights. 1982. *Unemployment and Under-Employment Among Blacks, Hispanics and Women*. Washington, DC: Clearing House Publication 74.

PETER DUIGNAN

BILINGUALISM. Language is an indelible aspect of our identities. It pertains simultaneously to the most private and the most public of our social existence. We cannot dissociate a person from their language, just as we cannot dissociate a nation from its national language(s). All the same, any given individual speaks several versions of the same language according to context and situation. Languages are not merely spoken; they also are performed and inflected. A personal or national language is already many: public, private, mundane, vulgar, informal, formal, academic, policed by royal academies of the language, cannibalized by sedition, appropriated in defiance, or simply renovated and transformed by the changing worlds of technology and politics. Bilingualism is not just what results from the proximity of two cultures, nations, countries, but also the result of the very logic of language use and enactment. It is more prominent when different cultures meet, as is the case in countries founded on immigrations and conquests, or in the shifting borderlands of countries that have negotiated peace with their neighbors. Language is a profoundly historical and political issue. It is historical because it harkens back to the very foundations of our cultural identity. The word "barbarian" was used by the Greeks to describe those who spoke a foreign language (i.e., not Greek). In countries whose frontiers wax and wane with the comings and goings of empires, national identity has been maintained through the preservation of local dialects and the maintenance of national tongues. In some cases, however, the languages that have been imposed are not necessarily those of the conquerors, but of the largest group of the dominated. This is what happened in Africa, India, China, and Latin America, where linguistic diversity remains vibrant.

The United States, which consolidated itself as a nation only in the second half of the nineteenth century, also underwent the process of affirming a national language. In addition to the many native tongues that were spoken in the North American continent (Iroquois, Cherokee, Osage, Sioux, etc.) before and after the landing of the pilgrims, there were also other European languages. Eventually, in the nineteenth century in particular, the waves of immigrants from Southern, Central, and Eastern Europe brought entire communities and towns with their languages (German, Polish, Italian in its many variants, Hebrew in its many diasporic inflections, and Yiddish). In the United States, as in Brazil and many Latin American countries that also received great waves of immigrants from Europe, many communities survived and flourished as late as the early part of the twentieth century. When Whigs, Know-Nothings, and similar "nationalistic" movements began to advocate the imposition of English as the national language, these anti-immigrant and nativist movements sought to reverse a long tradition of bilingualism that harkens back to the indigenous populations that existed in the American continent before the conquistadors and colonists arrived.

Bilingualism has been institutionally acknowledged in the United States. The Articles of Confederation were published in German in order to both inform and gain support from Germans in the colony of Pennsylvania. Pennsylvania, in turn, employed an official German press to print its official documents in German, not unlike how California prints today some of its most important official documents, as well as voting ballots, in Spanish, Mandarin, and Cantonese. The United States, as a nation that assimilated, incorporated, bought, and conquered territories colonized by other European nations, has had large groups of bilingual citizens in many of its regions: French in Louisiana and upper New England; German in Pennsylvania, Ohio, Indiana, and Kansas; Spanish in the South and Southwest, Puerto Rico, and Florida; Chinese in New York and San Francisco. In some midwestern states of the United States many towns had their own schools, newspapers, and local literary societies in German. In New York, for instance, there existed a vibrant Spanish literary community that published its own literary magazines and papers.

The two world wars exacerbated national linguistic chauvinisms and suspicion of anyone who retained his or her maternal language. Through a combination of war hysteria, militaristic jingoism, anti-immigrant feeling, racism, and lack of knowledge about the role of language in the education of children, the United States went from a multilingual to a monolingual nation. Yet, one may say that notwithstanding almost a century of "English-Only" initiatives, Spanish is still widely spoken in the major metropolises of the United States: Los Angeles, New York, Miami, Chicago, and San Francisco. In fact, the United States is on its way to becoming the fourth largest Spanish-speaking nation, after Mexico, Spain, and Colombia (in fact, according to some census projections, the United States may soon surpass Colombia). We find in some cities on the West Coast an ever-growing number of Chinese, Vietnamese, and Japanese speakers in addition to Spanish speakers. One may conclude that monolingualism as a national ideology might have been a brief episode in the process of national maturation.

This growing number of non-English speakers, as well as the important place of the United States in the global economy, has made it not just important but often necessary for residents of the United States to speak languages other than English. Such a shift has been institutionally acknowledged in at least three ways: the 1965 Voting Rights Act, the 1968 Bilingual Education Act, and the *Lau v. Nichols* Supreme Court decision. The 1965 Voting Rights Act sought to eliminate the literacy test used in the post–Civil War south to prevent blacks from voting. This act was amended in 1975 to expand its interpretation of what constituted exclusion from voting. Lack of proficiency in English was not to be a hindrance to participating in the rights of citizenship. In this way many ballots, federal policies, documents, and other types of public information were to be made available to citizens in their language of proficiency.

The 1968 Bilingual Education Act sought to extend equal protection to students whose maternal tongue was a non-English language. The goal of the act was to provide education in other languages besides English so as to maintain minimal levels of education in recent immigrants. The 1974 *Lau v. Nichols* Supreme Court decision ruled that non-native speakers were entitled to remedial courses. The ruling by the Supreme Court aims at ensuring that a guideline will be applied consistently and affirmatively: "Where inability to speak and understand the English language excludes national origin-minority group children from effective participation in the educational programs offered by a school district, the district must take affirmative steps to rectify the language deficiency."

Other forms of government acknowledgment and fomenting of bilingualism in the United States have come from presidential initiatives like President Jimmy Carter's Commission on Foreign Language and International Studies (1979) and other federal acts with bilingual components, such as the Emergency School Aid Act (ESAA) of 1972; the Vocational Education Act, amended in 1974 to include a bilingual component; the Adult Education Act; the Library Services and Construction Act (amended 1974); the National Defense Education Act (amended 1967); the National Reading Improvement Program (1974); the Indian Education Action (1972); and the Older Americans Comprehensive Services Amendments (1973) (Thernstrom 1980:619–629). During the 1980s 10 states had made bilingual education mandatory in districts that met certain criteria, and 16 other states had passed legislation that authorized local initiatives for bilingual programs. In this way, many districts became eligible for federal and local funds to develop bilingual programs. Such programs have become even more relevant in the first decades of the twenty-first century, when the United States has experienced a demographic explosion of Spanish and Chinese speakers. As of the early 1990s, according to the U.S. Census Bureau, close to 2 million New Yorkers spoke only Spanish, while in California close to 5.5 million spoke Spanish, and more than half a million spoke Chinese. The most recent U.S. census estimates reveal that 32.8 million Latinos in the United States constitute 12 percent of the U.S. population. According to projections, Latinos will account for 44 percent of the population growth in the United States by the year 2025. In the current national population of 262,375,152 individuals aged 5 and above, approximately 46,951,595 speak a language other than English at home. Of these, more than half speak Spanish.

A less historical, and more conceptual, approach to bilingualism must consider the reservations and objections that hold that neither the nation nor recent immigrants are served well by pursuing a bilingual educational policy. Critics of bilingualism point out that bilingualism hinders children from being assimilated and eventually marginalizes them and prevents them from appropriating the language in which politics and economics are spoken. These critics argue that pride in one's language is stubborn and detrimental. At best, these critics maintain, such maternal languages should be preserved but only for the home and the private realm (Rodriguez 1982). These objections and reservations may be well intentioned, but they are perhaps anachronistic. A national discourse about multiculturalism and cultural recognition has made it clear that one cannot be integrated into a polity that rejects one's cultural inheritance. One fundamental aspect of citizenship is respect toward the cultural integrity of all citizens. To negate and depreciate the language(s) of a nation's citizens becomes an assault and violation of the cultural integrity of its citizens, and thus a violation of their rights as citizens. Recent developments in cognitive psychology, sociolinguistics, neurobiology, and pedagogy have made it clear that children who are exposed to several languages in their early education develop better and stronger cognitive capabilities. Bilingualism has been shown to benefit not only the well-being of the social body but also the mental well-being of children (Portes and Rumbaut 1996:192–207).

As we look ahead to the twenty-first century, the preservation of languages will become a significant task, not only because languages are repositories of memories but also because they are tied to certain cultural practices. The death of a language may be compared to the extinction of a biological species. Both languages and biological species must be preserved not only for their worth today but also because of the benefit they harbor to future generations. *See also*: **Assimilation; Bilingual education; Citizenship.**

References

Anzaldúa, Gloria. 1987. *Borderlands/La Frontera: The New Mestiza*. San Francisco: Aunt Lute.

Arteaga, Alfred. 1994. *An Other Tongue: Nation and Ethnicity in the Linguistic Borderlands*. Durham, NC: Duke University Press.

Derrida, Jacques. 1997. *Monolingualism of the Other*. Stanford, CA: Stanford University Press.

Hakuta, Kenji. 1986. *Mirror of Language: The Debate on Bilingualism*. New York: Basic Books.

Kymlicka, Will. 1995. *Multicultural Citizenship*. Oxford: Oxford University Press.

Portes, Alejandro, and Ruben G. Rumbaut. 1996. *Immigrant America: A Portrait*. Berkeley: University of California Press.

Rodriguez, Richard. 1982. *Hunger of Memory: The Education of Richard Rodriguez*. Boston: D.R. Godine.

Takaki, Ronald. 1994. *From Different Shores: Perspectives on Race and Ethnicity in America*. New York: Oxford University Press.

Thernstrom, Stephan, ed. 1980. *Harvard Encyclopedia of American Ethnic Groups*. Cambridge, MA: Belknap Press of Harvard University.

Zinn, Howard. 1995. *A People's History of the United States: 1492 to the Present*. New York: HarperCollins.

EDUARDO MENDIETA

BIOLOGICAL RESPONSES. The conquest and colonization of the Americas was perhaps the greatest biological phenomenon in human history. Earliest immigrants brought with them diseases that were common in Europe, such as smallpox, measles, typhus, and plague, but unknown in the New World. People had little biological resistance to many diseases, nor did they have appropriate medical or public health knowledge of how to deal with the sick. The Maya, for example, were unprepared at every level to deal with these diseases. Estimated at 2 million people when the Spanish conquest began in the year 1520, the Maya population was reduced by 94 percent, to about 125,000 people, by the year 1625 (Lovell and Lutz 1994, 1996). With large numbers disabled by disease and racked with the fear of these epidemics and Spanish military attacks, everyday life collapsed. Food production stopped, and the sick died of hunger and thirst because there was no one to care for them. Families fell apart and the economic, social, and political system was in chaos. It took centuries for the Maya population to recover, until by 2000 the Maya population of Guatemala was estimated at 6 to 7 million.

The history of the Maya demonstrates the impact of immigration on the biological status of human populations. Health, disease, death, and fertility are broad categories that cover many of the biological responses to immigration. The movement of people from place to place rearranges the genetic, physiological, and morphological variability of the human population. These new combinations of biological variation, along with heterogeneity in the social and cultural practices of the immigrant and native populations, may lead to biocultural outcomes that are both novel and unexpected.

Biological responses to immigration may be grouped into three areas (the first two of which are discussed here): (1) health and disease, (2) demography (that is, fertility and mortality), and (3) physical growth and development responses.

The foreign-born are at risk for diseases from both their homeland and their new environment. Contemporary immigrants may be infected with tuberculosis, HIV/AIDS, and other diseases before arrival or contract these diseases after arrival. Either way, immigrants account for seven times as many cases of tuberculosis than the U.S.-born (CDCP 2002). Immigrants may also bring with them hepatitis, parasites, malaria, and other infections, particularly if coming from less developed areas (Adair and Nwaneri 1999:83–85).

Despite these risks, numerous regional and national studies in the United States show that the health of the recent immigrants is generally better than that of the U.S.-born population. A national survey of health finds that 12.1 percent of U.S.-born people over 18 years old report "fair-to-poor" health, nearly twice the proportion of immigrants residing in the United States less than five years (6.3 percent) who report "fair-to-poor" health. After 10 years or more in the United States the immigrants report higher "fair-to-poor" health, at 13.8 percent (Stephen et al. 1994), suggesting growing correspondence with the population at large. Once in the United States, immigrants are exposed to American biocultural environment and lifestyles, leading to new health problems. Acculturation to a pattern of high fat and high calorie diet along with low physical activity promotes lifestyle diseases. Immigrants' risks of smoking, obesity, hypertension, heart disease, diabetes, some cancers, and other chronic conditions, although substantially lower than those for the U.S.-born, increase with increasing length of U.S. residence (Bogin 2001; Singh and Siahpush 2002).

Social characteristics of immigrants and their place in American society exacerbate the risks for developing poor health. For example, immigrants are less likely to have graduated from high school than the U.S.-born (67 percent vs. 86.6 percent), although there is great variability, with 95 percent of African immigrants having a high school diploma (Schmidley 2001) compared with only 37.3 percent of immigrants from Mexico and Central America (Lollock 2001). Immigrants are more likely to earn less money, live in poverty, be unemployed, and live in inner-city neighborhoods than the U.S.-born (Lollock 2001). Each of these socioeconomic factors increases the risk for exposure to disease-causing agents and lifestyles and reduces the likelihood of effective treatment.

Fertility and mortality are also different for immigrants compared to the native-born in the United States. In the year 2000, the number of foreign-born and first-generation residents of the United States reached 56 million, or 20 percent of the U.S. population (Schmidley 2001). About 90 percent of the foreign-born were from Latin America and Asia, with 25 percent of all immigrants from Mexico. Both the sheer number of immigrants and their geographic origin have important impacts on the demographic structure of the United States. A greater percentage of foreign-born women (55.3 percent) than U.S.-born women (42.2 percent) are 15 to 44 years old, in the prime reproductive years, according to 2000 U.S. Census Bureau data. The foreign-born are also more likely to be married than U.S.-born (61 percent vs. 53.2 percent). Both age and marital status of women are strong correlates of fertility (Bogin 2001). Indeed, immigrant women give birth at higher rates in all age groups. In 2001, in a total population of 8.9 million foreign-born women, 637,000 women gave birth, which is a rate of 71 births per 1,000 women; the fertility rate for U.S.-born women was 60 births per 1,000 (U.S. Census Bureau 2001).

Mortality is generally lower at most ages in the foreign-born population than in the U.S.-born. In 1998, infant mortality for immigrants from Mexico, Central and South America, and Cuba was less than 6 per 1,000 live births. This was slightly lower than the rate for non-Hispanic whites at 6.0 per 1,000 and substantially lower than the rate for non-Hispanic Blacks at 14.2 per 1,000 (NCHS 2002; PEW Hispanic Center 2002). Infant mortality for Puerto Rican immigrants to the U.S. mainland was higher, at 7.8 per 1,000, than for other Latino immigrants.

Mortality for immigrants over 25 years old, analyzed using the National Longitudinal Mortality Study of 1979–1989, reveals that immigrant men overall had an 18 percent reduced risk of mortality and foreign-born women had a 13 percent lower risk of mortality (Singh and Siahpush 2001). Immigrants showed significantly lower risks of mortality from cardiovascular diseases, lung and prostate cancer, chronic obstructive pulmonary diseases, cirrhosis, pneumonia and influenza, unintentional injuries, and suicide, but higher risks of mortality from stomach and brain cancer and infectious diseases. Hispanic and Latino mortality follows the general trends except between ages 25 and 44, when the risk of death is higher for Latinos than for whites (PEW Hispanic Center 2002). These mortality trends are somewhat puzzling, as Latin American immigrants are more likely to be overweight and suffer from type 2 diabetes (adult onset) than U.S.-born whites. As with health and disease rates, sociocultural behaviors of immigrants, such as less smoking, less alcohol consumption, lower fat diets, and more physical labor, may account for their lower mortality.

The complexities of immigrant adaptation and adjustment to the American biocultural environment are far from being completely understood. A U.S. National Center for Health Statistics report (NCHS) explains that research relating to immigrants and their health has not attended to methodological issues, most notably the definition of an immigrant, changes in health or access to health care associated with changes in immigration status, and care in selection of samples to ensure validity of research (Loue and Bunce 1999). International migration is primarily a social and behavioral process. Migrants in general tend to be healthier, often better educated (though perhaps not highly educated), and younger than people who remain in the homeland. There is no evidence for the selection of genetic or biological "types" of migrants before they leave their homeland (Bogin 1988, 2001), but it is clear that social and cultural factors both lead to migration and impact immigrants in the new country. As shown here, these factors have appreciable consequences for human biology in terms of health, fertility, and mortality. *See also*: **Demography; Fertility; Growth and development; Health.**

References

Adair, R., and O. Nwaneri. 1999. Communicable Disease in African Immigrants in Minneapolis. *Archives of Internal Medicine* 159(1):83–85.

Bogin, B. 1988. Rural-to-Urban Migration. In *Biological Aspects of Human Migration.* C.G.N. Mascie-Taylor and G.W. Lasker, eds. Pp. 90–129. Cambridge: Cambridge University Press.

———. 2001. *The Growth of Humanity.* New York: Wiley-Liss.

Centers for Disease Control and Prevention (CDCP). 2002. Tuberculosis Morbidity among U.S.-Born and Foreign-Born Populations: United States, 2000. *Morbidity Mortal Weekly Reports* 51(5):101–104.

Lollock, L. 2001. The Foreign Born Population in the United States. U.S. Census Bureau. *Current Population Reports*, Series P20-534. Washington, DC: U.S. Government Printing Office.

Loue, S., and A. Bunce. 1999. The Assessment of Immigration Status in Health Research. *Vital Health Statistics* 2(127).

Lovell, W.G., and C.H. Lutz. 1994. Conquest and Population: Maya Demography in Historical Perspective. *Latin American Research Review* 29:133–140.

———. 1996. A Dark Obverse: Maya Survival in Guatemala, 1520–1994. *Geographical Review* 86:398–407.

National Center for Health Statistics (NCHS). 2002. *National Vital Statistics Report* 50(15), September 16.

PEW Hispanic Center. 2002. Hispanic Health: Divergent and Changing. http://www .pewhispanic.org/site/docs/pdf/health_pdf_version.pdf.

Schmidley, A.D. 2001. Profile of the Foreign-Born Population in the United States: 2000 U.S. Census. *Current Population Reports*, Series P23-206. Washington, DC: U.S. Government Printing Office.

Singh, G.K., and M. Siahpush. 2001. All-Cause and Cause-Specific Mortality of Immigrants and Native Born in the United States. *American Journal of Public Health* 91:392–399.

———. 2002. Ethnic-Immigrant Differentials in Health Behaviors, Morbidity, and Cause-Specific Mortality in the United States: An Analysis of Two National Data Bases. *Human Biology* 74(1):83–109.

Stephen, E., K. Foote, G.E. Hendershot, and C.A. Schoenborn. 1994. Health of the Foreign-Born Population: United States 1989–90. *Advance Data from Vital and Health Statistics*, No. 241. Hyattsville, MD: National Center for Health Statistics.

U.S. Census Bureau. 2001. Fertility of American Women: June 2000. http://www.census .gov. Retrieved December 20, 2004.

BARRY BOGIN

BORDER CONTROL. Immigration, along with two other agendas of the U.S. government, illegal drug interdiction and detection of terrorists and other political opponents of U.S. foreign policy, overlap in significant ways with immigration law enforcement as aspects of border control. Politically each constitutes a concern, even a fear, that blurs into the others (e.g., illegal immigrants as potential terrorists), thereby forming as a whole a compelling image of an imperiled national boundary. Organizationally, each initiative adds manpower, arms, and surveillance equipment to a small set of government agencies. Socially, their overlap adds to the legal and physical perils of migrants crossing borders.

Immigration and border control responsibilities were unified in 2003 under the Department of Homeland Security (DHS). However, important organizational boundaries were inherited from the past. Within DHS, U.S. Customs and Border Protection (CBP) includes what used to be the Border Patrol, which seeks to interdict the non-inspected movement of people and contraband along land boundaries between legal entry points. It also includes inspection of people and vehicles going through ports of entry (land, sea, and air), unifying what had previously been separate functions of Customs and Immigration and Naturalization Services (INS) inspections. Ports of entry are complicated since the flow of traffic is enormous, with hundreds of millions of annual entries and exits, and entrants may be law-abiding, fraudulent, or any number of ambiguous statuses in between. Also in DHS, U.S. Immigration and Customs Enforcement (ICE) performs interior immigration operations (such as serving orders of deportation) and customs law investigations, while also managing major control technologies along the border such as air surveillance. Finally, U.S. Citizenship and Immigration Services (USCIS) handles immigration and citizenship applications and other immigration benefits, such as work authorization (Andreas and Biersteker 2003).

Other branches of the government also play roles in border control. The Federal Bureau of Investigation (FBI) and the Drug Enforcement Administration (DEA) do not perform front-line border operations but have significant roles behind the scenes in investigations and surveillance. DEA, for example, coordinates multi-agency intelligence units that focus on the border. A complex network of U.S. and state attorneys, state and local police departments, courts, judges, and prisons also contribute to the border criminal justice-industrial complex, fed on a rich diet of budgeted monies and seized assets. Finally, there is a significant military presence in law enforcement at the border. In the 1990s, on-the-ground military surveillance operations verged on direct law enforcement, which stopped after shootings of U.S. citizens and migrants. But the national guard and other military units continue to supply logistical support to front-line border agencies, while electronic reconnaissance aircraft provide a curtain of surveillance above the boundary. Most important, military-civilian entities called "Joint Task Forces" (JTFs) are the centers of intelligence collection and dissemination in the region (Andreas and Biersteker 2003).

In addition to these organizations, numbering well over 20,000 troops and law enforcement officers, border control takes physical form on the landscape, especially at the southern boundary. The United States disproportionately enforces its immigration laws at the U.S.-Mexico border with more than 90 percent of immigration arrests taking place at or near that boundary. Any discussion of border control, therefore, must start with the southern border, before turning to enforcement at the Canadian land border, air and sea ports, and the interior.

In the 1990s, bent and torn fences in urban areas or densely settled rural areas were replaced by massive prefabricated walls of cast iron on the U.S.-Mexico border, reminiscent of the former Berlin Wall. One sees these makeshift walls and fences bathed in spotlights, while electronic motion sensors and television cameras flash activity back to Border Patrol stations and night vision scopes detect green glows flickering across the brush. Patrol officers stand guard, packed as tightly as several hundred yards apart in urban border areas, while other officers cruise dirt roads in the more open countryside. Helicopters and airplanes intermittently survey the landscape from the air. Night after night, little clusters of people throw ladders over the walls or slip through holes in the fence, hoping to evade the border surveillance and find the waiting van of the "coyote" (a term for those who help smuggle illegal immigrants across the U.S.-Mexico border), which transports them away from the border to other destinations.

Since the cessation of large-scale European immigration in 1924, government officials, politicians, the media, and public opinion have envisioned immigration as largely a matter of Mexican border crossers, whether permanent, with temporary labor contracts, or illegal, even though this is at best only half accurate. Most unauthorized Mexican border entrants are what one might characterize as small-scale law violators, moving as individuals and minuscule groups in search of jobs and kin. By contrast, single large employers (e.g., meatpacking plants), broad social classes (e.g., upper and upper middle class U.S. families that hire domestic workers), and migrant facilitating businesses (e.g., landlords) orchestrate large-scale violation of immigration laws. For many years, the law sheltered these major law-breakers, and even after 1986, when it turned against employers of illegal immigrants, the Immigration and Naturalization Service (INS, the antecedent of the immigration-oriented functions of Homeland Security) continued its focus on the low rather than the high scale (Andreas 2000). The portion of INS investigations devoted to enforcing employment laws in the interior was 10 percent or less of the operating workforce of the Border Patrol on the southern boundary, despite facing a nation of businesses. In the mid-1990s the INS largely abandoned investigating employers in favor of workplace raids centered on document checks. These actions resulted in the firing and arrest of workers with false documents, again persecuting small criminals and not large ones. Also, investigations focused more on rooting out immigration application fraud and deporting so-called criminal aliens from prisons, yet another example of the focus on the individuals rather than the migration system.

Because millions of unauthorized immigrants who cross the border are arrested, Homeland Security faces the logistical challenge of arraigning, detaining, trying, and deporting huge numbers of people. To escape this self-imposed dilemma, federal officers short-circuit formal deportation by offering most arrestees "voluntary departure," and most unauthorized Mexican migrants accept it (Massey et al. 2002). It makes good sense; they have almost no chance of winning in immigration court, and rapid return to Mexico facilitates their trying to enter the United States again. The loss of a legal hearing and quick removal do more harm to potential asylum seekers from Central America and other nations, however. Since Mexicans can and do re-enter repeatedly until they get past the Border Patrol, this "voluntary departure complex" means that a genuinely tough boundary enforcement system has little impact on the movement of labor across the border.

Despite this underlying flaw, border policing grows larger and more expensive by the year. The Border Patrol has grown dramatically, more than doubling in size in the 1990s to over 10,000 officers. Other control agencies have also grown and, as we have seen, added sophisticated weaponry and technologies. Normal operations have come to approximate military counterinsurgency operations both in terms of intelligence and deployment of small units and the effort to remold public opinion in the borderlands. This trend has been labeled the "militarization" of the U.S.-Mexico border (Dunn 1996). Meanwhile, the Illegal Immigration Reduction and Immigrant Responsibility Act of 1996 made deportation either mandatory or virtually not opposable in many situations such as previous illegal entry or non-immigration crimes. This act, together with national security concerns, justifies using networked databases to track individuals at the border, a trend strengthening as fingerprints and biometric data become more computerized. The effective and enduring labeling of people as criminals has been exacerbated by the rise of Mexico to pre-eminence as a transshipment point for illegal drugs, a trade in which some migrants work as petty carriers. Taken together, these trends constitute a sharp escalation of state and underworld threats at the U.S.-Mexico border.

Escalation of border control certainly has made covert border crossing harder, more risky, and more expensive, but it is unclear if it has actually reduced illegal entries. One reason is that the escalation of the police side has been met by adaptations on the part of migrants, especially through use of human smugglers (Andreas 2000). It is illuminating to think of border control not as a policing problem alone but as an evolving system of move and countermove on each side. Relatively little is known about smugglers at the border, but from what is known, their roles and behavior are more subtle than the stereotype of evil coyotes preying on helpless chicks. Smugglers form organizations, some loose and band-like, others larger and more hierarchical, and rely on referrals and return business as well as recruitment of newly arriving migrants. In this context, consistent disregard for the interests of migrants is not profitable, although in a pinch, smugglers think of themselves first and migrants second, if at all. Smugglers have valuable services to sell, for as U.S. control over the border throttles the easy places to cross, their knowledge and hidden connections become more needed (and more expensive) for migrants. This debunking of stereotypes is not to be taken as excusing the endangerment and exploitation that does occur, or the broader pattern of powerlessness among migrants engendered by the grand contest of police and underworld.

Surveying the impressive presence of the U.S. state and the wily tricks of smugglers, an obvious question is whether current border interdiction works to halt or significantly reduce illegal immigration. Visible, dense Border Patrol presence on the forward boundary line has reduced crossings in major urban areas, such as along the Pacific coast and in El Paso. This has somewhat reduced crossing by local illegal commuting workers, shoppers, thieves, and kids out for high jinx. Unauthorized migrants who come from the interior of Mexico and aim for destinations throughout the United States, however, have shifted entry points rather than being deterred, now crossing at smaller border towns and through ranch country, desert basins, and mountains, or use devices such as trucks and rail cars (Massey et al. 2002). The Border Patrol has followed, shifting intensive operations to key smuggling zones that have proven harder to blockade. This sequence of move and countermove started in 1994, and since then the rate of departure for the United States as measured in Mexico and the volume of arrests in the United States indicate that border enforcement has little or no effect on total unauthorized migration. In this era, many people in Mexico suffer economically from soaring debt and free-trade-driven job loss while the U.S.

economy has remained relatively stronger (e.g., in creating low-wage service jobs in urban and suburban areas, ones that migrants often fill). The most likely interpretation is that interlocking economies trump border control policies.

This views the question in narrow policy terms, but what are the human dimensions of border control? When tough but incomplete law enforcement faces off against the powerful motivations that drive migrants north (the need for family, the need for income), the result is extreme risk-taking. Recently, concerned scholars have drawn our attention to deaths of border entrants by heat exhaustion, exposure to cold, drowning, locked conveyances, and accidental falls. It is probable though not provable that this ongoing tragedy is worsened by law enforcement's shifting of undocumented migration from safe, walkable corridors to perilous vehicles and dangerous deserts and mountains. Human rights organizations have documented physical abuse and legal mishandling by the main U.S. and Mexican border agencies; again, it is possible that this has been worsened by quasi-militaristic border control. Death, injury, and abuse are low in frequency compared to the volume of border crossing (though not to be ignored for that reason), but other harms are more widespread. Successful defiance of tough law enforcement results in monetary and personal debts to questionable "friends," including smugglers and labor contractors. In turn, this exacerbates tendencies already present in immigrant life toward vulnerability, exploitability, and quiet, covert desperation.

There are also negative effects on border communities in both Mexico and the United States. This region is notable for widespread commercialization and industrialization. When immigration policy is displaced from its causes and consequences in the two nations' interiors, it is seen as primarily a "border problem." As smugglers profit and control bureaucracies bloat, the region becomes partly a no-man's land of police and thieves. All border regions face this risk, but the trend has been extreme on the U.S.-Mexico frontier, which is highly regrettable given the other positive developments in the area. One might seriously entertain the hypothesis that boundary policing and militarization serve less their ostensible purposes than as a means for the two nation-states to impose surveillance and regulation over a regional society that has mushroomed, largely unsupervised, in recent decades. Given the distortions of immigration control systems from rational policy (the disproportionate southern border focus, voluntary departure complex, and focus on petty rather than grand law-breakers), one might also conclude that border policy does not actually aim to halt illegal immigration so much as it helps (deliberately or accidentally) to facilitate the weakening and exploitation of such labor.

If this has been the situation on the border in the post-1965 period, it possibly is changing now. The United States is gradually expanding and diversifying its legal temporary labor programs. Though derailed by the terrorist attacks of 2001, the United States and Mexico have discussed a large-scale legalization of previously illegal migration. Meanwhile, terrorist attacks have partly shifted the emphasis among U.S. borders. While the Mexican boundary still has the largest police presence and regional ports have been subject to heightened control, international airports and the Canadian border are now experiencing some of the governmental surveillance that typifies the southern border. Previously, law enforcement at airports was tough on asylum applicants but other crossers, including those likely to overstay visas or work extra-legally, were rarely halted. The new border regime includes sophisticated biometric recording and data retrieval, computer-based watch lists for terrorists, smugglers, and political enemies, and possibly a comprehensive national identity card that potentially will transform migration control from the point of entrance to any place that such a card can be reviewed. New nationalities are targeted by immigration law enforcement, including men from Islamic countries. It may be that, in control systems as in so many other trends, the U.S.-Mexico border foretells the future of all ports of entry. *See also*: **Expedited entry and removal; Human smuggling; Ports of entry; Unauthorized immigration; U.S.-Canada border; U.S.-Mexico border.**

References

Andreas, Peter. 2000. *Border Games: Policing the U.S.-Mexico Divide*. Ithaca, NY: Cornell University Press.

Andreas, Peter, and Thomas J. Biersteker, eds. 2003. *The Rebordering of North America: Integration and Exclusion in a New Security Context*. New York and London: Routledge.

Chavez, Leo R. 1992. *Shadowed Lives: Undocumented Immigrants in American Society*. Ft. Worth, TX: Harcourt, Brace, Jovanovich.

———. 2001. *Covering Immigration: Popular Images and the Politics of the Nation*. Berkeley: University of California Press.

Chishti, Muzaffar, Doris Meissner, Demetrios G. Papademetriou, Jay Peterzell, Michael Wishnie, and Stephen W. Yale-Loehr. 2003. *America's Challenge: Domestic Security, Civil Liberties, and National Unity after September 11*. Washington, DC: Migration Policy Institute.

Dunn, Timothy J. 1996. *The Militarization of the U.S.-Mexico Border, 1978–1992: Low-Intensity Conflict Doctrine Comes Home*. Austin: Center for Mexican American Studies, University of Texas at Austin.

Eschbach, Karl, Jacqueline Hagan, and Nestor Rodriguez. 1999. Death at the Border. *International Migration Review* 33:430–454.

Haines, David W., and Karen E. Rosenblum, eds. 1999. *Illegal Immigration in America: A Reference Handbook*. Westport, CT: Greenwood Press.

Heyman, Josiah McC. 1998a. *Finding a Moral Heart for U.S. Immigration Policy: An Anthropological Perspective*. Washington, DC: American Anthropological Association.

———. 1998b. State Effects on Labor Exploitation: The INS and Undocumented Immigrants at the Mexico-United States Border. *Critique of Anthropology* 18:157–180.

———. 1999. State Escalation of Force: A Vietnam/US-Mexico Border Analogy. In *States and Illegal Practices*. Josiah McC. Heyman, ed. Pp. 285–314. Oxford: Berg.

Human Rights Watch. 1991. *Brutality Unchecked: Human Rights Abuses along the U.S. Border with Mexico*. New York: Human Rights Watch.

———. 1995. *Crossing the Line: Human Rights Abuses along the U.S. Border with Mexico Persist amid Climate of Impunity*. New York: Human Rights Watch.

Kahn, Robert S. 1996. *Other People's Blood: U.S. Immigration Prisons in the Reagan Decade*. Boulder, CO: Westview Press.

Kyle, David, and Rey Koslowski, eds. 2001. *Global Human Smuggling: Comparative Perspectives*. Baltimore, MD: Johns Hopkins University Press.

Massey, Douglas S., Jorge Durand, and Nolan J. Malone. 2002. *Beyond Smoke and Mirrors: Mexican Immigration in an Era of Economic Integration*. New York: Russell Sage.

Meyers, Deborah Waller. 2005. US Border Enforcement: From Horseback to High-Tech. *Insight* 7(1):1–29.

Nevins, Joseph. 2001. *Operation Gatekeeper: The Rise of the "Illegal Alien" and the Remaking of the U.S.-Mexico Boundary*. New York: Routledge.

U.S. General Accounting Office. 2001. *INS' Southwest Border Strategy: Resource and Impact Issues Remain after Seven Years*. Washington, DC: U.S. Government Printing Office.

JOSIAH McC. HEYMAN

BORDERLANDS. The idea of the borderlands in American scholarship has traditionally focused on the regions between Florida and California, which form the divide between the United States and Mexico. Historian Herbert Eugene Bolton introduced the term in 1921 in an attempt to give form to the long-neglected Spanish contribution to American civilization, dating the concept to the time of the conquest and predating English settlements in the United States. Bannon (1974) extended his work, detailing the differences between the Spanish frontier efforts and those of the French and British, primarily the mission and assimilation components of frontier settlements. McWilliams (1968) states the difference in a slightly different way, namely, that British influence was extended by immigrants and that Spain extended its influence through subjugation and conquest. Although Bannon stops short of Mexican influence on the borderlands once independence from Spain had been achieved, he makes clear that most of the geographic influence in the Southwest occurred through Mexico. McWilliams points out that Spanish influence in the Southwest has been romanticized while the Mexican influence has been denigrated.

The cultural component of U.S.-Mexico interaction is a central theme in borderlands studies. Now, however, this is augmented by the study of the effects of trade and migration which often have their source outside the region itself, in greater movements of people and things throughout Mexico and the United States, and indeed throughout the Western Hemisphere and the world. Thus the borderlands have become a unique venue for the study of globalization on a regional scale.

At the same time, the great majority of interaction in the borderlands continues to involve the peoples of the two nation-states that share the border. The relatively close proximity of the place of origin and the ever-present reality of a single geopolitical line ground the difference between migration studies in the area and diaspora studies, the latter involving a dispersal of people over longer distances, with less direct connection to their places of origin.

The 2,000-mile border between the United States and Mexico, established in 1848, both divides and unites residents on either side. Of the 13.4 million persons of Mexican descent who lived in the United States in 1990, at least 10.9 million lived in the four U.S. states that front the border (U.S. Bureau of the Census 1993). The border population is growing rapidly. Since 1950 the population of the U.S. border states more than doubled and the population of the six Mexico border states more than tripled (Lorey 1999:118). By 2000, 78 million people lived in these 10 border states, comprising 17 percent of the population of Mexico and 22 percent of the U.S. population, and 11.5 million people lived in counties and municipalities directly along the border. Although the Hispanic population, now estimated at 35 million, is rapidly dispersing throughout the United States, it is still heavily concentrated in states that once belonged to Mexico. Many residents are recent immigrants or retain strong ties to Mexico. This concentration, coupled with historical grudges about the manner in which the United States obtained the territory and how Mexicans were treated under U.S. rule, makes the border simultaneously more concrete and more abstract.

Much of the growth of the borderlands can be attributed to migration. The northern border cities of Mexico have been a magnet for rural and urban migrants, especially since 1965 when the Border Industrialization Program (BIP) was initiated, partly in response to the end of the Bracero program in the United States. The defining feature of the BIP was the introduction of the *maquiladora* assembly plant, sometimes shortened to *maquila* or twin plant (Stoddard 1987). These assembly plants laid the foundation for the North American Free Trade Agreement (NAFTA) of 1994. The cities of Tijuana and Ciudad Juarez have the largest number of maquilas, and migration effects in those cities have been the strongest. People migrate to these cities not only for permanent residence and employment, but also as a temporary place to live before crossing into the United States. This behavior is known as step migration. The population growth on the U.S. side of the border results from higher rates of natural increase resulting from both the age structure of migrants and immigrants and fertility differentials, and to a lesser extent, domestic migration tied either to the maquila industry or to the weather.

Geography, history, and economic exigencies have converged to create a rather unusual international phenomenon of twin cities along the border. Separated by long stretches of desert in the west and more closely spaced settlements in the less arid east, about a dozen cities in the United States are paired with their "twin" counterparts on the Mexican side. The proximity of these settlements to each other and relative isolation from other urban areas has, over time, cemented the interdependence of the region and increasingly of the two nations (Kearney and Knopp 1995).

It has been said that "demographically, economically, linguistically and culturally the U.S. border area is functionally an extension of Mexico, and in a similar fashion the Mexican border zone is an extension of the . . . United States" (Martínez 1995:145). Ironically, as Mexico and Americans of Mexican descent become ever more visible in the American economic, political, and cultural landscape, controversies over the security of the border, immigration policy, and bilingual education programs have intensified. NAFTA has created more economic interdependence between the two countries, but the border is currently less porous to the movement of people and more militarized than it has ever been, on both sides. This situation sharply contrasts with the climate on our northern border and third NAFTA partner, Canada. NAFTA and the growth of maquiladoras in border cities have also exacerbated environmental problems such as air quality and water scarcity.

Despite national policies, people continue to move to and across the border, and they do not leave their culture behind. With the movement of people and things comes the movement of ideas and cultural practices. If one major component of the borderlands is migration to the area, then the qualitative description and analysis of the cultural practices of these people must be taken into account. In addition, these practices are embedded not in one nation-state, but in the space where two nation-states collide. A set of cultural practices may be seen to emerge that is neither of one nation-state nor of the other, but a mixture of the two that is unique to the borderlands and transnational in its essence. The description and evaluation of these practices have become the subject of both empirical studies of borderlands culture and an offshoot of these evaluations, border theory. The latter, border theory, is an attempt to embed the development of a specifically borderlands culture in the larger theoretical framework of post-modern theories of culture and identity. In this discourse, the emergence of borderlands culture becomes a metaphor for cultural practices throughout the world that are not in the "center" of national cultural debates but instead exist at the edges or borders of these debates (Welchman 1996).

In a widely read commentary on the nature of borderlands culture, Gloria Anzaldúa (1987) argues that the value of this culture is the ability to shift between national discourses and to create a new, unique culture out of this shifting. She uses the example of Spanglish, the mixture of Spanish and English heard often on the border, as a model for the ability of the borderlander to shift between linguistic codes, creating a new, hybrid language in the process. Rather than a vulgarization of the national tongues, Anzaldúa points to this play of two languages as proof of the cultural fecundity of the area. She posits the idea that a mixed identity is an asset rather than a liability.

The validation of code-shifting between national languages and discourses (Spanish and English, Mexican and American) is at the heart of most contemporary descriptions of borderlands culture. At the same time, other commentators have pointed out the need to ground Anzaldúa's vision with a more critical attitude toward the history of political and cultural oppression in the area (Saénz 1997). Other researchers prefer to look closely at borderlands cultural productions, which may be seen as antagonistic (Vila 2000) as well as synthetic (Gómez-Peña 1996), as an antidote to the more sweeping comments of border theorists. Martínez (1994) uses oral histories to show that people living in the borderlands develop a range of responses from peripheral isolationism from the border to transnationalism. This variability within a supposed homogeneous ethnic group points to the need for additional research.

Recently scholars from Mexico have forcefully critiqued the U.S. bias of many earlier commentators and insisted on the recognition of a Mexican viewpoint in borderlands studies (Ruiz 2000). Generally, U.S. researchers fail to acknowledge how U.S. policies and practices have influenced life on the other side, nor have they queried their Mexican colleagues in border communities. Instead they have presumed that either they themselves, being of Mexican descent, or writers from Mexico City can speak authoritatively on conditions along the northern Mexico border. *See also*: **Demography**; **Migration processes**; **U.S.-Mexico border**.

References

Anzaldúa, Gloria. 1987. *Borderlands/La Frontera: The New Mestiza*. San Francisco: Aunt Lute.

Bannon, John Francis. 1974. *The Spanish Borderlands Frontier 1513–1821*. Albuquerque: University of New Mexico.

Bolton, Herbert Eugene. 1921. *The Spanish Borderlands: A Chronicle of Old Florida and the Southwest*. New Haven, CT: Yale University Press.

Byrd, Bobby, and Susannah Mississippi Byrd, eds. 1996. *The Late Great Mexican Border: Reports from a Disappearing Line*. El Paso, TX: Cinco Puntos.

Gómez-Peña, Guillermo. 1996. *The New World Border*. San Francisco: City Lights.

Kearney, Milo, and Anthony Knopp. 1995. *Border Cuates: A History of the U.S.-Mexico Twin Cities*. Austin, TX: Eakin.

Lorey, David E. 1999. *The U.S.-Mexican Border in the Twentieth Century*. Wilmington, DE: Scholarly Resources.

Martínez, Oscar J. 1994. *Border People*. Tucson: University of Arizona.

———. 1995. *Troublesome Border*. Tucson: University of Arizona.

McWilliams, Carey. 1968. *North from Mexico: The Spanish Speaking People of the United States*. New York: Greenwood Press.

Ruiz, Ramón Eduardo. 2000. *On the Rim of Mexico: Encounters of the Rich and Poor*. Boulder, CO: Westview Press.

Saénz, Benjamin Alire. 1997. On the Borderlands of Chicano Identity, There Are Only Fragments. In *Border Theory: The Limits of Cultural Politics*. Scott Michaelson and David E. Johnson, eds. Pp. 68–96. Minneapolis: University of Minnesota Press.

Stoddard, Ellwyn R. 1987. *Maquila: Assembly Plants in Northern Mexico*. El Paso: Texas Western.

U.S. Bureau of the Census. 1993. *1990 Census of Population, Social and Economic Characteristics, United States* (CP-2-1). Washington, DC: U.S. Government Printing Office.

Vélez-Ibáñez, Carlos C. 1996. *Border Visions: Mexican Cultures of the Southwest United States*. Tucson: University of Arizona.

Vila, Pablo. 2000. *Crossing Borders, Reinforcing Borders: Social Categories, Metaphors, and Narrative Identities on the U.S.-Mexico Frontier*. Austin: University of Texas.

Welchman, John C. 1996. The Philosophical Brothel. In *Rethinking Borders*. John C. Welchman, ed. Pp. 160–186. Minneapolis: University of Minnesota Press.

CHERYL HOWARD AND REX KOONTZ

C

CHILDREN. The 2000 census makes it clear that the children of immigrants are the fastest growing population in the United States. Twenty percent of children in the United States live in a household in which at least one parent migrated from another country (Suárez-Orozco and Suárez-Orozco 2001). The largest group of immigrants, numbering about 12.8 million, identified themselves on the census as Hispanic or Latino, and 36 percent of Latinos are under the age of 18.

In most research on immigration, however, children are invisible, especially as active participants in social processes. Where children's concerns are addressed, the focus is usually on individual measures of their health, psychosocial adjustment, and educational achievement. Attention is directed more to their futures, rather than their present realities, with concern for the problems and the challenges they present to schools and society rather than on their contributions to families and communities. Research on the children of immigrants falls into three general categories: (1) sociologically guided studies of broad social trends, often gathered through survey data, interviews, or structured questionnaires; (2) psychologically informed studies of individuals' process of adaptation, acculturation, identity formation, and school achievement, generally assessed through psychosocial measures; and (3) ethnographic research by anthropologists and sociologists in particular social and cultural contexts, highlighting local processes and practices that shape children's experiences.

The large body of sociological research on immigration patterns maps adults' (and usually men's) reasons for migrating, patterns of migration, work experiences, and material realities. Feminist scholars have highlighted gendered migration pathways. Only a few researchers have used the immigrant family as a central unit of analysis (e.g., Baca Zinn 1994; Booth et al. 1997). As Loucky (2001) points out, this is ironic considering that the "locus of human decision-making" usually happens within small groups such as families.

Qvortrup (1997) notes that children's activities are generally underrepresented in statistics and social accounting not because the methods preclude a child-centered perspective, but because questions are generally asked from an adult's standpoint, with adult activities privileged over children's. Take, for example, the U.S. Census report on "The Foreign-Born Population in the United States" (2000): the statistics, ranging from geographic residence to marital status to educational attainment, primarily focus on the foreign-born population aged 18–64. Other than stating that 10 percent of the foreign-born are under 18, the report states nothing about these first-generation immigrant children.

Immigrant youth *have* been studied in relation to their own pathways of adaptation to U.S. society. Sociologists Rubén Rumbaut and Alejandro Portés have written extensively about "the new second generation," describing the national, ethnic, and social class origins of the children of immigrant parents (Rumbaut 1994; Portés 1996). They and others have mapped large-scale social patterns, especially regarding educational attainment, processes of assimilation and cultural identification, and language use and loss.

These studies on immigrant youth and education have demonstrated that there is a negative association between the length of time families have resided in the United States and their children's school achievement (Rumbaut 1996; Suárez-Orozco and Suárez-Orozco 2001). That is, children who are born in the United States to at least one immigrant parent generally have lower grade-point averages and educational aspirations than their first-generation, foreign-born peers. However, as might be expected, extended length of residence in the United States is a predictor of children's improved English language skills. Five thousand eighth- and ninth-graders surveyed by Portés and Schauffler (1996), all of whom had at least one immigrant parent, showed an overwhelming preference for and dominance of English over their home language. Wong-Fillmore (1991) argues that such language loss within a single generation can have a disastrous impact on family communication patterns.

At the same time, many children of immigrants from non-English-speaking countries, both second-generation and foreign-born, serve as translators for their families, who often depend upon their English language skills for survival and daily life in public realms (Song 1999; Valdés 2002). Their bilingual skills may also become necessary for intergenerational communication within the family. Older children of immigrants sometimes translate between younger siblings who speak mostly English and their parents and grandparents who do not; in a survey conducted with 280 children of immigrants, 65 percent reported that they translate for their mothers and 31 percent for a younger sibling (Orellana et al. 2002). Such cultural brokers or "para-phrasers" may actually remain more closely tied to their home language than do their non-translator peers, and thus develop both their English and native-language abilities more extensively.

Early psychological research on immigrant youth was concerned with "assimilation" or "acculturation." Most of this work assumed models of cultural loss, conflict, and replacement. Other researchers have called for biculturation models, which assume additive, multidimensional frames, rather than subtractive, unidirectional ones. Portés (1996) and colleagues have extended this prior research by defining "segmented assimilation." They theorize that new immigrants no longer follow the pathways taken by earlier European migrants, who often adapted into middle-class circumstances by the second or third generation. Instead, some immigrants, including youth, are being assimilated into the urban poor. For example, Suárez-Orozco and Suárez-Orozco (2001) point out that many Latino youth have become part of black urban culture. They suggest three styles of adaptation that youth may employ as they develop a sense of self in cultures where patterned inequality shapes social interactions: "ethnic flight," in which children identify with the mainstream culture; "adversarial stance," in which they develop underground or rebellious identities; and "transcultural identity," in which children fuse aspects both of their parents' culture and traditions and of their new home.

Psychologists who study immigrant youths' processes of adjustment and identity formation certainly recognize the shaping effects of such social forces as the stressors of migration (Ahearn and Athey 1991), changes in family composition and family reunification processes (Rodriguez 1973), and shifting gender and generational roles. Suárez-Orozco and Suárez-Orozco, for example, have noted the gender and generational "role dissonance" that may result when families undergo rapid cultural changes in the process of immigration. They refer to the "Faustian bargain" that immigrant parents make: "although many immigrant parents are motivated by a desire for a better future for their children, the very process of immigration tends to undermine parental authority and family cohesion" (2001:6). As suggested by a number of researchers, when parents depend on their children to speak for them in an English-speaking world, this dependency or "role reversal" may help to undermine parental authority. Alternatively, because immigrants may operate with a cultural model that assumes children should contribute their skills to the good of the household, such acts may help to unite the family and operate against disintegrative forces.

Finally, we must not forget that children themselves actively engage in their own development. Loucky (2001) asked the immigrant children of Q'anjob'al Mayans living in Los Angeles, "What do you want to be when you grow up?" They responded with "stereotypical American answers"; for instance, 17 wanted to be teachers, 9 doctors, 8 police officers, and 3 fire fighters. They did not want to return to Guatemala, except for visits, and few wanted to continue speaking the Mayan language. Such personal desires likely influence the developmental pathways taken by these children, as well as their families' settlement processes.

Until the 1960s, few anthropologists studied immigrant communities in the United States; their focus instead was on studying cultural "others" in non-Western societies. This changed in the last quarter of the twentieth century, as some anthropologists joined sociologists in conducting ethnographic research on particular cultural subgroups within the United States, most notably Chicano and Mexican American communities. Since the 1980s some anthropologists have joined literary critics and cultural studies theorists to reframe the study of immigrant community experiences within the context of national debates concerning multiculturalism and identity politics. Other ethnographic projects took a political economic approach to immigrant community experiences to address how immigrant groups are structured along race and class lines of difference.

However, in all of these areas of study, as in anthropology in general, children's activities were largely overlooked. Immigrant youth do appear in language socialization studies (Zentella 1997) and in studies of education or school-like contexts (Delgado-Gaitan and Trueba 1991; Valdés 1996), but usually as the objects of adult socialization efforts. And when young people's actions and activities are given center stage, it is often as members of "deviant" or "gang like" subcultures (Moje 2000).

Other anthropological and sociological work is focused on border crossings, demonstrating that transnational practices have become a habitual part of life for some immigrant groups. Such practices and "transnational social fields" (Basch et al. 1994) have placed adults' economic, labor, and political transactions at the forefront, but a growing body of research highlights children within these social fields (Soto 1987; Olwig 1999; Orellana et al. 2001). Research has demonstrated that children may encourage or aid in the settlement process of immigrant families. Youth who are left behind, or sent ahead, may play an important role in facilitating connections between the old and new homelands. Families' lives are often defined by "here" and "there"; parents sometimes warn children they will send them "back home" for disciplinary purposes, while children may recognize their differing citizenship rights and threaten to use such U.S. practices as calling "911."

Continued exploration of immigrant youths' experiences will need to go beyond defining children as *future* citizens by measures of their health, psychosocial adjustment, and educational achievement. Research must also focus on their *present realities* and how they contribute to families and communities as they move from one homeland to another. *See also*: **Assimilation; Transnationalism.**

References

Ahearn, F.L., and J.L. Athey, eds. 1991. *Refugee Children: Theory, Research, and Services*. Baltimore, MD: Johns Hopkins University Press.

Baca Zinn, M. 1994. Adaptation and Continuity in Mexican-Origin Families. In *Minority Families in the United States*. R.L. Taylor, ed. Pp. 64–81. Englewood Cliffs, NJ: Prentice-Hall.

Basch, L., N. Glick Schiller, and C. Szanton Blanc. 1994. *Nations Unbound: Transnational Projects, Postcolonial Predicaments, and Deterritorialized Nation-States*. Amsterdam: Gordon and Breach.

Booth, A., A.C. Crouter, and N. Landale, eds. 1997. *Immigration and the Family: Research and Policy on U.S. Immigrants*. Mahwah, NJ: Lawrence Erlbaum.

Delgado-Gaitan, C., and H. Trueba. 1991. *Crossing Cultural Borders: Education for Immigrant Families in America*. New York: Falmer Press.

Loucky, James. 2001. Child and Family Well-Being in Settlement Decisions of Guatemalan Maya Women in Los Angeles. In *Negotiated Transnationalism*. Marycarol Hopkins and Nancy Wellmeier, eds. Pp. 182–201. Arlington, VA: American Anthropological Association.

Moje, E. 2000. To Be Part of the Story: The Literacy Practices of Gangsta Adolescents. *Teachers College Record* 102:651–690.

Olwig, K.F. 1999. Narratives of the Children Left Behind: Home and Identity in Globalised Caribbean Families. *Journal of Ethnic and Migration Studies* 25:267–284.

Orellana, M.F., J. Reynolds, L. Dorner, and M. Meza. 2002. In Other Words: Translating or "Para-Phrasing" as a Family Literacy Practice in Immigrant Households. *Reading Research Quarterly* 38(1):12–34.

Orellana, M.F., B. Thorne, A. Chee, and W.S.E. Lam. 2001. Transnational Childhoods: The Participation of Children in Processes of Family Migration. *Social Problems* 48:572–591.

Portés, A., ed. 1996. *The New Second Generation*. New York: Russell Sage.

Portés, A., and R. Schauffler. 1996. Language and the Second Generation: Bilingualism Yesterday and Today. In *The New Second Generation*. A. Portés, ed. Pp. 8–29. New York: Russell Sage.

Qvortrup, J. 1997. A Voice for Children in Statistical and Social Accounting: A Plea for Children's Right to Be Heard. In *Constructing and Reconstructing Childhood*. A. James and A. Prout, eds. Pp. 85–102. London: Falmer Press.

Rodriguez, R. 1973. Difficulties of Adjustment in Immigrant Children in Geneva. In *Uprooting and After*. C. Zwingmann and N. Pfister-Ammende, eds. Pp. 134–141. New York: Springer-Verlag.

Rumbaut, R.G. 1994. Origins and Destinies: Immigration to the United States Since World War II. *Sociological Forum* 9:583–621.

———. 1996. The Crucible Within: Ethnic Identity, Self-Esteem, and Segmented Assimilation Among Children of Immigrants. In *The New Second Generation*. A. Portés, ed. Pp. 119–170. New York: Russell Sage.

Song, M. 1999. *Helping Out: Children's Labor in Ethnic Business*. Philadelphia: Temple University Press.

Soto, I.S. 1987. West Indian Child Fostering: Its Role in Migrant Exchanges. In *Caribbean Life in New York City*. C.R. Sutton and E.M. Chaney, eds. Pp. 131–149. New York: Center for Migration Studies.

Suárez-Orozco, C., and M.M. Suárez-Orozco. 2001. *Children of Immigration*. Cambridge, MA: Harvard University Press.

U.S. Census Bureau. 2000. *The Foreign-Born Population in the United States*. Washington, DC: U.S. Department of Commerce, Economics and Statistics Administration.

Valdés, G. 1996. *Con Respeto: Bridging the Distances Between Culturally Diverse Families and School: An Ethnographic Portrait*. New York: Teachers College Press.

———. 2002. *Expanding Definitions of Giftedness: The Case of Young Interpreters from Immigrant Countries*. Mahwah, NJ: Lawrence Erlbaum.

Wong-Fillmore, L. 1991. When Learning a Second Language Means Losing Your First. *Early Childhood Research Quarterly* 6:323–346.

Zentella, A.C. 1997. *Growing Up Bilingual*. Malden, MA: Blackwell.

MARJORIE FAULSTICH ORELLANA, LISA M. DORNER,
AND JENNIFER F. REYNOLDS

CITIZENSHIP. In the liberal political tradition, citizenship is generally understood to connote full membership in a particular state and the specific rights, privileges, and duties entailed by state membership (Marshall 1992). Accordingly, U.S. citizenship law specifies the rules for the acquisition and loss of U.S. citizenship, as well as the rights, privileges, and duties of citizens and resident aliens. Since its inception, U.S. citizenship law gradually has been liberalized to extend citizenship to expanding categories of individuals. In recent years, public discussions about citizenship have proliferated, partly in response to this liberalization. Questions have been raised about the legitimacy of granting birthright citizenship to the children of undocumented immigrants and the integrity of the naturalization process. Debate remains contentious, particularly following Congress's 1996 decision to bar documented resident aliens from participating in most federal social welfare programs.

Acquisition of Birthright Citizenship

Individuals can acquire U.S. citizenship as a condition of birth or through the process of naturalization. The primary rule for the acquisition of citizenship by birth is jus soli (or right of soil), according to which citizenship is automatically conferred upon persons born within the territorial United States. Although the U.S. Constitution originally made no direct reference to jus soli, early Supreme Court decisions suggest that the principle was a part of the common law inherited from England (Aleinikoff 1998). For instance, the Supreme Court ruled in 1904 that "a person born in the territory of the United States who remained there after the war of independence was a U.S. citizen until such person expatriated himself" (Levy 2002:11). These decisions would seem to grant citizenship to all U.S.-born residents; however, the 1856 Dred Scott ruling excluded runaway slaves and free blacks from jus soli citizenship. The Citizenship Clause of the Fourteenth Amendment later remedied this discriminatory definition of citizenship by mandating that "all persons born . . . in the United States and subject of the jurisdiction thereof, are citizens of the United States and of the State wherein they reside" (Levy 2002:11–12).

The Citizenship Clause has long been understood as conferring citizenship upon all persons born on U.S. soil, including the children of resident aliens and temporary visitors. Current exceptions to the jus soli rule are few: birth to foreign diplomats and invading troops, and birth on a foreign public vessel. However, this inclusive interpretation of jus soli citizenship has been challenged on both theoretical and practical grounds. Critics argue that judicial precedent fails to support the application of jus soli citizenship to the children of undocumented aliens and temporary visitors, and that liberal political ideals weigh against such application (Schuck and Smith 1985:92–103). Moreover, they argue, full application of the jus soli principle provides an incentive for undocumented immigration and requires significant and avoidable expenditures of public resources in the form of education, medical care, and other social welfare benefits. These challenges have been criticized on the grounds that they contradict earlier judicial interpretations of the jus soli principle. Further, it is frequently argued that denying jus soli citizenship to the U.S.-born children of undocumented aliens would create a permanent subclass of resident aliens who are vulnerable to exploitation and mistreatment (Shulman 1995:720–721).

U.S. citizenship law also includes a second rule for the automatic acquisition of citizenship by birth. The jus sanguinis (or right of blood) principle confers citizenship upon children born abroad to parents, either one or both of whom are U.S. citizens. Congress has had discretion over jus sanguinis rules since they were first enacted in 1790. From the beginning, Congress sought to prevent transmission of jus sanguinis citizenship to expatriate generations who have no close contact with life in the United States. Thus, the first statute concerning jus sanguinis citizenship required at least one parent under whom citizenship is claimed to reside in the United States before the birth of the child. Beginning in 1934, Congress also required that children born abroad to one citizen and one alien parent reside in the United States for a specified number of years in order to retain their citizenship. The residency requirement on children was dropped in 1978. The parental residency requirement remains in effect, but the required lengths of residence were reduced by Congress in 1986. Under the current statute, if both parents are U.S. citizens, the child automatically acquires citizenship, provided that one of the parents resided in the United States at some point prior to the birth of the child; if one parent is an alien, then the citizen parent must have resided in the United States for a total of five years before the child's birth, including at least two years after the age of 14 (Aleinikoff et al. 1998a:25–27).

Congress consistently relaxed the requirements for the transmission of jus sanguinis citizenship during the twentieth century. Despite this liberalization, the jus sanguinis rules have been the subject of little controversy since 1934, when Congress eliminated the gender-based rule that allowed only U.S. citizen fathers (and not mothers) to transmit jus sanguinis citizenship (Aleinikoff et al. 1998a:14).

Naturalized Citizenship

The U.S. Constitution grants Congress control over the rules for naturalization, the process by which resident aliens acquire citizenship. Although U.S. naturalization law is currently among the most inclusive in the world, it has been characterized by racial, ethnic, and gender-based exclusions throughout most of its history. The original naturalization statute, enacted in 1790, explicitly restricted naturalization to "free white persons" (Aleinikoff et al. 1998a:15). The statute also implicitly excluded women from independent citizenship, as their citizenship was predicated on the citizenship of their husbands (DeSipio and de la Garza 1998:68). Congress extended naturalization eligibility to "persons of African nativity, . . . and descent" in the wake of the Civil War; however, the 1882 Chinese Exclusion Act, which prohibited the naturalization of Chinese nationals, initiated another 70 years of racial and ethnic exclusions (Aleinikoff et al. 1998a:15). The Cable Act of 1922 established the right of most married women to apply for naturalization on their own behalf, but the final overtly discriminatory aspects of U.S. naturalization law were not eliminated until the Immigration and Nationality Act of 1952 explicitly prohibited the use of race, national origin, and gender as criteria for determining naturalization eligibility (Aleinikoff et al. 1998b:48–49; Levy 2002:634).

For those persons eligible to apply for naturalization, the substantive requirements were fairly liberal, and they remain so today (Aleinikoff et al. 1998a:15). At present, in order to naturalize, a resident alien must meet certain threshold requirements: permanent resident status; five years of lawful residence in the United States; the ability to speak, read, and understand English; adherence to constitutional principles; knowledge of the fundamentals of U.S. government and history; "good moral character"; and a willingness to take an oath of allegiance to the United States (the oath suffices even if it does not effectively terminate the applicant's prior citizenship under the laws of the foreign state) (Levy 2002: 267–366). Although most naturalizations take place under these provisions, certain requirements are relaxed for special classes of applicants, including the spouses and children of American citizens, U.S. military personnel, and older and disabled persons (Aleinikoff et al. 1998a:15; Levy 2002:633). Other classes of resident aliens are automatically ineligible for naturalization based on their beliefs: communists, fascists, anarchists, and advocates of the forceful overthrow of the U.S. government. Also disqualified from naturalization are U.S. military deserters and aliens who have sought relief or have been relieved from U.S. military service on the grounds of alienage (Levy 2002:473–485). Naturalized citizens have the same basic legal rights and obligations as birthright citizens, except that they are ineligible for the presidency.

The 1990s witnessed a substantial increase in petitions for naturalization, nearly fourfold between 1992 and 1996 alone (Aleinikoff et al. 1998b:57), prompting national debate concerning the requirements, and ultimately the purpose, of the naturalization process. Some commentators expressed concern that the naturalization process fails to ensure that new citizens are sufficiently knowledgeable about and committed to the preservation of U.S. social and political culture. In a 1997 report to Congress, the U.S. Commission on Immigration Reform encouraged federal, state, and local governments to promote the "Americanization" of new immigrants by establishing orientation and educational programs to help recent immigrants to learn English and to develop shared commitment to the American values of liberty, democracy, and equal opportunity. The commission also recommended that the U.S. history, civics, and English portions of the naturalization examination be revised so as to more accurately measure applicants' knowledge and ability to communicate in English. This prompted a broad critique and cautions against the adoption of unduly restrictive naturalization requirements, such as literacy tests, that have functioned historically to exclude certain ethnic and racial groups from citizenship (Perea 1998:68).

Loss of U.S. Citizenship

The most common way that U.S. citizenship is lost is through expatriation, the voluntary relinquishment of citizenship. The law was unclear until Congress enacted legislation in 1868 explicitly guaranteeing the right of expatriation to all U.S. citizens (Aleinikoff et al. 1998a:21). It was not until the enactment of the 1907 Expatriate Act, however, that Congress set out the conditions under which U.S. citizens would be considered to have expatriated themselves (Levy 2002:873). The Supreme Court maintained, in its 1967 ruling in *Afroyim v. Rusk*, that the Fourteenth Amendment establishes a constitutional right to remain a citizen unless one voluntarily relinquishes that right. The Court's decision is currently reflected in the expatriation section of the Immigration and Nationality Act, which stipulates that expatriation is binding only if the expatriating acts are performed with the intention of relinquishing citizenship (Levy 2002:871–872). Citizenship may also be lost through denaturalization, which is the revocation of naturalized citizenship that was illegally or fraudulently obtained (Aleinikoff et al. 1998a:22). Citizenship is rarely terminated without consent, however. Some of its privileges can be unilaterally revoked under certain circumstances; for instance, both birthright and naturalized citizens lose their right to vote upon being convicted of a felony.

Rights, Privileges, and Obligations of U.S. Citizens and Resident Aliens

Resident aliens of the United States have most of the same obligations to the state as U.S. citizens. They must obey the same criminal and civil law as citizens, and documented resident aliens must pay taxes and register for the selective service if otherwise eligible. Some of the legal rights and privileges granted to citizens, however, are denied to resident aliens. These excluded rights and privileges fit broadly into three categories: political, occupational, and social welfare

(DeSipio and de la Garza 1998:95–103). All resident aliens—both documented and undocumented—are ineligible to vote in federal, state, and most local elections, to serve on federal and most state juries, and to run for certain high elective offices. Although documented aliens enjoy extensive employment privileges in the private sector, they are ineligible for most federal and many state civil service jobs, including police and fire protection and public school instruction. They are also ineligible for certain desirable professional licenses (e.g., medical and dental licenses) and for jobs requiring security clearances in many states. Undocumented aliens are altogether legally prohibited from obtaining employment in the United States. To discourage U.S. employers from violating this provision (and ultimately, to discourage undocumented immigration by removing the incentive of employment) the 1986 Immigration Reform and Control Act established employer sanctions to penalize employers who hire undocumented workers.

Undocumented aliens have long been barred from participating in most major social welfare programs, with the exception of emergency medical and disaster relief programs and public education. Documented resident aliens, on the other hand, were eligible for nearly all of the social services available to citizens until recently, when the Personal Responsibility and Work Reconciliation Act of 1996 (1996 Welfare Act) severely diminished their social welfare rights. With the exception of refugees, asylees, and U.S. veterans and soldiers, documented aliens who entered the United States after the enactment of this legislation are ineligible for virtually all federal means-tested programs for their first five years in the United States and are subject to state determinations of eligibility for most welfare programs, such as Temporary Aid to Needy Families (Acevedo-Garcia et al. 1997).

While some applauded the exclusion of documented aliens from eligibility for social welfare benefits as a justified way to reduce the cost of public assistance programs (Aleinikoff et al. 1998a:46), others have expressed humanitarian concerns about the way these changes have impacted the lives of individual immigrants. Feminists charge that the social costs of this legislation are borne disproportionately by poor female immigrants and their children (Fitzpatrick 1997:37–43). Critics also argue that if naturalization is the only way to gain access to social welfare benefits, immigrants will become citizens for purely instrumental as opposed to ideological reasons, such as an affinity with American values (DeSipio and de la Garza 1998:87). *See also*: **Dual citizenship; Employer sanctions; Jus soli; Legislation; Unauthorized immigration.**

References

Acevedo-Garcia, Dolores, Robin Omata, Deborah Ringel, Sharon Carothers, Christine Lee, and Amy Westpfahl. 1997. *Impact of the Federal Welfare Reform on Immigrants*. Washington, DC: U.S. Commission on Immigration Reform.

Aleinikoff, T. Alexander. 1998. *Between Principles and Politics: The Direction of U.S. Citizenship Policy*. Washington, DC: Carnegie Endowment for International Peace.

Aleinikoff, T. Alexander, David Martin, and Hiroshi Motomura, eds. 1998a. *Immigration and Citizenship: Process and Policy*, 4th ed. St. Paul, MN: West.

———. 1998b. *Immigration and Nationality Laws of the United States: Selected Statutes, Regulations and Forms*. St. Paul, MN: West.

DeSipio, Louis, and Rodolfo de la Garza. 1998. *Making Americans, Remaking America: Immigration and Immigrant Policy*. Boulder, CO: Westview Press.

Fitzpatrick, Joan. 1997. The Gender Dimension of U.S. Immigration Policy. *Yale Journal of Law and Feminism* 9(23):23–49.

LeMay, Michael, and Elliott Robert Barkan, eds. 1999. *U.S. Immigration and Naturalization Laws and Issues: A Document History*. Westport, CT: Greenwood Press.

Levy, Daniel. 2002. *U.S. Citizenship and Naturalization Handbook*. St. Paul, MN: West.

Marshall, T.H. 1992. Citizenship and Social Class. In *Citizenship and Social Class*. T.H. Marshall and T. Bottomore, eds. Pp. 3–51. London: Pluto Press.

Perea, Juan. 1998. Am I an American or Not? Reflections on Citizenship, Americanization, and Race. In *Immigration and Citizenship in the 21st Century*. Noah Pickus, ed. Pp. 49–75. Lanham, MD: Rowman and Littlefield.

Schuck, Peter, and Rogers Smith. 1985. *Citizenship without Consent: Illegal Aliens in the U.S. Polity*. New Haven, CT: Yale University Press.

Shulman, R. 1995. Children of a Lesser God: Should the Fourteenth Amendment Be Altered or Repealed to Deny Automatic Citizenship Rights and Privileges to American Children Born of Illegal Aliens? *Pepperdine Law Review* 22(2):669–725.

U.S. Commission on Immigration Reform. 1997. *Becoming an American: Immigration and Immigrant Policy*. Washington, DC: U.S. Government Printing Office.

SHELLEY WILCOX

CRIME. As the volume and composition of immigrants coming to the United States have changed, particularly since passage of the 1965 amendments to the Immigration and Nationality Act, the impact of immigration on American host society has been hotly debated. One of the most contentious issues in the debate is the effect of immigration on crime. The fear that immigrants contribute to high levels of crime is not new, but it has been a recurrent theme in American history. In the middle of the nineteenth century, nativist groups (e.g., the Know Nothings Party) that wanted restrictions on immigration argued that immigrants comprised an unusually high percentage of criminals and that they placed a burden on soup kitchens and other charitable organizations. Yet most of the alleged crimes ostensibly committed by immigrants were minor infractions, including public drunkenness (Haggan and Palloni 1998).

Although historically there has been some perception that immigrants contribute to crime, the debates or polemics took on added significance following the 1965 amendments to the Immigration and Nationality Act for two main reasons. First, a significant shift occurred in countries of origin. In most of America's history, immigrants had come primarily from Europe, especially northwestern Europe. These were more like white Americans, the dominant group, and it was presumed that since their human capital characteristics were generally high, they would not engage in street crimes. With changes in immigration laws after 1965, new entrants have been primarily from third world countries, with Latin American and Asian countries sending the bulk of immigrants. As national origins have shifted from Europe to less developed countries, mainly in Asia and Latin America, so too has the proportion of the population born outside the United States. In 2000, 10.2 percent of the U.S. population was foreign-born, up from 7.9 in 1990 (Bureau of Citizenship and Immigration Services 2004). There have been fears that these new immigrants, coming especially after the collapse of U.S.-sponsored regimes in Indochina, are not of high quality in terms of such human capital characteristics as education, occupation, and English proficiency. Without these, it is feared that the newcomers are not able to contribute much to

American prosperity and might become a burden on taxpayers. One consequence of this may well be crime.

A second and perhaps more sinister (but largely unspoken) reason for the heated debate about immigration and crime is the enduring legacy of racism in American culture. Whereas prior to 1965 most entrants were white, a considerable number of post-1965 immigrants are non-white. The latter are believed by some to be less easily assimilable and in some cases more inclined to speak languages other than English. There are concerns that if present trends continue, the United States might not remain a predominantly white country in the not-too-distant future.

Furthermore, there is an association of criminality with those who enter the United States without authorization. The U.S. Bureau of Citizenship and Immigration Services (BCIS) excludes from the definition of legal immigrant those individuals who enter the country without inspection at a U.S. consulate abroad or border crossings (illegal aliens), or those who enter legally (as non-immigrants) but stay beyond their allowed time (visa-overstayers). The perception held by many is that people who have already "broken the law" through such entry or overstaying are prone to do so again.

The controversies surrounding the immigration-crime relationship became even more potent and politically charged in the aftermath of the attacks on New York and Washington, D.C. in September 2001. Since the men who slammed passenger aircraft into the World Trade Center and the Pentagon were all foreigners, some have argued that this is proof that immigration causes crime, this time in the form of terrorism. Indeed, so frightened were politicians and the general public that immediately following the attacks, the U.S. Congress passed the now controversial USA Patriot Act.

An investigation of empirical evidence in the immigration-crime debate is imperative for various reasons. First, in American history, politicians have tended to overreact whenever the nation has been attacked or faced major challenges. As early as 1798, for example, Congress passed the Alien and Sedition Acts. These were actually three pieces of legislation passed in one session of the Congress. Two of them (the Aliens Act and the Enemy Alien Act) were aimed at "criminal" (potential terrorist) immigrants. During the undeclared war with France (a war fought entirely at sea) it was felt that some immigrants could not be trusted and that they were coming into the United States in order to aid the enemy. Consequently Congress empowered the president to imprison or deport out of the country any alien whom the president deemed dangerous to the peace and safety of the United States.

Following U.S. entry into World War I in 1917, animosity was directed at German immigrants, some of whom were thought to be enemy aliens or otherwise sympathetic to Kaiser Wilhelm II and his regime. A considerable number of Japanese immigrants (and even American citizens of Japanese ancestry) were forcibly removed from their homes and placed in detention centers following the Japanese attack on Pearl Harbor (Hawaii) in 1941. The internment of Japanese Americans for the duration of the war from 1942 was approved and ordered by President Roosevelt.

A second reason why obtaining empirical evidence in the immigration-crime debate is imperative is that frequently government overreaction to threats or perceived threats deemed to be stemming from immigrants (or abroad) leads to violation of civil liberties. In the aftermath of the September 11, 2001 attacks, but especially during the 9-11 Commission hearings, public officials (including Attorney General Ashcroft) called for the establishment of a domestic intelligence (spy) agency.

A third reason to focus on empirical evidence in the immigration-crime debate is closely related with the preceding second reason. Racial and ethnic profiling have been enduring practices in recent American history, but in the post–September 11 atmosphere, it is feared that profiling will become even more prevalent.

Most of the existing research on crime and immigration in the United States is based on information derived from persons in prison. One of the earliest works in this regard was that of the 1931 National Commission on Law Observance and Enforcement. The Wickersham Commission, as it was popularly known, studied arrest, conviction, and imprisonment statistics from 52 cities and reported that immigrants committed fewer major offenses, in proportion to their numbers, than did native-born persons. The commission observed that only in homicide arrest rates did the foreign-born approximate those of native-born Americans. The commission found that arrest rates for immigrants were much lower than those of native-born Americans.

Some researchers in the first half of the twentieth century advanced the view that in the process of international migration, immigrants transplant into the United States the types of crime and crime levels prevalent in their countries of origin. It was argued that due to cultural differences among nations, certain types of crime and delinquency might be expected among immigrants because behavior considered illegal in the United States might be considered normal in other countries (Sellin 1938).

In the period after 1965, one question that constantly emerges is whether crime is transmitted culturally in the process of immigration. A related question is whether or not there are criminal specializations based on national origin. Much of the research on these questions has not been based on empirical evidence, but often on innuendos and unsubstantiated allegations. Anti-immigration writers such as Tanton and Lutton (1993:217–218) describe "foreign crime syndicates" that are allegedly targeting the United States. They refer to "crime bosses in such places as Colombia, Mexico, Nigeria, South Korea, Japan, and Hong Kong viewing the U.S. as an especially inviting 'land of opportunity.'" Without providing empirical evidence, these authors claim that there exist in the United States criminal specializations on the basis of national origin. According to them, Colombians specialize in cocaine; Mexicans in marijuana, human smuggling, and auto theft; Nigerians in heroin, student-loan fraud, and credit-card fraud; Chinese in heroin and human smuggling; South Koreans in prostitution; Russians in drugs and insurance fraud; and Jamaicans in cocaine.

In a case study of South Korean immigrants and crime, Pogrebin and Poole (1989) argued that first-generation immigrants tend to show patterns of criminal involvement that were predominant in their countries of origin. They suggested that new immigrants import their own particular vices to the United States. These include gambling, prostitution, narcotics, and extortion. According to them, new immigrants perceive illegal markets as an opportunity structure within which they function to respond to demands for illegal goods and services.

There has been some interest in whether there is a link between immigration peaks and crime. The main finding is that decreases in crime rates have coincided with massive increases in immigration, and therefore, immigration per se does not cause crime. For instance, research by Butcher and Piehl (1998) using data from crime reports and the Current Population Surveys concludes that an influx of recent immigrants into a community had no association with local crime rates.

Immigration declined remarkably between 1930 and 1970. During this period, crime rates rose dramatically. Immigration has also been increasing since 1970, but it could hardly be argued that it was immigration that brought about elevations in the crime rates, for two reasons. First, crime rates were already on an upward swing when immigration began increasing after 1970. Second, since 1990 crime rates have been on a steady decline even though immigration has remained on an upward trend.

Some research has also been done on whether illegal immigration causes crime. Haggan and Palloni (1998:379) assessed the impact of illegal immigration and non-U.S. citizenship on arrest rates in 34 Metropolitan Statistical Areas in five southwestern states (Arizona, California, Colorado, New Mexico, and Texas). Their dependent variables were violent arrests, property arrests, and total arrests, all of which were log transformed. After doing regression analysis, they reported that illegal immigration had no significant effect on arrest rates, and proportionately non-citizens significantly influenced only property crimes. The authors concluded that there was no consistent or compelling evidence that immigration caused crime.

Researchers have studied the immigration-crime relationship using incarceration (prison) data as well as information in the FBI's Uniform Crime Reports. Despite shortcomings, the incarceration rate is a reliable measure of crime in the sense that those who end up in prison have usually been arrested, indicted, tried, and found guilty. Moreover, with the "war on drugs" declared over and over in the 1980s and an ever-skyrocketing prison population after 1980, if immigrants contributed to high crime rates, there should be an exceptionally high immigrant population in prison. After all, native-born citizens are arrested and imprisoned at a higher rate (2:1) than immigrants for all offenses except drug-related crimes, where immigrants outnumber natives by 2 to 1. Yet study after study employing incarceration data has found that the native-born are significantly more likely to be incarcerated than immigrants. In summary, empirical research contradicts in a radical fashion the popularly held belief that immigration contributes to street crime. There is no evidence for blaming high crime rates in the United States on immigrants or current immigration policy. *See also*: **Legislation; National security; Unauthorized immigration.**

References

Bureau of Immigration and Citizenship Services. 2004. *Immigrants Admitted to the United States, 2004*. Washington, DC: Department of Homeland Security.

Butcher, K.F., and A.M. Piehl. 1998. Cross-City Evidence on the Relationship between Immigration and Crime. *Journal of Policy Analysis and Management* 17:1–37.

Cole, D. 2002. Enemy Aliens. *Stanford Law Review* 54:953–965.

Haggan, J., and A. Palloni. 1998. Immigration and Crime in the United States. In *The Immigration Debate: Studies on the Economic, Demographic, and Fiscal Effects of*

Immigration. J.P. Smith and B. Edmonston, eds. Pp. 367–387. Washington, DC: National Academy Press.

Pogrebin, M.R., and E.D. Poole. 1989. South Korean Immigrants and Crime: A Case Study. *Journal of Politics* 17:47–79.

Sellin, T. 1938. *Culture Conflict and Crime*. New York: Social Science Research Council.

Sutherland, E.H., and D.R. Cressey. 1960. *Principles of Criminology*, 6th ed. New York: Lippincott.

Tanton, J., and W. Lutton. 1993. Immigration and Criminality in the U.S.A. *Journal of Social, Political and Economic Studies* 18:217–235.

Taylor, P. 1971. *The Distant Magnate*. London: Eyre and Spottiswoode.

U.S. Bureau of the Census. 1999. Profile of the Foreign Born Population of the United States: 1997. *Current Population Reports Special Studies* P23–195. Washington, DC: U.S. Department of Commerce.

Vigil, J.D. 2002. *A Rainbow of Gangs: Street Cultures in Mega-City*. Austin: University of Texas Press.

AUGUSTINE J. KPOSOWA

D

DEMOGRAPHY. Demography entails study of changes in the size, composition, and spatial distribution of human populations (Siegel and Swanson 2004), and is therefore a vital dimension of immigration. Demographic information informs business, service providers, and planners, and includes who is native versus foreign-born and proportions as well as proportions in different classes, ethnicities, religions, ages, literacy levels, and marital status. Demographers also determine numbers and territorial distributions, although this information is complicated by changes in composition and social mobility of populations. National censuses, registration records of vital events (such as births, deaths, marriages, and divorces, as well as migration), and sample surveys of specially selected populations, studied in more detail relative to particular issues, are the primary sources of information.

The initial push to record births, deaths, and population movement reflected an interest in social relationships such as who inherits, and was also in response to concerns about disease spread and its impact (Weeks 2001). John Graunt, the first to try to understand population growth, focused on migration of people from rural areas to London and also noted that deaths exceeded births in London in 1662. At the same time census taking was taking place in the colonies and was institutionalized by the fledgling United States in 1790, to occur every 10 years so the House of Representatives would accurately reflect population size and distribution. U.S. marshals counted people for the first century, followed by hired census agents beginning in 1880, and by 1902 the Census Bureau became a permanent part of the government.

Census queries focus on demographic and housing information, but additional questions can be added reflecting contemporary concerns. A continuing challenge is to determine whether to count individuals who are in a given territory on a given day (de facto population) or only those who have a legal right to be there (de jure population). The United States compromises with a count based on "usual" residence or where a person sleeps. Much controversy accompanied Census 2000 when it shifted from a single choice for racial or ethnic category to multiple choices for people of mixed ancestry, and also because statistically weightings were included to attempt to more accurately count more "hidden" populations such as homeless and transients, as well as undocumented immigrants who might be understandably reluctant to be interviewed on account of their status.

Demography is usually characterized in terms of three processes: mortality, fertility, and migration. Mortality is a significant indicator of the health of a population, and mortality rates (measured through crude death rate, infant mortality, and age-specific mortality rates) are likely increasing with the aging of world populations and spread of emerging diseases such as HIV (Siegel and Swanson 2004). Mortality and migration can be examined from several perspectives. There is risk of death during migration itself, and undocumented migration is particularly dangerous. Border enforcement intensified in urban areas along the southern U.S. border during 1993–1997, forcing migrants to more remote rural crossing areas and leading to perhaps at least 1,600 deaths from drowning, hypothermia, and dehydration (Eschbach et al. 1999). Even when relocated, migrants may still experience better or poorer health and associated rates of mortality during the adjustment process. Immigrants may endure long workdays and hazardous working conditions, gang activity and street crime in urban areas, and accumulating pressures of adjustment, expectations of generating remittances to send home, and insecurities associated with jobs and legal status. Thus environmental circumstances and lifestyles play a role in migrant health even after the move.

High fertility associated with low mortality is considered responsible for the population "explosion" that is widely perceived as the cause of many contemporary social problems. Immigrants are particularly singled out in public concern over how to control high fertility rates as well as the migrations that often follow economic shifts or population expansion abroad.

The third major demographic process, migration itself, strongly determines the number and distribution of populations, especially when movements are large as a result of volatile economic or social conditions. Demographers differentiate migration as being international (relocation between countries) or internal (moves within a country). International migration has received more research, media, and government attention, mostly from the perspective of peoples as immigrants to a receiving country rather than as emigrants from a country of origin. Measures of migration include crude net migration rate (CNMR, total immigrants – outmigrants × 1000 ÷ total midyear population) and migration ratio (MR, net migration × 1000 ÷ births – deaths).

Before World War I there were few restrictions on immigration to the United States. Mortality rates declined in Europe during the late 1800s and population growth coupled with poor wages and few jobs at home pushed folk to growing economies and temperate zones like the United States (Weeks 2001). While the Great Depression, more restrictive immigration laws, and World War II slowed migration dramatically during the 1930s and 1940s, immigration from Europe rose again after World War II, with subsequent replacement in recent decades by significant numbers of Latin Americans, especially Mexicans, and Asians, particularly from the Philippines, China, and India. Migration out of the United States is hard to track but most is due to either return migration after disillusionment or migrants who retire back to the country of origin.

Internal migration, migration within the United States, is a frequent occurrence (Weeks 2001). According to the Census Bureau, in 2000, about 16 percent of the population aged 1 year or older (43 million Americans) lived in a different house than the year before, and 17 million of those individuals crossed county lines, making them officially migrants. Historically, migration was toward industrial centers in the northeastern, north central, and midwestern states along with a largely westward push. The "Great Migration" occurred after 1910 as rural southern blacks and whites moved from the economically depressed South to the industrial cities in the North. Blacks were forced to settle mostly in urban centers and were not as successful as other immigrants economically (Tolnay et al. 2002; Tolnay 2003).

Since World War II the Pacific coast has been particularly popular, with many from northeastern and north central states heading west and south by the 1950s (Weeks 2001). The Sun Belt became particularly attractive to internal migrants and international immigrants alike. When California's economy suffered after the end of the Cold War, some started moving away, mostly to the nearby states of Arizona, Nevada, Utah, Idaho, and Washington (Gober 1993). This trend has included many immigrants, including Latin Americans who had settled in California, as well as new arrivals to the United States. As a result the face of the South and Midwest has changed profoundly, and the rate of population growth of Latinos, many foreign-born, in states like Georgia, North Carolina, Iowa, and Nebraska has been little short of breathtaking. International immigration continues at high rates, mainly for western states (Weeks 2001). Yet many, wanting to be near friends and relatives as much as for economic reasons (Kritz and Nogle 1994), are now drawn to new ports of entry in Texas, New York, Florida, and the U.S. interior, as well as urban centers like Los Angeles, Houston, New York City, and Miami (Frey and Liaw 1998).

Five trends help summarize the intricacies of population shifts in the United States (Frey 1995). First, some cities are experiencing an influx of migrants at the expense of other cities. Second, California, Texas, and New York have become particularly diverse ethnically thanks to immigrants from Asia and Latin America. Third, there are serious regional differences in skill levels, mirroring the widening gap between college-educated and non-college-educated individuals. Fourth, different birth cohorts are moving to different places, with older "Baby Boomers" moving west and south, while younger Boomers have to move to other places to succeed (Rogerson 1999) and the elderly continue to flock to the Sun Belt. Fifth, the suburbs have continued to grow the fastest with respect to residences and jobs (Rayer and Brown 2001), at least through the 1980s. *See also*: **Fertility**; **Health**.

References

Eschbach, Karl, Jacqueline Hagan, and Nestor Rodriquez. 1999. Death at the Border. *International Migration Review* 33(2):430–454.

Frey, William H. 1995. The New Geography of Population Shifts. In *State of the Union: America in the 1990s, Volume Two: Social Trends*. Reynolds Farley, ed. Pp. 271–336. New York: Russell Sage Foundation.

Frey, William H., and Kao-Lee Liaw. 1998. The Impact of Recent Immigration on Population Redistribution within the United States. In *The Immigration Debate: Studies of Economic, Demographic and Fiscal Effects of Immigration.* James P. Smith and Barry Edmonston, eds. Pp. 388–448. Washington, DC: National Academy Press.

Gober, Patricia. 1993. Americans on the Move. *Population Bulletin* 48:2–40.

Greenberg, Michael, and Dona Schneider. 1995. The Cancer Burden of Southern-Born African Americans: Analysis of a Social-Geographic Legacy. *Milbank Quarterly* 73(4):599–620.

Kritz, Mary M., and June Marie Nogle. 1994. Nativity Concentration and Internal Migration among the Foreign-Born. *Demography* 31(3):509–524.

Rayer, Stefan, and David L. Brown. 2001. Geographic Diversity of Inter-County Migration in the United States, 1980–1995. *Population Research and Policy Review* 20(3):229–252.

Rogerson, Peter A. 1999. Geography of the Baby-Boom Cohort. In *Migration and Restructuring in the United States: A Geographic Perspective.* Kavita Pandit and Suzanne Davies Withers, eds. Pp. 174–192. New York: Rowman and Littlefield.

Siegel, Jacob S., and David Swanson, eds. 2004. *Methods and Materials of Demography,* 2nd ed. San Diego, CA: Elsevier.

Tolnay, Stewart E. 2003. Trends in the Relative Occupational Status of African Americans and European Immigrants in Northern Cities, 1880–1970. *Social Science Research* 32(4):603–632.

Tolnay, Stewart E., Kyle D. Crowder, and Robert M. Adelman. 2002. Race, Regional Origin, and Residence in Northern Cities at the Beginning of the Great Migration. *American Sociological Review* 67(3):456–475.

Weeks, John R. 2001. *Population: An Introduction to Concepts and Issues,* 8th ed. Belmont, CA: Wadsworth.

JOAN C. STEVENSON

DIASPORAS. Diasporas have been defined as those "communities, migrant populations, ethnicities or nations that although separated from their home terrains...and scattered among other communities, imaginatively preserve and regenerate a set of distinctive cultural or ethnic identities" (Tedlock 1996:341). The traditional definition is based on the Greek origins of diaspora as a term for a "nation or part of a nation separated from its own state or territory and dispersed among other nations but preserving its national culture" (Dubnow 1930–1935:126). The Greeks in the ancient Roman Empire constituted a diaspora in the traditional sense as have the Armenian and Jewish people who have lived outside their original territory for centuries. The Jewish diaspora dating from the Babylonian captivity over 2,500 years ago has been the most notable and, until recently, the most analyzed diaspora. The impact of globalization on homogenization and assimilation has intensified the resurrection of transnational ethnic and cultural identities and thus the identification and self-identification of migrant populations as diasporas (Cohen 1997:131).

Current usages of the diaspora concept cover a broad range of situations, from its original use in ancient history to the cultural studies definition, which refers to a range of territorial "displacements, revivals, and reconfigurations of identities and traditions that characterize the contemporary global cultural landscape" (Subramaniam 1996:144). Some scholars have criticized this cultural studies usage as dehistoricizing the concept of diaspora and recommend that criteria be established for its usage. Richard Hovanissian of UCLA, an expert on the Armenian diaspora, believes the sense of attachment to a homeland, whether real or imaginary, is crucial for a migrant population group to constitute a diaspora

(Winkler 1999:A12). William Safran delineated several criteria that an expatriate community should satisfy in order to qualify as a diaspora. The criteria include being dispersed from a center to at least two peripheral places; believing that they can never be fully assimilated in their host nation; maintaining a "memory" or "myth" of a homeland; expecting eventual return to their ancestral home; being committed to maintaining or restoring the homeland; and having a group identity defined by this continuing relationship with the homeland. Though some legitimate diasporas may not meet all of these criteria, providing historical context for a diaspora prevents the term from becoming merely a metaphor for complex and multiple identities. In *Diaspora Politics*, Gabriel Sheffer remarks that the term "diaspora" has been applied to "various transnational formations espousing what has been termed 'deterritorialized identities'—that is, to groups whose hybrid identities, orientations and loyalties are not connected to any given territory" (Sheffer 2003:10). For that reason, he prefaces his use of diaspora with "ethno-national" to specify that he is discussing diaspora in the conventional use of this term.

> An ethno-national diaspora is a social-political formation, created as a result of either voluntary or forced migration, whose members regard themselves as of the same ethno-national origin and who permanently reside as minorities in one or several host countries. Members of such entities maintain regular or occasional contacts with what they regard as their homelands. (Sheffer 2003:9)

A distinction can be made between diaspora and borderlands in that the latter is determined by an "arbitrary geopolitical line" characterized by "legal and illegal practices of crossing and communication" whereas diasporas connect multiple communities of a population dispersed over longer distances (Clifford 1994:304). A distinction should also be made between diaspora as a dispersal of people to several places and migration as a movement of people from point A to point B.

Early examples of prominent diaspora populations in U.S. immigration history would include African Americans, Jewish Americans, and Irish Americans. The multicultural character of America as a "nation of nations" has made it possible for immigrants to become Americans without entirely abandoning their ethnic origins. The pan-African movement led by Marcus Garvey, W.E.B. Du Bois, and Paul Robeson in the 1920s and 1930s was a precursor for the activism of African Americans on behalf of the Comprehensive Anti-Apartheid Act (CAAA) passed by Congress in 1986. Irish Americans campaigned for home rule and in the 1860s even attempted to draw the United States into a war with the British empire (Shain 1994–1995:817). In the contemporary era, the Irish National Caucus and the Congressional Ad Hoc Committee on Irish Affairs have continued to lobby for reunification of Ireland (Arthur 1991:52). Jewish Americans lobbied for U.S. policy favorable to Israel as well as for the rights of Soviet Jewry. More recently, Palestinian and Arab Americans have crusaded for Palestinian self-determination.

The Immigration and Nationality Act of 1965 was not the sole factor in the changing composition of U.S. immigration. In fact, Soviet and Eastern Europe's restrictions on immigration as well as increased need for labor in Europe's expanding postwar economy reduced emigration from Europe. The 1965 act did lift the ban on Asian immigration, which increased when the United States' involvement in Southeast Asia obligated the United States to accept refugees forced to emigrate due to U.S. foreign policy. The 1980 Refugee Act also enabled large numbers of Cubans, Vietnamese, and other Southeast Asians to enter the United States. According to the 1990 census, Mexican immigration constituted 22 percent of the total, followed by Filipinos, Cubans, and Canadians.

Though Mexicans and Canadians are transnational populations that transcend one or more nation states, they constitute borderland communities rather than a diaspora, tending to cross over the arbitrary geopolitical line for economic opportunities. For most U.S. citizens of Mexican origin there was no original expulsion from a homeland or awareness of being dispersed to multiple locations that would represent a diaspora experience. However, the Mexican government has recently attempted to foster a stronger bond with Americans of Mexican ancestry because they constitute a market for Mexican products and a pressure group that can influence American policies. In 1996, Mexico's congress approved an amendment that provides for retention of Mexican nationality despite voluntary acquisition of another nationality. Other countries have a similar interest in developing stronger bonds with their diasporas. Taiwan intends to reach about 34 million Chinese living overseas—dispersed to the United States, Canada, South America, and Europe—with a new Chinese-language satellite television station. Since many Dominicans return home to vote, the two main contenders in the 1996 presidential campaign in the Dominican Republic targeted the diaspora community in New York City. Diaspora communities have financially assisted their home countries in the case of Eastern Europe, the former Soviet Union, Israel, and the emerging state of Palestine, and diaspora investment has benefited Central American countries, China, and Southeast Asian countries.

Recent diasporas to the United States are primarily Caribbean, Latin American, and Asian, the latter mainly Vietnamese, Cambodian, Laotian, and Hmong. The displacement of 1.7 million Indochinese refugees to Western Europe, North America, and Australia was a global diaspora. After China invaded Tibet in 1950, Tibetan refugees were dispersed to several locations, including Europe, India, Nepal, and North America. This community qualifies as a diaspora because its members have an attachment to their homeland and have attempted to influence U.S. policy toward China. Since the United States does not recognize Tibet's autonomy, it has denied refugee status to Tibetans.

There have been five major Caribbean migrations to the United States in the last century: Cubans, Dominicans, Haitians, Jamaicans, and Puerto Ricans. Cuban emigrés initially had the expectation of overthrowing Fidel Castro with U.S. assistance and returning to Cuba but instead have gradually evolved from exiles to immigrants. The Cuban-American National Foundation has lobbied effectively in Congress and is influential in Florida politics. The foundation members' efforts to unseat Castro have generally been compatible with U.S. foreign policy and led to passage of the 1992 Cuban Democracy Act, which tightened the economic embargo of Cuba (Shain 1994–1995:828). The Haitian diaspora community and African Americans were successful advocates on behalf of Jean-Bertrand Aristide, the president of Haiti who was deposed and exiled in 1991. The constantly changing global environment has also resulted in other new refugee migrations, such as the Kosovar-Albanian diaspora to which the United States responded by admitting approximately 20,000 refugees in 1999.

Whereas in the past diasporas have been viewed as homogeneous, recently there have been some efforts toward developing an analytical approach that addresses the internal complexities of diasporas by acknowledging the intersections of class, gender, and race within these migrant communities as well as in their relations with host nations. Since ethnic diasporas are not homogeneous, the members of such a group can encounter different receptions in the host nation depending on class, gender, education, and other differences. In addition, diasporas are often "composite formations" comprised of several migrations to various locations with each migration having a distinct history, such as the African, Chinese, Irish, Jewish, Palistinian, and South Asian diasporas.

The term "diaspora" also has gender implications, in part because its original meaning of "scattered seeds" relates to the metaphorical use of seed to designate male reproductive substance (Helmreich 1992:245). Sperm is etymologically derived from the same root as diaspora, suggesting that diaspora refers to a system of kinship traced through paternity. When diaspora is viewed in terms of "displacement rather than placement, traveling rather than dwelling," the male experience will predominate (Clifford 1994:313). Floya Anthias recommends "gendering" the diaspora by addressing relevant gender issues including the interaction of gender relations within the culture and those of the host society; women's labor market participation as family labor within their ethnic group; whether the nation is symbolized as woman; and whether women of the diaspora group are restricted to the private sphere or are allowed to participate in the political sphere (Anthias 1998:572–574).

In the future, investigations of diasporas will need to address their heterogeneous nature and the problems and concerns that affect these communities depending on class, race, and gender distinctions among their populations. Increased economic and political globalization will increase tensions between nation-states attempting to maintain their hegemony and ethnic groups hoping to preserve their cultural identity and political autonomy. According to Sheffer (2003), there is also a need to study the embryonic development of pan-ethnic transnational diasporas, mainly phenomena in North America and the European Union today, which may eventually appear in other host countries or regions. *See also*: **Borderlands; Gender; Refugee law and policy; Transnationalism.**

References

Anderson, Wanni W., and Robert G. Lee. 2005. *Displacements and Diasporas: Asians in the Americas*. New Brunswick, NJ: Rutgers University Press.

Anthias, Floya. 1998. Evaluating Diaspora: Beyond Ethnicity. *Sociology* 32(3):557–580.

Arthur, Paul. 1991. Diasporan Intervention in International Affairs: Irish America as a Case Study. *Diaspora* 1(2):143–162.

Clifford, James. 1994. Diasporas. *Cultural Anthropology* 9(3):302–338.

Cohen, Robin. 1997. *Global Diasporas: An Introduction*. Seattle: University of Washington Press.

Dubnow, Simon. 1930–1935. Diaspora. In *Encyclopaedia of the Social Sciences*. Edwin R. Seligman, ed. Pp. 126–130. New York: Macmillan.

Hall, Stuart. 1990. Cultural Identity and Diaspora. In *Identity: Community, Culture, Difference*. Jonathan Rutherford, ed. Pp. 222–237. London: Lawrence and Wishart.

Helmreich, Stefan. 1992. Kinship, Nation and Paul Gilroy's Concept of Diaspora. *Diaspora* 2(2):243–249.

Loucky, James, and Marilyn M. Moors. 2000. *The Maya Diaspora: Guatemalan Roots, New American Lives*. Philadelphia: Temple University Press.

Ram, Kalpana. 1998. Introduction: Migratory Women, Travelling Feminisms. *Women's Studies International Forum* 21(6):571–579.

Safran, William. 1991. Diasporas in Modern Societies: Myths of Homeland and Return. *Diaspora* 1(1):83–99.

Shain, Yossi. 1994–1995. Ethnic Diasporas and U.S. Foreign Policy. *Political Science Quarterly* 109(5):811–841.

Sheffer, Gabriel. 2003. *Diaspora Politics: At Home Abroad*. Cambridge: Cambridge University Press.

Subramaniam, Radhika. 1996. Diaspora. In *A Dictionary of Cultural and Critical Theory*. Michael Payne, ed. P. 144. Cambridge: Blackwell.

Tatla, Darshan Singh. 1999. *The Sikh Diaspora: The Search for Statehood*. Seattle: University of Washington Press.

Tedlock, Barbara. 1996. Diasporas. In *Encyclopedia of Cultural Anthropology*. David Levinson and Melvin Ember, eds. Pp. 341–343. New York: Henry Holt.

Tölöyan, Khachig. 1991. The Nation State and Its Others: In Lieu of a Preface. *Diaspora* 1(1):3–7.

Van Hear, Nicholas. 1998. *New Diasporas: The Mass Exodus, Dispersal, and Regrouping of Migrant Communities*. Seattle: University of Washington Press.

Vertovec, Steven, and Robin Cohen, eds. 1999. *Migration, Disasporas and Transnationalism*. Northampton, MA: Edward Elgar.

Winkler, Karen J. 1999. Historians Explore Questions of How People and Cultures Disperse Across the Globe. *Chronicle of Higher Education*, January 22, A11–12.

JEANNE ARMSTRONG

DOCUMENTATION. The wide use of the term "undocumented" reveals that documentation of non-citizens has long been part of immigration control in the United States, particularly for people seeking legal immigration. Historically, immigration arrival records, officially recording a person's admission to the United States, took different forms. Official arrival records were kept on big sheets called passenger lists, ship lists, or ship passenger manifests until 1924, after which visas became the official immigration records. Since 1944, the Immigration and Naturalization Service (INS), and now U.S. Citizenship and Immigration Services (USCIS), has had responsibility for maintaining files on all unauthorized people ("aliens") residing in the United States.

Most people in the United States have vague knowledge of "green cards," properly known as Alien Registration Receipt Cards (Form I-151 or I-551). Green cards, which actually are not green, document the status of permanent residents to travel, live, and/or work in the United States. These came as a result of the Alien Registration Act of 1940, a national defense measure which required all non-citizens within the United States, whether legal or illegal residents, to register with the U.S. government.

After World War II, immigration to the United States resumed and alien registration was standard immigration procedure. Aliens registered at the port of entry and the INS issued different documents to them according to their admission status: visitors received an I-94c, temporary foreign laborers received an I-100a, and permanent residents received the I-151. The I-151 status had the value of identifying its holder as a lawful permanent resident (LPR), who could live and work in the United States. In 1951, regulations were changed to allow aliens with legal status—those holding AR-3 cards—to have them replaced with a new Form I-151 (green card). Applicants who were unable to prove their legal admission into the United States did not qualify for LPR status and were subject to prosecution for violation of U.S. immigration laws (Smith 1993).

Some green card holders do so at the invitation of U.S. employers filing permanent employment-based visa petitions on their behalf. These include persons of extraordinary ability who are invited to the United States to share their expertise in a particular field, outstanding professors and researchers, and multinational executives or managers who apply for admission to the United States as priority workers. Others may receive visas through labor certification where there are shortages of qualified U.S. workers to fill positions.

Counterfeit green cards have been a continuing problem, leading the Immigration and Naturalization Service (INS) to issue 19 different designs of the I-151 between its initiation in the 1940s and its complete revision in 1977. Changing the color was one alteration implemented, but those who obtained and issued I-151s continued to refer to them as green cards (Smith 1993). During the mid-1970s, the INS studied methods to produce a counterfeit-proof Alien Registration Receipt Card for Legal Permanent Residents. The result, introduced in January 1977, was the machine-readable Form I-551.

The Bureau of Citizenship and Immigration Services (BCIS) and consular offices, now under the U.S. Citizenship and Immigration Services (USCIS), pay particular attention to the documents submitted by applicants given the possibility of deception and fraud. They assert that new rules strike an appropriate balance between the mission of ensuring that the nation's immigration laws are followed and illegal immigration stopped, and the need to welcome legitimate visitors to the United States (U.S. Immigration Attorneys 2003). Although there is wide recognition that most people who come to the United States as visitors are "honest and law abiding," the events of September 11, 2001, have increased the level of caution out of fears that some may seek to harm the United States and U.S. citizens.

Registry systems for non-citizens in the United States have become more stringent since the attacks of September 11, 2001. Prior to that, government manpower deficiencies made keeping track of visitors nearly impossible, and unknown numbers of unauthorized immigrants escaped detection. Some may not even have realized that the Illegal Immigration Reform and Immigrant Responsibility Act of 1996 created substantial new penalties for aliens who overstay their visas or enter the country illegally. Now, however, concerns for national security have increased, leading the new Department of Homeland Security to devote increasing attention to implementing registry systems that allow for more careful tracking of visitors.

Tracking systems have met with both cooperation and understandable anxieties, in large part because of fears of detention and deportations, especially of immigrants from countries that are considered bases for terrorism. An estimated 16 percent of Arab and Muslim men who came forward in 2004 to register with U.S. immigration authorities may, in fact, face deportation, even though only a handful have actually been linked to terrorism. But a system had to be enacted to pacify uneasy Americans as much as to guarantee that immigrants follow rules of admission to the United States and to rebuff those who might enter the United States with malevolent intentions. In September 2002, the INS (and now USCIS) began a program of fingerprinting nonimmigrant people that they considered to be potential security risks. An estimated 100,000 people per year are now required to periodically register with the INS. This represents a key first step toward development of a comprehensive entry-exit system applicable to all foreign visitors.

The USA Patriot Act also establishes new guidelines for monitoring international students and for disclosure of records within higher education. SEVIS (Student and Exchange Visitor Information System), instituted within the USA Patriot Act, is an Internet-based system which maintains immigration entry, personal, and academic information about students from beyond the United States and which is to be updated by schools if student information changes.

Tracking proposals extend beyond immigrants as well. A national registry and tracking system requiring everyone to carry a national identification card was proposed as early as the 1980s by several government agencies (including the Internal Revenue Service, State Department, and Central Intelligence Agency). While rejected in the past as a massive invasion of privacy, an automated entry-exit system (US-VISIT) is being implemented at all ports of entry. Coupled with enhanced surveillance powers of the executive branch, including ability to conduct covert searches, obtain personal records, and track e-mail and Internet usage, documentation and tracking of immigrants and even citizens may be growing in both technological and geographic scope.

Implementation of US-VISIT and collection of biometric data raises much concern, particularly in light of some prior excesses of immigration agencies. The American Immigration Lawyers Association (AILA) calls for reasonable immigration laws and reforming those that would facilitate flow of people for labor, commerce, and family matters while allowing the government to focus on potential security risks. Such reform involves opportunities for legalization for long-term unauthorized immigrants, facilitating family reunification and allowing businesses to bring in needed workers.

It is premature to tell whether increased tracking and documentation systems will result in enhanced security. The government's effort to register men from designated Muslim countries has resulted in few if any being charged with terrorism, though more than 83,000 persons have been registered under the National Security Entry-Exit Registration System (NSEERS) program. Whether tracking programs implemented at the borders result in any increased effectiveness against unwanted immigrants must be measured against additional burdens of travel delays, inconveniences to commerce, and costs of such programs. Furthermore, the costs, erosion of trust, and civil liberty concerns of such provisions must be considered, so that both public and congressional oversight of their implementation is paramount (Thal 2003). *See also*: **Border control; Expedited entry and removal; Legalization; Ports of entry; Unauthorized immigration; U.S.-Canada border; U.S.-Mexico border.**

References

American Immigration Lawyers Association. 2003. AILA Enumerates Concerns with the New "U.S. VISIT" Entry-Exit System. Press Release, May 21. http://www.aila.org.

Higher Education and National Affairs. American Council on Education. 2001. U.S. Patriot Act Includes Provisions on Student Records. Retrieved from http://www .acenet.edu/ on October 23, 2003.

Hing, B.O. 1999. *Immigration and the Law: A Dictionary.* Santa Barbara, CA: ABC-CLIO.

Immigration Law Group (ILG). Frequently Asked Questions (FAQ). Question 4. http:// immigrationgroup.com/main.htm.

Lemay, M., and E.R. Barkan. 1999. *U.S. Immigration and Naturalization Laws and Issues: A Documentary History.* Westport, CT: Greenwood Press.

National Immigration Forum (NIF). 2003. Immigration Basic Facts 2003:12. http:// www.immigrationforum.org/pubs/facts.htm.

Schwartz, Karyn. 2003. "Immigration and Registration." Online NewsHour. Paragraph 15. Retrieved from http://www.pbs.org/newshour/bb/terrorism/homeland/ir.html on November 14, 2003.

Smith, Marian. 1993. Why Isn't the "Green Card" Green? Interpreter Releases, Vol. 70, No. 30. August 7.

Thal, Steven C. 2003. Re: Why Isn't the "Green Card" Green? November 15.

Torpey, J. 2000. *The Invention of the Passport: Surveillance, Citizenship, and the State.* Cambridge: Cambridge University Press.

U.S. Citizenship and Immigration Services. 2003. Immigration Arrival Records. http:// www.uscis.gov/graphics/aboutus/history/immrecs/immrec.htm.

U.S. Department of Homeland Security, Office of the Press Secretary. 2003. US-VISIT Fact Sheet Press Release of October 28. http://www.dhs.gov/dhspublic/display?content= 2080.

U.S. Immigration Attorneys. 2003. Green Card Specialists for Family Members. Green Cards, http://www.familygreencards.com/greencard.html. Eligibility, http://www.family greencards.com/eligibility.html.

MARTINE HARVEY, MARGARET LOU FREKING,
AND STEVEN C. THAL

DOMESTIC WORK. Domestic work refers to housekeeping and childcare services individuals are paid to perform primarily in private homes. Throughout American history, domestic work has been, with few exceptions, performed by women of color and in the latter half of the twentieth century predominantly by immigrant women of color. Beginning in the 1970s, immigrant women from Mexico, El Salvador, and Guatemala have constituted the largest category of women entering the occupation in the United States (Romero 1992:71; Hondagneu-Sotelo 2001:7). There has also been a consistent flow of women from the Caribbean and the Philippines who have entered the domestic labor pool. The common bond of these diverse women is that they are economically motivated migrants who are sustaining emotional as well as monetary bonds across borders.

Contrary to the popular belief that women who migrate alone are young and single, studies now reveal that a large number of the Mexican, Central American, Filipina, and Caribbean immigrant women are married and have children back in their home countries (Colen 1989; Hondagneu-Sotelo and Avila 1997; Arat-Koc 2001; Parrenas 2001). For most of these women, their "undocumented" legal status poses many challenges, the largest being that this status restricts their ability to return home for family visits and emergencies. As "transnational mothers," immigrant women, who live apart from their children, state that caregiving is a defining feature of their mothering experiences. As part of this caregiving, immigrant domestic workers who have migrated without their children overwhelmingly cite monetary responsibility for their family as the primary reason for their migration. As transnational mothers they become focused on providing their children with better nutrition, clothing, and schooling through the monetary remittances they send home from each month's salary (Hondagneu-Sotelo and Avila 1997:562). It is this sense of responsibility that motivates immigrant women to take on seemingly exploitative, low-paying domestic jobs. In contrast to what the immigrant women earn in their home countries, the low wages paid by American domestic employers are initially appealing. Yet, this appeal ultimately wanes as they learn, generally from other domestics, that they are being underpaid and usually overworked (Wrigley 1995:27).

Much has changed in the structure of the domestic work market that receives these immigrant women. Far from a privileged staple reserved for the upper class of the United States a century ago, domestic services today are similarly sought by the expanding professional and middle classes. Although Mexican immigrant women have worked for decades as domestics in the Southwest, the mass entrance of American women into the U.S. labor force has dramatically increased the demand for domestic services (Hondagneu-Sotelo 1994:29). Today, many middle-class, dual-career parents struggling with the demands of competitive labor markets prefer the convenience and flexibility of having one person exclusively care for their children, cook their meals, and clean their homes. Furthermore, private caregiver arrangements, unlike day care, allow parents more control over the type and extent of care their children receive.

Not surprisingly, immigrant women have also filled this labor niche in other postindustrial societies such as Canada and parts of Europe and Asia where similar structural changes have created similar domestic needs (Hondagneu-Sotelo 2001:19). One striking example of this growing presence is the rising concentration of Filipino domestics throughout the 1980s in places such as Italy and Canada where immigrant women are formally recruited to come to work as in-home domestics for Canadian and Italian families (Hondagneu-Sotelo 2001; Parrenas 2001). However, unlike other countries where formal policies exist that allow for contracting with foreign domestic workers, most domestic workers in the United States are undocumented or in the country on a temporary visa (Hondagneu-Sotelo 2001:20–21).

Estimates on the number of domestic workers in the United States vary from state to state and even between various immigrant groups. Precise figures are obscured in part by the lack of legal documentation and unreliable census data on the sectors in which these women are employed (Hondagneu-Sotelo and Avila 1997). The unsystematic labels that are used by employers and researchers compound these fluctuating reports. While the term "domestic worker" is common within the academic literature, within the private, informal employment sector itself, the occupation is more commonly referred to as "housekeeper/ housekeeping" or "nanny or babysitting," underestimating the extent of the position.

Each domestic job is specific to the needs of the employer and the workload is structured accordingly. In general, domestic work may be categorized into three typical job arrangements:

1. *Live-in nanny/housekeeper.* In this arrangement, the employee lives and works with one family, caring for the children and performing most, if not all, of the household tasks including cleaning, cooking, and laundry. This arrangement may be highly demanding since the employee is often expected to be available 12 or more hours a day.

2. *Live-out nanny/housekeeper.* In this arrangement the domestic worker again works for one family; however, at the end of the workday she returns to her own home. This "live-out" domestic typically works a five-day workweek, starting each day before the employers leave for work and ending when they return. Similarly, tasks include housecleaning, cooking, laundry, and/or childcare.

3. *Housecleaner.* In this arrangement, the domestic worker cleans multiple houses for multiple employers and no childcare is involved. The employee generally cleans more than one house a day, thus increasing her potential to earn more money (Romero 1992:147; Hondagneu-Sotelo 2001:28).

Out of the three typical work arrangements, most women favor the housecleaner, as it allows a greater degree of flexibility and autonomy. However, for newly arriving immigrant women in need of a place to live and with little access to transportation to and from work, the live-in position may initially be the most suitable arrangement. Once established in a community, many immigrant women network with other domestics in order to identify new potential clients in an attempt to transition into housecleaner (Hondagneu-Sotelo 1994). This is especially true for most domestics who have brought their children over to the United States or who have started a family here and require the increased flexibility to tend to their own families and homes.

Beyond the physical labor that domestic work requires, it is important to understand that more often than not the job expectations involve *emotional* labor. In the same way that flight attendants and waitresses create exchange value from their own emotions, domestic workers must also manage their feelings in ways that fulfill the psychological expectations of their employers (Romero 1992). In particular, domestics who care for children must perform the emotional labor of mothering as part of their daily tasks. This qualitatively unique element of domestic work is only beginning to emerge in the research and has significant implications for redefining broad analytic categories of family and labor and for reconstructing policy decisions in light of such distinctions.

Although there is a wide range of pay within the occupation, many domestic workers, especially those who work as live-ins, earn less than the hourly minimum wage and rarely receive any benefits. One 1990s study indicated that nearly all live-in workers surveyed were earning less than $5 an hour, 79 percent below minimum wage, which was then $4.25. It is incorrect, however, to assume that rich employers pay more than middle-class employers (Hondagneu-Sotelo 2001:35). In fact, wealthier employers may have higher expectations and demand more for their money than their middle-class counterparts. Furthermore, the employer's word-of-mouth hiring practices produce an informal culture of expectations and standardized wages, thus making negotiations more difficult for employees.

While domestic work, as it is currently structured, allows immigrants with limited employment skills and tenuous legal status the opportunity to work in the United States, the real costs that immigrant domestic workers experience are often not fully known until they arrive. Paid domestic work, especially live-in arrangements, are generally incompatible with them being able to provide care for their own family, inadvertently fostering a long-term family separation. Furthermore, domestic work continues to be seen as unskilled, non-technical labor that is devalued and seen as relatively unimportant (Glenn 1986:167). Domestic workers, as a whole, are shown little respect and are often denied the rights and job benefits such as sick days, paid vacations, medical benefits, and employer-paid social security afforded other workers in the formal employment sector. Similarly, as members of an informal and nearly invisible labor market, domestic workers currently have no employment-related recourse from sexual harassment, threats of deportation, and loss of wages by employers who unjustifiably fire or refuse to pay them. In some parts of the United States, as well as in other countries (e.g., Canada), domestics have attempted to bring about change by collective organizing in order to educate domestic workers on their rights and employers on their responsibilities to their workers (Hondagneu-Sotelo 2001). There are great potential and need for future research to better understand the unanswered questions regarding the cultural, legal, and emotional impact of domestic work on immigrant women and their families, as well as the emergence of collective organizing and the policy implications around issues of pay equity and workers' rights.

Significant change can clearly come about once the occupation is formalized and regulated like other occupations. Reforming the occupation would benefit not only the worker, but also the families who employ domestic workers. Paying fair wages and allowing domestic workers to work fewer hours, to allow for better care of their own families, is likely to result in employers gaining better childcare and better services all around. By allowing workers more autonomy or at least input on how their jobs are structured, employers are likely to see that domestics will stay on the job longer. *See also*: **Gender; Transnationalism; Unauthorized immigration; Women.**

References

Arat-Koc, Sedef. 2001. *Caregivers Break the Silence*. Toronto: Intercede.

Colen, Shellee. 1989. Just a Little Respect: West Indian Domestic Workers in New York City. In *Muchachas No More: Household Workers in Latin America and the Caribbean*. Elsa M. Chaney and Mary Garcia Castro, eds. Pp. 171–196. Philadelphia: Temple University Press.

Ehrenreich, Barbara, and Arlie Russell Hochschild, eds. 2004. *Global Woman: Nannies, Maids, and Sex Workers in the New Economy*. New York: Owl Books.

Glenn, Evelyn Nakano. 1986. *Issei, Nisei, War Bride: Three Generations of Japanese American Women in Domestic Service*. Philadelphia: Temple University Press.

Hondagneu-Sotelo, Pierrette. 1994. *Gendered Transitions: Mexican Experiences of Immigration*. Berkeley: University of California Press.

———. 2001. *Doméstica: Immigrant Workers Cleaning and Caring in the Shadows of Affluence*. Berkeley: University of California Press.

Hondagneu-Sotelo, Pierrette, and Ernestine M. Avila. 1997. "I'm Here, but I'm There": The Meanings of Latina Transnational Motherhood. *Gender and Society* 11(5): 548–571.

Parrenas, Rachel. 2001. *Servants of Globalization: Women, Migration, and Domestic Work*. Stanford, CA: Stanford University Press.

Romero, Mary. 1992. *Maid in the U.S.A.* New York: Routledge.

Wrigley, Julia. 1995. *Other People's Children: An Intimate Account of the Dilemmas Facing Middle-Class Parents and the Women They Hire to Raise Their Children.* New York: Basic Books.

ERNESTINE M. AVILA

DUAL CITIZENSHIP. Dual citizenship refers to the legal status of persons who are citizens of two nations. Such persons may have two passports and can vote in the elections of the two countries of which they are citizens. In short, dual citizenship grants the rights and commands the duties of two different citizenships. Before dual citizenship can be discussed, citizenship as such must be studied.

Citizenship is one of the fundamental concepts in Western political thought. Most important, however, it is considered one of the most venerable institutions of Western societies, and perhaps its worthiest gift to humanity. It is as old as the notion of politics itself and, some even claim, as old as the very foundations of our most important institutions, namely, democratic self-ruling and public deliberation as a means to achieve a political consensus. Citizenship is a cognate of civic, civil, civilization, whose root is *civitas* (city). City, in turn, is the Latin translation for *polis*. From that Greek root are derived the cognates politics, police, and cosmopolitan.

A historical analysis of the development of the idea of citizenship would have to take into account not just the Greek, Roman, and early Christian appropriations of the idea, but also the Reformation in the sixteenth century, the French, Haitian, and American revolutions, the American Civil War, the Fourteenth Amendment to the Constitution of the United States, the women's suffrage movement, the civil rights movements in the United States in the second half of the twentieth century, the gay and lesbian movements, and finally the universal declaration of human rights after World War II. For this reason, citizenship may be seen as one of the most venerable political institutions. Citizenship has been the result of many long struggles that have shaped the character of our nation and given depth and shape to our institutions (Hindess 1993).

This history of citizenship as both a concept and an institution reveals that the "who" and the "what" or "how" of citizenship have both undergone expansion. With respect to the "who," it is to be noted that at first only very few were considered citizens: male, property-owning, educated whites. For a long time Asians were excluded from citizenship. Only after many struggles was citizenship extended to or acknowledged for all members of our nation.

The story of who is or can become a citizen in the United States is filled with not only shame and inequity but also struggles, triumph, and transformation. At first, citizenship was granted on the grounds of jus sanguinis, that is, by birth right and blood lineage. In this way, only descendants of the original inhabitants of the colonies could be citizens. Those who had no blood link to the inhabitants of the confederation and later United States of America could not be naturalized. This interpretation of citizenship has been in conflict with another that gave primacy to jus solis, or place of birth, meaning those born in the United States were citizens (Smith 1997).

The 1965 Immigration Act finally rejected and abandoned about a hundred years of explicitly racist policies that had excluded Native Americans, blacks, and

Chinese from citizenship on the principle of jus sanguinis. The Dred Scott decision of 1857 had ruled that blacks could not seek the benefits of courts because they were property; as property, they could not sue for their freedom, which meant refusal of citizenship to them (Zinn 2001:187). The Indian Removal Act of 1830 had also amounted to a rejection of citizenship rights and protection to Native Americans (Smith 1997:235–236). Only with the 1924 Indian Citizenship Act were Native Americans recognized fully as citizens (Smith 1997:459). The Immigration Act of 1875, which banned the importation of "orientals," had unleashed a series of anti-Chinese policies, which effectively prevented American-born Chinese people from being naturalized and future Chinese immigrant generations from ever obtaining citizenship. Such policies were amended and renewed successively in 1882, 1884, and 1902 (Smith 1997:326, 366–367, 442). The Guadalupe Hidalgo treaty with Mexico explicitly granted full citizenship to Mexicans in now U.S. territories, and Puerto Ricans were granted full citizenship through the 1917 Jones Act, but both groups continued to be treated as foreigners or second-class citizens (Smith 1997:446), including through unequal educational, employment, and residence opportunities.

With respect to the "what" or "how" of citizenship, it must be noted that to be a citizen or to have citizenship entailed a privilege and a series of duties. The innermost core or layer of citizenship is made up of what we can call civil rights: freedom of press and religion, privacy, right to a fair trial, and right to own private property (Marshall 1963). These are rights we associate with the inalienable autonomy and integrity of the individual person. They may be construed as rights against the state. The institutions that are associated with these rights are the national and international courts of law or justice: the supreme courts as well as international tribunals (nations can be brought before a court of law for their violations of the human rights of their citizens). The second layer is made up of what we can call political rights: rights to vote, to associate politically, and to participate in the bodies of self-legislation of a community. The institutions that are associated with these rights are parliaments, or what in the United States are better known as the senate, the house of representatives, and non-government organizations that lobby for certain bills or political causes as well as national parties. They might be construed as rights to the state, or rights that endow us with the power to participate in, shape, and direct the state. Social rights constitute the third layer: rights to a minimum wage, to public education, and to a minimum living standard.

In the United States, some of these institutions are as recent as the last quarter of the twentieth century. A fourth layer of citizenship, not foreseen by Marshall and most political thinkers in the early part of the twentieth century, but which has become one of the most debated areas of political theory, is constituted by what one might call cultural rights: rights to one's religion, language, and culture. While the first three groups of rights are granted or endowed upon individuals, the fourth group seems to be aimed at groups. This is one of the most serious issues facing contemporary social thinkers as well as multicultural societies, including the United States, where there are many immigrant and autochthonous cultural minorities. Thinkers like Will Kymlicka, John Rawls, Jürgen Habermas, Iris Marion Young, Amy Guttman, Seyla Benhabib, and David Ingram have developed analyses that aim at a multicultural citizenship. This, in turn, is related to the question of dual citizenship. It is against this background and series of challenges that we must think about the promises and perils of dual citizenship.

"The concept of dual nationality means that a person is a citizen of two countries at the same time. Persons may have dual nationality by automatic operation of different laws rather than by choice. For example, a child born in a foreign country to U.S. citizen parents may be both a U.S. citizen and a citizen of the country of birth" (U.S. Department of State). Dual citizenship developed in some cases out of agreements between two nations that found it advantageous to allow the unimpeded flow of citizens between their borders. Sometimes nations have unilaterally granted dual citizenship to their citizens because they found that some of their citizenry were an asset to their economies by being allowed to move back and forth without constraints. Mexico, the Dominican Republic, and Colombia allow dual citizenship. Those Mexicans who have become U.S. citizens since 1998 automatically retain their Mexican citizenship. As part of the change, the Mexican government also decided to set up a five-year program, from 1998 to 2003, allowing those Mexicans who became U.S. citizens before 1998 to reclaim their Mexican citizenship. Dual citizenship has been vigorously pursued by nations in the American continent who seek to derive benefits of a large transnational and migratory section of citizens. For example, more than 10,000 U.S. troops and civilian contractors lived in the Canal Zone before it was handed over to Panama, and children born there to two U.S. citizens retained the right to dual citizenship after the troops' withdrawal.

Federal statutes clarify how dual citizenship is retained.

> A U.S. citizen may acquire foreign citizenship by marriage, or a person naturalized as a U.S. citizen may not lose the citizenship of the country of birth. U.S. law does not mention dual nationality or require a person to choose one citizenship over another. Also, a person who is automatically granted another citizenship does not risk losing U.S. citizenship. However, a person who acquires a foreign citizenship by applying for it may lose U.S. citizenship. In order to lose U.S. citizenship, the law requires that the person must apply for the foreign citizenship voluntarily, by free choice, and with the intention to give up U.S. citizenship. (U.S. Department of State)

It is not clear yet what political impact dual citizenship has in both countries of citizenship. At the same time, it is unclear what role dual citizenship will have in light of the effects of globalization on national sovereignty. At worst, dual citizenship might be seen as a movement of accommodation to U.S. economic dominance in the continent. At best, dual citizenship in the American continent might be seen as a precursor of greater political, social, cultural, and economic integration, as in the European Union. There, citizens went from having two or even more passports to just one passport, although not the same rights and duties, across all the member nations of the union.

As a concept and as an institution, citizenship is once again undergoing transformation. Some of the most important factors and challenges directing that future evolution have to do with: (1) globalization, (2) its distinctive modern legalistic individualism, and (3) its role in a non-Eurocentric world. We are integrated not just economically, politically, and technologically, but also culturally.

Nation-states are unable any longer to control their national economies, borders, cultures, and other aspects of their peoples and territories. In its most recent versions (from the last 300 years), citizenship has evolved in tension with capitalism and constitutional, or rule of law, nation-states. One of the most fundamental aspects of capitalist and constitutional nation-states is their individualism. In this way, citizenship has been aimed and endowed upon "individuals." When persons contest before the courts and the political institutions of a state, they do so as individuals and on behalf of individuals. Yet, the persistence of **racism**, sexism, and ethnic and religious phobias even in constitutional and legalistic societies has made it clear that persons are discriminated against as members of a group or in groups.

The most important transformations of citizenship in the twentieth century were brought about because of the need to address the unique situations of persecuted, marginalized, disenfranchised groups such as the Jews, African Americans, Asian Americans, Latinos, or Mexican Americans in the United States. Perhaps the most serious challenge that citizens face in the United States at the dawn of a new century is how to maintain a common political culture as the country comes to terms with the cultural (religious and linguistic) plurality of its citizens. In the twenty-first century, most U.S. citizens will be either non-white or non-Protestant.

Finally, one of the consequences of globalization has been the localization of "Western" culture. In other words, in a global order, the "West" has become relativized as one among many cultures. It is contested and contestable just as any other culture is open to challenge and transformation. Like democracy, human rights, economic neoliberalism, women's rights, and privacy rights, citizenship has come under attack for being too mired in its Greek, Roman, and Christian roots to be of use to Confucians, Taoists, Buddhists, and others. At its core, citizenship is an institution that aims at universal equality, and this is a gift to present and future humanity, to all who have had to struggle and will have to struggle against inequality and inequity (Turner 1993:1–19). *See also*: **Citizenship**; **Jus soli**; **Transnationalism**.

References

Batstoned, David, and Eduardo Mendieta, eds. 1999. *The Good Citizen*. New York: Routledge.

Beiner, Ronald, ed. 1995. *Theorizing Citizenship*. Albany: State University of New York Press.

Benhabib, Seyla, ed. 1996. *Democracy and Difference: Contesting the Boundaries of the Political*. Princeton, NJ: Princeton University Press.

Dauenhauer, Bernard P. 1996. *Citizenship in a Fragile World*. Lanham, MD: Rowman and Littlefield.

Habermas, Jürgen. 1996. "Popular Sovereignty as Procedure (1988)" and "Citizenship and National Identity (1990)." In *Between Facts and Norms: Contributions to a Discourse Theory of Law and Democracy*. Jürgen Habermas. Cambridge, MA: MIT Press.

Hindess, Barry. 1993. Citizenship in the Modern West. In *Citizenship and Social Theory*. Bryan S. Turner, ed. Pp. 19–35. London: Sage.

Ingram, David. 2000. *Group Rights: Reconciling Equality and Difference*. Lawrence: University Press of Kansas.

Kymlicka, Will. 1995. *Multicultural Citizenship*. Oxford: Oxford University Press.

Marshall, T.H. 1963. *Sociology at the Crossroads and Other Essays*. London: Heinemann.

Portes, Alejandro, ed. 1996. *The New Second Generation*. New York: Russell Sage.

Rawls, John. 1993. *Political Liberalism*. New York: Columbia University Press.

———. 1999. *The Law of Peoples*. Cambridge, MA: Harvard University Press.

Shafir, Gershon, ed. 1998. *The Citizenship Debates: A Reader*. Minneapolis: University of Minnesota Press.

Smith, Rogers M. 1997. *Civic Ideals: Conflicting Visions of Citizenship in U.S. History*. New Haven, CT: Yale University Press.

Takaki, Ronald. 1993. *A Different Mirror: A History of Multicultural America*. Boston: Little, Brown.

Taylor, Charles. 1992. *Multiculturalism and "The Politics of Recognition": An Essay*. Ed. with commentary by Amy Gutmann et al. Princeton, NJ: Princeton University Press.

Turner, Bryan S., ed. 1993. *Citizenship and Social Theory*. London: Sage Publications.

U.S. Department of State Web site, http://travel.state.gov/dualnationality.html, accessed June 17, 2004.

Young, Iris. 2000. *Inclusion and Democracy*. Oxford: Oxford University Press.

Zinn, Howard. 2001. *A People's History of the United States: 1492 to the Present*. New York: HarperCollins.

EDUARDO MENDIETA

E

EFFECTS OF UNAUTHORIZED IMMIGRATION. Unauthorized (or alternatively, illegal or undocumented) immigrants are defined as foreign-born persons residing in the United States who are not refugees or legal temporary visitors and have not obtained legal permanent residence or U.S. citizenship status. A foreign-born person may become an unauthorized immigrant by entering the United States (1) "without inspection, using fraudulent documents, or violating the terms of border crossing cards," (2) "legally as a nonimmigrant [e.g., temporary tourist, business, or student visitor] and subsequently violating the terms of entry" (e.g., by failing to leave the country by the time a visa expires), or (3) "as a legal resident alien but subsequently violating the terms of entry," for instance, by committing a crime (Bean et al. 1998:32). Consequently, while economic opportunity and the possibility of reuniting with one's relatives remain prominent factors motivating international migratory flows into the United States, the details of U.S. immigration policy determine what proportion is unauthorized. Between 1789 and 1874, for example, the prohibition of the slave trade (commencing in 1808) and the implementation of individual state laws restricting the entry of paupers meant that both newcomer slaves and paupers could not reside in the United States or specific states legally (Heer 1996:27). Not until the passage of the federal Immigration Act of 1875, however, were convicts, paupers, and prostitutes officially, at the federal level, termed "illegal aliens" (Hutchinson 1981:63–70).

A full century would pass before the number of unauthorized immigrants residing in the United States began to be estimated empirically and before illegal immigration became a major concern of national policymakers. Coincidence had little to do with the 100 years of public disinterest. Rather, the termination of the Bracero program, through which the U.S. government secured a steady supply of Mexican migrant laborers for U.S. corporations, and the creation of the Western Hemispheric cap of 120,000 immigrants per annum in the mid-1960s—as well as the implementation of an immigrant quota system (limited to 20,000 immigrants per nation annually) biased against those nations most likely to be sending migrants—led to the criminalization of flows that had previously been institutionally encouraged by law (Heer 1996:54–58). Thus, accompanying individual desires for economic opportunity and familial association have been institutional forces influencing both legal and unauthorized international migration (Massey et al. 1993).

Initial speculative approximations of the number of unauthorized immigrants residing in the United States in the 1970s varied widely from 2 to 12 million and were not based on empirical evidence. In the early 1980s, however, a consensus emerged among researchers. This was based on more systematic, quantitative estimates produced by what has come to be known as the residual estimation methodology. By subtracting the number of foreign-born persons who were recorded in government administrative records (as either legal permanent residents or naturalized citizens) from the number of foreign-born persons enumerated in census data, researchers were able to obtain an estimate of the number of residual (or resident) unauthorized immigrants. The consensus placed the estimated number of unauthorized immigrants residing in the United States in 1980 between 2 and 4 million, with an additional 100,000 to 300,000 being added to the stock for each of the subsequent six years (Edmonston et al. 1990:27).

Most recent research has built on these earlier estimates and suggests that the estimated number of resident unauthorized immigrants in 1990 was approximately 3.5 million and about 5 million as recently as the mid-1990s, with approximately half of all unauthorized immigrants residing in California (Woodrow-Lafield 1998; Passel 1999). It is important to acknowledge that while these numbers are noteworthy, they represent a very small fraction of the entire U.S. and California populations. Public sentiment toward illegal immigration, as well as recent immigration policy, has been guided more by the ethnoracial composition, geographic concentration, and perceived economic effects of the unauthorized immigrant population. In short, unauthorized immigrants are more likely to be Latino, especially Mexican (Passel 1999); are more likely to be concentrated in relatively few urban-regional areas (Fix and Passel 1994; Marcelli 1999); and have been perceived by many, at least until very recently, to be competing with other lower-skilled U.S. residents for jobs (Bean et al. 1987; Bean, Lowell, et al. 1988; Marcelli 1999; Marcelli et al. 1999) and to be using public resources to which they are not entitled (Marcelli and Heer 1998).

Consequently, a large proportion of studies investigating the economic effects of unauthorized immigration have focused on unauthorized Mexican immigrants in the southwestern United States. Earlier exceptions concerning labor market effects include Grossman (1984), Bean et al. (1987), and U.S. General Accounting Office (1988), but these, as well as those estimating the impact of unauthorized Mexican workers alone, typically report negligible effects on other workers' wage and employment outcomes. More recent evidence for the 1990s in Los Angeles County, where most unauthorized Mexican immigrants reside, confirms these earlier findings (Marcelli 1999; Marcelli et al. 1999). Alternatively, passage of California's 1994 anti–illegal immigration initiative, Proposition 187, as well as the 1996 federal-level Illegal Immigration and Welfare Acts, were motivated by disquiet about unauthorized immigrants' putative use of public assistance, public school resources, and health services. This consensus about unauthorized rather than legal immigrants' socioeconomic costs outweighing their benefit to the United States, however, was based more on anecdotal rather than statistical data and quantitative analysis (Gimpel and Edwards 1999:1–26). This is not because no data or analyses of them existed, however.

Despite concerns of some researchers that "data obtained from survey items about legal status may be highly questionable if not worthless because unauthorized migrants wishing to escape detection may be unlikely to reveal their status in interviews and/or questionnaires" (Van Hook and Bean 1998:511), a series of legal status surveys during the past two decades suggests this is not necessarily the case (Heer 1990; Heer et al. 1992). That is, increasingly reliable survey-based estimates of the number, characteristics, and impact of unauthorized Mexican immigrants have been generated by Mexican and U.S. researchers collaborating in Los Angeles County (Marcelli and Heer 1997). In addition to the knowledge that the survey was sponsored by both Mexican and U.S. universities helping to convince Mexican-born respondents that their reported legal status would remain confidential, employing Mexican-origin interviewers only and having a series of specific legal status questions that could be cross-checked for inconsistencies helped generate data that have been used to produce estimates that are very similar to those using the more popular residual estimation methodology (Heer and Passel 1987; Marcelli 1999). Still, while both residual and survey-based approaches can generate comparable aggregate estimates of the number of unauthorized immigrants, systematic quantitative labor market and welfare impact studies are rarely possible without individual-level, survey-based data. Of course, even when reliable information about the demographic and economic effects of unauthorized immigrants is available, this does not guarantee that the public or their political representatives will heed it.

At least four lessons have emerged from residual and survey-based studies of unauthorized immigration during the past two decades. First, both the residual methodology, originally introduced by Heer (1979) and extended by others (Woodrow-Lafield 1998; Passel 1999), and the survey-based estimation methodology, again introduced by Heer et al. (1992) and developed further by Marcelli and Heer (1997, 1998) and Marcelli (1999), are needed for estimating the number, characteristics, and effects of unauthorized immigration to the United States.

Second, although most scholars do not separate the foreign-born by legal status when investigating the economic effects of immigration, it has become increasingly clear that legal status matters. One of the most prominent immigration scholars who has consistently argued that recent immigrants in the aggregate have a negative effect on U.S.-born workers, for instance, maintains that "illegal aliens surely improve the economic well-being of the many native households who hire them to tend the garden, do household chores, and care for the children" (Borjas 1999:88). Despite such claims even by those generally advocating a more restrictionist U.S. immigration policy, and contrary to existing evidence suggestive of the negligible or positive economic effects of unauthorized immigrants, it should come as no surprise that U.S. immigration policy became more restrictionist toward unauthorized immigration during the 1990s. As previously noted, most immigration impact research does not separate by immigrant legal status, so when negative effects from less-educated immigrant workers are detected, it is a short step to place the blame on unauthorized immigrants, who tend to have lower levels of educational attainment. This is called guilt by association. Lower-skilled U.S.-born workers are having some difficulty getting ahead even as the U.S. economy soars forward at an unprecedented pace. Consequently, those who are most likely to compete with them in the labor market, especially if unauthorized to work, are guilty. Precisely because of unauthorized immigrants' precarious legal status, they are an easy political target for those whose minds "are made up well in advance of any facts" (Gimpel and Edwards 1999:26).

Third, while studies using some variant of the residual estimation methodology provide information about the nations from which unauthorized immigrants come and to which states they enter (Passel 1999), most studies employing a survey-based estimation methodology focus on unauthorized Mexican immigrants residing in Los Angeles County only. Given that at least half of all unauthorized immigrants are of Mexican origin and a plurality resides there, it is both analytically sensible and economically feasible to do so. Nonetheless, because about half of all unauthorized immigrants are not of Mexican origin, the need to survey unauthorized immigrants from other nations is becoming increasingly obvious if an accurate demographic profile of all unauthorized immigrants is desired.

Fourth, given the spatial distribution of unauthorized immigrants in several regions (Passel and Woodrow 1984), there is a need to survey urban-regional areas outside of Los Angeles County. This has been recognized and currently researchers from the Urban Institute and UCLA are surveying foreign-born respondents in New York City as well as Los Angeles. Unauthorized immigrants are concentrated in other regions as well, however, and if we are to have a better understanding of their overall economic effects, surveys from additional regions will be necessary to both check and complement figures generated by residual estimation methodologies.

In sum, during the 1990s demographers significantly improved their methods of estimating the number and characteristics of unauthorized immigrants residing in the United States. While residual methodologies became more sophisticated and provided better national-level, state-level, and national-origin group estimates, survey-based estimation methodologies offered the first direct individual-level analyses of how other U.S. residents were being impacted economically. Most mainstream economists studying U.S. immigration, meanwhile, ignored such advances and did not incorporate the ability to separate by legal status into their research. The challenge that now confronts economists and other social scientists interested in how unauthorized immigrants impact the United States economically is to provide empirically based research that is guided by economic theory and employs either a survey-based or residual estimation methodology combined with census data. Until this is accomplished, public perception and policy most likely will continue to be guided more by anecdotal rather than systematic evidence. *See also*: **Demography; Legislation; Social benefits; Unauthorized immigration.**

References

Bean, Frank D., Rodolpho Corona, Rodolpho Tuirán, and Karen A. Woodrow-Lafield. 1998. The Quantification of Migration Between Mexico and the United States. In *Binational Study: Migration Between Mexico and the United States*. Mexican

Ministry of Foreign Affairs and U.S. Commission on Immigration Reform. Pp. 1–90. Austin, TX: Morgan Printing.

Bean, Frank D., B. Lindsey Lowell, and Lowell Taylor. 1998. Undocumented Mexican Immigrants and the Earnings of Other Workers in the United States. *Demography* 25:35–52.

Bean, Frank D., Edward Telles, and Lindsey Lowell. 1987. Undocumented Migration in the United States: Perception and Evidence. *Population and Development Review* 13(4):671–690.

Borjas, George J. 1999. *Heaven's Door: Immigration Policy and the American Economy.* Princeton, NJ: Princeton University Press.

Edmonston, Barry, Jeffrey S. Passel, and Frank D. Bean. 1990. Perceptions and Estimates of Undocumented Migration to the United States. In *Undocumented Migration to the United States: IRCA and the Experience of the 1980s.* Frank D. Bean, Barry Edmonston, and Jeffrey S. Passel, eds. Pp. 11–31. Santa Monica, CA: RAND Corporation and Washington, DC: Urban Institute.

Fix, Michael, and Jeffrey S. Passel. 1994. *Immigration and Immigrants: Setting the Record Straight.* Washington, DC: Urban Institute.

Gimpel, James G., and James R. Edwards Jr. 1999. *The Congressional Politics of Immigration Reform.* Boston: Allyn and Bacon.

Grossman, Jean Baldwin. 1984. Illegal Immigrants and Domestic Employment. *Industrial and Labor Relations Review* 37(2):240–251.

Heer, David M. 1979. What Is the Annual Net Flow of Undocumented Mexican Immigrants to the United States? *Demography* 16(3):417–424.

———. 1990. *Undocumented Mexicans in the United States.* New York: Cambridge University Press.

———. 1996. *Immigration in America's Future: Social Science Findings and the Policy Debate.* Boulder, CO: Westview Press.

Heer, David M., V. Agadjanian, F. Hammad, Y. Qui, and S. Ramasundaram. 1992. A Comparative Analysis of the Position of Undocumented Mexicans in the Los Angeles County Workforce in 1980. *International Migration* 3(2):101–126.

Heer, David M., and Jeffrey S. Passel. 1987. Comparison of Two Methods for Computing the Number of Undocumented Mexican Adults in Los Angeles County. *International Migration Review* 21:1446–1473.

Hutchinson, Edward P. 1981. *Legislative History of American Immigration Policy, 1798–1965.* Philadelphia: University of Pennsylvania Press.

Marcelli, Enrico A. 1999. Undocumented Latino Immigrant Workers: The Los Angeles Experience. In *Illegal Immigration in America: A Reference Handbook.* David W. Haines and Karen E. Rosenblum, eds. Pp. 193–231. Westport, CT: Greenwood Press.

Marcelli, Enrico A., and David M. Heer. 1997. Unauthorized Mexican Workers in the 1990 Los Angeles County Labour Force. *International Migration* 35:59–83.

———. 1998. The Unauthorized Mexican Immigrant Population and Welfare in Los Angeles County: A Comparative Statistical Analysis. *Sociological Perspectives* 41:279–302.

Marcelli, Enrico A., Manuel Pastor Jr., and Pascale M. Joassart. 1999. Estimating the Effects of Informal Economic Activity: Evidence from Los Angeles County. *Journal of Economic Issues* 33:579–608.

Massey, Douglas, Joaquín Arango, Graeme Hugo, Ali Kouaouci, Adela Pellegrino, and J. Edward Taylor. 1993. Theories of International Migration: A Review and Appraisal. *Population and Development Review* 19:431–466.

Passel, Jeffrey S. 1999. Undocumented Immigration to the United States: Numbers, Trends, and Characteristics. In *Illegal Immigration in America: A Reference Handbook.*

David W. Haines and Karen E. Rosenblum, eds. Pp. 27–111. Westport, CT: Greenwood Press.

Passel, Jeffrey S., and Karen A. Woodrow. 1984. Geographic Distribution of Undocumented Immigrants: Estimates of Undocumented Aliens Counted in the 1980 Census by State. *International Migration Review* 28:642–671.

Smith, James P., and Barry Edmonston, eds. 1997. *The New Americans: Economic, Demographic, and Fiscal Effects of Immigration*. Washington, DC: National Academy Press.

U.S. General Accounting Office. 1988. *Illegal Aliens: Influence of Illegal Workers on Wages and Working Conditions of Legal Workers*. Washington, DC: GAO/PEMD-88-13MB.

Van Hook, Jennifer, and Frank D. Bean. 1998. Estimating Unauthorized Mexican Migration to the United States: Issues and Results. In *Binational Study: Migration Between Mexico and the United States*. Mexican Ministry of Foreign Affairs and U.S. Commission on Immigration Reform. Pp. 511–550. Austin, TX: Morgan Printing.

Woodrow-Lafield, Karen. 1998. Undocumented Residents in the United States in 1990: Issues of Uncertainty in Quantification. *International Migration Review* 32:145–173.

ENRICO MARCELLI

EMIGRATION. With so much focus on immigration to the United States, it is easy to overlook the flow of people out of the country. Indeed, national data on emigration from the United States do not exist, leaving critical problems for demographic projections and national immigration policy (Woodrow-Lafield and Kraly 2004). Better knowledge of emigration would also inform our understanding of patterns of settlement and residence as well as the economics of transnational processes. What is the net gain or loss of population likely to be in future years? How likely are professionals to leave, or high-tech immigrant workers to remain? How predictable are future remittances? How do long-term intentions influence daily decisions or civic involvement? These are just a few of the questions that go unanswered, questions that appear even more significant after several decades during which migration became the key component in changing the contours of the world population (Massey 1995), and more heterogeneously complex in the United States in regard to ethnicity, generation, and citizenship.

Emigration entails departure by long-term residents from a country of settlement (like the United States) for long-term settlement in another country. In most nations there are few or no policies to intervene with individual decision-making to emigrate (United Nations 2002), and the United States is no exception. As a result, we have little clarity about what accounts either for departure of native-born and naturalized citizens or for emigration of foreign-born, or what is generally termed return migration (emigration of immigrants to their country of origin). Since migration so often involves clusters of people or families of varying places of origin and legal statuses, emigration decisions and dynamics are likely even more complicated than one might expect.

Like unauthorized immigration, emigration is inherently difficult to calculate. This is even more the case since collection of direct measures of emigration from the United States was stopped in 1957. Despite a lack of firm statistics, it is estimated that between 1900 and 1990, when roughly 38 million immigrants were admitted into the country, about 12 million (or 30 percent) subsequently emigrated. Emigration varies over time, however (Borjas and Bratsberg 1996). Until the 1920s, an era of high immigration to the United States was matched by frequent return, including one in three in the "great return" of European migrants (Warren and Kraly 1985). This was followed by a period of low immigration as a consequence of restrictive legislation, and apparently less emigration, perhaps because assimilation processes were generally effective. A growth of migration from Asia and Latin America following the immigration policy shift in 1965 and arrival and resettlement of Southeast Asian refugees in the 1970s–1980s appear to have been accompanied by less emigration at least at first, as immigrants had less time or inclination to reverse their decisions. Most analysts presume an increase in emigration by the late twentieth century.

Rates of emigration also vary widely depending on whether a person is foreign-born or native-born. During the 1990s, annual levels of emigration for foreign-born individuals (return migration) have been estimated at 220,000 compared to 48,000 for native-born; in other words, returning migrants constitute about four-fifths of all emigration (USCIS 2000). Not surprisingly, the destination countries of return migrants are generally those from which they migrated, the top five during the 1980s being Mexico, the United Kingdom, Germany, Canada, and Japan.

Both duration and rates of emigration are affected by many factors. Substantial costs, both economic and psychological, are implicit in waiting time, delayed family formation and childbearing, separation from family, changes in wages, and employment. Individual and family decisions are also influenced by sending countries' policies regarding remittances, dual citizenship, and the appropriateness of migration—ranging from vilification to Mexico's recent acknowledgment of migrants as "heroes." Prospective emigrants in home countries may do many things to absorb American culture in advance, what Gans (1999) terms "anticipatory acculturation." All of this may influence commitment to migrate to the United States, adaptive success, and intentions regarding long-term settlement as opposed to return migration. Emigration considerations are also heavily affected by level of receptivity in new settings, practical functionality of networks, and the presence and ages of children, not to mention political and economic conditions in countries of origin (Lindstrom 1996).

The substantial proportion of emigration represented by return migration encompasses arrangements ranging from short-term visits "home" to permanent return. Return visits may be occasioned by family crisis (such as death of a close family member), community solidarity (including participation in annual festivals or events in a home community), and legal and investment concerns. Desire to see relatives after long separation is of particular concern when separation involves spouses or parents and children. Return may also be an intrinsic part of plans to effect family reunification. Return migration often occurs during holidays, and travel during Christmas, in particular, is facilitated by seasonal slowdown in the pace of work in agriculture, canning, and apparel production in the United States. Many employees work out schedules and clear provisions with employers for reassuming work.

Longer-term or permanent return migration also occurs for a variety of reasons. Some immigrants are disillusioned with the opportunities and lifestyle offered in the United States or have run into financial, legal, or social problems.

Others have met their "target" income or other goals that motivated their migration in the first place. Still others may opt to return with new investment ideas and resources, or to "give back" some of what they have gained, including through emergent avenues of transnational philanthropy aimed at promoting development and democracy.

In the case of native-born, emigration has been part of U.S. migration history and mythology since the early days of the Republic. For example, the nineteenth-century short story "A Man Without a Country" recounts the hostile reception to an expatriate who returns from abroad. Popularly called "expats" by others as well as themselves, American expatriates include at least three main types: people in business who relocate to a different position or place of operations, entrepreneurs looking for opportunities abroad, and those who leave out of frustration with personal or political matters in the United States. Professionals may be most likely to be mobile, as well as privileged, while mid-range and independent-minded workers comprise some of the pioneering emigrants. Cities in Europe became havens for left-leaning expatriates throughout the twentieth century, including the "Left Bank" in Paris which became perhaps the most notable home away from home for socialists, jazz players, African Americans tired of discrimination, and others disaffected by social conditions in the United States. A wealth of literature and music records the angst of disaffection as well as distance. Not surprisingly, many of the same reasons motivating native-born emigrants from the United States resonate with similar motives and processes that surround people seeking to emigrate from other countries to the United States.

Communities, organizations, restaurants, sporting events, and holidays involving or operated by emigrants from the United States can be found across the globe (Bratsberg and Terrell 1996). From gated beach enclaves from Baja to Bali, to "hippie havens" in Panajachel and Kathmandu, emigrants contribute both directly and inadvertently to globalization processes that are distinctively "American," however much they may also mix in considerable local color.

Should levels of emigration increase in the future while levels of in-migration (immigration) remain constant, or even decline, the result would be a decline in the annual net migration to the United States—far different from the "out-of-control" immigration scenario often recounted today. Certainly linear calculations of either immigration or emigration levels are likely to greatly oversimplify or misrepresent actual human behavior. What is clear is that people can and do leave the United States, usually with the most admirable of intentions, and frequently with very positive results. *See also*: **Migration processes; Return migration.**

References

Borjas, George J., and Bernt Bratsberg. 1996. Who Leaves? The Emigration of the Foreign-Born. *Review of Economics and Statistics* 78:165–167.

Bratsberg, Bernt, and Dek Terrell. 1996. Where Do Americans Live Abroad? *International Migration Review* 30:788–802.

Gans, Herbert J. 1999. Filling In Some Holes: Six Areas of Needed Immigration Research. *American Behavioral Scientist* 42:1302–1313.

Lindstrom, David P. 1996. Economic Opportunity in Mexico and Return Migration from the United States. *Demography* 33:357–374.

Massey, D.S. 1995. The New Immigration and Ethnicity in the United States. *Population and Development Review* 21:631–652.

Reagan, Patricia B., and Randall J. Olsen. 2000. You Can Go Home Again: Evidence from Longitudinal Data. *Demography* 37:339–350.

United Nations. 2002. *National Population Policies*. New York: United Nations.

U.S. Citizenship and Immigration Services (USCIS). 2000. *Statistical Yearbook*. http://www.uscis.gov/graphics/shared/aboutus/statistics/Emigrat.htm.

Warren, R., and E.P. Kraly. 1985. The Elusive Exodus: Emigration from the United States. Population Trends and Public Policy Occasional Paper No. 8. Washington, DC: Population Reference Bureau.

Woodrow-Lafield, Karen A., and Ellen Percy Kraly. 2004. *Points of Departure: Emigration from the United States*. Boston: Population Association of America.

JAMES LOUCKY

EMPLOYER SANCTIONS. Employer sanctions are regulations imposed upon employers to prevent the hiring and employment of unauthorized or "illegal" workers. They are the major tool in the "control" component of the Immigration Reform and Control Act of 1986 (IRCA). Prior to IRCA it was illegal for undocumented (or unauthorized) immigrants to work in the United States, but it was not a violation of federal law to employ undocumented immigrants, resulting in a huge loophole that effectively condoned the hiring of undocumented workers.

Many factors contributed to the push for employer sanctions (Fix and Hill 1990). Principal was the perception that undocumented immigrant workers took jobs away from American citizens, especially those from low-income and minority backgrounds. Adverse job impacts, including unemployment and less favorable wages and working conditions, were deemed by proponents to be greater than the short-term advantages of "cheap" labor. These impacts in turn created greater burdens for taxpayers and social problems associated with unemployment and poverty. Another contributing factor that favored institutionalizing employer sanctions was xenophobia, whereby the general public believed that immigrants would not assimilate into American society, thereby threatening the unity and political stability of the country. There were perhaps as many organizations opposed to employer sanctions as there were groups calling for them. One of the main arguments against employer sanctions was that many businesses, especially in the agricultural section, relied heavily upon undocumented labor. It was argued that undocumented workers took jobs that no one else wanted and thus were not "stealing" jobs from other workers. Civil rights organizations and ethnic advocacy groups further argued that employers would discriminate against employees who appeared or sounded "foreign." Others voiced concern that the document requirements of employer sanctions would create a burden on businesses and might eventually lead to some form of national identification card.

IRCA sought to preserve jobs for those who were legally entitled to them: U.S. citizens and legal aliens. The main employment provision of IRCA requires employers to verify an employee's identity and eligibility to work in the United States. Every employee hired after November 6, 1986, must have an I-9 form kept on record with the employer, which verifies that an employee is eligible to work in the United States. At the time of hire, employees present a document that establishes both identity and employment eligibility, such as a U.S. passport, certificate of U.S. citizenship, certificate of naturalization, or unexpired Employment Authorization Card. Alternately, if an employee does not have one of these forms of identification, they can present two documents, one establishing identity and another which establishes employment eligibility. Examples of documents which establish identity include, but are not limited to, a driver's license or state-issued ID card, a school ID card with photograph, or a voter's registration card. Documents that establish employment eligibility include, but are not limited to, a U.S. social security card, a Native American tribal document, or an unexpired employment authorization document issued by the Immigration and Naturalization Service (INS). In major U.S. cities today, sophisticated identification and work documents can be obtained quite cheaply and in a matter of hours.

To combat the fear that employers would react to these new sanctions by discriminating against potential employees who appeared "foreign," IRCA included an anti-discrimination provision under which employers with four or more employees are prohibited from discriminating on the basis of citizenship or perceived citizenship. Employers are not allowed to ask to see a specific document or more than the minimum required documents. For example, employers may not refuse to hire asylees, refugees, or immigrants because their employment authorization documents contain expiration dates, nor are they to retaliate against employees who cooperate in an investigation, file a complaint, or testify at a hearing.

In reality employer sanctions resulted in considerable confusion at first and questionable effectiveness overall. The policy fails to provide clear means for employers to quickly and easily verify documents. There has been a surge of production and use of fraudulent documents resulting in burgeoning counterfeit operations. Given the wide array of identification and work-authorization cards, employers may not know which documents are legitimate and which documents are fraudulent, and in any case it is hard to prove that an employer knew the documents were not legitimate.

The Office of Special Counsel for Immigration-Related Unfair Employment Practices (OSC), Civil Rights Division, U.S. Department of Justice enforces the anti-discrimination provisions of IRCA, and the INS enforced the employer sanctions provisions. The enforcement priorities of the INS (and today, Bureau of Citizenship and Immigration Services [BCIS]) was another weakness, given that their enforcement responsibilities include removal of unauthorized immigrants found to be criminals, combating drug trafficking and human smuggling, and identifying immigration marriage fraud, as well as employer sanctions.

The enforcement of employer sanctions began with widespread education of employers. It was reasonable to think that employers would need education as they had become accustomed to and dependent upon hiring undocumented workers. Conducted by the INS, educational visits served to make employers aware of the new sanctions but ensure also that once employers were penalized by IRCA they could not claim ignorance. Another purpose of educational visits was to provide potential leads for violators. For example, foreign names on time cards could trigger a further investigation.

Penalties for violations of employer sanctions can be very harsh, ranging from $250 to $2,000 for each alien under a first offense, to as much as $10,000 per alien for the third and further offenses. Failure to fill out and maintain I-9's correctly can result in fines from $100 to $1,000 for each form. Nonetheless, it is difficult to prove that an employer knowingly employed an unauthorized alien. In 1996, the Illegal Immigration Reform and Immigrant Responsibility Act (IIRIR) added a small provision to the employer sanctions enacted under IRCA, one which prohibited employers from being fined for technical paperwork violations without the opportunity to correct the errors.

The main goal of employer sanctions is to protect American workers and other authorized workers, and selective high-profile cases have sought to demonstrate that sanctions work. However, if the United States sees more unauthorized immigrants within its borders, calls for tougher sanctions may ensue. By 2005, federal legislation was being proposed that could make it a felony not only to be in the United States without authorization but also to assist unauthorized immigrants, such as by offering employment. Many others, on the other hand, call for a humane policy based on evidence and practicality. As long as immigrant labor is so economically advantageous to employers and consumers alike, sanctions may serve mainly to affirm the government's recognition of the issue, while the overall system is allowed to continue. *See also*: **Immigration system; Legislation; Unauthorized immigration.**

References

Fix, Michael, and Paul T. Hill. 1990. *Enforcing Employer Sanctions: Challenges and Strategies*. Santa Monica, CA: RAND Corporation.

Kurzban, Ira J. 1998. *Kurzban's Immigration Law Sourcebook: A Comprehensive Outline and Reference Tool*. Pp. 876–882. Washington, DC: American Immigration Law Foundation.

U.S. Department of Agriculture, Office of the Chief Economist. 2002. Agricultural Labor Affairs, IRCA Anti-Discrimination Provisions. http://www.usda.gov/agency/oce/oce/labor-affairs/ircadisc.htm.

U.S. Department of Labor. 1991. *Impact of IRCA on the U.S. Labor Market and Economy*. Washington, DC: Bureau of International Labor Affairs.

JAMES LOUCKY

ENSLAVEMENT. Contemporary slavery has evolved into new forms that diverge from the ownership of humans as property characteristic of the pre–Civil War American South. Defining the new slavery as "complete control of a person for economic exploitation by violence or the threat of violence" (Bales 2000:462) reveals that slaves today are no longer kept as property, but as coerced labor to be used as a disposable work input on a limited time basis (Bales 1999, 2000). There are three major contemporary types of slavery. Traditional or chattel slavery is sometimes found today when "a person is born, captured or sold into permanent servitude and ownership is often asserted"; debt bondage, most common, occurs when "a person pledges him or herself against a loan of money, but the length and nature of the service is undefined, and the labor does not diminish the original debt"; and contract slavery occurs when an individual is offered a contract under misleading pretense, transported, threatened with violence, and enslaved to work without pay (Bales 2000:463). In the late twentieth and early twenty-first centuries, contract slavery is increasing and, notably, both debt bondage and contract slavery do not involve assertion of ownership, which was characteristic of slavery in the past.

Economic globalization is associated with an oversupply of labor in developing countries. This has resulted in a situation where workers, seen as of little intrinsic value, are used for a period of time while minimizing input of food, shelter, and other care, and then discarded when no longer of use. Kevin Bales (2000:466) identifies seven ways in which slavery of the pre–Civil War American South differs from the new slavery. Old forms were characterized by the assertion of legal ownership, high purchase cost, low profits, shortage of potential slaves, a long-term relationship, providing maintenance of slaves, and the importance of ethnic differences. By contrast, in new forms of slavery, legal ownership is avoided, purchase cost and profits are very high, there is a surplus of potential slaves, relationships are short term, slaves are disposable, and ethnic differences are generally unimportant.

Today contemporary workers are often tricked into enslavement through false contracts of debt servitude and then subject to violent control. Workers are often made responsible for their own upkeep and abandoned if unable to work. Furthermore, slavery today is based mainly on social inequalities of power and wealth rather than racial-ethnic differentiation. In the United States, Irish American employers and landlords may place undocumented Irish immigrants in sub–minimum wage jobs akin to involuntary servitude (Gozdiak 1999:268), whereas Eastern European and Russian immigrant women have been enslaved for prostitution (Hughes 2000).

Economic globalization has generated social conditions in developing countries which foster increased emigration. These include increased unemployment, the closing or reduction in enterprises producing goods for national use rather than export, and extensive government debt which in turn brings imposition of structural adjustment programs in which austerity measures limit education and social services. Households, communities, and governments are increasingly dependent on the remittance income of women abroad, as they used to be on male laborers in the past. This results in a "feminization of survival" and emergence of "counter-geographies of globalization," which are migration circuits associated with global economic conditions but "not typically represented or seen as connected to globalization, [which] often operate outside and in violation of laws and treaties, yet are not exclusively embedded in criminal operations as is the case with the illegal drug trade" (Sassen 2000:523). By entering into human trafficking, women become increasingly susceptible to enslavement as they search for survival income for themselves and households in their homeland.

Globalization has fostered transnational underground economies and organized criminal networks. Enslaved American immigrants originate from numerous countries, including Mexico, Poland, Russia, China, Thailand, India, Brazil, Ethiopia, Mauritania, Nigeria, and Cameroon. The most common method of enslavement is debt bondage. Contracts for being smuggled into the United States may require payments as high as $40,000 to $50,000, which lock undocumented workers in low-wage jobs into debt.

Immigration controls and resultant human trafficking, which is to be differentiated from human smuggling, is a major factor in the re-emergence of contract and debt servitude in the United States. Interpol has indicated that substantial sentences for drug trafficking have turned traffickers' attention to the equally profitable but less penalized transport of undocumented immigrants for the purpose of coerced labor (Bales 2000). Compared to human smuggling, which refers to the unlawful transport of people across borders for a fee, human trafficking involves smuggling plus coercion or exploitation. The United Nations draft Convention on Transnational Organized Crime delimits trafficking in people as "the recruitment, transfer, harboring or receipt of persons, either by the threat or use of abduction, force, fraud, deception or coercion, or by the giving or receiving of unlawful payments or benefits to achieve the consent of a person having control over another person" (Martin and Miller 2000:969–970). In practice, although some smuggling is individualized and does not involve coercion, as when aid is given to asylum seekers, it is difficult to draw a distinction between smuggling and trafficking, as both are illegal. An important method for enacting debt bondage is for human smugglers to "allow" individuals to contract for passage based on paying off the fee by work in the receiving country. Thus, human trafficking is intimately connected to enslavement, and smuggling operations can produce cases of enslavement.

Concerns about undocumented immigration and enslavement were addressed in the Trafficking Victims Protection Act of 2000, which authorized tougher penalties for human smugglers, including life imprisonment for individuals who engage in child sex-trafficking (Chaddock 2000:2). Previously, trafficking victims were likely to be punished and deported, discouraging them from taking action. To encourage enslaved immigrants to report this activity, visas are to be issued to undocumented immigrants who cooperate with law enforcement assistance provided to victims of traffickers regardless of immigration status.

The four main venues for enslavement of immigrants in the United States are: (1) child or adult domestic service, (2) farm workers kept in coerced labor camps under armed guard, (3) sweatshops, and (4) prostitution. The practice of enslavement varies from isolated individual cases to systematic exploitation of large numbers of workers. Locks, physical barriers, and verbal threats are common forms of coercion to effect enslavement, and abuse of human rights during enslavement may include physical abuse and rape.

The provision or hiring of undocumented immigrant women for domestic labor and childcare has produced a number of individualized cases of enslavement, sometimes including rape, by unscrupulous private household employers. In the Haitian migration stream, some immigrants bring *restavics* (child servants), importing a centuries-old practice (Cadet 1998). Another source of indentured servitude is the provision that foreign employers, such as embassy officials and those working for international organizations, may bring domestic servants to the United States (Branigan 1999). In the 1990s, 30,000 domestics were brought to the United States under special work visas which restrict them to a sponsoring employer, generally foreign diplomats or non-U.S. staff of international organizations. There is no monitoring of whether contracts are realized, and individuals may work hours well in excess of U.S. labor law and receive little or no pay. One method of employer abuse is impounding a servant's visa. In 2001, international organizations implicated in these abuses, particularly the World Bank and the International Monetary Fund (whose employees were a large group of those eligible to bring in foreign domestic workers), began generating codes of conduct to educate their employees about U.S. worker rights (*Washington Post* 2001). In addition, visa applicants are now being informed about worker rights by the State Department.

Many cases of enslavement take place in rural or farm work. Undocumented immigrants, along with citizen farm workers, have been found impounded in barricaded camps and forced to work for no pay in a state of debt bondage to the crew leader in isolated rural regions in the South (Rothenberg 1998). Similarly, undocumented immigrants from Latin America may be held in debt bondage to "pay off" a smuggling fee. Workers may also be "charged" for food, housing, and other necessities, thereby entering a condition of involuntary servitude. While previously those coerced into farm labor were primarily African Americans, and sometimes homeless, alcoholics, or drug addicts, today it is often immigrant Latino farm workers who receive very low wages and endure poor working conditions and quality of life.

Sweatshops, subcontracting factories in apparel and other industries, often violate labor laws such as the minimum wage and standards for working conditions. Because sweatshops are often underground, it is not surprising that conditions of indentured servitude and enslavement occur. Undocumented Chinese immigrants from the province of Fuzhou have been found indentured within the Fuzhounese Chinese ethnic enclave of New York's Chinatown (Kwong 1997), bound by smuggling debts as high as $30,000 which business owners pay "snakeheads" (smugglers) to sponsor clandestine immigration. With enforcement resources concentrated at the U.S.-Mexico border, there has been little left for prosecuting human smuggling, which is concentrated in global cities such as Los Angeles and New York.

Prostitution is a major form of enslavement in the United States, with close connection to sexually exploitative trafficking, defined as "any practice which involves moving people within and across local or national borders for the purpose of sexual exploitation" (Hughes 2000:627–628). It may be the result of "force, coercion, manipulation, deception, abuse of authority, initial consent, family pressure, past and present family and community violence, economic deprivation, or other conditions of inequality for women and children" (ibid.). It is estimated that 45,000 to 50,000 women per year are illegally brought into the United States, usually by crime rings.

Based on North-South disparities in assets, sexual enslavement provides a source of remittances and foreign exchange by violating women's basic humanity. Most enslaved women are from Southeast Asia or Latin America, but countries of the former Eastern Bloc and Soviet Union are now the world's chief suppliers of girls and women forced into prostitution. In some areas of the world, these women are so frequently involved in prostitution that they are stereotypically referred to as "Natashas" (Hughes 2000). Although some women are aware that they will become sex workers, most believe that they are emigrating to enter a legitimate form of work. These women are often deprived of their documents, and become subject to rape, sexual violence, and physical punishment. HIV protection and medical treatment are often denied, and underpaid or given no wages, these women become part of the global sex industry (Bertone 2000; Sassen 2000).

In addition, many girls and women are kidnapped or coerced into forced marriage. Mail-order brides can also be subject to domestic violence and involuntary servitude. The mail-order bride industry has been expanding in the United States, fueled by sex stereotyping of foreign women as more docile and compliant than U.S. women. The United States Citizenship and Immigration Services regulates international marriages through a "Marriage Viability Requirement," which places marriages on a conditional status for two years to prevent immigration fraud. Brides are subject to deportation if the marriage does not work out in a two-year period and need to provide substantial proof of maltreatment if battered by their husband, but viewed through the lens of gender this violates the immigrant bride's right to privacy, due process, and equal protection under the law (Simon 1999). There is little to deter organized crime; in fact, the International Organization for Migration (IOM) considers that all mail-order bride agencies in the former Soviet republics are connected to crime rings (Hughes 2000).

Strengthening education for girls in migrant sending countries, increasing awareness of sex trafficking among potential victim populations, and developing employment and income-earning opportunities for women are considered ways to reduce immigrant prostitution (Bertone 2000). Furthermore, extending care and assistance to sexually exploited women rather than simply deporting them is a more effective response on the part of the developed world. Despite these possibilities, current international treaties outlawing slavery and trafficking for the purpose of prostitution are ineffectively enforced and the global sex trade is increasing.

Key to anti-slavery efforts is global education, the strengthening of international laws regulating trade in "forced labor" (Kwong 1997), and global cooperation in enforcement of anti-slavery and indentured servitude laws (Bales 1999). Globalization facilitates the dissemination of knowledge that can influence practice, providing consumers and activists with the means to respond to this inhumanity. *See also*: **Domestic work; Human smuggling; Marriage; Sweatshops; Unauthorized immigration; U.S.-Mexico border.**

References

Anderson, Michelle J. 1993. A License to Abuse: Impact of Conditional Status on Female Immigrants. *Yale Law Journal* 102:1401.

Bales, Kevin. 1999. *Disposable People: New Slavery in the Global Economy*. Berkeley: University of California Press.

———. 2000. Expendable People: Slavery in the Age of Globalization. *Journal of International Affairs* 53(2):461–484.

Bertone, Andrea. 2000. Sexual Trafficking in Women: International Political Economy and the Politics of Sex. *Gender Issues* 18(1):4–22.

Branigan, James. 1999. Modern-Day Slavery? Imported Servants Allege Abuse by Foreign Host Families. *Washington Post*, January 5, A1.

Cadet, Jean-Robert. 1998. *Restavic: From Haitian Slave Child to Middle-Class American*. Austin: University of Texas Press.

Chaddock, Gail Russell. 2000. Congress Takes Aim at Modern-Day Slavery: Traffickers in Human Cargo for Sex Trade or Sweatshops Will Face Tougher Penalties. *Christian Science Monitor*, October 18, 2.

Gozdiak, Elzbieta M. 1999. Illegal Europeans: Transients Between Two Societies. In *Illegal Immigration in America: A Reference Handbook*. David W. Haines and Karen E. Rosenblum, eds. Pp. 254–273. Westport, CT: Greenwood Press.

Hughes, Donna M. 2000. The "Natasha" Trade: The Transnational Shadow Market of Trafficking in Women. *Journal of International Affairs* 53(2):625–651.

Kwong, Peter. 1997. *Forbidden Workers: Illegal Chinese Immigrants and American Labor*. New York: The New Press.

Los Angeles Times. 2001. Man Given 11 Years for Holding Illegal Immigrant in Slavery. April 17, B4.

Martin, Philip, and Mark Miller. 2000. Smuggling and Trafficking: A Conference Report. *International Migration Review* 34(3):969–975.

Richard, Amy O'Neil. 1999. *International Trafficking in Women to the United States: A Contemporary Manifestation of Slavery and Organized Crime*. Washington, DC: Center for the Study of Intelligence (newsletter).

Rothenberg, Daniel. 1998. *With These Hands: The Hidden World of Migrant Farm Workers Today*. New York: Harcourt, Brace.

Sassen, Saskia. 2000. Women's Burden: Counter-Geographies of Globalization and the Feminization of Survival. *Journal of International Affairs* 53(2):503–524.

Simon, Lisa. 1999. Mail Order Brides: The Legal Framework and Possibilities for Change. In *Gender and Immigration*. Gregory A. Kelson and Debra DeLaet, eds. Pp. 127–143. New York: New York University Press.

Su, Julie. 1997. El Monte Thai Garment Workers: Slave Sweatshops. In *No Sweat: Fashion, Free Trade and the Rights of Garment Workers*. Andrew Ross, ed. Pp. 143–150. New York: Verso.

Washington Post. 2001. Invisible Workers. June 25, A14.

JUDITH WARNER

ETHNICITY. "The word 'ethnic' derives via Latin from the Greek ethnikos, the adjectival form of ethnos, a nation or race. As originally used in English, ethnic signified 'not Christian or Jewish, pagan, heathen'" (Petersen et al. 1982). Although the term "ethnicity" was first used by David Riesman in 1953 to refer to cultural characteristics that distinguish a group of people, sociologists have long studied ethnic difference and ethnic groups since this occurs in most societies. Max Weber's classic definition of an ethnic group is one whose members have a "subjective belief in their common descent because of similarities of physical type or of customs or both or because of memories of colonization and migration" (Weber 1968). An ethnic group may share language, folklore, food, religion, country of origin, and social customs. The ethnicity-based approach to explain difference appeared in the early twentieth century to counter the biological approach, which was influenced by social Darwinism and eugenics. This biological paradigm assumed that race was a legitimate category that could be used to assert white superiority. The concept of ethnicity or ethnic groupings was popularized within academic circles and writings by the "Chicago School" of sociology during the 1920s and 1930s.

When some ethnic groups are perceived as having distinct physical traits, they may be seen as racial groups. Ethnicity can therefore be an identity claimed by members of a group, whereas "racial categories [are] seen as more imposed by outsiders" (Alba 2000). Omi (1994) suggests a definition of race as a "concept which signifies and symbolizes social conflicts and interests by referring to different types of human bodies." The distinction between race and ethnicity is often arbitrary and fluid as reflected in the ability of some immigrant groups such as Irish and Jews, which were originally categorized racially, to become "white" ethnic groups over time.

According to the ethnicity model, race was socially constructed and "ethnicity itself was understood as the result of a group formation process based on culture and descent" (Omi 1994). Since "descent" refers to heredity, ethnicity thus was initially viewed as biologically determined, but later ethnicity theory argued that ethnic categories were as much socially constructed as racial categories. This new approach emerged out of post–World War II reactions against racism as it appeared in Germany and a liberal ideal of racial/ethnic equality and incorporation. Structural racism continued to present obstacles for some groups' full participation in American society, however. "Many blacks . . . rejected ethnic identity in favor of a more radical racial identity, which demanded group rights and recognition" (Omi 1994). While liberal sociologists who originally espoused replacing the race paradigm with the ethnic group paradigm considered this a progressive move toward greater assimilation, some African Americans rejected that model as ignoring racist obstacles to a model of assimilation based on the experiences of predominantly European ethnic groups and instead espoused black nationalism. Another criticism of the ethnicity paradigm is that it does not recognize the unique experience of African Americans due to historical discrimination originating under slavery.

Over time members of the European ethnic groups that have immigrated to the United States became "assimilated" to varying degrees into the dominant society. Originally the assimilation approach dominated the study of immigration and ethnic relations in the United States. In the Anglo conformity model, the newcomers would gradually adapt the values and culture of the dominant group, which was defined as being primarily Protestant and having British ancestry. The "melting pot" model, however, whose name was first coined by playwright Israel Zangwill, gained recognition due to the increased waves of diverse ethnic groups immigrating into the United States. This model viewed American society and identity as formed by the biological and cultural fusion of different peoples (Alba and Nee 1997). Although the melting pot concept was challenged by Horace Kallen and other pluralists at the beginning of the twentieth century, the Anglo conformity and melting pot models became the dominant paradigms for "successful" assimilation during the early sociological studies of ethnic groups. It should also be noted that residential integration and intermarriage were seen as measures of assimilation and social integration.

The assimilation model used to describe the social process of immigration and Americanization of different ethnic groups fell into disrepute for awhile since it had acquired the connotation that ethnic groups should abandon their "inferior" or "parochial" cultures and adapt to the dominant Anglo-American culture. Cultural pluralism is a more recent model used to describe immigrants' adaptation in which groups may remain "socially differentiated, often with their own institutions and high rates of in group marriage" (Alba 2000). However, a modified concept of assimilation that recognizes the continuing heterogeneity of American culture while considering the process of socioeconomic and spatial assimilation is still relevant to an analysis of the immigration experience.

As immigrant groups become absorbed into American society through social mobility and intermarriage, maintaining ethnic identity and ethnic enclaves become less important to some groups, while others tenaciously cling to their ethnic and cultural heritage. Some scholars such as Andrew Greeley and Samuel

Huntington maintain that the persistence of ethnic differences and massive immigration has overwhelmed the ability of the dominant white, Anglo-Saxon, Protestant culture to absorb the subgroups, resulting in an American mosaic of subcultures. Some perceive this mosaic as a threat to E Pluribus Unum, a nation united under common values and a shared identity. This is the philosophy of Arthur Schlesinger Jr. in *The Disuniting of America: Reflections on a Multicultural Society*, who argues that too much emphasis on multiculturalism and bilingualism, which he refers to as the "cult of ethnicity," will create a fragmented United States (which some have termed "balkanization") in which immigrants will not be encouraged to assimilate, accepting the "language, the institutions and the political ideals that hold the nation together" (Schlesinger 1992).

Herbert Gans described "symbolic ethnicity" as the new expression of ethnic identity by third-generation Americans. He maintains that expressions of ethnicity have been used primarily by working-class groups as a "psychological and political defense against the injustices that they suffer in an unequal society" (Gans 1979). According to Gans, the third generation has usually lost contact with the language and customs that provide an ethnic identity and may join an ethnic organization or affiliate with an "abstract collectivity that does not exist as an interacting group" (ibid.). While symbolic ethnicity may be maintained from a sense of nostalgia for the immigrant culture and heritage, it may also be motivated by loyalty to a homeland afflicted by political conflicts as in the case of Ireland and Israel. Concerns about the homeland, as well as experiences of discrimination, have sometimes transformed an ethnic group into a political interest group (Glazer and Moynihan 1963).

Due to restrictive immigration policies implemented in the early twentieth century, the immigrants who arrived before 1965 were predominantly European. The major periods of immigration from the Asian countries were between the late nineteenth century and 1924. In 1882, Congress passed the Chinese Exclusion Act, which refused admission to Chinese laborers. This act was extended indefinitely with subsequent legislation in 1892, 1902, and 1904. The Gentlemen's Agreement was a diplomatic arrangement between Tokyo and Washington in 1907 that prevented Japanese laborers from leaving Japan for the United States. In 1921 Congress passed the First Quota Act, which favored immigrants from Northern and Western Europe, and in 1924 passed the Second Quota Act, which continued the exclusion of Asians (Ueda 1994). This restrictive legislation remained in effect until the Immigration and Naturalization Act of 1965, which abolished quotas on national origins, resulted in an increased admission of immigrants from non-European regions.

Many Chinese, especially Cantonese, had immigrated to the United States during the nineteenth century, however, before passage of exclusion acts and established Chinatowns in several cities with San Francisco's Chinatown being the most significant. Similarly, Japanese arrived in the United States initially as political refugees and later as agricultural workers in Hawaii. Prior to 1924, more than 300,000 Japanese came to the continental United States, settling in San Francisco, Seattle, and other Pacific Coast locations (Daniels 1991). Immigration from Mexico has proceeded almost without interruption since 1848 when Mexico ceded California, Arizona, and New Mexico to the United States. Likewise, after the United States acquired the Philippines in 1899, Filipino immigration was encouraged to fill a need for labor previously performed by the now-restricted Chinese and Japanese workers. A special Cuban Refugee Program admitted the hundreds of thousands of Cubans who left their country after Castro's 1959 revolution (Cordasco 1990). Nevertheless, the passage of the 1965 Immigration Act had a major impact on the diversification of the immigrant population, with the major increase coming from Asian and Latin American countries. The "top five sending countries from 1981 through 1995 were Mexico, the Philippines, China/Taiwan, the Dominican Republic and India, compared to Italy, Austria/Hungary, the Soviet Union, Canada, and the United Kingdom during the first two decades" of the twentieth century (Zhou 2001). In 2002, the top 10 countries sending immigrants to the United States were Mexico, India, China, the Philippines, Vietnam, El Salvador, Cuba, Bosnia-Herzegovina, the Dominican Republic, and Ukraine (USCIS 2003).

This shift in the origins of post-1965 immigrants from predominantly European to predominantly Asian or Latin American has challenged assumptions about assimilation theory based on the experience of earlier European immigrants. Upward mobility and migration to suburbs have not been equally available to all members of certain ethnic groups. African Americans have not experienced the same assimilation pattern, being visibly different due to skin color. Portes and Zhou (1993) have added the concept of "segmented assimilation" to address the fact that members of some groups assimilate into different strata of American society, depending on their skin color and social capital. Especially when their background is poor or working class, "children of nonwhite immigrants may not even have the opportunity of gaining access to middle-class white society, no matter how acculturated they become" (ibid.). Institutional racism has resulted in residential segregation, which demonstrates the persistent importance of racism in restricting opportunities for African Americans.

Waters's (1994) study of second-generation West Indian and Haitian Americans living in New York asserts that some first-generation black immigrants have distanced themselves from American blacks by emphasizing their Jamaican, Haitian, or Trinidadian identity, especially by maintaining their distinct accents. However, the second generation lacks this accent and must decide whether to identify as black American or as having Caribbean ancestry. Those who chose to identify as ethnic rather than African American were mostly from a middle-class background and accepted their parents' and society's negative stereotypes of inner-city blacks.

While some immigrants with little human capital continue to arrive and assimilate into the lower strata of society, many immigrants from Eastern Europe, India, and Korea, for example, are middle class with better education than many Americans and settle immediately into affluent suburbs. According to Portes and Zhou, Chinese and Koreans are examples of immigrants who develop strong ethnic enclaves. Groups who have strong ethnic networks and sufficient capital develop "linear ethnicity," which emphasizes "social capital—the networks of social ties from church and voluntary organizations" that create opportunities for jobs and upward mobility (Waters 1994).

While society has often used pan-ethnic categories such as Asian, Asian American, Hispanic, or Caribbean, a large number of immigrants do not view themselves as members of pan-ethnic categories but rather as specifically identified with their country of origin such as China, Japan, Korea, India, Vietnam, Trinidad, Jamaica, or Haiti. For example, Asian American or other pan-ethnic identities may be useful to organize groups for political purposes but not an especially meaningful designation for someone who sees herself as Japanese. While Asian Americans have been stereotyped as the model minority and seen as assimilating into "whiteness" through upward mobility, this does not apply equally to "predominantly uneducated, low-skilled refugees, such as Cambodians and Hmong" (Zhou 2004).

Today's stream of immigrants from Mexico and their descendants, especially those who arrive without documents, come from the "lower segment of Mexican society, which is stratified on the basis of color and class," and consequently they experience the segmented assimilation mentioned earlier, entering into a low socioeconomic strata with little opportunity for upward mobility aggravated by an experience of racist discrimination similar to that experienced by black Americans (Zhou 2001). Depending on whether immigrants arrive with few resources and settle in the inner city or whether they arrive with social capital and settle in white middle-class suburbs, their outcomes are vastly different. Mexican American students in the San Diego area showed lower achievement than other second-generation immigrant groups. As compared to well-educated upper-middle-class Asian immigrants, Mexican immigrants tend to have lower educational achievement and socioeconomic status, while additionally they experience the stigma of negative stereotypes long associated with Mexicans and Mexican Americans (Lopez and Stanton-Salazar 2001).

On the other hand, multiethnic middle-class Mexican Americans who have one Mexican American parent have the option of choosing to self-identify as Mexican American or multiethnic. In Jimenez's study, those light-skinned respondents without a Spanish surname were able to exercise greater freedom in choosing their identities. Many of these young people felt weak attachment to their other ethnic background but have had "considerable exposure to their Mexican background" which is made available through "school settings, travel to Mexico and extended family" (Jimenez 2004). However, some of them felt unwelcome in clubs or organizations of Mexican American students since they were perceived as not having experienced the same discrimination as those bearing clear markers of ethnicity in their appearance or surname.

While Spanish is stigmatized and banned in schools in Los Angeles, in Miami bilingualism and knowledge of Spanish are considered an asset (Zhou 2001). Cubans in Miami formed an enclave that included high-status professionals with social and economic capital and a lower status of workers. "While compensation may not be higher in the enclave, ethnic bonds provide for informal networks of support that facilitate the learning of new skills and the overall process of economic adjustment" (Perez 2001). Due to increased immigration from Cuba in the twenty-first century, Miami will become more Cuban but also more diverse with Haitians, Jamaicans, and Nicaraguans making immigrant culture dominant.

Alba and Nee (1997) predict that if the current rate of immigration continues, the large numbers of first- and second-generation immigrants will create "large, culturally vibrant and institutionally rich ethnic communities" that will provide opportunities for upward mobility. This will challenge U.S. society to embrace a more heterogeneous idea of American identity and to eradicate the institutionalized racism that still limits opportunities for full integration into American society. The shift from the Anglo conformity and melting pot models of assimilation to a social constructionist, pluralistic approach recognizes the malleability of ethnic boundaries and the varieties of adaptation available to diverse groups of immigrants (Alba 2000). *See also*: **Assimilation; Bilingualism; Interethnic relations; Marriage; Stereotypes.**

References

Alba, Richard. 2000. Ethnicity. In *Encyclopedia of Sociology*. Edgar F. Borgatta, ed. Pp. 840–852. New York: Macmillan.

Alba, Richard, and Victor Nee. 1997. Rethinking Assimilation Theory for a New Era of Immigration. *International Migration Review* 31:826–874.

Cordasco, Francesco. 1990. *Dictionary of American Immigration History*. Metuchen, NJ: Scarecrow Press.

Daniels, Roger. 1991. *Coming to America: A History of Immigration and Ethnicity in American Life*. New York: Harper.

Gans, Herbert J. 1979. Symbolic Ethnicity: The Future of Ethnic Groups and Cultures in America. In *Theories of Ethnicity: A Classical Reader*. Werner Sollors, ed. Pp. 425–459. New York: New York University Press.

Glazer, Nathan, and Daniel Patrick Moynihan. 1963. *Beyond the Melting Pot: The Negroes, Puerto Ricans, Jews, Italians, and Irish of New York City*. Cambridge, MA: MIT Press.

Jimenez, Tomas. 2004. Negotiating Ethnic Boundaries. *Ethnicities* 4(1):75–97.

Lopez, David, and Ricardo Stanton-Salazar. 2001. Mexican Americans: A Second Generation at Risk. In *Ethnicities: Children of Immigrants in America*. Ruben G. Rumbaut and Alejandro Portes, eds. Pp. 57–90. Berkeley: University of California Press.

Omi, Michael, and Howard Winant. 1994. *Racial Formation in the U.S.* New York: Routledge.

Perez, Lisandro. 2001. Growing Up in Cuban Miami: Immigration, the Enclave, and New Generations. In *Ethnicities: Children of Immigrants in America*. Rubén G. Rumbaut and Alejandro Portes, eds. Pp. 91–125. Berkeley: University of California Press.

Petersen, William, Michael Novak, and Philip Gleason. 1982. *Concepts of Ethnicity*. Cambridge, MA: Harvard University Press.

Portes, Alejandro, and Min Zhou. 1993. The New Second Generation: Segmented Assimilation and Its Variants. *The Annals of the American Academy of Political and Social Science* 530:74–96.

Schlesinger, Arthur M., Jr. 1992. *The Disuniting of America: Reflections on a Multicultural Society*. New York: W.W. Norton.

Thernstrom, Stephan, ed. 1980. *Harvard Encyclopedia of American Ethnic Groups*. Cambridge, MA: Belknap Press of Harvard University.

Ueda, Reed. 1994. *Postwar Immigrant America: A Social History*. Boston: Bedford Books, St. Martin's Press.

U.S. Citizenship and Immigration Services (USCIS). 2003. *2002 Yearbook of Immigration Statistics*. Washington, DC: U.S. Department of Homeland Security Office of Immigration Statistics.

Waters, Mary. 1994. Ethnic and Racial Identities of Second-Generation Black Immigrants in New York City. *International Migration Review* 28(4):795–820.

Weber, Max. 1968. *Economy and Society: An Outline of Interpretive Sociology*. New York: Bedminster Press.

Zhou, Min. 2001. Contemporary Immigration and the Dynamics of Race and Ethnicity. In *America Becoming: Racial Trends and Their Consequences*. Neil Smelser, William

Julius Wilson, and Faith Mitchell, eds. Pp. 200–242. Washington, DC: National Academy Press.
———. 2004. Are Asian Americans Becoming "White?" *Contexts* 3(1):29–37.

JEANNE ARMSTRONG

EXPEDITED ENTRY AND REMOVAL. Viewing migration across time and space reveals that immigrants follow multiple paths both for arriving and for departing. Some are chosen and others forced, some temporary and others cyclical. Return migration, for example, may be voluntary but it frequently occurs through enticed or coerced repatriation.

While most people in the United States have a rough understanding of deportation, fewer are aware that there are a number of policies and procedures by which either entry to or removal from the country may be expedited. Criteria for admissibility, and the experience of either inclusion or exclusion, vary depending on a person's country of origin, prevailing political and security conditions, and other economic and personal factors. In addition, some native peoples have designated rights to cross borders that transect traditional territories.

Removal

The Department of Homeland Security's (DHS) Bureau of Citizenship and Immigration Services, formerly the Immigration and Naturalization Service (INS), has responsibility for determining the admissibility of those who attempt entry into the United States. In response to concerns over "illegal immigration" and fraudulent asylum claims, Congress established the Illegal Immigration Reform and Immigrant Responsibility Act of 1996 (IIRIRA). Deportation and exclusion proceedings were consolidated as removal proceedings, creating new authority for expedited removals.

Expedited removal allows for the immediate removal of inadmissible persons termed "aliens," at the discretion of immigration officers, who can issue a removal order at any of the U.S. ports of entry, therefore bypassing review by an immigration judge. Aliens are considered inadmissible if they do not have a visa, possess false travel documents, have attempted illegal entry into the United States, or have a criminal history. In some cases, inadmissible aliens may be offered the option to withdraw their application or can be referred to an immigration judge for formal removal proceedings.

At first, expedited removal was relatively infrequent. In 1998, the INS claimed that out of 1 million people who attempted entry into the United States between September 1997 and February 1998, only about 30,000 were subjected to expedited removal proceedings, 90 percent of these being Mexican (Lobe 1998). In 2002, expedited removals accounted for 23 percent of all formal removals, with 50 percent occurring at southwest ports of entry (USCIS 2003). Most of those arriving who were determined to be inadmissible by immigration inspectors withdrew their application for admission or accepted the offer of voluntary departure. Nearly all (over 99 percent) of those who voluntarily departed the United States were apprehended by what was then the Border Patrol; most were Mexican and male, and median age was 24 years. Approximately 203,000 of the inadmissible persons were subject to the expedited removal process, but 155,000 were permitted to withdraw their application for admission to the United States.

Of the approximately 48,000 put into the expedited removal process, about 10,000 were referred to an asylum officer. Those who expressed fear of persecution were taken out of the expedited removal process and referred to an immigration judge.

To be authorized to order expedited removals, immigration and asylum officers complete an extensive basic training program and a one-year field training and probationary period. According to DHS, immigration officers who order expedited removal are monitored by supervisors on a regular basis to ensure that proper procedures are used. Immigration officers are expected to know how to identify indications of a fear of persecution and to follow procedures designed to protect the rights of asylum seekers, which include asking questions concerning credible fear of return. If a person shows indications of credible fear of return to their home country, the immigration officer is to refer that person to an asylum officer. Immigration asylum officers have the jurisdiction to interview people making asylum claims and refer them to an immigration judge so that they can make an asylum application (USCIS 2002).

The extent to which bona fide asylees and refugees are in fact granted full consideration of rights as stipulated by the law is a contentious matter. Paucity of hard data, institutional bias, and limited training of immigration decision makers in the past resulted in less-than-objective outcomes for applicants. Procedures in place today are, at least in part, a result of remedies that followed court rulings that determined that adjudication of asylum cases had often been influenced by political bias.

In August 2004, the Department of Homeland Security expanded the application of expedited removal to non-citizens found within the United States, not just at ports of entry. Expedited removal now applies to any non-citizen found within 100 miles of a U.S. border who cannot prove presence in the United States for 14 days or longer and who is deemed inadmissible due to misrepresentation or the lack of appropriate documentation.

This is a significant departure from past practice, for it means that non-citizens can be removed from the United States without a removal hearing, access to legal counsel, the right to challenge the government's witnesses and evidence, and opportunity to apply for relief from removal except in the case of credible fear of return. Because expedited removal proceedings do not allow for impartial adjudicators or appeals to the Board of Immigration Appeals (BIA), non-citizens essentially lose their rights and immigration officers' decisions are uncontested. Critics of the expedited removal expansion note that this opens considerable room for abuse, while not making the country safer or improving the legal entry process into the United States (American Immigration Lawyers Association 2004).

Besides giving immigration officers unprecedented authority, expedited removal procedures put asylum seekers at risk because of a lack of formal legal counsel at initial credible fear determination, the absence of third-party supervision, a shortage of language translators, and limited time available to prepare for credible fear interviews. Asylum seekers are referred to an asylum officer 48 hours after arrival, and credible fear of persecution often must be determined in less than an hour. Applicants deemed to have credible fear have only one week to seek review of their claim before an immigration judge. Such increased pace and pressure may decrease fair chances for acquiring access to formal asylum proceedings. Indeed, if credible fear is denied, the asylum seeker can be removed immediately. Not surprisingly, after the expedited removal process was initiated, applications for asylum decreased (Helton 1997).

Today, then, granting judicial power to immigration officers can result in the removal of bona fide asylum seekers. Whereas asylum seekers were guaranteed a hearing before an immigration judge prior to IIRIRA, the process now puts great responsibility on the applicant to be persuasive enough to convince an asylum officer of credible fear, an ordeal that may be inherently difficult if the asylum seeker is traumatized or lacks legal counsel or an adequate translator. Erroneous decision making by immigration officers and accounts of prolonged detention of asylum seekers, sometimes in poor conditions, have also surfaced. Rigorous and qualitative review of the process is needed to ensure the due process of those who are subjected to the procedures (Musalo 2001).

Entry

Entry into the United States has primarily been expedited for commercial reasons. Mexican and Canadian nationals may apply for expedited entry into the United States under NAFTA, which allows for the entry of temporary business visitors, specific professional categories cited in the treaty, business transferees, and investors. In practice, it may be easier for Canadian professionals to apply for expedited entry than it has been for Mexican professionals. Along the U.S.-Mexico border, DHS provides laser-readable visas and has extended the length of stay for Mexican nationals who hold a border crossing card (BCC), allowing 30 days within 25 miles of the border (75 miles from the border within Arizona), compared with a 72-hour stay that was formerly allotted (American Immigration Lawyers Association 2004).

In busy trade corridors, expedited entry for travel and commerce into the United States has been facilitated by the FAST/NEXUS programs. Regional arrangements, such as the PACE (Peace Arch Crossing Entry) program, started in 1992 to expedite faster border clearance at the Washington–British Columbia border for regular border commuters, were replaced by the border-wide NEXUS program in the aftermath of September 11, 2001. The NEXUS program allows greater focus on high-risk travelers while frequent and low-risk travelers can cross the U.S.-Canada border without being subject to regular customs and immigration questioning, thereby reducing overall delays at the border. Administered by both U.S. and Canadian inspection agencies, NEXUS grants pre-approved border crossers in passenger vehicles access to a commuter lane. To be eligible, a member must be a citizen or permanent resident of the United States or Canada and have demonstrated need for frequent crossings, such as because of business or government responsibilities. Security clearance includes an interview and biometric fingerprinting.

The FAST (Free and Secure Trade) program, initiated in 2002, expedites travel for pre-approved commercial drivers, carriers, and importers between the United States and Canada as well as between the United States and Mexico. Dedicated commercial lanes at the border facilitate trade in low-risk shipments by decreasing wait times. Like NEXUS, the FAST program is not trouble free. It works best for exporters of high-volume, low-risk commodities from a single source. The program remains relatively small, allowing 15,000 drivers to register each year between the United States and Canada, for example, only a small proportion of the 36,000 trucks that crossed the U.S.-Canada border daily in 2002. Costs of registering each driver, truck, cargo, and exporter are high, and bureaucratic delays persist.

Native Americans

A number of native peoples in North America live in ancestral territories that are today bisected by international borders. Some 24 Native American nations (known in Canada as First Nations), located along over 700 miles of border with Mexico and Canada, have had long-standing trade and ceremonial routes blocked and families and communities divided by either border. The Jay Treaty of 1794 was perceived by indigenous groups as giving them unconditional rights to cross borders, but it has not been consistently upheld by U.S. courts nor recognized by Canada. The Immigration and Nationality Act of 1924 also ensured the right to free passage for indigenous people across borders, but this is not recognized by Canada or Mexico, and not always in practice even in the United States.

To expedite crossing, both the U.S. and the Mexican governments have issued border crossing cards for indigenous peoples who reside on indigenous land now on the Mexican side. Native groups assert that tribal identity cards should function as sufficient identification for crossing borders. Indeed, members of the Tohono O'odham and Yaqui nations in Arizona and Sonora have long used these cards to cross at border checkpoints or elsewhere along their 90-mile border with Mexico, but now this violates U.S. laws. Heightened militarization and increased smuggling of contraband and people through Native American reservations have led to requirements for documentation, along with fines, confiscation of vehicles and goods, removal, arrest, and duties, not to mention humiliation for indigenous people in both northern and southern borderlands.

Native peoples are increasingly asserting their sovereignty as well as treaty rights to free passage without obstruction. They hold that they are entitled to cross freely without toll charges, to work on either side of the border, to carry sacred objects across the border without unnecessary inspection and mishandling by immigration officers, to engage in commerce on indigenous territory without the interference of national laws, to travel for internal and external government relations, to carry personal goods without paying duties, to hunt, fish, trap, and transport game across the border, and not have to declare U.S. or Canadian citizenship (IDLA 2004). Many tribes and human rights organizations have banded together to address treaty rights, human rights abuses, land claims, and indigenous heritage (Taliman 2001). Such problems are not limited to the United States; the Canadian government ruled in the landmark Mitchell case that it will not recognize tax and duty exemptions for indigenous peoples that cross the U.S.-Canada border (Barnsley 2003). As a result of the border problems experienced by indigenous people along the U.S.-Canada border, the Indian Defense League of America continues the annual Border Crossing Celebration, begun in 1928; this a mass demonstration every third week in July in solidarity with the struggle for free border crossing and the associated sovereignty rights of indigenous nations. *See also*: **Asylum; Border control; Documentation; Immigration system; International accords; Ports of entry; Return migration.**

References

American Immigration Lawyers Association. 2004. *Washington Update* 8(11). http://www.aila.org/fileViewer.aspx?docID=13889.

Barnsley, Paul. 2003. Government Applies Mitchell. *Wind Speaker* 21(7):12–14.

Canada Border Services Agency. 2004. http://www.cbsa-asfc.gc.ca.

Helton, Arthur C. 1997. U.S. Asylum Watch. *Migration World Magazine* 25(5):43.

Indian Defense League of America (IDLA). 2004. http://www.idloa.org.

Lobe, Jim. 1998. Immigration Rules Putting Asylum-Seekers at Risk. *Inter Press Service* 31 (March):1.

Musalo, Karen. 2001. Expedited Removal. *Human Rights* 28(1):12–13.

Taliman, Valerie. 2001. Borders and Native Peoples: Divided But Not Conquered. *Native Americas* 18(1):10–16.

U.S. Citizenship and Immigration Services (USCIS). 2002. Fact Sheet: Expedited Removal. http://www.uscis.gov/graphics/publicaffairs/factsheets/expeditedremoval_fs.htm.

———. 2003. *Yearbook of Immigration Statistics*. http://www.uscis.gov/graphics/shared/aboutus/statistics/Yearbook2002.pdf.

JAMES LOUCKY AND LEE LAWRENCE

F

FAMILIES. When immigrants move, in a primordial drive for a better life, families figure prominently in their goals as well as the setting and the means enabling their migration. Families are critical with respect to strategies, roles, identity, and loyalties. Nonetheless, immigration is often viewed, at least in the public mind, as essentially a matter of individual choices based on relative opportunities at home or in new destinations. The relative absence of a family perspective is ironic given that human decision making primarily occurs within small groups and especially families. Recent research reveals how critical family experiences are in the processes and changes entailed in moving and settling (Suárez-Orozco and Suárez-Orozco 1995; Foner 1997; Valenzuela 1999).

Focusing on the family dimension confirms how migration is as much a temporal as a spatial phenomenon. Adaptation and assimilation are neither simple nor linear, and the family experiences, roles, and relations that they entail also occur and change over time. This entry examines the role of the family in migration to and settlement in the United States, changes in composition and roles, the prevalence of household economic activities, and the critical issues relating to family life-cycle and second generation. This perspective is essential for a full understanding of U.S. immigration.

Families in the Migration Process

One of the ironies of migration is how often family members separate, through migrating, in an effort to strengthen and keep the family together in the long run. Improvement of life conditions for one's family and the well-being of children also underlie the strong efforts for family reunification (Rodriguez 1988; Malkin 2004). Families may move as intact entities, but frequently only some members move, generally those with ability to achieve quick stability and initiate generation of income. Subsequently, other family members may move, through various mixes of step- and chain-migration. Women, for example, often migrate to join husbands or other family members, depending on success of those who left earlier as well as practicality of achieving family reunification. Others directly enter the migration stream as the result of careful collaborative strategies, such as when there is likelihood of a job in domestic work or childcare (Hondagneu-Sotelo 1994, 2002). In virtually all cases, migration decisions are made by households with at least some kin advice or assistance, rather than by individual men or women.

Presence of women in migration to the United States has been increasingly recognized as allowing for expanded life choices for actual or potential families as well as wage-earning possibilities for themselves (Houstoun et al. 1984; Hondagneu-Sotelo 1994). Children continue to influence settlement and adaptation decisions of both women and men long after initial migration (Vlach 1992). Settlement decisions and adjustments of adults who either have or plan to have children may be best understood from a parental investment perspective, in which work, social networks, financial considerations, and planning are done with children's development and well-being as a primary priority.

Migration of younger members may occur as part of, or in continuing obligation to, the family of origin. However, migration may also involve leaving the parental home. Youth may head to the United States in an effort to gain independence or begin to establish new family. The incidence and risks associated with unaccompanied minors, who may be held in detention until family members are identified or willing to step forward, suggest the levels of motivation to flee endangerment at home or improve life chances (Ashabranner and Ashabranner 1987).

The family, oftentimes forms of the extended family, also frequently underwrites the expenses of migration both in the "launching" stages and for initial set-up costs on arrival. In turn, families generally incur expectations of shared advantage from the venture, most notably through remittances.

Family Size and Fertility

The growing proportion of the U.S. population represented by immigrants is revealed in a recent study that found nearly one in four births in the United States in 2002 was to an immigrant mother (Camarota 2005). The significance of this number is underscored by the policy of jus soli, where citizenship is conferred on anyone born on U.S. soil, inclusive of the children of illegal immigrants. The current increase of immigrant birthrates far exceeds that of the last great era of American immigration which took place in 1910. After 1910 immigration was curtailed drastically while the present pattern predicts even larger birthrates for immigrant families in the foreseeable future (Camarota 2005).

Immigration birthrates constitute a larger percentage of births because in general immigrants have higher fertility rates and are more likely to be in their reproductive years than native citizens. One of the greatest demographic shifts attributed to birthrates relates to regional and national identity. Hispanic immigrants accounted for 59 percent of all births to immigrant mothers in 2002. This constitutes the largest share of births to immigrants ever attributed to a specific cultural or linguistic group. Concomitantly, the growth in births to immigrants has also been accompanied by a decline in national diversity. In 1970 Mexico accounted for 24 percent of all births to immigrants increasing to 45 percent in 2002 (Camarota 2005).

Projections of immigrant families based on birthrate would predict a further Hispanicization of the United States in the years to come while Asians will continue to play a factor in the changing roles and makeup of the American family of the future. While immigration has had relatively little effect on the nation's age structure, new immigrants (legal and illegal) plus births to immigrants are forecasted to add nearly 2 1/2 million people to the nation's population each year. It should also be noted that census figures are likely to underreport immigrants and immigrant birthrates, because immigrants fear that participation may alert officials to possible illegal status. Such figures factor into the fears and warnings issued by some authors that the present immigration cycle coupled with immigrant birthrates will pose new barriers to Americanization and the assimilation and amalgamation process long adhered to by several American social theorists and policy makers.

New Family Patterns

Although immigrant families will assume newly adapted roles within American society, they will continue to rely and depend upon premigration family experiences, norms, and cultural frameworks that have proven useful to them within their own mother culture (Foner 1999). Strong immigrant communities and institutions coupled with dense ethnic networks and transnational ties to their mother country are part of the phenomenon coined "multilocal binational families" (Foner 1999). The availability of transportation, telecommunications, Internet technology, and in some cases border proximity all account for the maintenance of kinship ties as well as the reinforcement of family and communal values in many instances.

Faced with new surroundings and challenges in the United States, the belief structures, cultural symbols, behavioral patterns, and values of immigrant families often undergo fundamental as well as subtle changes and alterations. This is often expressed by differences between first and second generations in terms of language usage, dress, social customs, intermarriage, and even occupational choices. Many of these changes and new adaptations are part of an emerging process that is often termed segmented assimilation (Foner 1999). Segmented assimilation accounts for both integration of new values and patterns by families while preserving many of the older traditions and core family structures brought by the immigrant families from their original homeland.

Immigrant family patterns are also impacted by such factors as sex and age ratios. In certain instances an imbalance in sex ratio will foster marriage external to the national or ethnic group or consign many to remain single or searching for spouses in the home country. Family patterns and customs are also vulnerable to external economic and employment patterns that often predicate which family member seeks outside employment while the other spousal partner is charged with maintenance of the home and children. Immigrant family structure has been increasingly changing in line with employment availability that favors domestic and service workers that largely comprises a female workforce (Foner 1999).

The greatest influences upon immigrant families may come from dominant American cultural beliefs and values that relate to marriage, family, and kinship that are largely promulgated and disseminated by mass media, schools, and other institutions. Many of these values are embraced or consciously rejected by family members but have a tendency to break down across generational and gender lines. New norms are generally more accepted by children and by women when those values espouse greater freedoms, power, and mobility within ascribed roles and responsibilities. Legal mechanisms also may play a role in the changing of immigrant family patterns, especially those that relate to wife-beating, schooling, the legal age limit, and inheritance. Each immigrant family, depending upon its cultural and economic circumstances, will react differently to the forces placed upon them by the dominant society. However, their adaptations to or conformity with the prevailing social patterns will in turn determine the existing family norms for future generations.

Second Generation

The increase in immigration since 1965 has given rise to a record number of children who are raised in immigrant families. About one in every five individuals under 18 is either an immigrant or has parents who are immigrants (Schmid 2001). In 1997, there were approximately 3 million foreign-born children under 18, and nearly 11 million U.S.-born children under 18 who were living with at least one foreign-born parent (Alba et al. 1999). All projections indicate that this population will increase throughout the present century.

In certain respects second- and third-generation children of foreign-born parents face many of the same challenges and discriminatory patterns as that of their parents (Suárez-Orozco and Suárez-Orozco 1995). Children of immigrants may not share their parents' immediate connection to the past and their native country and culture, but many maintain "symbolic" ethnicity as a way of maintaining group identity or distinction from other ethnic and racial groups (Butterfield 2004). Unlike their parents, U.S.-born second generations are less likely to send money to relatives in their parents' native country. Nevertheless, second and third generations often face the same discrimination and economic difficulties that their parents faced while not necessarily perceiving the same benefits.

Many of the second-generation children struggle to integrate aspects of the two worlds they are faced with—that of their parents' native culture, and that of the dominant U.S. culture. Often cultural assimilation into the dominant culture by second-generation youths can lead to family conflict as well as isolation and alienation from parents and particular peer groups (Zhou 1997). Despite the fact that second-generation youths tend to identify more with the dominant culture than with their parents, perceived societal rejection or alienation on the part of second-generation youths can lead to participation in gangs and other ethnic-oriented groups (Suárez-Orozco and Suárez-Orozco 2001).

On average, second- and third-generation youths tend to complete school at a higher rate than their parents as well as new immigrants (Suárez-Orozco and Suárez-Orozco 2001). The difference between subsequent generations and new immigrants in terms of educational and even economic attainment can be largely attributed to aspects of psychological loss, culture shock, language, differences in culture, discrimination, and economic pressures that new immigrants face with greater frequency and severity.

Issues Impacting Immigrant Families

All families must confront positive and negative influences when raising children. This challenge poses even greater difficulties for immigrants, who must further negotiate the additional influences of culture and environment and incorporate their family history into their life in a new country and new surroundings. Research on immigrant families suggests that youth face multiple threats to their well-being, including substance use, poor school functioning, and early role taking. These risks may be particularly acute for children who immigrate later in childhood, especially during adolescence (Portes and Rumbaut 2001). Nevertheless, research would suggest that new immigrant families often possess certain cultural attitudes and norms that are protective against the many risks that accompany immigration (Chapman and Perreira 2005). Difficulties facing immigrant families and youth can often be mitigated when institutions and service agencies understand the inherent issues and problems that beset families who settle in a new community and who are confronted with often conflicting norms and values.

Poverty, a strong determinant of family and child well-being, is also closely linked to negative physical, developmental, and mental health–related issues. A family's socioeconomic status has a direct effect on their ability to access healthcare as well as other services. Children of immigrant and migrant families often are from racial or ethnic minority groups that face discriminatory treatment as well as racist patterns. Long-standing exclusionary practices often inhibit the full access and utilization of community resources and services that many immigrant families can opt for. Attempts to pass exclusionary legislation in California, Arizona, and other states seeking to curb illegal immigration have had a major impact on many immigrant families and their ability to obtain needed services and assistance. Most immigrant families will have similar challenges with regard to poverty, housing, and food, as well as existing physical, mental, and social health issues that are unique to each group (DuPlessis et al. 2005).

Within families, and through networks that link families as well as non-kin, values of interdependence are often visible, such as in pooling income to pay rent and other expenses. Families also provide "anchors" for newcomers, by extending temporary housing and job leads, as well as advice and social companionship that they themselves had received.

Immigrants in the United States demonstrate remarkable and diverse resourcefulness with which they both meet and modify new conditions that they experience, so as to sustain not only themselves but also their children (Suárez-Orozco and Suárez-Orozco 1995, 2001; Loucky 2001). Immigrant families constitute critical learning environments for both adults and children; children's experiences impact parents, and vice versa. Migration and settlement, which are imagined as much as they are experienced by families through expectations and dreams built up around children, contribute to the social cohesion of the family. Families will continue to be the integral force and in many cases the impetus for future immigration patterns that speak to trans-national, trans-communal, and trans-familial connections and support. *See also*: **Assimilation; Children; Family reunification; Jus soli; Marriage; Migration processes; Older persons; Social networks; Transnationalism; Women.**

References

Alba, Richard, Douglas S. Massey, and Ruben G. Rumbaut. 1999. *Immigration Experience for Families and Children*. Washington, DC: American Sociological Association.

Ashabranner, Brent, and Melissa Ashabranner. 1987. *Into a Strange Land: Unaccompanied Refugee Youth in America*. New York: Putnam.

Butterfield, Sherri-Ann P. 2004. Challenging American Conceptions for Race and Ethnicity: Second Generation West Indian Immigrants. *International Journal of Sociology and Social Policy* 24(7/8):75–103.

Camarota, Steven A. 2005. Births to Immigrants in America 1970 to 2002. Center for Immigration Studies. July. http://www.cis.org/articles/2005/back805.html.

Chapman, Mimi V., and Krista M. Perreira. 2005. The Well Being of Immigrant Latino Youth: A Framework to Inform Practice. *Families in Society* 86(1):104–112.

DuPlessis, Helen M., Suzanne C. Boulter, D. Cora-Bramble, Charles R. Field, et al. 2005. Providing Care for Immigrant, Homeless and Migrant Children. *Pediatrics* 115(4):1095–2001.

Foner, Nancy. 1997. Immigrant Family: Cultural Legacies and Cultural Changes. *International Migration Review* 31:961–974.

Gonzalez de la Rocha, Mercedes. 1994. *The Resources of Poverty: Women and Survival in a Mexican City*. Oxford: Blackwell.

Hareven, Tamara K., and John Modell. 1980. Family Patterns. In *Harvard Encyclopedia of American Ethnic Groups*. S. Thernstrom, ed. Pp. 345–354. Cambridge, MA: Belknap Press of Harvard University.

Hondagneu-Sotelo, Pierrette. 1994. *Gendered Transitions: Mexican Experiences of Immigration*. Berkeley: University of California Press.

———. 2002. Families on the Frontier: From Braceros in the Fields to Braceras in the Home. In *Latinos: Remaking America*. Marcelo M. Suárez-Orozco and Mariela M. Paez, eds. Pp. 259–273. Berkeley: University of California Press.

Houstoun, Marion F., Roger G. Kramer, and Joan M. Barrett. 1984. Female Predominance in Immigration to the United States since 1930: A First Look. *International Migration Review* 18:908–963.

Levitt, Peggy, and Mary C. Waters. 2002. *The Changing Face of Home: The Transnational Lives of the Second Generation*. New York: Russell Sage.

Loucky, James. 2001. Child and Family Well-Being in Settlement Decisions of Guatemalan Women in Los Angeles. In *Negotiating Transnationalism: Selected Papers on Refugees and Immigrants*, vol. 9. MaryCarol Hopkins and Nancy Wellmeier, eds. Pp. 184–204. Washington, DC: American Anthropological Association.

Malkin, Victoria. 2004. "We Go to Get Ahead": Gender and Status in Two Mexican Migrant Communities. *Latin American Perspectives* 31(5):75–99.

McAddo, Harriette Pipes, ed. 1999. *Family Ethnicity: Strength in Diversity*, 2nd ed. Thousand Oaks, CA: Sage.

Menjívar, Cecilia. 1999. The Intersection of Work and Gender: Central American Immigrant Women and Employment in California. *American Behavioral Scientist* 42:601–627.

Portes, Alejandro. 1995. *The New Second Generation*. New York: Russell Sage.

Portes, A., and R.G. Rumbaut. 2001. *Ethnicities: Children of Immigrants in America*. Berkeley: University of California Press.

Rodriguez, Julia E. Curry. 1988. Labor Migration and Familial Responsibilities: Experiences of Mexican Women. In *Mexicanas at Work*. Margarita B. Melville, ed. Pp. 47–63. Mexican American Studies Monograph No. 5. Houston, TX: University of Houston.

Schmid, Carol L. 2001. Educational Achievement Language-Minority Students, and the New Second Generation. *Sociology of Education*: 71–88.

Suárez-Orozco, Carola, and Marcelo Suárez-Orozco. 1995. *Transformations: Migration, Family Life, and Achievement Motivation among Latino Adolescents*. Stanford, CA: Stanford University Press.

———. 2001. *Children of Immigration*. Cambridge, MA: Harvard University Press.

Valenzuela, Abel, Jr. 1999. Gender Roles and Settlement Activities among Children and Their Immigrant Families. *American Behavioral Scientist* 42:720–742.

Vlach, Norita. 1992. *The Quetzal in Flight: Guatemalan Refugee Families in the United States*. Westport, CT: Praeger.

Zhou, Min. 1997. Growing Up American: The Challenge Confronting Immigrant Children and Children of Immigrants. *Annual Review of Sociology* 23:63–95.

LARRY J. ESTRADA AND JAMES LOUCKY

FAMILY REUNIFICATION. Family reunification is the principle within immigration policy by which foreigners who have become residents or citizens of a country may be reunited with their families. In democracies this principle is usually recognized, but legal definition of "family" and the conditions of reunification may be more or less generous. Immigration policy of the United States stands out for extending the list of family members entitled to reunification beyond the nuclear cell (father, mother, and children) and for the relatively large share of resident visas set aside annually for this type of immigration.

The main principles of the present system were laid out by the 1965 Immigration Act, but its roots are deeper: the federal immigration legislation has always allowed the entry of family members of U.S. citizens, even during its most restrictive periods. Under the national origin quota laws (passed in 1921 and 1924), wives and minor children of citizens were exempted from the quotas. In the decades before their abrogation in 1965, several loopholes were created to let in various family members, such as wives and children of servicemen (Reimers 1992:21–22, 25–26). In 1952, the McCarran-Walter Act created four preferential categories of immigrant visas within the quotas: 50 percent of those visas were attributed to workers with desirable skills in selected occupations, and the other 50 percent were divided among three other categories reserved to family members. The principle of the distinction between family and economic immigration was born.

The 1965 reform not only eliminated the discriminatory national origin quotas, it also created a system of admission based on that distinction (Reimers 1992:80). A new list of preferential categories was drawn, to be applied to the Eastern Hemisphere: one for refugees, a second for persons with desirable skills, another for training or education, and a fourth for close relatives of U.S. citizens. These were admitted within a limit of 170,000 visas per year, and no country was to receive more than 20,000 such visas. First preference was accorded unmarried sons and daughters over age 21 of U.S. citizens, for a maximum of 20 percent; second preference was granted spouses and unmarried sons and daughters of U.S. permanent residents (20 percent); third were members of the professions, scientists, and artists of exceptional ability (10 percent); fourth preference went to married sons and daughters over age 21 of U.S. citizens (10 percent); brothers and sisters of U.S. citizens were given fifth preference (24 percent); sixth preference was for skilled and unskilled workers (10 percent); and seventh preference went to refugees (6 percent). Spouses and minor children of U.S. citizens were still exempted from the ceilings and admitted without numerical limits, and so now were fathers and mothers of citizens (the "immediate family").

In the following decades a few further changes would be made. The preference system was extended to the Western Hemisphere in 1976, and in 1980, when Congress set up a separate admission program for refugee flows, it turned the second preference into the largest category. But by then family reunification had clearly become the cornerstone of the national immigration policy. Nearly three-quarters of all visas were now reserved for it, and only 20 percent were granted on economic grounds (Fuchs 1985:39; Lemay 1987:110–112).

There are several reasons for this choice, which marked a surprising change in the history of immigration policy. Indeed, in the project of reform that President Kennedy had sent to Congress in 1963, he had proposed attributing visas in equal numbers to family members and workers. The 1965 act therefore represented a reversal of priorities. Undoubtedly, this change corresponded to some deeply held values, which had thus been reflected in the 1953 report of the special commission appointed by President Truman to investigate immigration: that the great American stories of individual success remind us that we are a nation of immigrants, and that an important part of our moral and spiritual fiber is founded on the sacred place of the family in American life (U.S. President's Commission on Immigration and Naturalization 1953:119).

Nevertheless, the priority given to family reunification had more to do with political compromise. Organized labor had refused the initial proposal made by the Johnson administration of equally dividing the annual pool of visas, as they worried about the competition of immigrant workers. In order to quell their political opposition and ensure the passage of the most important reform, namely, the abolition of the national origin quotas, the administration had to sharply reduce the percentage of foreign workers in the annual inflow and to establish strict controls over economic immigration, such as the requirement of Labor Department certification. Such immigration was all the more reduced as the spouse and children (the dependents) of those obtaining visas under the third and sixth preference categories were counted in the same categories, so that the actual admissions of foreigners with skills, talents, or occupations would be less than 20 percent of the total.

Moreover, it was believed that the new emphasis on family reunification would not have a significant quantitative and qualitative impact on actual inflows. Only those national groups that already had a sizeable presence in the U.S. population would send new immigrants, namely, southern and Eastern Europeans rather than Asians, and once their families were joined, immigration would slow down. Thus, family reunification was conceived more as a means of controlling the entry of foreigners than as a way to reopen the doors.

The effects of such a complex system on the volume and composition of immigration were quite unexpected. In the decade following the implementation of the act an annual average of 90,000 aliens, twice what had been projected, entered as immediate family members (beyond the ceilings) and their total kept increasing every year, exceeding 200,000 annually by the mid-1980s (Reimers 1992:80). Moreover, people around the world rushed to take advantage of the new system of preferences, contrary to what supporters of the act had asserted. In the first years, Southern and Eastern Europeans used family reunification categories as expected. As soon as their numbers declined, they were replaced by rapidly growing flows of immigrants from the developing world, chiefly Asians and Latin Americans, who made up three-fourths of all admissions by the late 1970s (Keely 1971, 1975; Simcox 1988; U.S. General Accounting Office 1988; Reimers 1992; Hing 1993; Ueda 1998).

This dramatic shift in the national origin of immigrants is partly due to the reunification system. In the mid-1960s the situation in many developing countries was potentially conducive to emigration to the United States on account of a combination of political and socioeconomic factors. But it was the new system of visa distribution in the United States that made actual emigration possible. Applications for admission quickly grew when news about the implementation of the 1965 reform spread. At first, Asian countries that had a history of significant U.S.-bound migrations were at an advantage; Japanese and Chinese populations that were already established could send for their families. Other Asians, who lacked such a base, such as Filipinos, Koreans, and Indians, relied on the "economic" channel, using the third and sixth preferences, and after a while they too were able to use family reunification categories.

In fact, the system held a potential for chain migration that legislators had failed to anticipate. No large population base in the United States was necessary for immigration networks to develop. Under the 1965 act it was quite possible for a single immigrant to enable the entry of many others. The second preference could be used to bring over a spouse and children. Once they had become citizens, the couple could sponsor their brothers and sisters under the fifth preference; the latter could, in turn, use the second preference to be reunited with their own spouses, who might well have brothers and sisters who could be sponsored a few years later. For this reason, the U.S. program of family reunification is remarkable. Potentially, it allows a nearly endless chain of migration, all the more so as the new Asian and Hispanic immigrants are from cultures that traditionally attribute great importance to the extended family and to the links of obligations and solidarity among kin. That fact seems to have been overlooked by American legislators, who based the reform on Western conceptions where the nuclear family prevails.

The volume of immigration and the percentage of family visas within it thus soared. For major sending countries, it reached and even exceeded 80 percent in the 1980s, even those with a late start such as India. Mexico had the highest share, with over 93 percent of its immigrants using family preferences between 1980 and 1984. Awareness of this in a context of increasingly serious economic woes accounted for growing public uneasiness about immigration, contributing to the tenor of the public debate that emerged which centered on the need to control flows. Undocumented aliens were the first target of this restrictive surge. After Congress passed the Immigration Reform and Control Act to cope with this "problem" in 1986, legal, and in particular family, immigration also came under attack.

The Federation for American Immigration Reform (FAIR) and other similar anti-immigration organizations began to denounce the "snowball effect" of the preference system which, rather than simply reconstituting households as intended, created endless migration chains (Palmer and Lutton 1988:14). Those in favor of restrictions evoked catastrophic scenarios in which a single immigrant sponsored scores of relatives. Although studies conducted to assess the phenomenon generally reached moderate conclusions as to the effective family migration chains (Jasso and Rosenzweig 1986; U.S. General Accounting Office 1988), alarmist propaganda caught the public imagination. The legitimacy of extending the right to reunification beyond the nuclear family was questioned, and particularly criticized was the fifth preference reserved to brothers and sisters.

Such accusations did not go unanswered. Hispanic and Asian organizations, as well as church and civil liberties groups, denied the so-called snowball effect as pure speculation and stressed the special relationships between siblings in the immigrants' cultures. For them, reunion with extended family members was a right, the violation of which would be a form of racial discrimination. They pointed to the growing backlogs that considerably delayed the reunification of families from countries such as Mexico and the Philippines, and demanded a speeding up of the process.

Another criticism voiced against the existing system was that it almost totally barred entrance to "new seed" immigrants, that is to say, foreigners who had no family in the United States. Indeed the number of foreigners who received labor certification in the 1980s fell well below 10 percent of the total (U.S. Commission on Immigration Reform 1995). This bias had two disastrous consequences, critics claimed. On the one hand, it meant de facto exclusion of certain nationalities, since only those who already had a population base in the United States could benefit from the immigration system. Western Europeans, who had not used the opportunities offered when the program was implemented in 1965, were now the main victims. This point was made most forcefully by Irish American leaders. On the other hand, the bias in favor of families was said to lead to a decline in the "quality"—the education, skills, and training—of immigrants, as no selection of any kind was effected. Some economists published studies demonstrating such a negative evolution toward supposedly less "productive" immigrants, which they attributed chiefly to family reunion (Chiswick 1986; Borjas 1999). They and the business community advocated an immigration system that would be more finely geared to the country's real economic needs, allowing the United States to find more highly skilled labor (McConnel 1988:98). They also denounced the increased burden that family-sponsored immigrants were likely to have through the greater use of public social services.

Since there could be no question of significantly raising the ceilings to satisfy all the interests involved, the debate in the late 1980s took the form of a competition between the proponents of family reunification and those who preferred to develop economic immigration. The first bill introduced to reform legal immigration in 1988 included a provision significantly cutting the fifth preference. However, later attempts gave up this provision due to lobbying by ethnic organizations. For the same reason the Immigration Act that was finally passed in 1990 not only kept the fifth preference intact, it even raised the total for the second preference in an attempt to ease the backlogs in that category. Surprisingly, within a global ceiling of 700,000 annual visas for 1992–1994 and 675,000 after that transition period, every interest group obtained relative satisfaction. The act separated the family channel from two others, that of independent immigrants (the former third and sixth preferences) and a new category of "diversification," designed to facilitate entry for those nations adversely affected by the 1965 act (Schuck 1998).

As a consequence, the percentage of family immigration went down in the early 1990s, with "only" slightly more than half of all the visas granted within the numerical limits. But rather than leading to a decline in absolute numbers, this drop was due to the sharp increase of independent and diversity visas. Moreover, it was short-lived; in fiscal year 1997, family-sponsored immigrants and immediate relatives (well over 300,000 for that year alone) accounted for two-thirds of all legal immigrants.

Today family reunification continues to raise many fundamental issues such as the economic selection of immigrants, the definition of the family, and the affirmation of cultural differences. It also illustrates the continuing tensions between humanitarian goals and national interest that characterize the U.S. immigration policy: should immigrants be "productive," and in what sense? *See also*: **Legislation; Social networks; Unauthorized immigration.**

References

Borjas, George J. 1999. *Heaven's Door: Immigration Policy and the American Economy.* Princeton, NJ: Princeton University Press.

Chiswick, Barry R. 1986. A Troubling Drop in Immigrant Quality. *New York Times,* December 21, III 3.

DeJong, Gordon F., and Brenda D. Root. 1986. Family Reunification and Philippine Migration to the United States: The Immigrants' Perspective. *International Migration Review* 20(3):598–611.

Fuchs, Lawrence H. 1985. The Search for a Sound Immigration Policy: A Personal View. In *Clamor at the Gates: The New American Immigration.* Nathan Glazer, ed. Pp. 17–51. San Francisco: Institute for Contemporary Studies.

Hing, Ong Bill. 1993. *Making and Remaking Asian America Through Immigration Policy, 1850–1990.* Stanford, CA: Stanford University Press.

Jasso, Guillermina, and Mark R. Rosenzweig. 1986. Family Reunification and the Immigration Multiplier: U.S. Immigration Law, Origin-Country Conditions, and the Reproduction of Immigrants. *Demography* 23(3):291–311.

Keely, C.B. 1971. Effects of the Immigration Act of 1965 on Selected Population Characteristics of Immigrants to the United States. *Demography* 8(2):157–169.

———. 1975. Effects of U.S. Immigration Law on Manpower Characteristics of Immigrants. *Demography* 12(2):179–191.

Lemay, Michael C. 1987. *From Open Door to Dutch Door: An Analysis of U.S. Immigration Policy since 1820.* New York: Praeger.

McConnel, Scott. 1988. The New Battle over Immigration. *Fortune,* May 9, 98.

Palmer, Stacy, and Wayne Lutton. 1988. *The Immigration Time Bomb.* Monterey, VA: American Immigration Control Foundation.

Reimers, David. 1983. An Unintended Reform: The 1965 Immigration Act and Third World Immigration to the United States. *Journal of American Ethnic History* 3(1):9–28.

———. 1992. *Still the Golden Door: The Third World Comes to America.* New York: Columbia University Press.

Schuck, Peter H. 1998. The Politics of Rapid Legal Change: Immigration Policy, 1980–1990. In *Citizens, Strangers and In-Betweens: Essays on Immigration and Citizenship.* Peter Schuck, ed. Pp. 91–138. Boulder, CO: Westview Press.

Simcox, David E. 1988. *U.S. Immigration in the 1980s: Reappraisal and Reform.* Boulder, CO: Westview Press.

Ueda, Reed. 1998. The Changing Face of Post-1965 Immigration. In *The Immigration Reader: America in a Multidisciplinary Perspective.* David Jacobson, ed. Pp. 72–91. Oxford: Blackwell.

U.S. Commission on Immigration Reform. 1995. *Legal Immigration: Setting Priorities.* Interim Report. Washington, DC: U.S. Government Printing Office.

U.S. General Accounting Office. 1988. *Immigration: The Future Flow of Legal Immigration to the United States.* Washington, DC: U.S. Government Printing Office.

U.S. President's Commission on Immigration and Naturalization. 1953. *Whom Shall We Welcome?* Washington, DC: U.S. Government Printing Office.

DOMINIQUE DANIEL

FERTILITY. Fertility, the reproductive performance of a group or actual number of live births, is greatly affected by biological ability to reproduce, or fecundity, which of course varies by age (Ellison and O'Rourke 2000). If one is able to reproduce, the social and environmental context then determines whether one will have children and if one does, when and how many. So the locations and mobility associated with migration have a close association with fertility and, in turn, population growth and demographic profile.

Migration can have a significant impact on one's lifestyle and potentially one's reproductive decision making. There are four theoretical perspectives that try to account for why the fertility of migrants may differ from that of non-migrants (Brockerhoff and Yang 1994). The selectivity hypothesis proposes that fertility differences between migrants and non-migrants were in place before people migrated. Migrants often differ from the people that stay, and the characteristics that lead to migration may have a direct or indirect effect on fertility. Migration, when driven by a desire for a better life, may be coupled with the use of contraception. The relatively low fertility of immigrants from China, India, and Korea probably reflects their high levels of education and income (Kahn 1994).

The disruption hypothesis suggests that moving can get in the way of fertility either right before or during the change, or in the period of adjustment to a new location, especially if there is separation of mates (Brockerhoff and Yang 1994). Stress may also interfere with libido. Kahn (1994:512) found that during the 1980s, increases in the number of children born for women who were born between 1944 and 1962 were highest for most recent immigrants in the United States, a group with relatively low fertility in 1980, which likely reflects "catch-up" growth after disruption. This was particularly true for Mexican and Southeast Asian immigrants.

The adaptation hypothesis argues that people adjust to their new circumstances after arrival, including through changes in reproductive decision making. By the late 1980s, fertility of Southeast Asian immigrants was much lower than Mexican fertility, indicating that they were assimilating and adjusting their fertility to be more consistent with native fertility levels. Finally, the socialization hypothesis posits that fertility preferences are determined during one's development and thus that migrants would be expected to have fertility rates similar to the non-migrants in the country of origin. This is clearly evident in the "catch-up" fertility of Mexican women, which reflects Mexico's social and cultural beliefs regarding the importance of family and childbearing (Heim and Austin 1996).

Recently, immigrants have become more diverse than ever. The Immigrant Act of 1924 set quotas reflecting the proportion of national groups in the U.S. population, which meant that 84 percent of immigrants came from Northern and Western Europe (Ford 1985). During most of the twentieth century, the fertility of these immigrants was consistently lower than that of native-born women (Jasso and Rosenzweig 1990); census results for 1960, 1970, and 1980 showed that immigrant women at the end of their childbearing years had lower completed fertility than native-born women. Things began to change after 1965 when quotas became more equitable relative to sending countries and the number of immigrants admitted increased, reaching 800,000 annually by the early 1990s (Waldorf 1999). The proportion from Europe, a low fertility region, declined from 45 percent to 26 percent between 1970 and 1980 (Jasso and Rosenzweig 1990) and has since declined further. A much higher proportion of people are now coming from high fertility regions including Mexico, Latin America, and Asia, particularly Southeast Asia, and the ethnic composition of the country is changing profoundly as a result.

Most immigrant women in the United States are in their reproductive years, but there is considerable heterogeneity in fertility among different groups. In 1980, women from Cuba, the United Kingdom, and Canada had lower rates of current fertility than the native-born population (Ford 1990), as did Israeli immigrants in 1990 (Cohen and Haberfeld 1997). However, these immigrants are not typical, because during the 1980s the difference between immigrant and native fertility increased in part because of greater postponement of childbearing by native-born women (Waldorf 1999). In 1994, immigrant women, who comprised 9 percent of the women in the United States, had a fertility rate of 93 births per 1,000 women, relative to 62 births per 1,000 women in the native-born population.

Some argue that accepting immigrants from poorer, high fertility regions will increase fertility in the receiving countries and make it easier for those left behind to continue having larger families, thus exacerbating overpopulation and the associated negative economic impacts worldwide (Teitelbaum and Winter 1998). However, in many cases, fertility is actually lower for immigrants than for native born, as exemplified by Australia (Abbasi-Shavazi 1998). Overall, migration reduces population pressures in "overcrowded" developing nations and most immigrants, no matter what their destination, reduce their fertility relative to the sending country (Macunovich 1999). For example, while Turkish women in Germany have the highest fertility of all immigrants, it is much lower than the fertility rates of women living in Turkey, and their fertility in Germany declined in the 1980s as well (Waldorf 1999). This means that population growth worldwide is reduced and that immigrant children grow up in healthier surroundings with more educational opportunities, conditions associated with lower fertility. This portrait, however, presumes improved living conditions in receiving countries, which is not always the case. Downward assimilation brought on by racism and reduced economic opportunity can lead to a cycle of disadvantage that may be further exacerbated by premarital sexual activity and unplanned pregnancy (Singley and Landale 1998).

Women from Latin America exhibited the highest fertility rates through the 1980s, in addition to being the largest immigrant group in the 1990s (Waldorf 1999). In 1992, the total fertility rate of Hispanic women was significantly higher than that of non-Hispanic white women, at 2.7 (higher than the replacement level of 2) and 1.9, respectively. Overall, immigrant women in the 1990s expect to have more children than native-born. This likely reflects an attempt to recover from the disruption effect in order to achieve a family size more consistent with the attitudes and values of the sending country. Nonetheless, the longer immigrants stay in the United States the more likely fertility rates resemble those of native-born. This is especially true over several generations.

Because of international migration, then, the fertility of peoples from high fertility regions such as Mexico and Latin America will decrease, while fertility for people from low fertility regions such as the United States and Europe will tend to increase. Regardless of anti-immigrant fervor, countries with low fertility usually favor immigration because it can partly offset the negative impacts associated with such low numbers, including slower economic growth and a much larger proportion of aged retirees supported by a decreasing proportion of employed (Coale 1987). However, depending on how soon immigrants adopt similarly low fertility rates, they are likely to have decreasing impact on the aging of the overall population. *See also*: **Demography; Gender; Women.**

References

Abbasi-Shavazi, Mohammad Jalal. 1998. The Fertility of Immigrant Women in Australia. *People and Place* 6(3):30–38.

Brockerhoff, Martin, and Xiushi Yang. 1994. Impact of Migration on Fertility in Sub-Saharan Africa. *Social Biology* 41:19–43.

Coale, Ansley J. 1987. Demographic Effects of Below-Replacement Fertility and Their Social Implications. *Population and Development Review* 12:3–216.

Cohen, Yinon, and Yitchak Haberfeld. 1997. The Number of Israeli Immigrants in the United States in 1990. *Demography* 34(2):199–212.

Ellison, Peter T., and Mary T. O'Rourke. 2000. Population Growth and Fertility Regulation. In *Human Biology: An Evolutionary and Biocultural Perspective*. Sara Stinson, Barry Bogin, Rebecca Huss-Ashmore, and Dennis O'Rourke, eds. Pp. 553–586. New York: Wiley-Liss.

Ford, Kathleen. 1985. Declining Fertility Rates of Immigrants to the United States (With Some Exceptions). *Sociology and Social Research* 70(1):68–70.

———. 1990. Duration of Residence in the United States and the Fertility of U.S. Immigrants. *International Migration Review* 24(1):34–68.

Heim, Mary, and Nancy Austin. 1996. Fertility of Immigrant Women in California. *Population and Environment* 17(5):391–407.

Jasso, Guillermina, and Mark R. Rosenzweig. 1990. *The New Chosen People: Immigrants in the United States*. New York: Russell Sage.

Kahn, Joan R. 1994. Immigrant and Native Fertility During the 1980s: Adaptation and Expectations for the Future. *International Migration Review* 28(3):714–735.

Macunovich, Diane J. 1999. The Role of Relative Cohort Size and Relative Income in the Demographic Transition. *Population and Environment* 21(2):155–192.

Population Information Network (POPIN). 1999. *Dictionary of Demographic and Reproductive Health Terminology*. New York: United Nations. http://www.popin.org/~unpopterms/default.htm.

Singley, Susan G., and Nancy S. Landale. 1998. Incorporating Origin and Process in Migration-Fertility Frameworks: The Case of Puerto Rican Women. *Social Forces* 76(4):1437–1470.

Teitelbaum, Michael S., and Jay Winter. 1998. *A Question of Numbers: High Migration, Low Fertility, and the Politics of National Identity*. New York: Hill and Wang.

Waldorf, Brigitte. 1999. Impacts of Immigrant Fertility on Population Size and Composition. In *Migration and Restructuring in the United States: A Geographic Perspective*. Kavita Pandit and Suzanne Davies Withers, eds. Pp. 193–211. Lanham, MD: Rowman and Littlefield.

JOAN C. STEVENSON

FOOD. The familiar phrase "you are what you eat" suggests that food involves much more than nourishment alone. Food is an essential of life, fundamental to both survival and health. It is also central to human interaction, integral to everyday routines as well as to ritual events and special occasions of celebration or sorrow. As a universal need, food has generated considerable research in nutrition, anthropology, and related disciplines in regard to procurement and production, distribution, and consumption (Goodman et al. 2000; see also journals such as *Food and Foodways* and *Food, Culture, and Society*). Beyond food's dietary and economic dimensions, what is eaten, how ingredients are prepared, and when and how food is consumed also reveal the symbolic significance of food in serving to preserve cultural awareness, celebrate the past, and remind us of who we are.

In a country whose central ethos involves immigration and diversity, food is without doubt one of the most heralded and welcomed aspects of the rich cultural heritage that immigrants bring to the United States. As immigrants come to the United States, they bring with them food preferences and dietary patterns, as they have historically (McIntosh 1995). At the same time, they themselves adapt to the foods and the means of preparation and consumption that preceded them or that prevail in the United States (Jerome 1981; Jones 1990). This process has been lauded in the legendary Thanksgiving celebration of Pilgrims with the indigenous people of what came to be known as New England. The contemporary age of global migration entails similar processes of diffusion and blending, reminiscent of the "Columbian exchange" of innumerable plants, animals, and ideas associated with the transatlantic meeting of two hemispheres 500 years ago (Weatherford 1988).

The image of the "melting pot" brings food to mind, even though the metaphor originated from industrial foundries rather than the kitchen. Foods and their uses can denote belonging and being American, yet they may also represent substance and symbol for asserting cultural differences and group affinity. Ultimately, then, foods and their preparation, display, and sharing provide both means and settings for dynamic expression of identity and ethnicity, and therefore a vital key to understanding continuity as well as change in immigrants and immigrant communities (Brown and Mussell 1984).

When immigrating to the United States, people bring a desire for customary ingredients and cuisine, along with food preparation techniques and cultural and religious ideas concerning food. The diversity of dishes associated with immigrants is reflected in the array of cookbooks as well as reference volumes that are available (for example, the *Gale Encyclopedia of Multicultural America* and the *Encyclopedia of North American Eating and Drinking Traditions, Customs, and Rituals*). The predominant tendency is to pigeonhole groups according to broad labels and to assume homogeneity, for example, that all Mexicans eat tacos, tostadas, and enchiladas. Yet there is considerable intragroup variation, blending of ingredients and new forms of preparation, and a prevalence of syncretism overall. Furthermore, the regional dishes that have come to be associated with different areas of the United States arise largely as recipes brought by immigrants from native lands are modified with locally available foods and new cooking methods, and through different levels of isolation or intergroup exchange (McIntosh 1995).

Changes in foods within immigrant groups reflect shifting inclinations about maintaining traditional practices as well as the effects of generation and status (Kalcik 1984). In general, diet tends initially to change in an additive way, particularly through consumption of new beverages (such as soft drinks) and sweets. Breakfast foods tend to shift first, followed by lunch fare, both in association with greater limits on time. Dinners are slower to be altered since they hold much social and cultural significance. Not surprisingly, special or festival foods are those most likely to be retained. Foods and food preferences of immigrants groups are also greatly influenced by children, especially as they bring home "American ideas" gained from wider contacts than their parents may experience, especially those associated with school lunchrooms, lunch programs, and television and other media. Status has a direct bearing on changes in food choices, whether related to affordability or to the relative admiration or distaste expressed by others about what is considered food or its appropriate use.

New circumstances also result in modifications to familiar cooking methods, such as using woks atop electric ranges. Unavailability or expense of traditional ingredients may also result in substitutions, as seen in the phasing out of some darker grains in favor of wheat and corn among Germans in the Midwest, and fish replacing conch and lobster among West Indians. Styles of eating are also affected by migration. Eating on raised mats or with the hands, as is characteristic in much of Southeast Asia or the Middle East, may be replaced with tables and chairs and utensils. Both the transnational aspects of migration and the complex directionality and synergies of change are evident in changing tastes and food possibilities. Rice-cookers can be found alongside microwave ovens, just as chopsticks or low tables are common in many of the Asian restaurants that today are ubiquitous in cities across the country. And while many in the United States have come to relish chop suey, an Americanized version of "tsap soy" (miscellaneous leftovers), another distinctively American invention is now being exported in sizeable quantities to Asia and China itself: fortune cookies.

Changes in food marketed by grocery stores reflect the tremendous buying power of immigrants. The U.S. Hispanic population, representing 7.9 percent of total consumer spending in 2002 ($653 billion), is projected to be spending 9.6 percent by 2008 (Morley 2003). In some places, entire stores devoted to the immigrant population—including immense super-stores in cities like Los Angeles and Chicago—have followed the need for ethnic food aisles. Companies that have been providing food to immigrants for many years are expanding substantially. Major established firms like Coca-Cola, General Mills, Lipton, and Lean Cuisine are also entering the thriving "ethnic food market," developing product lines that include soft drinks with fruit flavors common in tropical home countries, reconstituted Asian side dishes, and frozen Thai and Chinese dinners. Trade agreements have also contributed to the inflow of ethnic foods, as food items previously unavailable in the United States are increasingly imported from different regions of the world. A sampling of recent business headlines from newspapers and trade publications (such as *Drug Store News*, *DSN Retailing Today*, *Progressive Grocer*, and *Chain Store Age*) reveal the tremendous growth and diversity associated with immigration today: "Albertson's Targets Hispanic Market," "From *Bodega* to Mega Store," "Goya Foods Leads an Ethnic Sales Trend," and "Supermarkets Offering Exotic Foods, Many Are from Foreign Countries."

The full array of world cuisine associated with large-scale immigration to the United States in recent decades increasingly encompasses the entire population and not just immigrants. The growing numbers of immigrants from Latin America, Asia, and elsewhere have stimulated considerable interest in new food varieties. This is clearly evident in restaurants as well as groceries. "Thai sounds good tonight" or "let's order Chinese" have become part of the American lexicon, while Ethiopian, Vietnamese, and Caribbean establishments also proliferate. Even large fast-food chains now offer egg rolls, teriyaki, or burritos as standard fare. The growing diversity of foods in stores, prevalence of television cooking shows, and travel experiences have all contributed to the significant growth of ethnic foods beyond the immigrant population. Sales of salsa, for example, have since 1991 outsold ketchup—the quintessential American condiment. Foods considered "foreign" not long ago are becoming mainstream, eaten by growing proportions of the overall population. In today's increasing variety of food offerings, items that were exotic only a few years ago (like papaya, yucca, chayote, and peppers) can now be found in the produce sections of most grocery stores. Consumption of mangos in the United States, for example, increased 40 percent in just the second half of the 1990s. Many meat and seafood departments offer marinated meat and whole or live fish, Latin American and Asian preferences that now extend to the wider public.

Some of the changes in consumption that involve immigrant and native-born Americans alike are increasingly problematic. Trends include growth in convenience foods, notably snacks and fast foods which tend to be high in fat content, carbohydrates, salt, and sweetness. This shift in nutrition has also been coupled with less physical activity as well as greater caloric intake, including the usual suspects: pizza, pastas, French fries, and hamburgers. Rising health concerns have accompanied growing evidence of unhealthy weight gains and even obesity among immigrant children the longer they are in the United States (Smith et al. 2000). The allure, and the deleterious impacts, of fast foods have led many educators to respond with healthier lunch programs. Ironically, though, children in high-density immigrant districts sometimes counter-respond with demands for "rights" to nachos and other high-fat foods, echoing the assertiveness of native-born youth. Concerns are also mounting regarding prevalence of health problems among immigrant adults, including chronic disease risks for diabetes and hypertension as well as being overweight, associated with dietary acculturation as well as lifestyle and environmental changes (Satia-Abouta et al. 2002). Growing restrictions on access to nutritional remedies like the Women, Infant and Children (WIC) program, food stamps, and healthcare and health insurance in general exacerbate the situation.

Of course, dietary shifts associated with urban lifestyles and global marketing mean that foods that predominate today in many countries may hardly be the "traditional" cuisine featured in cookbooks and romanticized in song (Belasco and Scranton 2002; Pilcher 2002). Many immigrants already bring a proclivity for processed foods since they are found so often on store shelves throughout the world as well as in the United States.

On the other hand, positive changes associated with the foods and nutrition of the immigrant population are also evident. In addition to greater diversity of foods, demand for plant foods by immigrants from places where meals are traditionally based on multiple vegetable dishes has encouraged broader awareness and experimentation. The rise in ethnic consciousness since the 1960s further renewed interest in heritage cuisine. Growing concerns for the environment, fitness, and food safety are also reflected in healthier food choices made by immigrants and their descendants, as well as the wider public.

The variety of new foods and novel combinations, stirred metaphorically by spatial mobility and ethnic mixing, is continuing to nurture a historical process whereby "ethnic" cuisine is incorporated into the "American" diet. The movement from ethnic foods to "nouvelle cuisine" is everywhere, from novel pizza toppings to newly invented wraps. Indeed today the boundary crossings inherent in migration, and in globalization generally, are those of cuisine as well as of ethnicities and geographies (McIntosh 1995; Anderson 2005). So while diet in the United States may be becoming more standardized and homogenous, it also remains highly diverse. As immigrant and ethnic groups seek to retain individuality, including through characteristic food patterns, the result is more of a smorgasbord than melting pot. *See also*: **Assimilation; Growth and development; Health; Transnationalism.**

References

Anderson, E.N. 2005. *Everyone Eats: Understanding Food and Culture*. New York: New York University Press.

Belasco, Warren, and Phillip Scranton, eds. 2002. *Food Nations: Selling Taste in Consumer Societies*. New York: Routledge.

Brown, Linda Keller, and Kay Mussell. 1984. *Ethnic and Regional Foodways in the United States*. Knoxville: University of Tennessee Press.

Goodman, Alan, D.L. Dufour, and G. Pelto, eds. 2000. *Nutritional Anthropology: Biocultural Perspectives on Food and Nutrition*. Mountain View, CA: Mayfield.

Jerome, N.W. 1981. The U.S. Dietary Pattern from an Anthropological Perspective. *Food Technology* 35(2):37–42.

Jones, E. 1990. *American Food*. Woodstock, NY: Overlook Press.

Kalcik, Susan. 1984. Ethnic Foodways in America: Symbol and the Performance of Identity. In *Ethnic and Regional Foodways in the United States*. Linda Keller Brown and Kay Mussell, eds. Pp. 37–65. Knoxville: University of Tennessee Press.

McIntosh, Elaine N. 1995. *American Food Habits in Historical Perspective*. Westport, CT: Praeger.

Morley, Hugh R. 2003. Secaucus, N.J.–Based Goya Fills Need for Authentic Hispanic Food. *Knight Ridder Tribune Business News*, November 2, 1.

Pilcher, Jeffrey M. 2002. Industrial Tortillas and Folkloric Pepsi: The Nutritional Consequences of Hybrid Cuisines in Mexico. In *Food Nations: Selling Taste in Consumer Societies*. Warren Belasco and Phillip Scranton, eds. Pp. 222–239. New York: Routledge.

Satia-Abouta, Jessie, Ruth E. Patterson, Marian L. Neuhouser, and John Elder. 2002. Dietary Acculturation: Applications to Nutrition Research and Dietetics. *Journal of the American Dietetic Association* 102(8):1105–1118.

Smith, Patricia K., Barry Bogin, M. Ines Varela-Silva, Bibiana Orden, and James Loucky. 2002. Does Immigration Help or Harm Children's Health? The Mayan Case. *Social Science Quarterly* 83(4):994–1002.

U.S. Census Bureau. 2000. The Foreign-Born Population. http://www.census.gov/prod/2003pubs/c2kbr-34pdf.

Weatherford, Jack. 1988. *Indian Givers: How the Indians of the Americas Transformed the World*. New York: Fawcett Columbine.

JAMES LOUCKY

FOOD PROCESSING. All segments of the North American food industry have attracted immigrant workers over the past two centuries, but the food processing industry consistently relied on immigrant labor through the twentieth century as both a supplementary and primary labor force. Following publication of *The Jungle*, Upton Sinclair's 1906 exposé of the meatpacking industry, a work he said was "aimed at the public's heart and hit its stomach," food processing underwent several structural and organizational changes that altered its relationship to the U.S. government and succeeded in upgrading and unionizing most meatpacking jobs. For several decades, these developments stabilized meatpacking employment, ushering in a period of reliance on domestic instead of immigrant labor. By World War II, the processing of beef and pork had entered a period of reduced turnover, higher wages, and somewhat more flexible working hours that was to last for two to three decades (Skaggs 1986). Packing houses in several large and small cities across the United States, including Chicago and Philadelphia, recruited from urban families without specifically targeting new immigrants.

Over this same time period, poultry processing grew throughout the U.S. South and southeastern United States, taking advantage of low land and labor costs and recruiting primarily African Americans and women. Seafood processing, more seasonal than either poultry or meatpacking, also recruited minorities and women, though in many areas—primarily California, Alaska, and New England—seafood firms utilized immigrant Asian, Portuguese, and Norwegian women during peak canning and processing periods. In California, seafood producers commonly used ethnicity to segment or divide the labor force in an effort to prevent unionization.

Several developments since the mid-1960s laid the foundation for increased use of immigrant labor in all branches of the food processing industry. Although the Civil Rights Movement did not immediately open up alternative economic opportunities for African Americans stuck in lower paying food processing jobs, it caused employers to consider alternative sources of labor. More directly, during the late 1960s and early 1970s, meatpackers began shifting production sites from large urban centers to smaller towns and rural areas closer to cattle and hog farms. In many cases, these new production sites were less strongly pro-union than urban areas; opportunities arose to replace union with non-union workers as well as negotiate less labor-friendly, sweetheart contracts.

The industry concentrated more food processing work in the plants during this time as well, moving many of the jobs that skilled butchers performed in grocery stores to rural processing plants. The production of new packaging techniques and value-added products such as boxed beef and boned chicken breasts both increased demand for low-wage, unskilled labor at processing plants and eliminated higher-paid, more skilled butcher jobs in retail food outlets. This set the stage for increased hiring of immigrant labor.

Since the late 1970s, the food processing industry has tapped all kinds of immigrant groups for labor: refugees, documented and undocumented immigrants, and temporary legal foreign workers imported with special H-class visas. In 1978, for example, after Governor Ray of Iowa responded to President Carter's call for assistance with Southeast Asian refugees by accepting all of the Tai Dam refugees from a single refugee camp in Laos, porkpacking plants in northwest Iowa aggressively recruited these refugees with the aid of refugee service bureaus and state employment agencies (Grey 1999). Similarly, through the 1980s, two beefpacking plants in Garden City, Kansas, filled over 4,000 jobs with a combination of Latino immigrants from Mexico and Central America, Lao and Vietnamese refugees, and local Kansans (Gouviea and Stull 1995). Beefpackers in another midwestern town, Lexington, Nebraska, followed suit in early 1990. During the first half of that decade, their hiring of native Nebraskan workers fell almost directly in relation to the hiring of Latino immigrants (Gouviea and Stull 1995).

The 1986 Immigration Reform and Control Act (IRCA) furthered the process of immigrants working in meatpacking and seafood and poultry processing, supporting developments occurring in the industry over the previous two decades. Latino immigrants in particular—most from Mexico and Central America—found work in the plants in large numbers following IRCA. As food processing companies across the country have increased their dependence on immigrant labor, they have, in many regions of the country, contributed to the Latinization of rural America (Griffith 1995). This has changed the face of food processing dramatically, altering ethnic compositions in most plants. At the same time, immigrants originally recruited into food processing have changed community and regional economies, cultures, and societies.

The two regions of the United States most affected by these changes are the South and the Midwest. Poultry plants in Texas, Arkansas, North Carolina, Alabama, and Georgia, as well as on the Delmarva Peninsula east of the Chesapeake Bay, have stimulated immigration primarily from Mexico and Central America, in some cases building housing for workers and using housing as a tool of labor control (Griffith 1993; Fink 2003). Pork and turkey processing plants in Iowa and Minnesota have hired more ethnically diverse populations, including Vietnamese, Thai, Hmong, Somali, and Latino workers. Small towns such as Marshalltown, Iowa, and Marshall, Minnesota, have been thoroughly transformed from these immigrations, with both positive and negative consequences. While high injury rates among food processing workers tend to stress local health systems, immigrants originally recruited to food processing have since moved on to open businesses and revitalize downtown areas. With increased family formation among immigrant workers, children born to immigrants have begun saving local school systems from closing or merging with other schools.

The industry, nevertheless, continues to prey heavily on the vulnerable attributes of immigrant workers, taking advantage of their undocumented status and the increased difficulty of crossing the U.S.-Mexico border since the terrorist attacks of 2001. A local observer in a small midwestern town reported in 2002 that superintendents at the porkpacking plant there have increased their use of threats of deportation since that time, facilitating compliance to plant discipline. Managers' reliance on fear is characteristic of labor relations in the worst of the plants, though some plants and some companies pride themselves on more enlightened labor relations, assisting workers in financial planning and with locating affordable housing, attending to their healthcare needs, and showing their appreciation through company picnics, English as Second Language classes, and cultural awareness training. For many immigrant workers, pay at the plants is relatively high compared to seasonal jobs in agriculture, hotels and restaurants, or other industrial sectors that routinely hire immigrants. Workers earn between

$7 and $15 per hour, depending on the region of the country, the industry sector, and the company for which they work. After 90-day waiting periods, most workers begin to accumulate vacation time and receive pension benefits and health insurance. Many plants are formally represented by the United Food and Commercial Workers Union, although in the right-to-work states (where most food processing plants are located), workers need not join the union. Union strength has waned since President Reagan's cavalier firing of the unionized air traffic controllers in the early 1980s, an act that a meatpacking worker in Minnesota described as opening the season on unions across the United States (Griffith 1993:19–21).

Intractable problems still plague food processing employment, particularly in the areas of health and safety and labor control (Schlosser 2001). Food processing jobs are among the most hazardous in the developed world, rivaling construction and agriculture in numbers of injuries per thousand workers. Food processing workers typically suffer from muscular trauma, repetitive motion disease, cuts, and strains. Amputations are not uncommon. Some of the most hazardous jobs are those on the crews that clean the plants, exposing workers to highly toxic chemicals and mechanical blades. Typically these crews are composed of undocumented immigrants hired through subcontractors. It is common for plant managers to hide or underreport occupational injuries to keep workman's compensation claims and insurance costs low. Injured workers are often encouraged to continue working, making their injuries worse, or are given jobs that, while not aggravating their injuries, keep them employed at the plant, absolving the plant of the responsibility of reporting their injury.

Labor control mechanisms used in the plants facilitate this approach to occupational injury. Plants use various social tools to enhance their control over their workers, including network recruiting and providing company housing to workers. The former allows managers to threaten workers with firing all members of a network for the infractions of a single member, leading members to police themselves. The latter enables managers to threaten workers with homelessness for disciplinary problems; company housing, usually close to the plant, also reduces workers' abilities to resist work at any time of the day or night that plant owners and managers need them.

Important mechanisms of labor control derive from the ethnic segmentation of plant labor forces, which provide managers opportunities to play different groups of workers off of one another, threatening to replace one group for another in preferred jobs in the plant or in the plant in general. Labor forces at the plants continue to be ethnically and legally mixed, with most plants having a core of stable workers surrounded by a shifting, high-turnover group, some of whom migrate from plant to plant within specific regions. Anthropologist Mark Grey, one of the nation's foremost experts on immigrants in meatpacking, argues that the practice of migrating among plants is common among Latino workers who are attempting to replicate patterns of migration they experienced while working in agriculture, where the work is highly seasonal (1999). At the same time, moving from plant to plant offers relief from the chronic muscular stress that accompanies meatpacking employment while also allowing workers to attend to the family responsibilities that enable their residence in the United States and their continued significant communication with villages in Mexico and Central America.

By means of such strategies, immigrant food processing workers have been able, in some instances, to shape employment in poultry, meat, and seafood processing to the contours of their own preferences and experiences. For example, the same networks that managers have been able to use as tools of labor control some workers now use to resist exploitative conditions in the plants. Through continued network recruitment since the immigration reforms of the late 1980s, more and more communities with large meatpacking employment have witnessed a shift from primarily single male workers to larger family groups settling and working in the plants. With more families and more women and children, immigrant groups have been able to become more enmeshed in community dynamics through churches, schools, and other organizations. Members of these organizations, in turn, have supported their attempts to break free of some of the labor control at work in the plants. It is likely that, as this process continues, the industry will seek new immigrant labor from other parts of the globe. *See also*: **Health; Labor organization and activism; Legislation; Social networks; Work.**

References

Fink, Leon. 2003. *The Maya of Morgantown: Work and Community in the Nuevo New South*. Chapel Hill: University of North Carolina Press.

Gouviea, Lourdes, and Donald Stull. 1995. Dances With Cows: Beefpacking's Impact on Garden City, Kansas and Lexington, Nebraska. In *Any Way You Cut It: Meat Processing and Small-Town America*. D. Stull, M. Broadway, and D. Griffith, eds. Pp. 85–107. Lawrence: University Press of Kansas.

Grey, Mark. 1999. Immigrants, Migration, and Worker Turnover at the Hog Pride Pork Packing Plant. *Human Organization* 58:16–27.

Grey, Mark, and Anne Woodrick. 2002. Unofficial Sister Cities: Meatpacking Labor Migration Between Villachuato, Mexico and Marshalltown, Iowa. *Human Organization* (61):364–376.

Griffith, David. 1993. *Jones's Minimal: Low-Wage Labor in the United States*. Albany: State University of New York Press.

———. 1995. Hay Trabajo: Poultry Processing, Rural Industrialization, and the Latinization of Low-Wage Labor. In *Any Way You Cut It: Meat Processing and Small-Town America*. D. Stull, M. Broadway, and D. Griffith, eds. Pp. 129–151. Lawrence: University Press of Kansas.

Schlosser, Eric. 2001. *Fast Food Nation: The Dark Side of the All-American Meal*. New York: Houghton-Mifflin.

Skaggs, J.M. 1986. *Prime Cut: Livestock Raising and Meatpacking in the United States, 1607–1983*. College Station: Texas A&M University Press.

Stull, Donald D., and Michael J. Broadway. 2004. *Slaughterhouse Blues: The Meat and Poultry Industry in North America*. Thomson-Wadsworth.

DAVID GRIFFITH

G

GANGS. Although migrations certainly include people of means looking for better opportunities, the large-scale movements of people in the nineteenth and twentieth centuries typically were represented by poorer populations seeking a better life. Immigration to the United States certainly has followed this pattern. With the closing of the western frontier, readily available land for settlers became increasingly scarce and newcomers consequently settled in urban environments lured by the promise of employment during the Industrial Revolution. Most were forced by their limited means to take up residence in rundown sections of these urban areas. The limited employment and limited overall opportunities, combined with the prejudices of earlier generations of Americans, made their task that much more difficult.

Beginning in the 1840s and continuing into the twentieth century, young immigrant men of Irish, Italian, German, Jewish, and Polish origin gathered on the street corners of their respective neighborhoods to form gangs and confront together the rigors of their new life in the industrialized cities of the eastern and midwestern United States. Later, other immigrant groups from Latin America, mainly Mexico, repeated this experience of establishing ethnic enclaves, or barrios (neighborhoods), characterized partly by youth gangs. In this context, a holistic, integrative assessment and interpretation of street gangs must recognize the many strands and sources of gang delinquency. For immigrants, adapting to a new culture and place affects family structure and stability, schooling readiness in the context of language and cultural differences, and level of involvement with police and the criminal justice system.

What is remarkable are the similarities then and now in how major pressures forced the children of immigrants into the streets. Moreover, the presence of immigrants has generally aroused resentment in some sectors of American society. Seldom, however, has this hostility reached such a high pitch, and what is different today is the amount and intensity of the anti-immigration backlash. These developments have led to the wholesale deportation of many gang youth, and in their wake, the exportation of gang culture to the home country.

Thus, immigration, both legal and illegal, and the experiences of immigrants adapting and adjusting to city life form the basis for all else that follows, including and especially the maladaptation that so often occurs among them. There are many areas in which immigrants and especially their children find themselves betwixt-and-between, beginning with where they settle, what jobs they fill, and how and why their social and cultural values and practices are challenged and typically undermined and revamped. A holistic perspective of gangs also takes into account when the social environment shapes personal identities with which the individuals interact. To broaden and deepen the picture many other factors need to be considered, such as ecological, socioeconomic, sociocultural, and sociopsychological, particularly in light of the immigrant experience. An analytic framework of what has been termed multiple marginality (Vigil 1988, 2002a) lends itself to a holistic strategy that examines linkages among the various factors, the actions and interactions between them, and notes the cumulative nature of urban street gangs. As immigrant families encountered problems in their adjustments to life in the new setting (due to poverty, lack of education, low-paying jobs, and discrimination), youths often sought respite in the streets from problems at home. Many of these street groups began as a small number of disaffected youth, usually undergoing the "storm and stress" of adolescence, whose street socialization and behavior over time evolved from a pattern of malicious mischief into a deadly and violent lifestyle. It is important to underscore that it is the most marginalized populations that are affected, as no more than 10 percent of the youths become gang members in most neighborhoods.

The contexts of time, place, and people are also an important part of the equation. For example, some gangs have been around for generations and are found in various large and middle-sized cities in the United States (Klein 1995). Studies in larger cities show a tradition of an age-graded gang structure (Moore 1978, 1991). This cohorting network works to maintain the size of the gang as older members "mature out" and the younger gang members, approximately from the ages of 14 to 18, are more likely to be led into and participate in unconventional and destructive behavior. Attention to female gangs and affiliates has also increased and helped broaden the discussion of gender roles. Newer gangs have emerged in different urban enclaves as a result of continuing large-scale immigration, where increasingly more street youth are opting for this lifestyle (Waters 1999). A few of these less rooted gangs have tried to play catch-up to the older gangs by becoming just as violent, and are succeeding.

In the context of Southern California today, this gang issue takes on special import when we consider whether immigration and the forces associated with it contribute anything to that difference. For example, is it true that it is the second generation of Mexicans and other immigrants that are prone to joining gangs (Waters 1999), and this only after experiencing devastating marginalization that undermines and destabilizes their adaptation to the United States (Vigil 1988, 2002a)? Or conversely, does the immigration experience alone generate enough stress and strain to pull immigrant youth into the streets and the gang life leading to violence? This seems to be the case with relatively recent arrivals from Central America, especially among the Salvadoran population in the Pico Union area of the near Westside of Los Angeles. With Asian Americans, especially the Vietnamese who fled a war-torn region, this also is the case but with a slight difference. The Vietnamese street gangs were largely formed from youth born in Vietnam but raised from an early age in the United States. These youth grouped together for self-defense because of pressure from Chicano gangs in the area.

Chicano youth gangs in Southern California originated among the second-generation offspring of those immigrant families that were less successful than most of those in the same neighborhoods. These families had major difficulties coping with pressures of poverty and social discrimination in employment, public services, housing, and other amenities and necessities of life. Youths from such backgrounds established the basic patterns of Chicano gang behavior, including violence, beginning in the 1930s and 1940s. In this, their actions in many ways paralleled what had occurred before (and later) among immigrant families' children in other U.S. cities. But whereas Irish and Italian immigrants to eastern seaboard cities soon ceased to arrive in large numbers and most families among them found their ways eventually into less crowded, rundown neighborhoods, Latino (mostly Mexican) immigrants have continued to pour into and beyond the *barrios* that generated the first Chicano street gangs. The conditions that gave rise to street socialization and gang participation have thus continued and, indeed, intensified (Moore et al. 1983).

Continuing large-scale immigration from Mexico in the last 75 years and from Central America more recently has ensured that a sizeable portion of the new population will be marginalized. The end result is second-generation youth who will have social control voids and wind up being socialized in the streets. As Waters (1999) has carefully documented for different ethnic groups, it is the second generation under intense marginalization pressures that generates gangs.

This relationship has been modified, however, in the last decade, as first-generation immigrant Latinos (Mexicans and Salvadorans mainly) have been subjected to accelerated street socialization in their home country before coming to the United States. For example, many Mexican bordertowns have street gangs, while San Salvador now has street gangs comprised of young people who were deported from the United States. For others, street socialization in the United States became tied to the drug trafficking that began to recruit heavily from the streets. Presently, the war on terrorism and the drug trafficking, as well as the continuing undocumented immigration from Mexico and other Latin American countries, has exacerbated matters to the point where various vigilante groups, such as the Minutemen in Arizona, have taken it upon themselves to prevent illegal immigration. Couching their stance on how these undocumented individuals might actually be a part of a terrorist infiltration, such groups have received strong tacit support from the U.S. citizenry who want to shore up the borders anyway. Anti-immigration attitudes and legislation have often been a part of the history of immigration to the United States, and the global terrorist threat and drug trafficking have added a new dimension to the story of antagonistic Anglo and Latino relations. This is particularly the case with the Central Americans, such as Mara Salvatruchas (MS 13), who have found their way back to the United States and are raising havoc in different regions. Surprisingly, some Salvadorans who have left the gang and opted for a conventional life have participated in the Homies Unidos (United Homeboys) organization in both countries to steer youth into pro-social behavior and away from the destructive gang lifestyle.

To reiterate, certain dynamics have changed. The line separating first from second generation and the propensity to join gangs and follow a different and often violent lifestyle is somewhat different today. This is not to say that new immigrants are not violent in their own right, irrespective of gang patterns, as street experiences are just one source of violence. Domestic violence, for example, is still a problem among Latinos. However, as Martinez (2002:139) has firmly stated: "It is worth noting that the advantages of immigration should be explored in more detail in the future so that scholars better understand how Latinos, a heavily immigrant group faced with adverse conditions, seem to endure violent crime better than native-born groups." *See also*: **Crime; Families; Social networks.**

References

Klein, M. 1971. *Street Gangs and Street Workers*. Englewood Cliffs, NJ: Prentice-Hall.
———. 1995. *The American Street Gang*. New York: Oxford University Press.
Martinez, R., Jr. 2002. *Latino Homicide: Immigration, Violence, and Community*. New York: Routledge.
Moore, J.W. 1978. *Homeboys*. Philadelphia: Temple University Press.
———. 1991. *Going Down to the Barrio: Homeboys and Homegirls in Change*. Philadelphia: Temple University Press.
Moore, J.W., J.D. Vigil, and R. Garcia. 1983. Residence and Territoriality in Chicano Gangs. *Social Problems* 31(2):182–194.
Vigil, J.D. 1988. *Barrio Gangs: Street Life and Identity in Southern California*. Austin: University of Texas Press.
———. 2002a. *A Rainbow of Gangs: Street Cultures in the Mega-City*. Austin: University of Texas Press.
———. 2002b. Community Dynamics and the Rise of Street Gangs. In *Latinos! Remaking America*. Marcelo Suárez-Orozco and M.M. Paez, eds. Pp. 97–109. Berkeley: University of California Press and The David Rockefeller Center for Latin American Studies, Harvard University.
Waters, T. 1999. *Crime and Immigrant Youth*. Thousand Oaks, CA: Sage.

JAMES DIEGO VIGIL

GENDER. Immigration scholars have been slow to recognize the extent and importance of women's immigration. Internationally, migrant women predominate among permanent settlers and men dominate migrant labor flows (Zlotnik 1995:231), and women are the majority of immigrants to developed countries (DeLaet 1999:2). During the twentieth century, immigration to the United States became increasingly feminized as well. Beginning in the 1930s, women have migrated more frequently to the United States than men (Houstoun et al. 1984). Yet the sex ratio (males per 100 females) of the 1997 legal foreign-born population in the United States remains skewed, with 101 males per 100 females as compared to 95 males per 100 females in the native-born population (U.S. Census Bureau 1998:26). The sex ratio of legal immigrants varies greatly by region of origin. African immigrants are characterized by the most skewed sex ratio, 162 males per 100 females, while Mexican males outnumber females by approximately 127 to 100 and Central American males outnumber females by 120 to 100. Among European and Canadian immigrants, women greatly outnumber men, with sex ratios of approximately 79 and 65 males per 100 females, respectively (U.S. Census Bureau 1998).

Women's international migration has often been a response to family reunification policy, and pro-family unity policies are a major reason for women's predominance in legal migration to the United States. Undocumented Mexican women and children, in particular, began to cross the border as a form of clandestine family reunion or to gain underground service sector employment (Hondagneu-Sotelo 1994) and later through legal entrance under family reunification provisions. Moreover, while the legalization program of the 1986 Immigration Reform and Control Act was gender-biased by favoring agricultural workers, who were primarily male sojourners, and setting terms of proof of illegal residency which men were more likely to be able to meet, women still comprised 45 percent of amnesty recipients (Zlotnik 1995:237).

Despite the importance of pro-family migration policies, however, women immigrants should not be viewed only as family dependents. For many decades, women migrants have been viewed largely as dependents rather than economically motivated individuals with personal agency. Although women may migrate to reunify families, their motives include obtaining work, escaping marital conflict, and obtaining personal independence (DeLaet 1999). While women are less likely to permanently immigrate for employment, many have come for both low-wage and professional work. Women immigrants to the United States have predominated in such low-wage employment as private domestic help (Hondagneu-Sotelo 1994) and subcontracted manufacturing, such as garments, footwear, textiles, and electronics, which has often reverted to sweatshop conditions (Bonacich and Appelbaum 2000). By 1993, women immigrants to the United States outnumbered males, a change related to an increase in underground service sector employment, such as domestic service (Bean et al. 1990). Professional occupations entered by immigrant women have included nursing, management, teaching, and administration.

Globally, women immigrants are a significant portion of undocumented entrants, including single women. The dynamics of both undocumented and legal immigration have been impacted by the globalization of the economy. Developed labor-receiving countries have a low-waged labor shortage, while the developing countries are dependent on migrant remittances as a source of foreign capital and a strategy for dealing with lack of employment. The demand for workers in gendered occupations in the service sector, retrograde manufacturing, private domestic employment, and the sex industry have contributed to the feminization of immigration (Cheng 1999:47).

The feminization of immigration has altered social reproduction in both sending and receiving countries by placing responsibility for subsidizing the cost of the next generation primarily on underdeveloped sending countries (Cheng 1999:49–50). Working, middle-class, and upper-class women have been able to enter the labor force by transferring gendered household work such as cleaning and childcare to immigrant women (Hondagneu-Sotelo 1994). This low-cost labor directly subsidizes the social reproduction of American families and the next generation of workers. Simultaneously, caretakers, most often grandmothers and other women relatives, raise the children of female domestics in the sending countries, subsidizing the cost of reproducing the next generation of migrant workers. One consequence is "transnational motherhood," a situation in which mothers have limited contact with their own children while they are growing up (Hondagneu-Sotelo and Avila 2002).

Women have been underrepresented among individuals entering as refugees and asylum seekers to developed countries, although, globally, women and children constitute a majority of refugees (DeLaet 1999:9). One of the reasons for low admittance of women to the United States has been a failure to recognize gendered persecution, such as domestic violence, genital cutting, and rape as human rights violations worthy of protection.

Anti-immigrant attitudes in the U.S. population are especially focused on women and children. The Personal Responsibility and Work Opportunity Reconciliation Act of 1996 (PRWORA) restricts provisions of many federal, state, and local services to undocumented immigrants, prompting debates about providing them with free and discounted healthcare. In California and some other states, propositions which sought to deny schooling and medical and welfare benefits for the undocumented portend especially negative impacts on women and children.

Denying access to affordable healthcare impacts undocumented immigrant children, many of whom are born in the United States and are therefore eligible for publicly funded healthcare programs. Immigrants are often confused by state and federal eligibility restrictions and fearful of being discovered and deported (Feld 2000). Thus many undocumented immigrants are prevented from seeking healthcare for their children by fear of authorities or a false belief that their children are not eligible for care, even though children born in the United States are eligible for government-funded health coverage and PRWORA allows for provision of discounted immunizations and emergency services. The argument that improving adults' access to services will improve children's access to care has been offered as a rationale for expanding public health insurance coverage to include parents of children enrolled in state health insurance programs. Another rationale might be that pregnant mothers should have prenatal care for children who will be U.S. citizens at birth and thus entitled to healthcare coverage.

In recent decades there are more female immigrants coming to the United States than to other "labor-importing countries," and women are the majority of immigrants from Asia, Central and South America, the Caribbean, and Europe (Donato in Pessar 1999). This increase in female immigrants is related to the increase of industries employing primarily female workers as, for example, service, healthcare, apparel, and microelectronics. While male immigrants from countries like India, Iran, and Japan have been able to use their education to move into a higher occupational status than native-born whites, female immigrants have not had the same success in converting high levels of education into managerial, professional, or entrepreneurial occupations (Pessar 1999).

Nevertheless, immigrant women's regular employment and wage-earning status have had an impact on gender relations in immigrant cultures. Despite their disadvantages in the labor market, immigrant women who are employed in the United States "generally gain greater personal autonomy and independence, while men lose ground" (Pessar 1999). Women who are wage earners and contribute to the household budget gain greater control over budgeting and decisions about managing the household. These women are also able to solicit male assistance with domestic tasks such as cleaning, shopping, and cooking. Considerable research has been reported on this shifting gender relationship among immigrant women of several countries from Vietnam to Mexico (Kabria; Guendelman and Perea-Itriaga in Pessar 1999). Exposure to American culture weakens the traditional patriarchal family structure and allows women to "assume more active public and social roles" that improve their status and allow them to contribute to the families' integration and in American society and potential for social mobility (Hondagneu-Sotelo in Pessar 1999). *See also*: **Family reunification; Social benefits; Sweatshops; Unauthorized immigration; Women; Work.**

References

Bean, Frank D., Barry Edmondson, and Jeffrey S. Passel. 1990. *Undocumented Migration to the United States: IRCA and the Experience of the 1980s*. Santa Monica, CA: RAND Corporation.

Bonacich, Edna, and Richard Appelbaum. 2000. *Behind the Label: Inequality in the Los Angeles Apparel Industry*. Berkeley: University of California.

Cheng, Shu-Ju Ada. 1999. Labor Migration and International Sexual Division of Labor: A Feminist Perspective. In *Gender and Immigration*. Gregory A. Kelson and Debra DeLaet, eds. Pp. 38–58. New York: New York University Press.

DeLaet, Debra L. 1999. Introduction: The Invisibility of Women in Scholarship on International Migration. In *Gender and Immigration*. Gregory A. Kelson and Debra DeLaet, eds. Pp. 1–20. New York: New York University Press.

Feld, Power B. 2000. *Immigrants' Access to Health Care after Welfare Reform: Findings from Focus Groups in Four Cities*. Washington, DC: Kaiser Commission on Medicaid and the Uninsured.

Hondagneu-Sotelo, Pierette. 1994. *Gendered Transitions: Mexican Experiences of Immigration*. Berkeley: University of California Press.

Hondagneu-Sotelo, Pierette, and Ernestine Avila. 2002. I'm Here But I'm There: The Meanings of Latina Transnational Motherhood. In *Families at Work: Expanding the Boundaries*. Naomi Gerstel, Dan Clawson, and Robert Zussman, eds. Pp. 139–161. Nashville, TN: Vanderbilt University Press.

Houstoun, Marion F., Roger G. Kramer, and Joan Mackin Barrett. 1984. Female Predominance in Immigration to the United States since 1930: A First Look. *International Migration Review* 18:908–963.

Pessar, Patricia R. 1999. The Role of Gender, Households, and Social Networks in the Migration Process: A Review and Appraisal. In *The Handbook of International Migration: The American Experience*. Charles Hirschman, Philip Kasinitz, and Josh DeWind, eds. Pp. 53–70. New York: Russell Sage Foundation.

U.S. Census Bureau. 1998. *Profile of the Foreign-Born Population in the United States: 1997*. Washington, DC: U.S. Government Printing Office.

Zlotnik, Hania. 1995. The South-to-North Migration of Women. *International Migration Review* 29:229–254.

JUDITH WARNER

GLOBAL ORIGINS: ASIA, AFRICA, AND EUROPE. After World War II, the United States experienced economic prosperity which, combined with the immigration issues resulting from the war, resulted in a relaxation of the restrictive immigration policy that had prevailed since the 1920s (Dinnerstein 1999). The War Brides Act of 1945 admitted 120,000 spouses and children of U.S. soldiers.

The Displaced Persons Act of 1948 admitted war refugees, but was written so that it could maintain restrictions on Jewish refugees. Immediately after the war, Europeans were the dominant immigrant group arriving in the United States. Then Congress began a special program in 1960 to help refugees from Communist countries, mostly Cuban refugees but later including refugees from Eastern Europe.

The number of European immigrants has steadily declined from 56 percent of all immigrants in the period from 1931 to 1960 to 34 percent during 1961–1970 and 15 percent during 1991–1998. In the past two decades, most European immigrants came from the United Kingdom, including Northern Ireland, the Republic of Ireland, Poland, Bosnia, the Soviet Union, and Russia and the Ukraine after the breakup of the former Soviet Union. During these same periods the number of Latin American and Asian immigrants has substantially increased so that Latin American immigrants represented 48 percent of the total number during 1991–1998 and Asian immigrants were 31 percent of all immigrants in this time period (Toro-Morn and Alicea 2004). Latin America and Asia are currently the two geographic regions sending the largest percent of immigrants to the United States.

Increased conflict in the Middle East has spurred immigration to the United States by Israelis, Palestinians, Lebanese, Jordanians, and Syrians. Most immigrants coming to the United States from Africa before 1971 were from North Africa, especially Egypt and Morocco, but this trend has been declining while immigration from Sub-Saharan Africa has increased. Ethiopians left their homeland after the 1974 Marxist revolution and the 1980s famine in that country. Other African immigrants are educated professionals from English-speaking nations like Nigeria. English-speaking West Indians who entered the United States were primarily from Jamaica at 1.9 percent of all immigrants in 2003. The largest non-English-speaking group of Caribbean immigrants came from the Dominican Republic at 3.7 percent followed by Haitians (1.7 percent), who were fleeing the repressive political situation and extreme poverty in Haiti.

Asia

In 2003, 34.7 percent of immigrants admitted to the United States came from Asia while only a slightly higher percent, 35.5 percent, came from North America, including Mexico and Canada. Of the sending countries, Mexico is number one with 16.4 percent of all immigrants in 2003 followed by India at 7.1 percent, the Philippines at 6.4 percent, and China at 5.8 percent. While some European countries benefited initially from the 1965 law (Italians, Portuguese, and Greeks), the most significant impact was on Asian countries. When U.S. immigration policy was changed by the 1965 Immigration and Naturalization Act of 1965, there were few indicators that there would be such a huge increase in Asian immigration since restrictive quotas of 100 admissions per year for most Asian nations discouraged Asians from even applying for the limited number of places (U.S. Department of Homeland Security 2003).

Immigration policy continued restrictions on Asian immigrants with the limited annual quotas of 100 immigrants per country until passage of the 1965 law, which allowed 170,000 admissions per year from the Eastern Hemisphere and 120,000 from the Western Hemisphere with a limit of 20,000 annual visas per country. Seventy-four percent of admissions were reserved for family reunification visas, 20 percent for occupational preference visas, and the rest for refugees (Dinnerstein 1999). After 1965, the higher country quotas and potential for chain migration using the new family reunification policy resulted in the steady increase of immigrants from Asian countries to reach 34.7 percent of all U.S. immigrants in 2003.

Among Asian countries, the Philippines was the major sending country of immigrants due to influence of U.S. colonization until 1946 and the operation of U.S. military bases there, which continued until 1992. Three other Asian countries with a high percent of immigrants coming to the United States, South Korea, China, and Vietnam, have also experienced U.S. political and military involvement with the "two Koreas, the two Chinas and the two Vietnams" (Kim 1974). Newcomers from Asia settled in a few cities such as San Francisco, New York, and Honolulu. The population of San Francisco's Chinatown doubled from 1952 to 1972, and the population of New York City's Chinatown grew from 33,000 in 1960 to 300,000 in 1990 (Dinnerstein 1999). While some Chinese immigrants struggled in these inner-city neighborhoods, others who were well educated and highly skilled settled in the suburbs. By the mid-1970s, 70 to 80 percent of the residents and interns in some New York City hospitals were immigrants due to a shortage of native-born doctors and the occupational preference visa category, which favored admission of scientists, engineers, doctors, and nurses (Kanjana-pan 1995).

By 1990, there were 800,000 East Indians in the United States. Their knowledge of English and educational background enabled them to have the highest income among immigrants. Some were professionals, while others started businesses, especially hotels and motels. Many Indochinese refugees, who were admitted after the failure of U.S. intervention in Southeast Asia, were in a very different situation since they were often poorly educated and lacked job and language skills. Despite their initial disadvantages and high rates of welfare recipients, Vietnamese immigrants often revitalized the slum neighborhoods where they settled in Chicago and San Francisco, while the second generation has succeeded academically (Dinnerstein 1999).

According to the 2000 census, the highest numbers of Asians in America are Chinese at 23.89 percent of the population, Filipinos at 18.3 percent, Asian Indians at 16.2 percent, Vietnamese at 10.9 percent, and Koreans at 10.5 percent. The percent of native-born Americans in these groups are 29.1 percent Chinese, 32.2 percent Filipinos, 24.6 percent Asian Indians, 23.9 percent Vietnamese, and 22.3 percent Koreans. Asian Pacific Americans will continue to be the fastest growing ethnic group in the United States with predictions that show 54 percent of Asian Pacific Americans will be foreign-born by 2020 (Hing 1997). Family reunification has been a major factor in this increase. In the late 1960s, about 45 percent of Filipino immigrants were entering through occupational preference and 55 percent through family reunification. By 1990 slightly over 8 percent came through occupational preference and 88 percent through family reunification. About 64 percent of Koreans entered through family reunification in 1969 compared to 90 percent in 1990. Between 1980 and 1990, there was a 134.8 percent growth in Vietnamese Americans with the majority entering as refugees after the U.S troop withdrawal following the Vietnam War (Hing 1997).

After passage of the 1965 immigration act, 4 million Asians immigrated to the United States between 1965 and 1992. Major sending areas have been the Philippines, the three Chinese-speaking regions (People's Republic, Taiwan, and Hong Kong), Vietnam, Korea, and India. The Asian American population in the United States, which had tripled by 1990, continues to cluster along the West Coast while nearly one-third of the population of San Francisco is Asian. Immigrants from Asia often leave their home countries because of the lower standard of living there and limited employment opportunities for the educated middle class. Post-1965 Japanese immigration to the United States, however, has remained low since Japan is on a par with other developed nations. Since 1965, two different categories of immigrants have developed with professional and highly skilled immigrants entering in the occupational category while semi-skilled or unskilled immigrants enter under family reunification policy and often experience a much higher poverty rate, nearly twice that of non-Hispanic whites (Liu 1995).

The top five Asian countries sending trained professionals to the United States are the Philippines, India, People's Republic of China, Taiwan, and Iran. As a result, there is a high representation of Asians among engineers, mathematicians, and computer science and health professionals. The Philippines sends a 68 percent majority of females since this country sends predominantly health professionals using the occupational preference category. For other countries, male immigrants predominate as engineers and generally enter the country under occupational preference status. Some students who enter with non-immigrant visas adjust their status. About two-thirds of Asian engineers using the occupational channel did so by visa adjustment. Health professionals, unlike engineers and scientists, are not likely to be visa adjustees. Approximately three-quarters of health professionals use family ties to get permanent resident status (Kanjanapan 1995).

Early Filipino immigrants were primarily single men recruited as laborers for Hawaiian sugar and pineapple plantations and later for California agricultural labor. The 1910 census counted 2,767 Filipinos, and 90 percent of these were males. By 1959, 58 percent of the Filipino labor consisted of farm workers or domestics (Lott 1997). In 1970, married couples were 86 percent of all Filipino families, which was approximately the same percent as for all U.S. families. By 1990 there was a higher percent of highly educated Filipinos than among the U.S. population in general. 39.3 percent of Filipino males and 41.4 percent of females were college educated compared to 20.3 percent of all U.S. males and 17.6 percent of all U.S. females. Median family income was $46,698 in 1990 compared to $35,225 for the U.S. population as a whole.

There is some indication of a trend for American men to seek Filipino women as mail-order brides. "For both Filipino women and American men, stereotyped and idealized images influence the decision to seek each other" (Ordonez 1997). American men may stereotype Filipino women as erotic, exotic, and more submissive and domestic than an American woman. However Filipino women come from a more matriarchal culture, are often independent and capable of earning a living for themselves, and expect to participate in family financial matters and other decisions.

Between 1960 and 1995, 1.3 million Filipinos arrived in the United States. Some were married to U.S. servicemen who returned in 1992 when the U.S.

military bases closed. Because of their fluent English and education, Filipinos could also enter the United States under occupational preference and easily assimilate. In "Dual Chain Migration: Post 1965 Filipino Immigration in the US," Liu et al. (1998) point out that there is one chain of Filipino immigrants deriving from those who entered before 1965 and use family reunification and a post-1965 chain of highly skilled immigrants using the occupational preference category. Before 1965 Filipino immigrants were often laborers recruited to replace Japanese and Asian Indian labor in Hawaii and the West Coast after passage of exclusionary laws. Chain B immigrants have higher education levels and a tendency to enter as families and lack ties to pre-1965 immigrants. Those in this post-1965 chain are often doctors or nurses and very soon brought in their parents. Chain A contributed to the revival of traditional Filipino communities while chain B created new communities.

In 1970 there were 70,000 Koreans in the United States, and by 1980 this had increased to 350,000. The number of Korean immigrants peaked in 1988 and then began to decline. Many Koreans could use occupational preference and enter as medical professionals or entrepreneurs. By the 1970s, many Koreans owned small groceries in black neighborhoods (Dinnerstein 1999). These immigrants were leaving Korea because of the division of the country, the military threat from North Korea, and the military dictatorships in South Korea. Recent social changes including democratization, economic development that has made Korea a relatively high-wage country, and the aftermath of the 1992 race riot in Los Angeles that destroyed 2,300 Korean stores have been responsible for this decline in Korean immigration. The 1990 census showed about 800,000 Koreans in the United States, and half of them resided in Los Angeles or the New York–New Jersey area (Barkan 1999). Since many husbands in Korean families have been underemployed due to limited English skills and discrimination, wives have sought employment.

Employed Korean immigrants tend to work in occupations that do not compete with white Americans. Korean physicians and nurses were employed due to shortages in these professions at certain periods. Korean small business owners serve mainly Korean enclaves and inner-city areas that white merchants tend to avoid (Barkan 1999). A study of Korean immigrants shows that the predicted probability of homeownership among Koreans increases by migration about 15 to 16 percent for women and 8 percent for men, which suggests that the goal of achieving a better standard of living has been realized for some Korean immigrants. Since Korean "society contains traditional and Confucian ideologies that are disadvantageous for women, there might be social and psychological advantages" for Korean women in the United States (Lee et al. 2005). Min finds that the increase in immigrant wives' economic role is often a source of marital conflict when their husbands have not changed their patriarchal attitudes about gender roles (Min 1998).

According to the 1990 census approximately 60 percent of Korean American married women participate in the labor force, and this figure would be higher if all those women who work for family businesses would have reported this employment on the census. Thirty-eight percent of Korean women work together with their husbands in the same business, with the wife usually managing the cash register. This is "one of the central factors that make Korean retail businesses, such as produce, grocery and liquor retail businesses successful" (Min 1998). Since Koreans are a more homogeneous group than other Asian immigrants, affiliate with Korean churches, and depend on Korean language newspapers, radio, and TV for information and 85 percent of them work in the ethnic economy, this cultural segregation allows males to retain their patriarchal views about gender roles and not adopt the more egalitarian gender role attitudes of the United States.

Chinese immigrants to the United States in the nineteenth century came to work in the mines and build railroads in the American West. Some later became tenant farmers, sharecroppers, and farm laborers or worked in small Chinese-owned businesses. The anti-Chinese movement that started in the early 1870s, fueled by an unstable economy and racism, eventually resulted in passage of the 1882 act that restricted admission of Chinese laborers. This act and subsequent legislation, which made it difficult for Chinese men to bring wives to the United States, resulted in limited growth of the Chinese American community (Tong).

More than two-thirds of the contemporary Chinese American population are foreign-born, while the rest are descendants of Chinese who have been in the United States for several generations. During 1979–1987 about 186,000 students came from Taiwan for education but only 12,000 returned to Taiwan. After the United States established diplomatic relations with the People's Republic of China (PRC) in 1979 and terminated the security treaty with Taiwan, the threat of a PRC takeover of Taiwan created uncertainty and encouraged Taiwanese to emigrate. While these initial Taiwanese immigrants had high levels of education and job skills, the family members sponsored by them were often not so highly educated. The years before 1997 reunification of Hong Kong with the PRC showed an increased immigration of "professionals and capitalists" from Hong Kong (Louie 2004).

Some of the Chinese arriving between 1965 and 1990 entered as refugees. Under the Displaced Persons Act of 1948, the Refugee Relief Act of 1953, and the Refugee-Escapee Act of 1957, approximately 32,000 Chinese escaping the communist regime of the PRC were admitted to the United States (Tong 2000). After normalization of relations with the PRC, mainland China, like Taiwan, had a separate yearly quota of 20,000. The Chinese Student Protection Act of 1992 allowed 48,212 students from mainland China to remain as legal immigrants because of the Tiananmen Square massacre of 1989.

In 1986 Hong Kong's quota was increased from 600 to 5,000. The Immigration Act of 1990 allowed additional increases in the quota for Hong Kong to 10,000 and later to 20,000 in 1995 in anticipation of the return of Hong Kong to the PRC in 1997. These 1990 immigration law reforms doubled visas for the occupational preference category and established categories for employment-based visas: (1) immigrants with extraordinary ability in arts, sciences, athletics, education, or business; (2) professionals with advanced degrees or special ability; and (3) skilled workers and professionals without advanced degrees. In 1990, about 31 percent of immigrants from the PRC were college graduates while 62 percent of immigrants from Taiwan and 47 percent of those from Hong Kong were college graduates (Portes and Rumbaut 2001).

There is also an influx of poor illegal immigrants mainly from Fujian province in mainland China who arrived on smuggling ships. After the Golden Venture incident, the use of the sea route diminished but smuggled Chinese still arrive in the United States by land or air routes. Some travel to Mexico or Canada and then cross the borders illegally. Typically illegal Chinese immigrants pay about $30,000 for the smugglers' services. These illegal immigrants typically have limited education, work at low-paid jobs in garment factories or restaurants, and live in Chinatowns or ethnic enclaves while the middle-class Chinese immigrants have highly paid professional jobs and live in suburban areas (Tong 2000).

Chinatown in New York City's Lower East Side tends to attract the greatest percentage of immigrants from the PRC, many of whom have little education and work low-level jobs with low wages. About 60 percent of the women work in the garment industry and there are now more pronounced class distinctions between workers and business owners than was formerly the case in this ethnic enclave. Sixty-five percent of the working-age population in Chinatown have little or no English and 70 percent have less than a high school education. Flushing, New York, meanwhile, has attracted well-to-do immigrants from Taiwan and has a substantially higher median income than Chinatown (Tong 2000).

Most of the post-1965 Chinese immigrants came as families and family chain migration, which has played a large role in the development of Chinese immigration. Chinese entrepreneurs and investors had more opportunity to emigrate after the 1990 immigration act increased the number of visas for skilled workers from 58,000 to 140,000. After Korean Americans, Chinese Americans have the highest self-employment rate of any immigrant group. Most businesses are small and rely on funding through kinship ties (Tong 2000).

Indochinese refugees in the United States arrived in three stages, each with different circumstances. The first group arrived during the emergency evacuation after the fall of Saigon in 1975. A second wave arrived when quotas were doubled to 1,400 per month in 1975, and the final group, with a greater proportion of Kampucheans and Laotians, entered after admissions were reduced in 1982. This third wave was mainly legal immigrants coming under the Orderly Departure Program or the Humanitarian Operation and often lived on welfare initially. Indochinese immigrants arriving in the second and third stages were less educated, less skilled, and often illiterate even in their native languages. Some of these refugees, like the Hmong, experienced a clash of values because their culture is extremely patriarchal and in the United States, women have access to the workforce (Mignot 1995).

Many children of these second and third waves of Vietnamese immigrants were living in poor neighborhoods with seemingly little prospect for upward mobility. Consequently studies have shown that selective assimilation or biculturalism, which maintains ethnic values while fostering economic assimilation, benefits these children. Vietnamese youth who have a "strong commitment to traditional Vietnamese values (Obedience and Hard work) and are highly involved in the ethnic community do better in school" (Killian and Hegtvedt 2003).

Initially there were no Indochinese communities like American Chinatowns and other ethnic enclaves. There was a government policy to disperse the refugees throughout the United States, but states west of the Mississippi had higher densities of Indochinese refugees, as did the four states (California, Arkansas, Florida, and Pennsylvania) with refugee camps. Secondary migration was influenced by movement from rural states to high-income states with better benefits.

Between 1820 and 1972 some 70,140 immigrants from India entered the United States. From 1907 to 1920, 6,400 Indians, mostly agricultural workers, entered and settled mainly in California. They experienced discrimination and often remained at a low socioeconomic status. Due to California's Alien Land Law that prohibited land lease or ownership by aliens ineligible for citizenship, some 3,000 East Indians returned to India from 1920 to 1940. Early immigrants from rural Punjab had intended to send for spouses, but later exclusion laws prevented this. Some Asian Indian lumberjacks were driven out of Washington State by racism early in the twentieth century (Hess 1998).

After 1965, East Indian immigrants who arrived in the United States were easily assimilated professionals. In 1980, the separate identity of immigrants from India was recognized for the first time as Asian Indians in the census. They are a rapidly expanding population group in the United States and hold 46 percent of the H-1B visas (non-immigrant classification used by an alien who will be employed temporarily in a specialty occupation) with education and income levels higher than those of most Asians (Das 2002). They come from the urban bourgeoisie and are engineers, doctors, scientists, and entrepreneurs. There is a growing preponderance of female immigrants from India, possibly widowed mothers or sisters coming under family reunification provisions. In general women from some Asian countries such as Korea, China, and India are attracted by more opportunities for women and less rigid gender roles than in their home countries.

By the 1990s 70 percent of Asian Indians settled in eight major urban states located in the East (New York, Pennsylvania, New Jersey), Southwest (Texas), Midwest (Michigan, Illinois, Ohio), and West (California) (Das 2002). Twenty percent of the Asian Indians were physicians, 26 percent were engineers, and 12 percent were in postsecondary education, and their median income was higher than that of the average U.S. household. On the other hand, many Asian Indians entered the hotel and motel business or operate businesses in ethnic enclaves. Increasingly, Asian Indians have entered the ranks of high-technology positions, computer programming, and telecommunications. Knowledge of English and familiarity with democratic institutions in their home country have facilitated assimilation for Asian Indians. According to Das, they often preserve cultural, social, and religious habits within the home and community while outwardly adapting in the workplace. The Asian Indians in this study agree that emigration to the United States has enhanced their professional and financial situation despite some problems with prejudice. The ability of professional and non-professional Asian Indian women to work outside the home has altered gender roles in the family.

Africa

During the first African diaspora, the slave trade brought from 400,000 to 500,000 Africans to the United States (Brownstone and Franck 2001). From 1900 to 1950, only 31,000 Africans immigrated to the United States. The new African diaspora after 1965 is a small percent of immigrants, only 3 percent in the 1980s and 1990s, mainly from Nigeria, South Africa, Liberia, Cape Verde, Egypt, Ghana, Kenya, Ethiopia, Somalia, and Eritrea. Before the 1990s many African immigrants were Egyptians. Then in the 1990s Nigerians and Ethiopians began entering. According to the Immigration and Naturalization Service (INS), between 1980 and 1993 more than 75 percent of all immigrants from Africa came from nine countries and only four countries, Egypt, Nigeria, Ethiopia, and South Africa, sent 53 percent. From 1974 to 1995, 17 percent of all African immigrants came from Nigeria, while 13 percent came from Ethiopia. In 2003, 6.9 percent of all immigrants to the United States came from Africa. In 2003 the four countries sending the largest number of immigrants were Nigeria with 7,892, Ethiopia with 6,643, Ghana with 4,416, and Egypt with 3,355. Many of these immigrants leave due to Africa's economic and political problems, for educational opportunities, or to reunite with family. Their low rate of naturalization suggests that they often view their residence in the United States as temporary and plan to return eventually (Arthur 2000).

Coming from countries where blacks are often the majority, African immigrants are confronted with "racial categorization and its economic and cultural results in the US" (Arthur 2000). African immigrants are often inexperienced with the racial stereotypes about anyone of African descent in this country and do not understand that a professional black person may be subjected to the same prejudice as a street vendor (Vesely 2005). By maintaining their accents and temporary status, African immigrants claim the status of foreigner hoping to avoid the discrimination experienced by African Americans who often have lower educational and income levels.

Many African immigrants would be unemployed or underemployed if they remained in their home countries (Arthur 2000). Some Africans have benefited from U.S. refugee law and policy that enabled them to leave Ethiopia, Somalia, Sudan, Eritrea, Ghana, and Liberia. Of those refugees admitted from Africa, the majority were coming from Marxist Ethiopia. Since U.S. national security issues play an important role in deciding whether to admit refugees, the other African countries sending refugees were Sudan and Angola, both Cold War allies of the United States, and Angola, a Marxist state (Gordon). Many immigrants from Anglophone West Africa as well as Ethiopia and South Africa came initially to study and then may have opted to stay for professional reasons. Thirty percent of Nigerians who were naturalized in 1991 were professionals and managers, though some immigrants work in restaurants, in convenience stores, or as street vendors (Bigman 1995).

From 1971 to 1996, about 85,000 Egyptians immigrated to the United States, the majority of them doctors, medical professionals, teachers, scientists, and technicians seeking employment opportunities that were not available in Egypt at that time (Brownstone and Franck 2001). This constituted a very small percentage, however, less than 1 percent of the total number of annual immigrants to the United States. Ethiopia is one of the poorest countries and suffered thousands of political mass murders during the dictatorship of Mengistu Haile Mariam from 1977 to 1991. During 1984–1985 many Ethiopians also experienced forced internal migration, drought, and famine, resulting in the death of approximately 2.5 million refugees. This hardship caused many of the most highly skilled and educated people to emigrate to the United States and other countries.

The Ethiopian and Eritrean refugees who came to the United States in 1992, for example, were 62 percent male and 38 percent female, since males more easily met the criteria for admission. The annual percentage of immigrants from

Ethiopia to the United States has never surpassed 1 percent (Brownstone and Franck 2001). Although their numbers were small, their immigration to the United States and Canada is significant because they were among the first Africans to voluntarily come to North America rather than being brought forcibly as slaves. After passage of the Refugee Act of 1980, which finally created a policy for admitting Africans to the United States as refugees, Ethiopians and Eritreans were the first large group of Africans to be resettled in the United States (Woldemikael 1996).

In 1980 the census recorded 25,528 Nigerians in the United States and by 1990 there were 91,688 of whom 55,350 were immigrants (Ogbaa 2003). During 1925–1952, Nigeria was still a British colony and most Nigerians went to the British Commonwealth for education, yet a small number did travel to the United States for their education, returning to Nigeria to assume leadership roles in the country. By 1952–1960, a more diversified group of Nigerians arrived in the United States, some of whom found jobs and decided to stay. Nigeria gained full independence in 1960. As a consequence Nigerians now possessed Nigerian passports, not British passports, and now could easily apply to the American Embassy for student visas to study in the United States. The University of Nigeria was founded with primarily American-style curricula and American professors and administrators. This increased acceptance of American-style education prompted more Nigerians to come to the United States for a university education.

The Nigeria Biafra civil war resulted in the sponsoring of immigrants by family members in the United States or by various religious groups that sponsored their members. The economic and political effects of the civil war caused more Nigerians to want to leave the country. Military dictatorships that came to power during and after the civil war caused political and economic conditions to further deteriorate. As a result, there was a huge exodus of professors and highly educated Nigerians. This more than doubled the U.S. Nigerian population between 1989 and 1990. Many hoped to and did return to Nigeria but left again under General Sani Abucha's dictatorship. Some 10,306 Nigerians were admitted in 1996 due to the peaking of the dictatorship's repression.

During the 1990s, "Statistics show that the percentage of foreign-born blacks rose from 4.9% to 7.3% overall, with cities like New York and Philadelphia registering one in three black residents as being born overseas" (Vesely 2005). Most of the new African immigrants live in two-parent families, are more highly educated than African Americans, and therefore are able to find more highly paid employment. Thus Africans in the second wave of migration may surpass African Americans just as earlier immigrant populations have. One explanation is that when blacks are living in an entirely black society, they do not have the same experience of racism that could lower their self-esteem.

Europe

From 1989 to 1997 the European countries sending the majority of immigrants to the United States were the United Kingdom (inclusive of England, Scotland, Ireland, and Northern Ireland), Poland, and the Soviet Union. The number of immigrants from Ireland peaked in 1994 at 17,256 and then began to decline as Ireland experienced a burgeoning economy. Immigrants from the Soviet Union to the United States reached an annual high of 56,980 in 1991. Since that year, the independent republics were no longer included in the count for the Soviet Union, and Russia and the Ukraine were among the major sending countries. With the exception of Ireland, with a substantial decrease in immigrants to the United States during 1998–2003, these 1989–1997 trends continued for the other countries during this later time period. From 1998 to 2003, 96,183 immigrants arrived from Russia, 87,239 from the Ukraine, 76,663 from Bosnia Herzegovina, 74,551 from the United Kingdom, and 62,471 from Poland. From 1993 to 1998, the number of annual refugees from Bosnia Herzegovina steadily increased to 30,906 in 1998 and then began to decline. The number of refugees from the Soviet Union peaked in 1992 at 61,298 and then began to decline. Data for refugees from the independent republics were not available until 1999 (U.S. Department of Homeland Security 2003).

The Irish immigrant has a long history in the United States. Pre-famine immigration was primarily composed of English-speaking farmers from the north and east with a higher concentration of Protestants than the famine immigrants. During the 1840s famine, 2.1 million people left Ireland and 1.8 million of them came to North America (1.5 million to the United States). This period of intensely concentrated Irish immigration provoked by a tragic situation in a homeland still under British domination had a major impact on Irish American history, including "Patterns of urban settlement and labour history, the expansion of the Catholic church, . . . rise of the Irish in municipal politics and the emergence of powerful Irish nationalist movements" in the United States (Kenny 2000). During the period from 1945 to 1980, immigration rates from Ireland varied as the country's economy fluctuated and Irish sought better economic opportunity in the United States. The 1965 immigration law did not especially benefit Irish immigrants since they did not have the connections to qualify for family reunification nor the skills to qualify for occupational preference. However, the Immigration Reform and Control Act of 1986 provided 40,000 special visas to countries that had traditionally sent immigrants to the United States and had been adversely impacted by the 1965 legislation (Kenny 2000). There were also thousands of Irish visitors who overstayed their visas and worked illegally, intending to return home eventually. The new wave of Irish immigrants was a mixture of middle-class university graduates or professionals and working class or lower-middle-class Irish who left because of the lack of work. Due to more economic stability in Ireland, the number of Irish immigrants has dwindled to approximately 1,000 per year since 1994.

The Polish diaspora is the largest and longest lasting emigration from Eastern European countries. Poles began emigrating after the breakup of the Polish homeland in 1795. The major period of Polish immigration to the United States lasted from the 1880s until passage of the restrictive immigration legislation in 1924. A wave of immigration from Poland occurred after the end of World War II and the installation of a Communist regime in Poland. Another wave came during political unrest of the late 1960s and early 1970s. The final groups of "post-Solidarity" refugees were admitted under the Refugee Act of 1980. Polish refugees in the mid-1980s had the lowest rate for public assistance among immigrants, although some had longer periods before becoming self-sufficient while retraining for better jobs. Over time the Polish refugees moved into "technical, administrative, sales and skilled trade positions" since most of them arrived with an educational level comparable to or higher than secondary school in the United States and some knowledge of English (Gozdziak 1996).

During the nineteenth century as a result of annexing Polish territory, Russia's Jewish population increased to approximately 4 percent of the total. The Russian State imposed restrictions on Jews, confining them within the Pale of Settlement, an area from the Black Sea to the Baltic, encouraging conversion to Christianity, and using other strategies in an attempt to dissolve the Jewish community. There were severe pogroms, violence against Jews, during 1881 and 1903–1905 (Holmes 1995). As a result of this repression and hostility, Russian Jews began to emigrate to other European countries and to the United States. The post-1965 period of Soviet Jewish emigration between 1968 and 1973 was mainly from the Soviet Union to Israel, but during the period from 1974 to 1979, Jews leaving the Soviet Union were heading to the United States, Canada, Australia, and New Zealand. By 1990, this had changed and 90 percent of all Soviet or Russian immigrants went to Israel, but this declined to 50 percent by early 1993.

The Soviet emigration is partly attributed to long-standing anti-Semitism, which was an official government policy referred to as "anti-Zionism" that was provoked by the 1967 Arab-Israeli War and Israel's invasion of Lebanon in 1982–1983 (Basok and Benifand 1995). Despite policies of glasnost and per-estroika that permitted Jewish cultural and religious life, anti-Semitism intensified and posed a threat to Jews in the Soviet Union. During the 1970s and 1980s Soviet Jews also emigrated due to dissatisfaction with the political system. Then political and economic instability combined with rising crime and violence shortly before, during, and after the breakup of the Soviet Union influenced Russian Jewish immigration in the late 1980s and 1990s. Family reunification and economic opportunities were other factors influencing the decision to emigrate. Soviet and post-Soviet Jews' adjustment to the United States has been successful because of their high levels of education and job skills. From 1965 through 1994, the Hebrew Immigrant Aid Society has settled 322,341 Jews in the United States with most entering as religious refugees from Russia and the Ukraine, which have the largest Jewish populations among the republics of the former Soviet Union (Gold 1996). In addition to Jews, other groups in the former Soviet Union that were identified since 1995 as eligible for refugee status include Evangelical Christians, Ukrainian Catholics, and followers of the Ukrainian Autocephalous Orthodox church (Gold 1996).

"Between 1992 and 1996, more than 1 million Bosnians became refugees as a consequence of ethnic cleansing, siege or war by extreme ethnic nationalists" (Weine et al. 2004). Many Bosnians immigrated to the United States as refugees during this time. Several studies have been concerned with the effects of post-traumatic stress on Bosnian refugees. One group of 34 Bosnian refugees that settled in Connecticut was found to have a high rate of Posttraumatic Stress Disorder, with symptoms such as "avoidance, numbing, splitting and denial to distance themselves psychologically from traumatic memories" during the first year after their arrival (Weine et al. 2004). These symptoms gradually diminish over time and with increased stability in family, work, and community. Though about 30,000 refugees settled in the Chicago area, it was estimated in 1999 that only about 7.5 percent of them received some mental health treatment. Despite challenging experiences with war, poverty, and immigration, the family support system remains an important factor in maintaining the mental health of Bosnian immigrants (Weine et al. 2004). *See also*: **Family reunification; Mental health problems; Ports of entry; Skilled migrants; Unauthorized immigration.**

References

Arthur, John. 2000. *Invisible Sojourners: African Immigrant Diaspora in the United States*. Westport, CT: Praeger.

Barkan, Elliott Robert, ed. 1999. *A Nation of Peoples: A Sourcebook on America's Multicultural Heritage*. Westport, CT: Greenwood Press.

Basok, Tanya, and Alexander Benifand. 1995. Soviet Jewish Emigration. In *Cambridge Survey of World Migration*. Robin Cohen, ed. Pp. 502–506. New York: Cambridge University Press.

Bigman, Laura. 1995. Contemporary Migration from Africa to the U.S.A. In *Cambridge Survey of World Migration*. Robin Cohen, ed. Pp. 260–262. New York: Cambridge University Press.

Brownstone, David M., and Irene M. Franck. 2001. *Facts about American Immigration*. New York: H.W. Wilson.

Carino, Benjamin, James T. Fawcett, Robert W. Gardner, and Fred Arnold. 1990. *The New Filipino Immigrants to the United States: Increasing Diversity and Change*. Honolulu: East West Center.

Das, Sudipta. 2002. Loss or Gain? A Saga of Asian Indian Immigration and Experiences in America's Multi-Ethnic Mosaic. *Race, Gender and Class* 9(2):131–155.

Desbarats, Jacqueline. 1998. Indochinese Resettlement in the United States in Asians. In *America: The History and Immigration of Asian Americans*. Franklin Ng, ed. Pp. 198–201. New York: Garland.

Dinnerstein, Leonard, and David Reimers. 1999. *Ethnic Americans: A History of Immigration*. New York: Columbia University Press.

Freeman, James. 1995. *Changing Identities: Vietnamese Americans 1975–95*. Boston: Allyn and Bacon.

Gold, Steven J. 1996. Soviet Jews in Refugees. In *America in the 1990s: A Reference Handbook*. David W. Haines, ed. Pp. 279–304. Westport, CT: Greenwood Press.

Gordon, April. 1998. The New Diaspora: African Immigration to the United States. *Journal of Third World Studies* 15(1):79–103.

Gozdziak, Elzbieta M. 1996. Eastern Europeans. In *Refugees in America in the 1990s: A Reference Handbook*. David W. Haines, ed. Pp. 121–146. Westport, CT: Greenwood Press.

Hess, Gary. 1998. The Forgotten Asian Americans: The East Indian Community in the United States. In *Asians in America: The History and Immigration of Asian Americans*. Franklin Ng, ed. Pp. 106–126. New York: Garland.

Hing, Bill Ong. 1997. Immigration Policy: Making and Remaking Asian Pacific America. In *New American Destinies: A Reader in Contemporary Asian and Latino Immigration*. Darrell Hamamoto and Rodolfo Torres, eds. Pp. 315–323. New York: Routledge.

Holmes, Colin. 1995. Jewish Economic and Refugee Migrations, 1880–1950. In *Cambridge Survey of World Migration*. Robin Cohen, ed. Pp. 148–153. New York: Cambridge University Press.

Kanjanapan, Wilawan. 1995. Immigration of Asian Professionals to the United States 1988–1990. *International Migration Review* 29(1):7–32.

Kenny, Kevin. 2000. *The American Irish: A History*. New York: Longman.

Killian, Caitlin, and Karen Hegtvedt. 2003. The Role of Parents in the Maintenance of Second Generation Vietnamese Cultural Behaviors. *Sociological Spectrum* 23(2):213–245.

Kim, Hyung-Chan. 1974. *Koreans in America 1882–1974*. Dobbs Ferry, NY: Oceana Publications.

Lee, Seong Woo, Dowell Myers, Seong-Kyu Ha, and HaeRan Shin. 2005. What If Immigrants Had Not Migrated? Determinants and Consequences of Korean Immigration to the United States. *American Journal of Economics and Sociology* 64(2): 609–636.

Liu, John. 1995. Comparative View of Asian Immigration to the USA. In *Cambridge Survey of World Migration*. Robin Cohen, ed. Pp. 253–259. Cambridge: Cambridge University Press.

Liu, John, Paul Ong, and Carolyn Rosenstein. 1998. Dual Chain Migration: Post 1965 Filipino Immigration in the U.S. In *History and Immigration of Asian Americans*. Franklin Ng, ed. Pp. 143–169. New York: Garland.

Lott, Juanita Tamayo. 1997. Demographic Changes: Transforming the Filipino American Community. In *Filipino Americans: Transformation and Identity*. Maria P.P. Root, ed. Pp. 11–20. London: Sage.

Louie, Andrea. 2004. *Chineseness across Borders: Renegotiating Chinese Identities in China and the United States*. Durham, NC: Duke University Press.

Mignot, Michel. 1995. Refugees from Cambodia, Laos and Vietnam 1975–93. In *The Cambridge Survey of World Migration*. Robin Cohen, ed. Pp. 452–456. Cambridge: Cambridge University Press.

Miller, Kenneth, and Lisa Rasco. 2004. *The Mental Health of Refugees: Ecological Approaches to Healing and Adaptation*. Mahwah, NJ: Lawrence Erlbaum.

Min, Pyong G. 1998. *Changes and Conflicts: Korean Immigrant Families in New York*. Boston: Allyn and Bacon.

Ogbaa, Kalu. 2003. *The Nigerian Americans*. Westport, CT: Greenwood Press.

Ordonez, Raquel Z. 1997. Mail-Order Brides: An Emerging Community. In *Filipino Americans: Transformation and Identity*. Maria P.P. Root, ed. Pp. 121–142. London: Sage.

Portes, Alejandro, and Ruben Rumbaut. 2001. *Legacies: The Story of the Immigrant Second Generation*. New York: Sage.

Tong, Benson. 2000. *The Chinese Americans*. Westport, CT: Greenwood Press.

Toro-Morn, Maura, and Marixsa Alicea. 2004. *Migration and Immigration: A Global View*. Westport, CT: Greenwood Press.

U.S. Department of Homeland Security. 2003. *Yearbook of Immigration Statistics*. Washington, DC: U.S. Department of Homeland Security, Office of Immigration Statistics. http://www.uscis.gov/graphics/shared/aboutus/statistics/ybpage.htm.

Vesely, Milan. 2005. Africans in the U.S.: Second Wave Migrants Outdo African Americans. *African Business* 309:38–40.

Weine, Stevan, Dolores Vojvoda, Daniel Becker, et al. 1998. PTSD Symptoms in Bosnian Refugees One Year after Resettlement in the United States. *American Journal of Psychiatry* 155(4):562–565.

Weine, Stevan, et al. 2004. Bosnian and Kosovar Refugees in the United States: Family Interventions in a Services Framework. In *The Mental Health of Refugees: Ecological Approaches to Healing and Adaptation*. Kenneth E. Miller and Lisa M. Rasco, eds. Pp. 263–294. London: Lawrence Erlbaum Associates.

Woldemikael, Tekle M. 1996. Ethiopians and Eritreans. In *Refugees in America in the 1990s: A Reference Handbook*. David W. Haines, ed. Pp. 147–169. Westport, CT: Greenwood Press.

JEANNE ARMSTRONG

GLOBAL ORIGINS: LATIN AMERICA AND THE CARIBBEAN. Shifting borders and recurrent human movements have characterized the Americas long before the contemporary era of global migration and regional trade accords. While the northward flow of people from Latin America and the Caribbean to the United States is nothing new, in the last century the character and intensity of such moves has changed dramatically. The trajectories and magnitude of international migration within the Western Hemisphere, especially from south to north into the United States, correspond closely to ebbs and flows in economic cycles and to associated shifts in public receptivity and immigration policy (Chavez 2001). The end of the 1924 National Origins Systems also played a pivotal role in transforming the composition of U.S. immigration. Consequently, the following decades experienced greater numbers of people arriving in the United States from developing countries, especially in Latin America, than from traditional European sending countries. U.S. immigration today, and the contentious debate that surrounds it, is for many people in the United States synonymous with Latin America, particularly Mexico (Bean et al. 1997).

What represents today a major area of the southwestern United States was, until little more than a century and a half ago, part of Mexico. The U.S.-Mexico border was, in fact, relatively porous and not perceived as a major "problem" until late in the twentieth century when it began to alter from a quiet, unpopulated region to one of concentrated, bustling economic activity and urban areas (Alvarez 1987). People and goods moved back and forth with relative ease, notwithstanding racism and double standards directed toward immigrants as well as border residents of Latin American heritage (Alvarez 1987; Martínez 1994; Velez-Ibáñez 1996). Beyond the fundamental reality of geographic proximity, in the famous lament, "Poor Mexico, so far from God, so close to the United States," the long history of laborers coming from Mexico to the United States to work in agriculture, mining, and railroads during the late nineteenth century set the stage for contemporary migration patterns. During World War II, U.S. labor demands in agriculture also brought serious numbers of Mexican workers north with the Bracero program, a contract-labor program that lasted from 1942 to 1964. This program led to large-scale permanent settlement of Mexican immigrants in the United States—a population that currently represents the most numerous Latin American immigrant group in the United States.

Since the mid-1960s, maquiladoras (assembly factories) established along the U.S.-Mexico border have greatly impacted out-migration from Mexico to the United States. A key question scholars and policymakers raise relates to whether maquiladora jobs inhibit or promote further migration to the United States. Recent studies suggest that maquiladoras, which in 2004 employed about 1.1 million workers, may serve as bridges to the United States (*Migration News* 2005).

A large body of work addresses Latin American migration to the United States, and immigration from Mexico in particular. The wealth of resources available includes research by scholars who work on either or both sides of the border (Massey et al. 1987; Heer 1990; Goldin 1999; Gonzáles 2000; Hirsch 2003; Adler 2004; Cohen 2004; Gutiérrez 2004). Many studies focus on Mexican northbound journeys and U.S.-Mexican border crossings and present this stream from three distinctive perspectives: (1) organizational (such as evaluating the immigration enforcement); (2) quantitative studies of undocumented border crossings; and (3) qualitative sources (Singer and Massey 1998). Latin American migration to the United States factors prominently in collections dealing with U.S. immigration trends and policy or with overall migration within the Western Hemisphere (Mitchell 1992; Hamamoto and Torres 1997; Goldin 1999). Considerable attention to Latin American immigration is also found within Latino and border studies (Alvarez 1987; Anzaldúa 1987; Martínez 1994; Alvarez 1995; Velez-Ibáñez 1996), as well as in the fields of education, language, and ethnic studies. Excellent migration scholarship is conducted in the countries and languages of Latin America and the Caribbean as well. Recent U.S. immigration from Latin America is also well represented in many other genres, including literature, autobiographies, and the arts (Siems 1992; Hart 1997; Marciel and Herrera-Sobek 1998; Martínez 2001).

As noted, the emphasis on Mexican migration occurs because of the much longer historical roots behind this population movement and proximity to the United States. Examinations of the overland, and often clandestine, trip to the United States by Central American, South American, and Caribbean migrants remain scant. Given such magnitude and coverage of Mexico elsewhere, this entry focuses on U.S.-bound migration from Central and South America as well as the Caribbean—places of origin of many of the "other than Mexican," or OTMs, currently arriving in the United States.

Shifting Origins of U.S.-Bound Immigration from Latin America

While Mexican laborers headed earlier immigration trends from Latin America to the United States, increasingly inflows from other regions in the Western Hemisphere have become more pronounced. In the 1960s, there were fewer than 1 million Latin American immigrants in the United States. During the decade of the 1990s, at least 4.6 million immigrants from Latin America entered the United States. Mexico is still the Latin American country that sends the largest number of immigrants to the United States, followed by the Central American countries (Hamilton and Chinchilla 1997; Office of Immigration Statistics 2004). In 2000, South American immigrants living in the United States had come primarily from Colombia (435,000), Peru (328,000), Ecuador (281,000), and Venezuela (126,000). From the Spanish-speaking Caribbean, there were 952,000 persons of Cuban origin and 692,000 from the Dominican Republic in 2000 (Gutiérrez 2004).

In the nineteenth and early twentieth centuries, most Latinos were located in the border states, South Florida, and the New York and Chicago metropolitan areas. More recent trends, however, reveal that the Latino population is found dispersed throughout most of the United States. Median income for Latino households reached a high of $31,663 in 1999, but among all Latino households almost one-quarter of them were below the poverty level ($7,463) according to the 2000 census. Also in 2000, 43 percent of all Latinos did not have a high school education and less than 11 percent had a college degree (Gutiérrez 2004).

U.S. economic and political involvement in Mexico and Central America influenced the early immigration from Central America. Capitalist penetration, industrialization, and land pressures contributed to internal migration, usually from rural to urban areas. These dislocations, combined with the presence of U.S.

corporations that employed local residents, made migration to the United States seem feasible. Political and economic instability, civil wars between leftist guerrillas and authoritarian regimes, and brutal state-sponsored campaigns that resulted in over 600 massacres (primarily targeting the huge indigenous population in Guatemala and entire villages in El Salvador) led staggering numbers of undocumented Salvadorans and Guatemalans to come to the United States in the 1970s and 1980s (Hamilton and Chinchilla 1997; CEH 1999). In 2003, the leading number of Central American immigrants continued to be from El Salvador at 28,296 and the next largest group came from Guatemala at 14,415. This does not include the significant number of undocumented immigrants from these countries, however.

In 1981, 40,000 Central American refugees applied for asylum and by 1983 this number had increased to more than 140,000. Despite dangerous and repressive conditions in El Salvador and Guatemala, less than 0.5 percent of Guatemalan applicants and less than 2.5 percent of Salvadoran applicants were granted asylum in 1984. In turn, hundreds of thousands of undocumented Central American refugees lived in the United States with limited access to social services. Church and community groups responded to this situation, and eventually the sanctuary movement included 300 churches, synagogues, and community groups. The 1990 Immigration Act established Temporary Protected Status for people forced to leave their countries due to ongoing conflict, an environmental disaster, or some other "extraordinary and temporary" condition. Approximately 180,000 immigrants from El Salvador took advantage of Temporary Protected Status (Ferris 1995).

In the case of Guatemala, U.S. census data and immigration records reveal that Guatemalan emigration to the United States gradually emerged in the 1960s, but escalated in the 1980s. Out-migration from Guatemala to the United States in the 1990s increased due to political strife, poverty, scarcity of employment opportunities in both rural and urban areas, and the country's persistent inequalities in wealth and land ownership (Loucky and Moors 2000; Taylor et al. 2006). Such conditions also ring true for El Salvador (Mahler 1995; Menjívar 2000).

U.S.-bound migration from Central America has yielded both positive and negative outcomes. One way that northbound migrant flows have helped Central American countries, especially those that experience large out-migration—Guatemala, El Salvador, and Nicaragua—is in the way of cash remittances. Remittances, or simply put, the monies that migrants earn, save, and send back to their families in their places of origin, play a key role in the economies of these sending countries. The volume of these economic resources, compared with that generated through other income flows (e.g., export cash crops, tourism), currently constitutes the largest source of foreign currency funneled into this region.

By contrast, Guatemala, El Salvador, and Honduras have experienced some of the negative effects of migration. Because of recent deportations of young individuals back to their home countries, gangs or *maras*, such as the *Mara Salvatrucha* and 18th Street gangs which initially formed in Los Angeles, are now present in towns throughout Central America, contributing to a rise in crime rates and becoming an acute dilemma in these Latin American societies. Global restructuring of capitalism exacerbated deplorable economic conditions and gave way to capital investment in export processing industries, food importation, and agribusiness in many Latin American countries. These broad structural changes not only altered local economies, but also increasingly incited many individuals to look north, to *el norte* (Sassen 1988; Robinson 2003).

Sending countries that export workers from South America today include Colombia, Ecuador, and Brazil. Early immigrants from South America were urban, educated, and upper-middle class, but the current migratory flow is more diverse, with more immigrants coming from rural areas. Unstable economic conditions encouraged a brain drain of educated professionals as well as migration of rural and working-class individuals, who had lost jobs. Repressive regimes, military coups, drug wars, and guerrilla conflicts in countries such as Argentina, Chile, Peru, and Colombia caused many people to leave these countries (Espitia 2004).

Brazilian migration, especially to New York City, began to gain momentum during the 1980s (Margolis 1994). By 2005, Brazilians figured as the most numerous of OTMs crossing the U.S.-Mexican border. Much of U.S.-bound migration originating from Colombia and Ecuador headed to New York City too. Whereas several recent ethnographic studies explore various aspects of Ecuadorian transnational migration such as families and ethnic entrepreneurship (Kyle 2000; Miles 2004), considerably less attention is given in the migration literature to the Colombian flow. The Colombian immigrant population tends to be more dispersed than any other major Latin American immigrant group living and working in the United States (Guarnizo et al. 1999).

As the numbers and origins of individuals migrating to the United States shift further south, greater attention is being paid to their step-migration as well as the dangers and uncertainties inherent in their movement, including through Ecuador, Central America, and Mexico. There is evidence of abuses at borders and, in particular, human rights abuses continue to be on the rise at the Guatemalan-Mexican border. Shipwrecks of unseaworthy and overladen vessels of would-be immigrants that embark from Ecuador and the Dominican Republic signal many others who may have been lost at sea without record. There is also growing awareness that Latin America serves as a staging region for U.S.-bound migrants from more distant places, such as China (Anderson and Lee 2005).

In contrast to Central and South American migration studies, there exists an extant body of work that attends to Caribbean migration to the United States. Such a trend may prevail due to the longer and more established flows of people leaving that region to work elsewhere. During the period between 1950 and 1980 about 4 million people migrated from the Caribbean to Europe and North America (Chaney 1987). In 2003, the largest number in the United States came from the Dominican Republic at 26,205, followed by Jamaica at 13,384 and Haiti at 12,314. Immigration from Cuba seems to have temporarily peaked at 28,272 in 2002 and then declined in 2003 to 9,304. British West Indians in the United States are concentrated in professional and skilled occupations, and their median income had surpassed that of African Americans in New York City in 1970 (Peach 1995).

A striking difference exists between the English-speaking Caribbean and other non-English-speaking Caribbean countries. Whereas the English-speaking area began to experience temporary out-migration during the nineteenth century, particularly to England and the United States, emigration on a large scale from the Spanish Caribbean, for instance, the Dominican Republic, only began in the 1960s. As with many other Central American–sending countries, the Dominican Republic first experienced out-migration due to political reasons. A plethora of studies examine U.S.-bound Dominican migration (Hendricks 1974; Sutton and Chaney 1987; Georges 1990; Gmelch 1992; Grasmuck and Pessar 1992). Additionally, a number of studies incorporate a transnational perspective to examine U.S.-bound Dominican flows (Guarnizo 1994; Pessar 1997; Levitt 2001).

Cuban migration to the United States mainly began in the late 1950s due to revolutionary upheaval (Portes and Bach 1985; Grenier and Perez 2003). Portes and Bach (1985) indicate, for instance, that between 1958 and 1980 about one-tenth of the island's population left—a migratory flow that for the most part has been recognized as a one-way flow. Cuban immigrants have been coming to the United States since the nineteenth century. The first immigrants who left Cuba before 1860 were mainly white and middle class. Later Cuban migrants included those who were attracted by the potential of earning higher incomes in the United States. In the 1940s and 1950s, Cuban immigrants originated from all social classes, leaving their home country for economic and/or political reasons. After Fidel Castro came to power, the first wave of 248,070 Cubans arrived in the United States during the period between 1959 and 1962. Some folks were associated with the overthrown Batista government; others sought to escape economic problems and political repression as Castro's regime transformed Cuban society. From 1962 to 1965 an estimated 56,000 Cubans came to the United States either via another country, such as Spain or Mexico, or on small boats and rafts (García 2004).

In September 1965, after Castro gave permission for Cubans with relatives in the United States to leave, the second wave of migration commenced. The United States, using the new 1965 Immigration Act, limited immigration to immediate families of Cubans residing in the United States. Women and workers comprised a large percent of this wave, including 57 percent blue collar, service, or agricultural workers. The third wave took place in 1980 when about 120,000 Cubans arrived through the Mariel boatlift. The government announced in 1980 that all Cubans who wanted to leave could do so if their relatives from the United States could come to Mariel with boats. However, Castro used this plan to rid Cuba of dissidents and "undesirables" who were removed from hospitals or jails. Many of those released had infectious diseases, alcohol or drug problems, or criminal records (García 2004).

Another Caribbean sending country that can be described as a country on the move is Haiti. As is the case with many other Latin American countries, large-scale Haitian migration to the United States began due to political unrest in the late 1950s (Basch et al. 1994; Stepick 1998). While U.S. Cold War policy welcomed Cubans who were refugees from the Castro government, this policy was not so welcoming toward Haitians who sought to escape persecution under the Duvalier regime. By 1979 when Haitian boats started arriving in South Florida, the Immigration and Naturalization Service initiated a Haitian policy to detain and deport asylum seekers from Haiti. The 1980 Refugee Act adopted the United Nations' definition of refugee and removed the previously anti-Communist bias from refugee and asylum decisions. Haitians were still viewed as voluntary immigrants, however, not refugees (Zucker and Zucker 1995). The Justice Department decided in 1984 that the Cuban Adjustment Act of 1966 entitled all Cubans arriving in the United States to permanent resident status, but this provision was denied to Haitians until the general amnesty under the Immigration Reform and Control Act of 1986.

A reign of terror followed the overthrow of President Jean Bertrand Aristide shortly after he was elected president in 1991. The army was killing a large number of civilians and starvation threatened. Haitians again began fleeing their country. At first the United States allowed them to be detained at Guantanamo, where their asylum claims were screened. Fear of political fallout similar to the Mariel boatlift, however, prompted President Bush to issue the Kennebunkport Order, which provided that the coast guard would intercept Haitians and return them to Haiti. Although the UN Protocol prohibits returning individuals to a country where they face a "well founded fear of persecution," this in fact has been U.S. policy toward Haitian refugees (Zucker and Zucker 1995).

Puerto Rico represents a very different case from other Caribbean sending countries. Since 1898, Puerto Rico has been a territory of the United States. Thus, Puerto Ricans can and do move between the island and the mainland without legal constraints. While Puerto Ricans cannot be categorized in the same vein as migrant flows evident among other Latin American places of origin, this migrant group nonetheless plays an important role in strengthening Latino society in the United States, particularly in New York City and other northeastern cities.

Although the bulk of migrants coming to the United States are from Latin America, many of these national groups differ in multivariate ways: by class, ethnicity, occupations, religion, gender, color, and rural or urban backgrounds. Among some Latino national groups such distinctions may also be true for the kinds of differences that emerge within migrant groups with similar national origins. Of concern here, too, are the different destination sites that the various Latin American immigrant groups reach in the United States. Mexican migration to the United States is mainly associated with urban and rural areas located in the southern states of California, Arizona, and Texas.

U.S.-bound Central American migration, however, is more scattered. It is typically associated with North American "gateway cities" such as Los Angeles, Houston, San Francisco, Washington, D.C., and New York. Several studies examine, for example, how different Central American national groups incorporate in Los Angeles (Hart 1997; Hamilton and Chinchilla 2001), Houston (Hagan 1994), San Francisco (Menjívar 2000), Washington, D.C. (Repak 1995), and New York (González 1988; Mahler 1995). More recently, second-tier cities, such as Phoenix, increasingly are receiving Central American immigrant groups (Moran-Taylor and Menjívar 2005). While the largest concentration of Salvadorans and Guatemalans are found in Los Angeles, Nicaraguans mostly head to Miami, Hondurans to New Orleans, and Belizeans to New York City.

South American migration to the United States is primarily associated with the northeastern region. Many Ecuadorians, Brazilians, Peruvians, and Colombians gravitate to Washington, D.C., and New York City. Miami is an attractive destination for many Central and South American folks too, but for the most part

Cuban and Haitian immigrant groups have settled in that city (Portes and Bach 1985; Stepick 1998; Grenier and Pérez 2003).

Looking Ahead

Many immigrants coming to the United States from Latin America do so not through legal channels, but through clandestine means. This unauthorized migration adds fuel to the immigration debate and will continue to play a critical role in future policymaking related to U.S. immigration concerns.

While recent economic reforms have been promoted as means to improve local economies, there appears to be growing frustration among many Latin Americans who have suffered the pain of neoliberal policies and as yet only the slim benefits these changes bring. Such negative effects derive primarily from market-oriented economic policies that tend to be focused on the upper rungs of society. In turn, governments offer little to cushion the impact of privatization and trade on the poor who are saddled with lofty debts. These outcomes are likely to continue to spur further out-migration from Latin America to the United States. On the other hand, tangible improvements in economic opportunities in the region, and clear signs of a slowing population growth in Mexico and elsewhere, could portend a potential dwindling of south to north migration in years ahead, beyond whatever U.S. immigration policies seek to accomplish. *See also*: **Migration processes; Ports of entry; Remittances; Skilled migrants; Transnationalism; Unauthorized immigration.**

References

Adler, Rachel H. 2004. *Yucatecans in Dallas, Texas*. Boston: Allyn and Bacon.

Alvarez, Robert. 1987. *Familia: Migration and Adaptation in Baja and Alta California, 1800–1975*. Berkeley: University of California Press.

———. 1995. The Mexican-U.S. Border: The Making of an Anthropology of Borderlands. *Annual Review of Anthropology* 24:447–470.

Anderson, Wanni W., and Robert G. Lee, eds. 2005. *Displacements and Diasporas: Asians in the Americas*. New Brunswick, NJ: Rutgers University Press.

Anzaldúa, Gloria. 1987. *Borderlands/La Frontera: The New Mestiza*. San Francisco: Aunt Lute.

Basch, Linda, Nina Glick Schiller, and Cristina Szanton Blanc. 1994. *Nations Unbound: Transnational Projects, Postcolonial Predicaments and Deterritorialized Nation-States*. Amsterdam: Gordon and Breach.

Bean, Frank D., Rodolfo de la Garza, Bryan R. Roberts, and Sidney Wientraub. 1997. *At the Crossroads: Mexico and U.S. Immigration Policy*. Lanham, MD: Rowman and Littlefield.

CEH (Commission for Historical Clarification). 1999. *Guatemala Memory of Silence*. Guatemala City: CEH.

Chaney, Elsa M. 1987. The Context of Caribbean Migration. In *Caribbean Life in New York City: Sociocultural Dimensions*. Constance R. Sutton and Elsa M. Chaney, eds. Pp. 3–14. New York: Center for Migration Studies.

Chavez, Leo. 2001. *Covering Immigration: Popular Images and the Politics of the Nation*. Berkeley: University of California Press.

Cohen, Jeffrey H. 2004. *The Culture of Migration in Southern Mexico*. Austin: University of Texas Press.

Espitia, Marilyn. 2004. The Other "Other Hispanics": South American–Origin Latinos in the United States. In *The Columbia History of Latinos in the United States since 1960.* David G. Gutierrez, ed. Pp. 257–280. New York: Columbia University Press.

Ferris, Elizabeth G. 1995. Central American Refugees to the USA. In *Cambridge Survey of World Migration.* Robin Cohen, ed. Pp. 226–228. New York: Cambridge University Press.

Foner, Nancy, ed. 1987. *New Immigrants in New York.* New York: Columbia University Press.

———. 2000. *From Ellis Island to JFK: New York's Two Great Waves of Immigration.* New York: Russell Sage.

Garcia, Maria Cristina. 2004. Exiles, Immigrants, and Transnationals: The Cuban Communities of the United States. In *The Columbia History of Latinos in the United States since 1960.* David G. Gutierrez, ed. Pp. 146–186. New York: Columbia University Press.

Georges, Eugenia. 1990. *The Making of a Transnational Community: Migration, Development, and Cultural Change in the Dominican Republic.* New York: Columbia University Press.

Gmelch, George. 1992. *Double Passage: The Lives of Caribbean Immigrants Abroad and Back Home.* Ann Arbor: University of Michigan Press.

Goldin, Liliana R. 1999. *Entities on the Move: Transnational Processes in North America and the Caribbean Basin.* Albany: Institute for Mesoamerican Studies, State University of New York.

González, Juan. 2000. *Harvest of Empire: A History of Latinos in America.* New York: Viking.

González, Nancie L. 1988. *Sojourners of the Caribbean: Ethnogenesis and Ethnohistory of the Garifuna.* Urbana: University of Illinois Press.

Grasmuck, Sherri, and Patricia Pessar. 1992. *Between Two Islands: Dominican International Migration.* Berkeley: University of California.

Grenier, Guillermo J., and Lisandro Perez. 2003. *The Legacy of Exile: Cubans in the United States.* Boston: Allyn and Bacon.

Guarnizo, Luis. 1994. Los Dominicanyork: The Making of a Binational Society. *Annals of the American Academy of Political and Social Science* 533:70–86.

Guarnizo, Luis, Arturo Sanchez, and Elizabeth Roach. 1999. Mistrust, Fragmented Solidarity, and Transnational Migration: Colombians in New York City and Los Angeles. *Ethnic and Racial Studies* 22:367–396.

Gutiérrez, David G. 2004. Introduction. Demography and the Shifting Boundaries of "Community": Reflections on "U.S. Latinos" and the Evolution of Latino Studies. In *The Columbia History of Latinos in the United States since 1960.* David G. Gutierrez, ed. Pp. 1–42. New York: Columbia University Press.

Hagan, Jaqueline. 1994. *Deciding to Be Legal: A Maya Community in Houston.* Philadelphia: Temple University Press.

Hamamoto, Darrell Y., and Rodolfo D. Torres, eds. 1997. *New American Destinies: A Reader in Contemporary Asian and Latino Immigration.* New York: Routledge.

Hamilton, Nora, and Norma Stoltz Chinchilla. 1997. *Central American Migration: A Framework for Analysis in New American Destinies.* Darrell Y. Hamamoto and Rodolfo D. Torres, eds. Pp. 91–122. New York: Routledge.

———. 2001. *Seeking Community in a Global City: Guatemalans and Salvadorans in Los Angeles.* Philadelphia: Temple University Press.

Hart, Dianne Walta. 1997. *Undocumented in L.A.: An Immigrant's Story.* Wilmington, DE: Scholarly Resources.

Heer, David M. 1990. *Undocumented Mexicans in the United States.* Cambridge: Cambridge University Press.

Hendricks, Glenn. 1974. *The Dominican Diaspora: From the Dominican Republic to New York City—Villagers in Transition.* New York: Teachers College Press.

Hirsch, Jennifer. 2003. *A Courtship after Marriage: Sexuality and Love in Mexican Transnational Families*. Berkeley: University of California Press.

Kyle, David. 2000. *Transnational Peasants: Migrations, Networks, and Ethnicity in Andean Ecuador*. Baltimore, MD: Johns Hopkins University Press.

Levitt, Peggy. 2001. *The Transnational Villagers*. Berkeley: University of California Press.

Loucky, James, and Marilyn Moors, eds. 2000. *The Maya Diaspora: Guatemalan Roots, New American Lives*. Philadelphia: Temple University.

Mahler, Sarah. 1995. *Salvadorans in Suburbia: Symbiosis and Conflict*. Boston: Allyn and Bacon.

Manz, Beatriz. 1988. *Refugees of a Hidden War: The Aftermath of Counterinsurgency in Guatemala*. Albany: State University of New York Press.

Marciel, David R., and María Herrera-Sobek. 1998. *Culture across Borders: Mexican Immigration and Popular Culture*. Tucson: University of Arizona Press.

Margolis, Maxine. 1994. *Little Brazil: An Ethnography of Brazilian Immigrants in New York City*. Princeton, NJ: Princeton University Press.

Martínez, Oscar. 1994. *Border People: Life and Society in the U.S.-Mexico Borderlands*. Tucson: University of Arizona Press.

Martínez, Ruben. 2001. *Crossing Over: A Mexican Family on the Migrant Trail*. New York: Henry Holt.

Massey, Douglas, Rafael Alarcon, Jorge Durand, and Humberto Gonzalez. 1987. *Return to Aztlán: The Social Process of International Migration from Western Mexico*. Berkeley: University of California Press.

Menjívar, Cecilia. 2000. *Fragmented Ties: Salvadoran Immigrant Networks in America*. Berkeley: University of California Press.

Migration News. 2005. Mexico: Legalization, Brazilians, Economy. July, vol. 12, no. 3. http://migration.ucdavis.edu/mn/more.php?id=3114_0_2_0.

Miles, Anne. 2004. *Cuenca to Queens: An Anthropological Story of Transnational Migration*. Austin: University of Texas Press.

Mitchell, Christopher, ed. 1992. *Western Hemisphere Immigration and United States Foreign Policy*. University Park: Pennsylvania State University Press.

Moran-Taylor, Michelle, and Cecilia Menjívar. 2005. Unpacking Longings of Return: Guatemalan and Salvadoran Migrants in Phoenix, Arizona. *International Migration* 43(4):91–121.

Office of Immigration Statistics. 2004. *2004 Yearbook of Immigration Statistics*. Washington, DC: U.S. Department of Homeland Security. http://www.uscis.gov/graphics/shared/statistics.

Peach, Ceri. 1995. Anglophone Caribbean Migration to the USA and Canada. In *Cambridge Survey of World Migration*. Robin Cohen, ed. Pp. 245–247. New York: Cambridge University Press.

Pessar, Patricia. 1997. Introduction: New Approaches to Caribbean Emigration and Return. In *Caribbean Circuits: New Directions in the Study of Caribbean Migration*. Patricia Pessar, ed. Pp. 1–11. New York: Center for Migration Studies.

Portes, Alejandro, and Robert Bach. 1985. *Latin Journey: Cuban and Mexican Immigrants in the United States*. Berkeley: University of California Press.

Repak, Terry A. 1995. *Waiting on Washington: Central American Workers in the Nation's Capital*. Philadelphia: Temple University Press.

Robinson, William I. 2003. *Transnational Conflicts: Central America, Social Change, and Globalization*. London: Verso.

Sassen, Saskia. 1988. *The Mobility of Labor and Capital: A Study in International Investment and Labor Flow*. New York: Cambridge University Press.

Siems, Larry. 1992. *Between the Lines: Letters Between Undocumented Mexican and Central American Immigrants and Their Families and Friends*. Tucson: University of Arizona Press.

Singer, Audrey, and Douglas Massey. 1998. The Social Process of Undocumented Border Crossing among Mexican Migrants. *International Migration Review* 32(3):561–592.

Stepick, Alex. 1998. *Pride Against Prejudice: Haitians in the United States*. Boston: Allyn and Bacon.

Sutton, Constance, and Elsa Chaney. 1987. *Caribbean Life in New York City: Socio-cultural Dimensions*. New York: Center for Migration Studies.

Taylor, Matthew, Michelle Moran-Taylor, and Debra Rodman Ruiz. 2006. Land, Ethnic, and Gender Change: Transnational Migration and Its Effects on Guatemalan Lives and Landscapes. *Geoforum* 37(1):41–61.

Velez-Ibáñez, Carlos. 1996. *Border Visions: Mexican Cultures of the Southwest United States*. Tucson: University of Arizona Press.

Zucker, Naomi Flink, and Norman L. Zucker. 1995. U.S. Admission Policies towards Cuban and Haitian Migrants. In *Cambridge Survey of World Migration*. Robin Cohen, ed. Pp. 447–451. New York: Cambridge University Press.

MICHELLE J. MORAN-TAYLOR AND JAMES LOUCKY

GROWTH AND DEVELOPMENT. The earliest studies of the biology of migrants to America deal with physical growth. Even today it is common for anthropologists, public health workers, physicians, economists, and historians to use measures of physical growth and development in their research. This is so because the physical growth of an individual, and the aggregate growth of the population of which they are members, is highly sensitive to the overall quality of the environment. Today we know that human biological and cultural environments influence human growth and development because of factors that promote either health or disease and condition nutritional status. Human biocultural environments also include social, educational, economic, psychological, and political forces that shape human biology (Tanner 1981; Bogin 1999).

Measures of the growth of the general population in the United States, dating to the late 1800s, were originally taken to survey the health of children in urban schools, but the data became part of a highly contentious political debate about race and immigration. In studies of height and weight of Boston school children which assessed differences in growth associated with sex, nationality, and socioeconomic level, Henry Pickering Bowditch found children of immigrants to be taller than similarly aged children in their countries of origin. He also found that working-class children were smaller, and explained this as environmental, attributing the height of children of non-laboring classes to the greater comfort in which they lived and grew up (Boyd 1980:469).

This conclusion ran counter to the work of Francis Galton, whose book *Natural Inheritance* (1889), demonstrating the heredity of stature and other physical traits, was used to support the eugenics movement, a pseudo-scientific political movement that claimed to be able to improve the human species by controlled breeding. Franz Boas, a German-born anthropologist working in the United States, used the Bowditch studies, as well as his own research with immigrants from Eastern and Southern Europe, to demolish the position of the eugenicists (Boas 1910). Boas found that children of recent immigrants grew up to look much like "good old Americans," and ascribed this plasticity in growth of migrants to the better healthcare and nutrition they received in the United States.

Despite this work, many eugenicists and politicians continued to call for quotas on the immigration of so-called inferior peoples into the United States. By mid-century, however, the work of Boas had led to a number of studies of immigrant and native-born children in the United States and other countries, studies which confirmed the nature of human developmental plasticity.

Immigrant growth studies in the United States usually depend on who is immigrating, so not surprisingly recent studies mostly involve foreign-born children from Latin America and Asia. Survey data from the National Center for Health Statistics (NCHS) reveal generally shorter statures of Mexican American children, compared with non-Hispanic whites and blacks, a difference which increases with age. While it is possible that Mexican Americans may inherit a genetic predisposition to shorter stature, it is even more probable that older Mexican American children (12–19 years old) spent less time in the United States compared to the younger Mexican Americans (6–11 years old). The earlier and the longer their exposure to the U.S. environment, the more likely that growth in height of Mexican Americans will converge on that of whites and blacks. Mexican American boys and men also tend to be heavier and fatter than whites and blacks, group differences in fatness which are due primarily to lifestyle factors, such as total food intake and levels of physical activity. Of additional concern is the fact that all groups show higher than expected rates for being overweight. This is a serious concern for the health of all U.S. children, as early overweight tends to lead to adult health problems.

Research on Guatemalan Maya immigrants to the United States replicates and extends the findings for Mexican Americans (Bogin and Loucky 1997; Bogin et al. 2002; Smith et al. 2002). Virtually all of these Maya immigrants arrived since 1979, which makes them more homogeneous in terms of time in the United States than the Mexican Americans. Most of the Maya families were refugees from civil war in Guatemala. The parents were very poor and poorly educated, placing their children at risk for poor growth and health. Measures of height, weight, and sitting height (length from buttocks to top of head) of children of Maya immigrants (93 percent born in the United States) living in California and Florida in 1999 and 2000 were measured and compared to school-aged children measured in Guatemala in 1998. Maya American children are on average 10 centimeters taller than Maya children in Guatemala. This suggests that better nutritional status and health and are associated with greater economic productivity in adulthood, while it is widely known that the Maya in Guatemala suffer from undernourishment and high levels of infectious disease. So while increases in stature and leg length of the Maya Americans are not unexpected, the magnitude of these increases is the largest ever recorded for any group of immigrants, revealing how rapidly and powerfully human plasticity can be expressed. Not all the growth changes are positive, however, as nearly half the Maya American children are overweight (and 42 percent obese), which increases the likelihood of health problems later in life, such as hypertension and diabetes. Growing acculturation to American lifestyles of watching TV or playing computer games, fat-laden foods, and less walking tend to lead to more overweight children.

Like Latin Americans, the rate of Asian immigration to the United States grew rapidly in the last 30 years. Like the Maya, many of these Asians are refugees from warfare and terrible living conditions. Not surprisingly, Asian refugee adults and children tend to be of low socioeconomic status and poor health, with the first generation born in the United States showing high prevalence of low birth weight as well as poor growth during infancy and childhood. Within a decade, however, these problems began to show improvement, until today the growth status of Asian children was near that of low-income white, black, and Hispanic children (Yip et al. 1992).

The growth of U.S.-born children from two immigrant Asian ethnic groups, Lao and Hmong, shows similar differences (Hyslop et al. 1996). Both the Hmong and Lao children were short relative to American reference data, growing between the 10th to 25th percentile of the NCHS references. The Lao children were also proportionally light relative to reference data, but the Hmong children were disproportionately heavier, reaching about the 75th percentile of the NCHS references. The short but heavy physique of Hmong children was also found in an independent study (Gjerdingen et al. 1996). All of the families of these children lived in low-income neighborhoods and the mothers and children received medical care at public clinics.

The growth of immigrants shows that human biology, as measured in centimeters and kilograms, is intertwined with social, economic, and political forces. To understand human growth requires a biocultural perspective (Bogin 1999). Much cooperation between human biologists and social scientists will be required to eventually unravel how biological, social, and cultural factors interact and influence the growth of immigrants and succeeding generations of their children born in the Americas. *See also*: **Demography; Fertility; Health.**

References

Boas, F. 1910. Changes in the Bodily Form of Descendants of Immigrants. Report submitted to the Congress of the United States of America.

———. 1940. *Race, Language, and Culture*. New York: Free Press.

Bogin, B. 1999. *Patterns of Human Growth*, 2nd ed. Cambridge: Cambridge University Press.

Bogin, B., and J. Loucky. 1997. Plasticity, Political Economy, and Physical Growth Status of Guatemala Maya Children Living in the United States. *American Journal of Physical Anthropology* 102:17–32.

Bogin, B., P.K. Smith, A.B. Orden, M.I. Varela Silva, and J. Loucky. 2002. Rapid Change in Height and Body Proportions of Maya American Children. *American Journal of Human Biology* 14:753–761.

Boyd, E. 1980. *Origins of the Study of Human Growth*. B.S. Savara and J.F. Schilke, eds. Eugene: University of Oregon Press.

Gjerdingen, D.K., M. Ireland, and K.M. Chaloner. 1996. Growth of Hmong Children. *Archives of Pediatrics and Adolescent Medicine* 150(12):1295–1298.

Goldstein, M.S. 1943. *Demographic and Bodily Changes in Descendants of Mexican Immigrants*. Austin, TX: Institute of Latin American Studies.

Hyslop, A.E., A.S. Deinard, E. Dahlberg-Luby, and J.H. Himes. 1996. Growth Patterns of First-Generation Southeast Asian Americans from Birth to 5 Years of Age. *Journal of the American Board of Family Practice* 9(5):328–335.

Lasker, G.W. 1952. Environmental Growth Factors and Selective Migration. *Human Biology* 24:262–289.

Lasker, G.W., and F.G. Evans. 1961. Age, Environment and Migration: Further Anthropometric Findings on Migrant and Non-Migrant Mexicans. *American Journal of Physical Anthropology* 19:203–211.

National Center for Health Statistics web site, http://www.cdc.gov/nchs/about/major/nhanes/growthcharts/datafiles.htm.

Smith, P.K., B. Bogin, M.I. Varela Silva, A.B. Orden, and J. Loucky. 2002. Does Immigration Help or Harm Children's Health? The Mayan Case. *Social Science Quarterly* 83:994–1002.

Tanner, J.M. 1981. *A History of the Study of Human Growth*. Cambridge: Cambridge University Press.

Yip, R., K. Scanlon, and F. Trowbridge. 1992. Improving Growth Status of Asian Refugee Children in the United States. *Journal of the American Medical Association* 267:937–940.

BARRY BOGIN

GUESTWORKERS. The term *guestworkers* is an official designation for state-authorized, temporary foreign workers who must ultimately return to their countries of origin when their legal status expires. The admission of migrant workers under fixed-term visas has been observed in the latter half of the twentieth century in various world regions including Europe, South Africa, the United States, the Middle East, and East Asia. In the United States, guestworker programs have received mixed reviews because of the possibility that workers will refuse to return to their countries of origin and instead remain as undocumented workers. However, these concerns become less pronounced during periods of economic upswing which prompt employers to demand the authorized entrance of foreign labor. After tracing the historical changes in U.S. guestworker programs and examining the characteristics of guestworkers involved in these programs, current proposals about impending change are described.

The history of guestworkers in the United States is associated with broad migration policies that emerged from the need to restrict the entrance of some individuals in the late 1880s, resulting in the establishment of a quantitative quota system in 1921. The United States and Mexico first established a formal labor agreement in 1917–1921, but it was in 1942 that the labor agreement popularly referred to as the Bracero program was signed, allowing for the temporary migration of an unspecified number of Mexicans to work in the agricultural sectors (Oliveira 2002). Initially, the federal government exercised direct control of the program but dropped out of this role in 1947, allowing employers to recruit temporary workers privately if the labor department certified their needs. Some authors have suggested that the conditions of the workers who participated in this and subsequent guestworker programs were similar to those of indentured servants (Hahamovitch 2003; Hall 2002). Guestworkers are expected to work for only one employer who often provides housing below quality standards and away from the mainstream community, and to be healthy during the work period. Workers who jump their contracts and join the ranks of undocumented migrants could be pursued by the Immigration and Naturalization Service (INS; since 2003, the U.S. Citizenship and Naturalization Services), and if caught are automatically returned to Mexico (Oliveira 2002; Hahamovitch 2003).

The basic framework for present-day guestworker programs was provided by the Immigration and Naturalization Act (INA) of 1952. The INA implemented a requirement for employers to apply for labor certification of their guestworkers and expanded quotas allotted to specific skills and occupations. This act established a guestworker program under the H-2 section which details a process that should be followed to fill up empty jobs with foreign workers. Today the H-2 program is recognized as the official guestworker program featuring workers with fixed-term visas. By the early 1960s, up to 400,000 Mexicans and 15,000 workers from the British West Indies were entering the United States each year under the protection of the Bracero program and the H-2 section of the INA. However, the Bracero program was discontinued in 1964, in part because the secretary of labor was pressured by U.S. farm workers to deny labor certification to employers in California and other states, prompting Congress to stop renewing the program. The H-2 program of the Caribbean was allowed to continue because sugar producers convinced the Secretary of Labor that U.S. citizens would not be attracted to sugar harvesting jobs (Hahamovitch 2003).

Additional specification of the H-2 program was included in the provisions of the Immigration Reform and Control Act (IRCA) of 1986, which differentiated between H-2A visas reserved for workers in the agricultural sector and the H-2B visas provided to non-agricultural temporary workers (Chang 2002; Meyerle 2002). An H-1B guestworker program was expanded for professionals with "specialty occupations" in 1991. These guestworker programs are jointly administered by the Department of Labor, Employment and Training Administration, and the Department of Justice, U.S. Citizenship and Naturalization Services. Although the statutes did not determine the number of workers that could be admitted under the H-2 program, this number was limited to 40,000 H-2A and 66,000 H-2B awards annually. Guestworker visas are awarded to fill temporarily vacant jobs if (1) U.S. workers are not available for the jobs and (2) the presence of foreign workers will not have negative effects on similar native workers (Martin 2002).

The specific conditions associated with the H-2 program indicate that employers in the agriculture and hotel and restaurant business should apply for labor certification of workers who would enter the country to fill temporary jobs in these sectors and return to their country when the contract is fulfilled (Chang 2002; Oliveira 2002). Under this program, the employer is expected to provide workers with Adverse Effect Wage Rate, prevailing, or minimum wages whichever is higher, free and approved housing, and transportation from the country of origin. However, the actual process of acquiring the visa is left to workers, who must request the visa in the U.S. consulate in the countries of origin. This visa is issued only for the length of time required for employment and while the worker continues working for the employer who requests the visa. In this process, the workers carry some of the costs, which include paying for the visa and accompanying documentation and return transportation when employment has expired. As they enter the United States, guestworkers are contracted to work for only one employer, which creates possibility for abuse by employers (Hall 2002).

In a related development, some 1.3 million legalization applications were filed under the Special Agricultural Worker (SAW) provisions associated with the Immigration Reform and Control Act of 1986, of which 1.2 million were awarded (Martin 2002). Because of the geographic proximity, most guestworkers who benefit from the H-2 program have traditionally come from Mexico and the Caribbean. This workforce has been almost exclusively male, reflecting a perception that agricultural jobs are unsuitable for women and the problem of birthright citizenship for children born in the United States (Hahamovitch 2003). In addition, guestworkers are more likely to end up in those regions of the country that require the kinds of labor that they are able to offer. In 2001 more than 25 percent of H-2A visa holders were attracted into North Carolina, making it the leading state that has benefited from a guestworker program. In the same year, the actions of the North Carolina Grower Association (NCGA) were influential in sponsoring 10,500 workers who came to work in tobacco and vegetable farms, orchards, nurseries, and Christmas tree farms (Hall 2002).

The global competitive environment of the 1980s prompted the U.S. government to expand the H-1B guestworker program for skilled labor to meet the demands in important technological sectors with apparent need for trained workers. The Immigration Act of 1990 (IA90) established a cap for H-1B visas of 65,000 annually reserved for workers in "specialty occupations." In addition, the IA90 included specific provisions for employers, including (1) that they must offer at least 95 percent of prevailing wages for the specialty occupation; (2) that the hiring should not adversely affect U.S. workers and must have taken place in the absence of any strike or lockout; (3) that the employer cannot have laid off any U.S. worker 90 days prior to or following the filing of an H-1B visa; and (4) that there must have been a previously failed attempt to recruit U.S. workers. These only apply to a small fraction of all U.S. employers. Unlike other guestworker programs, the length of stay of guestworkers with H-1B status is predetermined to a period of three years with a possibility to renew it once, and workers can apply for renewal without the need to leave the country to obtain their visas. They may also apply for permanent residency after obtaining labor certification from the Department of Labor (DOL), based on sponsorship by their employers.

Presently the H-1B guestworker program has received its greatest support from the American Competitiveness in the Twenty-First Century Act (AC21), which expanded the cap to 195,000 each year between 2001 and 2003. In addition, the AC21 allowed employers to pay a fee of $1,000 to obtain faster services in a 15-day period (Carpenter 2003). According to the INS, of the 257,640 H-1B approved petitions in 2000, 136,787 (53 percent) were initial employment applications while the remaining 120,853 were petitions for continuing employment.

An interpretation of the descriptive characteristics of approved applications in 2000 demonstrates the selectivity of this guestworker program. First, almost one-half (48 percent) of petitions went to individuals from India. The participation of Indian citizens is staggering when compared to the 8.8 percent of visas for Chinese citizens that comprise the second largest group receiving approval. Second, nearly 69 percent of the applicants were between 25 and 34 years of age and 98 percent of the applicants had earned at least a bachelor's degree. Third, computer-related occupations account for 68 percent of the petitions that were approved followed by occupations in architecture, engineering, surveying, and administration. Finally, the general median annual income that workers expect to earn is $53,000, although this amount varies by type of occupation and whether the applicant was applying for the first time or was renewing the status (INS 2002).

Early in 2001, Presidents George Bush from the United States and Vicente Fox from Mexico had begun bilateral talks to discuss a legalization program for Mexican temporary workers in the United States. However, these efforts were hampered by attacks on the World Trade Center and the Pentagon on September 11, 2001, and the subsequent passage of the USA Patriot Act in Congress that placed restrictions on immigration and immigrant populations (Hines 2002). As a result, the attention of the federal government turned to increased border enforcement by enhancing the budget of the INS for the hiring of additional border patrol agents.

Supporters and opponents of the guestworker program expect that U.S.-Mexico talks will resume in the future and have laid out several proposals about the future of guestworkers in the United States. Some propose a temporary guestworker program that would allow some guestworkers to obtain permanent residence over a period of time (Hines 2002). Other beneficiaries of this program would be unauthorized workers who did at least 100 days of farm work in the previous year and continued in that sector for at least 360 more days over the next six years (Martin 2002).

A different proposal has been put forward by opponents of the guestworker program; they support a policy that resembles the current guestworker program with some minor changes. Under this program undocumented workers who are already in the country would be allowed to obtain seasonal work permits that would allow them to return to the United States indefinitely. However, these workers would be allowed to work consecutively for three years but must remain in the place of origin for at least one more year after this period (Martin and Teitelbaum 2001).

A third proposal, proposed by independent professionals and supported by the AFL-CIO, envisions the legalization of undocumented immigrants and some guestworkers. The program would cover unauthorized workers and guestworkers who were in the United States before a predetermined date. The legalization date would be rolled forward a year each of the next five years, eventually encompassing all undocumented residents.

Whether one of these proposals becomes crystallized, or what the future holds for authorized employment of foreign workers, will depend on how important immigration issues are in further electoral campaigns. Guestworker policy will undoubtedly continue to shift along with shifting labor demands of industrial, agricultural, and service sectors, which are steadily taking on a more global character. *See also*: **Agricultural workers; Expedited entry and removal; Legislation; Mexico-U.S. migration; Skilled migrants.**

References

Basok, Tanya. 2002. *Tortillas and Tomatoes: Transmigrant Mexican Harvesters in Canada.* Toronto: McGill–Queen's University Press.

Carpenter, Leah. 2003. The Status of the H-1B Visa in These Conflicting Times. *Tulsa Journal of Comparative and International Law* 10:553–578.

Chang, Howard. 2002. Liberal Ideals and Political Feasibilities: Guest-Workers Program as Second Best Policies. *North Carolina Journal of International Law and Commercial Regulation* 27:465–481.

Hahamovitch, Cindy. 2003. Creating Perfect Immigrants: Guestworkers of the World in Historical Perspective. *Labor History* 44:69–94.

Hall, Mary. 2002. Defending the Rights of H-2A Farmworkers. *North Carolina Journal of International Law and Commercial Regulation* 27:521–535.

Hines, Barbara. 2002. So Near and Yet so Far Away: The Effect of September 11 on Mexican Immigrants in the United States. *Texas Hispanic Journal of Law and Policy* 8:42–54.

Lowell, B. Lindsay, ed. 1999. *Foreign Temporary Workers in America: Policies That Benefit the U.S. Economy*. Westport, CT: Quorum.

Martin, Phillip. 2002. Legalizing Farmworkers: The 2002 Outlook. *Migration World* 30:19–23.

Martin, Phillip, and Michael Tietelbaum. 2001. The Mirage of Mexican Guest Workers. *Foreign Affairs* 80:117–125.

Meyerle, Michael. 2002. Proposed Guest Worker Statutes: An Unsatisfactory Answer to a Difficult, If Not Impossible Question. *The Journal of Small and Engineering Business Law* 6:559–580.

Oliveira, Laura. 2002. A License to Exploit: The Need to Reform the H-2A Temporary Agricultural Guest Worker Program. *The Scholar: St. Mary's Law Review on Minority Issues* 55:157–189.

U.S. Immigration and Naturalization Service (INS). 2002. *Report on Characteristics of Specialty Occupation Workers (H-1B): Fiscal Year 2002*. Washington, DC: U.S. Government Printing Office.

LUIS ALFREDO POSAS

H

HEALTH. Although the U.S. Public Health Service requires the evaluation of immigrants and refugees before exiting their country of origin or being given asylum, undocumented immigrants do not pass through this filter and logistical difficulties sometimes prevent everyone from being assessed (Walker and Jaranson 1999; Goodridge 2002). Guidelines set by the Centers for Disease Control (CDC) emphasize checking for disorders that might lead to harmful behavior, drug abuse, or addiction and infectious diseases that threaten public health (such as tuberculosis, hepatitis, and Hansen's disease or leprosy). Healthcare workers employed by the International Organization for Migration (IOM) follow these guidelines, along with conducting a chest x-ray for individuals older than 2 years and laboratory testing for venereal disease and HIV for individuals older than 15 years, when administering a physical exam and history to immigrants. Immigrants are not tested for chronic conditions such as malaria or parasites, however, and year-long approval of entry can be problematic if immigrants are exposed to infectious disease during that year. If tests are positive, individuals are prevented from entering the United States or are allowed to enter after treatment. The federal Office of Refugee Resettlement and the CDC also advise immigrants to have a health screen within 90 days of arrival or within one month if a problem is identified. Ideally, new refugees obtain assistance and medical attention from a voluntary resettlement agency (VOLAG). In addition, Title VI of the Civil Rights Act of 1964 mandates that healthcare providers receiving federal funding provide translation services to clients with poor English skills to facilitate better access (Moua et al. 2002).

Barriers to healthcare for immigrants and refugees have been erected in recent years, however. Proposition 187 would have made undocumented residents in California ineligible for non-emergency publicly funded healthcare services, social services, and public education (Mizoguchi 1999), had it not been struck down in the courts. Similarly the Personal Responsibility and Work Opportunity Reconciliation Act, passed into law by Congress in 1996, made immigrants ineligible for Supplemental Security Income or food stamps and requires a 5-year wait before qualification for federal health benefits (Moua et al. 2002). Some public health services are still available, including communicable disease services, immunizations, emergency medical services, emergency Medicaid, the Women, Infants, Children (WIC) program, and some mental health and abuse services. Yet unfortunately the general perception is that immigrants are not eligible for anything for five years, so even these services are often not used. Public health suffers when immigrants, unaware they can receive immunizations, succumb to infectious diseases such as rubella. In addition, non-citizen immigrants and their children, and particularly the poor, are often uninsured, further reducing their access to healthcare (Ku and Matani 2001).

Surprisingly, immigrants experience better health than the U.S.-born population. They often exhibit better self-assessed health, and lower numbers of restricted activity days, bed disability days, work-loss days, physician visits, and hospitalizations (Singh and Siahpush 2002). Foreign-born status is also associated with reduced risk for infant mortality and low birth weight, particularly true for Africans, Cubans, Mexicans, and Chinese (Singh and Yu 1996). Comparison of mortality risks by ethnicity of immigrants relative to U.S.-born reveals that foreign-born individuals have mortality risks that are significantly lower (by 16 percent to 45 percent, depending on group), compared with U.S.-born whites of similar social and economic backgrounds (Singh and Siahpush 2002). There were also significant differences in mortality rates for cancer, cardiovascular disease, respiratory and infectious diseases, and injury, with Asians, Pacific Islanders, and Hispanics having the lowest risks. Lower morbidity and mortality risks of immigrants and their children likely reflect better health and fitness of those migrating to the United States than those who stay behind in the country of origin, though family case studies would lead to a better understanding of this health advantage.

The adjustment of immigrants has been studied within an assimilation framework, which assumes that the longer immigrants are in the country the more similar they become to native populations. This process varies because highly educated immigrants with resources may adjust more quickly. Certainly immigrants vary dramatically in terms of education and skills when they arrive in the United States (Landale et al. 1999). In addition, spending more time in the country does not necessarily mean leaving one's culture behind. Sizeable ethnic communities permit many to remain bicultural. Unfortunately, risk of smoking, obesity, hypertension, and chronic conditions do increase the longer immigrants reside in the United States (Hernandez and Charney 1998). Chronic disease risk increases when immigrants adopt U.S. dietary patterns (dietary acculturation) with foods high in fat and low in fruits and vegetables (Satia-Abouta et al. 2002).

Not surprisingly, immigrants with fewer resources have more difficulties. For example, in their assessment of three migratory streams of agricultural workers, many based in Mexico, through California, Texas, and Florida, Benavides-Vaello and Setzler (1998) find that health problems vary depending on the characteristics of each "stream," but also that the constant mobility of these populations makes it difficult to manage health issues. Overall low education levels of the migrants and underfunded clinics that do not share information exacerbate health problems. Thus, the health status of these groups is much worse than that of the general population of U.S.-born. The border with Mexico is particularly problematic; communicable diseases thrive thanks to poor living conditions, including the inadequate housing in many *colonias* (unincorporated settlements on both sides of the border) that often lack running water and plumbing, electricity, sewage, or drainage systems.

The globalization of health problems associated with human movement became an acute concern with the virulent spread of Severe Acute Respiratory Syndrome (SARS) from Asia in February 2003. This resulted in travel advisories issued by the World Health Organization and the Centers for Disease Control for Beijing, Hong Kong, Taipei, and other regions in China, and rudimentary health screenings of passengers on planes going to or coming from SARS-affected areas. The rapid appearance of masks on travelers worldwide, and deaths from China to Canada, showed how intertwined contagious and communicable diseases are with international and internal migration.

Individuals who emigrate under traumatic circumstances are a particularly high-risk group. Posttraumatic Stress Disorder and expression of depression and other mental disorders, including substance abuse, are common in such people (Kramer et al. 1999; Eisenman et al. 2003). What is considered salient in one's experience with physical or mental illness, or mentioned to a healthcare provider, is conditioned by one's culture. Since illness is ultimately both a biological and a social construct, cultural sensitivity to different worldviews and familiarity with the healthcare systems of the originating countries would more effectively influence response to treatment recommendations and facilitate better healthcare for immigrants and refugees in general (Lewis-Fernández and Kleinman 1995; Loue 1998; Miller 2000; Andresen 2001; Goodridge 2002). *See also*: **Biological responses; Growth and development; Mental health problems.**

References

Andresen, Jensine. 2001. Cultural Competence and Health Care: Japanese, Korean, and Indian Patients in the United States. *Journal of Cultural Diversity* 8(4):109–121.

Benavides-Vaello, Sandra, and Heather Setzler. 1998. Migrant and Seasonal Farmworkers: Health Care Issues. In *U.S.-Mexico Border Health: Issues for Regional and Migrant Populations.* J. Gerard Power and Theresa Byrd, eds. Pp. 224–249. Thousand Oaks, CA: Sage.

Eisenman, David. P., Lillian Gelberg, Honghu Liu, and Martin F. Shapiro. 2003. Mental Health and Health-Related Quality of Life among Adult Latino Primary Care Patients Living in the United States with Previous Exposure to Political Violence. *Journal of the American Medical Association* 290(5):627–634.

Goodridge, Elizabeth. 2002. Meeting the Health Needs of Refugees and Immigrants. *Journal of the American Academy of Physician Assistants* 15(1):20-2, 25-6, 31-2.

Harborview Medical Center. 1995–2003. Ethnomed. Seattle: University of Washington. http://www.ethnomed.org.

Hernandez, Donald J., and Evan Charney, eds. 1998. *From Generation to Generation: The Health and Well-Being of Children in Immigrant Families.* Washington, DC: National Academy Press.

Kramer, Elizabeth J., Susan L. Ivey, and Yu-Wen Ying, eds. 1999. *Immigrant Women's Health: Problems and Solutions.* San Francisco: Jossey-Bass.

Ku, Leighton, and Sheetal Matani. 2001. Left Out: Immigrants' Access to Health Care and Insurance. *Health Affairs* 20(1):247–256.

Landale, Nancy S., R.S. Oropesa, and Bridget K. Gorman. 1999. Immigration and Infant Health: Birth Outcomes of Immigrant and Native-Born Women. In *Children of*

Immigrants: Health, Adjustment, and Public Assistance. Donald J. Hernandez, ed. Pp. 244–271. Washington, DC: National Academy Press.

Lewis-Fernández, Roberto, and Arthur Kleinman. 1995. Cultural Psychiatry: Theoretical, Clinical and Research Issues. *Cultural Psychiatry* 18(3):433–448.

Loue, Sana. 1998. *Handbook of Immigrant Health.* New York: Plenum Press.

Miller, Nikki Levy. 2000. Haitian Ethnomedical Systems and Biomedical Practitioners: Directions for Clinicians. *Journal of Transcultural Nursing* 11(3):204–211.

Mizoguchi, Nobuko. 1999. Proposition 187: California's Anti-Immigrant Statute. In *Immigrant Women's Health: Problems and Solutions.* Elizabeth J. Kramer, Susan L. Ivey, and Yu-Wen Ying, eds. Pp. 72–77. San Francisco: Jossey-Bass.

Moua, Mee, Fernando A. Guerra, Jill D. Moore, and Ronald O. Valdiserri. 2002. Immigrant Health: Legal Tools/Legal Barriers. *Journal of Law, Medicine and Ethics* 30(3):189–196.

Satia-Abouta, Jessie, Ruth E. Patterson, Marian L. Neuhouser, and John Elder. 2002. Dietary Acculturation: Applications to Nutrition Research and Dietetics. *Journal of the American Dietetic Association* 102(8):1105–1118.

Singh, Gopal K., and Mohammad Siahpush. 2002. Ethnic-Immigrant Differentials in Health Behaviors, Morbidity, and Cause-Specific Mortality in the United States: An Analysis of Two National Data Bases. *Human Biology* 71(1):83–109.

Singh, Gopal K., and Stella M. Yu. 1996. Adverse Pregnancy Outcomes: Differences between U.S.- and Foreign-Born Women in Major U.S. Racial and Ethnic Groups. *American Journal of Public Health* 86(6):837–843.

Walker, Patricia F., and James Jaranson. 1999. Refugee and Immigrant Health Care. *Travel Medicine* 83(4):1103–1121.

JOAN C. STEVENSON

HUMAN SMUGGLING. Human smuggling into the United States across land, sea, and air borders involves significant numbers of immigrants as well as operators. Profits from illegally transporting human beings worldwide are estimated to top $10 billion annually (Fennell 1999). Smugglers target in particular migrants who seek economic opportunities in developed countries. Consequently human smuggling has grown in scope, from 9 percent to 14 percent between 1997 and 1999 alone (International Organization for Migration 2000), to become the third-highest illegal income source in the United States today (Edwards and Harder 2000).

In its various forms, human smuggling is a lucrative and illicit industry, often demeaning and criminal as well, that is fueled by an increasingly interconnected world of easy travel, rapid communications, and quick profits. The nature of smuggling ranges from short rides by back or boat across the Rio Grande into Texas to the threat and use of violence, abduction, or coercion in trafficking people. The U.S. government recently estimated that 18,000–20,000 people are trafficked annually into the United States (U.S. Department of State 2003). Estimates of all who pay for cross-border passage are considerably higher as well as indeterminable, since reporting and investigation are inherently difficult.

Human smuggling along the U.S.-Mexico border is especially pronounced given the scope of labor migration between the two countries. Since the early twentieth century, employers in the United States informally recruited Mexicans for agricultural labor, and at times mass labor migration was institutionalized through formal means such as the Bracero program between 1942 and 1964. However, because immigrants entered the United States relatively easily, smugglers were in little demand and hired mainly when women, children, the elderly, and non-Mexican nationals were involved. Growth in immigration in recent decades, however, contributed to the public perception that immigration was "out of control," particularly along the southern border. By the mid-1990s, more than 7 million Mexican nationals had illegally entered and settled in the United States (Spener 1999). Greater surveillance and interdiction came through expansion of the Border Patrol following the Immigration Reform and Control Act of 1986 (IRCA), and increasing hours of linewatch duty were designed to assure the security of the border (Dunn 1996).

Not unexpectedly, accompanying the rise in numbers of immigrants as well as in border enforcement, networks of kin groups providing assistance along with "professional" smugglers developed accordingly. In turn, the number of agents was doubled to 10,000 through the Illegal Immigration Reform and Immigrant Responsibility Act of 1996 (Andreas 2001), which also attempted to restrict unauthorized entry along with organized smuggling by increasing penalties, including up to five years in prison for entering the United States illegally.

Those who smuggle people do not fit a uniform pattern but instead range from friends and family members who are an intrinsic part of migration networks, to local guides who assist in crossing a border, to people who assist with transportation within the interior, using private vehicles along with trains, buses, and planes. In Texas, Spener (1999) differentiates between *pateros* (those who help migrants across the river), local interior guides, friends and family, and commercial smugglers. Smugglers are often referred to as *coyotes*, revealing that they may be either feared or admired, as is the cunning of the four-legged variety. Immigrants may also be called *pollos* (chickens) and their guides *polleros*. In other words, while shakedowns and detentions are common, both immigrants and smugglers may see this as providing an essential human service (Spener 1999). Conover (1987), among others, chronicles eloquently both the dangers and the dynamics of arranging crossings and transportation, payments of bribes, and collection of fees from relatives.

Human smuggling of unauthorized immigrants into the United States, estimated to generate about $3 billion a year, involves as many as 75 percent of undocumented immigrants from Latin America (Andreas 2000:95). As increasing enforcement pushes entrants into more remote areas along the U.S.-Mexico border, there is more use of scouts to run interference with border agents in order to make the crossing more assured. Tunnels, packed vans and 18-wheeler trucks, and automobile trunks each bring with them their own levels of endangerment to immigrants. While many smugglers are concerned with the welfare of their clients, others prey on them or leave them abandoned if the journey becomes perilous or apprehension likely (Rotella 1998).

The U.S.-Canada border has also seen increasing evidence of professional human smuggling in recent years. Most notable are organized networks from China, with smugglers given the ominous name "snakeheads" in recognition of their common connection to the Chinese mafia. News accounts of the recruitment of immigrants from Fujian province, the sale of false documents throughout Asia, and the harrowing tales of entombment in cargo containers for a transoceanic voyage add greater urgency to the immigration debate within Canada and in turn in the key destination cities of Vancouver, Toronto, and Montreal. In turn, the secondary smuggling from Canada across the long and porous border with the United States has risen to become one of the contentious issues between two countries that have long prided themselves on having few border problems.

Smugglers generally work in teams, many of them international. These may include recruiters in sending countries, persons accompanying groups through intermediate countries or across borders, and those who provide safe houses during transit or near the destination. Networks of human movement are often community- or ethnic-specific, and rely on personal acquaintances as well as local and language knowledge to instill trust. Others promise a "full service," from town or village to U.S. destination, even advertising such guarantees in newspapers as well as through word-of-mouth. Costs have risen dramatically in recent years, to thousands of dollars a person. Heightened border security accounts for this at least in part. The high costs as well as vulnerabilities lead to widespread exploitation, ranging from threats to separation of families and de facto kidnappings when payment is delayed.

Trafficking is a particularly worrisome phenomenon insofar as it often entails smuggling of women and clear violations of human rights. Richard (1999) estimates that 45,000 to 50,000 women have been trafficked to the United States, primarily for sex industries, but also for sweatshop labor, domestic servitude, agricultural work, maid work in hotels, trinket selling, and begging. Many of the women trafficked to the United States are from Asia, and most are young, in search of better opportunities, and, unfortunately, therefore highly vulnerable. Urban centers in New York, California, and Florida are frequent destinations of trafficked women.

Organizations which direct attention to the problems of trafficking include the International Office for Migration, Human Rights Watch, and the Civil Rights Division of the U.S. Department of Justice. The Protection Project of Johns Hopkins University has identified Mexico and Japan as having some of the most extensive rings dedicated to recruitment, transport, hiding, and even selling of people, including for prostitution and other forms of near-slavery, sometimes within the United States. A variation of human smuggling also occurs with "mail-order" bride operations, including a growing number of international matchmaking organizations.

Unaccompanied minors (persons under the age of 18 who enter the United States without a parent or legal guardian) often cross with non-relatives, including human smugglers (Ashabranner and Ashabranner 1987; Thompson 2003). The endangerment of children was highlighted by the November 1999 case of Elian Gonzalez, who was rescued off the Florida coast after his mother and others drowned when attempting entry from Cuba in a small boat. Recent attention suggests that up to 48,000 unaccompanied minors attempt entry into the United States each year, 3 of 4 in order to reunite with mothers (Nazario 2006). In the hands of smugglers, or when detained by immigration authorities, as are up to 5,000 are each year (Solomon 2002), these smallest immigrants are clearly among the most imperiled.

As long as the United States remains such a large labor-receiving country, policies for understanding what motivates use of smugglers as well as for effectively combating the harmful forms of smuggling will continue to be required. We should also be cautious about overgeneralizations. Giving housing or similar help to those in need is a far cry from exploiting vulnerable people who lack documentation, and extending the human smuggling label or potential prosecution to those who provide humanitarian assistance would hardly be appropriate. *See also*: **Enslavement; Marriage; Social networks; Transnationalism; Unauthorized immigration; U.S.-Canada border; U.S.-Mexico border.**

References

Andreas, Peter. 2000. *Border Games: Policing the U.S.-Mexico Divide*. Ithaca, NY: Cornell University Press.

———. 2001. The Transformation of Migration Smuggling across the U.S.-Mexico Border. In *Global Human Smuggling*. David Kyle and Rey Koslowski, eds. Pp. 107–125. Baltimore, MD: Johns Hopkins University Press.

Ashabranner, Brent, and Melissa Ashabranner. 1987. *Into a Strange Land: Unaccompanied Refugee Youth in America*. Canada: Dodd, Mead and Company.

Conover, Ted. 1987. *Coyotes: A Journey through the Secret World of America's Illegal Aliens*. New York: Vintage.

Dunn, Timothy. 1996. *The Militarization of the U.S.-Mexico Border, 1978–1992*. Austin: University of Texas Press.

Edwards, Catherine, and James Harder. 2000. Sex-Slave Trade Enters the U.S. *Insight on News* 16(14):14–17.

Fennell, Tom. 1999. The Human Smugglers. *Maclean's* 112(47), November 27, 18.

International Organization for Migration. 2000. *Alien Smuggling: Management and Operational Improvements Needed to Address Growing Problem*. Washington, DC: General Accounting Office. http://www.iom.int.

Kyle, David, and Rey Koslowski, eds. 2001. *Global Human Smuggling: Comparative Perspectives*. Baltimore, MD: Johns Hopkins University Press.

Nazario, Sonia. 2006. *Enrique's Journey*. New York: Random House.

Richard, Amy O'Neil. 1999. International Trafficking in Women to the United States: A Contemporary Manifestation of Slavery and Organized Crime. http://www.cia.gov/csi/monograph/women/trafficking.pdf.

Rotella, Sebastian. 1998. *Twilight on the Line: Underworlds and Politics at the U.S.-Mexico Border*. New York: Norton.

Solomon, Alisa. 2002. The INS v. Juvenile Justice. *Amnesty Now* (Fall):8–11.

Spener, David. 1999. This Coyote's Life. Contested Terrain: The U.S.-Mexico Borderlands. *Report on the Americas* 33(3):22–23.

———. 2001. Smuggling Migrants through South Texas: Challenges Posed by Operation Río Grande. In *Global Human Smuggling*. David Kyle and Rey Koslowski, eds. Pp. 129–165. Baltimore, MD: Johns Hopkins University Press.

Thompson, Ginger. 2003. Littlest Immigrants, Left in Hands of Smugglers. *New York Times*, November 3, A1.

U.S. Department of Justice, Civil Rights Division. http://www.usdoj.gov/crt/crim/trafficking summary.html.

U.S. Department of State. 2003. Assessment of U.S. Activities to Combat Trafficking in Persons. http://www.state.gov/g/tip/R/S/tiprpt/2003.

JAMES LOUCKY

I

IMMIGRANT EDUCATION. If we understand "immigrant student" to mean any foreign-born immigrant residing in the United States who is involved in or eligible for public education services, then the immigrant student population would comprise those with either legal or unauthorized residence. Immigrant students come from a variety of different social, political, and cultural backgrounds. Whether they arrive as refugees from countries imbued with political turmoil or cross the border illegally with a parent seeking employment, they often find themselves enrolled in schools that are insensitive to their previous experiences. Adjusting to such marked differences and sudden change of social environments may be very emotionally and psychologically trying. As students, they are expected to overcome personal issues and smoothly acclimate to new instructors, peers, language, and indeed perhaps a wholly different educational system. Problems arise when school personnel in the United States do not sufficiently take into consideration the best means of educating individuals from varied backgrounds.

This discussion focuses on the issues that immigrant students have faced historically and the current direction in which the American sociopolitical system is directing them. International students studying on temporary student visas may face similar issues of enculturation or discrimination, but the two groups differ due to the disparity in the social and economic support available from their countries of origin. Because the principal objective of international students is based on education, they are not therefore considered here, whereas the situations of immigrant students are subsumed under the larger context of immigration.

Even though immigrant students face a myriad of social and cultural obstacles throughout their academic careers, educators commonly elect to categorize them according to linguistic abilities. Immigrant students and programs dedicated to their education are frequently labeled as English Language Learners (ELL), Limited English Proficient (LEP), English as a Second Language (ESL), bilingual education, or language minority students. The very tenor of some of these terms suggests remediation and problem, rather than affirmation and potential.

The main focus of immigrant education revolves around the nature of language. Considerable recent debate about the most sound methods for teaching non-English speakers includes practitioners whose benevolent intentions may mask underlying biased language policies. One problem is that assimilationist intentions are often conflated with practical issues of bilingual education. Groups and ideologies in dominant positions channel the legislation, policies, and pedagogy dealing with immigrant education, with language serving as the fulcrum upon which the enculturation or acculturation of immigrant students pivots. This is evident in the turbulent evolution of language policy in education over the past 40 years.

In spite of the fact that the Bilingual Education Act (Title VII of the Elementary and Secondary Education Act, 1968) was initiated to address the needs of the language minority population, it did not specifically require schools to use a language other than English for instruction in order to receive funding. Without direct federal guidance, language issues were further disputed in state courts (Crawford 1999). Unanimously ruled on by the U.S. Supreme Court in 1974, *Lau v. Nichols* is the defining court case for language minority children. This decision provided guidelines for school districts on how to evaluate language minority students and offer instructional options for them. The Office of Civil Rights used the *Lau* decision to police school districts around the country and to make sure that they were providing adequate services.

Due to misunderstandings or misapplications of bilingual education pedagogies, many disputes arose over services offered to immigrant students during the subsequent decades. Xenophobic sentiments began to surface as bilingual education programs were described as impeding English acquisition by cultivating native languages instead. Shortly after taking office, President Reagan announced that "it is absolutely wrong and against American concepts to have a bilingual education program that is now openly, admittedly dedicated to preserving their native language and never getting them adequate in English so they can go out into the job market and participate" (Crawford 1999). Not only do statements like this effect political mandates, they contribute to the corpus of commonly shared social knowledge that is reproduced and perpetuated (van Dijk 1987, 2000), such as that immigrant students and their parents are not interested in or have good abilities for learning English.

Siphoning the negativity from debates over these misdiagnosed programs, proponents of the "English-Only" (U.S. English, English First) movement were able to gain considerable public support for their misguided language policies (Crawford 1992). In fact, many researchers agree that the most effective means of eradicating other languages is to halt future speakers from learning them. Such fervent attitudes toward language issues not only suggest deeper seated sentiments of xenophobia, even racism, they are even more troubling since groups active in the language debates are expending increasing energy and financial resources into shaping the education system.

Institutions such as education are used to shaping society through the implementation of policy that reflects dominant belief systems (van Dijk 1987). One need not look very far to see manifestations of this in education. Cummins explains educational ideology as *coercive relations of power*, which are realized through overtly biased educational structures such as (1) English submersion programs for bilingual students that actively suppress their first language and cultural identity; (2) exclusion of culturally diverse parents from participation in their children's schooling; (3) tracking or streaming practices that place subordinated groups of students disproportionately in lower-level tracks; (4) use of biased standardized tests for both achievement monitoring and special education placement; (5) teacher education programs that prepare teachers for a mythical monolingual monocultural white middle-class student population; and (6) curriculum content that reflects the perspectives and experiences of dominant groups and excludes those of subordinated groups (Cummins 1999b).

> Since 1997, three states have passed anti–bilingual education laws that prohibit schools from utilizing a language other than English for instruction. In California (1997), Arizona (2000), and Massachusetts (2001), millionaire Ron Unz successfully bankrolled an "English for the Children" campaign and convinced voters to limit options for the language minority population. According to his program, after one year of an English immersion class, students are mainstreamed into regular classes without further instruction in their native tongue. To exacerbate the situation, the laws hold teachers personally liable for speaking only English. (Crawford 2004)

Even though alternative forms of bilingual education (two-way, early exit, late exit, ESL) have proven culturally and linguistically beneficial to language minority students (Krashen 1998; Crawford 1999), teachers in California, Arizona, and Massachusetts are legally fettered to the guidelines of a law that was politically and financially propagated by the dominant class (Crawford 1999). Whereas the research literature supporting bilingual education is quite extensive, opponents easily convinced the public of its alleged disabilities by exaggerating the few published failures of bilingual methodologies (Crawford 1999). The irony in this battle of ideologies is that the "research" supporting the English-Only campaign in many cases actually provides evidence of the success of bilingual education (Cummins 1999a). Regardless of what the research purports, politicians in these states have cajoled voters into passing anti–bilingual education legislation in order to disenfranchise the linguistic minority.

Critics contend that current federal education policy also reflects apathy toward nurturing the native language skills of non-English speakers. In 2002, Title VII (the Bilingual Education Act) was eliminated by the Bush administration as part of the new No Child Left Behind education reform. Under No Child Left Behind, Title III outlines the federal language policy for immigrant students (U.S. Department of Education 2000). While the new Title III will continue to support the education of language minority students, it places more emphasis on rapid English acquisition, accountability of schools on standardized assessment, stronger state control of resources, less focus on the development of native language skills, and funding for program development based on "scientifically based research." What is considered "scientific research," however, can easily be misconstrued to justify allocation of funds or policy implementation, as in California, Arizona, and Massachusetts.

According to the U.S. Department of Education (2000), the number of limited English proficient children attending American schools has grown dramatically, primarily because of immigration. State education agencies reported that limited

English enrollment rose from 2.1 million in the 1990–1991 academic year to more than 3.7 million in 1999–2000. A congressionally mandated study found that these students receive lower grades, are judged by their teachers to have lower academic abilities, and score below their classmates on standardized tests of reading and math. While standardized assessments might be efficient for large-scale comparison purposes, more than test scores need to be investigated to support serious accusations like these.

Although often framed in the context of linguistic difficulties, the challenges facing language minority students also stem from a cultural gap experienced in the classroom. Surrounded by students that have had up to 12 years of academic and social enculturation, a non-English-speaking student may feel lost or confused while processing even basic school traditions (such as taking roll, tardiness, and lunch procedures). As argued by Cummins (1999a), "socio-cultural determinants of minority students' school failure are more fundamental than linguistic factors." Such practices, and teachers' exercise of authority, may so demean students' self-concept that they withdraw from the educational environment, thereby appearing unmotivated or "lazy."

Immersed within a hierarchy based on linguistic prowess, language minority children, then, are often torn between the dominant language and their mother tongue. Described by Cummins (1999a) as having *bicultural ambivalence*, they may simultaneously feel aggression toward the dominant culture and shame toward their own. Policies that openly reject a student's native language, then, both invalidate and demean students' cultural background and contribute to delaying their academic advancement.

These attitudes often intensify when students are placed into academic classes with lower expectations. Lower-track and retained students are likely to experience learning environments that carry a stigma, further undermining their self-concept as learners. Such classes may be less stimulating and less likely to provide opportunities to develop higher-order thinking and problem-solving skills (Montgomery and Rossi 1994). Building upon or acknowledging the presence of the cultural knowledge that students bring to the classroom, on the other hand, can mitigate frustration and encourage success.

An effective education is achieved through a combination of social, political, pedagogical, and cultural determinants. Even though immigrant students experience many of these factors differently than their American classmates, the language issue continues to be the most scrutinized. Ignoring other aspects of the education process can have deleterious effects. Considering some of the basic trends in dropout rates further illuminates this problem. The attrition rate for foreign-born Hispanic students (ages 16–24), a stifling 44.2 percent (U.S. Department of Education 2000), demands a more holistic approach to immigrant education. Basing public instruction on valid research and observable results, rather than rhetoric, is essential for fully enfranchising the immigrant students who are so predominant and critical for the country's future. *See also*: **Bilingual education; Bilingualism.**

References

Crawford, Jim. 1992. *Hold Your Tongue: Bilingualism and the Politics of "English Only."* Los Angeles: Bilingual Education Services.

————. 1999. *Bilingual Education: History, Politics, Theory and Practice*. Trenton, NJ: Crane.

Cummins, Jim. 1999a. Rights and Responsibilities of Educators of Bilingual-Bicultural Children. http://www.iteachilearn.com/cummins/rightsresponsbilinged.html.

————. 1999b. Rossell and Baker: Their Case for the Effectiveness of Bilingual Education. http://www.iteachilearn.com/cummins/rossellbaker.html.

————. 2004. *Educating English Learners: Language Diversity in the Classroom*, 5th ed. Los Angeles: Bilingual Education Services.

Krashen, Stephen D. 1998. *Under Attack: The Case Against Bilingual Education*. Culver City, CA: Language Education Associates.

Montgomery, Alesia F., and Robert J. Rossi. 1994. Education Reforms and Students at Risk: A Review of the Current State of the Art. American Institutes for Research, http://www.ed.gov/pubs/EdReformStudies/EdReforms/chap1a.html.

Nieto, Sonia. 2004. *Affirming Diversity: The Sociopolitical Context of Multicultural Education*, 4th ed. New York: Longman.

Olson, Laurie. 1997. *Made in America: Immigrant Students in Our Public Schools*. New York: The New Press.

Rodríguez, Tomás D. 2002. Oppositional Culture and Academic Performance among Children of Immigrants in the USA. *Race, Ethnicity and Education* 5(2):199–215.

Rong, Xue Lan, and Judith Preissle. 1998. *Educating Immigrant Students: What We Need to Know to Meet the Challenges*. Thousand Oaks, CA: Corwin Press.

Trueba, Enrique T., and Lilia I. Bartolomé. 2000. *Immigrant Voices: In Search of Educational Equity*. Lanham, MD: Rowman and Littlefield.

U.S. Department of Education. National Center for Education Statistics. 2000. http://nces.ed.gov.

Van Dijk, Teun A. 1987. *Communicating Racism: Ethnic Prejudice in Thought and Talk*. Newbury Park, CA: Sage.

————. 2000. *Discourse as Social Interaction*. London: Sage.

ERIC JOHNSON

IMMIGRATION SYSTEM. The context of law and practice comes from diverse and energetic people, both immigrants and established populations, who use or violate the law to their own ends. Four broad categories of people figure in U.S. immigration law and its enforcement: citizens, who have largely unlimited rights to move about, settle, and work, as well as to participate in politics; permanent residents (legal immigrants), who lack political rights and can be deported, but who otherwise have rights of mobility, residence, and work similar to citizens; temporarily visiting non-immigrants of various sorts (tourists, students, international business people, contract workers, etc.); and persons violating the borders, literal and figurative, of these categories, who are often called undocumented or illegal aliens. The immigration system is best understood as an attempt, in the face of social complexity, to regulate the categorization among and transition between these statuses.

Naturalization, the transition to citizenship, exhibits the interplay of law and society especially well. People who have been legal immigrants for at least five years can petition the U.S. Citizenship and Immigration Services (USCIS), formerly the Immigration and Naturalization Service (INS), to naturalize. Their record may be reviewed for deportability and they have to pass a test in English on U.S. history and government. The USCIS has about a year's backlog of naturalization petitions. One cause of the delay is chronic underfunding of this benefit-awarding role of government, because it does not involve law enforcement at borders. Another cause is the USCIS political mandate to scrutinize naturalization applicants for fraud and criminal records. Although transition to citizenship is cherished in the United States, there is also a politically influential fear of outsiders illicitly gaining this hallowed insider status—a typical paradox of American immigration attitudes. Nor are the barriers to naturalization only a matter of government inaction. The choice to change identity in law and self is a profound personal choice toward which immigrants do not move easily. However, the 1996 Illegal Immigrant Responsibility and Immigration Reform Act (IIRIRA) and welfare reform laws threatened legal residents with facile deportation and loss of social security and food stamps, causing a rapid increase in applications for naturalization. Thus, understanding the bureaucratic and legal process of naturalization requires attention to a wide range of social and political variables, both among existing citizens and among immigrants, a lesson that applies generally.

Before people naturalize, they must legally immigrate. They do this at the rate of 800,000 to 1 million per year, an addition of approximately a third of a percent to the U.S. population. U.S. law presents three main paths to immigrant visas, along with some odd short-cuts. The largest set of visas, roughly 600,000 per year, are reserved for close relatives by blood and marriage of U.S. citizens and legal residents, the family or kinship preferences. They are graded by relative speed of entry and number of visas, so that spouses of citizens can get immigrant visas quite rapidly—by bureaucratic standards—while adult siblings of citizens face delays of many years waiting for their visas.

Just as family visas paradoxically serve economic roles, employment and skill visas, explicitly devised for U.S. economic benefit, also support extensive family migration. Like the kinship preferences, employment visas present a daunting set of legal rules. Under some categories, sheer educational accomplishment or comparable distinction justifies an immigrant visa, while in other categories (e.g., software engineers and computer technicians), the U.S. Department of Labor has to certify a lack of domestic workers at the prevailing wage rate. Because there are in some cases significant numbers of domestic workers with the same skills and preparation, the allocation of visas indicates the triumph of employer over labor definitions of national interests and needs. In all these instances, however, if a permanent immigrant visa is awarded, additional visas are allocated for family members, who make up the majority of the nearly 200,000 visas annually.

The third, and smallest, of the three main categories of legal immigrants are refugee visas and adjudicated asylum cases resulting in visas. Refugees are people the U.S. government commits to shelter from well-founded fear of persecution in another country, while asylees arrive unwanted, even actively interdicted by arms of the U.S. government like the Border Patrol or the Coast Guard. If asylees run that gauntlet, they may also gain temporary shelter from an immigration court. Initially, refugees and asylees are temporary residents, but with time some are permitted to adjust their status to legal permanent immigrant. This, of course, depends on whether the situation in their homeland has changed or continues to present a well-founded fear to them. Geopolitical considerations often operate within the formal laws and judicial rulings governing refuge. Weighing State Department recommendations and advocacy group lobbying against anxiety about immigrant "waves," Congress sets an annual number of visas for refugees (70,000 is a recent figure) that in no way matches global numbers of refugees or their geographic distribution. Likewise, the ratings of nations according to the degree of persecution, the categorization of kinds of persecution, and the application of asylum rulings to the details of people's stories demonstrably follows the vagaries of U.S. foreign policy, favoring the victims of enemies and neglecting the victims of friends.

In awarding immigrant visas, the U.S. government has a stated policy of treating each nation of origin equitably. Certain visas are not subject to per nation limits, such as spouses of citizens, but for most family preferences each nationality has the same potential number of visas allocated to it. The intent is to avoid racist quotas or bans on certain nations of origin. The reality, however, is that some nations send many more legal immigrants than others, though U.S. immigration is so diverse that one encounters visas—and hence immigrant communities—for almost every nation. To understand this, one must keep in mind that an immigrant does not apply for a visa, but rather a petitioner already legally in the United States—say, a citizen mother or the Motorola corporation— asks the USCIS for a visa for the intended immigrant. The family preference system requires the petitioner to be a close family member, which reinforces movements from nations where many have legally come before, such as Mexico. On the other hand, employers using the job or skill visas target nations such as India that produce significant numbers of educated and eager technical specialists.

Non-immigrant visas may not appear to relate in any way to the immigration system, and indeed, millions of visitors—tourists, cross-border shoppers, traveling performers, and so forth—come and go without migrating in a social sense. However, non-immigrant visa holders slip into many migration situations. This is sometimes envisioned in law, as when non-immigrant fiancées become immigrated spouses. In other cases, non-immigrant visas are a first step toward incorporation in the new society, say, when an engineering student graduates and her employer petitions for her. Because these non-immigrants are already in the United States, they obtain their immigrant visa through an adjustment of status; in recent years over half of the new permanent immigrants adjusted their status, indicating the importance of this immigration path. Other non-immigrant statuses allow de facto long-term residence in U.S. society, such as foreign traders and managers or religious figures. Finally, temporary labor visas (the "H" visas) include agricultural laborers, certain seasonal unskilled employees, and skilled technical employees in occupations where debatably domestic workers are scarce.

Illegal or undocumented immigration is entrance, residence, or work in the United States outside these visa and citizenship categories. Although undocumented immigration is outside the legal system in formal terms, there is in reality extensive institutionalized support for undocumented immigration from people situated inside the legal framework, including employers large and small, landlords, charitable groups, and legal immigrant friends and relatives. There are two basic forms of illegal migration: entering without being inspected, the stereotypical crossing of border fences and wading of rivers, and entry on a legal nonimmigrant visa whose terms are then violated by not leaving upon the expiration of the visa. People generally assume that "illegal aliens" are Latin American border crossers, but recent research indicates that over half of all undocumented U.S. residents have overstayed temporary visas, and as such are much more diverse in national origins than just Mexican border entrants. The estimated annual increment of settled undocumented residents is approximately 500,000 per year, roughly half of legal immigrant numbers and only a small fraction of the overall U.S. population.

Undocumented immigrants may be prevented from entering or may be removed from the United States, but so may legal non-immigrants and even legal "permanent" immigrants. The legal action halting entry is "exclusion" and that of removal is "deportation." Obviously, entering without inspection or without a proper visa or overstaying a visa can result in exclusion or deportation, if detected by the U.S. government. Employment of unauthorized aliens is illegal according to the Immigration Reform and Control Act of 1986, but its sporadic enforcement mainly results in migrant deportations and rarely in employer penalties. Exclusion and deportation grounds represent a map of the moral anxieties of the U.S. polity, which views foreigners as a potential danger to national security and has a bias toward prosecuting minor criminals over influential and established ones.

Most arrests for deportations (exclusions are much rarer) take place at or near the U.S.-Mexico border, at a rate of over a million a year. The vast majority of arrests do not enter the legal process of deportation, but instead are short-circuited by the arrestee voluntarily departing the United States. Many interior arrests also end in voluntary departure. Formal deportations have been increasing, however, and now total over 100,000 annually. Deportation has significant punitive effects, since it removes the right to future legal entry (visiting or immigrating) for at least seven years, sometimes longer. Likewise, being caught as an unauthorized immigrant is enough to result in loss of future rights to legal immigration even without formal conviction. Deportation falls under "administrative law," meaning that immigrants do not have a right to counsel (it must be purchased or volunteered), trials are not by jury, proof involves preponderance of evidence rather than going beyond reasonable doubt, prosecutorial conduct is less constrained, and appeals are more so.

The USCIS is the principal but not exclusive arm of the government in immigration affairs. Also in Homeland Security, the Border Patrol and Customs and Border Protection agencies control entry, while Immigration and Customs Enforcement investigates immigration violations and enforces deportation orders within the United States. The Department of State, via its consulates, issues non-immigrant visas and officially issues immigrant visas overseas after the petition is approved by the USCIS. The Department of Labor certifies skills or education, the shortage of labor, and prevailing wage rates for occupational visas and temporary labor non-immigrant visas. Deportation and exclusion proceedings, asylum proceedings, and appeals of USCIS decisions enter the immigration courts and can be appealed to the Bureau of Immigration Appeals, which are internal to the Department of Justice, rather than forming an independent judiciary. In very limited circumstances, federal courts review immigration cases.

A typical problem, within the formalized process, is the loss of essential records, bringing proceedings to a grinding halt in immigration court. This fumbling is a result of the low status accorded to the immigration process and immigrants by the U.S. government, which results in scarce resources, excessive workloads, failed reforms, and discouraged workers. It is compounded by a subtle but pervasive mandate to view immigrants suspiciously, on the grounds that they might maneuver their way into possession of a jealously guarded good, U.S. residence and citizenship. At the same time, many specific interests and broad attitudes in the United States favor immigration (both legal and unauthorized), meaning that bureaucrats also seek to avoid offending powerful legislators and lobbying groups, and more generally need to facilitate a huge volume of transit in and out of the nation. The result is spotty and clumsy immigration regulation, reflecting the ambivalence about immigration in U.S. society as a whole. *See also*: **Border control; Expedited entry and removal; Family reunification; Legislation; Migration processes; National security; Unauthorized immigration.**

References

Aleinikoff, T. Alexander, David A. Martin, and Hiroshi Motomura. 1998. *Immigration and Citizenship: Process and Policy*. St. Paul, MN: West.

Chavez, Leo R. 2001. *Covering Immigration: Popular Images and the Politics of the Nation*. Berkeley: University of California Press.

Fix, Michael, and Jeffrey S. Passel. 1994. *Immigration and Immigrants: Setting the Record Straight*. Washington, DC: Urban Institute.

Haines, David W., and Karen E. Rosenblum, eds. 1999. *Illegal Immigration in America: A Reference Handbook*. Westport, CT: Greenwood Press.

Heyman, Josiah McC. 1995. Putting Power into the Anthropology of Bureaucracy: The Immigration and Naturalization Service at the Mexico-United States Border. *Current Anthropology* 36(2):261–287.

———. 1998. *Finding a Moral Heart for U.S. Immigration Policy: An Anthropological Perspective*. Washington, DC: American Anthropological Association.

———. 2000. Class and Classification on the U.S.-Mexico Border. *Human Organization* 60(2):128–140.

Magaña, Lisa L. 2003. *Straddling the Border: Immigration Policy and the INS*. Austin: University of Texas.

Massey, Douglas S., Jorge Durand, and Nolan J. Malone. 2002. *Beyond Smoke and Mirrors: Mexican Immigration in an Era of Economic Integration*. New York: Russell Sage Foundation.

U.S. General Accounting Office. 1991. *Immigration Management: Strong Leadership and Management Reforms Needed to Address Serious Problems*. Washington, DC: Government Printing Office.

JOSIAH McC. HEYMAN

INFORMAL ECONOMY. The informal sector is a major and yet poorly understood part of contemporary American economic experience. Estimates of its magnitude have ranged widely, from less than 5 percent to greater than 25 percent of the total U.S. economy, with similar discrepancies in assessments of total revenues that are generated from the varied forms of informal economic ventures. Due to its nature as involving production and exchange of goods and services outside government regulation and lacking formal boundaries and organizations, it is also next to impossible to determine how many people are involved. What we do know is that a large majority of those involved are immigrants and unauthorized entrants to the country, whose lack of work permits or proper identification may preclude them from seeking employment through usual channels.

The informal economy spans a wide number of industries. Construction, apparel, footwear, furniture-making, in-home retail sales, and electronics assembly are six industries that have been specifically cited as entailing a considerable amount of informal activity (Sassen 1988). With activities in so many different sectors, it has proven difficult to even define the term "informal economy." Instead, studies have focused on the main criteria that tend to accompany work and jobs performed "off the books."

To begin with, a distinction is usually be drawn between legal and illegal activities. Some scholars distinguish the informal economy as comprising legal activities occurring outside regulations or institutional frameworks, from the underground economy as constituting all income not measured by official figures, including clearly illegal activities (Valenzuela 2001). For example, food, clothing, and childcare services are legal commodities, but may be produced through unregulated or informal means. Thus, these activities are not automatically illegal, but may not adhere to regulations or labor laws. This is in contrast to the overtly illegal activities and criminal activities of some underground sectors, such as the drug trade, gambling, or prostitution (Butcher and Piehl 1998).

A second key characteristic of the informal economy is the use of cash as a medium of payment. This focus on cash payments is tied to the extralegal nature of the informal economy. This often relates to efforts by employers or workers to avoid paying taxes. But cash also permits work by those who may otherwise have difficulty securing employment, such as immigrants who lack work authorization. Transactions may be "under the table," or even take the form of exchange or barter, with services performed in exchange for a future return. These informal structures often evolve in the closely knit communities of immigrants or low-income workers, with persons offering one kind of skill or services in exchange for different work.

A final common characteristic of the informal sector is its capacity for worker abuse. In addition to the societal stigma associated with informal work, there are few labor rights or legal protections for informal workers. Because of the lack of governing institutions or regulations, informal markets are often rife with abuses. Individuals may be forced to work without the minimal level of protection offered by the legal system, and political mobilization of workers through unions is restricted. Such is the case for the growing phenomenon of subcontracting (Ciscel et al. 2003). Informal workers often also face long hours, sub-minimum wages, unpaid overtime, and hazardous working conditions. For this reason, the informal economy has been classified as a new form of worker exploitation (Raijman and Tienda 2000).

At the same time, there are those who defend the informal economy for its role in providing opportunities for employment to marginalized portions of society. These groups, including both documented and undocumented immigrants, might not have access to the formal sector and would otherwise be unable to find any employment at all (Ferman et al. 1987). For them, the informal sector may provide the only chance to earn a living and support a family.

Two of the more visible kinds of informal sector workers are street vendors and day laborers. Vendors can be seen in many major U.S. cities, selling everything from candy to batteries to various fruits and vegetables at traffic intersections or door-to-door. Thousands of vendors are estimated to be working in the Los Angeles area alone. Vendors, who earn between $10 and $50 on a good day, face hundreds of dollars in fines and possible jail time if targeted by the police. Many come from countries where street vending is an accepted part of the local economy (Austin 1994). Others turn to street vending as a last means of survival after finding themselves unable to secure other work. Despite the low overhead, street vendors face a number of obstacles and hazards, including police crackdowns, customers who renege on payment or pay with counterfeit currency, and theft of goods. Furthermore, many are dependent on a patron, either a boss or subcontractor, for their supply of goods and for transportation, often having to split their earnings accordingly.

Immigrants also predominate in day labor, as they have throughout American history. Day labor is often difficult, irregular, and even dangerous (Valenzuela 2001, 2003). Laborers are sometimes refused pay by employers or receive less than the agreed-upon amount; some have been dropped off in remote areas without transportation, or threatened with exposure to the authorities if they complain about work conditions or remuneration. The first systematic study of day laborers in the United States, drawing on a national survey of 2,660 day laborers, shows the enormous breadth of such work, the tremendous potential for rights violations, and rising community tensions based largely on misperceptions (Valenzuela et al. 2006). Many, for example, move on to more secure work as opportunities arise. Debate about day labor is often contentious, as seen in the controversy that arises about whether to set up specific hiring locations, with an informal agreement with authorities to forgo prosecution of the laborers in order to help prevent traffic accidents and control the spread of temporary workers (Tambini and Sandoval 2004). These issues have provoked communities from Long Island to Los Angeles, with some angry voices claiming that day laborers steal jobs from American workers.

Informal sectors also rely heavily on social networks for their activities and workers. Immigrants are hypothesized to reproduce in the host society forms of economic activity that were common in their countries of origin. These include informal activities, which account for a high proportion of the economics in third world countries. Furthermore, people can be recruited into informal self-employment through providing products and services to family, friends, and neighbors in ethnic residential communities (Raijman and Tienda 2000:48). Tightly knit communities, such as immigrant enclaves, use informal ties to marshal resources and provide employment in response to family or community needs. These exchange networks become a potential source of economic support in case of hard times, and can be called upon to provide employment in times of need. Recent arrivals to the United States are usually given their first job through such social networks, often in the informal sector. For immigrants for whom social connections or other methods have failed to secure a job, the informal sector becomes an essential source of temporary employment, and a possible springboard into longer-term or formal work.

Finally, there is a strong link between informal activities and gender, with various types of informal activities remaining almost exclusively the domain of one gender or the other. Childcare and housecleaning, for example, are considered "women's work," and account for a large percentage of the informal occupation for women. Some studies suggest that women are more likely to work in the informal sector because it allows them to work around their prior responsibilities of household and children. Informal employment, through additional domestic tasks of cleaning, laundry services, or childcare, allows women to supplement family income (Fernández-Kelly and Garcia 1989).

The informal sector, including both street vendors and day laborers, thus represents a form of self-employment as immigrants carve out their own economic niche in an environment of scarce opportunities (Kelly 1990; Jossart et al. 1999). These forms of work serve as a crucial employment and wage-earning strategy for immigrants, many of whom are both underemployed in the formal sector and poor relative to the population as a whole. Informal work also promotes training in new fields, resulting in entrepreneurial activity and even business creation. In the aggregate, of course, informal work cumulates tremendous income, albeit mostly unreported, into the economy and society. However, informal work can also open the door for violations and fraud, as reported in garment sweatshops and garment homework, for example (Kwong 1998; Light et al. 1999; Bonacich and Appelbaum 2000).

From the unlicensed taxi cab driver in New York, to the producer of black market clothing goods, to the housekeeper in a wealthy household, there are many faces of the informal economy. Despite the social stigma and possibility of abuse, the informal sector remains a possibility for employment for those who would otherwise have no hope, and thus will remain a major source of income, employment, and support for immigrants across the nation. *See also*: **Crime; Effects of unauthorized immigration; Gender; Social networks.**

References

Aponte, R. 1997. Informal Work in the U.S.: Case Studies and a Working Typology. *International Journal of Sociology and Social Policy* 17:18–36.

Austin, Regina. 1994. An Honest Living: Street Vendors, Municipal Regulation, and the Black Public Sphere. *Yale Law Journal* 103:2119–2131.

Bonacich, Edna, and Richard P. Appelbaum. 2000. *Behind the Label: Inequality in the Los Angeles Apparel Industry*. Berkeley: University of California Press.

Butcher, Kristin F., and Ann Morrison Piehl. 1998. Recent Immigrants: Unexpected Implications for Crime and Incarceration. *Industrial and Labor Relations Review* 51(4):654–679.

Ciscel, David H., Barbara Ellen Smith, and Marcela Mendoza. 2003. Ghosts in the Global Machine: New Immigrants and the Redefinition of Work. *Journal of Economic Issues* 37:333–341.

Cross, J. 1998. The Informal Sector. In *Encyclopedia of Political Economy*. Philip Anthony O'Hara, ed. London: Routledge.

Ferman, L., S. Henry, and M. Hoyman. 1987. Issues and Prospects for the Study of Informal Economies: Concepts, Research Strategies, and Policy. *Annals of the American Academy of Political Science* 493:154–172.

Fernández-Kelly, M. Patricia, and Anna M. Garcia. 1989. Informalization in the Core: Hispanic Women, Homework and the Advanced Capitalist State. In *The Informal Economy*. Alejandro Portes, Manuel Castells, and Lauren Benton, eds. Pp. 216–227. Baltimore, MD: Johns Hopkins University Press.

Gaughan, J., and L. Fermand. 1987. Toward an Understanding of the Informal Economy. *Annals of the American Academy of Political and Social Sciences* 493:15–25.

Gerber, J. 1999. Measuring the Informal Economic Sector. San Diego Dialogue Report. *Cross Border Economic Bulletin* 3(1):5–6.

Jossart, Pascale M., Enrico A. Marcelli, and Manuel Pastor Jr. 1999. Estimating Effects of Informal Economic Activity: Evidence from Los Angeles County. *Journal of Economic Issues* 33:579–607.

Kelly, Bruce. 1990. El Mosco: It Means Day Labor, and, Increasingly, All the Controversies and Conflicts That Surround Latin American Immigration in Southern California. *Los Angeles Times Magazine*, March 18.

Kwong, Peter. 1998. *Forbidden Workers: Illegal Chinese Immigrants and American Labor*. New York: New Press.

Light, Ivan, Richard B. Bernard, and Rebecca Kim. 1999. Immigrant Incorporation in the Garment Industry of Los Angeles. *International Migration Review* 33(1):5–25.

Raijman, R., and M. Tienda. 2000. Training Function of Ethnic Economies: Mexican Entrepreneurs in Chicago. *Sociological Perspectives* 43(3):439–456.

Sassen, Saskia. 1988. *The Mobility of Labor and Capital: A Study in International Investment and Labor Flow*. New York: Cambridge University Press.

Tambini, Catherine, and Carlos Sandoval, Directors. 2004. *Farmingville*. Amagansett, NY: Camino Bluff Productions.

U.S. Department of Labor. 1992. The Underground Economy in the United States. Washington, DC: U.S. Government Printing Office. Occasional Paper Series on the Informal Sector, Occasional Paper No. 2.

Valenzuela, Abel, Jr. 2001. Day Laborers as Entrepreneurs? *Journal of Ethnic and Migration Studies* 27(2):335–352.

———. 2003. Day-Labor Work. *Annual Review of Sociology* 29(1):307–333.

Valenzuela, Abel, Jr., Nik Theodore, Edwin Melendez, and Ana Luz Gonzales. 2006. On the Corner: Day Laborers in the United States. Working Papers. Center for the Study of Urban Poverty. Los Angeles: University of California.

Wiles, P. 1987. The Second Economy: Its Definitional Problems. In *The Unofficial Economy: Consequences and Perspectives in Different Economic Systems*. Alessandri Sergio and Bruno Dallago, eds. Pp. 21–33. London: Gower.

JAMES LOUCKY AND JAIME LOUCKY

INTERETHNIC RELATIONS. An ethnic group is defined as "individuals who consider themselves or are considered by others, to share the common characteristics which differentiate them from the other collectivities in a society, within which they develop distinct cultural behavior" (Lehman 1994:157). Ethnicity can but does not always include race as a distinct characteristic. It would be useful to consider geographic location, national origin, language, foods, and cultural traditions in understanding what constitutes an ethnic group. According to Max Weber's classic definition, an ethnic group is one whose members "entertain a subjective belief in their common descent because of similarities of physical type or of customs or both, or because of memories of colonization and migration" (Alba 2000:841).

Interethnic contact has been stormy and tumultuous throughout the history of the United States. Early destruction of Native American cultures by the arrival of waves of European immigrants was followed by the importation of African slaves who helped to build the emerging nation's strong economy. Cheap labor was also supplied by Chinese and poor from Europe. Interethnic conflicts usually result when ethnic groups are played against each other for the purpose of economic exploitation. In the past, the melting pot theory was generally considered as the most appropriate way of becoming an American. Recently, there is recognition of a multicultural or pluralist society, where diversity is both embraced and encouraged. However, the struggle for equality along ethnic and racial lines remains an ongoing challenge for the United States.

Interethnic conflict may be defined as "disputes between contending groups who identify themselves primarily on the basis of ethnic criteria and who make group claims to resources on the basis of their collective rights" (Henderson 1999:751). Interethnic relationships often begin with conflict, which may or may not lead to violence, followed by cooperative relationships between primarily non-white ethnic groups. Settings are often urban. While much recent attention has been devoted to the study of conflict in the social science literature, it appears that cooperation merits much of the discussion of interethnic relations in the United States. Perhaps this is because violent disputes occur on a greatly reduced scale when compared to other parts of the world, such as in Rwanda or the former Yugoslavia or East Timor. Examples of conflict in the United States are mainly due to the result of sudden influx of a new ethnic group combined with adverse economic circumstances affecting the established group.

The passage of the Immigration and Nationality Act of 1965 opened the door to Asian immigrants, and this new wave of Asian immigrants included Filipinos, Chinese, Koreans, Indians, and refugees from Southeast Asia. U.S. residents have sometimes experienced tensions with newcomers, perhaps most notably friction between African Americans and Korean shop owners. Due to language, educational, and licensing barriers and discrimination in the labor market, many Koreans chose to be self-employed shop owners in the retail trade. Koreans comprise about 30 percent of small business owners in urban centers like New York, Los Angeles, and Atlanta (Perry 2000:308). Blacks' hostility toward Asian shop owners continued to grow in major cities. Incidents included the fire-bombings of Korean businesses in the black neighborhoods of Washington, D.C. Korean shop owners were shot and killed in robbery attempts and hate **crimes** committed against Asian Americans (Perry 2000:309) and the boycotts of Korean stores became endemic. The tension reached a boiling point with the outbreak of the Los Angeles riots of 1992, following the Rodney King verdict, when rioters targeted, looted, and burned Korean-owned businesses in South Central Los Angeles and elsewhere in Los Angeles. Although many African American, white, and Chinese-owned businesses did not escape the same fate, Korean businesses suffered the most damage.

Using a case study of the Los Angeles riots, it becomes apparent that several factors explain the conflict between African Americans and Asian Americans. Demographic change occurred in both the number and composition of Los Angeles. Asian and Latino populations increased markedly between 1980 and 1990. One outcome of the Immigration Act of 1965 was significant growth of the Korean population, which increased by 140 percent between 1980 and 1990 as the population rose from 60,618 to 145,421 persons (Umemoto 1994:97). At the same time, African American population decreased. As a result, the characteristics of many African American communities were changed drastically. These non-white ethnic groups compete for limited jobs, housing, political powers, and government services. Ethnic groups also misunderstood each other and often accepted the stereotypes of other groups. "Asians see African Americans as criminals, as welfare cheats, as threats in their economic and physical well being.

African Americans see Asians as 'perpetual foreigners,' as unsavory business men" (Perry 2000:308). Korean shop owners are seen as forcing the black business owners out of the neighborhood and as being unwilling to hire blacks. In reality, Koreans have assumed "the role of commercial 'middle-men' between corporations reluctant to locate in the inner city, and their low-income, non-white clientele" (Perry 2000:308). In addition, the model minority image of Asian Americans contributed to the creation of anti-Asian sentiment.

High unemployment and poverty rates continued to increase in black communities. High unemployment was due to plant closings, industrial firms relocating to the third world, and inability to find new jobs in the field of high technology or in advanced services, as well as downgraded manufacturing and services sectors. For example, over 70,000 heavy manufacturing jobs were lost during the 1970s due to plant closings. Furthermore, over 200 Los Angles–based firms, including Hughes Aircraft, Northrop, Rockwell, and a number of smaller firms, have relocated their production facilities in Mexican border towns, primarily in Tijuana, Tecate, and Ensenada (Johnson and Oliver 1989:451). In addition, the media focus on interethnic tensions instead of interethnic reconciliation, and the highly publicized police brutality led to an escalation of tensions.

Some of the key issues behind black and Latino conflicts are illustrated by Miami. Its diverse Hispanic population includes Cuban Americans, Puerto Ricans, and other Latinos such as Nicaraguans, Colombians, Venezuelans, Dominicans, and Brazilians. Cuban Americans are the most dominant group. They have had open conflicts with African Americans ever since Cuban migration started growing dramatically in 1959 due to Fidel Castro's revolution. First came approximately 3,000 supporters of the deposed dictator Fulgencio Bastista following the victory of Fidel Castro, followed by Cubans who opposed Castro's socialist government. Between 1959 and 1962, about 250,000 Cubans fled Cuba. Between 1965 and 1973 almost 300,000 newcomers arrived. The Mariel Boat Lift of March–October 1980 brought another 125,000 Cuban refugees (Buffington 2000:475).

The clashes between blacks and Cubans were the result of the sizeable influx of refugees. Local blacks felt they had received disparate treatment because special classes were developed for Cuban children at a time when black children were still prohibited from attending integrated schools. Local blacks faced fierce competition with the newcomers over jobs, political power, housing, and government services. While the Civil Rights Movement opened up opportunities for blacks, the Cuban migration was seen to interfere with blacks' economic and political progress in Miami (Mohl 1990:40). The entrepreneurial success of Cubans created a sense of powerlessness in the black communities. Police violence against blacks supplied fuel for the conflict, which erupted in a number of riots in the 1980s. While these regions are the most visible examples of interethnic conflict, tensions have surfaced in other large cities.

While journalists and much of the academic literature on ethnic conflict give an opposite impression, peaceful and generally cooperative relations between ethnic groups are far more common than large-scale violence (Fearon and Latin 1996). The "Community Control Movement" in the Lower East Side of New York City in the early 1970s is an example of a political coalition comprised of various ethnic backgrounds. This political collaboration of Latino, black, and Asian parents sought the power to mold public school policies. As a result of the coalition, the city addressed the needs and well-being of ethnic minority children (Jennings 2002:15).

Another positive example of political collaboration between blacks and Latinos was the election in 1983 of Harold Washington as the first black mayor of Chicago. Washington envisioned that he could develop the downtown while maintaining the economic well-being in Chicago neighborhoods at the same time. His policies gained wide support from the same coalition which supported his election and reelection in 1987. Black and Latino leaders realized that they must cooperate in the electoral arena (Jennings 2002:15). Another politician, David Dinkins, the first black mayor of New York City, won his election in part due to the support of the Latino voters.

Many examples of effective community-oriented inter-minority coalitions and public policy coalitions, collaborative efforts between independent groups, and government-related agencies can be found in the Inter-Relations Collaborative report. For example, New York Civil Rights Coalition (NYCRC) is a multiracial coalition which includes 33 legal and advocacy organizations. The NYCRC was formed in 1986 in response to the "Howard Beach Incident." The incident occurred on December 20, 1986, in Howard Beach, New York. A small white mob brutally beat three black men who were stuck in a predominantly white neighborhood when their car broke down. One of the black men, Michael Griffith, was killed when he tried to escape the attackers and was hit by a car. The coalition speaks out against incidents of violence and promotes education and mutual understandings among ethnic minorities in the city. A civil rights curriculum was successfully introduced in the public schools by NYCRC. The Hoboken Tenants Union in New Jersey and Concerned Community Adults in New York City are other examples of community-oriented coalitions.

The Black-Korean Alliance (BKA) is a public-policy coalition, formed in 1985, in respond to a series of violent incidents in Los Angeles. Black and Korean businessmen, church representatives, and community activists all work together to encourage ongoing dialogue, community education, and cultural exchange between these two groups (Yun 1993:33).

Cooperation is the most powerful way to prevent interethnic conflicts from erupting into violence. The history and cultures of a wide variety of ethnic minority groups needs to be taught in schools. Mutual understanding and ongoing dialogue among the communities of color is important. Government leaders should be committed to banning discriminatory policies, providing economic and political opportunities for the ethnic minorities, and cultivating a multiethnic environment (Henderson 1999:763). As America's population becomes more racially, ethnically, and culturally diverse, pluralism is being embraced. Therefore, interethnic relations will continue to be an important area for research in the new century. *See also*: **Ethnicity; Political participation; Racism; Stereotypes.**

References

Alba, Richard D. 2000. Ethnicity. In *Encyclopedia of Sociology*. Edgar F. Borgatta and Rhonda J.V. Montgomery, eds. Pp. 575–584. New York: Bedminster.

Buffington, Sean. 2000. Cuban Americans. In *Gale Encyclopedia of Multicultural America*. Jeffrey Lehman, ed. Vol. 1. Detroit: Gale Group.

Fearon, James, D., and David D. Latin. 1996. Explaining Interethnic Cooperation. *American Political Science Review* 90(4):715–736.

Harris, Daryl. 1994. Generating Racial and Ethnic Conflict in Miami: Impact of American Foreign Policy and Domestic Racism. In *Blacks, Latinos, and Asians in Urban America: Status and Prospects for Politics and Activism*. James Jennings, ed. Pp. 79–94. Westport, CT: Praeger.

Henderson, Errol A. 1999. Ethnic Conflict and Cooperation. In *Encyclopedia of Violence, Peace, and Conflict*. Lester Kurtz and Jennifer Turpin, eds. Pp. 751–764. San Diego, CA: Academic Press.

Jennings, James. 2002. Political Coalitions between Communities of Color: The Glue of Social Justice. *SAGE Race Relations Abstracts* 27(1):7–20.

Jennings, Keith, and Clarence Lusane. 1994. The State and Future Black/Latino Relations in Washington, DC: A Bridge in Need of Repair. In *Blacks, Latinos, and Asians in Urban America: Status and Prospects for Politics and Activism*. James Jennings, ed. Pp. 57–78. Westport, CT: Praeger.

Johnson, James H., and Melvin L. Oliver. 1989. Interethnic Minority Conflict in Urban America: The Effects of Economic and Social Dislocations. *Urban Geography* 10(5):449–463.

Lehman, Jeffrey. 1994. Ethnicity, Ethnic Group. In *The Concise Oxford Dictionary of Sociology*. Gordon Marshall, ed. Pp. 157–158. Oxford: Oxford University Press.

Mohl, Raymond A. 1990. On the Edge: Blacks and Hispanics in Metropolitan Miami since 1959. *Florida Historical Quarterly* 69:37–56.

Perry, Barbara. 2000. Beyond Black and White: Ethnoviolence Between Oppressed Groups. *Sociology of Crime, Law and Deviance* 2:301–323.

Umemoto, Karen. 1994. Blacks and Koreans in Los Angeles: The Case of LaTasha Harlins and Soon Ja Du. In *Blacks, Latinos, and Asians in Urban America: Status and Prospects for Politics and Activism*. James Jennings, ed. Pp. 95–118. Westport, CT: Praeger.

———. 1996. Washington, D.C. In *The Latino Encyclopedia*. Richard Chabrán and Rafael Chabrán, eds. Pp. 1702–1703. New York: Marshall Cavendish.

Yun, Grace. 1993. *Intergroup Cooperation in Cities: African, Asian and Hispanic American Communities*. New York: Inter-Relations Collaborative.

CECILIA SIU-WAH POON

INTERNATIONAL ACCORDS. The United States is signatory to a number of international economic, humanitarian, and security agreements that have direct or indirect implications for immigration. While humanitarian accords have a long history, economic accords have gained the lion's share of attention in recent years.

In an era of economic integration, Free Trade Agreements (FTAs) have been debated vigorously with respect to immigration as well as labor rights and economic justice. FTAs liberalize the movement of investments, goods, services, and trade exchanges, but they also limit the movement of people. Essentially, new international trade policies echo the right for governments and investors to participate in markets regardless of location, in order to take advantage of the most profitable conditions, while the same rights to freely work and live without discrimination of placement are not legally allocated to individuals.

The U.S.-Canada Free Trade Agreement was the most comprehensive trade agreement between any two countries when signed into law in 1988. In addition to abolishing most tariffs and trade barriers, it recognized that the interdependent trade reliance between the partners in the world's biggest trade relationship should allow Canadian and U.S. non-immigrants reciprocal access and free movement across the border for making sales and investments. Immigration provisions entailed temporary entry of persons categorized as business visitors, traders and investors, intracompany transferees, and professionals (Thompson and Frankel 1989).

The North American Free Trade Agreement (NAFTA), the most notable FTA in U.S. history, was implemented as a free trade agreement between Canada, the United States, and Mexico in 1994, in the hopes that all three countries would experience an increase in economic growth and income levels. Indirectly, it was also an instrument designed to stem the flow of immigrants, principally from Mexico into the United States. With Mexico being the poorer economic partner, the United States hoped to strengthen the Mexican economy, and in turn increase jobs within Mexico, through the free flow of goods, services, investment, and access to labor markets, such that growth of in-country jobs would make migration to the United States less necessary. While the agreement included few explicit provisions regarding labor migration, then-President Salinas openly advocated its passage as an implement to decrease illegal Mexican immigration to the United States (Weinfeld 1995).

Trade policies like NAFTA, then, are an indirect approach to curb migration by encouraging capital flows to developing countries that send emigrants, which would theoretically both increase wages in the sending country and decrease the demand for unskilled labor in receiving countries. In reality, NAFTA seems to have added impetus to emigration from Mexico because of the great difference in income levels between the two nations. The shift of investment to Mexico by the United States increases the demand for high-skilled labor in both the United States and Mexico. Jobs that are considered low skilled in the United States may be viewed as high skilled as well as higher paying from a Mexican perspective, displacing even more workers in Mexico. Further, with the import of U.S.-subsidized produce such as corn, NAFTA has undermined much of Mexico's domestic agriculture, adding even more Mexican farm workers to the northward push for jobs. The youthfulness of Mexico's population and the relatively high rates of unemployment and underemployment also continue to motivate emigration to the United States, particularly as long as wages in Mexico continue to remain substantially less than wages paid in the United States for the same labor (Markusen and Zahniser 1999).

NAFTA does include immigrant-related provisions for business professionals and intracompany transferees. During the first decade of NAFTA (1994–2003), visas for Mexican professionals were limited to a total of 5,500 annually. Beginning in January 2004, Canadians and Mexicans were allowed an unlimited number of TN-visas (trade visas), now called Free Trade Nonimmigrant Visas (U.S. Citizenship and Immigration Services 2003). Treaty-NAFTA (TN) classification is available to individuals who qualify as members of one of more than 60 designated professions, from accountants to zoologists, who seek to engage in professional activities in the United States. Nonetheless, more restrictive interpretations of various TN professions along with new security concerns continue to affect both policy and practice.

NAFTA, then, has resulted in a dramatic increase in trade as well as professional connections and social relations, through business, tourism, and scientific and cultural exchanges, but it does not seem to have decreased the push and pull factors of migration. In 2000, an estimated 150,000 migrants entered the United States from Mexico without inspection, adding to the estimated 3 million Mexicans living in the United States without authorization, as people put into practice a demand for entry that is far more than the allotment of immigrant visas of only 20,000 per year (Massey et al. 2002). So while NAFTA was touted as a means to reduce incentives for migration, emigration from Mexico persists despite limited avenues for safe and legal entry and employment. Furthermore, the agreement is in place during a time of increasing militarization of the U.S.-Mexico border and de facto criminalization of immigration (Flynn 2002), whose consequences have often been tragic. Since the beginning of Operation Guardian, created in 1994 to limit the entry of illegal immigrants, at least 2,300 Mexican migrants have died trying to cross the border (Eschbach et al. 2001).

Trade agreements beyond North America also affect immigration. The General Agreement on Trade in Services (GATS), introduced in 1995 by the World Trade Organization, marked the beginning of visa regulations for foreign workers in global trade agreements. This treaty requires the United States to admit nonimmigrant specialty workers and intracompany transfer employees as part of international trade agreements. U.S. immigration laws reflect admittance for foreign workers under this treaty in the allotment of H-1B visas with a limit of 65,000 visas annually, with a limited stay of three years with a renewal for three additional years. An unlimited number of L-1 visas are also available and permit a stay of five to seven years.

Critics argue that trade agreements are not an appropriate way to modify immigration policy since they undermine the authority of Congress to amend policies if economic conditions change. GATS, for example, allows for foreign competition for diminishing numbers of professional jobs in the United States, even requiring some American workers to train their foreign replacements before being laid off. Similar controversy accompanies discussion of a Free Trade of the Americas Agreement (FTAA) among 34 nations in the Western Hemisphere. With immigration provisions limited to business professionals, government officials, and executive administrators, similar immigration impacts as in NAFTA may follow from the absence of legal provisions relating to the forced mobility of unskilled labor. If only workers with higher income levels and advanced academic degrees have the right to pursue employment across borders, then Latin American economies stand to lose both employees and viability to the forces of disequilibrium and displacement (Ponicki 2002).

Other new and projected trade accords are also expected to have cross-border immigration effects. The Central American Free Trade Agreement, modeled after NAFTA and raising similar controversy, may stimulate additional labor migration when its trade liberalization provisions are implemented. Immigration provisions for the Chile and Singapore Free Trade Agreements, which went into effect in January 2004, provide a model likely to be replicated. Non-immigrant (H-1B1) visas are available for professionals who, like holders of other Free Trade Nonimmigrant Visas, are persons involved with a "specialty occupation requiring theoretical and practical applications of a specialized body of knowledge." The individual must be able to prove the attainment of a postsecondary degree or equivalent and ceilings pertain; Chile initially gets 1,400 visas while Singapore receives 5,400.

With respect to humanitarian concerns, the United States has numerous international obligations. Key among these are protocols for the protection and processing of refugees. The United States is signatory to international provisions (known commonly as the Geneva Accords) which established the right to not be sent back to one's country if there is credible reason to fear persecution. Subsequent agreements held that deportation could involve a second country only if they offered "safe haven."

Rising concerns for the serious abuses associated with the trafficking of people across borders, and continued abuses and potential enslavement of unauthorized immigrants within the United States, have resulted in both Congressional and executive proclamations in recent years. Commitment to upholding the well-being of families involved in international migration is evident in accords that facilitate family reunification as well as adoption. More recently, and particularly in the aftermath of the tragedies of September 11, 2001, the United States has advocated for international accords aimed at reducing the threat of terrorism through immigration or settlement. Canada and Mexico have been pressured to tighten control of their own borders, airports, and seaports. Both countries have also been involved in discussions of whether and how to implement a North American perimeter, whereby potential terrorists would be identified and precluded from entry at travel points prior to departure for North American destinations.

As with international trade agreements, humanitarian accords have both direct and indirect implications for immigration. Underlying further development is a growing conundrum: how much demographic, economic, and multinational realities will be acknowledged by a global superpower that has so much to gain, or to lose, through international partnerships. *See also*: **Adoption; Enslavement; National security; Refugee law and policy; Rights.**

References

Eschbach, Karl, Jacqueline Hagan, and Nestor Rodriguez. 2001. *Causes and Trends in Migrant Deaths Along the U.S.-Mexico Border: 1985–1998*. Houston: University of Houston, Center for Immigration Research.

Flynn, Michael. 2002. Donde esta la Frontera? *Bulletin of Atomic Scientists* 8(4):24–36.

Global Exchange. 2004. Central American Free Trade Agreement. http://www.global exchange.org/campaigns/ftaa/cafta.

Markusen, James R., and Steven Zahniser. 1999. Liberalization and Incentives for Labor Migration: Theory with Applications to NAFTA. In *Migration: The Controversies and the Evidence*. K.F. Zimmerman, R. Faini, and I. De Melo, eds. Pp. 263–293. Cambridge: Cambridge University Press.

Massey, Douglas S., Jorge Durand, and Nolan J. Malone. 2002. *Beyond Smoke and Mirrors: Mexican Immigration in an Era of Economic Integration*. New York: Russell Sage.

Ponicki, Maureen Heffern. 2002. Linking the Free Trade Area of the Americas and Immigration. http://www.citizenstrade.org/pdf/ftaa_imm.pdf.

Thompson, Elizabeth, and Asher I. Frankel. 1989. *Immigration Guide to the United States–Canada Free Trade Agreement*. Washington, DC: American Immigration Lawyers Association.

U.S. Citizenship and Immigration Services. 2003. North American Free Trade Agreement between the Government of Canada, the Government of the United Mexican States, and the Government of the United States of America. http://www.sice.oas.org/trade/NAFTA/NAFTATCE.asp.

Weinfeld, Morton. 1995. North American Integration and the Issue of Immigration: Canadian Perspectives. In *NAFTA in Transition*. Stephen J. Randall and Herman W. Konrad, eds. Pp. 237–251. Calgary: University of Calgary Press.

JAMES LOUCKY AND LEE LAWRENCE

J

JUS SOLI. The Latin phrase *jus soli* (literally, the "right of land") refers to one of the ways of acquiring the citizenship of a country, by birth within its national territory. It is the most common way of obtaining U.S. citizenship: any child born in the United States, even to foreign parents, automatically becomes a U.S. citizen. There are two other ways by which U.S. citizenship can be obtained: *jus sanguinis* (the right of blood, i.e., birth to one or two citizen parents, even outside the national territory) and naturalization (Brubaker 1989).

Nonetheless, the United States is noteworthy for its exceptional reliance on unconditional jus soli: geography, or place of birth, is a sufficient criterion, so that citizenship is a right that is extended to children of temporary sojourners, visitors, and even illegal aliens. The only exceptions are children born on foreign ships or to foreign diplomats with an assignment within the United States and children born to enemies occupying the national territory in times of war.

Jus soli in the United States was inherited from the English legal tradition: that of the common law, according to which all persons born within the dominions of the Crown, whether of English or foreign parents, were English subjects, owing allegiance to the sovereign by the mere circumstances of their birth (Schuck and Smith 1985). Surprisingly, however, it took over a century to complete the U.S. laws of citizenship. The Constitution of 1787 gave no definition of federal citizenship. It was not until 1866 that Congress enacted a Civil Rights Act that for the first time formalized citizenship by birth inside the country. Two years later this principle was enshrined into the Constitution by the Fourteenth Amendment of 1868: "All persons born or naturalized in the United States, and subject to the jurisdiction thereof, are citizens of the United States and of the State wherein they reside." Although the amendment was clearly intended for the benefit of the emancipated slaves, it had a broader significance: a constitutional guarantee of unconditional birthright citizenship that has since then consistently been recognized by the courts.

Even when Congress decided that certain national or racial groups were ineligible for naturalization, their American-born children automatically became citizens. In the landmark *U.S. v. Wong Kim Ark* case of 1898, the Supreme Court ruled that a child born in San Francisco to Chinese immigrants was a U.S. citizen even though his parents could never acquire that status. For this ruling the Court reviewed the whole history of U.S. citizenship, confirming its common law origin, providing long and precise analyses of the Fourteenth Amendment and its legislative history, and discussing the incorporation of jus soli into the American jurisprudence. For nearly a century, this interpretation was unchallenged.

In the 1980s and 1990s, however, jus soli increasingly came under attack as a group of political leaders expressed serious doubts about its application to children of illegal immigrants. These critics—mostly anti-immigrant activists and Republican Congressional representatives from states with large immigrant populations such as California, Texas, and Florida—proposed to modify automatic birthright citizenship, through either federal legislation or a constitutional amendment, by excluding those children born in the United States but whose parents had entered illegally and had not regularized their status. Two phenomena played a determining role in the emergence of this reform movement: the rise in illegal immigration and the public awareness of it, and the development of the welfare state in the two preceding decades. In California, some began to worry that the undocumented population's use—and abuse—of public social services and benefits was imposing a heavy fiscal and social burden on certain states. In the media the image of hordes of heavily pregnant Mexican women, secretly crossing the border so as to give birth to American citizens entitled to American welfare in American clinics, began to take shape (Jost 1995). The issue gained prominence on the national agenda in the mid-1990s. Yet although numerous bills have been introduced in Congress to deny citizenship to U.S.-born children of illegal aliens—either by statute or a constitutional amendment—no action has been taken on any of them, since they ran too radically counter to the practice and accepted constitutional interpretation of unconditional jus soli (Daniel 2000).

The challenge to jus soli does raise significant questions in the enduring debate on membership in and definition of the national community, and therefore on the Americans' national identity. Should the national community be closed, or at least well circumscribed so as to prevent the "dilution" or devaluation of citizenship? Should the distinction between citizens and non-citizens be strengthened? In that case, where should the line be drawn between members and outsiders? From the point of view of political philosophy, what is at stake is the role of government. Is it or is it not part of its exclusive, sovereign powers to ascribe citizenship to those individuals it has selected, or should men and women have the right and liberty to choose their own citizenship? In fact, the issue of automatic birthright citizenship illustrates once more the tensions between the inclusive and exclusionary tendencies that have long characterized U.S. immigration policies. The "restrictive nationalism" (Schuck 1998:20) manifested by the opponents of automatic birthright citizenship is opposed to the American tradition of welcome and of citizenship as a universal natural right, not to be regulated by a government's whims (Jacobson 1996; Chavez 1997).

To be sure, some American lawyers and philosophers have pointed out the oddity of the attachment to jus soli in the United States: in this liberal democracy the main political tradition relies on the principle of the consent of the governed, and therefore conceives of the relationship between individuals and their government as a symbolic contract of mutual recognition. Yet jus soli leaves no room for consent, because of its automatic, not to say arbitrary, character. In this perspective, Schuck and Smith (1985) argued in favor of a more consensual form of U.S. citizenship. The essay triggered heavy criticism, based on the liberal argument that jus soli helps thwart any temptation of exclusion and restrictions the government might have toward aliens (Carens 1987; Martin 1995; Aleinikoff 1997).

Ultimately, beyond the intellectual reflection and the political controversy it has stirred, jus soli remains the rule in the United States and appears as one of the manifestations of the national tradition of open immigration. *See also*: **Citizenship; Unauthorized immigration.**

References

Aleinikoff, Alexander. 1997. The Tightening Circle of Membership. In *Immigrants Out! The New Nativism and the Anti-Immigrant Impulse in the United States*. Juan Perea, ed. Pp. 324–332. New York: New York University Press.

Brubaker, William Rogers. 1989. Citizenship and Naturalization Policy and Politics. In *Immigration and the Politics of Citizenship in Europe and North America*. William Brubaker, ed. Pp. 99–127. Lanham, MD: University Press of America.

Carens, Joseph H. 1987. Who Belongs? Theoretical and Legal Questions about Birthright Citizenship in the United States. *University of Toronto Law Journal* 37(4):413–443.

Chavez, Leo. 1997. Immigration Reform and Nativism: The Nationalist Response to the Transnationalist Challenge. In *Immigrants Out! The New Nativism and the Anti-Immigrant Impulse in the United States*. Juan Perea, ed. Pp. 61–77. New York: New York University Press.

Daniel, Dominique. 2000. Automatic Birthright Citizenship: Who Is an American? In *Federalism, Citizenship, Collective Identities in U.S. History*. Cornelius van Minnen, ed. Pp. 246–267. Amsterdam: VU University Press.

Jacobson, David. 1996. *Rights Across Borders: Immigration and the Decline of Citizenship*. Baltimore, MD: Johns Hopkins University Press.

Jost, Kenneth. 1995. Cracking Down on Immigration. *Congressional Quarterly Researcher* 103 (February).

Lacey, Mark. 1995. Move to Limit Citizenship Gains Support. *Los Angeles Times*, June 15, A1.

Martin, David A. 1994. The Civic Republican Ideal for Citizenship and Our Common Life. *Virginia Journal of International Law* 35(4):301–320.

Schuck, Peter. 1998. *Citizens, Strangers, and In-Betweens: Essays on Immigration and Citizenship*. Boulder, CO: Westview Press.

Schuck, Peter, and Rogers Smith. 1985. *Citizenship Without Consent: Illegal Aliens in the American Polity*. New Haven, CT: Yale University Press.

Verhovek, Sam Howe. 1994. Texas and California: Two Views of Illegal Aliens. *New York Times*, June 26, A12.

DOMINIQUE DANIEL

L

LABOR ORGANIZATION AND ACTIVISM. The U.S. labor movement has experienced drastic changes throughout the history of the United States. The level of political tolerance to labor unions and pro-labor legislation can be traced by patterns of global and national economies. Economic shifts today are felt throughout the world as the global economy has come to play the dominant role within most national economies. The organization of labor within the United States is responding to these economic transitions, and must also adjust to the repercussions that the global market economy has had on the lives and roles of immigrants within the U.S. workforce.

Since the mid-1960s the American workplace has witnessed the concomitant phenomenon of large influxes of immigrant laborers and at the same time the decline in numbers and power once attributed to American organized labor. Related to this process has been the continued debate that immigrant labor has had a debilitating affect on union propagation and organizing while others would contend that immigrant labor has brought a new vitality and revitalization to the American workplace as well as labor organization. Regardless of the view projected toward immigrant laborers, diverse social and environmental conditions faced by workers in the latter part of the twentieth century have spawned new and innovative strategies and coalitions that often transcend national identity and race (Park 2004). In large response to this a number of labor unions presently have adopted strategies that transcend national boundaries and forge cross-national strategic alliances.

Background of U.S. Labor Positions

Traditionally, organized labor in the United States has viewed immigrant laborers as a cheap and manipulated workforce that threatened the economic and political power of native workers. More often than not the most prominent labor unions employed exclusionary and racist policies and restrictions that lasted well into the 1960s and beyond (Almaguer 1994). In contrast to this, immigrant workers in many instances became the backbone and driving forces within the

American labor movements of the nineteenth and twentieth centuries that brought about the enactment of fairer, more humane working conditions and living wages.

The early U.S. immigrants, particularly the German, English, and Irish, integrated the socialist and labor union activist parts of their European heritage within the new country. The industrial and working-class atmosphere in the United States at that time encouraged labor rights movements. As most immigrants, until the mid to late 1800s, came with labor activist sentiments and did not threaten the heavy influence of U.S. labor unions on the national economy, there was minimal discussion of limiting immigration. Beginning in the mid-1800s labor organizations began to take on exclusionist attitudes against the newly arriving Chinese, and later Japanese, immigrants. Hate crimes and racist policies were especially prevalent in California and other West Coast states (Daniels 2002).

In the twentieth century, the Immigration Act of 1965 heralded the rise of a new immigrant workforce while the power of organized labor was starting to decline. According to Milkman (2000), the rate of unionization in the private sector declined from 30 percent to 9 percent from 1960 to 2000. During this same period, the numbers of newly arrived immigrants rose dramatically. Between 1960 and 2001, over 24 million immigrated to the United States, with the greatest number of immigrants arriving from Asia, Mexico, and Central America. The state of California received the largest number of immigrants, helping to transform the size of the workforce within a 30-year period (1970–2000) from 6 million to 13.5 million workers and transforming the California economy as a result. During this same period the number of Latino workers grew over 500 percent while the number of Asian American workers grew over 800 percent. By 2000, 30 percent of the California workforce consisted of Latino and Asian immigrant workers (Lopez and Feliciano 2000).

Globalization

The decades since World War II saw advances in U.S. economic integration within the global economy. As more businesses looked to invest outside U.S. borders, international institutions, such as the International Monetary Fund (IMF), the World Bank, and the World Trade Organization (WTO), have sought to promote global trade through international agreements and deregulation of trade barriers.

The impact of greater economic integration, or globalization, can be felt by U.S. laborers today. Many firms, such as in the manufacturing sectors, are relocating outside the United States where production costs are lower. Simultaneously, the U.S. economy is experiencing a transition from jobs previously concentrated in production to those centered in retail trade, business, and consumer services. This deindustrialization process has resulted in an expansion of the upper and lower tiers of occupations, along with a reduction of the middle class. With more people working in higher-paid jobs, more demands are made for services supplied by the lower-class tier. Many of these jobs exist within the informal economy, where they escape regulations on wages and working conditions normally applied to similar occupations. As laws protecting labor rights are more easily dismissed in the light of global economic competition, workers find it increasingly difficult to organize (Ness and Unger 2001).

Current Challenges to U.S. Immigrant Labor Organization

The struggles immigrant workers face in achieving a safe and secure workplace are acute. A history of union intolerance of immigrant workers, a changing U.S. economy, and immigration enforcement have all shaped the immigrant experience in the U.S. workforce.

National unions have a history of exclusion based on race and incompatibility with immigrant workers. Unions, having faced large influxes of immigrants willing to work for low wages, long hours, in unsafe conditions, and without union representation, have traditionally advocated for immigrant exclusion from the United States. In 1986, the American Federation of Labor–Congress of Industrial Organizations (AFL-CIO) pronounced support for the Immigration Reform and Control Act (IRCA) that included an employer-sanctions provision that enabled, for the first time, employers to be punished for hiring undocumented immigrants. IRCA generated fear among immigrants and employers alike and increased likelihood of discrimination against people of color, both foreign and native-born. On the other hand, cessation of illegal immigration, the provision's initial intention, has not occurred to any notable degree (Daniels 2004).

With the legal immigration of almost 10 million people in the 1990s (surpassing the former peak of 8.8 million immigrants in the first decade of the twentieth century), immigrants are now considered the future for labor unions (Macias 2001). In October of 1999, the AFL-CIO rescinded its earlier support of IRCA. In a vote to recommend repeal of the employer-sanctions provision, the AFL-CIO declared the provision a barrier to immigrant membership with unions. This vote is significant in that it highlights the changing attitude of unions, especially national ones, concerning immigration at the turn of the twentieth century.

Aside from adaptations that unions are undertaking to accommodate greater immigrant populations, changes in the U.S. economy require unions to shift their traditional presence within manufacturing sectors to the growing private and service sectors. New immigrants, especially, may be crowded into easily exploitable private-sector occupations that are more resistant to unionization. Since the 1990s, private contractors and subcontractors have been increasingly employing people, and especially immigrants, in small or medium-sized facilities dispersed throughout cities, causing a separation between the workplace and the ethnic community. This weakens workers' ability to band together and organize (Ness and Unger 2001).

The Immigration and Naturalization Service (INS) has had a very strong presence in the lives of immigrant workers and those organizing for labor rights. While the INS (U.S. Citizenship and Immigration Services, or USCIS, since March 1, 2003) has decreased the number of raids (arrests for deportation went from 22,000 in 1997 to 8,600 in 1999), their connection with the U.S. workforce remains strong (Ness and Unger 2001). The USCIS is currently focusing on dissolving the main motivation for illegal immigration: work, based on a new mantra that available work breeds undocumented immigration (Bacon 2000). The new strategy of "interior enforcement" includes such tactics as more vigilantly checking workers' I-9 (work authorization) forms.

Immigrant Presence in the U.S. Labor Movement

Despite numerous barriers, immigrants have played an incredibly important part in the U.S. labor movement. The commonly held belief that immigrants are more difficult to organize than native workers is a disempowering and often incorrect view. In fact, some survey evidence suggests that foreign-born workers have more favorable attitudes toward labor unions than many native-born workers (Milkman 2002). There are credible reasons for this. Many recent immigrants, such as many from Central America, have had a positive union experience in their home country and often arrive in the United States with a history of union leadership. The intricate ethnic communities in which many immigrants live also provide fertile ground for organizing. Close ties and shared living and financial and occupational resources appease the effort needed to recruit members. Finally, the harsh atmosphere in which immigrants enter the labor market encourages union involvement. Crowded into specific occupations, and excluded from alternative community labor or legal resources, immigrants are left with few options but a union (Forester 2004).

There have been numerous actions taken by immigrant workers to ensure their rights as U.S. laborers. Many have centered in large cities that serve as ports of entry for immigrants, notably Los Angeles, New York, and Miami. As early as 1906, Japanese immigrant workers had created a whole network of independent trade unions and small business associations with enough power to set prices and wages with mainstream native unions (Lowenberg 2000). A more recent successful drive, initiated in 1990, was the Justice for Janitors campaign in Los Angeles. In Washington State, there was a successful strike in 1999 of a meatpacking plant, where 90 percent of the workers were foreign-born. That same year, in Kannapolis, North Carolina, there was a union victory at the Fieldcrest Cannon textile plant; the union had tried repeatedly over 20 years to organize the workers, but succeeded only with the increasing numbers of union-supportive immigrant workers (Milkman 2002).

Immigrants have led strikes and organizing drives as carpenters, harbor truckers, garment workers, factory hands, and tortilla delivery drivers in the absence of labor law protection and local union support. Nationally, unions see immigrants as the base for rebuilding the labor movement, especially in industries such as meatpacking, food processing, and residential construction where union presence has been eroded (Bacon 2000). Yet this appraisal of immigrant worker organization is still relatively shallow among local unions throughout the nation, and immigrant and non-immigrant workers alike face many challenges in their effort to transform traditional labor unions.

Challenges and Direction for Labor Organization

A number of factors have affected the willingness of unions to incorporate immigrants as members and as leaders. These include the structure of unions, how readily they respond to changes in the labor force, their leadership and ideology, and internal organizational practices.

The structure of unions heavily influences how they are run and who is included. Most U.S. unions can be divided into two categories, based on mission and internal structure. Unions traditionally founded on exclusion, such as building trade unions that follow "craft union conservatism," generally believe that immigrants or minorities would jeopardize union stability (Nissen 2002a, 2002b) and consequently have put forth little effort to recruit immigrant members. A second class of unions comprises those that have survived by keeping admission open. These include most industrial unions, particularly apparel and hotel unions. They have generally been more progressive in ensuring representation of immigrant workers within the union. The Union of Needletrades, Industrial, and Textile Employees (UNITE), for example, has been a national leader in reaching out to immigrant workers, by creating support for a diversity of cultures and celebrations, devoting time and money to broader issues that concern members, adapting to changing economic pressures that affect job location, and keeping a consistent vision of having representational leadership (Nissen and Grenier 2001).

Another factor that influences union receptiveness to immigrants is how quickly unions can respond to changes in the labor force or employer characteristics. As unions experience decline in industries that were traditionally unionized as well as decreasing membership, they have responded in several ways. One route is to organize an industry outside the traditional union jurisdiction. Such "organize or die" sentiment can be related to loss of traditional membership, requiring effort to organize the new workforce of immigrant workers, or risk economic collapse. Unions may also turn to building better connections within a particular ethnic group rather than an industry, seeing value in developing a relationship of trust among members rather than focusing on a specific industry. UNITE, originally a garment industry union, now also organizes workers in the service sector, while the Hotel Employees and Restaurant Employees (HERE) union has expanded beyond lodging and eating establishments to also represent workers employed in other service sector jobs (Nissen and Grenier 2001). Larger unions, on the other hand, may not face sufficient pressure to lead to outreach or union transformation; some are at times structurally inflexible and may also harbor nativist sentiments (Ness and Unger 2001).

Union leadership may play a significant role in responding to immigrant workers. After a leadership change in 1995, the AFL-CIO initiated the "New Voice" team that has made organizing the unorganized its top priority. In 2000, the AFL-CIO confirmed support for amnesty of 6 million undocumented workers. National and regional leaders of unions of other sectors have also reached out to immigrant workers by holding constant cultural, community, religious, and similar activities within the workplace (Nissen 2002a, 2002b).

Internal organizational practices generally foretell how well a union is accommodating immigrant workers. This can be seen in the special programs, cultural events, and educational campaigns sponsored by some unions in an effort to make immigrant workers truly welcome (Nissen 2002a, 2002b).

Success in recruiting today's changing labor force has also been possible by acting strategically, not defensively, when accommodating immigrants within the union. Educational campaigns that reach the majority of the members can relay the importance of immigrant workers to the labor movement. Having leaders who are committed to cultural and ethnic diversity, representational leadership, and structural flexibility also allow unions to respond to members. Adopting bottom-up strategies to incorporate immigrants into leadership positions reaches out to more people, while intercultural interaction enables the union membership to experience broader issues affecting fellow workers and those in other occupations.

Continued Efforts Toward Activism and Organization

Harsh conditions still exist for many immigrant workers within the United States. The concepts of the sweatshop and work houses long eulogized as passing stages of the nineteenth and early twentieth centuries still can be encountered in communities where immigrants are forced to pay off smuggling debts, debt obligations, and rent for substandard housing, while facing in many cases the possibilities of physical and emotional abuse (Kwong 2002). Newspapers across the country have heralded the vast and complex human smuggling rings and their American accomplices that have operated with near impunity from Latin America, Asia, and Eastern Europe, often with the sole purpose of smuggling and exploiting immigrants for their labor and commodification within the American workplace.

Despite their legal status, more and more workers are uniting to address the injustices and inequities that confront them. Cross-national and cross-racial unionization efforts in cities such as Los Angeles, New York, and Miami are fusing together garment workers, hotel workers, and other service laborers in efforts to demand livable wages and humane working conditions (Nissen and Grenier 2001; Kwong 2002; Park 2004).

A historic event occurred at the 2005 50th anniversary of the AFL-CIO in Chicago when dissident unions decided to boycott the convention. Two unions, Service Employees International Union and the Teamsters, quit the federation while Unite Here and the United Food and Commercial Workers announced that they were delaying their decision. These four unions, together with the Laborers Union and the United Farm Workers, formed the "Change to Win" coalition (Fournier 2005). One of the factors causing the split is that the dissident unions want to prioritize increasing union membership by organizing more service industry workers, many of whom are women as well as immigrants and ethnic minorities. How this division will affect the future of the labor movement is difficult to predict. The continued vibrancy of America's immigrant communities and the strong work ethic that permeates them will likely provide a continued stronghold for collective action and unity when addressing social injustices within the American workforce. *See also*: **Human smuggling; Informal economy; Unauthorized immigration.**

References

Almaguer, Tomas. 1994. *Racial Fault Lines: The Historical Origins of White Supremacy in California*. Berkeley: University of California Press.

Bacon, David. 2000. Immigrant Workers Ask Labor "Which Side Are You On?" *Working USA* 3(5):7.

Cuoto, Richard. 2001. Leadership, Activism and Public Life: Lessons from Community Health as Social Justice. *Journal of Family and Community Health* 23:1–17.

Daniels, Roger. 2002. *Coming to America: A History of Immigration and Ethnicity in American Life*, 2nd ed. New York: Perennial Press.

———. 2004. *Guarding the Golden Door: American Immigration Policy and Immigrants Since 1882*. New York: Hill and Wang.

Foley, Michael. 2001. Religious Institutions as Agents for Civic Incorporation: A Preliminary Report on Research on Religion and New Immigrants. Working Paper No. 2 presented at the American Political Association Annual Meeting, August 30, 2001, San Francisco.

Forester, Amy. 2004. Race Identity and Belonging: "Blackness" and the Struggle for Solidarity in a Multiethnic Labor Union. *Social Problems* 51:386–409.

Fournier, Ron. 2005. Teamsters Are Part of Historic Defection at the AFL-CIO. *The Record*, July 25, A1.

Kwong, Peter. 2002. Forbidden Workers and the U.S. Labor Movement: Fuzhounese in New York City. *Critical Asian Studies* 34:69–88.

Lopez, David, and Cynthia Feliciano. 2000. Who Does What? California's Emerging Plural Labor Force. In *Organizing Immigrants: The Challenge for Unions in Contemporary California*. Ruth Milkman, ed. Pp. 25–28. Ithaca, NY: Cornell University Press.

Lowenberg, Cathy Malia. 2000. Still a Community of Laborers. *International Examiner*, Seattle, WA, 27(5):11.

Macias, Tom. 2001. Impact of Immigration on the American Economy. In *Encyclopedia of American Immigration*. James Ciment, ed. Pp. 591–596. Armonk, NY: M.E. Sharpe.

Milkman, Ruth. 2000. Introduction. In *Organizing Immigrants: The Challenge for Unions in Contemporary California*. Ruth Milkman, ed. Pp. 1–24. Ithaca, NY: Cornell University Press.

———. 2002. New Workers, New Labor and the New Los Angeles. In *Unions in a Globalized Environment*. Bruce Nissen, ed. Pp. 103–129. Armonk, NY: M.E. Sharpe.

Ness, Immanuel, and Nech Unger. 2001. Unions and Union Organizing. In *Encyclopedia of American Immigration*. James Ciment, ed. Pp. 686–692. Armonk, NY: M.E. Sharpe.

Nissen, Bruce, ed. 2002a. *Unions in a Globalized Environment: Changing Borders, Organizational Boundaries, and Social Roles*. Armonk, NY: M.E. Sharpe.

———. 2002b. Unions and Immigrants in South Florida. In *Unions in a Globalized Environment*. Bruce Nissen, ed. Pp. 130–162. Armonk, NY: M.E. Sharpe.

Nissen, Bruce, and Guillermo Grenier. 2001. Union Responses to Mass Immigration: The Case of Miami, USA. *Antipode* 33:567–592.

Park, Edward J.W. 2004. Labor Organizing beyond Race and Nation: The Los Angeles Hilton Case. *International Journal of Sociology and Social Policy* 24(7–8):137–152.

LARRY J. ESTRADA

LEGALIZATION. Legalization refers to the process of granting legal status to immigrants residing in the United States without legal documents. The Immigration Reform and Control Act of 1986 (IRCA) allowed for the legalization or "amnesty" of undocumented residents with a rationale of reducing the undocumented population without deportation; integrating them into federal, state, and local tax systems; and improving wages and working conditions for legalized and resident aliens or citizen employees by eliminating a category of people subject to employer exploitation due to lack of papers.

Legalization of undocumented workers under IRCA was, at best, a "cautious welcome" (Baker 1990) because of restrictions on proof for qualification. IRCA contained provisions for legalization of two major categories of undocumented individuals. The largest group comprised those who could establish that they had resided in the United States prior to the cut-off date of January 1, 1982, a five-year residency requirement. A second group, designated Special Agricultural Workers (SAWs), was composed of undocumented individuals who could show that they had worked in U.S. agriculture for 90 days or longer in the one-year period ending May 1, 1986, a comparatively easy hurdle.

IRCA was implemented in two phases: phase one involved the application process, while phase two required that individuals meet an English language and civics requirement through taking an exam or attending 40 hours of classes. The Immigration and Naturalization Service (INS) was selected to implement legalization even though they were ordinarily involved in deportation that could frighten away potential applicants. "Qualified Designated Entities," such as church and social service agencies, also enrolled amnesty applicants and became involved in immigrant advocacy (Berardi 1990; Hagan and Baker 1993). Ultimately, approximately 1.6 million were legalized under pre-1982 provisions and over 1 million as a part of the SAW program (U.S. Department of Labor 1996). IRCA was designed to limit fraudulent applications. In fact, it appears that there was a low rate of fraudulent application and that both categories of individuals under-applied despite eligibility (Donato and Carter 1999). The goal of reducing the undocumented population was temporarily met, but continued illegal immigration allowed a new, unregistered group to form. In 1995, the size of the undocumented population in the United States, estimated at 5.1 million, was certainly greater today than in 1986, when IRCA was passed, and individuals without papers were thought to number 3 to 5 million (Passel 1999). About 8.5 million undocumented immigrants lived in the United States in 2000, according to the best available evidence from estimates that draw largely on data from Census 2000. Reducing the undocumented population through legalization has not, therefore, significantly worked to control unauthorized workers.

Amnesty requirements and the process through which individuals illegally entered produced lop-sided national, gender, and age distributions of amnesty and SAW recipients (Arp 1990; Baker 1997). Surveys of applicants and recipients, compiled into administrative files known as the Legalization Application Processing System (LAPS), show that 69 percent of pre-1982 and 81 percent of SAW legalized aliens had emigrated from Mexico, with 15 percent from Central America (U.S. Department of Labor 1996). Males constituted 56 percent of legalized applicants, while 44 percent were female. Those attaining legal status also tended to be young: 31 percent were 17 years old or younger upon arrival, 38 percent aged 18–24 years, 21 percent 25–34 years, and only 10 percent 35 years or older. The criteria for amnesty were clearly tilted toward admitting Mexican undocumented workers, as individuals entering without inspection (EWIs) were clearly eligible while those overstaying visas had greater difficulty obtaining legalization (Baker 1997).

One of the reasons for "gender skewing," or a disproportionate sex ratio, is that the SAW program favored temporary male migrants (Arp 1990; Warner and Snowden 1998). IRCA was based on the assumption that most undocumented Mexicans in the United States were male workers who either were single or had economically dependent wives in Mexico (Mattingly 1997). Rules for determining amnesty eligibility facilitated incorporation of immigrant men but made it hard for immigrant women, working or not, to prove residency. Men were more likely to have such proof of residence as rent and utility receipts and could get employer verification more easily than many women who tended to work in less visible positions. Domestic workers, for example, were often isolated in private households and less likely to be connected to immigrant social networks familiar with the legalization process (Hagan 1994). Economically dependent wives and undocumented women who headed households were also disadvantaged by the rule permitting rejection of applications of those likely to become a public charge. In addition, undocumented women who had received Aid for Dependent Children were barred from applying (Chang 1994).

IRCA is thought to be the cause of the skewed population estimate for undocumented individuals in the 1990 census (Passel 1999). Forty-three percent of those undocumented were male, indicating that males were in a better position to legalize than females, who became a majority of those without papers. Because of gendered assumptions built into IRCA, issues of family reunification were by and large overlooked by the legislators who drafted it as well. These issues were at least partially addressed by later family reunification legislation (U.S. Department of Labor 1996). Amnesty recipients were concentrated in three states: California (58 percent), Texas (13 percent), and New York (7 percent) (U.S. Department of Labor 1996).

As of 1992, the legalized adult population also appeared to be less educated than the general U.S. population. Lower levels of education presented a constraint on social mobility for the newly legalized population (Baker 1997). While legalizing aliens were expected to meet an English language and civics requirement, this did not seem to have substantial impact on legalized individuals' English-speaking capabilities, since the goal was not to achieve functional competency in English. Nonetheless, about half of legalized aliens have since supplemented English ability through additional training (U.S. Department of Labor 1996). Although English language skills in the legalized population varied widely, lack of English proficiency remained an obstacle for social mobility for some amnesty recipients during the initial years of legalization (Chiswick and Miller 1998). Blue collar work, especially production and service jobs, predominated among legalizing Mexican immigrants (Borjas and Tienda 1993), while there was a wider spread across categories among European legalizing individuals. Africans tended to be at the top or bottom of the occupational hierarchy, while one-half of Asians held white-collar jobs.

Social mobility, however, occurred within a very limited range of traditional immigrant occupations: food preparers, farm workers, groundskeepers, janitors, miscellaneous machine operators, construction laborers, textile machine operators, non-construction laborers, cooks, handlers and helpers, assemblers, hand packers, other metal machine operators, vehicle washers, construction painters, punch press operators, other construction trades, freight handlers, auto mechanics, welders, and solderers (Kossoudji and Cobb-Clark 1996). Some changes of employment within these occupations occurred, and pre-legalization mobility occurred mainly into skilled work such as carpenter, production supervisor, shipping clerk, and brick mason jobs. Change that occurs within such a limited range of occupations suggests "occupational churning" (Kossoudji and Cobb-Clark 1996), with job changes not representing assimilation per se, but pre-legalization efforts to seek improved position within the unauthorized job market. Workers tried to exit jobs with a higher probability of apprehension or a high wage penalty for lacking documents. In this unauthorized market, U.S. labor market experience, education, and even English language proficiency did not predict occupational mobility, suggesting that the unauthorized labor market did not operate according to conventional criteria associated with worker mobility.

Legalization does appear to have positively impacted wage rates, although wages for legalized immigrants still tend to remain lower than those for other U.S. workers. As legalizing workers and SAWs found higher paying employment, wages for undocumented workers declined and working conditions worsened due to employer discrimination and the sudden increase in the supply of legal workers. Research on pre- and post-IRCA wages indicates that the integration of the legalized population into the labor market resulted in the development of a sizeable wage penalty for undocumented immigrants, estimated at 22 percent (Phillips and Massey 1999). Downward pressure on wages in agriculture, which has become predominately an undocumented employer after departure of the SAWs, was estimated at 33 percent.

Increased employer ability to exploit undocumented workers, especially those hired through subcontractors without having protective social ties, continues. Post-IRCA employers may be less likely to hire "foreign-looking" workers, which suggests that IRCA's sanctions against employers hiring undocumented workers have impacted the entire population, including legalized immigrants (Lowell et al. 1995).

Legalized women immigrants' wages are not clearly related to English proficiency, labor market experience, and other human capital variables before or after legalization (Cobb-Clark and Kossoudji 1999). The exception is English proficiency, which is associated with small wage increases after amnesty. One factor that may explain wage stability among legalizing women is their concentration in traditional immigrant jobs after amnesty, which have been associated with lower wages. Mobility for these women, then, is similar to the "occupational churning" of legalized men. In other words, amnesty did not appear to further development of human capital or labor market mobility among legalized immigrant women.

Legalization proposes to integrate undocumented workers into the tax and social security systems of the United States. This goal does not reflect the reality that amnesty recipients previously had payroll deductions and the challenge to access these accounts, even in cases where workers had been in industries that primarily employed illegal workers. Legalization has succeeded in diminishing many workers' vulnerability to exploitation as more skilled workers in better jobs became legal and as those acquiring skills began an exodus from agriculture, domestic service, and other low-wage employment. Unskilled workers with limited English language proficiency, however, have largely remained in lower-paying work.

Legalization has been an important tool to integrate an undocumented population of workers into U.S. society. The chief incentives for amnesty applicants, however, proved to include international travel authorization and the ability to apply for legal admission of relatives, not just work authorization (Baker 1997). Thus, legalization has actually functioned to strengthen ties to families in sending countries. Those who are legalized also became aware of their rights as workers and permanent legal residents (Baker 1997). Legalization works to promote permanent settlement of amnesty applicants and their spouses and children.

Fostering continued immigration for family reunification is an unexpected by-product of legalization which will continue to influence and strengthen immigrant communities in the United States in the foreseeable future. *See also*: **Family reunification; Gender; Legislation; Social mobility; Unauthorized immigration.**

References

Arp, William, III. 1990. Immigration Reform and Control Act of 1986: Differential Impacts on Women? *Social Justice* 17:23–39.

Baker, Susan Gonzalez. 1990. *The Cautious Welcome: The Legalization Programs of the 1986 Immigration Reform and Control Act*. Washington, DC: Urban Institute.

———. 1997. The Amnesty Aftermath: Current Policy Issues Stemming from the Legalization Programs of the 1986 Immigration Reform and Control Act. *International Migration Review* 31(1):5–27.

Berardi, Gayle. 1990. The Role of Church Amnesty Assistance Programs in the Implementation of the 1986 Immigration Reform and Control Act. *Journal of Borderland Studies* 4(2):59–69.

Borjas, George J., and Marta Tienda. 1993. The Employment and Wages of Legalized Immigrants. *International Migration Review* 27(4):712–747.

Chang, Grace. 1994. Undocumented Latinas: The New "Employable Mothers." In *Mothering: Ideology, Experience and Agency*. Evelyn Nakano Glenn, Grace Chang, and Linda Rennie Forcey, eds. Pp. 259–285. New York: Routledge.

Chiswick, Barry R., and Paul W. Miller. 1998. Language Skills Definition: A Study of Legalized Aliens. *International Migration Review* 32(4):877–900.

Cobb-Clark, Deborah, and Sherrie A. Kossoudji. 1999. Did Legalization Matter for Women? Amnesty and the Wage Determinants of Formerly Unauthorized Latina Workers. *Gender Issues* 17(4):3–14.

Donato, Katherine, and Rebecca S. Carter. 1999. Mexico and U.S. Policy on Illegal Immigration: A Fifty-Year Retrospective. In *Illegal Immigration in America: A Reference Handbook*. David W. Haines and Karen E. Rosenblum, eds. Pp. 112–129. Westport, CT: Greenwood Press.

Hagan, Jacqueline Maria. 1994. *Deciding to Be Legal: A Maya Community in Houston*. Philadelphia: Temple University Press.

Hagan, Jacqueline Maria, and Susan Gonzalez Baker. 1993. Implementing the U.S. Legalization Program: The Influence of Immigrant Communities and Local Agencies on Immigration Policy Reform. *International Migration Review* 27(3):513–536.

Kossoudji, Sherrie A., and Deborah A. Cobb-Clark. 1996. Finding Good Opportunities within Unauthorized Markets: U.S. Occupational Mobility for Male Latino Workers. *International Migration Review* 30(4):901–924.

Lowell, B. Lindsay, Jay Teachman, and Zhongren Jing. 1995. Unintended Consequences of Immigration and Hispanic Employment. *Demography* 32(4):617–628.

Martin, Philip S. 1999. Unauthorized Workers in U.S. Agriculture: Old versus New Migrations. In *Illegal Immigration in America: A Reference Handbook*. David W. Haines and Karen E. Rosenblum, eds. Pp. 133–156. Westport, CT: Greenwood Press.

Mattingly, Doreen J. 1997. "Working Men" and "Dependent Wives": Gender, "Race," and the Regulation of Migration from Mexico. In *Women Transforming Politics: An Alternative Reader*. Cathy J. Cohen, Kathleen B. Jones, and Joan C. Tronto, eds. Pp. 47–61. New York: New York University Press.

Passel, Jeffrey S. 1999. Undocumented Immigration to the United States: Numbers, Trends and Characteristics. In *Illegal Immigration in America: A Reference Handbook*. David W. Haines and Karen E. Rosenblum, eds. Pp. 27–111. Westport, CT: Greenwood Press.

Phillips, Julie A., and Douglas S. Massey. 1999. The New Labor Market: Immigrants and Wages after IRCA. *Demography* 36(2):233–246.

U.S. Department of Labor. 1996. *Characteristics and Labor Market Behavior of the Legalized Population Five Years after Legalization*. Washington, DC: U.S. Government Printing Office.

Warner, Judith Ann, and Lynne Snowden. 1998. Gender Skewing and Migration: U.S. Immigration Policy's Impact on the International Reproduction of Unskilled Labor. Paper presented at the annual meeting of the American Sociological Association, San Francisco.

JUDITH WARNER

LEGISLATION. Immigration law has traditionally been defined as "the policies of the federal government toward the admission of foreigners who intended to become permanent residents of the United States" (Lee 2001:118). Usually this referred specifically to congressional legislation; however, many scholars would include judicial cases and administrative decisions affecting admission or deportation of aliens as well as local, state, and federal policy that affect eligibility for social services.

Immigration was regulated by state governments until 1875, although naturalization was controlled by the federal government since the Naturalization Act of 1790, which provided that "free white persons" who resided in the United States for at least two years could become naturalized citizens. The first legislation that regulated and restricted immigration was the Page Law of 1875, which forbade entry of "Chinese, Japanese and other Asian laborers brought to the United States involuntarily and women brought for the purpose of prostitution" (Lee 2001:118).

The United States has been and continues to be fundamentally a country of immigrant and immigrant descendant populations. However, recent immigration policy and legislation have failed to safeguard the rights of particular immigrant groups. American perspectives and conversely legislation have changed considerably over the past few decades. Presently, there is a marked focus both in the political arena and in public discourse on the "crisis" caused by illegal immigration from Central and South America, and especially from Mexico, to the United States. The U.S. government estimates that over 200,000 Mexican immigrants entered the United States in 2001 alone, and that following 1996 half of the undocumented population or more than 2.7 million immigrants were from Mexico. Census 2000 figures indicate that 30 percent of all foreign-born people in the United States are from Mexico, making this population the largest group of immigrants, both legal and illegal, in the country (Daniels 2004).

The bulk of recent American legislation that has been enacted to control immigration patterns has largely been projected toward maintaining the integrity of the U.S.-Mexico border. As a result, American policymakers in the 1990s and into the twenty-first century, addressing immigration issues, have been almost singularly focused in their efforts to control immigration principally from Latin America. Legislative measures enacted and proposed during this period have largely sought to strengthen border security, expand human resources involved with border surveillance, levy employer sanctions, and increase infrastructure designed to impede border trafficking (Aleinikoff et al. 2003a).

Overview of U.S. Immigration Policy and Legislation

Mexican immigration into the United States during the late 1800s and early 1900s was relatively unrestricted and fed into the economic boom-and-bust cycle along the U.S.-Mexico border. After the adoption of the Chinese Exclusion Act of 1882, American employers in the Southwest and parts of the Midwest began to recruit increased numbers of Mexican laborers to lay rails and harvest America's crops. The legislation passed during this period reflected a pronounced preference for Mexican immigrants over those from other regions of the globe.

While the Chinese Exclusion Act provided Mexican migrants a certain degree of protection, U.S. policies in respect to Mexican immigration tended to change in direct response to fluctuations within the American economy. As a result, the Border Patrol was created by Congress to control illegal immigration into the country. The 1924 National Origins Act also established for the first time a visa requirement for all people wanting to immigrate into the United States. Despite these legislative provisions, Mexican immigration continued relatively unabated while most Mexicans crossed the border without the needed papers or documentation.

The deportations of the 1920s marked a high point in restrictive U.S. immigration policy, but the creation of the Bracero program less than 20 years later signified yet another shift toward a more liberal posture regarding immigration from Mexico. In response to the labor shortages and the demand for increased manpower during World War II, Congress entered into a series of bilateral agreements with the Mexican government that provided for the importation of temporary laborers into the United States. The Bracero program was to be regenerated and modified over three decades in line with American agricultural and industrial needs. At its height in 1959 over 450,000 Mexican migrant workers entered the United States.

Unlike the permissive immigration patterns of the late nineteenth century, the Bracero period did not provide for unrestricted migration. In 1952 Congress passed the "Wetback Act," which aimed to discourage illegal Mexican immigration by criminally sanctioning anyone who smuggled or harbored aliens who had not been inspected and legally admitted. The United States in 1954 alone deported over 300,000 Mexicans. The Bracero program was terminated in 1964, in large part due to employer abuses and opposition campaigns waged by labor unions and civil rights groups.

On the heels of the passage of the Wetback Act Congress also implemented the McCarran-Walter Act, which is commonly referred to as the Immigration and Nationality Act (INA). The INA continued to support the national origins system, but it was progressive in its removal of racial bars to immigration and naturalization. Preferential treatment was given to those who possessed needed skills in line with the U.S. economy while barring those with unwanted political profiles and beliefs. The INA was destined to create years of debate and discussion by Congress over immigration policy, which eventually culminated in the passage of new immigration reforms in 1965. Present visa systems and temporary worker visa permits all to a great degree owe their genesis to the INA and later amendments.

Post-1965 Legislation

The passage of the Hart-Cellar Immigration Act of 1965 officially ended the structure established by the National Origins Acts of 1921 and 1924. Although the 1965 act purported to eliminate the practice of regulating immigration, based on race and discrimination, by shifting the emphasis of immigration away from economic concerns to family reunification, the net effect was to curtail overall immigration from Central and South America. In this respect the legislation ended the "Good Neighbor" policy of past U.S. immigration legislation policy and the Kennedy administration by limiting immigration from the Western Hemisphere. Largely as a result of this legislation, an increased backlog of Latin American and Caribbean immigrants seeking entry into the United States often delayed family reunification, which in turn resulted in augmenting illegal immigration coming from these affected regions.

Reacting to the increased illegal immigration patterns of the late 1960s and 1970s, policymakers and the general public perceived that the United States had lost virtual control of its border. As a result, Congress passed the Immigration Reform and Control Act (IRCA) in November 1986. This piece of legislation represented a complete reconstruction of immigration policy and effectively supplanted most of the provisions established within the 1965 act. The major provisions of this act were intended to curtail illegal immigration by the legalization of illegal immigrants already residing within the country, leveling harsher sanctions on employers who hired undocumented workers, and allocating increased resources to the Immigration and Naturalization Service for border enforcement and security. Nearly 90 percent of the 1.7 million people who applied for general amnesty under this particular legalization provision were Mexican and Central American immigrants.

The decade of the 1990s was to witness ever-increasing legislation aimed at controlling the spiraling immigration flow into the United States. Much legislation sought to bring about long-lasting reforms in immigration policy while creating an efficient border policy that would curtail drug and human trafficking. The Immigration Act of 1990 established major revisions within U.S. immigration laws while providing a higher, more flexible annual ceiling on immigration levels. Through the adoption of a federal diversity policy, Congress gave priority in terms of work visas and legal residency to immigrants from countries that had demonstrated low levels of immigration to the United States subsequent to the 1965 act and who were underrepresented within the overall U.S. population. Congress was to later amend this act to restrict anyone from a foreign state contiguous to the United States entrance into the United States through a diversity visa. This had the effect of making both Mexicans and Canadians ineligible for utilization of the diversity policy.

Even though the North American Free Trade Agreement (NAFTA) was signed and ratified in 1994 and ostensibly was an economic pact between Mexico, Canada, and the United States, the real expectation was that NAFTA would serve U.S. interest in reducing illegal immigration from Mexico through the stimulation of economic growth and development. In reality, NAFTA produced variable results in terms of the Mexican economy and failed to resolve the severe economic issues of the border region.

NAFTA had no real effect in easing illegal immigration or human trafficking across the U.S.-Mexico border. In September 1996 Congress enacted the Illegal Immigration Reform and Immigrant Responsibility Act, which was intended to stop the rising tide of illegal migration across the U.S.-Mexico border through the expansion of the Border Patrol, increased personnel within the INS, the imposition of new sanctions for smuggling and hiring of illegal aliens, revision of the removal and deportation procedures, and the restriction of benefits previously accessible to illegal immigrants. These reforms provided the basis to deport thousands of illegal immigrants to their home countries. However, the net result still accomplished little in curtailing the continuous flow of illegal crossings across the southern border.

During the 1990s federal initiatives such as Operation Gatekeeper in San Diego, Hold the Line in El Paso, and Safeguard in Tucson were to further militarize the U.S.-Mexico border while providing for the construction of extensive physical barriers and the increased use of technology to patrol both the southern and northern borders. Along with these new efforts, vigilante groups such as the Minutemen and other more localized citizen militias have attempted to apprehend illegal immigrants as they are forced to cross more desolate parts of the U.S.-Canada and U.S.-Mexico borders.

Events stemming from September 11, 2001 brought about the next period of major changes to immigration policy and enforcement. Establishment of the Department of Homeland Security in conjunction with the creation of the USA Patriot Act was to revise the entire structure of governmental agencies and border enforcement in line with the War on Terror. Immigration and Naturalization Services once housed within the Department of Justice eventually became the United States Citizenship and Immigration Service as an arm of the Department of Homeland Security. Under this new realignment Congress promulgated antiterrorism legislation that has ostensibly led to the broadened investigative powers of the Attorney General and the Department of Justice related to intelligence activities and the surveillance of individuals. Broader legislative interpretation also has led to increased discretion in the apprehension and detention of any immigrant who is suspected of abetting or engaging in terrorist activities.

Conclusion

Possibly the greatest impact of 9/11 stems from the resultant breakdown in amnesty talks between President George W. Bush and President Vicente Fox of Mexico. Projected legislation between the two countries prior to 9/11 favored plans to develop increased labor migration, a new sweeping guestworker bill, and regularization of undocumented Mexicans already residing within the United States. Bilateral agreement on these provisions seemed almost inevitable up to the morning of September 11, 2001.

While asylum, family reunification, and economic factors, especially the need for low-skilled and unskilled labor, will continue to influence immigration policy, this will be balanced by the post-9/11 environment, which requires tighter restrictions in terms of heightened security measures at borders and ports of entry and apprehension and detention of illegal immigrants across the country.

The appointment of Michael Chertoff as Secretary of the Department of Homeland Security in February 2005 suggests an intensified enforcement of restrictions against illegal immigrants, since Judge Chertoff, as Assistant Attorney General in charge of the Justice Department's Criminal Division, played a major role in the post-9/11 detention of more than 800 mainly Arab Muslim and South

Asian men who were often held incommunicado without being charged or having access to legal counsel (Civilrights.org 2005).

On the other side of this trend, this stronger enforcement is complemented by a renewed plan to grant temporary work permits, or guestworker status, to illegal workers. This plan recognizes that illegal workers fill a need for low-paid labor in the U.S. economy. In early 2005 the Bush administration recommended bringing this shadow labor market into the open in order to eliminate the illegal market and the network that specializes in providing false identities and protection for illegal immigrant workers. This illegal "subculture" is said to provide access for potential terrorists and is therefore a threat to national security. Senators Edward Kennedy and John McCain co-sponsored a bill on May 12, 2005 that would provide illegal workers and their employers with an alternative. Illegal workers can apply for temporary work permits and employers can hire immigrant workers if they can prove that there are no Americans to fill these jobs. However, illegal immigrants will face heavy fines and will be put at the end of the queue for green cards.

According to recent data from the Department of Homeland Security, there are an estimated 8 to 11 million illegal immigrants currently in the country. Of those, approximately 400,000 have standing deportation orders and another 15,000 may pose a national security risk. In December 2005 the U.S. House of Representatives passed the Border Protection, Antiterrorism, and Illegal Immigration Control Act of 2005 (H.R. 4437), which still awaits discussion, formal adoption, and ratification by the U.S. Senate.

Major provisions of H.R. 4437 would require that the U.S. Department of Homeland Security and the Department of Defense develop a joint strategic plan that will provide the Border Patrol with military support and increased state-of-the-art surveillance technology consisting of added cameras, sensors, radar, satellite, and unmanned aerial vehicles. It would further authorize 1,000 new, full-time port of entry inspectors over the next four years and the training of 1,500 K-9 units over the next five years. This legislation also seeks to increment physical barriers and the expanded construction of a wall along a sizable portion of the U.S.-Mexico border. Effectively it would also put an end to the catch-and-release practice along the southern border when there is a lack of detention space.

H.R. 4437 would require mandatory detention for all illegal immigrants who are apprehended at U.S. land borders attempting to cross illegally by October 1, 2006. This particular legislation further authorizes new detention space for the holding of illegal immigrants. Additionally, by October 1, 2006, illegal immigrants who are released pending an immigration removal hearing would have to post a minimum bond of at least $5,000.

H.R. 4437 would further enact increased sanctions on employers hiring illegal workers, smugglers involved in human trafficking, and illegal gang members. One of the most controversial aspects of this legislation relates to the imposition of criminal felon status on all individuals who enter the United States illegally and those who are presently residing in the country illegally. The logistical demand inherent in the apprehension and incarceration of 8–12 million new felons would literally strain the nation's resources presently devoted to the entirety of law enforcement and prison facilities. Added to this would be the countless moral and legal implications as to the status of children born in the United States to illegal immigrants.

Immigration legislation has nearly always been predicated upon the perceived benefit or threat of immigrants to the nation's security, culture, and economy. This cycle would appear to remain intact in the foreseeable future. Future debates on immigration policy will have to continue to weigh the various national interests in line with moral and economic considerations. There is little doubt that policymakers and legislators will have to stake out pronounced positions and clear stances on the issue of immigration in the years to come. *See also*: **Immigration system; Legalization; National security.**

References

Aleinikoff, T.A., David A. Martin, and Hiroshi Motomura. 2003a. *Immigration and Citizenship: Process and Policy*, 5th ed. St. Paul, MN: West Publishing Co.

———. 2003b. *Immigration and Nationality Laws of the United States: Selected Statutes, Regulations and Forms*. St. Paul, MN: West Publishing Co.

Civilrights.org. 2005. With Questions Unanswered, Senate Confirms Chertoff. February 16. http://www.civilrights.org/issues/enforcement/details.cfm?id=28337.

Daniels, Roger. 2002. *Coming to America: A History of Immigration and Ethnicity in American Life*, 2nd ed. New York: HarperCollins.

———. 2004. *Guarding the Golden Door: American Immigration Policy and Immigrants since 1882*. New York: Hill and Wang.

Dunn, Timothy. 1996. *The Militarization of the U.S.-Mexico Border, 1978–1992: Low-Intensity Conflict Doctrine Comes Home*. Austin: University of Texas Press.

Lee, Erika. 2001. U.S. Immigration and Naturalization Laws and Issues: A Documentary History. *Journal of American Ethnic History* 20(2):118.

LeMay, Michael C. 2004. *U.S. Immigration: A Reference Handbook*. Santa Barbara, Calif.: ABC-CLIO.

LoBreglio, Kiera. 2004. The Border Security and Immigration Improvement Act: A Modern Solution to a Historic Problem? *St John's Law Review* 78(3): 933–964.

Portes, Alejandro, and Rubén Rumbaut. 1996. *Immigrant America: A Portrait*, 2nd ed. Berkeley: University of California Press.

United States: On the Border; To Come. 2005. *The Economist* 375(8427):58.

Volpp, Leti. 2005. Impossible Subjects: Illegal Aliens and Alien Citizens. *Michigan Law Review* 103(6):1595–1631.

LARRY J. ESTRADA AND JEANNE ARMSTRONG

LITERATURE AND FILM. Immigrant literature and film is not an easily defined category. Most critical overviews of immigrant literature include literature by immigrants and their descendants if the theme treats issues relating to immigration, such as assimilation or cultural identity differences between generations. Roberta Simone, in *The Immigrant Experience in American Fiction*, defines immigrant literature as a "branch of ethnic writing distinguished by the choice to relocate to the United States and [that] concerns the process of becoming American" (Simone 1995:vii). While there can be some ambiguity about what constitutes immigrant literature as compared to ethnic literature, some criteria may include literature written by first-generation immigrants and their descendants and representing themes and values typical of that group. Simone's annotated bibliography, however, includes literature with immigrant themes not authored by members of the ethnic group. Both Roberta Simone and Alpana

Sharma Knippling, editor of a resource entitled *New Immigrant Literatures in the United States*, exclude Native American literature because it is produced by the indigenous peoples of America and African American literature because it is created by people and their descendants who were forcibly relocated to America as slaves. Some critical collections, such as Knippling's, include autobiographies and memoirs as well as works of fiction. Currently diaspora literature may be an increasingly appropriate term for some immigrant literature. In the transnational environment of the twenty-first century, many immigrants maintain ties with their homelands, are often mobile between different continents, and publish in a global marketplace.

Among the earliest works of immigrant literature are Irish novels, such as Father Hugh Quigley's *The Cross and the Shamrock* (1853) about exploitation of Irish laborers and persecution of their Catholicism and Mary Anne Sadlier's *Confession of an Apostate* (1864) about an Irish American who hides his Catholicism to succeed in America. Most immigrants before World War II were Western Europeans who had assimilated fairly easily, but some groups were less easily assimilated because of religion, such as Irish Catholics and Jews. The earliest immigrant literature, from 1890 to 1914 in particular, was usually written by the second or third generation because the first generation lacked the time, education, and often the literacy to produce such works. The xenophobic and nativist atmosphere of this era was also generally unreceptive of ethnic and immigrant literature. Such literature did not conform to standards of the standard literary canon, which required universal themes rather than specific ethnic topics. Some immigrant novels, however, have become classics of the genre. Examples included the works of Anzia Yezierska, a Russian-born Jewish writer who wrote about the struggle by young immigrant women against Jewish patriarchal restrictions and for acceptance in their new homeland in New York's Lower East Side in the early twentieth century. Norwegian-born Ole Roelvaag's *Giants in the Earth* is also a classic about the hardships of immigrant farm families on the prairies.

After World War II, ethnic groups from Eastern Europe, especially Jews, were admitted under special provisions for displaced persons. The 1965 Immigration and Nationality Act, which reversed the restrictions of the 1882 Chinese Exclusion Act and the 1924 quota law, admitted immigrants from Central and South America, the Caribbean, and Asia. Because of the 1960s civil rights movements, the climate became more accepting of the United States as a pluralist country and more open to literatures representing this diversity. New immigrants producing recent immigrant fiction are often well educated even in the first generation. Bharati Mukherjee from India has a doctorate from the University of Iowa and Cristina Garcia, born in Cuba, was educated at Barnard and Johns Hopkins.

While themes in earlier first-generation literature addressed the culture shock and homesickness of immigrants and their adaptation to a new home and conflicting values, literature by third- and fourth-generation immigrations often concerns recovering lost roots and ancestry. In comparison, literature by more recent immigrants often examines the multiple identities of groups inhabiting cultural borderlands, issues of racism and postcolonialism, and, especially in women's literature, gender dynamics. Recent immigrant literature is a respected area of scholarship and finds a more favorable publishing market than earlier literature.

Some characteristics of recent immigrant literature include cultural mingling, the blending of coexisting cultures from two or more cultural identities, and an often critical stance toward American violence, racism, and materialism (Payant 1999). This literature represents the desire to maintain complex cultural identities rather than to assimilate. Another current trend in immigrant literature is the flourishing of women writers. Whereas in the past male writers often predominated, currently women writers outnumber men in immigrant authors being studied. These women are often writing in a postcolonial or postmodernist style with a feminist perspective on gender problems within their original culture as well as in their adopted American culture.

Some ongoing issues in immigrant literature include the tendency of ethnic authors to stereotype or exoticize themselves. Lin Yu Tang's *Chinatown Family* represents Chinese Americans as the model minority, and Maxine Hong Kingston has been criticized for exoticizing Chinese American culture. Mario Puzo's novel *The Godfather* about the Mafia underworld was a success, but not his earlier novel *The Fortunate Pilgrim* about a typical immigrant family in New York's Little Italy. Frank Chin, who was an early voice of Chinese American literature, has criticized more recent authors as inauthentic in their Americanized writing. Yet some disagree with Chin's attempt at establishing a cultural hegemony. Another concern is the marginalization of literatures written in native languages. Asian language texts are especially excluded. Some Spanish language literature is available through publishers such as Bilingual Press and Arte Publico. The Society for the Study of the Multi-Ethnic Literature of the United States and its journal, *MELUS*, are a valuable resource on ethnic and immigrant literature.

Film

The U.S. film industry had a number of Irish American actors such as Pat O'Brien, Spencer Tracey, and James Cagney and some notable Irish American directors such as John Ford and John Huston. These two directors, however, made only three films dealing with Irish themes. John Ford, originally Sean O'Feeney, directed *The Informer* (1935) based on Liam O'Flaherty's novel and *The Quiet Man* (1952) based on a short story by Maurice Walsh. The latter film had a significant impact on images of Ireland as as well as on the subsequent development of the Irish film industry. Although some of the characters are stereotypical, there is some treatment of authentic issues, such as return migration and Irish dowry customs. John Huston, an Irish American who resided in Western Ireland for 20 years, made a film based on James Joyce's story *The Dead*, which was released posthumously to critical acclaim. Recent Irish films suggest the difficulty of categorizing films in an increasingly globalized industry. *The Playboys* starred the Irish American actor Aidan Quinn, was directed by a Scottish-born director, and was written and filmed in the home town of Shane Connaughton using American financing.

Films by such directors as Ang Lee, Christine Choy, Trinh T. Minh-ha, and Mira Nair could also be considered transnational rather than immigrant. Ang Lee, born in Taiwan, directed the award-winning trilogy *Pushing Hands* (1992), *Wedding Banquet* (1993), and *Eat Drink Man Woman* (1994) that undermines racial, cultural, and sexual categories in their treatments of contemporary Asian American immigrants. His films are financed by Central Motion pictures in Taiwan and made in collaboration with a New York production company, "produced and consumed in the world market, with a multinational crew, story-line, and marketing strategies" (Ma 1998:145). Christine Choy, born in China of a Chinese mother and Korean father, has lived in Korea and the United States. Her films are somewhat autobiographical with themes of immigration, cultural identity, and racism. *Who Killed Vincent Chin?* was based on the true story of a Chinese man murdered by white unemployed auto workers in the Midwest who mistook him for being Japanese.

Trinh T. Minh-ha, born in Vietnam and educated in the United States and France, has made films about African women, *Naked Spaces: Living Is Round* (1985); Vietnamese women, *Surname Viet Given Name Nam* (1989); and Chinese women, *Shoot for the Contents* (1991). Trinh uses strategies of l'ecriture feminine as well as hybridity, occupying the space between categories of fiction and nonfiction, subject and object, viewer and viewed (Foster 1997:95). Mira Nair, born in India, educated at Harvard, and living in Africa, has made documentaries about India such as *Salaam Bombay!* and *India Cabaret* as well as other feature films. Her *Mississippi Masala* is the story of a forbidden love between an Indian woman whose family was forced out of Africa and an African American man. "The film caters to an audience eager to celebrate exotic Otherness in the form of sexuality between brown bodies . . . yet it delivers a political examination of race and colonialism as they have been positioned in Western filmic practice" (Foster 1997:121).

Gregory Nava is a Mexican American director whose films include *El Norte* and *Mi Familia, My Family*. *El Norte* is a story of two illegal immigrants from Guatemala and *Mi Familia* is a film about three generations of a Mexican American family. Wayne Wang, born in Hong Kong, has made *Dim Sum*, *Eat a Bowl of Tea*, and *Chan Is Missing*, as well as the mainstream film *Maid in Manhattan*. There are also many other examples of Hollywood films based on immigrant literature, such as *Enemies: A Love Story* (Isaac Bashevis Singer), *A Thousand Pieces of Gold* (Frank Chin), *Mambo Kings* (Oscar Hijuelos), *The Joy Luck Club* (Amy Tan), and *Picture Bride* (Yoshiko Uchida). In addition to such feature films, there are numerous documentaries on immigrants. The chapter "Documentary Films about Refugees" in *Refugees in America in the 1990s* is recommended as a good overview of some documentaries with suggestions on locating documentary films about refugees. *See also*: **Diasporas; Transnationalism.**

References

Aranda, José, Jr. 2003. *When We Arrive: A New Literary History of Mexican America.* Tucson: University of Arizona Press.

Di Pietro, Robert J., and Edward Ifkovic. 1983. *Ethnic Perspectives in American Literature: Selected Essays on the European Contribution.* New York: Modern Language Association.

Ferraro, Thomas. 1993. *Ethnic Passages: Literary Immigrants in Twentieth-Century America.* Chicago: University of Chicago Press.

Foster, Gwendolyn. 1997. *Women Filmmakers of the African and Asian Diaspora: Decolonizing the Gaze, Locating Subjectivity.* Carbondale: Southern Illinois University Press.

Kafka, Phillipa. 2003. *On the Outside Looking In(dian): Indian Women Writers at Home and Abroad*. New York: Peter Lang.

Knippling, Alpana Sharma. 1996. *New Immigrant Literature in the United States: A Sourcebook to Our Multicultural Literary Heritage*. Westport, CT: Greenwood Press.

Ma, Sheng-mei. 1998. *Immigrant Subjectivities in Asian American and Asian Diaspora Literatures*. Albany: State University of New York Press.

MacKillop, James. 1999. *Contemporary Irish Cinema*. Syracuse, NY: Syracuse University Press.

Muller, Gilbert H. 1999. *New Strangers in Paradise: The Immigrant Experience and Contemporary American Fiction*. Lexington: University Press of Kentucky.

Payant, Katherine B., and Toby Rose. 1999. *The Immigrant Experience in North American Literature: Carving Out a Niche*. Westport, CT: Greenwood Press.

Ruoff, A. LaVonne Brown, and Jerry W. Ward Jr. 1990. *Redefining American Literary History*. New York: Modern Language Association.

Simone, Roberta. 1995. *The Immigrant Experience in American Fiction: An Annotated Bibliography*. Lanham, MD: Scarecrow.

JEANNE ARMSTRONG

M

MARRIAGE. The historical and contemporary experience of the United States has been one of considerable cross-ethnic mixing, particularly during lengthening settlement and for subsequent generations. Marriage is one of the primary ways in which immigrants both retain and shape family patterns. Endogamy prevails among most immigrant groups, and arranged marriages, like those found in South Asian immigrant communities, may also persist. However, the urban contexts, continuing mobility, and exposure to people of diverse backgrounds in work, school, and social settings combine to make for greater influence of personal choices in partner selection in new generations.

The connection of immigration and marriage also comes into play through the presumed right of spouses to be together. The ability for spouses of American citizens and permanent residents to enter the United States has long been assumed to be a customary right of citizens to be reunited with family members. However, this privilege was not clearly articulated and codified until the Immigration Act of 1965. Prior to this, alien dependents and spouses were frequently granted admittance, but such an opportunity was often contested by Congress and the court system and subject to issues of patriarchy, nativism, racism, and international affairs. Congressional efforts to bar the importation of women for the purposes of prostitution (Page Law of 1875), for example, became a legal weapon to exclude lower-class women who sought to join their husbands. Changing racial criteria for American citizenship also became the basis on which to exclude immigrant spouses. For example, because Chinese aliens were deemed ineligible to become U.S. citizens (1882 Exclusion Act), Chinese immigrants—including spouses of Americans—were denied admittance as of the 1924 Immigration Act.

Fortunately, Congressional intervention has been swayed by other influences as well. Political and legal challenges from citizens and immigrant spouses have affected legislation, which has benefited new arrivals to these shores. The phenomenon of war brides and mail-order brides reveals how citizens' desires and demands have effectively widened aspects of immigration law in the mid-to-late twentieth century. Most important, these examples demonstrate how a customary right in terms of immigration became a set of legal rights for both citizens and immigrant spouses.

Intermarriage

Intermarriage, the popular term for exogamy, means marrying outside one's ethnic, racial, and religious group or marrying someone of a different nationality. In the United States, there has been a long history of intermarriage because of the tremendous diversity. With at least 249 different racial and ethnic groups noted in the 2000 census, intermarriage is not only possible but also highly probable. Demographic studies confirm the large increase in interethnic and interracial couples; in 1960 there were about 150,000 interracial couples, while there were 1 million mixed race and ethnic couples in 1990 (Waters 2000).

The earliest documented intermarriages were between European fur traders and Native American women in the 1600s, but mixed marriages were hardly limited to Europeans and Natives. Though custom and law often forbade such unions, intermarriages occurred frequently. By the nineteenth and twentieth centuries, mixtures widened to include unions between Chinese and Irish, Japanese and Anglo, Filipino and French, and Mexicans and Sikhs (Lee 1999; Nash 1999). Today intermarriages transcend nearly all racial, ethnic, and religious boundaries.

Responses to intermarriage have often been extreme. Certain legends, such as the union between Pocahontas of the Algonquian tribe and John Rolfe, a Virginia tobacco planter, paint intermarriage as an example of love triumphing over any and all differences in culture and custom. However, intermarriage has generally been considered a threat because of its potential to weaken a group's cultural and social identity (Sung 1990). The degree to which groups have resisted, condemned, ignored, or begrudgingly accepted intermarriage has varied depending on time period, regional location, the particular ethnic and gender groups involved, and the sociopolitical and economic interests at stake. However, the greatest legal resistance has been directed toward marriages between whites and non-whites (Nash 1999).

Criminalizing intermarriages is certainly not a new practice, but the United States stands out for marriage laws that criminalized unions based on skin color, even between parties of equal social status. Long after passage of the Fourteenth and Fifteenth Constitutional amendments, state laws still prohibited African American men and women from marrying whites. By the early twentieth century, other racial groups were included in anti-miscegenation laws. For example, the California Civil Code barred Asians, referred to as "Mongolians," from marrying whites. Some 30 states maintained anti-intermarriage laws on their books in the mid-twentieth century and a handful actively enforced them. It was not until 1967 that the Supreme Court ruled all anti-miscegenation and anti-intermarriage laws unconstitutional (*Loving v. Virginia*, 388 U.S. 1). Intermarriage has thus been legally protected for less than 50 years in the United States, though this has become a demographic reality for hundreds of thousands of immigrants and children of immigrants.

Mail-Order Brides

"Mail-order brides" is the popular name for foreign-born women who marry American men after brief correspondence and refers less to a "pen-pal" courtship than to a process through which couples meet. Men who are interested in finding a wife or partner select from catalogs, magazines, and Internet Web sites operated by international dating services. Once the men make a selection, they pay a fee, ranging up to hundreds of dollars, for the addresses of the women. After contact, a man often travels to meet the woman and arranges for her to relocate to the United States as soon as legally possible.

The mail-order bride system became popular in the United States during the late twentieth century. By 1998, 4,000 to 6,000 mail-order brides were arriving annually, double the number in 1990 (Scholes and Phataralaoha 2002). Though mail-order brides hail from nearly every country in the world, an overwhelming number come from Southeast Asia, China, the Philippines, and the former Soviet Union. Because so many of the women come from East Asia, "mail-order marriages" commonly refers to the union between Asian women and white American men.

The profile of participants reveal that men tend to be 10–15 years older than women, politically conservative, financially secure, and having some college education. Some men go abroad in search of an "old-fashioned" wife, or because they find American women to be "pushy" or mainly interested in having someone to father their children or provide for them. Many women abroad are from poor backgrounds and countries that are politically and economically struggling. In the Philippines, because of financial difficulties, political turmoil, and cultural traditions, economic and educational opportunities are not readily available to women (Pizarro 2002). Under such conditions, options for young women are often limited, including in domestic service and sex industries, and many see foreign marriage as a key to a "better life" with financial security, educational opportunities, and a safe, stable home.

Supporters of mail-order matrimony argue that most agencies are simply international matchmaking services and work along the lines of domestic dating agencies, while opponents argue that there are major differences between the domestic and international dating services. Local dating and matchmaking services require that all parties disclose information about themselves, but in the mail-order business only the women who are advertised provide photographs and personal details. Until recently there have been few regulations to prevent fraud, whereas many states regulate dating services through consumer protection agencies.

No doubt both parties can, and often do, provide false information about themselves. However, the mail-order bride industry itself falsely advertises the women by painting them in stereotyped terms. Many agencies claim Asian women are solely interested in being wives and not career women, desiring primarily to cater to their husbands' needs and wishes. For example, one agency claims a Filipina will make her husband more comfortable by anticipating his needs, a character trait said to be ingrained in the mind of the average Filipina. Such stereotypes reinforce expectations and can have long-term negative consequences.

The degree of control husbands have in such marriages is potentially harmful. Men sometimes take extreme steps to prevent their wives from gaining independence. As new immigrants, women are vulnerable to abuse and exploitation as they often lack proficiency in English, job skills for the American labor market, and familiarity with U.S. customs and laws. Because of their circumstances, they tend to be highly dependent on their husbands for material needs. This leaves them vulnerable to physical, emotional, and psychological violence and even death, as evidenced by the death of Susana Blackwell, a Filipina bride, and two of her friends at the hands of Blackwell's estranged husband in 1995 (Lloyd 2000).

The legal response to the mail-order bride industry has been somewhat misguided and has frequently protected the wrong parties. The 1986 Immigration and Marriage Fraud Amendments sought to regulate mail-order marriages to protect American men from being deceived and manipulated into fraudulent unions, although the Immigration Act of 1990 acknowledged the greater risk to women in these unions (Anderson 1993). The new law created opportunities for women, particularly those who have been battered and abused, to separate from their husbands without the threat of deportation. Since 2000, additional acts have further eased the process for battered mail-order brides to escape abuse, and forced mail-order agencies to disclose criminal information and marital histories of potential grooms to women in their native languages.

War Brides

"War brides" are foreign national women who marry members of the American military personnel while they are stationed abroad. Courtships and marriages between foreign-born women and U.S. soldiers occurred prior to World War II, but it was not until 1945 that Congress amended immigration restrictions to allow alien spouses and children to enter the country. Public Law 271, passed on December 28, 1945, became popularly known as the War Brides Act. With the G.I.'s Fiancees Act of 1946, Congress further modified immigration regulations to allow the fiancées of U.S. military men to enter the country on the premise that they would marry soon after arrival. Estimates suggest that nearly 1 million war brides from more than 50 countries came to the United States during World War II and during the postwar occupation of Japan and Germany (Shukert and Scibetta 1988).

Explanations for wartime romances and marriages widely vary; some scholars, and many brides themselves, suggest that marriage was a natural result of throwing together bachelor American soldiers and young single foreign women at a time when the local native men were abroad fighting. Other explanations include economic motivations. Impoverished socioeconomic conditions in Japan following the country's defeat, for example, prompted some women to marry U.S. soldiers for greater physical and economic security (Spikard 1989). Anti-German and anti-Japanese sentiment in the United States further encouraged some Americans to view the brides and fiancées as opportunists, gold-diggers, home-wreckers, or worst, as spies (Shukert and Scibetta 1988).

Suspicions about war brides even led military authorities to deter soldiers from wedding local women by making the bureaucratic procedure terribly complicated: personnel had to receive permission from their commanding officers, file numerous papers, obtain many signatures, and complete a series of interviews. Even then couples had to wait from a few months to full year. Marriage petitions from Japanese women and American soldiers were not even considered by commanding officers in 1945. According to the War Brides Act, alien spouses who were excluded by the Immigration Act of 1924—which included nearly all

Asian groups—were not eligible to enter the country as war brides. Though Congress extended the law to admit Chinese and Filipina brides of U.S. soldiers, Japanese women did not receive the same recognition until 1947, amid mounting pressure (Spikard 1989; Takaki 1989; Simpson 2001).

War brides who survived the bureaucratic obstacles and finally made it to the United States still faced many other challenges. Brides experienced culture shock, loneliness, and homesickness for family and friends. They were often isolated from others like themselves. Living situations were the worst for Japanese, German, and Italian brides because they had to contend with language differences as well as enmity toward "enemy nationals."

The war bride experience has had measurable demographic impact on the United States. In particular, the entry of Asian war brides helped rejuvenate the Chinese and Filipino communities. Because of immigration restrictions, many young Chinese and Filipinos were forced to marry outside their ethnic group or remain single. The War Bride Act helped adjust the sex imbalance by allowing young Asian soldiers to marry Chinese and Filipina women and bring them back to the United States. According to one source, between 1946 and 1953, over 7,000 Chinese war brides entered the United States (Takaki 1989).

While the term "war bride" has historically referred to immigrant wives of U.S. soldiers during the World War II era, it has since been expanded to include the foreign-born wives of military personnel wherever American troops are stationed. Military conflicts involving the United States—in Korea, Vietnam, and most recently the Middle East—have greatly increased the number of immigrant spouses of U.S. military service personnel. *See also*: **Families; Family reunification; Interethnic relations.**

References

Anderson, Michelle J. 1993. A License to Abuse: The Impact of Conditional Status on Female Immigrants. *Yale Law Journal* 102(6):1401–1430.

Cott, Nancy F. 2000. *Public Vows: A History of Marriage and the Nation.* Cambridge, MA: Harvard University Press.

Lee, Robert G. 1999. *Orientals: Asian Americans in Popular Culture.* Philadelphia: Temple University Press.

Lloyd, Kathryn A. 2000. Wives for Sale: The Modern International Mail-Order Bride Industry. *Northwestern Journal of International Law and Business* 20(2):342.

Nash, Gary. 1999. The Hidden History of Mestizo America. In *Sex, Love, Race: Crossing Boundaries in North American History.* Martha Hodes, ed. Pp. 10–34. New York: New York University Press.

Pascoe, Peggy. 1999. Miscegenation Law, Court Cases and Ideologies of "Race" in Twentieth-Century America. In *Sex, Love, Race: Crossing Boundaries in North American History.* Martha Hodes, ed. Pp. 464–490. New York: New York University Press.

Pizarro, Gabriela Rodriguez. 2002. Specific Groups and Individuals: Migrant Workers. Report to the Commission on Human Rights, Economic Social Council, United Nations, November 1. http://www.unchr.info/statement/I14-0408-SP%20on%20HR%20of%20Migrants-Spanish.pdf, accessed April 21, 2005.

Scholes, Robert J., and Anchalee Phataralaoha. 2002. The "Mail-Order Bride" Industry and Its Impact on U.S. Immigration. http://uscis.gov/graphics/aboutus/repsstudies/Mobappa.htm, accessed March 21, 2005.

Shukert, Elfrieda Berthiaume, and Barbara Smith Scibetta. 1988. *War Brides of World War II*. Novato, CA: Presidio Press.

Simpson, Caroline Chung. 2001. *An Absent Presence: Japanese Americans in Postwar American Culture, 1945–1960*. Durham, NC: Duke University Press.

Spikard, Paul R. 1989. *Mixed Blood: Intermarriage and Ethnic Identity in Twentieth-Century America*. Madison: University of Wisconsin Press.

Sung, Betty Lee. 1990. *Chinese American Intermarriage*. New York: Center for Migration Studies.

Takaki, Ronald. 1989. *Strangers from a Distant Shore: A History of Asian-Americans*. Boston: Little, Brown.

Waters, Mary C. 2000. Immigration, Intermarriage and the Challenges of Measuring Racial/Ethnic Identities. *American Journal of Public Health* 90(11):1735.

MIDORI TAKAGI

MENTAL HEALTH PROBLEMS. Immigrants in the United States, and particularly refugees, are at particularly high risk for mental health problems and have a high need for mental healthcare because of their pre-immigration traumatic experiences. Coming to another country, immigrants often experience "culture shock" or "acculturative stress," which involves psychological stress created by external stressors. In this case, difficulties are relatively moderate and may include somatic symptoms, mild depression, and worries. Acculturative stress tends to be high in the first three years after arrival in the United States. Refugees often experience a U-shaped curve of adjustment, where they experience an initial euphoria in the first year of migration, followed by a strong disenchantment and demoralization reaction during the second year, with a gradual return to well-being and satisfaction in the third year (Rumbaut 1989).

When difficulties are beyond the individual's coping capacity during migration or adaptation, symptoms such as depression, anxiety, and psychosis may be experienced. Posttraumatic Stress Disorder (PTSD) is the most prevalent mental health problem among refugees. Many Southeast Asian refugees, for example, have been found to be at risk for PTSD associated with the trauma they experienced before they immigrated to the United States. One study found that pre-migration traumatic events and refugee camp experiences predict psychological distress even five years after migration (Chung and Kagawa-Singer 1993). Similarly, among Central American adults attending three schools in Los Angeles who were examined for symptoms of PTSD and depression, half reported symptoms consistent with a diagnosis of PTSD (Cervantes et al. 1989). Another study found 60 percent of adult Central American refugee patients as diagnosed with PTSD (Michultka et al. 1998). High rates of major depression, anxiety disorder, and somatoform disorders are also common (Kroll et al. 1989). Furthermore, a high percentage of refugees had depression along with PTSD, and most had experienced premigration trauma including starvation, torture, and loss of family members to war (Blair 2000). Refugees who have lost children are particularly likely to have significantly more health-related concerns, a variety of somatic symptoms, and culture-bound conditions of emotional distress such as "a deep worrying sadness not visible to others" (Caspi et al. 1998).

Distress among refugee youth is also quite high. Central American immigrant children seeking care at refugee services centers had high rates (33 percent) of

PTSD (Arroyo and Eth 1984), while Cambodian high school students had PTSD symptoms and mild but chronic depressive symptoms (Kinzie et al. 1986). Among Cambodian adolescents who survived Pol Pot's concentration camps, Kinzie and colleagues (1989) found high rates of PTSD and depression even ten years later. Unaccompanied minors, adolescents, and young adult refugees from Vietnam have also been found to have high levels of anxiety (Felsman et al. 1990). Rates of depression and PTSD, then, appear to be extraordinarily high among both adult and youth refugees because so many experienced trauma prior to immigrating to the United States.

The scope and intensity of adjustment and mental health problems create an urgent need for valid assessment and intervention methods as well as public policies (Marsella et al. 1994). However, there are substantial challenges to conducting assessment and providing treatment for the mental health problems that the immigrants bring, particularly since culture influences manifestations of illness as well as other aspects of psychopathology (Kleinman 1988). Culture even determines whether an individual seeks help in the first place, what types of help are sought, and how much stigma and meaning a person may attach to mental illness. Presentation of symptoms could be different from what U.S.-trained clinicians expect. A good illustration of different symptoms is Kinzie's (1982) validation study of the Beck Depression Inventory (BDI), where researchers ended up creating a Vietnamese Depression Inventory (VDI) that replaced almost entirely the items of the original BDI.

Another issue is using criteria that were developed within a framework of U.S. culture. For example, the *Diagnostic and Statistical Manual of Mental Disorders*, 4th edition (DSM-IV) sets criteria for mental illness to be "distress" and "disability," which creates difficulty in assessing individuals from different cultures since degree of stress reporting varies among cultures. Some cultures encourage people to self-disclose while the others discourage this (Kleinman 1988), so the applicability of DSM-IV criteria across cultural borders is thus questionable.

The mental health services system in the U.S. system serves many different populations that require mental health services, and has been criticized for not successfully addressing the needs of those people with the most complex needs and those with the fewest financial resources. In fact, it has been called a "de facto mental health system" (Regier et al. 1993). The problem is only magnified for minority groups, including immigrants and refugees. First, it is difficult to find a practitioner of the same ethnic background of many patients. There are, for example, only about two Hispanic psychiatrists for every 100,000 Hispanic residents, making it difficult to find a nearby ethnically matched provider (Manderscheid and Henderson 1999). Second, evidence-based treatment methods, those based on current scientific evidence which are found to significantly improve treatment outcomes, are often not available in community-based treatment centers. While a gap between research and practice exists for the general population, it is even worse for ethnic minorities. In all clinical trials reporting data on ethnicity, very few minority patients were included, and not a single study analyzed the efficacy of the treatment by ethnicity or race (U.S. Department of Health 2001). The APA reached a similar conclusion on psychotherapies: that there is no research showing treatment efficacy for ethnic minority populations (Chambless et al. 1996).

A third issue is ethnopsychopharmacology. Ethnopsychopharmacologists investigate ethnic variations of medication dosage and other aspects of pharmacology. There is a growing body of research on genetic differences in the process of metabolizing medications in certain ethnic populations. Related studies also focus on how drug metabolism is affected by lifestyle choices, such as diet, rates of smoking, and alcohol consumption, along with use of alternative or complementary treatments. These factors can interact with drugs to alter their safety or effectiveness. One danger uncovered by this line of research is that individual differences among an ethnic group may be overlooked, leading potentially to more medication side effects, patient non-adherence, and possibly greater risk of long-term, severe side effects (Lin and Cheung 1999).

Immigrants and refugees in the United States are at risk of various mental health problems, from acculturative stress to depressive and anxiety symptoms. Prior research consistently indicates the existence of these symptoms and need for treatment. Research, however, is lacking in the area of appropriate treatment and outcome of these mental health problems. Marsella et al. (1996) argue that cultural factors need to be considered even in conceptualization, diagnosis, and treatment, since culture is an essential part of the etiology, expression, course, and outcome of mental illness. This statement presents a tremendous, if not insurmountable, challenge to researchers as well as U.S.-trained mental health practitioners who provide treatment to culturally different populations. Moreover, the applicability to immigrants in general of our growing knowledge of the mental health problems found in refugees in the Unites States is an area that merits considerably greater attention. *See also*: **Health; Posttraumatic Stress Disorder.**

References

Arroyo, William, and Spencer Eth. 1984. Children Traumatized by Central American Warfare. In *Posttraumatic Stress Disorder in Children*. Spencer Eth and Robert S. Pynoos, eds. Pp. 101–120. Washington, DC: American Psychiatric Press.

Blair, R.G. 2000. Risk Factors Associated with PTSD and Major Depression among Cambodian Refugees. *Health and Social Work* 25:23–30.

Caspi, Y., C. Poole, R.F. Mollica, and M. Frankel. 1998. Relationship of Child Loss to Psychiatric and Functional Impairment in Resettlement. *Journal of Nervous and Mental Disease* 186:484–491.

Cervantes, R.C., V.N. Salgado De Snyder, and A.M. Padilla. 1989. Post Traumatic Stress in Immigrants from Central America and Mexico. *Hospital and Community Psychiatry* 40:615–619.

Chambless, D.L., W.C. Sanderson, V. Shorham, S. Bennett Johnson, K.S. Pope, P. Crits-Christoph, M. Baker, B. Johnson, S.R. Woody, S. Sue, L. Beutler, D.A. Williams, and S. McCurry. 1996. An Update on Empirically Validated Therapies. *The Clinical Psychologist* 49:5–18.

Chung, R.C., and M. Kagawa-Singer. 1993. Predictors of Psychological Distress among Southeast Asian Refugees. *Social Science and Medicine* 36:631–639.

Felsman, J.K., F.T.L. Leong, M.C. Johnson, and I.C. Felsman. 1990. Estimates of Psychological Distress among Vietnamese Refugees: Adolescents, Unaccompanied Minors and Young Adults. *Social Science and Medicine* 31:1251–1256.

Kinzie, J.D., S.M. Manson, D.T. Vinh, N.T. Tolan, B. Anh, and T.N. Pho. 1982. Development and Validation of a Vietnamese-Language Depression Scale. *American Journal of Psychiatry* 139:1276–1281.

Kinzie, J.D., W.H. Sack, R.H. Angell, G. Clarke, and B. Rath. 1989. A Three-Year Follow-up on Cambodian Young People Traumatized as Children. *Journal of American Academy of Child and Adolescent Psychiatry* 28:501–504.

Kinzie, J.D., W.H. Sack., R.H. Angell, S. Manson, and R. Ben. 1986. The Psychiatric Effects of Massive Trauma on Cambodian Children. *Journal of the American Academy of Child and Adolescent Psychiatry* 25:370–376.

Kleinman, Arthur. 1988. *Rethinking Psychiatry: From Cultural Category to Personal Experience.* New York: Free Press.

Kroll, J., M. Jabenicht, T. Mackenzie, M. Yang, S. Chan, T. Vang, T. Nguyen, M. Ly, B. Phommasouvanh, H. Nguyen, Y. Vang, L. Souvannasoth, and R. Cabugao. 1989. Depression and Post-Traumatic Stress Disorder in Southeast Asian Refugees. *American Journal of Psychiatry* 146:1592–1597.

Lin, K.M., and F. Cheung. 1999. Mental Health Issues for Asian Americans. *Psychiatric Services* 50:774–780.

Manderscheid, Ronald, and Marilyn J. Henderson, eds. 1999. *Mental Health, United States: 1998.* Rockville, MD: Center for Mental Health Services.

Marsella, Anthony, Thomas Bornemann, Solvig Ekblad, and John Orley, eds. 1994. *Amidst Peril and Pain: The Mental Health and Well-Being of the World's Refugees.* Washington, DC: American Psychological Association.

Marsella, Anthony, Matthew Friedman, Ellen Gerrity, and Raymond Scurfield. 1996. Ethnocultural Aspects of PTSD: Some Closing Thoughts. In *Ethnocultural Aspects of Posttraumatic Stress Disorder: Issues, Research, and Clinical Applications.* Anthony J. Marsella, Matthew Friedman, Ellen Gerrity, and Raymond Scurfield, eds. Pp. 529–538. Washington, DC: American Psychological Association.

Michultka, D., E.B. Blanchard, and T. Kaloous. 1998. Responses to Civilian War Experiences: Predictors of Psychological Functioning and Coping. *Journal of Traumatic Stress* 11:571–577.

Regier, D.A., W.E. Narrow, D.S. Rae, R.W. Manderscheid, B.Z. Locke, and F.K. Goodwin. 1993. The de facto U.S. Mental and Addictive Disorders Service System: Epidemiologic Catchment Area Prospective 1-Year Prevalence Rates of Disorders and Services. *Archives of General Psychiatry* 50:85–94.

Rumbaut, Ruben G. 1989. *Patients, Patterns, and Predictors of the Refugee as Immigrants: Cambodians, Laotians and Vietnamese in America.* Totowa, NJ: Rowman and Littlefield.

U.S. Department of Health. 2001. *Mental Health: Culture, Race and Ethnicity.* A Supplement to *Mental Health: A Report of the Surgeon General.* Rockville, MD: U.S. Department of Mental Health and Human Services, Public Health Services; Washington, DC: Office of the Surgeon General.

YOKO SUGIHARA

MEXICO-U.S. MIGRATION. In 1970, when Mexico's population was just over 50 million, there were about 750,000 Mexican-born residents of the United States. In 2000, when Mexico's population was just over 100 million, there were over 8 million Mexican-born U.S. residents (Escobar et al. 2003). This means that the number of Mexican-born persons in the United States increased over 10 times, while Mexico's population doubled. Mexicans pioneered the now "normal" way to immigrate to the United States—arrive in another status, usually unauthorized, and adjust to immigrant status in the United States, as over half of U.S. immigrants have done in recent years.

The Mexican-born U.S. population continues to increase by about 500,000 a year, a result of the unification of families of settled Mexican immigrants as well as unauthorized Mexican-born workers spreading throughout the United States, including in construction and services in the Midwest and Southeast (Lowell 2004). During the twentieth century, California agriculture was the major port of entry for Mexicans coming to the United States as sojourners and settlers, but in the twenty-first century, construction, meatpacking, and services throughout the United States have overtaken agriculture in offering first jobs to Mexican newcomers. Of the 6 to 7 million Mexican-born workers in the U.S. labor force, only 25 percent are employed in agriculture, where as seasonal workers they are employed about half the year for hourly earnings that are about half the U.S. average, giving them incomes that are a fourth of the U.S. average, $8,000 versus $32,000 a year (Martin 2003).

Mexican-born U.S. residents now come from virtually every Mexican state and most of Mexico's 2,400 *municipos*, or counties, and migrating to the United States has become a "rite of passage" especially for male youth turning 16 to 18 in rural Mexico. The networks that link Mexican workers to U.S. jobs have been strengthened by decades of cross-border movement, so that Mexicans thousands of miles from U.S. workplaces may learn about new U.S. jobs before local U.S. workers. Migration can beget more migration, as U.S. employers adapt their employment systems to the Spanish-speaking newcomers they prefer and Mexicans become dependent on the U.S. labor market.

Evolution of Mexico-U.S. Migration

Migration has been a defining feature of Mexico-U.S. relations for most of the twentieth century, but legal immigration remained low until recently. Some 36 percent of twentieth-century Mexican immigrants arrived in the 1990s, and 34 percent of the apprehensions of unauthorized Mexicans were in the 1990s. During most of the twentieth century, Mexican migrants were negatively selected, meaning that emigrants had less education and fewer skills than the average Mexican, largely because U.S. farmers recruited rural Mexicans willing to accept seasonal farm jobs (Martin 1993). There were bilateral agreements to regulate Mexico-U.S. labor migration between 1917–1921 and 1942–1964, but most twentieth-century Mexican migrants arrived and were employed outside these guestworker or Bracero programs.

Many Mexicans and Americans continue to associate migrants with Braceros (strong arms), the Mexicans admitted "for the purpose of accepting employment in agricultural pursuits." Mexican workers were admitted to help win World War I, but their number peaked after the war ended—18,000 were admitted in 1917, and 52,000 in 1920. Recession in 1921 and Mexican government dissatisfaction with the treatment of Braceros on some U.S. farms allowed the program to end (Binational Study on Migration 1997).

Mexicans who continued to migrate north found few obstacles to entry, as the U.S. Border Patrol was not established until 1924. Mexican-born workers became the core of the seasonal farm workforce in California, but during the 1930s, when displaced white farmers joined Mexicans in the fields, southwestern agriculture's dependence on migrants came under attack. John Stein-beck's 1940 novel *The Grapes of Wrath* gave an emotional impetus to the call for farm labor reform—namely, to restructure southwestern agriculture in a manner that reduced its dependence on migrant and seasonal workers. Alternatively, if factories in the fields persisted, reformers wanted farm workers to be treated as factory workers and covered under nonfarm labor laws, including minimum wages, unemployment insurance, and the right to form unions (Martin 2003).

The outbreak of World War II allowed farmers to win a new Bracero program, and between 1942 and 1945, Braceros, prisoners of war, interned Japanese, and state and local prisoners "supplemented" the U.S. hired farm workforce, sending an unmistakable signal to U.S. farm workers—getting ahead in the U.S. labor market usually meant getting out of farm work. Bracero admissions rose in the 1950s, when federal and state irrigation projects opened new land for farming, the cost of shipping produce by truck from west to east fell with the interstate highway system, and the baby boom increased the demand for fruits and vegetables. Western farmers made business decisions assuming that Braceros would continue to be available, and when the Bracero program ended in 1964, there was a wave of labor-saving mechanization spurred by the higher wages (Martin and Olmstead 1985).

Mexico-U.S. migration remained low between the end of the Bracero program in 1964 and peso devaluations in the late 1970s. During this "golden age" for U.S. farm workers, Cesar Chavez and the United Farm Workers (UFW) won a 40 percent wage increase for grape pickers, increasing entry-level wages from $1.25 to $1.75 an hour in the UFW's first contract in 1966, when the federal minimum wage was $1.25 an hour (Martin 2003). However, U.S. immigration law allowed U.S. employers to issue letters asserting that a foreigner was "essential" to fill even a seasonal farm job, enabling Mexicans to get immigrant visas printed on green cards. Many became green-card commuters who lived in Mexico and worked seasonally on U.S. farms. When the UFW called strikes in support of another 40 percent wage increase in 1979, growers turned to labor contractors, many of whom were green-card commuters, and they recruited replacement workers from their villages in Mexico. Contractors soon replaced the UFW as the major supplier of farm workers, and the number of workers under UFW contract fell, from 60,000 to 70,000 in the early 1970s to 6,000 to 7,000 by the mid-1980s (Martin 2003).

From IRCA to NAFTA

The Immigration Reform and Control Act of 1986 (IRCA, also known as the Simpson-Mazzoli Act) aimed to reduce illegal immigration, largely from Mexico, by imposing sanctions on U.S. employers who knowingly hired unauthorized foreigners and by legalizing some unauthorized foreigners in the United States. Contrary to expectations, the IRCA actually increased Mexico-U.S. migration, in part because of large-scale legalization combined with ineffective border and interior enforcement.

The IRCA included two legalization or amnesty programs, and over 70 percent of the appellants in each were from Mexico. The legalization program for unauthorized farm workers—the Special Agricultural Worker program (SAW)—was rife with fraud. Over 1 million Mexican men became U.S. immigrants under the SAW program by presenting letters from U.S. farm employers saying they had done at least 90 days of farm work in 1985–1986, a sixth of the adult men in rural Mexico. Their families were excluded from legalization, under the theory that SAWs wanted to commute to seasonal farm jobs as had earlier green-card commuters (Martin 1994).

However, many SAWs found non-farm jobs and settled in U.S. cities with their families. As state and local government outlays for education, health, and other public services rose during the recession of the early 1990s, there were suits against the federal government seeking reimbursement for the costs of caring for unauthorized foreigners. The impetus for these lawsuits was the theory that these migrants would not be in the United States if the U.S. government had prevented their unauthorized entry and stay. The perception that immigrants did not pay their way culminated in California's Proposition 187 in 1994 and federal welfare reforms in 1996 that restricted the access of legal and unauthorized foreigners to tax-supported benefits.

U.S. legalization programs encouraged more Mexico-U.S. migration during a time of rapid change in Mexico. Mexico has often defined itself in opposition to the United States and a common Mexican saying is, "Poor Mexico, so far from God, and so close to the U.S." Beginning in the mid-1980s, Mexico's economic policies changed from inward-oriented import substitution to an outward-oriented trade model, which led to the government encouraging foreign investors to create jobs in Mexican factories producing goods for export. The result of this first wave of structural reforms was reduced employment in previously protected sectors such as agriculture and textiles, where workers were displaced. The North American Free Trade Agreement (NAFTA), which went into effect on January 1, 1994, accelerated the restructuring of the Mexican economy (Hufbauer and Schott 1992; U.S. Commission 1990).

The upward slope of the Mexico-U.S. migration hump in the 1990s was due primarily to previous demographic growth and insufficient job creation in Mexico as well as a strong and spreading U.S. demand for Mexican workers. The downward slope of the hump is expected when the number of new entrants to the Mexican labor market falls and economic growth creates more and better-paid jobs in Mexico. The critical questions are how much additional migration results from the economic integration of Mexico and the United States, how soon Mexico-U.S. migration returns to its normal or status quo level, and how much migration is eventually avoided by NAFTA. There was more Mexico-U.S. migration during the 1990s than anticipated. With lower fertility promising significantly fewer new Mexican labor force entrants after 2010, the keys to Mexico-U.S. labor flows will be formal sector job growth in Mexico, demand for Mexican workers in the United States, and U.S. border and interior enforcement policies.

Developments since 2000

The elections of Mexican President Vicente Fox and U.S. President George Bush in 2000 were expected to lead to a new era in Mexico-U.S. migration, as they agreed to develop "an orderly framework for [Mexico-U.S.] migration that ensures humane treatment [and] legal security, and dignifies labor conditions."

Fox subsequently proposed a four-point migration plan that included legalization for unauthorized Mexicans, a new guestworker program, cooperative measures to end border violence, and changes in U.S. law that would exempt Mexicans from U.S. immigrant visa ceilings. In presenting Mexico's proposal, Foreign Minister Jorge Castaneda said, "It's the whole enchilada or nothing." During the summer of 2001, the U.S. government seemed willing to embrace historic changes in Mexico-U.S. migration management, although perhaps not the "whole enchilada."

The September 11, 2001, terrorist attacks froze Mexico-U.S. migration discussions, and the U.S. focus shifted to security. Mexico-U.S. migration continued after September 11 at historically high levels despite stepped-up border controls. President Fox called Mexican migrants in the United States heroes for the $1 billion a month in remittances they sent to Mexico in 2003, and instructed Mexico's 47 consulates in the United States to issue *matricula consulars*, or identification cards. These provided Mexicans with the needed documentation to open bank accounts in a security-conscious United States.

Future Scenarios

There are two extremes along the spectrum that defines future Mexico-U.S. migration flows: stay-at-home development and increased Mexican dependency on the U.S. labor market. In the first scenario, especially rural Mexico may run out of young workers eager to migrate to the United States because of the drop in fertility and if good jobs become available in Mexico. At the other extreme, Mexicans may continue to live on small farms in rural areas but become dependent on remittances from family members with jobs elsewhere in Mexico or the United States. This could lead to rural Mexico becoming a place of "nurseries and nursing homes" producing workers for urban Mexican and U.S. labor markets.

Few observers predicted the large Mexico-U.S. migration hump in the 1990s. A combination of continued U.S. job growth, the diffusion of migration networks within the United States and Mexico, and the rise of China as an alternative place to locate factories makes it hard to predict future Mexico-U.S. migration flow. Slower growth of the Mexican labor force combined with faster economic growth could create good jobs that keep potential Mexican migrants at home. If this is indeed the case, the past quarter century may have seen the peak of the Mexico-U.S. migration. *See also*: **Border control; Legalization; Legislation.**

References

Binational Study on Migration. 1997. *Migration between Mexico and the United States.* Washington, DC and Mexico City: Commission on Immigration Reform. http://migration.ucdavis.edu/mn/cir_mn.html.

Escobar, Agustin, Philip Martin, Peter Schatzer, and Susan Martin. 2003. Mexico-US Migration: Moving the Agenda Forward. *International Migration* 41(2):125–137.

Hufbauer, Gary, and Jeffrey Schott. 1992. *North American Free Trade: Issues and Recommendations.* Washington, DC: Institute for International Economics.

Lowell, B. Lindsay. 2004. *Managing Mexican Migration to the United States: Recommendations for Policymakers.* A Report of the U.S.-Mexico Binational Council. Washington, DC: Center for Strategic and International Studies.

Martin, Philip L. 1993. *Trade and Migration: NAFTA and Agriculture*. Washington, DC: Institute for International Economics.

———. 1994. Good Intentions Gone Awry: IRCA and U.S. Agriculture. *Annals of the Academy of Political and Social Science* 534:44–57.

———. 2003. *Promise Unfulfilled: Unions, Immigration, and Farm Workers*. Ithaca, NY: Cornell University Press.

Martin, Philip L., and Alan L. Olmstead. 1985. The Agricultural Mechanization Controversy. *Science* 227(4687):601–606.

Migration News. 2001. Fox Visits Bush. *Migration News*, October. http://migration.ucdavis.edu/mn/more.php?id=2463_0_2_0.

U.S. Commission for the Study of International Migration and Cooperative Economic Development. 1990. *Unauthorized Migration: An Economic Development Response*. Washington, DC: U.S. Government Printing Office.

U.S.-Mexico Binational Council. 2004. Managing Mexican Migration to the United States: Recommendations for Policymakers. http://www.csis.org/americas/mexico/binational_council_migration.pdf.

PHILIP MARTIN

MIGRANT EDUCATION. In 1960, Congress appropriated $6.5 million to preserve wildlife, yet in the same session declined to appropriate $3.5 million for the education of migrant children. That same year, on Thanksgiving weekend, CBS aired a documentary by Edward R. Murrow entitled *Harvest of Shame* that exposed the treatment of migrant workers and their children.

Five years after the Murrow documentary, President Johnson's war on poverty led Congress to pass the Elementary and Secondary Education Act (ESEA) which would, it was hoped, help bridge the gap between the needs of the children of migrant farm workers and what schools were ready to provide. Unfortunately, most Title I funds went to urban districts while migrant students attended rural schools, so ESEA was soon amended to authorize the Migrant Education Program (Perry 1997:13). Since 1966, the Office of Migrant Education (OME) has helped states that apply to provide services to these children.

A migrant child is defined in Section 1309(2) of the Elementary and Secondary Education Act as a child who is (or whose parent, spouse, or guardian is) a migratory agricultural worker, including a migratory dairy worker or a migratory fisher, and who has moved from one school district to another in the preceding 36 months in order to obtain temporary or seasonal employment in agriculture or fishing. These children change schools frequently, affecting their education. Their needs are also unique. Researchers have noted that half are in low-income families, and that they enroll late in school, fall below the 35th percentile in reading, and require free or reduced meals (Perry 1997:7). Another 40 percent fall below the 35th percentile in math, many have not reached fluency in English, and they have health characteristics similar to those in many developing countries, leading to high rates of absence.

Travel during the year can be in the thousands of miles, and children may leave school in the spring, enter another for the final months of the year, and be in another school in the fall, before returning home, changing schools yet again. There are few studies on the impact of mobility and even fewer on migrant children. One, which examined the impact of family relocation on children's development and functioning in school, concluded that a family move disrupts the routines, relationships, and attachments that define the child's world. Children of families who move often were between 50 and 100 percent more likely to have a delay in growth or development or to have a learning disorder, among other problems (Wood et al. 1993:1337).

John Perry describes why schools are not organized to meet the needs of migrant students: "The typical elementary and secondary school in the United States is organized for a stable population of resident students. It is assumed students will enroll in the fall and be in attendance for the full year and that most of the students will continue in the school during the succeeding year. The curriculum is sequential from fall to spring. Records of student progress and problems are easily available to teachers and guidance counselors" (Perry 1997:8). Thus migrant students might be taught some skills in more than one place, yet miss other critical skills entirely. Schools come to expect parents to be aware of their children's progress as well as the school's activities, which is almost impossible for workers whose schedule may begin with the sunrise and end after the sun sets. Adding lack of public transportation and distance required to travel to some rural schools, we can see the challenges both parents and migrant educators face in meeting the educational needs of the farm workers' children.

For many people it is hard to understand why workers do not stay for the entire school year in one place. Because adult members of migrant families seldom have advanced skills, and therefore enter unskilled agricultural labor to sustain themselves, work and economic necessity are primary factors in family decision making. Migrant programs therefore must help children adjust to constant changes in schools. Teachers also know that at the present time, many migrant families do not speak English at home, so children may have additional pressure to "help their parents make sense of the life in the United States . . . [and] translate letters, read instructions, pay bills, and sometimes negotiate with growers" (Rothenberg 1998:276).

In 1969, a national system to count migrant students and transfer their school records was established as part of the Migrant Education Program. It operated for 25 years until almost all states had applied for a Migrant Program. By then costs of the Migrant Student Records Transfer System (MSRTS) had become too high, and in 1994, MSRTS was discontinued. The Migrant Education Program continues to require that every state maintain and transmit student records in a timely manner.

It used to be thought that farm workers tended to follow three main routes, the Eastern Coast Stream, the Mid-Continent Stream, and the Western Coast Stream, but new studies indicate that farm worker routes are not as clear-cut as once thought. Along their routes, nonetheless, schools can be divided into "sending schools," considered the home base by migrant families, and "receiving schools," which serve migrant children for a shorter time. In either case the students' records are crucial for placing the students at the appropriate level. For this reason, migrant teachers encourage parents to take a copy of their children's records before they leave.

In 1994, a General Accounting Office Report documented that "a child's records often take two to six weeks to arrive in a new school" (GAO 1994:2). But because of privacy and confidentiality laws, there is opposition to a national database to share students' education and health records. In 1999, the National

Association for Migrant Education recommended the "contract for a national data exchange system that could also be used for maintaining student counts" (Resendez et al. 1992). Some of the reasons given were that when the records are late or non-existent, students may receive inappropriate levels of instruction and delayed access to special education services, in addition to being immunized repeatedly and not receiving credit for completed courses because they left before the term came to a close, and the information was not shared.

At the present time OME administers four programs. The Basic State Formula Grant provides funds (more than $350 million in 2000) to be used for supplemental education and support services. The awards are based on the number of students served per state, with part of the funds covering Consortium Arrangements awarded as incentive grants to encourage states to work together and reduce administrative costs, thus increasing funds available for direct services to children. Other funds support projects from across the country aimed at exploring how technology can be used to combat the problems of educational disruption, lack of resources, and language difficulty that traditionally plague children in migrant worker families.

A second OME program is the Migrant Education Even Start, a family literacy program focusing on families who perform migrant agricultural work and related processing activities. The program is designed to assist parents in obtaining their high school diploma or GED, prepare them to be their child's first teacher, and support developing reading skills in young children, thus helping families break the cycle of poverty and illiteracy. Third, the High School Equivalency Program provides funds through institutions of higher education to provide academic and support services like counseling, health services, and job or education placement to eligible migrant youth 16 years and older. Lastly, the College Assistance Migrant Program assists migrant first-year college undergraduates.

One of the biggest challenges for migrant students today is the national movement for school accountability. Most states and national leaders have focused their attention on higher academic standards for all the children in the public schools. As state reforms have created a way to ensure accountability they have also created additional barriers to the graduation of migrant students in American schools (GAO 1994).

Today local Migrant Education Programs must adapt their strategies to a changing farm worker force. Farm workers are young, averaging 31 in age, and half are married. Half of all farm worker parents are accompanied by their children (U.S. Department of Labor 2000:9). In addition, the vast majority of all farm workers, 81 percent in 1997–1998, were foreign-born; 77 percent of all farm workers were Mexican-born (U.S. Department of Labor 2000:5). In some areas the majority of workers may be from Haiti or Central America; in others, the majority may be indigenous Mexican or Guatemalan families who do not speak Spanish or have previous schooling. To this challenge is added the pressure of the anti-immigrant feelings that continue to increase in many American communities.

Since most public schools are already crowded, new students with limited resources but with a great amount of needs are sometimes not welcomed. When children do not speak English at home, schools usually label them as Limited English Proficient (LEP). This is a derogatory label. The alternate designation

English Language Learner focuses on what students are accomplishing, rather than on their limitations (Exum-Lopez 1999:7).

While anti-immigrant advocates add up the cost of providing health and educational services to the children of "foreigners," most growers find it impossible to find American workers willing to plant, tend, harvest, and pack fruits and vegetables. As an example, the state of Virginia appointed a study to determine the economic impact of migrant and seasonal farm workers. Since states cannot deny undocumented children access to public education, taxpayers continue to be billed over $6,000 per student, but this was found to be offset by migrant workers' contribution to the economy including approximately $284 million annually in cash receipts to Virginia farmers (Trupo 1998).

In an effort that grew to become the Binational Program, California Migrant Teachers have since 1976 attempted to improve communication between the U.S. and Mexican schools where cross-border migrant students spent most of their time. Currently this involves over 45,000 students. While the program does not involve any money, it helps both school systems in the transmission of students' records and other initiatives that make the students' lives easier when migrating every year. One of the components is the binational document, written in both English and Spanish, which allows teachers in either country to write the subjects and grades that the student achieved until his departure date. A chart explains how the American grading system (A, B, C) equates to the Mexican system (0–100), making it easier for both parents and teachers and counselors who may not be with the other school system.

The topic of education for the children of migrant workers is increasingly significant, in part because it is not exclusive to the United States. As the National Institute of Adult Education in Mexico views the future, "As we see a few decades into the next century, with their veritable rivers of migrants going to the stronger economies, the [education] problem becomes one for the developed countries with their aging populations in dire need of migrants" (Díaz de Cossio 1999:13). *See also*: **Agricultural workers; Bilingual education; Immigrant education.**

References

Ashabranner, Brent. 1985. *Dark Harvest*. Hamden, CT: Linnet Books.

Díaz de Cossio, Roger. 1999. *Adult Education, Migration, and Immigrant Education*. http://www.ed.gov/pubs/HowAdultsLearn/DiazdeCossio.pdf.

Exum-Lopez, Marianne. 1999. *When Discourses Collide*. New York: Peter Lang.

Hart, Elva Treviño. 1999. *Barefoot Heart*. Tempe, AZ: Bilingual Review/Press.

Office of Migrant Education. n.d. Harvest of Hope: Guide to the Program Services of the Office of Migrant Education. U.S. Department of Education. www.ed.gov/offices/OESE/MEP.

Perry, John D. 1997. Migrant Education: Thirty Years of Success, but Challenges Remain. Position Paper. ERIC Digest.

Pindus, Nancy M., et al. 1993. *Services for Migrant Children in the Health, Social Services, and Education Systems*. Washington, DC: Urban Institute.

Resendez, I., W. Miller, T. Reyna, V.A. Rivera, and A. Wright. 1992. *A Comprehensive Plan for the Education of America's Migrant Children Through Elementary and Secondary Education Programs Scheduled for Reauthorization in 1993*. Sunnyside, WA: National Association of Migrant Educators.

Romo, Harriet. 1999. *Reaching Out: Best Practices for Educating Mexican-Origin Children and Youth*. Charleston, WV: ERIC and Clearinghouse on Rural Education and Small Schools.

Rothenberg, Daniel. 1998. *With These Hands*. New York: Harcourt Brace and Company.

Trupo, Paul. 1998. *The Impact of Migrant, Seasonal, and H-2A Farmworkers on the Virginia Economy*. Blacksburg: Virginia Tech, Department of Agricultural and Applied Economics.

U.S. Department of Education. 1999a. *Directory of Services for Migrant and Seasonal Farmworkers and Their Families*. Washington, DC: U.S. Department of Education.

———. 1999b. *Handbook of Effective Migrant Education Practices*. Washington, DC: U.S. Department of Education.

———. 2000. *Participation of Migrant Students in Title I Migrant Education Program Summer-Term Projects, 1998*. Statistical Analysis Report, January. Washington, DC: U.S. Department of Education.

U.S. Department of Labor. 2000. *Findings from the National Agricultural Workers Survey (NAWS) 1997–98, Research Report No. 8, A Demographic and Employment Profile of United States Farmworkers*. Washington, DC: U.S. Department of Labor.

U.S. General Accounting Office. 1994. *Elementary School Children: Many Change Schools Frequently, Harming Their Education*. Report No. GAO/HEHS-94-45. Washington, DC: General Accounting Office.

Wood, David, Debra Scarlata, Paul W. Newacheck, and Sharon Nessim. 1993. Impact of Family Relocation on Children's Growth, Development, School Function, and Behavior. *Journal of the American Medical Association* 270(11):1334–1337.

VERONICA L. DONAHUE AND ELVA TREVIÑO HART

MIGRATION PROCESSES. Looking around the United States at the opening of a new century, we see many recent immigrants representing a remarkable variety of world cultures. Such vistas, common to many nations, give the misleading impression that extensive migration is new. In fact, continual comings and goings have marked human history from the beginning. Settlers energized by new crops expanded, merchants and artisans voyaged, empires introduced colonists and slaves, and so forth. Migration has helped spread world religions and other cultural transformations. The present is not distinctive for migration but for the bounded nation-state with defined rights to residence. Today, migrants come from one country, go to another, and stand out as such.

Migration processes thus include not only migrants but also the contexts that surround contemporary migration: capitalist economies, advanced communications and transportation technologies, and the ruling ideas of various nations. Modern political developments, such as mass citizenship, public education, social services, and military duty, help define a "host" population vis-à-vis newcomers. Cultural issues in immigration are shaped by our contemporary assumption that nations share cultures, languages, and identities, a concept of community that would have been foreign to the highly segmentary societies of the past. Contemporary asylum law has emerged from the post–World War II development of international human rights ideals, in the modern context of total warfare, including war against civilians, and the tight interweaving of political-military relations among distant world locations.

Much, though not all, migration occurs through the growth and diversification of the capitalist economy opening money-earning opportunities to newcomers.

Hot spots of capital investment and economic growth combine with mobile populations to create foci of intensive settlement. This scenario begs two questions: how are people "mobilized," and why do some elements of the modern economy attract and accept newcomers while others specialize in established populations?

The answer to the first question is that employers initiate migration by recruiting labor in previously untouched places; in the twentieth century, large government temporary contract worker (guestworker) programs have also spread the word. Once initial recruitment ends, migrants do the rest themselves: personal information and expectations are more than enough to mobilize relatives and hometown mates. The answer to the second question is more complex than just that generic jobs and money in rich countries attract migrants. Jobs and small businesses are highly differentiated by educational requirements, pay scales, working conditions, contractual rights, and degrees of personal status. We refer to this feature of the capitalist economy as "segmentation," and like the flow of money in general, segmentation is dynamic, closing up old labor markets and opening new ones. While many migrants enter the segments most exploited and least respected by society at large, the "dirty, dangerous, and demeaning" jobs, some skilled job sectors also attract immigrants. Job segmentation is in some part dictated by market processes, but to a considerable extent it is a matter of politics, in which firms, labor unions, politicians, and bureaucrats negotiate specific patterns of official or even covert immigrant access. Furthermore, migration between nations is profoundly shaped by globalization, not only in obvious ways, such as the ease of air transportation across vast distances, but also in subtle ones, including the use of immigrants by domestic industries in globally competitive situations to keep down costs, and the emergence of cities (New York, Miami, Los Angeles, San Francisco) whose commerce and culture substantially aim at international rather than domestic markets.

Hosts assist migrants without obvious material benefits in return, such as churches serving community needs and established ethnic organizations advocating for co-ethnics who encounter police or immigration officials. Migration is inextricably woven into society, a process memorably termed "institutionalized support for immigration." As institutionalized support has grown, deliberate migrant recruitment has declined, though not disappeared, partly because such movement becomes self-perpetuating. Thus, for migration to continue, pro-immigration interests do not always have to have their way politically, which results in a disparity between immigration reality and immigration policy.

According to the push-pull forces that influence immigration, where immigrants come from is as important as their destination. It is true that most migrants seek to earn money (the exceptions being refugees forced from home and those whose main motivation is joining other family members), but the converse is not true, that each and every poor person in an impoverished country compares the local money-making capacity with that available in a wealthy nation, and on this basis decides to move. If that were the case, there would be far more migrants than there actually are. The person contemplating a move needs information: possible ways to earn money, places to live, ways to cross the border, and so on. This requires the help of those already in the new locale, or who have gone and returned. In turn, the person who takes this dramatic step becomes a resource for others back home. Migration thus takes place through networks rather than by decisions of free-floating individuals.

Furthermore, the weighing of options ("should I stay or should I go?") takes place in a web of commitments and perceptions that envelop the individual. The most important commitment is to the household, especially on the part of adult sons and daughters and young husbands. Earnings from migration often shelter domestic economies from sudden risk (whether a slumping national economy or a family illness), in a context where few people have insurance. Such earnings also fund investments and subsidize day-to-day expenses. In other words, families try to maintain and improve themselves over time, with migration as just one of their options.

Gender and generation are factors influencing migration processes. In migration-prone regions, there often is an idealization of migratory adventure (sometimes called a "culture of migration") as a rite of passage in young men's lives as well as a household economic obligation to their mothers and fathers. Likewise, women often migrate due to circumstances in which men have abandoned women with children. A young mother, then, might go to earn money cleaning U.S. motels while a grandmother watches over the grandchildren back in Mexico.

In opting to move, the possibility of change through migration needs to be meaningful to people. What opens such possibilities? Besides deliberate recruitment, we notice that out-migration typifies nations that are rapidly developing (not, as one might expect, the poorest and most stagnant ones). Why should this be? Commercialization of agriculture breaks the old ties between patrons and peasants; landlords may no longer sharecrop land that now can be farmed by tractor. Local inequalities worsen; the very poorest can rarely afford to migrate internationally but the beleaguered lower and middle ranks of the peasantry find migration a defense against declining relative position. People are exposed to new consumer goods, which become essential to daily life. Such goods both take income to purchase and appear to originate in the wealthier nations of the world. Population surges; the global development process has sparked rapid population growth in the past two centuries.

Though the increase in population is leveling off today, most migrant-sending nations have a young population seeking jobs as domestic agriculture and industry become more capital intensive, reducing their need for labor. Education also widens the horizons of youth, while at the same time few educated jobs are created locally. Finally, global and national economic cycles, spurts of growth followed by bitter depressions, spur migration; terrible waves of unemployment, farm decline, and business failure particularly stimulate departure. Migration is part and parcel of modern economic, social, and political change, not poverty, isolation, and stagnation.

Most people who migrate intend to return. With time, however, commitments to the new society intervene—steady and fulfilling jobs, satisfying homes, children speaking English and going to local schools, and, for women, relatively less belabored life. Such processes of "incorporation" take place independent of both initial migrant intentions and the receiving nation's legal approval or disapproval. Many, if not most, migrants return before such attachments set in place, but the "settlers" gradually form an immigrant community. One might note the distinction drawn here between migrants, who go back and forth, and immigrants, who spend extended periods of time in the new society. Efficient transportation and communication in the current era permit some people to hold strong attachments across borders, which is referred to as transnationalism, but this seems less common than either endpoint.

Migration, then, is more like a glacier—slow, accumulative, and quite powerful—than an invasion. Migration processes humble public policy's ambition to design and control. Nevertheless, an involved public might consider four options, not mutually exclusive. First, the sending and receiving nations can together organize the temporary or permanent movement of people. This can make part of the flow safe and subordinate, but experience shows that unofficial migration always accompanies it. Second, the receiving nation can unilaterally determine numbers and kinds of people who migrate legally, while using police or military force to interdict those people who migrate outside such rules, resulting in a massive control bureaucracy. This is the pattern of most nations in the world today, and it certainly guides and affects migration, but experience shows that extra-legal migration persists despite intensive law enforcement, and brings in its wake smuggling, accidental deaths, underworlds, exploitation, and other negative consequences.

Third, the sending and receiving societies can bolster their communities and institutions to temper the dynamism of the capitalist economy. In part, this requires stronger mutual relations between newcomers and established residents. This might involve altering the contexts of migration, including resisting the drastic recessions in developing economies caused by international private and public banks, promoting more equal and less capital intensive forms of development, and altering the conduct of foreign policy to reduce refugee-producing activities, including arms sales, military advisors, and support for guerrilla and anti-guerrilla wars. Finally, hosts can support the self-organizing actions that immigrants undertake to give security and dignity to their lives, such as forming effective unions, neighborhood and ethnic associations, and so on, which reduce exploitation, crime, and misery, benefits in which the entire society shares.

Migration is forging the contemporary world. In part through migratory processes, both hosts and migrants are reformulating their activities and the symbols that surround them; we perceive this as the development of new identities in the course of conflict and compromise. Major blocs of nations, such as the European Union and potentially the North American Free Trade area, are making internal movement easier and more open, while stigmatizing and interdicting migrants from the poorer nations that border them. Thus, the present relationship of migration and citizenship to the system of nations may be changing, but in so doing creating new forms of stratification. The question whether migration reduces or reinforces global inequality remains vital, yet unanswered; a reasonable case can be made that migrant sending countries, and the families and communities inside them, expend effort and resources to bring up future migrants as children, to give them rest while returning from foreign labors, and to shelter them once retired. The money sent home helps, especially when there are vibrant commercial and agricultural economies in which to invest it, but in many cases it just enables survival in areas ignored by national and global capitalization. *See also*: **Gender; Return migration; Social networks; Transnationalism.**

References

Brettell, Caroline B., and James F. Hollifield. 2000. *Migration Theory: Talking Across Disciplines*. New York and London: Routledge.

Brubaker, William Rogers, ed. 1989. *Immigration and the Politics of Citizenship in Europe and North America*. Lanham, MD: University Press of America.

Cornelius, Wayne A., Philip L. Martin, and James F. Hollifield, eds. 1994. *Controlling Immigration: A Global Perspective*. Stanford, CA: Stanford University Press.

Heyman, Josiah McC. 1998. *Finding a Moral Heart for U.S. Immigration Policy: An Anthropological Perspective*. Washington, DC: American Anthropological Association.

Hondaganeu-Sotelo, Pierrette. 1994. *Gendered Transitions: Mexican Experiences of Migration*. Berkeley and Los Angeles: University of California Press.

Massey, Douglas, Rafael Alarcón, Jorge Durand, and Humberto González. 1987. *Return to Aztlán: The Social Process of International Migration from Western Mexico*. Berkeley and Los Angeles: University of California Press.

Massey, Douglas, Joaquín Arango, Graeme Hugo, Ali Kouaouci, Adela Pellegrino, and J. Edward Taylor. 1998. *Worlds in Motion: Understanding International Migration at the End of the Millennium*. Oxford: Clarendon Press.

Meillassoux, Claude. 1981. *Maidens, Meals, and Money: Capitalism and the Domestic Community*. Cambridge: Cambridge University Press.

Piore, Michael. 1979. *Birds of Passage: Migrant Labor and Industrial Societies*. Cambridge: Cambridge University Press.

JOSIAH McC. HEYMAN

MUSIC. From the beginning of European settlement, the United States has been a mecca for immigration from various regions of the world, with each group bringing its own distinctive music, both as a cultural link to its place of origin and as a means for enjoying accessible entertainment. Over the first 300 years of its existence, from Spanish settlement in Florida in 1565 through the establishment of British colonial government beginning in 1617 to increasing waves of immigration of the nineteenth century encouraged by the doctrine of manifest destiny that pushed the frontiers of the country to achieve transcontinental reach, the development of music in the United States was largely the provenance of ethnic groups that remained relatively independent from cross-cultural interaction. This involved both the music of the people—so-called ethnic or folk music—as well as more sophisticated styles of classical music.

Examples can be seen in the westward migration of the Scots-Irish, who formed the bulk of early settlers of the British colonies. Their folk tunes, often performed on improvised instruments to accompany the voice, include hymns, work songs, lullabies, and other pieces of social music in the Appalachian hinterlands, passed on as immigrants continued to move farther west. Immigrants from Bohemia and Moravia formed colonies in North Carolina and Pennsylvania by 1750, where a vibrant musical life surrounded the Moravian Church. The deportation in 1756 of French Acadians to Louisiana, then a largely unexplored French territory, brought the rhythmically vital secular dance music in dialect that served as the foundation for modern Cajun styles, such as Zydeco, nourished over almost two centuries of cultural isolation. Finally, the importation of slaves, mostly from West Africa by way of the Caribbean islands, brought a polyglot of musics from the various tribes and kingdoms of a region that stretched from Mauritania and Senegal in the north to Nigeria and Cameroon in the south. These included rhythmic drumming of an additive sort (whereby rhythms shift over time by altering strong and weak beats), choral singing (either monophonic chanting of work songs or polyphonic social songs of more than 200 ethnic groups), and, with the rise of Christianity among this group, creation of hymns that reflected a mixture of Protestant homophony with ethnic melodies and rhythms. This later became organized into the African American spiritual.

During the nineteenth century, waves of principally European immigration brought the popular music of each group, resulting in notable regional preferences, depending on patterns of settlement. For example, Germans in the upper Midwest developed the ubiquitous town band with genres such as the waltz and polka, both of which are heard frequently today in those regions. Further derivatives of the Scots-Irish tradition were created to accommodate the new territories, resulting in Gold Rush songs of 1849 California and the so-called Cowboy songs of 1875–1910, both of which feature nostalgic texts and lyrical melodies. The rise in status of the African American during this time also resulted in a corresponding development of popular ethnic music, ranging from romanticized parodies of songwriters such as Stephen Foster in the 1860s and the ragtime of Scott Joplin around 1900 to the development of largely improvisational blues and jazz idioms in the twentieth century. Settlement of Hispanic areas of the Southwest from Texas to California included the importation of dance music like the Habañero or Zapatillo, as well as mariachi bands.

For the bulk of the twentieth century the music of immigrants shifted dramatically from self-contained cultural entertainment toward a more integrated polyglot style that infused both classical and popular music with new idioms, even as it began to dissolve the boundaries of what could be considered ethnic. This was due largely to the notion of fusion, wherein certain elements of music could be studied, absorbed, and re-formed to serve new musical forms and styles. For example, the music of Southeast Asia, particularly Indonesia, which consists mainly of marimbas and xylophones repeating modal phrases that change from one to another subtly over time, became the basis for the Minimalism espoused by Philip Glass and John Adams. Similar evolution of beat patterns in West African drumming served Terry Riley and Steve Reich in the same way. Blues and jazz continued to evolve, with elements such as the gliding of notes, driving rhythms, and improvisatory call-and-response forms becoming mainstream and helping to bridge the divide between popular and classical.

In the mid-1960s, associated with the development of "youth culture" as well as a time of social challenges and rapid change, many in different immigrant groups tended to amalgamate into homogenous forms that incorporated many cultures without necessarily distinguishing any particular element. For music, particularly popular music, this meant that genres of particular immigrant communities were absorbed into more generic developing styles such as rock and pop. This in turn was intensified by the development of mass media, particularly the recording and broadcast by way of radio, film, and television, through which the world's music became accessible instantaneously by electronic means. The advent of the driving rock style of British rock groups such as the Beatles and Rolling Stones, for example, began a wave of American imitations. While few of these bands immigrated permanently to the United States, there were many cross-Atlantic visits, and the resulting influence was incalculable in further directing the development of the music business and thus popular music.

The pervasive spread of American popular culture beginning with this period, as both reaction to and consequence of the Cold War, also had the effect of spreading the media globally. For immigrants, however, the homogenization of popular music meant that ethnic musical roots were seen as becoming endangered, particularly as second and third generations became Americanized. Immigrant communities that were self-contained, whether in urban or rural areas, began serious study of their own musical-cultural roots, with the intent both of preserving this heritage and of reinventing their music for presentation to the musical world at large.

It was during this period that a dual identity was created. In the "Latin" (Latin American) barrios of New York, for example, Cuban folk music, derived from the mixed Caribbean heritage of Hispanic and African music, was combined with both jazz and native Puerto Rican folk idioms such as the jibaro, bomba, and call-and-response plena. The result was a particularly rhythmically incisive style that came to be known as *Salsa*. Since dance was a social outlet for many communities, music derived from a rhythmic richness of conga, rumba, and mambo became commonplace. The spread to American culture at large came when these ethnic genres were infused into the mainstream by the media, particularly film. Popular Latin stars, ranging from sophisticated singers like Desi Arnaz to popular artists like Gloria Estefan, Ricky Martin, and Selena, have since not only catered to their own immigrant communities but also achieved popular general success with music that largely fuses the Hispanic style with more generic popular trends.

The 1960s and the internal political situation also helped to create a style of popular music that was derived from both past folk traditions and immigrant forms. Sometimes, this included secondary sounds of non-Western instruments as backdrops to popular music. For instance, Paul Simon imported pan pipe players from the Andes as well as South African choral singing to enhance his performances of politically charged songs.

Perhaps the most important of the immigrant musical contributions came from the island of Jamaica. The civil rights movements of the 1960s led African Americans to explore their own musical heritage. Since many of the former styles, such as jazz, ragtime, blues, and spirituals, either already had been absorbed into the national musical language or were associated with the oppression of slavery, a new African American style emerged that was modern, yet contained melodic and ethnic historical roots and could serve as a musical messenger. This was found in two places: the resurrection of indigenous groups such as the Gullah of the sea islands off South Carolina, and the creation of a non-Hispanic Caribbean style, principally from islands such as Jamaica and Barbados where Spanish influence was minimal. These resulted in an amalgam of strong island traditional music and modern rock, called hip-hop. Early hip-hop music by Jamaican immigrant DJ Cool Herc incorporated a Rastafarian style called reggae into a style of music emphasizing rapid-fire spoken-sung dialogue about 1975, at the same time legitimate practitioners like Bob Marley began to introduce the genre in its native form. Both forms embodied political commentary, and as they were meant to reflect society in minority (including immigrant) communities, their content further developed during the 1970s to include rap, soul, and funk. Rap in particular relies heavily on vocal traditions that emphasize rhythmic-melodic chanting with verse phraseology derived from West Africa by way of slaves and immigrants of the Caribbean.

Since 1980, immigration statistics demonstrate that many new arrivals from Asia and Latin America either have been imbued with the global American popular musical style or have tended to remain largely isolated and self-contained. While these immigrants bring with them the belief that their ethnic cultural identity (including music) needs to be preserved, this often occurs without much attempt to provide further musical techniques to the general world of popular (or classical) music. For instance, immigrants from various Asian communities, from China to Korea, India to the Philippines, have native-language television- or radio-stations in major areas of settlement, such as Seattle or Los Angeles—or in the case of Vietnamese immigrants, as far afield as Garden City, Kansas. These stations broadcast cultural programs and music for a specific and limited audience, and there is little known about how this might influence or reach out to a broader section of the public.

Many immigrant groups, however, form ensembles to perform folk music of their native regions at specific ethnic gatherings and larger venues. There are over 50 national folk festivals, with some of the most important held annually in Boston, Minneapolis, New Jersey, Philadelphia, and Seattle. These concentrate almost exclusively on traditional ethnic music, emphasizing less of an evolving style than a preservative approach. Such events serve to broaden musical spread as folk ensembles are asked to perform publicly at a variety of venues having nothing to do with their own communities. They also introduce new ethnic music to the national scene. Whether Russian balalaika ensembles, Jewish Klezmer bands, or, for general entertainment purposes at ubiquitous occasions like graduation ceremonies and county fairs, Scottish pipe bands, the contribution to the musical sound-scape is auto generative, whether or not immigrant musicians are themselves involved.

Certain immigrant groups do continue to participate in the development of American music. Celtic bands, popularized by the extensive use of Irish and Scottish music in mass media such as film scores, have proliferated and offer popular entertainment based to some extent on the sentimental nature of the lyrics and use of unusual ear-catching instruments like uilleann pipes, the tin whistle, and the Celtic harp. Polyrhythmic music derived from Middle Eastern Arabic genres such as the maqam and taksim can occasionally be found in popular music, such as Queen's "We Will Rock You."

The influence of immigrant music has been most obvious in the world of popular music over the past 25 years, thanks in part to the global mass marketing of popular styles such as rock and country and western. Beginning with the international tours of pop groups like the Beatles in the early 1960s, the style has become endemic in all parts of the globe, so that immigrants arriving from virtually any country to the United States are familiar with the majority of popular American groups or songs. The effect of this mass media is that immigrant music is largely localized, either with traditional groups or in academic institutions, while their contribution to the development of American music in general has become a much more subtle and less overt process than it has been prior to the last two or three decades. *See also*: **Global origins: Asia, Africa, and Europe; Global origins: Latin America and the Caribbean.**

References

Encyclopedia of Popular Music. 1998. London: Macmillan.
Garland Encyclopedia of World Music. 2002. Particularly vol. 3: *The United States and Canada.* New York: Routledge.
Guinness Encyclopedia of Popular Music. 1992–1995. Enfield, U.K: Guinness.
World Music: The Rough Guide. 1995. London: Penguin Books.
http://www.encyclopedia.thefreedictionary.com/music.
http://www.fact-index.com/m/mu/music.

BERTIL VAN BOER

N

NATIONAL SECURITY. The constant policy and political challenge of balancing border enforcement while reaping the economic benefits of immigration intensified on September 11, 2001. While the hijackers on September 11 were not illegal immigrants, all were foreign-born, and most held legally issued visas. As a consequence, legislative and judicial action ensued which underscores the indelible mark that these terrorist attacks have left on the immigration history of the United States (Chishti 2002). The impacts on immigration are more process- and technology-oriented than the sweeping "prevention through deterrence" border enforcement changes in the 1990s; nevertheless, the disruption to foreigners and effect on immigration have been clear as well as controversial (Cornelius 2004).

Factors such as high unemployment rates in Mexico, a burgeoning service sector, and reliance on foreign-born skilled labor in the technology industry provide the requisite supply and demand scenario for continuing to fuel the employment of foreign-born workers. A major portion of these workers come from Mexico. Consequently, the U.S.-Mexico border serves as the stage for dramatic increases in border security and is a vivid example of the tensions between homeland security and immigration. Even the Mexican government concurred, when publicly acknowledging the impossibility of dealing with migration issues without taking into account security considerations (Carral 2003).

The misconception remains that post–September 11 policies were the first to be aimed at heightening border enforcement; in fact, increased border security began during the first term of the Clinton administration. With fast growth of the immigrant worker population and fears that U.S. natives were being displaced from jobs, anti-immigration fervor and political pressure mounted, particularly in states bordering Mexico. "Operation Gatekeeper" in San Diego, in concert with operations "Blockade" in El Paso and "Safeguard" in Arizona, were launched in order to seal popular urban crossing points, in hopes that mountains and desert would guard the rest of the border naturally and curb the influx of unauthorized immigrants through deterrence (Cornelius 2004). Immigration policy in the 1990s was characterized by increased border enforcement, with patrol hours along the U.S.-Mexico border tripling between 1994 and 1999. Passage of the Illegal Immigration Reform and Immigrant Responsibility Act (IIRIRA) in 1996 increased the number of Border Patrol agents, lengthened the list of deportable crimes, and rescinded rights of unauthorized immigrants to judicial review prior to deportation (Orrenius 2003).

Scholars have highlighted the paradoxical relationship between heightened border enforcement and the immigration boom (Cornelius 2004). The Urban Institute estimates that 9.3 million undocumented immigrants are currently in the United States. Critics of concentrated border enforcement also underscore the unintended consequences. From 1995 to 2004, more than 2,640 migrants have died in border crossing–related incidents, a tenfold increase since the strategy was initiated. Moreover, these policies have fueled the human smuggling industry along with the number of vigilantes. Critics and proponents alike point to the lack of workplace enforcement as the main reason for ineffectiveness of border enforcement; in 2001, there were only 124 immigration agents focused on workplace enforcement compared to 9,500 on the U.S. border (Cornelius 2004).

With both sides of the immigration debate demanding reform and candidates attempting to court the Hispanic vote, President George W. Bush proposed guestworker and amnesty programs during the 2000 presidential campaign. These programs would have regularized the status of millions of unauthorized workers. However, the events of September 11 caused these pending immigration proposals to be dropped from his political agenda (Orrenius 2003). Proposals for a guestworker program still resurface, but disagreements about an amnesty program and the potential impact of policy changes on overall immigration continue (Leiken 2002).

While September 11 did not provide the initial impetus to enhance U.S. border security or reform immigration policy, it has affected the personnel, processes, and technology associated with entering and exiting the country, primarily through three congressional acts: the USA Patriot Act, Enhanced Border Security Act, and Homeland Security Act. Impacts of this legislation are manifested through changes in non-citizen detainment, screening of foreign visitors and students, and technological advances in surveillance, biometric identification, and tracking of visitors.

In the days following September 11, particular scrutiny was directed at the Immigration and Naturalization Service (INS). Notoriety surrounding the agency's bureaucratic system and propensity for mistakes, prevalent well before September 11, exploded into furious criticism when it was revealed in March of 2002 that INS had issued student visas to two of the hijackers who had trained at a Florida flight school (Leiken 2002). Legislative changes and executive orders to alter visa issuance and application rules as well as detainment and deportation regulation began soon after the attacks.

Perhaps the most controversial changes have come as a consequence of the USA Patriot Act. Passed overwhelmingly by Congress just one week after September 11, the USA Patriot Act has been hailed as a key tool in the war on terror, and as a frontal assault on civil liberties. The Department of Justice was given broad new powers to conduct searches, employ electronic surveillance, and detain suspected terrorists. Exclusive power was granted the attorney general to certify an alien as a terrorist simply on "reasonable grounds to believe" that the alien is a terrorist or has committed an act of terrorism, leading to mandatory detention (Greenya 2003; Migration Policy Institute 2003). The indefinite detainment of over 1,250 people since September 11, mostly for violations of immigration law, and harsh and seemingly permanent imprisonment of non-citizens in Guantanamo Bay, Cuba, alarm numerous civil rights and legal organizations and call into question fundamental commitments to Constitutional rights as well as international treaties (Chishti 2002).

Aside from detainment, the most obvious changes have been in the area of visa requirements and stricter background checks for visa applicants. Length of time that tourists and business people may stay in the United States has been limited to 30 days, and application rules for student visas have been tightened. These changes have resulted in drastic declines in visas issued for tourism and business from 3.5 million in 2001 to 2.2 million in 2003 (Orrenius 2003). After the Enhanced Border Security and Visa Entry Reform Act was signed into law in May of 2002, a new foreign student reporting system, the Student and Exchange Visitor System (SEVIS), was unveiled as part of the Enhanced Border Security law. This system mandated all schools to report enrollment and progress information for all international students, while required background checks and stricter overall requirements effectively reduced the total number of student visas issued by 26 percent from 2001 to 2003 (Orrenius 2003). Further sharp reduction in numbers of students and scholars have led higher education and business alike to predict significant future impacts on quality of research as well as international understanding.

Refugee resettlement has also decreased substantially, with number of refugee approvals accepted in 2002 (18,653) representing a 72 percent decline from the previous year (Kerwin 2002). This reflects a global retrenchment on commitments to refugee protection as well as implementation by the Justice Department of the National Security Entry-Exit Registration System (NSEERS) a month after SEVIS was announced. NSEERS requires certain non-immigrants deemed to be a national security risk to register and submit fingerprints as well as photographs upon their arrival. It has been vehemently criticized for infringing on civil liberties, and particularly for allowing racial profiling of particular immigrant communities (particularly Muslim, Arab, and South Asian) for harsh and selective application of immigration laws based on nationality and religion, while failing to really address the threat of terrorism and reduce the number of undocumented immigrants (Sherer 2004).

All of these programs were eventually moved, either entirely or partially, into the jurisdiction of the Department of Homeland Security (DHS). As part of the largest government reorganization in 50 years, DHS brings together 22 disparate agencies (including a portion of the abolished INS), 180,000 government employees, and a $40 billion budget. This has brought several former border and security agencies under one umbrella, Immigration and Customs Enforcement (ICE). In combining the resources, jurisdictions, and functions of the U.S. Customs Service, the Immigration and Naturalization Service, the Federal Protective Service, and later the Federal Air Marshals Service, ICE has become Homeland Security's largest investigative bureau. Its responsibilities include securing the nation's long, porous borders, tracking smuggling and shipment of weapons and "dual-use" equipment that could be used as weapons, and increasing numbers of interdiction teams to coordinate air and land responses to border threats. ICE continues to oversee SEVIS and the US VISIT program launched in 2004 that requires visa holders to be photographed and fingerprinted before entering the country. In addition to overseeing programs and immigration policy that pre-dated the department's existence, DHS has also launched further projects, such as Operation Liberty Shield, a policy allowing detention of asylum seekers from countries where al-Qaeda is said to have operated.

The interrelationship between immigration and security continues to compli-cate reform within the intelligence community as well as the very nature of the democratic system. The legacies of September 11 continue to reverberate through impacts on immigration policy and immigrants themselves. National intelligence legislation continues to be formulated, and on December 8, 2004, the Intelligence Reform bill passed Congress, adding 10,000 more border guards, 4,000 more border inspectors, and 40,000 beds to detention centers housing illegal immigrants over the next five years (Barrett and Henry 2004). Ultimately, as researchers and policymakers alike have asserted, the immigration system is broken. There ap-pears to be no end in sight for unilateral concentrated border enforcement strat-egy, despite the fact that it has not addressed the increase in undocumented immigrants nor proven to prevent terrorism. The federal government and the American public are likely to have a continuing and contentious struggle to bal-ance border and immigration enforcement in a time when security and economic and social gains seem to be at great odds. *See also*: **Border control; Employer sanctions; Unauthorized immigration; U.S.-Mexico border.**

References

Barrett, Ted, and Ed Henry. 2004. Senate OKs Intelligence Overhaul Bill. http://www.cnn.com/2004/ALLPOLITICS/12/08/intelligence.bill/index.html.

Carral, Magdalena. 2003. Migration and Security Policy Post-9/11: Mexico and the United States. Paper presented at the 2nd North American Meeting of the Trilateral Commission, New York, November 14–16.

Chishti, Muzaffar. 2002. Immigration and Security Post-Sept. 11. http://www.migration information.org/feature/display.cfm?ID=46.

Chishti, Muzaffar, Doris Meissner, Demetrios G. Papademetriou, Jay Peterzell, Michael J. Wishnie, and Stephen W. Yale-Loehr. 2003. America's Challenge: Domestic Security, Civil Liberties, and National Unity after September 11. http://www.migrationpolicy.org/pubs/Americas_Challenges.pdf.

Cornelius, Wayne. 2004. Evaluating Enhanced U.S. Border Enforcement. http://www.migrationinformation.org/feature/display.cfm?ID=223.

Greenya, John. 2003. Immigration Law in Post-9/11 America. http://www.dcbar.org/for_lawyers/washington_lawyer/august_2003/immigration.cfm.

Kerwin, Donald. 2002. Migrants, Borders and National Security: U.S. Immigration Policy Since September 11, 2001. CMS occasional paper no. 12. New York: Center for Migration Studies.

Kraly, Ellen Percy, Mary G. Powers, and William Seltzer. 2004. IRCA: Lessons of the Last U.S. Legalization Program. http://www.migrationinformation.com/Feature/display.cfm?ID=233.

Leiken, Robert. 2002. Mexican Immigration after 9/11: New (and Old) Challenges. http://www.cis.org/articles/2002/meximmpanel.html.

Maxwell, Kenneth. 2003. *Review of* Operation Gatekeeper: The Rise of the "Illegal Alien" and the Remaking of the U.S.-Mexico Boundary. *Foreign Affairs* 82(2):158.

Migration Policy Institute. 2003. Chronology of Events since September 11, 2001 Related to Immigration and National Security. http://www.migrationinformation.org/chronology.pdf.

Orrenius, Pia. 2003. U.S. Immigration and Economic Growth: Putting Policy on Hold. Federal Reserve Bank of Dallas, *Southwest Economy* 6:1–7.

Rohde, David. 2003. Threats and Responses: Crackdown; U.S.-Deported Pakistanis: Outcasts in Two Lands. *New York Times*, January 20, A1.

Sherer, Paul M. 2004. Targets of Suspicion: The Impact of Post-9/11 Policies. http://www.ilw.com/lawyers/articles/2004,0721-Sherer.shtm.

LARRY M. ESTRADA JR.

O

OLDER PERSONS. Over 3 million older immigrants and refugees comprise a substantial segment of America's population aged 65 and over. Much information on the immigrant population is available in federal government documents under the category "foreign-born" (Schmidley 2002). The Bureau of Citizenship and Immigration (formerly the Immigration and Naturalization Service) does not include undocumented immigrants in its statistics. Since few in the older age category are undocumented, the numbers cited here encompass the vast majority of immigrants aged 65 and over.

Older immigrants and refugees in the United States vary in terms of their national and cultural backgrounds and face different challenges adapting to American society (Haines 1996). The proportion of older to younger immigrants approximates the proportion of older to younger native-born Americans. Older immigrants constitute 11 percent of the total foreign-born population, according to the 2000 census, while the older native-born make up close to 13 percent of the native-born population. Among newer arrivals the average age is younger.

From 1970 to 1999, the overall number of new arrivals to the United States tripled what it had been in the previous 30-year period. The influx of immigrants after 1970 consisted largely of young Latin Americans and Asians, who contributed to a sharp decrease in the average age of America's immigrants (He 2002). The median age of the foreign-born dropped from 52 in 1970 to 38 in 2000. Despite the recent increase in non-European immigration, the older population from abroad consists largely of immigrants who came from Germany, Italy, Britain, and other European countries over the first seven decades of the twentieth century. Europeans make up more than one-third of the older foreign-born population. As a result of the most recent immigration patterns, however, the older foreign-born population will be less European in origin and more Latin American and Asian within a few years.

Immigration of the past 35 years brought numerous speakers of new languages to the United States. Most from Latin America speak Spanish, while Asians come from a number of countries, such as Vietnam, China, India, and the Philippines, where distinct languages are spoken. Many of the Asians are refugees who fled hostile political regimes in Southeast Asia following the end of the Vietnam War. Other refugees, such as Ethiopians and Afghans, also arrived in the wake of violence. Special programs, under the guidance of social science practitioners with expertise in intercultural understanding, have helped some groups, such as Bosnians, to move beyond some of the obstacles to adaptation in the United States (Gozdziack and Tuskan 2000).

Immigrants, old and young, are distributed unevenly throughout the country. In large cities, such as New York, ethnic and language diversity associated with immigration is highly visible. In the homes and on the streets of Los Angeles, where older immigrants are a conservative force for the retention of pre-immigration speech patterns, over 100 languages are spoken. Immigrants tend to be concentrated in cities that serve as major ports of entry, with the result that they contribute to the cultural diversity of certain regions such as the western and northeastern states and Florida (Longino 2001).

In addition to the stress of trying to adjust to a new culture, a large percentage of older American immigrants, such as Puerto Ricans in New York City, live in overcrowded, urban housing where they encounter serious problems with living arrangements that include inadequate heating and cooling, broken appliances, difficult access, and insufficient furniture (Friedenberg 2000). Many older refugees live in multi-generational immigrant households; others alone in low-income, single-room-occupancy dwellings. Sources of considerable anxiety for older immigrants are safety, housing affordability, periodic cutbacks in government support, and unpredictable shifts in immigrant and refugee policies and laws.

Studies of non-European immigrant families reveal that older family members tend to have much more difficulty adjusting to life in America than younger people. Older family members are unlikely to find employment. Living in poor and sometimes violent inner-city neighborhoods exacerbates the problems they face. Older immigrants, who diligently served their own parents and parents-in-law, find that American culture does not emphasize filial obligations. In most cultures older people have special privileges, which include the utmost respect from the young. Family discord among the foreign-born is common as younger family members aspire to participate in America's youth-oriented culture, which precludes their providing the time and services to older parents or grandparents that the elders expect. That problem among Afghan refugees is explored in detail by Omidian (1996).

Older migrants usually experience frustration and stress as young family members adopt American values such as individualism and the right to make their own decisions (Harman 1996). Intergenerational conflict sometimes leads to serious interpersonal disputes. Older people leaving the homeland to settle in America lose much more than younger generations in terms of prestige and control over their lives. The later in life that people immigrate, the more problems they face. Research on a sample of several hundred Mexican immigrants showed conclusively that immigrating later in life was associated with economic well-being and mental health problems (Angel and Angel 1997).

The ability to understand and speak the host country's language is a critical attribute for successful adaptation in a new country. Lack of English language skills in the United States hampers the adjustment of older immigrants as members of their generation tend to spend more time at home and in other settings where the natal language is spoken. Many older immigrants rely on children and grandchildren to translate for them outside the home. Elder dependence applies also to transportation, and older family members become even more reliant upon younger ones when the latter acquire automobiles.

Unlike young immigrants who must learn language skills and other American cultural norms in order to succeed at school and work, many older immigrants assume a retired status upon arriving in the United States. Without a pension they often become dependent on children and grandchildren for financial support. Late-middle-aged immigrants sometimes work at entry-level jobs, at least until their children are old enough to earn a living at higher wages and fulfill their cultural obligation to support the parents. Older immigrant women who arrive in the United States as widows, or become widowed soon after arrival, are particularly vulnerable if left without spousal pension benefits.

A large percentage of older women contribute childcare and cooking skills to the extended family household as they would in the homeland. Traditional family and community leadership roles for older men, which were established norms in the home countries of most immigrants, can quickly dissolve in the United States. Role reversal in decision making and control over household resources can be psychologically devastating to older men as younger household members become more adept at maneuvering in the American society. Older immigrant men may additionally be deprived of the former daily social support of local male friends in public settings like coffee houses. Informal community leadership privileges of older men, which are viable in most neighborhoods of the world, are rarely present in the United States.

In the United States, a large formal sector provides health services and meets most other basic needs of older persons. Outside services, however, do not satisfy the emotional needs of older people. Loneliness and isolation contribute to a high rate of depression in recent older immigrants.

Older immigrants and refugees, like other older Americans, require more healthcare than younger people. They are covered for many healthcare services under two major acts of legislation passed in 1965. The Immigration and Nationality Act of 1952 was substantially amended in 1965 to abolish previous quotas that favored Europeans. That legislation enabled entirely new populations to migrate to the United States. The Older Americans Act of 1965 provided all American residents 65 and over, including legal immigrants, a substantial number of benefits. It also created the Administration on Aging. Approximately 7 million older persons, including large numbers of immigrants, are served by the Administration on Aging, which had a 2003 budget appropriation of nearly $1.4 billion. The agency has an official policy to ensure that people with limited English skills have access to health and social services, and also provides outreach to family providers.

Despite the institutions previously mentioned, some older immigrants, and supporting family members, feel that their healthcare is inadequate. The healthcare system does not reach all the aged immigrants. Some prefer traditional treatments in a familiar home setting over Western medicine, which is offered in a clinic or hospital, and emphasizes efficiency over personalized care. The lack of English language skills among many older immigrants also contributes to a discomfort with American physicians. Older people may not understand the regimen for certain medications and face disapproval when failing to follow physicians' orders. It can also be difficult to arrange transportation for scheduled appointments.

Older immigrants often face difficulties in finding meaning to their lives in the United States. Some become preoccupied with death, especially when ill with chronic ailments. Others seek to return to their home countries to complete their lives surrounded by relatives and friends. Many people also wish to return to the homeland when death is imminent to arrange culturally prescribed funerary practices that dispose of the body properly and guide the soul or spirit to its proper destination (Becker 2002).

Further research is needed to inform us more precisely how diverse older immigrants and refugees are adapting in America. As recent immigrants and refugees age, additional large-sample and in-depth long-term qualitative studies are essential for data that will provide more effective policymaking. *See also*: **Assimilation; Families; Health; Mental health problems.**

References

Angel, Ronald J., and Jacqueline L. Angel. 1997. *Who Will Care for Us? Aging and Long-Term Care in Multicultural America*. New York: New York University Press.

Becker, Gay. 2002. Dying Away from Home: Quandaries of Migration for Elders in Two Ethnic Groups. *Journal of Gerontology* 57(2):79–95.

Friedenberg, Judith N. 2000. *Growing Old in El Barrio*. New York: New York University Press.

Gozdziac, Elzbieta M., and John J. Tuskan Jr. 2000. Operation Provide Refuge: The Challenge of Integrating Behavioral Science and Indigenous Approaches to Human Suffering. In *Rethinking Refuge and Displacement*. Elzbieta Gozdziac and Dianna J. Shandy, eds. Pp. 194–222. Arlington, VA: American Anthropological Association.

Haines, David W. 1996. Patterns in Refugee Resettlement and Adaptation. In *Refugees in America in the 1990s: A Reference Handbook*. David W. Haines, ed. Pp. 28–59. Westport, CT: Greenwood Press.

Harman, Robert C. 1996. Intergenerational Relations Among Maya in Los Angeles. In *Selected Papers on Refugee Issues*, vol. 4. Ann Rynearson and James Phillips, eds. Pp. 155–173. Arlington, VA: American Anthropological Association.

He, Wan. 2002. *The Older Foreign-Born Population in the United States, 2000*. Washington, DC: U.S. Census Bureau.

Longino, Charles F., Jr. 2001. Geographical Distribution and Migration. In *Handbook of Aging and the Social Sciences*, 5th ed. Robert H. Binstock and Linda K. George, eds. Pp. 103–124. San Diego: Academic Press.

Omidian, Patricia A. 1996. *Aging and Family in an Afghan Refugee Community*. New York: Garland Press.

Schmidley, Dianne. 2003. The Foreign-Born Population in the United States: March 2002. *Current Population Reports*. Pp. 20–539. Washington, DC: U.S. Census Bureau.

ROBERT C. HARMAN

P

POLITICAL PARTICIPATION. Among the many challenges and opportunities faced by new immigrants to the United States, voting and political participation may not necessarily be the first to come to mind. However, both are indispensable to the functioning of American government, which is viewed widely as resting upon the consent of the governed. Voting and participation provide a key linkage between the people and elected officials. For those who dislike government's current policy direction, periodic elections provide a means of removing elected officials and replacing them with new ones. Election outcomes, in turn, depend in part on voter turnout: who votes, who does not, and social and demographic characteristics of both groups.

Inevitably, the policies adopted by national and state governments affect immigrants. In the 1920s, the U.S. government adopted highly restrictive immigration laws, which remained in effect for four decades. In 1994, California voters approved Proposition 187, which sharply curtailed social services to illegal immigrants and their families, although the courts later struck it down. "Official English" laws have been passed in some states and proposed in others, drawing strong opposition from immigrant advocacy groups. Governments frequently make choices that affect immigrants' access to public education, housing assistance, and other social services. Voting is perhaps the key means individuals have of influencing these and other government policies that affect immigrants' daily lives. Thus it is important to consider the conditions under which immigrants are eligible to vote and factors that may affect voter turnout among voting-eligible immigrants.

The U.S. Constitution charges individual states with supervising elections. The rules governing who is eligible to vote are also set by states, but are subject to some uniform federal standards. In general, U.S. citizens aged 18 or over who are not institutionalized or convicted felons are eligible to vote in federal elections. The Voting Rights Act of 1965 (and its later amendments) prohibits racial discrimination in voting and voter registration. The Nineteenth Amendment (1920) prohibited gender discrimination in voting. Within these guidelines, states may decide other particulars, such as how often to remove non-voters from regis-tration rolls, how to register voters, and the deadline for registration. One state, North Dakota, has no voter registration requirement; the other 49 states require voters to register by a certain deadline, ranging from election day in Minnesota and six other states to up to 30 days before election day in many states. Election day registration appears to raise voter turnout, and conversely, voter turnout is lower in states where the registration deadline is well before election day (Mitchell and Wlezien 1995). Clearly, stricter election laws tend to lower turn-out, while more relaxed election laws tend to raise turnout, among immigrants and non-immigrants alike.

To be eligible to vote in federal elections, an immigrant must become a U.S. citizen. A person born on U.S. soil is automatically a U.S. citizen, even if both parents are illegal immigrants. To become a naturalized (not natural-born) American citizen, one must also demonstrate an understanding of the English language, including "ability to read, write, and speak . . . in ordinary usage in the English language." Even so, once immigrants become citizens, language can re-main a hindrance to the meaningful exercise of their voting rights. Election ballots printed only in English pose a significant barrier to voting for immigrants whose first language is not English. In 1975, Congress amended the Voting Rights Act to require bilingual ballots in any political district where residents for whom English is not the first language make up at least 5 percent of the total population, and where less than half of the district's citizens were either regis-tered to vote or had voted in the 1972 presidential election. Congress also re-quired that bilingual election materials be made available to voters in every county above the national average in the proportion of the non-native-English-speaking population that had not completed the fifth grade. Conversely, the use of English-only ballots is likely to suppress immigrant voting, to the extent that some immigrants are not English proficient.

Restrictive 1920s immigration laws drastically reduced immigration until their repeal in the 1960s. This four-decade period was sandwiched by two periods of sustained high immigration rates: the 1840–1920 period, and the 1960s to the present. During the era of "old immigration" to the United States (1840 to 1920), most immigrants came from European nations, initially Ireland, Italy, Germany, and the Scandinavian nations, and later from Russia and Eastern and Southern European nations such as Greece, Poland, and Czechoslovakia. These immigrants settled heavily in northern and midwestern cities, where urban political machines provided housing, jobs, language training, and other assistance, and also mobi-lized them as pro-machine voters (Crotty 1994). First-generation European im-migrants tended to become U.S. citizens and learn English quickly—and to pass their citizenship and English language to their children. Thus, future generations were natural-born U.S. citizens and more English proficient, meaning that for the second and later generations of European immigrants, both language and citi-zenship became less of a hindrance to voting.

The period from the 1960s to the present can be characterized as a period of "new immigration." Although European immigration has not ceased, the new immigrants have arrived heavily from nations in Latin America, Asia, and Africa. For these immigrants, language is often a greater hindrance to voting than for their European counterparts, underlining the importance of multilingual ballots and other accommodations for those whose first language is not English. In addition, some Mexican and other immigrants come to the United States as guestworkers without becoming U.S. citizens. Accordingly they cannot vote in federal elections. Thus, two important differences arise between "old" and "new" immigrants. First, new immigrants find language differences a more significant barrier to voting, especially where election laws provide for English-only election ballots. Second, new immigrants are less likely to become U.S. citizens than old immigrants are, at least in the short term. The upshot is that new immigrants' political power (through voting) lags behind their actual share of the voting-eligible population, more so than for today's descendants of old immigrants.

Other factors may encourage immigrant voting. The old immigrants settled largely in major midwestern and northeastern cities such as Chicago, New York, and Kansas City. In these and other cities, politics was often dominated by urban political party machines, which sought out immigrants, assisted them in finding jobs and housing, and successfully encouraged them to become loyal machine workers—and machine voters. Urban machines, then, provided the means and support to bring the largely European immigrant population into full participation in American politics (Crotty 1994). Among the famous machines that mobilized immigrants were the Irish-dominated Tammany machine in New York City and the Anton Cermak and Richard J. Daley machines of Chicago. Today the political power of urban party machines has faded; only widely scattered remnants of their influence remain.

A more recent incentive for immigrant voting has been the presence of anti-immigrant legislation or ballot initiatives on the local or national agenda. In 1994, California voters passed Proposition 187, which cut off social services to many illegal immigrants. One study concluded that the prominence of Proposition 187 in the 1994 California elections mobilized first- and second-generation immigrants to vote. The perceived anti-immigrant nature of Proposition 187 seems related to a doubling of voter turnout among first-generation immigrants in California compared with first-generation immigrants elsewhere, where no anti-immigrant legislation was on the ballot (Ramakrishnan and Espinshade 2000). Another study concluded that anti-immigrant rhetoric and Proposition 187 in California contributed strongly to the naturalization and subsequent political mobilization of Latinos in that state (Pantoja et al. 2001). This effect was much weaker among Latino natural-born citizens in California and among Latinos in Florida and Texas, suggesting that a situation of perceived political threat, as found in California, was a strong impetus for Latinos to naturalize and vote.

A third influence on immigrant voting is socioeconomic status (SES, a combination of education, income, and occupation). Much voting research has shown that higher-SES persons are more likely to vote than lower-SES persons (Rosenstone and Hansen 2003). First-generation immigrants, facing adjustment to life in a new country and often learning a new language, tend to be less well-off economically than later generations. Thus, the socioeconomic profile of later generations of immigrants favors voting more than for the first generation. This effect is amplified further by the greater likelihood that second-generation and later-generation immigrants will learn and speak English—a valuable resource in understanding political issues and in the voting booth on election day.

In the future, immigrants are likely to become an increasingly important electoral force in U.S. politics. The U.S. population, around 288 million as of July 2002, continues to grow. According to the U.S. Census Bureau's middle-range projection, the U.S. population may reach 404 million by the year 2050. The same Census Bureau projection indicates that immigration will account for 63 percent of U.S. population growth between now and 2050. That would translate into 73 million new immigrants between 2002 and 2050. Not all of these immigrants will become citizens—but most will. Language and other obstacles are likely to hinder their voting somewhat, more so for the first generation and less so for later generations.

Moreover, the recent new immigration has not been uniformly distributed across the country. During the 1980s, over 75 percent of new immigrants went to six states: California, New York, Texas, Florida, New Jersey, and Illinois—and heavily to urban areas. Immigrants have long been attracted to areas where communities of others like themselves already exist. Mexican immigrants tend to seek out areas where many others of Mexican ancestry already live, such as Los Angeles, Tucson, and El Paso. A large Arab American community has taken root in Dearborn, near Detroit. Asian immigrants have concentrated heavily in West Coast cities, such as the Los Angeles, San Francisco, and Seattle metropolitan areas. Cuban American immigrants are a major political force in the Miami area and in Florida politics statewide. Immigrants' voting power is likely to be felt first in these immigrant-heavy urban areas, and increasingly in state politics in immigrant-rich states. Conversely, in states that attract fewer immigrants, found heavily in the Great Plains, northern mountain states, and much of the South (outside Florida and Texas), immigrants should wield less influence.

As more new immigrants move to the United States, as more current immigrants become citizens, and as more learn English and become accustomed to parties, candidates, and issues, immigrants are likely to become an increasingly potent force in U.S. politics. *See also*: **Assimilation; Bilingualism; Citizenship; Rights.**

References

Crotty, William. 1994. Urban Political Machines. In *Parties and Politics in American History: A Reader*. L. Sandy Maisel and William G. Shade, eds. Pp. 131–155. New York: Garland.

Hansen, Kristen A., and Carol S. Farber. 1996. *The Foreign Born Population*. Current Population Reports. Washington, DC: U.S. Bureau of the Census.

Mitchell, Glenn E., and Christopher Wlezien. 1995. The Impact of Legal Constraints on Voter Registration, Turnout, and the Composition of the American Electorate. *Political Behavior* 17:179–202.

Pantoja, Adrian D., Ricardo Ramirez, and Gary Segura. 2001. Citizens by Choice, Voters by Necessity: Patterns in Political Mobilization by Naturalized Latinos. *Political Research Quarterly* 54:729–750.

Ramakrishnan, S. Karthick, and Thomas Espinshade. 2000. *Immigrant Incorporation and Political Participation in the United States*. Princeton, NJ: Center for Migration and Development, Princeton University.

Rosenstone, Steven J., and John Mark Hansen. 2003. *Mobilization, Participation, and Democracy in America*. New York: Longman.

FRED SLOCUM

PORTS OF ENTRY. Ports of entry function both as gateways and gatekeepers, controlling traffic of people and goods entering the United States, regulating admission of immigrants and screening out those excluded. From 1892 to 1924, Ellis Island in New York was the major port of entry, admitting three-quarters of all immigrants to the United States. Due to World War I and restrictive quotas, immigration declined in subsequent years. During its years of operation from 1892 to 1954, 12 million immigrants, most from Southern and Eastern Europe, were processed at Ellis Island, which became a museum in 1990. On the West Coast, Angel Island in San Francisco was an immigration station from 1910 to 1940. The mostly Asian immigrants entering at Angel Island were often detained and denied entry because of anti-Asian exclusionary laws. One hundred thousand people, 60,000 of them Chinese, passed through Angel Island. Other early ports of entry included Boston, Philadelphia, and Baltimore on the East Coast and Seattle, Portland, and Los Angeles on the West Coast. After its 1898 U.S. acquisition, Hawaii admitted large numbers of Asians, especially Japanese.

Since the early years of immigration, when most immigrants arrived by boat, the nature and number of ports of entry have substantially changed. Now immigrants might cross the U.S. northern and southern borders by car, on foot, or at official or unofficial ports of entry, or they might arrive by planes at any number of international airports. The 4,121-mile-long northern border between the mainland United States and Canada has an estimated 130 official ports of entry and more than 300 unofficial crossing areas where it is illegal to cross. This border is the world's busiest in terms of volume of trade. The 2,062-mile-long southern border with Mexico has 30 official ports of entry and numerous unofficial crossing points. Unauthorized entries are far more numerous along the border with Mexico than along the border with Canada. Additionally, the United States has 12,353 miles of marine shoreline and approximately 300 seaports.

The top ten land border crossings for people are El Paso, Texas; San Ysidro, California; Hidalgo, Texas; Brownsville, Texas; Laredo, Texas; Detroit, Michigan; Buffalo, New York; Calexico, California; Nogales, Arizona; and Otay Mesa, California. The top ten airports for international passengers are New York (JFK), Los Angeles, Miami, Chicago (O'Hare), Newark, San Francisco, Atlanta, Houston, Honolulu, and Dallas/Ft. Worth.

In 2001, the Border Patrol apprehended over 1.2 million illegal immigrants. Forty-one percent of illegal immigrants entered legally but overstayed visas. As of 2001, there were between 5 and 9 million illegal immigrants living in the United States. This figure increases by approximately 275,000 per year. Illegal immigration occurs through the smuggling of aliens, often in cargo containers, the use of false papers, and extending the stay of legal short-term visits.

The Immigration Act of 1990, which revised the previous 33 grounds for exclusion into nine categories, describes the still-current immigrant and non-immigrant classifications and numerical ceilings that serve as guidelines at ports of entry. It was the most comprehensive revision of U.S. immigration laws since the Immigration and Nationality Act of 1952 (Ciment 2004). Categories for exclusion include: (1) persons who have a health-related disease of a physical or mental nature that may pose a threat to the personal safety or welfare of others; (2) persons convicted of certain crimes, involved in moral turpitude, prostitution, and commercialized vice or terrorist activities, and members of a totalitarian party;

and (3) laborers: any alien laborer who seeks to enter the United States is excludable unless its determined that their employment will not adversely impact wages or working conditions of similar workers in the United States.

The role of inspectors at ports of entry in determining whether or not foreign nationals should be allowed to enter the United States was studied by Gilboy (1991), who chose a metropolitan airport in the central United States with heavy international traffic. Citing Van Vleck's study of Ellis Island processing during the 1930s, she reports that inspectors still use a standard routine of questions in order to work rapidly. An individual who is categorized from a "high-risk" nation is automatically referred for further questioning. A high-risk nation might be one whose travelers claim to be tourists but are actually coming for temporary work or whose travelers often have fraudulent documents. Other possible triggers for secondary inspection include requests to stay in the United States for many months, touring without a destination, lack of plane tickets, or tickets without a return date.

Due to backlogs in processing asylum claims and increased fear of terrorism in the early 1990s, the Immigration and Naturalization Service (INS) began to institute reforms. Congress, however, still concerned with immigration problems, passed the 1996 Illegal Immigration Reform and Immigrant Responsibility Act, which included expedited removal provisions. INS officers were empowered to issue a summary order for the deportation of any alien considered inadmissible for lack of suitable documents. This expedited removal procedure, originally intended to address false asylum claims, was reported to have mainly impacted Mexican nationals, most of whom were not seeking asylum. During 1997–1999, 90 percent of an estimated 190,000 persons deported under expedited removal were Mexican nationals.

The U.S. Customs Service, long a branch of the U.S. Department of the Treasury and now part of the Department of Homeland Security, has existed since 1789. Customs enforces laws and regulations on behalf of more than 40 federal agencies on the borders, along the coasts, and at the ports of entry, but its stated primary responsibilities are to collect tariffs and fees from importers and to prevent the smuggling of contraband into the United States. Inspectors at ports of entry are responsible for inspecting all goods entering the United States, whether commercially or by individual travelers. They conduct inspections of commercial cargo on trucks, trains, sea carriers, and air carriers as well as inspections of passengers entering on foot or by passenger vehicles, airplanes, rail, ferries, and cruise ships. Customs often uses canine inspectors to detect narcotics, weapons, and other contraband. The alleged "millennium bomber," Ahmed Ressam, was caught by a customs inspector at the passenger ferry port of entry at Port Angeles, Washington. After Ressam was referred for a secondary inspection due to suspicious behavior, inspectors discovered a bomb in the trunk of his car.

Since the terrorist attacks of September 11, 2001, there has been a complete reorganization of government agencies dealing with immigration and national security. President Bush decided that 22 agencies needed to be coordinated under the Department of Homeland Security (DHS). On March 1, 2003, responsibility for managing immigration was transferred from the INS to the U.S. Citizenship and Immigration Services, a bureau of the DHS. The enhanced border security and visa entry reform act of 2002 made several changes that impact procedures at ports of entry. The Department of Homeland Security was given permanent authority to retain and use Machine-Readable Visa fees. Law enforcement and intelligence agencies are now required to share information needed for visa adjudications through an interoperable database. Requirements for the Visa Waiver Program (VWP) were changed to specify that participating countries must incorporate biometrics that meet international standards in their passports by October 26, 2004, report thefts of blank passports, and be reviewed for compliance with program requirements every two years. Closer monitoring of foreign students in the United States was instituted, including establishing an electronic tracking system. Security-related controls were imposed on issuance of visas to non-immigrants from countries that are state sponsors of international terrorism.

Additionally, there are plans to implement a high-tech visa system that includes biometric measurements. This plan was originally proposed in 1996 but postponed because of opposition by business groups. This system would allow government agencies to track entry and exit and pursue those overstaying visas as well as allowing more thorough background checks before issuing visas. Previously there was no method of determining whether those who entered the United States ever exited. Since August 2003, airlines and cruise ships must provide data to U.S. authorities on arriving and departing passengers, and foreign visitors from 27 countries were required to have machine-readable passports or obtain a visa in order to enter the United States. Latin American and Caribbean nationals who were already required to have visas may be required to have personal interviews (Hoag 2003).

As of January 1, 2004, all foreigners entering the United States from countries that sponsor terrorism are being fingerprinted and photographed and entered into a computer database to track their entry and exit. As of December 31, 2004, the 50 highest volume ports of entry and exit were to have an electronic recording system called US-VISIT. All other ports had until December 31, 2005, to implement this system (Perry 2003). The US-VISIT program, which was implemented pursuant to a Department of Homeland Security interim rule, requires that travelers to the United States have passports with biometric identifiers, such as facial bone structure characteristics in a chip in the document (Hoag 2003). The transit without a visa program allowed foreign travelers to change flights at U.S. airports without a visa. The visa waiver program allowed citizens of 28 countries to visit the United States for as along as 90 days without a visa. As of August 2003, these programs were temporarily suspended until new security measures preventing admission of terrorists are implemented. *See also*: **Border control; Legislation; National security; U.S.-Canada border; U.S.-Mexico border.**

References

Ciment, James, ed. 2004. *U.S. Immigration Reference Handbook*. Santa Barbara, CA: ABC-CLIO.

Gilboy, Janet. 1991. Deciding Who Gets In. *Law and Society Review* 25(3):571–599.

Heyman, Josiah McC. 2001. Ports of Entry on the Mexican Border. In *On the Border: Society and Culture Between the United States and Mexico*. Andrew Grant Wood, ed. Pp. 221–240. Lanham, MD: SR Books.

Hoag, Christina. 2003. Passport Rules to Get Stricter. http://www.miami.com/mld/miamiherald/6253243.htm?1c.

McLaughlin, Abraham. 2002. Immigrant Visa Card Can Only Buy So Much Security; with $380 Million and a Post-9/11 Mandate, Washington May Check Fingerprints of US Visitors. *Christian Science Monitor*, December 2, 2.

Perry, Daniel. 2003. McAllen, Texas Leaders Concerned about National Entry Exit Control System. *Knight Ridder Tribune Business News*, July 15, 1.

U.S. House of Representatives, Committee on Government Reform. 2003. *Federal Law Enforcement at the Borders and Ports of Entry*. Washington, DC: U.S. Government Printing Office.

Van Vleck, William. 1932. *The Administrative Control of Aliens: A Study in Administrative Law and Procedure*. New York: Commonwealth Fund.

Zeidel, Robert. 2001. Immigration Stations. In *Encyclopedia of American Immigration*. James Ciment, ed. Armonk, NY: M.E. Sharpe.

JEANNE ARMSTRONG

POSTTRAUMATIC STRESS DISORDER. A high prevalence of Posttraumatic Stress Disorder (PTSD) among refugee populations in the United States has been confirmed in various research findings. Refugees who come to the United States have often experienced trauma before and during migration and have suffered from various psychological symptoms. Trauma may arise from combat, incarceration, reeducation camps, mass genocide, deprivation, physical injury and torture, and death of loved ones and friends. Due to these kinds of traumatic experiences, refugees develop PTSD symptoms such as re-experience of trauma in flashbacks and dreams, avoidance behavior, and depression. To the extent that immigrants experience significant uprooting from family and homeland, dangers of the journey, and insecurities in new situations, they may also suffer some PTSD symptoms.

Emotional reactions to trauma have been documented for over 4,000 years. During the American Civil War, symptoms similar to PTSD were named "Soldier's heart" because autonomic cardiac symptoms such as elevated heart rate and high blood pressure were observed among soldiers who experienced trauma during the war. The syndrome was called shell shock during World War I because brain trauma due to explosion of shells was considered to be responsible for the condition. A similar condition called combat neurosis was observed among World War II veterans, survivors of Nazi concentration camps, and survivors of atomic bombings in Japan.

In 1980, the condition was recognized as Posttraumatic Stress Disorder in the *Diagnostic and Statistical Manual of Mental Disorders*, 3rd edition (DSM-III), which described PTSD as emotional reactions after experience of trauma that is outside the range of human experience. More recent findings indicate PTSD symptoms also occur due to rape, criminal victimization, and natural and technological disasters. The modified definition of PTSD is a psychological disorder in which after being exposed to a trauma where an individual experiences or witnesses an event that involved actual threat to his or her life or serious injury and has intense fear and helpless feelings, he or she re-experiences the trauma accompanied with avoidance and increased arousal (APA 1994). Prevalence varies widely, from 1 percent to 14 percent for the general population to 3 percent to 54 percent for at-risk populations such as combat veterans and victims of natural disasters and criminal assaults.

Studies of PTSD among refugees in the United States are infrequent, and focus mainly on prevalence of PTSD in specific groups rather than ethnocultural aspects. Available research suggests cultural differences in manifestation of symptoms and relatively high prevalence of PTSD symptoms in refugees from both Southeast Asia and Latin America. Research regarding PTSD among Asians mostly concerns Southeast Asians who have settled in North America. The Vietnamese were among the earliest of Southeast Asian refugee groups, arriving in considerable numbers in 1975. Their traumatic experiences included not only life-threatening experiences in their own country, but also multiple traumas associated with forced labor, starvation, torture, and imprisonment in refugee camps in Thailand, Hong Kong, Indonesia, Malaysia, and the Philippines. Prevalence rates of PTSD, from 8 percent (Kroll et al. 1989) to 54 percent (Kinzie et al. 1990) in clinical populations, were often accompanied by other psychological distress such as depression, anxiety, and poor general health (Felsman et al. 1990). Despite such high levels of psychological and physical distress, overall adjustment of Vietnamese appears better than that of other Southeast Asian refugees due to their already established support system in the United States (Chung and Kagawa-Singer 1993).

Cambodian refugees exhibit the greatest psychological problems, manifested by high level of depressive and anxiety symptoms, dissociation, and chronic psychotic symptoms (Chung and Kagawa-Singer 1993; Kinzie and Boehnlein 1999). Prevalence of PTSD among Cambodian refugees varies from 22 percent (Kroll et al. 1989) to 92 percent (Kinzie et al. 1989) in clinical samples. Yet despite their high level of psychological distress due to multiple traumatic experiences, they reported the highest life-satisfaction among Southeast Asian refugees (Rumbaut 1985). This might be attributed to their Buddhist beliefs that life-events are manifestations of their *karma* (fate) and therefore meaningful and important to their present and future lives. In Laos, massive immigration started when the Pathet Lao gained control over Laos in 1979 after American troops withdrew from Southeast Asia. Laotians also experienced multiple traumas before migration to new countries. Prevalence rates of PTSD among Laotians vary from 20 percent (Kroll et al. 1989) to 68 percent (Kinzie et al. 1990) in clinical populations.

Refugees may continue to have psychological problems and difficulty adjusting even years after immigration. Many Southeast Asian patients "who continue to seek mental health care years after entry into the United States have not made successful adjustments...may not have learned English, may not have found jobs, may be dependent on government welfare and, worst of all, may be in despair that their children, once their hope for the future, are delinquent" (Kroll 2003).

Research on PTSD in Latin American refugee populations is mostly limited to descriptive studies. Studies examining ethnocultural aspects of symptoms caused by traumatic experiences are rare. An anecdotal study indicated that alexithymia (inability to label emotions) is more frequently seen among Hispanic males who suffered from PTSD symptoms than among other populations (Hough et al. 1996), suggesting that a desire to be in control may cause extreme difficulty in accepting conditions that may include helplessness.

Cultural concepts of both psychological and physical illness among Hispanics include *ataques de nervios,* or "nerve attacks." These include a range of stress symptoms including tremor, heart palpitations, memory loss, dizziness, difficult breathing, and fainting (Canino and Canino 1993). It might be expected, because of this high frequency of *ataques* symptoms among Puerto Ricans, that Hispanics with PTSD display more dissociative symptoms than other populations. Garrison (1977) suggested that *ataques* might be associated with PTSD in Hispanic populations since they are a culturally acceptable way to express a need for help. The research findings, however, are not conclusive. Somatization is also commonly observed among Hispanics. Among Hispanic groups, Puerto Ricans reported the highest level of somatic symptoms (Fabrega 1991; Canino et al. 1992). It would be expected that societal views of mental illness and low availability of mental health treatment and services are among the factors affecting manifestation of PTSD symptoms among Latin American and other refugee and immigrant groups.

The prevalence of exposure to torture among refugees is another factor in the likelihood of PTSD. One study of 1,134 East Africans in Minnesota discovered that torture survivors were more likely than other refugees to experience physical and psychological problems, especially showing an increase in PTSD symptoms (Jaranson et al. 2004). Their findings recommend screening refugees, especially women, for a history of torture and following up with referrals to mental health services. Although there are 31 torture rehabilitation centers in the United States, they cannot treat all torture survivors and less than 1 percent of survivors actually request referral (Jaranson et al. 2004).

Assessing and treating PTSD patients who come from non-Western cultures present considerable challenges. Barriers in communication and establishment of trust as well as utilization of community mental health services and acceptance of different forms of treatment such as individual and group therapy are common issues. Particularly, non-Western patients tend to avoid coming for treatment earlier, and severe depression, dissociation, and even paranoid symptoms may develop by the time they seek treatment.

Cultural understanding and therapist sensitivity are extremely important in treating clients from different cultures. Family therapy is implicated as a treatment of choice for Central American refugees with trauma experiences (Arredondo et al. 1989). Kinzie and Fleck (1987), in treating Cambodian refugees, emphasized the importance of establishing a long-term supportive relationship, paying attention to present stressors, educating patients about medications, and empowering them to strengthen their traditional value system, social support, and ties in their own communities.

Overall, research on PTSD among refugee and immigrant populations is limited, and only a few studies have examined the important issues of cultural manifestations and culturally appropriate treatments. Insofar as diagnostic criteria of PTSD have been developed in Western cultures and standardized primarily for majority populations in the United States, applying Western theories and concepts to non-Western cultures entails serious risk because norms and standards in Western cultures might not be applicable to the other cultures. While findings indicate consistent symptoms in these Western measures across different refugee populations, few have tapped into ethnocultural aspects of PTSD. The findings, therefore, might miss a wide variety of culturally specific aspects of PTSD symptoms in different groups. Available literature suggests that PTSD has been relatively common among refugee populations and that the symptoms have been developed in close relationship to cultural experiences and practices. Thus, research on culturally sensitive and appropriate therapeutic interventions is imperative. *See also*: **Mental health problems; Refugee law and policy.**

References

American Psychiatric Association (APA). 1994. *Diagnostic and Statistical Manual of Mental Disorders*, 4th ed. Washington, DC: American Psychiatric Association.

Arredondo, P., E. Orjicla, and L. Moore. 1989. Family Therapy with Central American War Refugee Families. *Journal of Strategic and Systematic Therapies* 8:41–50.

Canino, I.A., and G.J. Canino. 1993. Psychiatric Care of Puerto Ricans. In *Culture, Ethnicity, and Mental Illness*. A.C. Gaw, ed. Pp. 467–499. Washington, DC: American Psychiatric Press.

Canino, I.A., M. Rubio-Stipec, G.J. Canino, and J.I. Escobar. 1992. Functional Somatic Symptoms: A Cross-Ethnic Comparison. *American Journal of Orthopsychiatry* 62:605–612.

Chung, R., and M. Kagawa-Singer. 1993. Predictor of Psychological Distress among Southeast Asian Refugees. *Social Science Medicine* 36:631–639.

Fabrega, H., Jr. 1991. Psychiatric Stigma in Non-Western Societies. *Comprehensive Psychiatry* 32:823–829.

Felsman, J.K., F.T.L. Leong, M.C. Johnson, and I.C. Felsman. 1990. Estimates of Psychological Distress among Vietnamese Refugees: Adolescents, Unaccompanied Minors, and Young Adults. *Social Science Medicine* 31:1251–1256.

Garrison, V. 1977. The Puerto Rican Syndrome in Psychiatry and Espiritismo. In *Case Studies in Spirit Possession*. V. Crapanzano and V. Garrison, eds. New York: John Wiley.

Helzer, J.E., L.N. Robins, and L. McEvoy. 1987. Posttraumatic Stress Disorder in the General Population. *New England Journal of Medicine* 317:1630–1634.

Hough, R.L., G.J. Canino, F.R. Abueg, and F.D. Gusman. 1996. PTSD and Related Stress Disorders among Hispanics. In *Ethnocultural Aspects of Posttraumatic Stress Disorder: Issues, Research, and Clinical Applications*. A.J. Marsella, M.J. Friedman, E.T. Gerrity, and R.M. Scurfield, eds. Pp. 301–338. Washington, DC: American Psychological Association.

Jaranson, James M., James Butcher, Linda Halcon, et al. 2004. Somali and Oromo Refugees: Correlates of Torture and Trauma History. *American Journal of Public Health* 94(4):591–598.

Kinzie, J., and J.K. Boehnlein. 1989. Post-Traumatic Psychosis among Cambodian Refugees. *Journal of Traumatic Stress* 2:185–198.

Kinzie, J., and J. Fleck. 1987. Psychotherapy with Severely Traumatized Refugees. *American Journal of Psychotherapy* 141:82–94.

Kinzie, J., J.K. Boehmlein, P.K. Leung, L.J. Moore, C. Riley, and D. Smith. 1990. The Prevalence of Posttraumatic Stress Disorder and Its Clinical Significance Among Southeast Asian Refugees. *American Journal of Psychiatry* 147:913–917.

Kroll, J., M. Habenicht, T. Mackenzie, M. Yang, S. Chan, T. Vang, T. Nguyen, M. Ly, B. Phonnasouvanh, H. Ngyen, Y. Vang, L. Souvbannasoth, and R. Cabugao. 1989. Depression and Posttraumatic Stress Disorder in Southeast Asian Refugees. *American Journal of Psychiatry* 146:1592–1597.

Kroll, Jerome. 2003. Posttraumatic Symptoms and the Complexity of Responses to Trauma. *Journal of the American Medical Association* 290(5):667–671.

Kulka, R.A., W.E. Schlenger, J.A. Fairban, R.L. Hough, B.K. Jordan, C.R. Marmar, and D.A. Weiss. 1990. *Trauma and the Vietnam War Generation*. New York: Brunner and Mazel.

Rumbaut, Ruben. 1985. Mental Health and the Refugee Experience: A Comparative Study of Southeast Asian Refugees. In *Southeast Asian Mental Health: Treatment, Prevention, Services, Training, and Research*. T.C. Owan, ed. Pp. 433–486. Rockville, MD: National Institute of Mental Health.

YOKO SUGIHARA

PUBLIC CHARGE. Public charge doctrine has been part of American immigration law since colonial days. A public charge is someone who cannot provide for his or her own livelihood and thus relies on public assistance (Gimpel and Edwards 1999:78). Those individuals deemed as likely to be charges of the public are excluded from entry or, if already present in the United States, stand subject to being deported.

The reason for excluding potential public charges is to ensure that individuals unable or unwilling to sustain themselves not burden society. Immigration has to do with selecting which foreigners to admit, and thus designating public charges as excludable falls within the sovereignty of a nation. A major "long-standing concern from the time of provincial and state regulation of immigration was with the coming of persons who might become a burden to the community; . . . both colonies and states sought to protect themselves by exclusion of potential public charges" (Hutchinson 1981:410). The chief goal of American immigration policy has always been to admit productive, self-reliant individuals who positively contribute to society (e.g., settling frontiers, building commercial enterprises, paying taxes, displaying republican virtues). Public charges fall under the category of "undesirables."

The earliest public charge laws date to 1645 in Massachusetts, as colonists were increasingly reluctant to extend a welcome to impoverished foreigners and "Rogues and vagabonds" that England decided she could spare (Baseler 1998:71). The primary approaches taken to protect against public charges were mandatory reporting of passengers, immigrant screening and exclusion upon arrival of designated "undesirables," and requiring bonds for potential public charges (Hutchinson 1981:397). For example, colonial Massachusetts enacted a law in 1700 keeping out the infirm who had no security against their becoming public charges (Hutchinson 1981:390). Ship captains were required to post bonds for "lame, impotent, or infirm" passengers who were "incapable of maintaining themselves," or the vessel had to carry the person back home (Baseler 1998:1). A 1691 New York law required an immigrant to have "a visible Estate" or "a manual occupation" or "give sufficient surety, that he shall not be a burden or charge to the respective places, he shall come to Inhabit." A 1740 law in Delaware sought to "Prevent Poor and Impotent Persons being Imported," including "any such infant, lunatick [*sic*], aged, maimed, impotent or vagrant person" (Hutchinson 1981).

Following independence, states either automatically continued to enforce colonial-era public charge laws or reaffirmed such laws. With ratification of the U.S. Constitution, the federal government gained a role in immigration policy, beginning in 1808 with Article I, Section 9, Clause 1. Yet states continued to strengthen their own public charge laws, apparently in accord with the Constitution; states also retained jurisdiction over the allocation of their public resources and the control of their populations. New York, for instance, in 1827 passed a law that fined anybody who brought into the state a "poor or indigent person, not having legal settlement therein" (Hutchinson 1981:398). However, state head taxes on able-bodied immigrant arrivals, intended to fund public relief costs imposed by immigrant "paupers," brought public charge doctrine to a federal-state confrontation; in 1849, the U.S. Supreme Court overturned New York and Massachusetts head taxes as unconstitutional.

Congress and the states concurrently acted within their respective jurisdictions to control immigration throughout much of the nineteenth century. However, a Supreme Court decision struck down certain state laws restricting immigration, resulting in passage of the federal Immigration Act of 1882. This law included the first federal public charge measure, excluding from entry any immigrant "unable to take care of himself or herself without becoming a public charge." This provision essentially adopted at the federal level the same exclusion policy states had had, and also carried a head tax "to meet the expenses of regulating immigration and caring for needy immigrants on arrival" (Hutchinson 1981:412).

The Immigration Act of 1891 provided for the deportation, or removal to one's country of origin, of public charges and members of other excludable classes. This law also called for the deportation of "any alien who becomes a public charge within one year after his arrival in the United States from causes existing prior to his landing therein" (Hutchinson 1981:449). The time in which public charges faced deportation was successively extended, culminating in the 1917 Immigration Act's 5-year period after arrival. The 1917 act also placed the burden on the immigrant to prove that the causes of his becoming a public charge arose after arriving here.

The Immigration and Nationality Act, the basic U.S. immigration statute (enacted in 1952 and heavily amended in 1965), contains both exclusion and deportation provisions under public charge doctrine. Inadmissible is "[a]ny alien likely at any time to become a public charge" (Immigration and Nationality Act Section 212(a)(4)), and deportable are immigrants who become public charges within five years of entry unless they prove the causes of reliance on public assistance developed after entry (Immigration and Nationality Act Section 241(a)(5)).

More recently, the 1996 Illegal Immigration Reform and Immigrant Responsibility Act strengthened public charge doctrine. It raised the qualifications and obligations of individuals who sponsor, or petition as the one assuming financial responsibility for, an immigrant. These requirements include filing a legally binding affidavit of support, earning an income at least a quarter above the federal poverty line, and reimbursing any government agency that supplies the sponsored alien with a means-tested benefit, public assistance for which one qualifies based on low income (Wheeler 1998; Gimpel and Edwards 1999:292). When applying for immigration at a U.S. consular office abroad, consular officers assess a would-be immigrant's application on a number of factors. Besides the affidavit of support, officers consider "the applicant's age, health, family status, assets, resources, financial status, education, and skills" (Interpreter Releases 1999:1414). Such determinations in one's home country relate to whether or not an individual is excludable on public charge grounds. Most public charge actions occur in terms of excludability rather than by deportation.

After the 1996 immigration reform and welfare reform laws limited immigrant eligibility for public assistance (Gimpel and Edwards 1999:284), the Immigration and Naturalization Service (INS) in its regulatory authority defined public charge in 1999, in order to clarify the grounds for inadmissability and deportation. The INS rule defined "public charge" as an alien who has become or likely will become "primarily dependent on the government for subsistence, as demonstrated by either: (i) the receipt of public cash assistance for income maintenance purposes, or (ii) institutionalization for long-term care at government expense" (Joaquin and Cancilla 1999:886–887; Vialet 1999:1). The INS definition lists a number of non-cash benefit programs that it deems not to be counted toward a public charge determination, and even receipt of cash assistance does not automatically render an alien a public charge.

Other nations besides the United States require assurance that prospective immigrants will not become public charges. For example, Australia demands that an immigrant's sponsor post a refundable bond and repay the government for public assistance the immigrant receives (Shroff 1999a:1). Canada requires immigrant sponsors to provide for the financial needs of the immigrant for ten years, with provincial governments able to enter into more limited pledges of support (Clarke 1999:1). The United Kingdom may, within its discretion, require immigrant sponsors to promise to assume financial responsibility for a prospective immigrant, although sponsors may count their own entitled public assistance as income in declaring that their income is sufficient to maintain the immigrant (Shroff 1999b:1). The Netherlands may impose conditions on prospective immigrants, including guaranteed payment for return fare to another country, securing a sponsor who pledges responsibility for the costs the immigrant places on public entities, and evidence of health insurance (Wennick 1999:1).

Concern over the high likelihood of immigrant usage of welfare benefits in the United States led to the limitations of welfare eligibility and tightening of public charge doctrine in the 1996 immigration and welfare reform laws. Documented resident aliens were eligible for nearly all of the social services available to citizens until the Personal Responsibility and Work Reconciliation Act of 1996. Except for refugees, asylum seekers, and U.S. veterans and soldiers, documented aliens who entered the United States after passage of this legislation are ineligible for almost all federal means-tested programs for their first five years in the United States, and are subject to state determinations of eligibility for most social welfare programs, such as Temporary Aid to Needy Families (Acevedo-Garcia et al. 1997).

Public opinion subsided somewhat amid the sustained strong U.S. economy and low unemployment rate at the turn of the twenty-first century. However, increased responsibility placed upon immigrant sponsors and higher eligibility requirements for immigrant participation in public assistance programs will likely serve as the immigration standard for some time to come. It appears that, as long as times are good, Americans are more willing to tolerate higher levels of immigration, so long as those most likely to rely on public assistance are excluded from entry and those who are admitted look to their legally responsible sponsors for support before turning to government programs. This attitude is affected by other concerns, such as heightened emphasis on homeland security. Still, public charge doctrine remains one of America's fundamental immigration policies. *See also*: **Expedited entry and removal; Social benefits.**

References

Acevedo-Garcia, Dolores, Robin Omata, Deborah Ringel, Sharon Carothers, Christine Lee, and Amy Westpfahl. 1997. *Impact of the Federal Welfare Reform on Immigrants*. Report prepared for the U.S. Commission on Immigration Reform.

Aronson, David. 1996. Immigrants and Welfare. In *Research Perspectives on Migration* 1:1 (September/October). http://www.ceip.org/rpm1main.

Baseler, Marilyn C. 1998. *Asylum for Mankind: America, 1607–1800*. Ithaca, NY: Cornell University Press.

Clarke, Stephen F. 1999. *Canada*. Law Library of Congress (October).

Gimpel, James G., and James R. Edwards Jr. 1999. *The Congressional Politics of Immigration Reform*. Boston: Allyn and Bacon.

Hutchinson, E.P. 1981. *Legislative History of American Immigration Policy, 1798–1965*. Philadelphia: University of Pennsylvania Press.

Interpreter Releases. 1999. State Dept. Finalizes Affidavit of Support Regulations. *Interpreter Releases* 76(37):1413–1414.

Joaquin, Linton, and Braden Cancilla. 1999. Protecting Immigrants and the Community: A New Approach to Public Charge Determinations. *Interpreter Releases* 76(22):885–895.

Shroff, Kersi. 1999a. *Australia. Migration Regulations: Assurances of Support*. Law Library of Congress (November).

———. 1999b. *United Kingdom*. Law Library of Congress (October).

U.S. House of Representatives. 1995. *Immigration and Nationality Act*, 10th ed. Committee Print of the Committee on the Judiciary. Washington, DC: U.S. Government Printing Office.

Vialet, Joyce. 1999. Immigration: INS's Proposed Public Charge Rule. Congressional Research Service, Library of Congress, RS20265 (July 16).

Wennick, Karel. 1999. *The Netherlands*. Law Library of Congress (October).

Wheeler, Charles. 1998. Affidavit of Support and Sponsorship Requirements. *Immigration Briefings* 98 (June 6).

JAMES R. EDWARDS JR.

R

RACISM. The Statue of Liberty, beckoning all who yearn to be free, stands in sharp contrast to the rejection and aspersions many immigrants experience in the United States. In adjusting to life in a new place, immigrants face numerous challenges, including language barriers, pressure to secure work and housing, and anxieties associated with maintaining cultural traditions while fitting in with new cultural norms. Sometimes they are also targets of racism, either as individuals or as members of an ethnic group. The hostilities they may encounter, including both subtle and overt discrimination, compound the cultural and economic adjustment they must make.

Racism refers to beliefs in, and assumptions about, racial superiority. The concept of race is problematic, with little biological basis; in fact, more genetic variation exists between individuals within a single racial group than between groups (American Anthropological Association 1998). However unscientific, notions about race are widespread in the United States. Race is generally associated with visible biological differences—particularly combinations of skin color, hair color and texture, and facial features—as well as geographic origin. It is a convenient way of classifying and categorizing peoples based on observable physical attributes. Race is thus culturally constructed, through a process of "racialization" whereby ethnic or biological differences are perceived to be fixed, immutable qualities which are then used to define people and demarcate groups. Not only are qualities said to define a group as different, or "other," but the representation of difference as natural and inherent also gives rise to stereotypes. Not surprisingly, the social, political, and economic factors that may have created differences upon which stereotypes are based tend to be glossed over or incorporated directly into the stereotypes themselves.

Based on the belief that attributes such as intelligence, cultural qualities, and even moral character are physically determined, race and its resulting stereotypes in turn become a rationale for separation and maintaining "purity," as well as for justifying distinct and often inequitable treatment. The result of racism, then, is often discrimination, which can be overt or covert, on the basis of characteristics like "race" which are perceived as natural and fixed. Racism can also be seen to some extent as an extension of ethnocentrism, the view of one's own culture or group as "best." Most anthropologists and psychologists believe that all peoples are ethnocentric to some extent, since viewing one's own culture favorably is necessary for generating allegiance on which cultural continuity and social cohesiveness depend (LeVine and Campbell 1972). However, ethnocentrism has also been hypothesized to be grounded in sociobiology, as well as relative difference, degree of interaction, compatibility of goals, and competition for resources. Like racism, ethnocentrism may have negative implications, particularly when it leads to subjecting people to unequal and even harmful treatment.

Expression of racist views also results largely from daily exposure to beliefs and influences that are so ubiquitous that they come to be seen as part of a person's rational perception of the world (Crenshaw et al. 1995). Situations that are atypical compared to mainstream culture are deemed alien and wrong. This makes it easy, in turn, to blame failure, anti-assimilation, dropout rates, and ethnic enclaves on immigrants or minorities themselves. Socially constituted stereotypes become common viewpoints as well through the inundation of media images, many visceral and deliberately slanted, which further galvanize popular conceptions and antipathy (van Dijk 1987; Chavez 2001).

Because they often look, speak, and act differently, immigrants are common targets of racism, along with its permutations in stereotypes, ethnocentrism, and the like. Mexicans and Arabs may be feared, caricatured, and threatened today, as Irish, Italians, Germans, Jews, and Slavs have been in the past. Over the years, newspapers editorialized, politicians lambasted, and citizens slandered against immigrants deemed too dangerous or "un-American" for the good of "our" country. Today racist undertones may be seen when immigrants are referred to as "aliens" or have imputed to them unsavory habits and maleficent motives.

U.S. immigration policy in general has had at least an implicit racial basis insofar as it favored people from certain countries, particularly from countries in Western Europe, until only a few decades ago. This is evident in quota systems, policies of targeted exclusion or deportation, and biased consideration of asylum applicants. Thus institutionalized, discrimination in policy and practice accompanies prevailing public prejudice based on race, notably against immigrants from Latin America, Asia, and Africa. Defining race and determining immigration policy through biological and geographical criteria are additionally problematic insofar as this can create categories that are highly arbitrary. This is exemplified by the mid-nineteenth-century designation of Irish immigrants as part of an inferior "Celtic" race, rather than "white" (Roediger 1999). It is also evident in U.S. Census forms that have placed individuals of Japanese, Mongolian, Hmong, and Punjabi origin within a single "Asian" racial category.

Immigrants are also particularly imperiled by xenophobia and nativism. Closely related to racism, xenophobia refers to attitudes and behaviors that vilify and often reject or exclude people based on the perception that they are foreigners or outsiders to a community, society, or nation. In their extreme forms, such as when isolationism prevails in a country's international relations, racism and xenophobia can manifest themselves in nativism—assertions of superiority and actions of vigilant separatism against "foreigners" and foreign cultures because they threaten cultural integrity. Nativism is not simply a dislike or distrust of immigrant minorities, but asserts that non-natives have the potential to undermine core values and basic customs of a country, including through the introduction of new languages, social customs, familial patterns, and religion, not to mention demographics. In a contemporary age of considerable global migration, coupled with deeper security concerns, immigrants are said to endanger not only American "way of life" but also cultural integrity in Europe and elsewhere (Pettigrew 1998; Stolke 1999).

Reinforced by stereotypes, xenophobia and nativism mark some of the more ignoble periods in U.S. history (Jenness and Broad 1997). Immigrants, along with blacks and Jews, were targets of the hatred and violence perpetrated by the Ku Klux Klan and other nativist groups, for example. Anti-immigrant violence also emerged in the aftermath of the Rodney King verdict in 1992, when Koreans— and to a lesser degree, Latinos—were the targets of violence. Some of this violence was perpetrated by African Americans who resented the expansion of both groups in Los Angeles neighborhoods which were once predominantly African American—and which, not coincidentally, had lost much economic vitality through the exodus of jobs and stores. Recent nativist tendencies are also seen in "English Only" proposals, which attempt to block multilingual education in schools and legislate English as the official language (Crawford 1992). Legislation proposed at the state level includes Proposition 187 in California, which sought to deny virtually all social services (except emergency medical care) to undocumented immigrants, while effectively deputizing school and health personnel as immigration officials by forcing them by law to reveal the whereabouts of "illegal immigrants" among their students, patients, and clients. Ideas of racial distinctiveness motivate some proponents of such activities, while also playing on racist (and erroneous) stereotypes that immigrants come to the United States to feed off the generosity of the welfare state while contributing little in return (Sanchez 1997).

Immigrants may also face segregation through practices and policies that physically separate them, often residentially. In Los Angeles, for example, racism and segregation in what had been touted as a modernistic multicultural metropolis were unmasked not only by the conflagration in 1992, but also by subsequent reports that the city was becoming increasingly divided by income and ethnicity. Countervailing vibrant intermixture was growing hyper-segregation of schools and neighborhoods. Segregation, then, may be promoted in both insidious and institutionalized ways, such as through the practice of "profiling" by ethnicity or race during real estate or employment inquiries.

A pernicious face of racism, and racial persecution, is seen in the flight of refugees. The enormity of what today is increasingly referred to as a "refugee crisis" is a measure of human intolerance as well as indifference. Echoing a history of blaming victims, the influx of refugees is often cited as justification for growing xenophobia. In the United States, as well as in Europe and elsewhere, refugee claims are increasingly doubted and denied. Refugees are, like immigrants in general, also targets of racism and stereotyping not only for their appearance and cultural differences, but also because their needs and frequent poverty reinforce a perception that they are an economic drain on the host country's resources and generosity.

One of the more blatant recent examples of racism in immigration policy is the vastly different receptivity that has faced Cubans and Haitians (Haines 1996).

Until the mid-1990s anyone reaching U.S. soil from Cuba was almost automatically granted refugee status. By contrast, Haitians arriving in the United States were routinely judged to be coming for economic reasons rather than because they feared persecution. Most Haitians have darker skin, at least as compared to many of the Cuban exiles. Haitians were further stigmatized as health risks, and especially as carriers of AIDS or tuberculosis. Despite ample evidence of serious human rights abuses in Haiti, the specter of illiterate, impoverished boatloads of Haitians who would drain public resources contributed to a policy which led many to be turned back at sea or otherwise not accorded due process of law. Haitians and human rights advocates alike have decried the discrimination and racism inherent in U.S. policy, and strenuous legal battles resulted in the right to have their cases for asylum considered, yet generally held conceptions of race result in a continuing ambivalence about the acceptability of Haitians becoming Americans.

The most strident anti-immigrant, and now anti-refugee, rhetoric is usually directed at the poorest groups. While often working in the lowest-paid, least desirable jobs, they are nonetheless routinely accused of "taking" jobs from native-born workers. Immigrants from Mexico, and refugees from Central America, provide a clear example of how the process of racialization—expressed as racism—works. Seeking work or safety in the United States as a result of economic hardship or political repression, they generally receive low wages, poor housing, and harsh working conditions, as well as finer scrutiny. Stereotypes depicting Mexicans and Latin Americans as naturally suited to agricultural "stoop labor" and content with squalid living conditions persist to this day and continue to rationalize low status and poor treatment in general (Gamboa 1990; Velez-Ibanez 1996; Foley 1997).

Racism thus provides a rationalization for poor treatment of immigrants, both "naturalizing" their socioeconomic inferiority and disarming them politically, oftentimes in the name of cultural supremacy or national security. In a modern world of unprecedented migration, as well as inter-group and international relations, racism and xenophobia are not only closely related but perhaps increasingly endemic as well (Lee et al. 2003). Ethnocentric and racist reactions are also linked with religious views, political affiliation, or patriotism. Arguments for the need to guard borders and our way of life against potential enemies are increasingly aimed at home as well as afar, often toward non-citizens. We see this reflected most strikingly in the post–September 11, 2001, suspicion directed toward Muslims in the United States. On the other hand, growing recognition of commonalties and understanding of the mutual benefits of pragmatic alliances and citizen empowerment are likely to continue to bring together immigrants and non-immigrants alike in the common pursuit of building effective communities. *See also*: **Ethnicity; Interethnic relations; Refugee law and policy; Rights; Stereotypes.**

References

American Anthropological Association. 1998. Statement on "Race." http://www.aaanet.org.

Chavez, Leo R. 2001. *Covering Immigration: Popular Images and the Politics of the Nation*. Berkeley: University of California Press.

Chinea, Jorge L. 1996. Ethnic Prejudice and Anti-Immigrant Policies in Times of Economic Stress: Mexican Repatriation from the United States, 1929–1935. *East Wind/West Wind* (Winter): 11.

Crawford, James. 1992. *Language Loyalties: A Source Book on the Official English Controversy.* Chicago: University of Chicago Press.

Crenshaw, Kimberle, Neil Gotanda, Gary Peller, and Kendall Thomas. 1995. *Critical Race Theory: The Key Writings That Formed the Movement.* New York: New Press.

Foley, Neil. 1997. *The White Scourge: Mexicans, Blacks, and Poor Whites in Texas Cotton Culture.* Berkeley: University of California Press.

Gamboa, Erasmo. 1990. *Mexican Labor and World War II: Braceros in the Pacific Northwest, 1942–1947.* Austin: University of Texas Press.

Haines, David W., ed. 1996. *Refugees in America in the 1990s: A Reference Handbook.* Westport, CT: Greenwood Press.

Jenness, Valerie, and Kendal Broad. 1997. *Hate Crimes: New Social Movements and the Politics of Violence.* Hawthorne, NY: Aldine deGruyter.

Lee, Y-T., J. Quinones-Perdomo, and E. Perdomo. 2003. An Integrative Model of Ethnic Contact, Identity and Conflict (CIC): Application to U.S. Immigration and Naturalization. *Ethnic Studies Review* 26(2):57–80.

LeVine, Robert A., and Donald T. Campbell. 1972. *Ethnocentrism: Theories of Conflict, Ethnic Attitudes, and Group Behavior.* New York: John Wiley and Sons.

Pettigrew, Thomas F. 1998. Reactions Towards the New Minorities of Western Europe. *Annual Review of Sociology* 24:77–103.

Roediger, David R. 1999. *The Wages of Whiteness: Race and the Making of the American Working Class.* New York: Verso.

Sanchez, George J. 1997. Face the Nation: Immigration and the Rise of Nativism in Twentieth Century America. *International Migration Review* 31:1009–1030.

Stolke, Verena. 1999. New Rhetorics of Exclusion in Europe. *International Social Sciences Journal* 159:25–35.

van Dijk, Teun. 1987. *Communicating Racism: Ethnic Prejudice in Thought and Talk.* London: Sage.

Velez-Ibanez, Carlos G. 1996. *Border Visions.* Tucson: University of Arizona Press.

JAMES LOUCKY

REFUGEE LAW AND POLICY. During the twentieth century, U.S. refugee law and policy developed from ad hoc preferential schemes to institutionalized legal procedures. The Refugee Act of 1980 introduced systematized processes, and brought U.S. refugee law substantially in line with international standards. However, the 1996 Illegal Immigration Reform and Immigrant Responsibility Act included many provisions that violate the rights of refugees under domestic and international law. In the wake of September 11, 2001, under the guise of preventing terrorism, Congress and the executive branch threaten to unravel the advances made in protecting refugee rights in the United States.

Prior to 1965, refugee processing in the United States was undertaken through temporary, ad hoc admissions programs. There were no permanent mechanisms to process refugee admissions; groups of refugees were brought into the United States as one-time responses to specific crises. These admissions were often instituted by the State Department to address particular foreign policy concerns. As a result, the groups of refugees admitted in this era were largely Jews fleeing Nazi persecution and political dissidents fleeing from communism in Eastern Europe and Latin America (Loescher and Scanlan 1986:1–2, 49–67).

The first U.S. legislation relating to refugees was the Internal Security Act of 1950, which declared that refugees were exempted from deportation to a country in which they would be subject to physical persecution. In 1952, the Immigration and Nationality Act granted the attorney general a discretionary authority, or "parole power," to withhold deportation in such cases (Aleinikoff et al. 1995:760). Refugees were admitted under this parole power of the attorney general or through specific legislation providing for one-time admission. This meant that refugees were not technically admitted to the United States, and could therefore be excluded from entry (rather than deported after entering). Moreover, refugees could not adjust status to permanent residence unless specific legislation was passed to authorize this change, or adjustment, of immigration status (Aleinikoff et al. 1995:736). This status, now known as withholding of removal, still exists.

The 1965 Immigration Act amendments began to systematize refugee admissions into the United States. The amendments eliminated the policy of national origins quotas, although geographic caps on refugee admissions remain to this day. Furthermore, the new act provided that 6 percent of visas under the new immigration system would be reserved for individuals fleeing Communist or Middle Eastern countries (Loescher and Scanlan 1986:73). The amendments intended to terminate the use of parole admissions for refugees, but failed in this regard (Aleinikoff et al. 1995:737). Thus the act represented an initial step toward the creation of a coherent and systematic refugee admissions policy.

On November 1, 1968, the United States acceded to the United Nations Protocol Relating to the Status of Refugees. The Protocol incorporated Articles 2 through 34 of the United Nations Convention Relating to the Status of Refugees, so the United States essentially signed on to the Refugee Convention as well. The Refugee Convention defines a refugee as an individual who is unable or unwilling to return to her country of origin "owing to well-founded fear of being persecuted for reasons of race, religion, nationality, membership of a particular social group or political opinion" (United Nations 1951: Art. 1(A)(2)). The Refugee Convention further provided for numerous civil, political, and social rights of refugees, including the right to freedom of movement, primary education, and access to courts. Most important, the convention enshrined the principle of non-refoulement, the cornerstone of refugee protection. This rule provides that member states must not return or "refoule" refugees to a country in which they fear persecution.

The Refugee Act of 1980 incorporated the convention definition of a refugee into United States law. This was a further step toward the systematization of U.S. refugee law and policy, ending a longstanding practice of "geographical and ideological preferences" (Anker and Posner 1981:11). Most important, the act constructed regularized procedures, many of which are still in place today, for the asylum application process. The Refugee Act also terminated the strict numerical limits of the 1965 amendments and created a broader admission structure. The act created the distinction between refugees and asylees, asylees being individuals who apply for asylum within the borders of the United States and refugees being those who claim asylum under the overseas refugee processing program (Anker 1999:4–5). Finally, the Refugee Act made provisions for the adjustment of status of refugees and asylees to permanent residence status after one year (Aleinikoff et al. 1995:762).

Throughout the 1980s, however, the asylum process in the United States was still tainted by political influence. The starkest example of politically motivated discrimination is that of Salvadoran and Guatemalan asylum seekers. Despite brutal government terror campaigns in both countries, the Immigration and Naturalization Service (INS) granted asylum to less than 3 percent of applicants from each country. Not coincidentally, the U.S. government was politically aligned with the governments of both El Salvador and Guatemala and provided military support to the Salvadoran regime (Blum 1997:43–44). Finally, a class action lawsuit, *American Baptist Churches v. Thornburgh*, was filed on behalf of these asylum seekers. The INS acknowledged the flaws in its asylum process, and settled the case by re-adjudicating all Salvadoran and Guatemalan asylum claims from that era.

Immigration legislation since 1980 has been characterized by efforts to make the asylum process more stringent and to address the large backlog of asylum applications. In 1986, the Immigration Reform and Control Act instituted employer sanctions for individuals who hire undocumented immigrants (Martin 1990:1290–1292). This was the first of many efforts to close loopholes in the asylum system that attracted numerous fraudulent claims to asylum.

The 1990 Immigration Act created two programs in order to decrease the asylum backlog and to regularize the asylum process. First, the act established Temporary Protected Status, or TPS, which permits nationals of selected countries to remain in the United States for a specified period of time, usually one year (McBride 1999:3). Congress grants TPS to individuals from nations such as Liberia and Ethiopia, which are in the throes of widespread civil unrest and human rights abuses or natural disasters. Second, the act constructed the "affirmative" asylum procedures that remain in place today, and the corps of specialized asylum officers (Rogers 1998:791–793). Under this system, asylum seekers who are not in deportation proceedings have their cases heard by asylum officers, who make an initial determination on their case. If the asylum officer does not grant the case, or the applicant is placed in deportation proceedings before seeking asylum, the case is heard by an immigration judge. These measures have proven both effective and often beneficial to asylum seekers.

In 1994, Congress strictly limited the ability to work while applying for asylum. Employment authorization is now granted only to asylum seekers whose cases have been pending for more than 180 days (Rogers 1998:795–796). Any delay caused by the asylum seeker does not count toward this 180-day timeframe, also known as the employment authorization "clock." This further effort to discourage fraudulent asylum claims has led to a large decrease in the number of asylum applications.

Despite the effectiveness of earlier legislation, the Illegal Immigration Reform and Immigrant Responsibility Act of 1996 (IIRIRA) enacted further, harsh restrictions on the rights of refugees. The expedited removal provision provides for speedy status determination without proper procedural safeguards as well as mandatory detention of refugees whose papers appear fraudulent. These provisions of the law are in direct violation of Article 31 of the Refugee Convention, which prohibits the imposition of penalties on refugees who enter illegally. They also pose a threat to the principle of non-refoulement and the due process rights of refugees under the Constitution. The IIRIRA also established a one-year filing deadline for asylum applications, which has no grounding in the Refugee Convention and risks refoulement of genuine refugees. The IIRIRA strictly limits judicial review of asylum determinations, thereby threatening the due process rights of refugees under the Constitution and Article 32 of the Refugee Convention. Finally, the IIRIRA imposes bars to asylum and withholding of removal for individuals who have committed certain crimes and have been members of organizations designated as "terrorist" by the State Department. While the U.S. government has the right under the Refugee Convention to exclude individuals who have committed serious non-political crimes or who pose a threat to national security or public order, such determinations must be made on a case-by-case basis, rather than through a blanket denial of protection. IIRIRA's bars to asylum again violate the due process rights of refugees and risk refoulement of genuine refugees. While it is important to discourage fraudulent asylum applications, the changes made by IIRIRA violate the rights of refugees under international law (Ramji 2001).

In 1999, the United Nations Convention Against Torture (CAT) was incorporated into U.S. law. Article 3 of the CAT prohibits member states from returning an individual to a country where there are "substantial grounds for believing" that she or he risks being tortured (United Nations 1984:Art. 3). Individuals who qualify for relief under the Convention Against Torture are allowed to remain in the United States under withholding of removal status. This means that they do not have the right to adjust to permanent residence and lack many of the other rights granted to refugees and asylees. Withholding of removal is also granted to individuals who are excluded from asylum but can establish that they have a "more likely than not" chance of being persecuted if returned to their country of origin (Ramji 2001). The new CAT-based protections help to ameliorate the harsh impacts of IIRIRA but do not fully mitigate its detrimental aspects.

U.S. refugee law and policy have improved dramatically since their introduction in the 1950s. An institutionalized system of refugee and asylee admissions is now in place, and ideological and geographical preferences have largely been eliminated. However, U.S. law still fails to protect all of the legal rights accorded to refugees under international law, and the gains that have been made are tenuous in the current political climate. *See also*: **Asylum; Expedited entry and removal; International accords; Rights; Temporary Protected Status.**

References

Aleinikoff, Thomas Alexander, David A. Martin, and Hiroshi Motomura. 1995. *Immigration: Process and Policy*, 3rd ed. St. Paul, MN: West.

American Baptist Churches v. Thornburgh, 760 F. Supp. 796 (N.D. Cal. 1991).

Anker, Deborah E. 1999. *Law of Asylum in the United States*. Boston: Refugee Law Center.

Anker, Deborah E., and Michael H. Posner. 1981. The Forty Year Crisis: A Legislative History of the Refugee Act of 1980. *San Diego Law Review* 19:9.

Blum, Carolyn Patty. 1997. A Question of Values: Continuing Divergences Between U.S. and International Refugee Norms. *Berkeley Journal of International Law* 15:38.

Loescher, Gil, and John A. Scanlan. 1986. *Calculated Kindness: Refugees and America's Half-Open Door, 1945–Present*. New York: Free Press.

Martin, David A. 1990. Reforming Asylum Adjudication: On Navigating the Coast of Bohemia. *University of Pennsylvania Law Review* 138:1247.

McBride, Michael J. 1999. The Evolution of U.S. Immigration and Refugee Policy: Public Opinion, Domestic Politics, and the UNHCR. United Nations High Commissioner for Refugees, Working Paper No. 3 (May).

Ramji, Jaya. 2001. Legislating Away International Law: The Refugee Provisions of the Illegal Immigration Reform and Immigrant Responsibility Act. *Stanford Journal of International Law* 37:117.

Rogers, Andrea. 1998. Exploitation v. Expulsion: The Use of Expedited Removal in Asylum Cases as an Answer to a Compromised System. *William Mitchell Law Review* 24:785.

United Nations. 1951. Convention Relating to the Status of Refugees (28 July).

———. 1967. Protocol Relating to the Status of Refugees (4 October).

———. 1984. Convention Against Torture and Other Cruel, Inhuman or Degrading Treatment or Punishment (10 December).

JAYA RAMJI

RELIGION. Throughout its history, the United States has experienced a wide and rich religious diversity. Into a continent with deep spiritual traditions of many different native peoples came millions of immigrants from Europe, representing an array of Christian faiths that encompassed Spanish, French, and Irish Catholics, British Anglicans, and Dutch Reformers. Many fled religious persecution, including significant numbers of Congregationalists, Mennonites, and Quakers, as well as Pilgrims and Puritans who garnered prominence in the lore of American history. The Jewish diaspora generated additional immigrants from Europe and the Middle East during the last two centuries. As many as 500,000 people were brought involuntarily from Africa and the Caribbean until trafficking of slaves into the United States was abolished in 1808; they, too, enriched the religious pulse of the emerging country.

The role of religion in the lives of new immigrants has only recently come under close scrutiny, in comparison to the considerable attention devoted to researching the cultural and ethnic diversity of immigrants in the United States. Many dimensions of the immigrant experience are, in fact, intertwined with religion, perhaps most notably some powerful motives for moving, means of facilitating adaptation, and avenues for expressing continuing as well as new forms of identity and social cohesion. Greater attention to these dynamics is certain to affirm further the overall significance of religion in the American experiment of democracy as well as in individual lives (Leonard et al. 2005).

Despite being characterized as a melting pot of three faiths, Protestant, Catholic, and Jewish, the United States has long manifested considerable religious diversity. This diversity has deepened rapidly and profoundly in recent decades, so much so that the United States today is the most religiously diverse of industrialized nations and perhaps the most religiously diverse of any nation in the world (Eck 2001). In addition to wars and political violence that have led large numbers of refugees and asylum seekers to the United States, major shifts in global economic processes and domestic labor markets and consumption patterns have increased the numbers and origins of people on the move. The demographic and religious face of the country has also been significantly affected by legislation, particularly the Immigration Act of 1965, which replaced national and ethnic quotas with a quota system based on occupational preference and family reunification. This led to significant increase in immigration from Latin America and Asia, regions which account for the majority of today's immigrants. Provisions of the Immigration Reform and Control Act of 1986 enabled still further numbers of immigrants from these regions to remain, ultimately deepening their contributions to the religious as well as cultural mix of the United States.

Today's immigrants bring with them myriad expressions of Christianity, Islam, Hinduism, Buddhism, and Sikhism, along with Afro-Caribbean and other religious traditions. While statistics are ever changing, immigrants and their descendants comprise substantial and growing portions of the estimated 62 million Catholics, 10 million Methodists, 6 million Jews, and 4 million Mormons (members of the Church of Jesus Christ of Latter Day Saints) in the United States (Glenmary Research Center 2000). Perhaps most dramatic is how migration is transforming the Catholic Church into a predominantly Hispanic American institution, as it had earlier been largely Irish, Italian, and Polish. As emptying pews are filled by immigrants, parishes are being reinvented from the bottom up, resulting in Spanish language liturgies, emotion-filled and charismatic services, and growing Hispanic pastoral and youth ministry. While overall membership in "mainstream" Protestant congregations has been declining in recent decades, growth of evangelical Pentecostalism has been substantial, especially among immigrants from Latin America, where roughly one-third of those who identify as Christian are now Pentecostal (Deck 1989). The replication of storefront evangelical Protestant churches has added even more challenge to the Catholic Church to speak to the needs of new immigrants.

The growth of American Muslims has also been equally remarkable, with perhaps 1.5 million of 5 million being recent immigrants. Today there are more Muslim Americans in the United States than Episcopalians and Presbyterians, and their number—between 5 and 7 million—is roughly that of the Jewish population (Eck 2001). Asian immigrant communities, which are growing faster than almost any other immigrant population, account for much of the growth in other religions. Hindus in the United States now number about 1 million, Buddhists roughly 700,000, and Sikhs possibly 100,000. The significant increases in Islam and other religions, through immigration as well as conversions, mean that these religious denominations are ceasing to be associated only with ethnic enclaves and increasingly becoming "native" to the United States, coexisting with previous Christian and Jewish religious communities.

While immigrants transform denominations and churches in multiple ways throughout the nation, the impact is most apparent in major gateways such as New York City, Washington, Miami, Chicago, Houston, Los Angeles, and San Francisco. New York, for example, has 600 Protestant and Catholic Korean churches, while Chicago has 70 mosques and a half million Muslims (Eck 2001). The presence of immigrants is visible in religious symbols that dot the landscape. Converted stores and hotels and apartments become new worship places, businesses and homes include shrines to gods and spirits, and groups may form within evangelical mega-churches. The experience of Muslim taxi drivers in New York and elsewhere reflects true "religion without walls," as drivers stop in restaurants or along street corners to pray five times a day.

Los Angeles, a quintessential global city, is the world's most religiously pluralistic metropolitan region in the world, with 10,000 congregations representing 600 different faiths (Eck 2001). In this most complex Buddhist city in the world, Chinese, Vietnamese, Cambodian, Lao, Japanese, and Korean temples exist alongside Tibetan communities and native-born American Buddhists. Filipinos outnumber white American worshipers in many Catholic churches. Some arch-dioceses are among the most diverse in the world, composed of congregants from Mexico, Puerto Rico, Central America, and Korea who may worship together or in services devoted to their own nationalities and languages. Muslims from the Middle East, Africa, and Asia who gather at Friday prayer services may be Egyptian, Saudi, Persian, Lebanese, and Thai, as well as African American.

Similar changes are evident in other cities. Houston, Pittsburgh, Nashville, and Atlanta have Hindu temples and temple consecration rites that surpass what most immigrants ever witnessed in India. For example, within a five-mile radius in Houston, where 20 years ago the only religious buildings were a dozen Protestant churches and a few Catholic ones, there are now at least 30 temples, mosques, churches, Sikh gurdwaras, storefront worship places, faith-based com-munity centers, and homes where immigrant religious groups meet (Ebaugh and Chafetz 2000).

For many immigrants, churches, synagogues, mosques, and other religious institutions serve as conduits for migration networks, providing an anchor and safety net for new arrivals. During the period of transition, religion can play a critical role by giving tangible support along with a reinforcement of self and place. In Brooklyn's Catholic Migration Office, where lawyers and counselors annually handle over 3,000 immigration cases from more than 160 countries and in over 80 languages, immigrants say that what they most want from their re-ligious institutions is "home"—a comforting sense of "belonging" that comes through affirmation of shared religious beliefs as well as emerging multiethnic identities. Cultural identity and sense of "home" are supported through worship services that include familiar rituals, traditions, and language, as well as through social interaction and sharing food in the gathering spaces.

Beyond serving religious and spiritual needs, then, religious organizations are crucial to healthy cultural adjustment. Upon arrival, immigrants generally learn that Americans tend to be more tolerant of religious differences than of ethnic diversity. This enables them to use religion as a socially tolerated avenue for expressing identity and culture (Carnes and Karpathakis 2001). Religious orga-nizations contribute to civic education and incorporation as they develop lay leadership and volunteerism. At times they facilitate understanding of the problems that immigrants face, including through public education events, classes, and individual advisement about legal, employment, and other challenges of adapting to American life and its morals and values. Since September 2001, for example, the mosque has been playing an important new role as a place where both "being a Muslim" and "being American" are being redefined. Open-house activities may expose people of other faiths to their Muslim neighbors, who inform them about "true Islam" and what "true Muslims" do or do not do. At the same time, Friday sermons are now also occasions to inform Muslims that as Americans they have a duty to fully participate in civic and political arenas.

The social services offered by religious organizations depend on the needs of immigrants, including whether they come highly educated or with limited edu-cation, are documented or not, have suffered the trauma of persecution, or are in need of re-socialization to new forms of government. They may offer translation services, aid in navigating the confusing sea of immigration processes, advocate and defend immigrant rights, or provide ministry to those in prison. Many churches also provide English lessons or parenting classes, addressing concern about pressures children face and potential discontinuities between home and school.

Many congregations have also established means to ensure economic support including through economic development funds or corporations that provide affordable housing to families and revolving credit for small businesses. African American churches have led the way and pastors of immigrant congregations are following, including Latin Americans who are often co-resident in the same urban neighborhoods. Many churches also offer grassroots community organizing that benefits their neighborhoods.

The increasingly transnational nature of contemporary immigration is also reflected in religious practice. The ubiquitous image of the Virgin of Guadalupe now seen well beyond Mexican immigrant churches and communities alone reveals her elevated status as a transnational symbol of immigrant hope. Immigrants often arrange return visits to coincide with religious events, including annual celebrations for a patron saint. Many Salvadorans have returned to commemorate the assassination of Archbishop Romero, while in reverse direction some have even traveled with a six-foot replica of "El Salvador"—Jesus, the Saviour—back to their new church in Los Angeles (Center for Religion and Civic Culture 2001). Young Vietnamese, for example, may return to a country of origin for church marriage, while community members pool resources to enable their dead to be shipped back for burial in family plots (Ebaugh and Chavetz 2002).

Hometown associations that are common to immigrant populations often have a religious dimension, sometimes coinciding with or complementing efforts to raise money for community needs. Remittances help support church reconstruction projects, schooling, and support of clerics, along with public works projects such as schools, potable water, roads, clinics, or libraries in a home village or town. Immigrant faith congregations are also key contributors in disaster relief. In Los Angeles, Korean churches help ease economic hardships in North Korea, Salvadoran and Taiwanese congregations have sent aid following earthquake disasters, and Armenian churches funnel thousands of dollars to relief and development projects back home, in addition to their long history of adopting orphans.

Many immigrant congregations also invest in the healing process of immigrants coming from situations of torture and horrific suffering due to dictatorships and war. During the 1970s and 1980s, the U.S. government requested the support of church agencies such as the U.S. Catholic Conference, Lutheran Social Services, and Mennonites, among others, in the settlement of refugees from Vietnam and Cambodia. At other times, churches have challenged U.S. foreign or domestic policy affecting immigrants. Especially notable is the Sanctuary movement of the 1980s, during which over 400 congregations offered refuge to Salvadorans and Guatemalans fleeing war in their countries. Hearing the stories of refugees, people of faith chose to follow their conscience and compassion, even in the face of immigration policy that precluded most Central Americans from finding protection in the United States. Clergy and laity alike even risked prosecution for providing shelter in churches, synagogues, and homes to those fleeing persecution.

Since September 11, 2001, the U.S. government has implemented policies that conflict with religious freedom. In the deepened climate of fear, many Muslim and Arab immigrants have been the target of questioning, secret profiling, and even detention. Just as atheists were excluded in the past, visas are today revoked for those whose views are deemed "dangerous," as in the 2004 case of Tariq Ramadan, a leading European Muslim intellectual. Concerns for violation of civil rights extend from stereotyping to security measures directed toward people of a particular faith or ethnicity. Faith traditions of new immigrants may arouse fears for the loss of "common"—predominantly European or Anglo-centric—heritage. By contrast, and largely in response to growing public fear and even support for monitoring Muslims, interfaith alliances of immigrants and non-immigrants alike are responding with new efforts to herald the contributions of immigrants today and their commonalties with immigrants in the past.

The religious diversity of immigrants in the United States today raises a number of significant issues. Continuing research and debate will revolve around the impacts of immigrants on various denominations, and particularly the growth of non-Christian faiths and future of ecumenism. As religion increasingly enters the political arena, new avenues for advocacy and influence may open for immigrants themselves, in addition to longstanding roles of churches and religious organizations in facilitating adaptation, and replicating cultural and religious values. Also in question is the role of government in upholding rights to free expression of religion, including of immigrants, while respecting separation of church and state. In a new security era, it remains to be seen how more fundamentalist beliefs of all kinds might be tolerated. In regard to immigration and religion, then, the ever-changing American people continue to face multiple challenges associated with how assimilation and multiculturalism are perceived as well as the extent to which there is real commitment to pluralism in a democratic society. *See also*: **Assimilation; Ports of entry; Social networks.**

References

Buck, Fielding. 2004. Religious Diversity Works to Define 21st Century America. http://www.facsnet.org.

Carnes, Tony, and Anna Karpathakis, eds. 2001. *New York Glory: Religions in the City.* New York: New York University Press.

Carnes, Tony, and Fenggang Yang, eds. 2004. *Asian American Religions: The Making and Remaking of Borders and Boundaries.* New York: New York University Press.

Center for Religion and Civic Culture. 2001. *Immigrant Religion in the City of Angels.* Los Angeles: University of Southern California.

Deck, Allan Figueroa. 1989. *The Second Wave. Hispanic Ministry and the Evangelization of Cultures.* New York: Paulist Press.

Ebaugh, Helen Rose, and Janet Saltzman Chafetz. 2000. *Religion and the New Immigrants: Continuities and Adaptations in Immigrant Congregations.* Walnut Creek, CA: AltaMira Press.

———. 2002. *Religion Across Borders: Transnational Immigrant Networks.* Walnut Creek, CA: AltaMira Press.

Eck, Diana. 2001. *A New Religious America: How a Christian Country Has Now Become the World's Most Religiously Diverse Nation.* New York: HarperCollins.

Glenmary Research Center. 2000. *Religious Congregation Membership: 2000.* Nashville, TN: Glenmary Research Center.

Golden, Renny, and Michael McConnell. 1986. *Sanctuary: The New Underground Railroad*. Maryknoll, NY: Orbis.

Hackett, David G., ed. 1995. *Religion and American Culture*. New York: Routledge.

Haddad, Yvonne Yazbeck, Jane Smith, and John Esposito, eds. 2002. *Religion and Immigration: Christian, Jewish and Muslim Experiences in the United States*. Walnut Creek, CA: AltaMira Press.

Lawrence, Bruce. 2002. *New Faiths, Old Fears: Muslims and Other Asian Immigrants in American Religious Life*. New York: Columbia University Press.

Leonard, Karen I. et al., eds. 2005. *Immigrant Faiths: Transforming Religious Life in America*. Walnut Creek, CA: AltaMira Press.

Min, Mira Pyong Gop, and Jung Ha Kim, eds. 2002. *Religions in Asian America*. Walnut Creek, CA: AltaMira Press.

Tweed, Thomas. 2003. *Our Lady of Exile of the Exile: Diaspora Religion at a Cuban Catholic Shrine in Miami*. New York: Oxford University Press.

Warner, Stephen, and Judith Wittner. 1998. *Gatherings in Diaspora: Religious Communities and the New Immigrants*. Philadelphia: Temple University Press.

Wellmeier, Nancy. 1998. *Ritual, Identity and the Mayan Diaspora*. New York: Garland.

Williams, Raymond. 1988. *Religions of Immigrants from India and Pakistan: New Trends in the American Tapestry*. Cambridge: Cambridge University Press.

SHIRLEY OSTERHAUS AND JAMES LOUCKY

REMITTANCES. As population movements from developing to developed localities due to wage work in labor markets intensify, and become more complex, the flow of cash remittances—migrants' earnings sent back home—also increases. According to recent reports, remittances that migrant workers sent back to their home countries in 2004 were estimated to total $120 billion (Migration News 2005a). Economic remittances affect migrants' places of origin in multivariate ways, but also contribute immensely to the balance of payments in many sending countries. As a result of the massive flows of remittances that enter migrant sending countries, the relationship between international migration and development looms as a significant matter, one that has emerged as a "hot" topic in many scholarly arenas. Hence, a key question arises: do economic remittances that migrants send back home promote local development?

Two competing views emerge in the debate about the nature of changes associated with remittances. One camp highlights the negative effects for local development and emphasizes that migration aggravates unequal conditions in migrant-sending countries. Scholars supporting this view claim that cash remittances lead to greater social inequality (Georges 1990); generate an increased economic dependency among those who migrate (Grasmuck and Pessar 1991; Rubenstein 1992); or increase consumption patterns without aiding local development (Gmelch 1980; King 1986; Georges 1990). By contrast, a divergent axis of this debate contends that economic remittances and migration yield positive outcomes and help solve economic, social, and political problems for some migrant-sending regions. These scholars argue that remittances invested in migrants' places of origin help promote local development (Durand et al. 1996); support, create, and revive it (Smith 1995); and propel self-advancement of households, families, and villages (Cohen 2002). While past studies have analyzed the effects of migrants' savings as well as the linkage of migration and development, conflicting views persist regarding the nature of outcomes and effects in sending regions. As Grasmuck and Pessar (1991) observe in their study of U.S.-bound Dominican migration, the debate is further exacerbated by a lack of systematically collected data on the frequency and amount of cash remittances transferred. Findings from ethnographic studies indicate that significant remittances are generated even by migrants with minimal wage jobs, such as one report that migrants send home on average $200–300 each month (Taylor et al. 2006).

Remittances constitute a leading source of income in the economy of many sending countries. India, for instance, receives the greatest amount of migrant remittances of any sending country. While India received $23 billion from its migrant workers abroad in 2004, Mexican migrant workers in the United States sent back home $17 billion (*Migration News* 2005a). Cash remittances currently comprise the largest source of foreign currency funneled into Latin America and are quintessential for the development of many stagnant economies in the area. According to the Inter-American Development Bank, remittances reaching Latin America in 2004 amounted to $45.8 billion U.S. (Migration News 2005b).

In Guatemala, as is the case for many other migrant-sending regions in Latin America, the Bank of Guatemala and the popular press proudly report that economic remittances now form the most important source of income for the country. In fact, "*migra* dollars" (i.e., cash remittances) far exceed earnings from traditional money-making export crops such as coffee, bananas, and sugar. Guatemala's largest circulating newspaper, *Prensa Libre*, now runs daily reports on migrants living and working in the United States, including visible impacts of cash remittances. Glossy color photographs depict mansions in rural areas built through the sweat of migrant brows. Western Union plasters Guatemalan roadsides with bright yellow billboards that advertise the ease of money transfers.

But in spite of the increasing importance of remittances in many migrant-sending regions like Guatemala, places where the culture of migration and the ritual of remitting money back home permeates, little attention is paid to cash remittance patterns at the individual and household levels. A recent study conducted in Mexico even challenges current assumptions made about money remitted to Mexican families and argues that only about half of the monies sent actually reach folks at home. This same study also points to some of the deleterious effects of remittances in Mexico, for while the Mexican government has become overly dependent on such resources, these monies at the same time help mask a decline in foreign investment and serve as a substitute for broader anti-poverty programs (Malkin 2005).

Clearly, strong transnational ties between migrants' places of origin and destination help maintain and perpetuate the transfer of economic remittances. The maintenance of transnational ties becomes easier with the innovative and efficient kinds of transportation, telecommunications, and technology available today. With cheaper technology, increasing purchasing power (among more financially prosperous individuals and those who remain behind and receive cash remittances), and greater global flows and consumption of electronics (e.g., televisions, stereos, video recorders, cameras, cellular telephones, and cassette recorders), transnational linkages endure and are kept alive.

Increasingly, transnational ties and sending cash remittances back home are also encouraged and become reinforced through practices at the grassroots level.

Hometown associations, sport-based organizations (most notably soccer), and church-based groups help sustain transnational bonds between migrants' homeland and their adoptive country (e.g., Popkin 1995; Hamilton and Chinchilla 1999; Moran-Taylor 2005). Such organizations look for beneficial ways to impact and change their home communities through a wide range of transnational activities and relations. Typically, they are formed by groups of people from the same community of origin and migrants with shared ethnic identities. Nagengast and Kearney (1990) observe, however, that pan-Mixtec transnational associations formed in the United States crosscut migrants' places of origin and instead base themselves on a shared ethnicity. These associations promote development projects along with such concerns as discrimination, exploitation, and human rights abuses in migrants' destination sites. In metropolitan Los Angeles, for example, several hundred associations for villages in Mexico and Central America exist. The Mexican Consulate registers 170 hometown associations, 60 from the state of Zacatecas alone. As a whole, cash remittances become a creative and vital source of economic development in many migrant places of origin, yielding new opportunities for migrant households, promoting the enhancement and continuity of life-cycle events, and, perhaps most important, providing a means for survival for the vast majority of those who stay behind. *See also*: **Social networks; Transnationalism; Work.**

References

Cohen, Jeffrey. 2002. Migration and "Stay at Homes" in Rural Oaxaca, Mexico: Local Expressions of Global Outcomes. *Urban Anthropology* 31(2):231–259.

Durand, Jorge, Emilio A. Parrado, and Douglas Massey. 1996. Migradollars and Development: A Reconsideration of the Mexican Case. *International Migration Review* 30(2):423–444.

Georges, Eugenia. 1990. *The Making of a Transnational Community: Migration, Development, and Cultural Change in the Dominican Republic*. New York: Columbia University Press.

Gmelch, George. 1980. Return Migration. *Annual Review of Anthropology* 9:135–159.

Grasmuck, Sherri, and Patricia Pessar. 1991. *Between Two Islands: Dominican International Migration*. Berkeley: University of California.

Hamilton, Nora, and Norma Stoltz Chinchilla. 1999. Changing Networks and Alliances in a Transnational Context: Salvadoran and Guatemalan Immigrants in Southern California. *Social Justice* 26(3):4–26.

King, Russell. 1986. *Return Migration and Economic Problems*. London: Croom Helm.

Malkin, Elisabeth. 2005. Study Challenges Assumptions about Money Being Remitted to Mexico. *New York Times*, July 7, C4.

Migration News. 2005a. India: Remittances, High-Tech. *Migration News* 12(2).

———. 2005b. Latin America. *Migration News* 12(2).

Moran-Taylor, Michelle. 2004. Crafting Connections: Maya Linkages between Guatemala's *Altiplano* and *el Norte*. *Estudios Fronterizos* 5(10):91–115.

Nagengast, Carole, and Michael Kearney. 1990. Ethnicity: Social Identity, Political Consciousness, and Political Activism. *Latin American Research Review* 25(2): 61–91.

Popkin, Eric. 1995. Guatemalan Hometown Associations in Los Angeles. The Center for Multiethnic and Transnational Studies, Los Angeles, 1995, pp. 35–40. Occasional Paper Series, Monograph Paper No. 1, Central Americans in California: Transnational Communities, Economies, and Cultures.

Rubenstein, H. 1992. Migration, Development and Remittances in Rural Mexico. *International Migration* 30(2):127–141.

Smith, Robert C. 1995. *Ausentes Siempre Presentes*: The Imagining, Making and Politics of a Transnational Community Between Ticuani, Puebla, Mexico and New York City. Ph.D. Dissertation, Columbia University.

Taylor, M., M.J. Moran-Taylor, and D. Rodman Ruiz. 2006. Land, Ethnic, and Gender Change: Transnational Migration and Its Effects on Guatemalan Lives and Landscapes. *Geoforum* 37:41–61.

MICHELLE J. MORAN-TAYLOR

RESIDENTIAL PATTERNS. In the twentieth century, immigration in the United States has primarily been an urban affair. For the most part, immigrants first come to the port cities, seaports early in the century and airports at the end, and spread out from there to other urban locations. There is, of course, some overland migration from Mexico and Canada, but even in those cases the end of the journey in most cases is still an urban area.

Recent history of U.S. immigration falls into three phases: the "classic" era (1901–1930) of mass European immigration, a "long hiatus" (1930–1970) of limited movement, and the "new immigration" (1970 to the present) of large-scale, non-European migration resulting from changes in immigration laws in 1965 (Massey 1995). In the classic era, as natives moved to the suburbs, immigrants settled in central cities and moved through a cycle of contact, competition, accommodation, and eventually assimilation with the culture they found in their new home (Park 1930). It usually took several generations for a group to go through this cycle, moving from an ethnic enclave in the central city until finally becoming absorbed into a generalized American identity in the suburbs. A classic study in this genre was Louis Wirth's *The Ghetto* (1928).

Over time, this framework for understanding the classic era of immigration came under increasing scrutiny. Recent research has found that often the "ethnic enclaves" (places with names like "Bohemian town" and "the Jewish section") were not as ethnically homogeneous in their residents as they were a visible location for ethnic social institutions such as churches, businesses, and clubs (Chudacoff 1973). Baltimore's ethnic structure in 1870 has been described as more a "social quilt of heterogeneous neighborhoods" than a tiling of distinct ethnic enclaves (Garonzik 1976), for example. While Cuban immigrants to Miami during the 1950s became economically assimilated and moved from the central city to the suburbs, they did not move to heterogeneous communities but created suburban ethnic enclaves instead (Winsberg 1979).

Nonetheless, Park's spatial assimilation theory has continued to be the dominant framework for explaining the residential patterns of immigrants, sometimes modified by a "segmented assimilation" approach. Residential or "spatial" assimilation is an intermediate step toward full or "structural" assimilation (Alba and Nee 1997). Individuals convert occupational mobility and economic success into "residential gain," in effect using their economic success to move into more socially advantageous locations. The term "spatial assimilation" has been used with three related, but distinct, meanings. In one sense, it occurs when the immigrant group attains the same residential distribution as the majority group, with the immigrant group becoming indistinguishable from the majority. In another less restrictive sense, it occurs when group members with similar resources demonstrate the same residential opportunities as majority group members; in other words, individuals from the immigrant group become indistinguishable from the majority. In the third sense, it occurs when there are neighborhoods which provide economic, social, and cultural supports for ethnic identity. These are the ethnic enclaves where immigrants retain their separate identity but achieve the same material conditions as the majority. At issue here is whether the salient dimension in assimilation is suburban location with its correlates, such as lower residential densities, better schools, and higher-income neighbors, or majority-dominated suburban location with the implications of social acceptance (White and Sassler 2000).

While Park felt that assimilation was inevitable, others have argued that the process might be more contingent. Racial and ethnic stratification may limit the ability of some immigrant groups or subgroups to convert their economic gains into residential gain (Alba and Logan 1991; White et al. 1993; Rosenbaum 2001). What occurs in this case is "segmented assimilation," a modification of spatial assimilation theory (Zhou 1997), in which not all immigrant groups experience the same patterns of adaptation to the majority culture. Some might achieve "upward mobility" and be assimilated into the majority culture; this is particularly true of immigrant groups with a significant portion entering middle class communities directly upon or shortly after arrival. Others might experience "downward mobility" and be acculturated into the underclass; this would be particularly true for immigrant groups which arrive with a significant portion of unskilled laborers. Still others might achieve economic assimilation while maintaining a distinct cultural identity; this is the case for groups which come with strong economic and educational resources, but whose social opportunities are limited by racial or ethnic discrimination.

Although previous, classic immigration had been mostly to cities, the new immigration has been primarily to a few specific cities. Most of the new immigration came to five cities: Los Angeles, New York, Chicago, San Francisco, and Miami (Waldinger 1989). Between 1965 and 1980, 94 percent of new immigrants lived in metropolitan areas, and fully 40 percent lived in two cities, Los Angeles and New York, which accounted for only 7 percent of the total U.S. population.

To a certain extent, concentration of immigrants is inevitable. Boyd (1989) has pointed out that migration choice is mediated by kinship, friendship, and acquaintance, and immigrants do better initially when migrating to an ethnic enclave. Light has underscored the importance of "place entrepreneurs" (realtors and developers) to the provision of residential opportunities to members of their own group (Light 2002). More than 50 percent of immigrant Koreans in Los Angeles and Portuguese in Toronto moved up and out from their original place of settlement through the services of a realtor from their native ethnic group.

Some research on the new immigrants supports the residential assimilation model. Alba has found evidence that, except for Latinos who are 53 percent of all immigrants, most immigrants are only moderately segregated from the non-Latino white majority (Alba and Logan 1991; Alba and Nee 1997). Myers and Lee (1996) found a link between income growth and decline in overcrowding—except for Hispanic immigrants. White et al. (1993) used census data to show that Asian immigrants have successfully converted economic achievement into residential assimilation.

On the other hand, Waldinger (1989) has found wide diversity in new immigrant settlement patterns, often at odds with assimilation theory. While there have been Korea towns and Little Havanas, there also have been major immigrant settlements outside the core city, such as Mexicans in East LA (a mostly unincorporated area outside the center of Los Angeles) and Dominicans and Chinese in the outer boroughs of New York. In Miami, as Cubans moved out of Little Havana, they settled in homogeneous suburban enclaves rather than assimilating into majority-dominated suburban neighborhoods. Differences in the housing and real estate markets may explain at least part of this difference. Frey (1996) found evidence in some cities of domestic out-migration away from high immigration areas. White and Sassler (2000) found that, at least in some cities, ethnic group membership was more important than immigration status in residential attainment. For example, immigrants who appeared to be black displayed assimilation patterns similar to those of black Americans.

In addition, many researchers have expressed concern that previous experience with residential assimilation may not necessarily predict what is happening recently (Alba and Logan 1991; Massey 1995; Alba and Nee 1997; Zhou 1997). Two structural conditions of the classic period of immigration that facilitated assimilation, the long hiatus in immigration from 1930 to 1970 and the economic boom following World War II, may not be present for the "new immigration." As a result the residential patterns of immigrants in the last third of the century may not be following the "traditional" pattern. Massey (1995) has suggested that there is no reason to anticipate any significant decline in the number of immigrants for the foreseeable future. This will result in much greater generational complexity than was experienced earlier in the twentieth century. As cohorts adapt to the culture and move away from ethnic enclaves, their spaces are filled by continuing waves of others from their country. As a result, the character of each ethnic group is likely to be determined by this continuing inflow of immigrants, rather than by the assimilating generations. Nor is there any guarantee of upward social mobility. The current trends of a hollowing out of middle-management jobs and the loss of low-skilled manufacturing jobs may be knocking out several rungs at the center of the upward-mobility ladder. While this "hour-glass" trend affects the entire U.S. society, it could also have noticeable effect on cohorts of immigrants and their ability to "move up" by "moving out."

There are other ways in which the new immigration is different from the classic model. A growing number of immigrants are locating in suburban communities immediately upon, or shortly after, arriving (Alba and Logan 1991). In some cases, this is because they arrive with significant economic or human resources, which permit them to move directly into middle-class employment. In other cases, immigrants move into older, first-ring suburbs which majority former residents have left. In either case, the residential environments are less dense than central city locations and spread farther apart from the enclaves of other immigrant groups. This results in a different dynamic of adaptation and acculturation, possibly making it more difficult to maintain former behavior patterns and increasing the inroads of the majority culture.

On the other hand, increasing segregation by race and ethnicity may limit assimilation (Frey 1996). Hispanic segregation increased in 60 metro areas from 1970 to 1980 and there is evidence that Asian enclaves may be forming more readily as well (Massey and Denton 1987). While cross-sectional analysis of 1990 census suggests residential assimilation, longitudinal comparison with 1980 showed less consistency (Alba et al. 2000). In another study, while Latino and Asian segregation *increased* in all U.S. cities from 1980 to 1990, it *declined* in multiethnic metro areas (Frey and Farley 1996). While there is an increase in multiethnic neighborhoods, entailing greater diversity and assimilation, they are also increasingly non-majority multiethnic (Alba et al. 1995).

Finally, Latinos may be more resistant to linguistic assimilation which could limit the range of acceptable residential choices and slow the process of residential gain (Alba and Nee 1997). Massey (1995) found that nearly 40 percent of new immigrant cohorts come from Spanish-speaking countries, more than twice the rate of any single language spoken during the classical period of immigration, and further evidence reveals delay in Hispanic language acculturation (Alba 2002) and correlation between suburbanization and language acculturation (Alba and Logan 1991).

Forces driving the U.S. experience appear to be similar to forces elsewhere in the world, although the effects may be different. Studies in Sweden, Australia and Canada have found the spatial assimilation model useful, and have noted the importance of networks and ethnic enclaves as attractors for immigrants. At the same time, some Canadian research suggests increasing ethnic segregation is not inevitable. While Asian immigration has increased into Canada, for example, and immigrants show distinct preferences for particular cities (Balakrishnan 2001) Canada's multiculturalism policies have prevented increasing concentration or segregation of Asian immigrants. *See also*: **Assimilation; Migration processes; Social mobility.**

References

Alba, Richard D. 2002. Only English by the Third Generation? Loss and Preservation of the Mother Tongue among the Grandchildren of Contemporary Immigrants. *Demography* 39:467–484.

Alba, Richard D., Nancy Denton, Shu-yin Leung, and John Logan. 1995. Neighborhood Change under Conditions of Mass Immigration: The New York City Region, 1970-1990. *International Migration Review* 29:625–656.

Alba, Richard D., John Logan, and Brian Stults. 2000. The Changing Neighborhood Contexts of the Immigrant Metropolis. *Social Forces* 79:587–621.

Alba, Richard D., and John R. Logan. 1991. Variations on Two Themes: Racial and Ethnic Patterns in the Attainment of Suburban Residence. *Demography* 28(3):431–453.

Alba, Richard D., and Victor Nee. 1997. Rethinking Assimilation Theory for a New Era of Immigration. *International Migration Review* 31:826–874.

Balakrishnan, T.R. 2001. Residential Segregation and Socio-Economic Integration of Asians in Canadian Cities. *Canadian Ethnic Studies* 33:120–131.

Boyd, Monica. 1989. Family and Personal Networks in International Migration: Recent Development and New Agendas. *International Migration Review* 23:638–670.

Chudacoff, Howard P. 1973. A New Look at Ethnic Neighborhoods: Residential Dispersion and the Concept of Visibility in a Medium-Sized City. *Journal of American History* 60:76–93.

Frey, William H. 1996. Immigration, Domestic Migration, and Demographic Balkanization in America: New Evidence for the 1990s. *Population and Development Review* 22:741–763.

Frey, William H., and Reynolds Farley. 1996. Latino, Asian, and Black Segregation in US Metropolitan Areas: Are Multiethnic Metros Different? *Demography* 33:35–50.

Garonzik, Joseph. 1976. The Racial and Ethnic Make-up of Baltimore Neighborhoods, 1850–1870. *Maryland Historical Magazine* 71(3):392–402.

Light, Ivan. 2002. Immigrant Place Entrepreneurs in Los Angeles, 1970–1999. *International Journal of Urban and Regional Research* 20:215–228.

Lobo, Arun P., Joseph Salvo, and Ronald Flores. 1999. Immigration to the New York Metropolitan Region in the 1990s. *Migration World Magazine* 27:5.

Massey, Douglas S. 1995. The New Immigration and Ethnicity in the United States. *Population and Development Review* 21(2):631–652.

Massey, Douglas S., and Nancy A. Denton. 1987. Trends in the Residential Segregation of Blacks, Hispanics, and Asians: 1970–1980. *American Sociological Review* 52:802–825.

Myers, Dowell, and Seong Woo Lee. 1996. Immigration Cohorts and Residential Overcrowding in Southern California. *Demography* 33:51–65.

Park, Robert E. 1930. Assimilation, Social. In *Encyclopedia of the Social Sciences*. E. Seligman and A. Johnson, eds. Pp. 281–283. New York: Macmillan.

Rosenbaum, Emily. 2001. Differences in the Locational Attainment of Immigrant and Native-Born Households with Children in New York City. *Demography* 38(3):337–348.

Waldinger, Roger. 1989. Immigration and Urban Change. *Annual Review of Sociology* 15:211–232.

White, Michael J., Ann L. Biddlecom, and Shenyang Guo. 1993. Immigration, Naturalization, and Residential Assimilation among Asian Americans in 1980. *Social Forces* 72:93–117.

White, Michael J., and Sharon Sassler. 2000. Judging Not Only by Color: Ethnicity, Nativity, and Neighborhood Attainment. *Social Science Quarterly* 81(4):997–1014.

Winsberg, Morton D. 1979. Housing Segregation of a Predominantly Middle Class Population: Residential Patterns Developed by the Cuban Immigration into Miami, 1950–1974. *American Journal of Economics and Sociology* 38:403–418.

Wirth, Louis. 1928. *The Ghetto*. Chicago: University of Chicago Press.

Zhou, Min. 1997. Segmented Assimilation: Issues, Controversies, and Recent Research on the New Second Generation. *International Migration Review* 31:975–1008.

ANTHONY J. FILIPOVITCH

RETURN MIGRATION. In 1885, the British scholar E.G. Ravenstein delineated the notion of return migration in *The Laws of Migration*. Return migration is generally defined as the movement of individuals back to their places of origin. Despite early recognition of return migration or counter-flows, migration scholarship emphasizes the assimilation of immigrants, that is, the process of being incorporated into the "melting pot" or the "salad bowl" and of ultimately finding success in America. The focus on assimilation derives from prior ideas that Europeans who engaged in the transatlantic trip from the Old World to the New World did not go back to their homeland. In recent studies, however, scholars highlight how immigrants who headed to America during the era of 1880–1930 sustained strong connections with their home countries through various means—such as sending remittances (migrants' earnings), written correspondence, journeying back and forth, and even returning to stay in their homeland—much more than previously thought (Wyman 1993; Foner 2000). In fact, nearly one-third of all European immigrants (e.g., Irish, Italians, Polish) to America from the period between 1880 and 1930 "turned their backs on the promised land" and permanently headed back to their homeland (Wyman 1993:14).

The notion of return migration is problematic. In anthropology, for example, Wiest (1979) states that until the late 1970s little work conceptualized the meaning of return migration. When referring to return migration in contemporary (post-1965) U.S. immigration history, scholars employ several labels. King notes that a seasonal returnee migrates back and forth between his or her community of origin and destination and that circular migration may become seasonal "if the movements are regular, dictated perhaps by climate or the seasonal availability of certain types of work" (1986:6). Another term closely related to return migration is repatriation. Repatriation usually develops when the return is forced on migrants by political events, authorities, or some personal or natural disaster, rather than being the initiative of the migrants themselves.

In refugee studies where the focus is non-voluntary migration, scholars often employ the concept of repatriation. Chavez (1988) differentiates between settlers and sojourners when considering Mexican and Central American migrant populations in California. He views settlers as individuals who reside in the United States on a more or less permanent basis, regardless of their U.S. immigration status, while calling temporary migrants sojourners. In another study, Margolis (1994) discusses return migration among Brazilians who migrate to New York and employs the concepts of commuters and sojourners. She describes sojourners as people who remain in the United States long enough to save money for a particular objective (mainly to gain social status back home) and then return to their homeland. In contrast, she defines commuters as individuals who make trips back home for varying lengths of time but repeatedly engage in this migratory pattern.

Recent migration studies pay much attention to directionality, that is, to the back and forth movements of migrants, within the parameters of globalization and transnationalism. Pessar (1997:3), for example, views return migration as "one episode in an ongoing process of migration." In research embracing a transnational approach to migration, Levitt (2001) makes distinctions of various types of returnees in her study of Dominican "transnational villagers" in Boston and the Dominican Republic, and describes how individuals change once they go back home. Among Central Americans, one of the newest and fastest growing Latino populations in the United States since the 1980s, Mahler (1999) finds that two kinds of Salvadoran return migrants emerge in her research. While permanent returnees typify individuals who desire not to go back to the United States, recurrent migrants constitute people journeying between their places of origin and destination with some regularity, despite their undocumented status. Some academics suggest using the label of transmigrants to capture how folks regularly participate in activities that transcend national borders and individuals who shuttle back and forth (Glick Schiller et al. 1992; Guarnizo 1997). Still others use the term "return migrant" but view counter-flows of U.S.-bound migrants within the context of transnationalism (Espinosa 1998).

In efforts to capture divergent return migration practices, some studies draw typologies and examine migratory patterns, length of time migrants intend to remain abroad, and reason(s) migrants return to their homeland (González 1961; Gmelch 1980; King 1986). Brettell (1979) suggests that there are analytical distinctions that must be explored between an intention to return and physical return. Factors that influence an actual return include: (1) immigration policies of migrants' destination localities, (2) out-migration policies of sending countries, (3) employment possibilities upon return in migrants' places of origin, and (4) demographic conditions. In contrast, an intention or desire to return varies from a physical return in that it considers a number of social, cultural, and historical traditions or perceptions about migration.

Ideology of return, a notion that represents an important element in return migration, strongly sways how migrants feel and think about their places of origin and arrival and the different attachments they develop (Moran-Taylor 2001). Past usages of perceptions and attitudes concerning return migration examine these ideas under rubrics such as "institutionalized return," "return illusion," "myth of return," "ideology of return," "mirage of return migration," "nostalgia," and "longings of return." Brettell (1979) demonstrates that even after many years of living in France, Portuguese migrants retain an "ideology of return." Many lower-class Portuguese migrants embrace strong intentions to return to their homeland, send their earnings to relatives back home, and invest much of their savings in building homes in Portugal. Despite the strong ideology of return among Portuguese migrants, few actually journeyed back home. More recently, like in the early days of the turn of the twentieth century, Irish living and working in the United States (such as in Boston) are now embarking on their eastward trip. Because of Ireland's booming economy, many Irish are not only thinking and reminiscing about their return, but actually do.

But why do returnees go back to their places of origin? As in previous historical times, times when Europeans journeyed back home in large numbers, primary reasons propelling a return home deal with non-economic factors such as familial social obligations, cultural motives, and discrimination and racism in migrants' places of destination. Economic factors, including failure to complete financial goals, usually arise as less significant in migrants' decisions to go back home.

Return migration may be the most difficult aspect of the migration cycle to quantify (Gmelch 1980:135; Wyman 1993). Though it is difficult to "count" returnees, the movement back home affects the sending country in a variety of ways, especially migrants' communities of origin and people's livelihoods. Thus, future research needs to pay more attention to material and non-material as well as visible and invisible changes related to return migration. A better understanding of return migration is also important to migrant sending countries because of its great potential to affect development, such as through different kinds of investments that returnees may opt to make in their native land. *See also*: **Diasporas; Emigration; Remittances; Transnationalism.**

References

Brettell, Caroline. 1979. Emigrar para Voltar: A Portuguese Ideology of Return Migration. *Papers in Anthropology* 20(1):1–20.
Chavez, Leo. 1988. Settlers and Sojourners: The Case of Mexicans in the United States. *Human Organization* 47(2):95–108.

Espinosa, Victor M. 1998. *El Dilema del Retorno: Migración, Género y Pertenencia en un Contexto Transnacional*. Zamora, Michoacán: El Colegio de Michoacán.

Foner, Nancy. 2000. *From Ellis Island to JFK: New York's Two Great Waves of Immigration*. New York: Russell Sage Foundation.

Glick Schiller, Nina, Linda Basch, and Cristina Blanc-Szanton, eds. 1992. *Towards a Transnational Perspective on Migration: Race, Class, Ethnicity, and Nationalism Reconsidered*. New York: New York Academy of Sciences.

Gmelch, George. 1980. Return Migration. *Annual Review of Anthropology* 9:135–159.

González, Nancie. 1961. Family Organization in Five Types of Migratory Wage Labor. *American Anthropologist* 63:1264–1280.

Guarnizo, Luis. 1997. The Emergence of a Transnational Social Formation and the Mirage of Return Migration Among Dominican Transmigrants. *Identities* 4(2):281–322.

King, Russell. 1986. *Return Migration and Economic Problems*. London: Croom Helm.

Levitt, Peggy. 2001. *The Transnational Villagers*. Berkeley: University of California Press.

Mahler, Sarah. 1999. Engendering Transnational Migration: A Case of Salvadorans. *American Behavioral Scientist* 42(4):690–719.

Margolis, Maxine L. 1994. *Little Brazil: An Ethnography of Brazilian Immigrants in New York City*. Princeton, NJ: Princeton University Press.

Moran-Taylor, Michelle J. 2001. Nostalgia por la Tierra, Nostalgia por el Dólar: Guatemalan Transnational Lives and Ideology of Return. *Estudios Fronterizos* 2(4): 65–114.

Pessar, Patricia. 1997. Introduction: New Approaches to Caribbean Emigration and Return. In *Caribbean Circuits: New Directions in the Study of Caribbean Migration*. P. Pessar, ed. Pp. 1–11. New York: Center for Migration Studies.

Wiest, Raymond. 1979. Anthropological Perspectives on Return Migration: A Critical Commentary. *Papers in Anthropology* 20(1):167–187.

Wyman, Mark. 1993. *Round-Trip to America: The Immigrants Return to Europe, 1880–1930*. Ithaca, NY: Cornell University Press.

MICHELLE J. MORAN-TAYLOR

RIGHTS. Immigrant rights have evolved from the notion that all non-citizens are afforded due process under the U.S. Constitution into a movement to ensure that all non-citizens are treated equally and justly under the law. Today immigrant rights entail safeguarding fairness in the adoption, implementation, and application of immigration laws and procedures. The definition of immigrant rights also extends beyond the realms of immigration benefits and into other areas of basic freedoms such as equal access to government services, quality healthcare, education, and employment.

Non-citizens who are not yet legally admitted to the United States have limited rights. Although all persons in the United States sustain basic rights under the Constitution, such as the freedom of religion, speech, and association, non-citizens do not enjoy all of the same protections and benefits as citizens. Non-citizens may not vote or hold particular government positions or jobs. They face the threat of losing immigration status if any of the grounds for deportation are triggered. Congress, which has unfettered power over immigration, may promulgate laws that further broaden or restrict the rights of immigrants as they pertain to immigration status. Immigrant rights are often curtailed in immigration proceedings. Even though the right to due process under the Fifth Amendment applies to all persons within the United States who are placed in immigration proceedings

(Kurzban 2004:29), non-citizens do not necessarily enjoy the same privileges in immigration proceedings as in other court proceedings.

Most defenses to deportation involve discretionary benefits that give immigration judges and officials broad discretion when determining the outcome of a case. Non-citizens are entitled to having an attorney represent them in immigration matters, but not at government expense. Non-citizens may be detained for immigration violations or specific grounds of deportation. Non-citizens' liberty interests are limited under immigration law in that non-citizens may be detained without the opportunity to post bail for even minor crimes for which incarceration in the criminal justice system would not be required. This is known as mandatory detention (INA 236(c)).

Constitutional challenges to the application and interpretation of immigration laws are regularly made both at the administrative level and in immigration courts. Courts have held that non-citizens do not share the same rights as citizens in some instances. For example, the mandatory detention of lawful permanent residents with certain criminal convictions was challenged before the Supreme Court in the case *Demore v. Kim* (538 U.S. 510, 123 S.Ct. 1708). In that case, the Supreme Court held that lawful permanent residents who are in removal (deportation) proceedings could be incarcerated throughout the immigration process without the opportunity to apply for bail, essentially acknowledging that "Congress makes rules that would be unacceptable if applied to citizens" (Kurzban 2004:33).

Immigration policies and reform have historically been based on providing affirmative benefits despite an underlying principle of exclusion. For a century, immigration benefits were unrestricted. Immigration status and entry into the United States were afforded to those fleeing persecution or economic devastation (Weissbrodt 1998). Discontent with America's "open door policy" emerged as certain groups of people became "undesirable." The first statutes to exclude specific groups were passed in the 1800s, and included convicts, prostitutes, "idiots," lunatics, and those likely to become a public charge. These statutes were followed by laws that barred persons of specific nationalities from entry into the country. The Chinese Exclusion Act, for example, did not allow persons from China to obtain immigration status. Quotas began to be implemented in the 1900s, becoming an important way to control the numbers of people who could immigrate. The quota system and the classification of "undesirable groups" continue to exist under immigration law today. For example, the numbers of refugees permitted to enter each year as well as the number of individuals permitted to immigrate through a family member are subject to caps based on country of origin.

In addition, the Immigration and Nationality Act prevents people from immigrating who fall within specific classifications under the act. Such grounds of exclusion have become known as the grounds of inadmissibility. Some of the common grounds of inadmissibility are: (1) health related, such as those with certain communicable diseases; (2) criminal grounds, which include numerous categories and types of crimes that would render someone inadmissible even if the crime would be minor under criminal law; (3) security; (4) public charge, which prevents those who would likely become financially dependent on public resources; (5) prior immigration violators, including, for example, those who have entered the United States without inspection or who may have been deported before.

The ability to pass immigration measures without limitation stems from the principle of plenary power, which grants Congress exclusive power over other government entities such as states and municipalities. The first signs of Congress's plenary power over immigration emerged in the 1800s with the case *Henderson v. City of New York* (Sup.Ct. 1875) where the Supreme Court declared that states did not have the authority under the Constitution to infringe on the federal government's authority over foreign commerce (Weissbrodt 1998:4), although whether or not foreign commerce included immigration matters was not clear. In the well-known Chinese Exclusion Case, the Supreme Court explicitly ratified the concept of plenary power in 1889 (Gordon et al. 2004: 1.03[1].1.02[2][3][b]). Here, the Supreme Court held that the federal government has exclusive authority over matters of national interest while states are to deal with local concerns. Because immigration is an area of national interest, then, the federal government retains sole power to regulate this area (Sup.Ct. 1889).

Over time immigration law and policy have developed into a highly complex area that is constantly changing and is discretionary in nature. Sweeping reforms in the law have led to great restrictions on migration, while emphasis has been placed on enforcement rather than benefits. In March of 2003, in the "largest government reorganization since World War II" (Gordon et al. 2004:SA1-1), the Immigration and Naturalization Service (INS) was abolished and replaced with the Department of Homeland Security (DHS). Whereas the INS had become a large bureaucracy plagued with inefficiency, backlogs, and red tape (Johnson 1993:1174), DHS today has become a symbol of enforcement, with millions of dollars appropriated into agencies responsible for enforcement (Jachimowicz and Margon 2004).

Numerous immigrant rights groups have emerged over time to challenge restrictive measures and harsh enforcement policies. Immigrant advocacy organizations have been a vital force in influencing legislative change and have served as "watchdogs" for ensuring that basic constitutional rights of non-citizens are protected both in and outside of the legal system. A prime example of the success such groups have had in impacting change is during the "sanctuary movement." During the 1980s, as the Central American nations of Guatemala and El Salvador were engulfed in civil wars, thousands of people fled their home countries in search of safe haven. Many came to the United States in the hope of being afforded protection through the asylum process, only to find obstacles throughout the legal process. Churches and immigrant advocates throughout the United States joined together in providing basic essentials to Guatemalan and Salvadoran refugees such as food and shelter. In addition, immigrant and refugee organizations collaborated with religious groups and denominations in filing a nationwide class action suit against the federal government challenging the systematic discrimination in the asylum process. The class action suit resulted in a settlement that ultimately granted benefits to over 250,000 Guatemalans and Salvadorans nationwide (Rosenblum 2004).

Recently immigrant rights has become a growing area of concern because of deepening national security concerns, economic uncertainty, and growing anti-immigrant sentiment which have given rise to highly restrictive policies and procedures affecting immigrants at both the state and federal levels. Following the tragic events of September 11, 2001, several security measures were implemented in the form of executive orders, legislation, and regulations. In April 2002, for example, the Department of Justice issued a legal opinion stating that state and local law enforcement officials have the authority to enforce federal immigration laws.

Civil rights groups continue to regard some of these actions as infringements on individual civil liberties that primarily target non-citizens (Akram and Johnson 2002). Seattle became the first city to adopt an ordinance prohibiting local police and other city officials from inquiring into immigration status from those seeking city services. In response to current immigration policies, 100,000 people united across the country in one of the largest immigrant rights protests in U.S. history. The Immigrant Workers Freedom Ride was another national event, sponsored by immigrant rights groups, unions, and businesses, which bused immigrant rights advocates as well as both documented and undocumented workers to the U.S. capitol in an effort to encourage reform in immigration laws and policies. Immigrant rights has also taken center stage in the national debate because of the deaths of many people while crossing the U.S. border in search of employment, for family reunification, or to flee persecution.

Today the area of immigrant rights encompasses many new and critical issues, including: whether non-citizens who are undocumented should be afforded immigration status through measures such as amnesty; whether non-citizens regardless of immigration status should have access to driver's licenses, medical care, public benefits, and bilingual education; and whether non-citizen children who are placed in deportation proceedings should be provided with legal representation. Because immigrant rights signify human dignity and respect for all persons irrespective of immigration status, the resolution of such issues will affect receptivity and diversity of the country for years to come. *See also*: **Agencies; Expedited entry and removal; Legislation; National security; Public charge.**

References

Akram, Susan M., and Kevin R. Johnson. 2002. Race, Civil Rights, and Immigration Law after September 11, 2001: The Targeting of Arabs and Muslims. *New York University Annual Survey of American Law* 58:345–377.

Gordon, Charles, Stanley Mailman, and Stephen Yale-Loehr. 2004. *Immigration Law and Procedure*, Rev. ed. Albany, NY: Matthew Bender.

Jachimowicz, Maia, and Sarah Margon. 2004. Bush Boosts Immigration Enforcement in FY2005 Budget. http://www.migrationinformation.org/feature/display.cfm?ID=207.

Johnson, Kevin R. 1993. Los Olvidados: Images of the Immigrant, Political Power of Noncitizens, and Immigration Law and Enforcement. *Brigham Young University Law Review* 1139.

Kurzban, Ira J. 2004. *Immigration Law Sourcebook*, 9th ed. Washington, DC: American Immigration Law Foundation.

Murthy, Sheela. 2000. Overview of Immigration Law: A Brief History. http://www.murthy.com.

Rosenblum, Marc R. 2004. Moving Beyond the Policy of No Policy: Emigration from Mexico and Central America. *Latin American Politics and Society* 46(4):91–124.

Weissbrodt, David S. 1998. *Immigration Law and Procedure in a Nutshell.* St. Paul, MN: West.

NEHA V. CHANDOLA

S

SEXUAL ORIENTATION. In sharp contrast to the generally liberalizing impulse behind the 1965 Immigration Reform Act as a whole, Congress used that revision to strengthen the existing exclusion against lesbian and gay aliens. That exclusion began in 1917 when Congress relied on Public Health Service (PHS) definitions for exclusionary categories, lumping "persons with abnormal sexual instincts" under the rubric "constitutional psychopathic inferiority" (Bogatin 1981).

Revisiting the topic in the 1952 McCarran-Walter Act, Congress again relied on the PHS to provide the term "psychopathic personality" for the 1917 language (*Congressional Digest* 1977). They refined the exclusion again in 1965 in part because a Canadian citizen had filed suit challenging the term "psychopathic personality" as unconstitutionally vague. In 1967, the case *Boutilier v. INS* produced a decision from the Supreme Court upholding the 1952 language. Not knowing the ultimate outcome, Congress in the 1965 act revised the possible bases for exclusion of aliens to include "sexual deviation" (U.S. House of Representatives 1965).

The statutory exclusion of lesbian and gay aliens affected relatively few people, but it rankled lesbian and gay civil rights activists who saw in the exclusion the belief that no lesbian or gay man could make a valuable citizen of the United States. The most recent scholarship on this topic, currently mostly unpublished, has begun to identify heterosexuality as an implicit requirement for citizenship during much of the twentieth century.

That Congress reinforced, rather than relaxing or eliminating, the lesbian and gay exclusion in 1965 illustrates the fact that lesbian and gay civil rights activists had not yet succeeded in climbing aboard the civil rights bandwagon (Frank 2000). Their increasingly successful efforts over the next 25 years would include attacks on both the statutory exclusion of lesbian and gay aliens and the presumption that evidence of lesbian and gay identity or sexual practices should invalidate an application for citizenship on the grounds of moral turpitude. The Immigration and Naturalization Service (INS) would drop its policy barring citizenship applications by lesbian and gay aliens in 1975 in response to a federal court decision.

The statutory prohibition on admitting lesbian and gay aliens remained, however. Lesbian and gay civil rights activists first gained major access to federal policymakers during Jimmy Carter's presidential administration (1977–1981). While they failed to persuade INS Commissioner Leonel Castillo to eliminate the lesbian and gay exclusion administratively, they did persuade Surgeon General Julius Richmond to announce in 1979 that the PHS would no longer conduct medical examinations of incoming aliens whom INS officials suspected to be lesbian or gay. Richmond made this decision in response to the case of a British man whom INS officers detained because he was wearing a "Gay Pride" button (Turner 1995, 2000). He noted that his decision was consistent with the American Psychiatric Association's removal of "homosexuality" from its official nosology, the *Diagnostic and Statistical Manual of Mental Disorders*, in 1973 (Bayer 1981).

Richmond's decision rendered immigration policy toward lesbian and gay aliens absurdly inconsistent, but little changed during the next 11 years. INS officials continued to insist that, although Congress had relied on PHS definitions and advice in excluding lesbian and gay aliens, the surgeon general's decision was not a sufficient basis for changing policy administratively because Congress had created an exclusionary standard, not a medical category, and Congress has plenary power to exclude aliens.

This situation produced conflicting federal court decisions that the Supreme Court chose not to resolve. In 1981, the Board of Immigration Appeals decided the case of the British man, finding that the INS did not need a PHS certificate in order to exclude a lesbian or gay alien when the alien had made "an unsolicited, unambiguous admission that he is a homosexual and where the current U.S. Public Health Service position that homosexuality cannot be medically diagnosed is a matter of record." The Ninth Circuit court of appeals overturned the board's decision, finding that the statute clearly required a PHS certificate any time they wished to exclude an alien on medical grounds. The next month, however, in an unrelated case, the Fifth Circuit found just the opposite.

By forcing debate on the issue, lesbian and gay civil rights activists also produced clear evidence that the ban on lesbian and gay aliens created opportunities for discriminatory treatment, including potential harassment, by INS officers. Responding to the surgeon general's decision in 1979, Commissioner Castillo adopted an interim policy according to which all suspected lesbian and gay aliens would be admitted provisionally, pending a final decision by the INS on how to proceed. But the National Gay Task Force and the National Organization for Women received complaints from women who tried to enter the country to attend the Michigan Women's Music Festival that year. They claimed that INS officers had refused to allow them into the United States after asking them whether they slept with men or women and other, similarly intrusive questions. Another widely reported episode involved the detention in January 1980 of a Mexican man who spoke no English but whom INS officers persuaded to sign a statement that he was gay. They had initially stopped him because he wore makeup and an engagement ring.

As a result of the debate over immigration policy that extended throughout the 1980s, the lesbian and gay exclusion was removed from the 1990 immigration reform. Numerous factors contributed to this success, including considerable changes in public attitudes toward lesbian and gay civil rights issues between 1965 and 1990 and the central role of Congressman Barney Frank (D-MA) in the entire process of writing new immigration law. With the anti–lesbian and gay exclusion removed, Frank next asked for inclusion of persecution on the basis of sexual orientation as grounds for granting asylum. The Bush administration refused, but President Clinton's attorney general, Janet Reno, complied (Frank 2000).

Immigration policy has broadly mirrored changing attitudes on matters of sexual orientation in the larger culture and the fortunes of the lesbian and gay civil rights movement since the passage of the 1965 immigration reform. Future research will fill in the continuing gaps in our knowledge of how this exclusion affected particular individuals. It will also continue to elaborate on the notion of sexuality as a criterion for citizenship in the United States. *See also*: **Asylum**; **Legislation**.

References

Bayer, Ronald. 1981. *Homosexuality and American Psychiatry: The Politics of Diagnosis.* New York: Basic Books.

Bogatin, Marc. 1981. The Immigration and Nationality Act and the Exclusion of Homosexuals: *Boutilier v. INS* Revisited. *Cardozo Law Review* 2.

Congressional Digest. 1977. Evolution of U.S. Immigration Policy. *Congressional Digest* 56.

Frank, Barney. 2000. American Immigration Law: A Case Study in the Effective Use of the Political Process. In *Creating Change: Sexuality, Public Policy, and Civil Rights.* John D'Emilio, William B. Turner, and Urvashi Vaid, eds. Pp. 208–235. New York: St. Martin's Press.

Hutchinson, E.P. 1981. *Legislative History of American Immigration Policy, 1798–1965.* Philadelphia: University of Pennsylvania Press.

Levy, Daniel. 1991. Exclusion Grounds Under the Immigration Act of 1990. *Immigration Briefings: Practical Analysis of Immigration and Nationality Issues* 91(8):4–12.

Lubheid, Eithne. 2002. *Entry Denied: Controlling Sexuality at the Border.* Minneapolis: University of Minnesota Press.

Turner, William B. 1995. Lesbian/Gay Rights and Immigration Policy: Lobbying to End the Medical Model. *Journal of Policy History* 7(2):208–225.

———. 2000. Mirror Images: Lesbian/Gay Civil Rights in the Carter and Reagan Administrations. In *Creating Change: Sexuality, Public Policy, and Civil Rights.* John D'Emilio, William B. Turner, and Urvashi Vaid, eds. Pp. 3–28. New York: St. Martin's Press.

U.S. House of Representatives. 1965. Hearings on H.R. 2580, Committee on the Judiciary, Subcommiteee on Immigration and Naturalization. 89th Congress, 1st Session, March 4.

WILLIAM B. TURNER

SKILLED MIGRANTS. The United States accepts about half of the world's anticipated legal immigrants and more than half of the world's professionals who settle in other countries. In many cases, skilled migrants arrive as temporary visitors and do not leave. For example, foreign students may wind up as foreign workers who find U.S. employers to sponsor them for immigrant visas—about 90 percent of the foreigners granted immigrant visas in the United States for employment reasons in recent years already had been in the United States. Even when they do not settle in the country, foreigners who visit, engage in business, play on U.S. sports teams, or perform in the arts do much to enrich U.S. society and its economy.

Professionals or skilled migrants can be defined in several ways (Lowell 2001), including level of education, so that persons with higher education are considered professional or skilled. This is a supply-side approach, since it defines skills by educational levels. Other analysts use a demand-side approach, asking where people work or how much they earn. For example, all persons in computer engineering occupations could be defined as professionals, or all those earning $50,000 a year or more could be defined as skilled (average earnings are about $34,000 in 2005). There is no consensus on whether skilled should be defined by personal characteristics, occupation, earnings, or some combination of these factors.

Foreigners enter the United States via three major doors: as immigrants, non-immigrants, and unauthorized foreigners. Immigrants are citizens of other countries who have been granted a visa that allows them to live and work permanently in the United States and, generally after five years, to become naturalized U.S. citizens. Immigrant visas used to be green, and immigrants are still often referred to as "greencard holders." In the past, most immigrant visas were issued to foreigners at U.S. consulates in their home countries. In the 1990s, this changed, and today most immigrant visas are issued to foreigners inside the United States.

Non-immigrant visa holders are foreigners who are granted temporary entry into the United States for a specific purpose, such as visiting, working, or studying. About 30 million non-immigrants a year are admitted, over 90 percent as temporary visitors for pleasure (tourists) or business. Non-immigrants who enter and leave the United States several times during a year are counted each time in these data, but Mexicans with border crossing cards that allow shopping visits and Canadian visitors are not included in non-immigrant admissions data.

Unauthorized, undocumented, or illegal migrants are foreigners in the United States without valid visas. The best estimates are that the number of unauthorized immigrants doubled from 3.5 million in 1990 to 7 million in 2000, and have risen to 11 million in 2005. About 60 percent of the unauthorized are Mexicans, and many who elude the Border Patrol and enter the United States stay because it has become more difficult and costly to cross the border. The United States permits non-immigrant and unauthorized foreigners to become immigrants if they find U.S. employers to sponsor them, and options for a regularization program for at least some of the unauthorized are under discussion.

Skilled Immigrants

Immigration averaged about 920,000 a year over the past decade, and would have been higher if the government had been faster in dealing with the 1.2 million applications for immigrant visas that were pending in 2005 (almost all the pending applications are expected to result in the issuance of an immigrant visa). The rising number of immigrants and the significant backlog reflect primarily family unification, as when a U.S. citizen or legal immigrant relatives already in the United States petition for the admission of a foreigner.

About a seventh of U.S. immigrants (including their family members) are admitted because they have extraordinary ability or because U.S. employers sponsor them for immigrant visas. The employment door to the United States admits up to 140,000 foreigners a year (including family members) or 10 to 15 percent of the immigrant flow, versus half in Australia and Canada. Most economists advocate a higher percentage of immigrant visas for the highly skilled (Borjas 1999).

Three features of the U.S. employment-based immigration system merit attention. First, three-fourths of the employment-related visas involve a U.S. employer proving to the satisfaction of the U.S. Department of Labor that U.S. workers are not available to fill the job for which the employer is seeking an immigrant. Second, there are relatively few admissions of "global talent," foreigners with extraordinary ability, outstanding professors, and executives and managers—fewer than 1,000 a month. Third, if the U.S. share of global talent is about the same as its share of immigration, half, then not many highly talented people are eager to settle in other countries.

In recent years, an average 55,000 "principals" a year obtained employment-related immigrant visas (the other visas in the employment category were given to their family members). First-preference immigration is supply driven, meaning that a foreigner with "extraordinary ability," which U.S. regulations suggest means receiving a Nobel prize or having a worldwide reputation, can obtain an immigrant visa by presenting her credentials, and the United States admits an average 2,200 such foreigners a year. Outstanding professors and multinational executives must have U.S. job offers, but their U.S. employers do not have to prove that U.S. workers are not available, and the number admitted has recently averaged 2,400 and 6,700 a year, respectively.

There are more second-preference immigrants, an average 13,000 a year. They are professionals with advanced degrees who must undergo labor certification, meaning that the U.S. employers who want to hire them must prove to the satisfaction of the U.S. Department of Labor that U.S. workers are not available. Third-preference immigrants, an average 27,000 a year, must have at least a college degree and must also undergo labor certification. A maximum 10,000 immigrant visas a year are available to unskilled workers, so that the wait for U.S. employers sponsoring their maids and gardeners for immigrant visas is often a decade or more.

The final two categories of employment-related visas are for religious workers and investors. Religious worker immigrants are sponsored by U.S. churches, while foreign investors undergo an investment and job creation test, with most investing at least $500,000 to create or preserve at least 10 full-time jobs (at least 35 hours a week) in "targeted employment areas," including rural and urban areas with unemployment rates that are 150 percent of the U.S. average. After making the investment (most are passive investments in which the foreigner is not an active manager), the foreigner receives a probationary immigrant visa that converts to a regular immigrant visa after two years.

In the mid-1990s, the inspector general of the U.S. Department of Labor issued a report that was very critical of the labor certification process (U.S. Department of Labor 1996). The inspector general found that 99 percent of the foreigners being requested for an immigrant visa by employers were already in the United States, and that 74 percent were already employed by the sponsoring employer. Some 165,000 U.S. workers applied for the 24,000 jobs examined, almost seven U.S. applicants per job, but in virtually every case, the U.S. workers were found not qualified, and the foreigners were hired. The report concluded that U.S. employers sponsor foreigners for immigrant visas to "reward" them.

Employment-based immigration is a contentious but low-profile issue. Academic studies conclude that the net economic benefits of immigration, estimated to add one tenth of one percent to U.S. GDP of about $11.5 trillion, would be higher if the United States shifted the composition of immigrants toward the highly skilled. Employers who seek immigrant visas for foreigners and the lawyers who advise them express dissatisfaction with the delays and costs of the current systems, but have been unwilling to shift toward a pay-to-prove-that-you-need-immigrants system, with the funds collected used to subsidize training in occupations with labor shortages.

Migrant Professionals

Immigration is sometimes referred to as the front door to the United States, which makes non-immigrant admissions the side door and illegal immigration the back door. Non-immigrants are foreigners in the United States for a specific time and purpose. The number of non-immigrants tripled in the past 20 years, primarily because of the growing number of tourists and business visitors, but there has also been significant growth in admissions of temporary foreign workers—over a million a year have been admitted in recent years, although the same individual could be counted several times in admission data.

The non-immigrant program closest to "global talent" offers O-1 visas for foreigners with "extraordinary ability in the sciences, arts, education, business or athletics" further defined as "a level of expertise indicating that the person is one of the small percentage who have risen to the top of the field of endeavor." The supporting documentation for applicants for O-1 visas includes national and international prizes, scholarly publications, or "evidence that the alien has or will command a high salary."

A third of the temporary foreign worker admissions in the late 1990s were for foreign professionals with H-1B visas. Half of those are from India, and over half of the H-1Bs work in information technology–related fields while they stay in the United States for up to six years. The H-1B program allows most U.S. employers to attest that they are paying prevailing wages and that there is no strike that has made a job vacant, and then foreigners with at least a bachelor of arts degree are permitted easy entry for up to six years to fill a U.S. job that normally requires its holder to have a B.A. degree. The U.S. employer completes an online Department of Labor form and, with only minimal checks, the Department of Labor approves the employer's request, which is then submitted to immigration authorities and to consular officials overseas, so that the foreigner or beneficiary can receive the H-1B visa inside or outside the United States.

Complaints about the H-1B program center on displacement of U.S. workers and the activities of intermediaries. The trade-off embodied in the H-1B program is that employers face few barriers to hiring H-1Bs, but there is a cap of 65,000 H-1B visas a year. The assumption was that U.S. workers with college degrees would complain loudly against abuses, so the H-1B program did not include provisions that, for example, prohibited employers from displacing U.S. workers in order to hire H-1Bs. Some did just that, as when American International Group in September 1994 laid off 130 U.S. programmers and outsourced the **work** they did to Syntel, an Indian-American firm; the laid-off U.S. programmers protested that they had to train the workers who replaced them in India and the United States. Only H-1B–dependent employers, those with 15 percent or more H-1B workers, must certify that they did not lay off U.S. workers to hire H-1B workers.

The second major complaint involves the intermediaries who recruit workers for U.S. jobs. These so-called body brokers aim to maximize their revenues, which are obtained from migrants and employers, and often involve charging migrants fees, bringing them to the United States, and then sending them to employers and profiting from the difference between what an employer pays and what the migrant receives.

The next largest group of foreign professionals is so-called NAFTA (North American Free Trade Agreement) professionals. Chapter 16 of NAFTA created almost freedom of movement for Canadian, Mexican, and U.S. workers with a college degree or more by allowing employers to hire workers from other NAFTA countries easily if they have a college degree or more. Employers in the three countries can offer an unlimited number of jobs requiring college degrees to NAFTA nationals with college degrees; unlike the H-1B program, there is no requirement that an employer pay at least the prevailing wage. The number of Canadian professionals entering the United States with NAFTA-TN visas almost tripled since 1995, from about 25,000 entries a year to 70,000 entries, but the number of Mexican entries remains low, generally less than 2,000 a year.

Foreign professionals can also enter the United States with L-1 visas for up to seven years if they are managers or have specialized knowledge of the company's products or processes, were employed at least one year abroad, and are transferred by multinationals from a foreign to a U.S. branch, and they may adjust to immigrant status while in the United States on an L-1 visa. There is no ceiling on the number of L-1 visas that can be issued, and in FY04, some 57,245 L-1 visas were issued, about the same as in previous years, including a third to persons from India.

The final non-immigrant door is for foreign students. Some 637,954 foreigners with student visas entered the United States in FY2002, led by students from India and China. Foreign students must be admitted or accepted by accredited U.S. institutions, and then must convince consular officials that they have sufficient funds to study in the United States and that they intend to return at the end of their studies. Foreign students may work on campus (including for off-campus firms that provide on-campus services such as food or janitorial services), up to 20 hours a week while studying and full time during breaks. Foreign students can and do find U.S. employers to sponsor them for immigrant and non-immigrant visas, and many remain in the United States, including 90 percent of mainland Chinese students, although recent reports suggest that more Chinese graduates of U.S. universities are now returning to China.

Conclusions

The United States sees itself as a nation of immigrants that is open to newcomers who benefit by immigrating while conferring benefits on the U.S. economy and society. Most political leaders thus assert that the best way to attract global talent is to maintain an open and free society that maximizes freedom and opportunity and minimizes taxes.

In response to economists' recommendations to accept more highly skilled immigrants as well as requests from particular groups of employers, the United States more than doubled the number of economic immigrants in 1990, from 54,000 to 140,000 (including family members). Only 11,000 of these immigrants a year qualify as global talent, in the sense that there is no need to test the U.S. labor market to determine if U.S. workers are available. Instead, most are admitted after a U.S. employer sponsors them by proving, to the satisfaction of the U.S. Department of Labor, that U.S. workers are not available to fill the job for which the foreigner is being requested.

There are far more non-immigrants admitted to fill vacant U.S. jobs, and U.S. employers must satisfy a wide range of criteria to have visas issued to the foreigners they want to employ. The largest program issues H-1B visas to foreigners with at least college degrees coming to the United States for up to six years to fill jobs requiring college degrees. This program more than tripled to more than 195,000 admissions a year at the height of the information technology boom in 2000, but has since shrunk to about half that level. The other large program is for foreign students, many of whom stay in the United States and work after graduation, though the number of foreign graduate students appears to have fallen significantly in the aftermath of new security measures instituted since 2001. *See also*: **Documentation; Effects of unauthorized immigration; Immigration system; Work.**

References

Borjas, George. 1999. *Heaven's Door: Immigration Policy and the American Economy.* Princeton, NJ: Princeton University Press.

Cornelius, Wayne A., Thomas J. Espenshade, and Idean Salehyan, eds. 2001. *International Migration of the Highly Skilled.* San Diego, CA: Center for Comparative Immigration Studies, University of California.

Lowell, B. Lindsay. 2001. Skilled Temporary and Permanent Immigration to the United States. *Population Research and Policy Review* 20(1–2):33–58.

Martin, Philip. 2004. Migration. In *Global Crises, Global Solutions.* Bjorn Lomborg, ed. Pp. 443–477. Cambridge: Cambridge University Press.

Martin, Philip, Manolo Abella, and Christiane Kuptsch. 2005. *Managing Labor Migration in the Twenty-First Century.* New Haven, CT: Yale University Press.

Martin, Susan, Lindsay Lowell, and Philip Martin. 2002. US Immigration Policy: Admission of Highly Skilled Workers. *Georgetown Immigration Law Journal* 16(3):619–636.

Organisation for Economic Cooperation and Development. 2002. *International Mobility of the Highly Skilled.* Paris: Organisation for Economic Cooperation and Development.

U.S. Department of Labor. 1996. The Department of Labor's Foreign Labor Certification Programs: The System Is Broken and Needs to Be Fixed. Report. 06-96-002-03-321. http://www.oig.dol.gov/public/reports/oa/pre_1998/06-96-002-03-321s.htm.

U.S. General Accountability Office. 2000. *H-1B Foreign Workers: Better Controls Needed to Help Employers and Protect Workers.* GAO-HEHS-00-157.

———. 2002. *Highlights of a GAO Forum: Workforce Challenges and Opportunities for 21st Century: Changing Labor Force Dynamics and the Role of Government.*

————. 2004. *H-1B Foreign Workers: Better Tracking Needed to Help Determine H-1B Program's Effects on U.S. Workforce*. GAO-03-883.

PHILIP MARTIN

SOCIAL BENEFITS. For at least a decade preceding the welfare provisions of the 1996 Welfare Act and the 1996 Immigration Act, there was debate about the use of social, including medical and educational, services by immigrants, especially the undocumented. Some scholars and policymakers claimed immigrants consumed more tax monies through the services they accessed than they paid in income taxes. Others argued that immigrants paid far more in income taxes than they received in benefits, and that without their tax contributions, the current social security system could not be maintained (Hayes-Bautista et al. 1988). Legislation in the 1990s concerning immigrants was predicated on the former argument and viewed immigrants, especially the undocumented, as a cost to the system. California's Proposition 187, passed in 1994, denied undocumented immigrants an array of educational, medical, and welfare services. Attendance in public schools was to be restricted to children of U.S. citizens and lawfully admitted immigrants. Although Proposition 187 was eventually declared unconstitutional, primarily on the grounds that legislation concerning immigrants must be promulgated on the federal level, it signaled widespread public perception that costs of immigration were "out of control," or at least needing some curtailment.

The federal government generated similarly restrictive legislation in the form of the Personal Responsibility and Work Opportunity Reconciliation Act of 1996 (PRWORA). This "welfare act" dovetailed with the immigration reform acts of 1996 (Fragomen 1997; Gimple and Edwards 1999), and differed from Proposition 187 in two ways. First, it does not deny free K–12 schooling for undocumented immigrant children. Second, it does not demand that medical care, school personnel, and law enforcement personnel inform the Immigration and Naturalization Service (INS) of suspected undocumented immigrants who utilize their services. It does, however, cut off both undocumented and some legally resident immigrants from an array of publicly funded social services.

PRWORA is notable in its targeting of immigrants in a number of its provisions. First, it is to be circulated to all consular officials, who are in charge of deciding whether potential immigrants will receive documentation to enter the United States, or if there is a chance they will become a public charge. Second, it incorporates a number of assumptions and provisions included in California's Proposition 187 and makes legal immigrants, for the first five years after their entry, as well as undocumented immigrants, ineligible for a number of federally funded welfare benefits. Noting that immigrants are increasingly using public benefits at federal, state, and local levels, PRWORA indicates a traditional preference for self-sufficient immigrants and calls for the removal of incentives for undocumented immigrants to come to the United States to avail themselves of these benefits, the assumption being that this is why the undocumented are arriving, rather than to seek work in the many industries that employ them. Third, it permits state and local governments to restrict public benefits, including subsidized housing, to legal permanent residents, as well as to the undocumented. There are exceptions to restrictions on both federal and state or local levels: refugees, asylees, and those immigrants who have received a stay of deportation are eligible for public benefits for the first five years after their entry; veterans and those on active duty are exempted from restriction as are immigrants who have worked for 40 qualifying quarters "as defined under Title II of the Social Security Act" (Section 402 (a)(ii)(I)). Fourth, eligibility of a legal permanent resident for federal or state means-tested public benefits will be determined not only by his or her own income but by spouse's income and the "income and resources of any individual who executed an affidavit of support" (Section 421 (a)(1)).

The sponsor's affidavit of support, necessary for legal immigration to the United States, is to be taken as a contract guaranteeing that the immigrant will not become a public charge, a contract "which is legally enforceable against the sponsor by the sponsored alien, the Federal government, and by any State (or any political subdivision of such state) which provides any means-tested public benefits program" (Section 423 (A)). Thus undocumented workers and legal permanent residents for their first five years in the United States are ineligible for food stamps and social security benefits, including "any retirement, welfare, health, disability, public or assisted housing, post secondary education, food assistance, unemployment benefit, or any similar benefit" (Section 401 (c)(1)(B)). In sum, there are five-year restrictions on eligibility for Medicaid, Supplementary Security Income, the Food Stamp Program, State Children's Health Insurance Program (SCHIP), and Temporary Assistance to Needy Families (TANF). Eligibility, however, was maintained for both undocumented and legally admitted immigrants for non-cash disaster relief, the National School Lunch Act, immunizations and treatment for communicable diseases, and such things as soup kitchens or temporary shelter under conditions determined by the attorney general.

The ineligibility provisions appear to be a response to the growing number of immigrant settlers, especially from Mexico and Central America. Prior to the termination of the Bracero program in 1964, most immigrants from Mexico were recurrent immigrants, coming to the United States to work, and then returning home. The costs of raising the labor force, including medical and educational expenses, and the costs of maintaining the labor force in times of unemployment, sickness, disability, or old age were borne by the sending state. As more and more Mexican, and later Central American, immigrants—dislocated from their home countries by civil strife and economic dislocations—arrived to stay permanently or semi-permanently, their dependents (especially wives and children) came to join them, putting pressure on educational, medical, and other services. The costs of reproduction and maintenance of the immigrant labor force began to take place not abroad, but within the United States. Nativist movements and immigration-control advocates sought to deny immigrants the benefits needed for their social reproduction, despite the fact that most of these immigrants, undocumented or documented, pay at least the federal level income taxes. Title IV of PRWORA attempts to re-export from the U.S. economy the costs of reproduction and maintenance once more, but now internally, by "deeming" the income of spouse and sponsor (often the same person) in determining eligibility of public benefits and by denying public benefits outright to undocumented immigrants and for five years to the majority of legal permanent residents.

Nonetheless, humanitarian considerations have led to the introduction and passage of some legislation that modifies provisions of the 1996 Welfare Act. Social Security Insurance and Medicaid were restored for legal immigrants residing in the United States prior to the passage of PRWORA by the Balanced Budget Act of 1997. The Agricultural Research, Extension and Education Act of 1998 restored food stamps to disabled, aged, or child immigrants present before the passage of PRWORA. Food stamps were also reinstated for legal immigrants meeting the means test who had been in the country for five years by the Farm Security and Rural Investment Act of 2002. Undocumented immigrants remain outside the social safety net. However, as of 2003, under consideration is the DREAM (Development, Relief and Education for Alien Minors) Act which would legalize students over the age of 12 and of "good moral character" who have lived in the United States for at least five years and permit undocumented students to be eligible for in-state tuition at institutions of higher education in the states where they reside.

The costs and benefits of immigration have long been disputed, elsewhere (Burawoy 1976) as well as in the United States (Portes 1978). These issues will continue to be debated, particularly in times of tight budgets and in association with rising nativist impulse (Perea 1997; Wilson 1999, 2000). While some new analyses of 2000 census data reveal less use of public assistance as incomes rise, conflictive public perspectives are likely unless and until good empirical research replaces more ambiguous media accounts. *See also*: **Effects of unauthorized immigration; Public charge; Social mobility.**

References

Burawoy, Michael. 1976. The Function and Reproduction of Migrant Labor: Comparative Material from Southern Africa and the United States. *American Journal of Sociology* 81(5):1050–1087.

Fragomen, Austin T. 1997. Illegal Immigration Reform and Immigrant Responsibility Act of 1996: An Overview. *International Migration Review* 31(2):438–461.

Gimple, James G., and James R. Edwards Jr. 1999. *The Congressional Politics of Immigration Reform*. Boston: Allyn and Bacon.

Hayes-Bautista, David E., Werner O. Schink, and Jorge Chapa. 1988. *The Burden of Support: Young Latinos in an Aging Society*. Stanford, CA: Stanford University Press.

Perea, Juan F., ed. 1997. *Immigrants Out! The New Nativism and the Anti-Immigrant Impulse in the United States*. New York: New York University Press.

Portes, Alejandro. 1978. Toward a Structural Analysis of Illegal Immigration. *International Migration Review* 12(4):469–484.

Wilson, Tamar Diana. 1999. Anti-Immigrant Settlement and the Process of Settlement Among Mexican Immigrants to the United States: Reflections on the Current Wave of Mexican Immigrant Bashing. *Review of Radical Political Economics* 31(2):1–26.

———. 2000. Anti-Immigrant Sentiment and the Problem of Reproduction/Maintenance in Mexican Immigration to the United States. *Critique of Anthropology* 20(2):181–213.

TAMAR DIANA WILSON

SOCIAL MOBILITY. Within the broad term of social mobility, there are many contexts and specific types of mobility such as economic, occupational, educational, spatial, and geographic. Attempts to understand the social mobility of contemporary American immigrants have included comparing and contrasting ethnic groups' cultural values, group social pressures, social structure, level of educational attainment, occupational attainment, income levels, levels of assimilation, and the dominant culture's perceptions and openness to immigrants. It becomes difficult to determine an ethnic immigrant group's overall social mobility in America because all the various components are interrelated and essential to understanding the larger picture. Although the research on social mobility of contemporary immigrant groups is overwhelmed by debates as to which factors best determine levels of mobility and also various assimilation theories, there are numerous patterns and trends to the American immigration process since 1965.

Economic Factors

The liberalization of immigration policy following the 1965 Immigration and Naturalization Act dramatically changed the immigrant composition in America. In the 1960s, the traditional dominance of European immigration began to decline. By the 1980s, only 11 percent of the total immigration came from Europe, whereas in 1900 they made up 90 percent of total immigration (Ueda 1998). After this reversal, the majority of immigrants coming to the United States were from Asia and Latin America. Whereas immigrants before the Great Depression were almost entirely working-class, all the immigrants of the 1970s through the 1990s can be divided into two economic classes, either highly skilled or poorly skilled. Many post-1965 immigrants were highly educated and trained workers. In the 1970s, 25 percent of immigrants were professionals and often more than 40 percent were white-collar workers. This trend continued into the 1980s. From 1976 to 1990, more than 35 percent of employed immigrants were in professional and other white-collar jobs, and an additional 12 percent were in skilled crafts (Ueda 1998).

This human capital migration was counteracted by a large group of low-skilled workers. Service workers, laborers, and semiskilled operatives composed about 46 percent of employed immigrants in this same time period. The flow of the low-skilled and under-educated immigrants rose in numbers and in percentages in the 1980s and 1990s. Hispanic, Asian, and West Indian workers moved into the service and semi-skilled job markets in large cities like Los Angeles and New York, causing increasing friction and conflict with native black workers (Ueda 1998).

Frey (1996) focuses on the demographic and economic "balkanization" patterns occurring with post-1965 immigrant groups. Largely the result of de facto as well as self-imposed segregation patterns, new immigrants and ethnic groups have become segregated across neighborhoods or between central cities and suburbs. Recent trends see the emergence of entire metropolitan areas or labor market regions that are distinct from the rest of the country in their race, ethnic, and demographic composition.

The notion of self-imposed segregation as it relates to immigrant enclaves speaks to an urban model in which ethnic enclaves or neighborhoods in cities can also serve relatively impoverished new arrivals for a period of time and then later provide a base for spatial assimilation and entry into integrated suburban areas (Logan et al. 2002).

Although the development of extended communities for immigrants provides in some cases a jump-off point for later integration into the American mainstream, the social inequality and mobility of recent immigrant groups are still largely affected by enduring racial disparities in class and economic structures.

Non-white immigrant groups are impacted by diverse mechanisms of control (e.g., "glass ceilings" and cultural attacks on racial self-esteem), different economic strategies and structures (e.g., unpaid family labor and dual wage–earning households), inconsistencies in status and occupation (e.g., occupational segregation and disparities between educational achievement and occupational or income status), heterogeneous modes of incorporation (e.g., segmented assimilation), cultural stereotypes that shape public perceptions and behavior (e.g., model minority and illegal aliens), international systems of dominance (globalization and geopolitical relationships), and new racialized standards in education and employment (e.g., Asian quotas and ideologies of meritocracy used to create divisions between Asians and Latinos versus blacks).

Despite the touted socioeconomic advances of a few immigrant groups and individuals, the social mobility of immigrant populations are still by and large directed by long-established social patterns that act to stratify new immigrants (Allen and Chung 2000). The impact of these patterns can be vividly seen by the fact that in 1990, British immigrants on average earned 40 percent more than the typical native worker, while Mexican immigrants as a whole earned 40 percent less. If the recent historical pattern holds, a century from now the third-generation descendants of today's British immigrants will earn about 10 percent more than the typical native worker, while the descendants of today's Mexican immigrants will earn about 10 percent less (Borjas 2004).

Education and Self-Employment

Several studies show that Mexican Americans and Mexican migrants fare better socially than native blacks of comparable or higher education. Michael Greenwood and Marta Tienda (1997) report that male Mexican migrants were disadvantaged relative to native blacks in terms of educational attainment and language skills, yet in most states they had higher rates of labor-force participation and usually lower unemployment rates. This suggests that some employers prefer Mexican immigrants as workers because they allegedly assume that Mexicans have better work habits and attitudes than blacks due to a continuation of racist stereotypes in American society (Raijman and Tienda 1999). This systemic racism can also adversely impact opportunities for very dark-skinned immigrants from some Caribbean and Asian nations.

Immigrants' changing educational composition is crucial for understanding processes of economic assimilation and socioeconomic mobility. In general, immigrants from Latin America exhibit the lowest educational levels, on average, while immigrants from Asia are the most highly educated. Nevertheless, these percentages can vary distinctly when allowing for particular cultural and nationalistic differences. Proportions of Laotian, Cambodian, Italian, and Haitian immigrants who completed high school and college degrees fell below the U.S. average, while Peruvian, Cuban, Colombian, and Nicaraguan immigrants attained high school or college graduation rates similar to the U.S. average (Raijman and Tienda 1999). Nigerian immigrants appear to be the most educated because nearly 100 percent are high school graduates; however, Asian Indians hold the top position when considering college graduation rates.

Mexican immigrants have the lowest level of schooling in terms of high school and college graduation, and also years of graded schooling. One reason for this might deal with the educational setting where most Mexican and Latino immigrant children find themselves. In their study of Spanish-speaking, "Limited English Proficiency" students, Van Hook and Balistreri (2002) mention that Hispanics bear the brunt of institutional disadvantage partly because of their demographic circumstances. Among immigrants, Hispanics are the most numerous, tend to be poor, and tend to be residentially segregated and isolated along the lines of both ethnicity and poverty. These characteristics produce a situation in which it is nearly impossible for Hispanic-dominated school districts not to be mostly poor, mostly minority, and mostly non–English speaking. Smaller immigrant groups, such as some Asian subgroups like the Vietnamese, may be as poor and residentially segregated, but due to their smaller size, do not dominate entire school districts and attend schools that are similar in low-income composition to those attended by non-Hispanic white children (Van Hook and Balistreri 2002).

One of the most important variables of social mobility and assimilation is economic status; the narrowing of what might be called the "opportunity gap" between immigrants and natives. Immigrants generally enter the United States with substantially lower skills than the native population and encounter initial difficulties in terms of economic opportunities. At the beginning of this millennium, a newly arrived worker earned about 34 percent less than the typical American-born worker. Over time, the acquisition of increased skills and English language proficiency can narrow the opportunity gap significantly for immigrant groups, but in many cases equal access to societal goods and opportunities are realized only after the progression of two to three generations (Borjas 2004).

Socioeconomic status has an independent effect on mobility outcomes because it influences where people live, where they go to school, with whom they socialize, and what kind of family and community resources are available (Zhou 2000). Some well-educated immigrants, arriving from India, for example, may settle immediately in affluent communities, bypassing the earlier process of trans-generational residential upward mobility. Numerous researchers have reported impressive patterns of educational and economic social mobility among Asian Americans. As a result, there has been a notable change in perceptions of Asian Americans; the unfavorable stereotypes that were widely adopted by white Americans before, during, and immediately after World War II have transformed into the controversial characterization of Asian Americans as the "model minority." Today the educational levels of Chinese, Japanese, and Asian Indians, as well as native-born, equal or exceed those of native and European immigrant groups (Yetman 1999).

Sociological research has also shown that self-employment is an important avenue for immigrants' labor market assimilation (Portes and Stepick 1985). Except for very recent arrivals (less than five years of U.S. residence), rates of self-employment are systematically higher among the foreign-born. There are also visible concentrations of immigrants in small businesses in large, metropolitan, immigrant-receiving areas like New York, Los Angeles, Miami, Houston, and Chicago. Generally, self-employment rates are the highest for Asian immigrants (especially Koreans), but for white immigrants the highest self-employment rates are found among Russians, Armenians, and Greeks, and among Hispanics, Cubans exhibit the highest self-employment rates. Among all foreign-born groups, Mexicans exhibit the lowest rates of self-employment.

Gender

Additionally, it is important to note that a significant number of the U.S. informal-sector occupations that grew during the 1970s and 1980s—paid domestic work, childcare, garment and electronic assembly—recruited primarily female immigrant workers. Some assert that the range of immigrant social networks expands with the entry of each new migrant into the migration process; however, it is important to add that the networks themselves do not automatically become equally accessible to women and men. Immigrant social networks are highly contested social resources, and they are not always shared, even in the same family. Hondagneu-Sotelo (1999a, 1999b) argues that women and men do not share the same experiences with migration, and their gender relations—patterns of separation, conflict, and cooperation—produce distinct migration patterns.

Patriarchal gender relations undergo continual renegotiation as women and men rebuild their families in the United States. Gender is reconstructed in different ways, imposed by particular contexts and patterns of migration, but family and community relations tend to display a general shift in the direction of gender egalitarianism. The level of improvement women experience when they migrate, to a large extent, depends on their role in production and their social status in the home country as well as their economic role in the host country (Foner 2000). The trend toward more egalitarian patterns of shared authority can occur because immigrant women become more autonomous and assertive through their immigration and settlement experiences. Egalitarianism is also promoted by the relative increase in women's contributions to the family income. As the balance of resources and contributions changes, women can assume more active roles in key decision-making processes, leading to an increase in women's social mobility within the family (Hondagneu-Sotelo 1999a, 1999b).

Although women's employment opportunities can provide a source of independence from family constraints, the alternative is only likely to be attractive when the immigrant group has low expectations of family-based mobility. When group support for family-based mobility is greater, as is the case of the Cuban immigrants, then women may prefer to stay at home. Children being educated in American schools are often taught that the path to social mobility is through educational achievement, not family cohesion. Therefore, these children who go to school with other ethnic students whose native-born parents are economically unsuccessful may serve as ethnic role models and could potentially pass on their anti-school feelings because of poor prospects for social mobility. Thus, the process of socialization and the psychological effects of race and ethnicity in America, consistently dependent on immigration, can significantly affect group or individual social mobility. *See also*: **Assimilation; Ethnicity; Gender; Skilled migrants; Women.**

References

Allen, W.R., and A.Y. Chung. 2000. "Your Blues Ain't Like My Blues": Race, Ethnicity, and Social Inequality in America. *Contemporary Sociology* 29(6):796–805.

Berreman, G.D. 1999. Race, Caste, and Other Invidious Distinctions in Social Stratification. In *Majority and Minority: The Dynamics of Race and Ethnicity in American Life*. N.R. Yetman, ed. Pp. 39–56. Needham Heights, MA: Allyn and Bacon.

Borjas, G.J. 2004. Economic Assimilation: Trouble Ahead. In *Reinventing the Melting Pot*. T. Jacoby, ed. Pp. 199–210. New York: Basic Books.

Foner, N. 2000. Immigrant Women and Work in New York City, Then and Now. In *Mass Migration to the United States: Classical and Contemporary Periods*. P.G. Min, ed. Pp. 231–249. Walnut Creek, CA: AltaMira Press.

Frey, W.H. 1996. Immigration, Domestic Migration, and Demographic Balkanization in America: New Evidence for the 1990's. *Population and Development Review* 22(4):741–763.

Greenwood, Michael, and Marta Tienda. 1997. U.S. Impacts of Mexican Immigration. In *Binational Study: U.S.-Mexico Migration*. Washington, DC: U.S. Commission on Immigration Reform.

Hondagneu-Sotelo, P. 1999a. Gendered Immigration. In *Majority and Minority: The Dynamics of Race and Ethnicity in American Life*. N.R. Yetman, ed. Pp. 485–497. Needham Heights, MA: Allyn and Bacon.

———. 1999b. Introduction: Gender and Contemporary U.S. Immigration. *The American Behavioral Scientist* 42(4):565–576.

Logan, J.R., W. Zhang, and R.D. Alba. 2002. Immigrant Enclaves and Ethnic Communities in New York and Los Angeles. *American Sociological Review* 67(2):299–322.

Mac Thomais St.-Hilaire, A. 2001. Segmented Assimilation. In *Encyclopedia of American Immigration*. J. Ciment, ed. Pp. 460–467. Armonk, NY: M.E. Sharpe.

Nagel, J. 1999. Constructing Ethnicity: Creating and Recreating Ethnic Identity and Culture. In *Majority and Minority: The Dynamics of Race and Ethnicity in American Life*. N.R. Yetman, ed. Pp. 57–71. Needham Heights, MA: Allyn and Bacon.

Portes, A., and R.G. Rumbaut. 1996. *Immigrant America: A Portrait*. Berkeley: University of California Press.

———. 2001. *Legacies: The Story of the Immigrant Second Generation*. Berkeley: University of California Press.

Portes, A., and A. Stepick. 1985. Unwelcome Immigrants: The Labor Market Experiences of 1980 (Mariel) Cuban and Haitian Refugees in South Florida. *American Sociological Review* 50(4):493–514.

Raijman, R., and M. Tienda. 1999. Immigrants' Socioeconomic Progress Post-1965: Forging Mobility or Survival? In *The Handbook of International Migration: The American Experience*. C. Hirschman, P. Kasinitz, and J. De Wind, eds. Pp. 239–256. New York: Russell Sage Foundation.

Roberts, B.R. 1995. Socially Expected Durations and the Economic Adjustment of Immigrants. In *The Economic Sociology of Immigration*. A. Portes, ed. Pp. 42–86. New York: Russell Sage Foundation.

Ueda, R. 1994. *Postwar Immigrant America: A Social History*. Boston: Bedford Books of St. Martin's Press.

———. 1998. The Changing Face of Post-1965 Immigration. In *The Immigration Reader: America in a Multidisciplinary Perspective*. D. Jacobson, ed. Pp. 72–91. Malden, MA: Blackwell.

Van Hook, J., and K.S. Balistreri. 2002. Diversity and Change in the Institutional Context of Immigrant Adaptation: California Schools 1985–2000. *Demography* 39(4):639–654.

Yetman, N.R. 1999. *Majority and Minority: The Dynamics of Race and Ethnicity in American Life*. Needham Heights, MA: Allyn and Bacon.

Zhou, M. 2000. The Changing Face of America: Immigration, Race/Ethnicity, and Social Mobility. In *Mass Migration to the United States: Classical and Contemporary Periods*. P.G. Min, ed. Pp. 65–98. Walnut Creek, CA: AltaMira Press.

LARRY J. ESTRADA AND ANGELA KRATTIGER

SOCIAL NETWORKS. Social networks—the informal ties constituted by family, friends, neighbors, co-workers, and coreligionists, to name a few—are central in the process of migration. These ties allow migrants to draw upon obligations implicit in these relationships to initiate their migration, to undertake the journey, and to settle in the host society (Boyd 1989). The presence of friends and family is evident from the moment a person plans to migrate. It is well known that potential migrants often base their decision to move to a particular destination on whether they have friends or relatives there who can assist them upon arrival. Often these initial contacts place a job within the migrant's reach, sometimes even before the actual move is realized (Massey and Espinosa 1997). Through these ties migrants obtain information about how to undertake the journey, job opportunities in the place of destination, housing, and everyday aspects of life, which facilitate settlement. Thus, these ties are catalysts for migration and important vehicles for settlement.

The very nature of family reunification in U.S. immigration law is predicated on the notion that migrants have extensive informal networks. Immigrants can petition for close family members to immigrate because it is assumed that family members already settled and with permanent immigration statuses will assist their newcomer relatives in their settlement. Thus, thousands of migrants from all over the world immigrate to the United States every year as relatives of U.S. citizens or of permanent residents. In some cases migrants have relatives who can petition for them, but the waiting periods to obtain family reunification visas for some countries are extremely long (for instance, if a Mexican petitions a sibling it may take up to 16 years for that person to obtain a visa; for a Filipino the waiting period is approximately 20 years). In these cases, migrants end up entering the country without inspection or overstay their visas, thus becoming undocumented immigrants.

When individuals travel without a visa, family and friends often mobilize resources to make the journey possible. Importantly, informal networks are vital in cases of family reunification and labor migration, but also when migration occurs from politically conflictive regions, or refugee migrations. For instance, the migration of thousands of Guatemalans and Salvadorans who fled political turmoil in their countries was made possible by their families and friends, as the U.S. government would not accept them as refugees because of its support to the Guatemalan and Salvadoran governments. In fact, an important reason why so many of these Central Americans ended up settling in the United States and not in adjacent countries (for instance, other Central American countries) is that many migrants already had friends and family in the United States (Menjívar 2000). Friends and family often lend the migrants money to initiate the journey (or sometimes pay for the trip themselves, particularly when it is a close family member who is traveling), and in case they run into difficulty during the long journeys by land, informal ties continue to assist them financially until they arrive safely. There are many cases that exemplify this point from other migrant-sending countries, such as from Southeast Asia, the Caribbean, and Africa. In all these cases, the centrality of friends and family in determining the migrants' decision to migrate, their eventual destination, and the resources available to them there is evident.

A move to a foreign land often entails a heavy toll on the migrants—psychological, financial, and social—but the presence of family and friends at the place of destination can lower such costs. Newcomers tend to rely on people familiar to them for a range of material and emotional needs. For those migrants with few resources, a friend or a relative can allow them to share a room in an apartment or to share a meal, or can lend them small sums of money for the migrants' initial few days. For migrants who join relatives who have more material and financial resources, these contacts can facilitate the newcomer's settlement by making available similar paths to economic integration. For instance, Korean migrants often rely on rotating credit associations made up of friends and family, as well as on their know-how to set up successful businesses (since friends and relatives already know the inner workings of this economic niche). Similarly, Vietnamese migrants have been known to lend money to one another or pool resources to be able to open up a restaurant or a store (Kibria 1993). For all immigrants, friends, family, co-workers, neighbors, and others provide vital information, including information about how to enroll in English language classes or professional training, or where to obtain a driver's license or a social security card.

Indeed, the concentration of certain migrant groups in a few industries or commercial enterprises reveals the centrality of their social networks as facilitating the migrants' entry in those occupations (Massey et al. 1987). This has been particularly the case when migrants have faced exploitation and discrimination upon arrival. In these cases, people familiar to the migrants (or with whom they live in close proximity) have been pivotal in shaping the migrants' economic integration. There are some contemporary examples that come to mind—for instance, the case of Asian Indians in the motel and hotel industry in different U.S. cities, of Ethiopian and Somali taxi drivers in Washington, D.C., of Latinos (mainly Guatemalans) in the roofing industry in Phoenix, Arizona, and of Latina (mainly Central Americans and Mexicans) in housekeeping and baby-sitting jobs in Southern California, to name a few. However, there are many other examples from other historical periods, such as Italians in construction jobs, Jews working as tailors, Irish women working as domestics, and Chinese in laundromats.

The migrants' networks are not only limited to providing financial or material assistance, as they are also an important source of social, emotional, and moral comfort for the newcomers. In many cases, migrants live and work among their compatriots, for those settings provide familiarity with customs and language, as well as opportunities. Often newcomers initially live with family or friends, and then move to an apartment or a house nearby, sometimes because the housing market does not permit them to move any further, or because they opt for staying in a familiar environment close to friends and family. Thus, the high residential concentration of many migrant groups is another piece of evidence of the central place of social networks in the migrants' settlement. Even in cases where migrants do not live in the same neighborhoods with compatriots, such as in the case of Asian Indians or Filipinos—two of the most geographically dispersed migrant groups—they remain connected with family and friends in other ways, such as through hometown or professional associations and, importantly, through religious organizations. Indeed, the church has been a central place for migrants to connect with one another and to obtain varied forms of assistance. Today, as in the past, we see many "immigrant churches"—sometimes created by the immigrants themselves, in other cases expanded by the presence of migrants—in the major receiving U.S. cities.

Friends and family are also important sources of emotional or moral solace, as they often provide a crucial word of advice or consolation to a newcomer in need. Often migrants create "hometown" associations, through which they send assistance to their communities of origin and remain emotionally linked to their natal lands. Thus, migrants' networks are not only crucial catalysts for migration and vital for settlement, but also critical links to the migrants' homelands.

The Underside of Immigrant Networks

Although migrants often obtain substantial help from their relatives to undertake the journey, this vital channel of support sometimes weakens during settlement. This tends to happen when the newcomer arrives to join friends or relatives who are already overwhelmed by their own financial and legal difficulties. When the newcomers arrive to join relatives who live in extreme poverty and have uncertain legal statuses and their communities are resource poor, their networks sometimes weaken (Menjívar 2000). It is often assumed that informal networks among poor migrants (or the poor in general) can guard them against the difficulties of their conditions. However, when the receiving and the arriving migrants face the same confluence of adverse factors in their resettlement, they often do not have enough resources even for themselves, much less to share with others, even if this goes against the migrants' cultural dictates. In these circumstances, the migrants may not be able to restructure the solid ties that made the newcomers' migration possible in the first place. Too many demands on already overburdened friends and family put too much pressure and the networks may weaken. The result tends to be a weakening, not a permanent break, in these informal ties.

Gender and Immigrant Networks

Just as networks can be affected by the financial ability and material conditions of migrants, they can also be influenced by gender. In fact, the very nature of women's and men's networks is different. For instance, among Lao refugees it was observed that men tended to create networks in a patron-client fashion, whereas women accomplished everyday tasks without focusing on power or competition but rather on cooperation (Muir 1988). Some studies have found that women tend to form stronger networks than men; other research indicates that women's networks are not necessarily stronger, that they are simply different because men and women have access to different resources on the basis of their sex (Menjívar 1999). Also, it has been observed that men and women derive unequal benefits from their networks. Women may obtain a smaller share of the benefits—or fewer economic advantages—from networks than do their male counterparts and end up with not-so-desirable resources, and thus it is more difficult for them to help others (Hagan 1998). Other times it appears as if women derive considerable benefits from their own networks. Interestingly, research indicates that women often mobilize their informal networks to obtain assistance for others in their family, particularly their children, as indicated in a study of Puerto Ricans in Chicago (Pérez 2004). Different societal and cultural expectations of men and women often contribute to differences in social networks, as women are often called on to assist in the household or family-oriented issues more frequently than men are (Menjívar 2002). Such differences in network dynamics may account for divergences in the social, economic, and legal incorporation of immigrant women and men.

Although the networks of men and women may differ because they are organized differently, and often for dissimilar purposes, the fact remains that social networks are crucial in the lives of both immigrant men and women, though these are not consistently havens of support. These social relations do not work independently of the context in which they are created, and thus the conditions immigrants face and the opportunity structure available to them shape in vital ways the form, continuity, and composition of migrant social networks. *See also*: **Families; Family reunification; Gender; Migration processes.**

References

Boyd, Monica. 1989. Family and Personal Networks in International Migration: Recent Developments and New Agendas. *International Migration Review* 23:638–670.

Hagan, Jacqueline Maria. 1998. Social Networks, Gender, and Immigrant Incorporation: Resources and Constraints. *American Sociological Review* 63:55–67.

Hondagneu-Sotelo, Pierrette. 1994. *Gendered Transitions: Mexican Experiences of Immigration*. Berkeley: University of California Press.

Kibria, Nazli. 1993. *Family Tightrope: The Changing Lives of Vietnamese Americans*. Princeton, NJ: Princeton University Press.

Krissman, Fred. 2005. Sin Coyote Ni Patrón: Why the "Migrant Network" Fails to Explain International Migration. *International Migration Review* 39:4–44.

Massey, Douglas S., Rafael Alarcón, Jorge Durand, and Humberto González. 1987. *Return to Aztlan: The Social Process of International Migration from Western Mexico*. Berkeley: University of California Press.

Massey, Douglas, and Kristin Espinosa. 1997. What's Driving the Mexico-U.S. Migration? *American Journal of Sociology* 102(4):939–999.

Menjívar, Cecilia. 1999. The Intersection of Work and Gender: Central American Immigrant Women and Employment in California. *American Behavioral Scientist* 42:601–627.

———. 2000. *Fragmented Ties: Salvadoran Immigrant Networks in America*. Berkeley: University of California Press.

———. 2002. The Ties that Heal: Guatemalan Immigrant Women's Networks and Medical Treatment. *International Migration Review* 36:437–466.

Muir, Karen L.S. 1988. *The Strongest Part of the Family: A Study of Lao Refugee Women in Columbus, Ohio*. New York: AMS Press.

Pérez, Gina E. 2004. *The Near Northwest Side Story: Migration, Displacement, and Puerto Rican Families*. Berkeley: University of California Press.

CECILIA MENJÍVAR

STEREOTYPES. America has been idealized as a nation of immigrants, where freedom, democracy, and unlimited economic opportunities are readily available to all newcomers, regardless of one's country of origin, racial and ethnic background, or religious affiliation. For years, this powerful, romanticized imagery has served to attract millions of people from all corners of the globe. Today, the foreign-born comprise roughly 11.1 percent (31.1 million) of the U.S. population (Singer 2004). Like their predecessors, recent immigrants continue to make innumerable contributions to society. Despite this fact, however, many continue to struggle for recognition and acceptance. As their numbers continue to grow, they increasingly face varying forms of prejudice and discrimination (e.g., stereotypes, ethnophaulisms, and anti-immigration policies). The current wave of anti-immigration sentiment, like earlier waves, is primarily rooted in economic uncertainty and uneasiness about shifting demographics.

This entry specifically focuses on the nature and content of stereotypes and myths that have been leveled against immigrant groups, both past and present. The discussion is couched in the notion that stereotypes and myths are defensive reactions by the dominant group when they believe that members of the subordinate group threaten their group interests. Stereotypes and myths routinely serve as justification for more severe forms of prejudice and discrimination. Take, for instance, the Chinese Exclusion Act of 1882. Immigrant Chinese workers, once heralded as hard-working laborers, were maligned by dominant group members as heathen, dirty, "mice-eaters," and cunning when the economic situation took a turn for the worse (beginning in California). The increasing wave of negative stereotypes in conjunction with the poor economic climate and racial hatred led to the passing of the Chinese Exclusion Act that precluded Chinese immigration. As is frequently the case, economic competition breeds prejudice and discrimination, a pattern that has repeated itself throughout history.

One of the earliest characterizations of stereotypes was provided by Walter Lippmann in 1922, who described stereotypes as being "pictures in people's heads" that are not acquired through personal experience, but rather second-hand. Unlike rational generalizations, stereotypes exaggerate and inaccurately represent social reality by attributing certain characteristics or traits (mostly negative) to an entire group of people without recognizing individual differences within the group. For instance, during the first great wave of immigration (1820s to the 1890s), Irish newcomers were characterized as "apelike," emotionally unstable, and morally primitive. Italian immigrants were similarly viewed as degenerate, superstitious, and criminally oriented. Although stereotypes such as these misrepresent sociocultural truth, they are socially approved descriptions held by one group about another (Parillo 2002).

At the same time, stereotypes are routinely incorporated into myths, which are popular beliefs or traditions (fiction or half-truth) that explain a natural phenomenon or delineate the customs or ideals of a society. Myths are social products that typically form part of a dominant ideology. Similar to stereotypes, they try to show what people are really like (although usually from the dominant group's point of view). For example, in the 1960s, the dominant group via the press began popularizing the notion that Asian immigrants were successful in achieving the American dream because they possessed certain positive characteristics. Asians were viewed (and still are) as frugal, industrious, and possessing a strong achievement orientation. However, the "model minority" myth, which is empirically inaccurate and racially stereotypic, serves to mask the diversity that exists among Asian immigrants. For instance, in regard to social disadvantage, in

1998, approximately 18 percent of Asians under the age of 18 (many of whom are immigrants) lived below the poverty line (U.S. Bureau of the Census 1999).

Once stereotypes and myths become ingrained in the dominant culture, they become extremely difficult to eradicate. Although they may wax and wane over time, they may never disappear entirely. Stereotypes and myths tend to be passed down from one generation to the next (they are collectively shared), thus ensuring their existence over time. Their pervasiveness and longevity can be attributed to the different psychological needs, at both the individual and group level, that stereotyping and myth construction seemingly fulfill (Kposowa and Tsunokai 2002; Parrillo 2002).

For instance, at the individual level, stereotypes are frequently employed as mental shortcuts that facilitate information processing and response generation. They are often triggered automatically, below the level of consciousness, and applied in judgmental tasks when processing the social environment becomes too complicated and time consuming. Thus, in an effort to make the world more manageable, some individuals make judgments about groups of people and then consciously or unconsciously generalize their oversimplified ideas or beliefs (which also become myths) to all persons who fit within that particular group or category (Ryan et al. 1996). For example, it may be less taxing for some individuals to view diverse Asian ethnic groups (e.g., Vietnamese, Filipinos, Asian Indians, and Taiwanese) as simply being a single homogenous group, who possess indistinguishable physical features, common traditions and customs, and a unifying language (a common stereotypical view that "all Asians look and act alike").

At the group level, stereotyping and myth construction may often serve as a way for groups to establish a sense of their social position or identity relative to one another (Quillian 1995). Viewed under the lenses of group-threat theory, stereotypes and myths become more negative and persistent when the size of an out-group (e.g., an immigrant group) increases to a point where the dominant group believes their proprietary claim to certain areas of advantage or privilege are being threatened. This perceived collective threat routinely translates into prejudice and discrimination against the subordinate or out-group. For example, studies show that Americans who feel that immigrants threaten domestic jobs have a greater likelihood of expressing a hostile "immigrant orientation" (Hoskin 1991; Fetzer 2000). More often than not, stereotypes and myths provide false justification for reactive policies or actions that seek to curb or eliminate the perceived threat.

It is important to note that the content or intensity of stereotypes and myths may change occasionally, and sometimes radically, depending on the social, economic, and political conditions or circumstances in effect at a given time. Take for instance the current situation of Arab and other Muslim immigrants who must carefully navigate their existence in a post–September 11, 2001, atmosphere. The events that occurred on September 11 changed America's sociopolitical landscape. Hate crimes and anti-Arab sentiment increased to record levels. A recent telephone interview found that a significant percent of Americans stated that they would keep their eye on Arabs in public places (Levin et al. 2003). Many of these same respondents supported questioning Arabs as long as necessary in airports. The Federal Bureau of Investigation reported that anti-Islamic incidents, previously the least recorded type of religious-based hate crime, became the second-highest reported type of religious-based incident after September 11 (Kaufman 2002).

The events of September 11 have intensified pre-existing stereotypes and myths surrounding Arab and other Muslim groups. Prior to September 11, Arabs and Muslims were consistently portrayed by the media, especially in American films (e.g., *Network*, *True Lies*, and *The Siege*), as villains or terrorists. Not surprisingly, public opinion polls conducted prior to September 11 found that more than half of the respondents felt that Arabs were cruel and treacherous (Shade 1981). These negative mental images in conjunction with the perceived threat of terrorism have led to widespread prejudice and discrimination against Arab immigrants (from "suspicious looks" to racial profiling by the criminal justice system).

As we enter the twenty-first century, the wave of unprecedented immigration in the United States has once again raised the question, "Is immigration an asset for America?" As in days past, this topic remains extremely volatile. Predictions by demographers that the United States will continue to grow even more diverse in population have some people concerned. For many of these individuals, immigrants pose a threat to their economic well-being and collective American identity (with the assumption being that there is in fact a common American identity). These unfounded fears have manifested themselves in various myths that serve to distort public debate and policies concerning immigration. As outlined by Cole (1994), current myths include: (1) America is being overrun by immigrants; (2) immigrants take jobs from U.S. citizens; (3) immigrants are a drain on society's resources; (4) aliens refuse to assimilate, and are depriving us of our cultural and political unity; and (5) immigrants have a higher propensity to commit crime than the native-born.

These current myths reflect attitudes and beliefs that are shrouded in fear and intolerance. When one takes the time to examine existing empirical evidence, it becomes clear that the major myths concerning immigration are unsubstantiated. For instance, the vast majority of newcomers who immigrate to the United States have entered legally under the strict standards imposed by the Immigration and Nationality Act (ACLU 1997). At the same time, studies continue to show that immigrants promote economic growth. For example, a 1994 American Civil Liberties Union Immigrants' Rights Project report demonstrated that immigrants actually generate more job positions than they fill (Cole 1994). Moreover, four recent Federal Reserve studies warned that restricting immigration could stifle business expansion plans and hurt the profitability of American businesses (Catillaz 2000). In regard to social services, this research has shown also that immigrants pay considerably more in taxes each year than they receive in social services, such as welfare benefits.

Once embedded in the dominant discourse or culture, stereotypes and myths are very difficult to eliminate. Although some may remain dormant for a period of time, when conditions are right, they reemerge (oftentimes via the media). When used, stereotypes and myths deny immigrants the right to be judged and treated as individuals. They mask the diversity that exists within each group. Moreover, as history has shown, these oversimplified generalizations are frequently used as a justification for discriminatory behavior. By reducing prejudice and discrimination (an extremely difficult task), however, it is possible that stereotypes and myths will someday no longer be a part of the immigration experience. *See also*: **Ethnicity**; **Racism**.

References

American Civil Liberties Union (ACLU). 1997. *The Rights of Immigrants*. New York: ACLU.

Catillaz, Margaret. 2000. *Immigrants Help Our Economic Boom*. AILA InfoNet, Doc. No. 38me0090.

Cole, David. 1994. The New Know-Nothingism: Five Myths about Immigration. In *Taking Sides*, 5th ed. Raymond D'Angelo and Herbert Douglas, eds. Pp. 34–37. Dubuque, IA: McGraw-Hill/Duskin.

Fetzer, Joel. 2000. *Public Attitudes toward Immigration in the United States, France, and Germany*. Cambridge: Cambridge University Press.

Hoskin, Marilyn. 1991. *New Immigrants and Democratic Society*. New York: Praeger.

Kaufman, Stephen. 2002. *U.S. Government Fights Hate Crimes in September 11 Aftermath*. Washington, DC: U.S. Department of State, Bureau of International Information Programs.

Kposowa, Augustine, and Glenn Tsunokai. 2002. Searching for Relief: Racial Differences in Treatment of Patients with Back Pain. *Race and Society* 5:193–223.

Levin, Jack, Gordana Rabrenovic, Janese Free, Colleen Keaney, and Jason Mazaik. 2003. *Flag-Waving as a Form of Self-Presentation in the Aftermath of September 11*. Boston: The Brudnick Center on Violence and Conflict, Northeastern University.

Parrillo, Vincent. 2002. *Understanding Race and Ethnic Relations*. Boston: Allyn and Bacon.

Quillian, Lincoln. 1995. Prejudice as a Response to Perceived Group Threat: Population Composition and Anti-Immigrant and Racial Prejudice in Europe. *American Sociological Review* 60:586–611.

Ryan, C., C. Judd, and B. Park. 1996. Effects of Racial Stereotypes on Judgments of Individuals: The Moderating Role of Perceived Group Variability. *Journal of Experimental Social Psychology* 32:71–103.

Shade, Shelly. 1981. The Image of the Arab in America: Analysis of a Poll on American Attitudes. *Middle East Journal* 35:143–162.

Singer, Audrey. 2004. *The Rise of New Immigrant Gateways*. Washington, DC: The Brookings Institute.

U.S. Bureau of the Census. 1999. *The Asian and Pacific Islander Population in the United States*. Washington, DC: U.S. Government Printing Office.

GLENN T. TSUNOKAI

SWEATSHOPS. Sweatshops are "workplaces where employees are paid low wages, with few benefits and little employment security, under poor occupational conditions of light, health and safety" (Lin 1998). The re-emergence of sweatshops is connected to the economic restructuring of urban employment. Deindustrialization, or the relocation of traditional manufacturing to less developed countries with cheaper labor, has resulted in a reorganization of manufacturing, including the proliferation of sweatshops and industrial homework (Sassen 1988). American "global cities," major financial centers involved in control and management of the world economy, increasingly host downgraded manufacturing sectors which do not meet the labor law standards (Sassen 1991). New York and Los Angeles are among primary locations of low-wage immigrant labor (Bonacich and Appelbaum 2000). Post-1965 unauthorized immigration to the United States is said to have made "the new immigrant sweatshop ... [a] major central city employment growth sector" (Smith 1988). It should be understood, however, that a return to sweatshop or low-wage labor has occurred in global cities across the First World, from London to Tokyo (Sassen 1991).

International competition has produced economic restructuring of labor-intensive manufacturing, such as apparel, footwear, toys, and electronics, and has resulted in the increased utilization of low-wage women workers (Lin 1998). Brand-name manufacturers have taken advantage of the capital mobility facilitated by free trade to pit impoverished workers in developing countries against American subcontracting firms employing immigrant women as their primary labor supply (Enloe 1993). Globalization of economic competition and market changes create job instability in sweatshop industries like apparel (Zhou 1992). In a global economy, both worker and subcontractor profits are minimal while brand-name product owners make record profits.

The garment industry is typical of U.S. sweatshop manufacturing. Garment sweatshops have developed in immigrant enclaves such as New York City (Kwong 1997) and in the Greater Los Angeles immigrant economy (Bonacich and Appelbaum 2000). Three trends led to the downgrading of apparel jobs in New York City: (1) competition due to incorporation of jobs by newly automated factories in the Sun Belt and labor-intensive manufacturing overseas; (2) loss of medium-sized, often unionized operations; and (3) re-growth of sweatshops and industrial home work (Sassen 1988). Later, the Sun Belt itself suffered job loss in the clothing sector to developing countries. Competition occurs in a world market with wages as low as 50 cents per hour. The United States has retained that portion of apparel manufacturing that is "transient, unstandardized and susceptible to the quick-changing vagaries of fashion" (Zhou 1992). Garment shops with mechanized production were most likely to relocate, while less mechanized and smaller shops remained in the United States. Many of the remaining shops are owned by immigrant entrepreneurs who employ immigrant women at low wages (Sassen 1988).

Sweatshops violate American labor laws and regulations, but a major enforcement problem is that they can shift location to evade investigation. Production is easy to relocate because (1) only a small investment is required; (2) workers do not need to be highly skilled; and (3) activities requiring high skill can be separated from the basic production process. Today, brand-name manufacturers use subcontractors who allocate section work which allows for replacing a skilled worker who would make an entire garment with several semi- or unskilled workers who mass produce one piece (Sassen 1988). New York City and Los Angeles continue to host small subcontractor apparel firms because of an abundant low-wage immigrant labor supply.

At the beginning of the twenty-first century, the U.S. Department of Labor estimated that over one-half of American garment factories violate minimum wage and overtime pay laws (White 2000). In the late 1990s, the U.S. Department of Labor found that over 60 percent of garment firms in New York City and Los Angeles were in violation of wage and labor laws (Houghteling 1999). Extensive publicity occurred in the El Monte, California, sweatshop case, where 72 undocumented Thai immigrants worked without pay for long hours and in substandard working conditions (Su 1997; Schoenberger 2000). Involuntary servitude, or enslavement, had returned to the United States.

This retrograde garment production is largely dependent on the labor of immigrant women, often Chinese. Jan Lin (1998) points out that managers explain that they hire women because of their "nimble fingers," patience, and attention to detail. The reality, however, is that as secondary earners in patriarchal households, many women will accept lower wages and are willing to accept less stable work because their wages are viewed as supplemental (Zhou 1992). Gender discrimination, lack of support for equal educational opportunity in Chinese culture, and their dependent status as wives of immigrants leave them little choice but to work in apparel.

Since the early twentieth century, wages and working conditions within the traditional manufacturing sector have varied by the degree to which workers are unionized and labor laws are enforced (Howard 1997). Yet even where unions survive, their bargaining tactics have been undermined. In New York City, a majority of the over 20,000 Chinese garment workers are members of UNITE, formerly the International Ladies Garment Worker Union (ILGWU) (Waldinger 1996). Unfortunately, UNITE's Chinese garment workers are organized from the top down, and the rank-and-file workers still lack effective representation in pursuing labor violations (Kwong 1997). Despite such obstacles, UNITE members have organized militant demonstrations to protest the use of non-union contractors in the New York apparel trade.

New York revitalized prosecution for labor law violations in an effort to prevent sweatshop conditions as the state approached the twenty-first century. Yet the New York State Apparel Industry Task Force fields only five inspectors. Nationally, the U.S. Department of Labor is charged with enforcement of labor laws and pledged to work with the Immigration and Naturalization Service (INS), now the U.S. Citizenship and Immigration Service (USCIS), in locating undocumented immigrants working in violation of labor laws. There remain problems with labor law enforcement in the current legal structure, however. First, the INS typically deports workers instead of detaining them to give evidence against employers in court. Second, negative media publicity about undocumented immigrants frightens them into keeping quiet about violations for fear of deportation. Third, there is no motive for undocumented immigrants to testify since, because of the employer sanctions provision of the Immigration and Reform Act of 1986, they must be deported, not reinstated. Finally, a major undersupply of federal labor inspectors ensures that many violations remain undetected. Currently, fear of INS deportation is a major factor in keeping unauthorized immigrant workers quiet about labor violations. If a violation is reported, the New York judiciary typically sends guilty employers to educational seminars on labor rights rather than imposing monetary fines (Kwong 1997).

The Thai and Filipino immigrants found held in involuntary servitude were working to pay off large human smuggling debts and, theoretically, to send remittances to their families. Wages were withheld while they labored for extremely lengthy work days in unhygienic compounds encircled with barbed wire. Withholding wages is a standard strategy for controlling workers and "sweating" further profit, but it is difficult to prosecute this violation.

The U.S. problem of labor law violations has also been exported in a novel ramification of globalization. Overseas sweatshop conditions have received extensive publicity. Media coverage and union publicity prompt Americans to search for U.S.-made garments, but that is still not always a guarantee of human rights for workers. Throughout the 1990s, apparel has been subcontracted to subcontractors on Saipan, an island in the U.S. territory of the Marianas in the South Pacific (Schoenberger 2000). Technically, this clothing can still be labeled "Made in the USA."

During the Clinton administration, the Fair Labor Association (FLA) was organized on the basis of the White House Apparel Industry Partnership to monitor wages and working conditions of subcontractors in the United States and abroad in the $70 billion American apparel industry (Schoenberger 2000). Sneaker and apparel makers such as Nike, Reebok, and L.L. Bean have joined with human rights and college student organizations in this effort. Goals include abolishing involuntary servitude and child labor, providing the right of free association for labor organizing, an end to physical abuse at work, and a maximum 60-hour work week. In New York City's Chinatown, however, Chinese garment workers, who belong to UNITE, continue to work 60-hour weeks with no overtime pay (Kwong 1997).

Anti-corporate protests challenging American and global income gaps have also generated a campus movement. Groups like the Worker's Rights Consortium and United Students Against Sweatshops have protested the making of college logo clothing, a $2 billion industry, under conditions that violate human rights or labor laws (Houghteling 1999; Cray 2000). Drawing on concepts like joint moral and legal accountability of corporations and subcontractors regarding compensation and working conditions that come into play, the ability to monitor assembly plants, referred to as "transparency," is integral to the effort to attain moral and legal accountability to end worker abuse (Schoenberger 2000). Because shareholders, multinational employees, and consumers are increasingly concerned about growing workplace abuses, pressure can be placed on corporations to end violation of labor laws by subcontractors in an effort to protect brand names. Action can also come at the state level, as has occurred in California since 2000, with bills strengthening the monitoring and legal enforcement of American labor laws. The California Sweatshop Reform Bill, for example, requires that manufacturers, subcontractors, and retailers share legal responsibility in guaranteeing that workers are compensated at minimum wage or higher and given overtime pay (Foo and Su 2000).

The use of overseas labor in such industries as apparel has depressed wages and working conditions in remaining American garment industries, a situation exploited by contractors utilizing immigrant labor. Since U.S.-based multinational corporations are involved in producing for American consumers, attempts at establishing a subsistence wage and humane working conditions have targeted inspection of overseas subcontracting firms as well as trying to enforce U.S. labor law. Consumer boycotts of brand labels known to utilize sweatshop labor is another practice to bring positive global change in working conditions both internationally and in the United States. *See also*: **Gender; Women.**

References

Bonacich, Edna, and Richard P. Appelbaum. 2000. *Behind the Label: Inequality in the Los Angeles Garment Industry*. Berkeley: University of California Press.

Cray, Charlie. 2000. Students Against Sweat. *Multinational Monitor* 21(4):4.

Enloe, Cynthia. 1993. *The Morning After: Sexual Politics at the End of the Cold War*. Berkeley: University of California Press.

Foo, Lora Jo, and Julie A. Su. 2000. Let the Sweatshops Reform Law Work: Garment Workers Have a Right to Minimum Wages and Overtime. *Los Angeles Times*, April 7, B9.

Hapke, Laura. 2004. *Sweatshop: The History of an American Idea*. New Brunswick, NJ: Rutgers University Press.

Houghteling, Charles. 1999. Sweat and Tears. *Harvard International Review* 21(4):10–12.

Howard, Alan. 1997. Labor, History and Sweatshops in the New Global Economy. In *No Sweat: Fashion, Free Trade and the Rights of Garment Workers*. Andrew Ross, ed. Pp. 151–172. London: Verso.

Kwong, Peter. 1997. *Forbidden Workers: Illegal Chinese Immigrants and American Labor*. New York: The New Press.

LaFeber, Walter. 1999. *Michael Jordan and the New Global Capitalism*. New York: W.W. Norton.

Lin, Jan. 1998. *Reconstructing Chinatown: Ethnic Enclave, Global Change*. Minneapolis: University of Minnesota Press.

Ross, Andrew, ed. 1997. *No Sweat: Fashion, Free Trade and the Rights of Garment Workers*. London: Verso.

Safa, Helen. 1981. Runaway Shops and Female Employment: The Search for Cheap Labor. *Signs* 7:418–433.

Sassen, Saskia. 1988. *The Mobility of Labor and Capital: A Study in International Investment and Labor Flow*. New York: Cambridge University Press.

———. 1991. *The Global City: New York, London, Tokyo*. Princeton, NJ: Princeton University Press.

Schoenberger, Karl. 2000. *Levi's Children: Coming to Terms with Human Rights in the Global Marketplace*. New York: Atlantic Monthly Press.

Smith, Michael Peter. 1988. *City, State, and Market: The Political Economy of Urban Society*. New York: Basil Blackwell.

Su, Julie. 1997. El Monte Thai Garment Workers: Slave Sweatshops. In *No Sweat: Fashion, Free Trade and the Rights of Garment Workers*. Andrew Ross, ed. Pp. 143–149. London: Verso.

Waldinger, Roger. 1996. From Ellis Island to LAX: Immigrant Prospects in the American City. *International Migration Review* 30(4):1078–1087.

White, Heather. 2000. Disturbing Trends in Global Production. *USA Today* 128 (2660):26–28.

Zhou, Min. 1992. *Chinatown: The Socioeconomic Potential of an Urban Enclave*. Philadelphia: Temple University Press.

JUDITH WARNER

T

TEMPORARY PROTECTED STATUS. Mass exoduses, such as those resulting from natural disasters, warfare, and major political turmoil, confound immigration policies, and U.S. responses have varied widely depending on historical period as well as place of origin and causative factors (Churgin 1996). Refugee relief acts allowed the admission of more than 200,000 people from Europe after World War II. Cubans, by virtue of geographic proximity and the vexing nature of the Cuban-U.S. relationship during the Cold War, also benefited from the extension of preferential treatment, resulting in 370,000 becoming permanent residents by 1978. The fall of Saigon raised the issue again, resulting in the entry of some 750,000 refugees from Southeast Asia by 1990. When dangerous or inhospitable conditions arise, then, and if they persist, humanitarian concerns generally come up against political ones, with rights to safety mixing with those of return (Frelick 1990).

The executive branch has responded through refugee policies as well as by creating various categories for temporary status until conditions ameliorate. One of these is Temporary Protected Status (TPS) grants a stay of removal plus work authorization to people with non-immigrant visas in the United States who are temporarily unable to return to their homeland because of ongoing armed conflict, environmental disasters, or other extraordinary and temporary conditions. By providing a temporary immigrant status that allows people to remain in the United States, TPS may be viewed as a sound and humanitarian emergency relief measure intended to assist nationals of a given country who are already in the United States at the time of designation.

TPS designation is made when the attorney general, after consultation with appropriate agencies, determines that a country or part of a country is experiencing conditions that would pose a serious hardship or threat to the personal safety of nationals if returned (INA Sec. 244 1A, B). For example, some 82,000 Hondurans and 5,000 Nicaraguans were granted TPS designation to remain and work in the United States in the wake of the devastation of Hurricane Mitch in 1998. TPS may also be granted if a foreign state is unable to handle the return, generally through the deportation of nationals of the state, and officially requests such designation (INA Sec. 244 2C). After El Salvador suffered severe earthquakes in early 2001, undocumented citizens of that country were granted TPS, a designation later extended into 2005. Before the end to the TPS designation period, the secretary of the Department of Homeland Security reviews the conditions in the designated state to determine whether the conditions that led to the TPS designation continue to be met.

The concept of TPS was debated repeatedly in Congress in the 1980s before being enacted in 1990 as part of Immigration Act 244. Prior to 1990, the only legal way people could remain in the country under such circumstances was by requesting asylum. The need for an intermediate immigration status was recognized as long ago as 1960, when the Department of Justice created the status of Extended Voluntary Departure (EVD), later called Deferred Enforced Departure (DED). In effect, this enabled the attorney general to exercise prosecutory discretion to not remove nationals from particular countries. The impetus for the TPS provision of the 1990 Immigration Act was the desire for some kind of regularized vehicle to avoid having to deport tens of thousands of illegal people from El Salvador. They had come to the United States during years of conflict for which the United States bore some responsibility through the provision of substantial military aid to successive military-dominated governments. Faced with a potential return of so many to a country already suffering high rates of unemployment and poverty, the president of El Salvador campaigned vigorously with the U.S. government to hold off with such deportations. TPS thus serves, in effect, as a temporary response to humanitarian need for which granting refugee status could be technically or politically difficult.

In 2003, responsibilities for administering the TPS program were transferred to the Bureau of Citizenship and Immigration Services (BCIS). However, the mechanism for TPS remained essentially unchanged. TPS is usually granted in 12- to 18-month increments but may be renewed at the discretion of the U.S. government, currently through the secretary of the Department of Homeland Security. Once TPS is terminated, people revert to their previous immigration status. An application for TPS does not affect an application for asylum or any other immigration benefit, and people may simultaneously apply for both asylum and TPS. TPS can be a first step in becoming a U.S. citizen (Lowell 1999). Some, in fact, criticize TPS as being a de facto amnesty or asylum program due to the long lengths of some designations and poor tracking of outcomes.

Refugee status and asylum status are granted similarly to TPS in that candidates are unable or unwilling to return to their home country because of persecution or a well-founded fear of persecution on account of race, religion, nationality, membership in a particular social group, or political opinion. However, refugee and asylum status differ in regard to where the individual is when applying for status; asylum status is obtained within the United States, while refugee status is obtained outside the United States. Asylum and refugee status differ from TPS in that they are seen as more long-term. They allow the individual to live and work in the United States and, after one year, to be able to apply for permanent residency. The goal of TPS is to temporarily provide a safe place for individuals of another nation with the aim of returning the individual to their country.

When TPS is designated for a particular country, the number of eligible people is estimated by the government. Countries currently or recently listed under TPS designation include: Burundi, Liberia, Sierra Leone, Somalia, and Sudan in Africa; El Salvador, Honduras, and Nicaragua in Latin America; and Montserrat in the Caribbean.

Like TPS, Deferred Enforced Departure (DED) is a temporary protection from removal granted to people from a designated country, in this case by the president of the United States as part of the office's constitutional powers to conduct foreign relations. First used in 1990, it appears to provide some flexibility to TPS designation. After El Salvador's TPS ended in 1992, the president still chose not to deport and reverted to Extended Voluntary Departure (EVD), though the name has since been changed to Deferred Enforced Departure (DED). Liberian nationals in the United States were granted DED from 1999 to 2002, after which they were designated under TPS status, due to ongoing armed conflict in their homeland.

Temporary Protected Status has been both praised as a humanitarian relief measure and criticized as an invitation to fraudulent non-immigration visa abuse. It was devised to be a humanitarian response as well as to ease potential deportation burdens on various government agencies. Given incomplete tracking of people with non-immigrant visas, it remains uncertain how many people remain in the United States after their TPS designation ends, how many return to their homelands, who may receive amnesty, and whether some people change their non-immigrant visa status in other ways (Lowell 1999). *See also:* **Expedited entry and removal; Refugee law and policy; Unauthorized immigration.**

References

Churgin, Michael J. 1996. Mass Exoduses: The Response of the United States. *International Migration Review* 30:310–324.
Frelick, Bill. 1990. The Right of Return. *International Journal of Refugee Law* 2:442–447.
Lowell, B. Lindsay, ed. 1999. *Foreign Temporary Workers in America: Policies That Benefit the U.S. Economy.* Westport, CT: Quorum Books.

JAMES LOUCKY

TRANSNATIONALISM. Much confusion and debate emerge in the literature over the specific meanings of transnationalism. As Kearney (1995) observes, transnationalism is limited to behavior across nation-states. Increasingly researchers focus on transnationalism as a process, a phenomenon, and an approach. Transnational migration approaches draw from world systems theory to redress concepts dealing with migration processes, migrant incorporation, and migrant identity. Various perspectives associated with transnational migration have developed over the last decade that cut across different disciplines.

Pathfinders of transnational perspectives include both anthropologists and researchers in cultural studies. In particular, scholars of cultural studies examine the cultural aspects of transnational practices (e.g., Gupta and Ferguson 1992; Appadurai 1996; Clifford 1997). Anthropologists, though, are at the forefront in studies of transnational migration. One of the first studies to address the tenets behind this approach is the well-recognized work of Glick Schiller, Basch, and Blanc-Szanton (1992). Shortly thereafter, Basch, Glick Schiller, and Szanton

Blanc (1994) published the first major study on this topic. According to transnational migration proponents (e.g., Rouse 1991; Glick Schiller et al. 1992; Basch et al. 1994; Kearney 1995), this approach looks at the bidirectional flow of people, commodities, ideas, and behavior. This approach, however, also inherently includes the notion that migrants construct hybrid identities and spaces that span the community of origin and arrival due to the dynamic nature of the outcomes and effects that this back-and-forth movement generates. As Georges (1990:233) describes for Dominican migrants: they are people with "*un pie aquí, el otro allá*." In other words, migrants maintain one foot here and the other over there. Similarly, Chaney (1979:290) observes that Dominicans are "people with feet in two societies." In short, folks tend to simultaneously hold a sense of belonging to two different places.

An important question is whether transnationalism represents a new or old phenomenon. This issue has been a subject much debated in the literature. Critics, for example, challenge the originality of transnational migration and stress that it occurred a century ago among European immigrants (e.g., the Irish, Italians, and Polish) to the New World (Goldberg 1992; Wyman 1993; Foner 1997, 2002; Mintz 1998). Transnational migration scholars (e.g., Glick Schiller et al. 1992; Portes, Guarnizo, and Landolt 1999), however, contend that it is indeed a relatively new phenomenon. Portes et al. (1999), for example, argue that what signals truly original phenomena, and thus a new line of inquiry, includes the high rate of exchanges, the new ways of transacting, and the myriad activities that entail regular cross-border travel and contacts.

Some critics also question transnationalism's concepts and new lexicon. Mintz (1998), for example, argues that transnationalism does not sufficiently account for reversible processes. For Mintz, transnational migration scholars emphasize the rapid, intensive movement of people on a global scale, but neglect to address how such flows may dwindle or even reverse when conditions alter. He points out that it is not *how* things happen, but *what* happens that becomes significant. What may be new of transnationalism are the relatively open conditions in which processes unravel and thus help shape the ways people construct their identities and conceptualize place. He adds that studies, which embrace new theories of transnationalism and globalization, are ahistorical. Goldberg (1992:201) also emphasizes "an ongoing re-reading of the past." He points out the failure of transnational migration approaches to account for past studies and calls attention to Bourne's (1916) earlier observation on the transnational character of earlier immigration waves. Goldberg (1992) goes on to argue that in contrast to past migrants—who were considered "children of capitalism"—those of today epitomize offshoots of the broader structural forces of American globalism and hegemony of European colonial powers. More recently, and according to Foner (2002), to understand what is truly novel about the new immigration, comparisons between past and present immigration trends are important. A historical comparison reveals whether models and social constructs currently used, such as transnationalism, are unique to the present or whether they also pertain to the past.

What do historians say about living in both worlds, transnationally? Cinel (1991) and Wyman (1993), for instance, show that during the nineteenth and early twentieth centuries, the waves of migration between the Old World and

New World represented a way of life—as it is for many folks today who move from developing to developed countries. Migrants who came to America in previous times left their home countries with their heads dancing with stories of extraordinary wages earned abroad (Wyman 1993). Present-day migrants to the United States, particularly those from Latin America and Asia, are also lured by better wages and economic prospects than those available in their native land. Moreover, those who embarked on the westward journey from the Old World to the New World continued to participate in the social, economic, and political activities of their homeland while still living abroad—akin to many current migrants. Similar to migrants today, those of the past sent their earnings (i.e., remittances) back home—thus making economic remittances a vital source of revenues for sending countries and deeply impacting the dynamics of social and economic life in the homeland.

While similarities arise between earlier and present transnational processes and practices, key distinctions also emerge. Great differences exist with regard to communications and modes of transportation. Current rapid and innovating modes of transportation allow many individuals (particularly those with legal documentation) to move back and forth with ease between their places of origin and destination. Additionally, the loyalties and orientations that individuals maintain toward their homeland, as well as the transnational bonds sustained, become easier to foster and to be kept alive due to the sophisticated technology and electronic communications available today. The role that hometown associations, informal organizations, and migrant leadership play in transnational connections between those who stay and those who go is crucial to consider too (Popkin 1995; Chinchilla and Hamilton 1999; Moran-Taylor 2004). Hometown associations, for instance, which often take shape as sport-based organizations or church-based organizations, typically are created by a migrant group from the same community in the homeland in their destination localities and by individuals with a shared identity. Importantly, a goal among such hometown associations is to search for meaningful ways to help their people and their places of origin.

Another disparity that sets apart past and present immigration trends involves the sociocultural, political, and economic conditions in the homeland that migrants leave behind. Previously, migrants departed from places in the midst of their nation-building processes. Thus, many of these folks maintained little or no sense of a modern national identity (Foner 1997). Now we see a different picture. Contemporary migrants typically move from places well developed as modern nation-states—albeit some from places imbued with economic chaos and political violence.

A large body of interdisciplinary work now analyzes the divergent kinds of transnational practices, relations, outcomes, and effects evident among different migrant communities. Much work explores the ways in which migrants and non-migrants participate in the social, cultural, religious, and political affairs of their communities. Recently, in a special issue on transnational migration that the journal *International Migration Review* published in 2003, scholars came together to assess U.S. and European research in this field to date. As the editors Levitt, DeWind, and Vertovec (*International Migration Review* 2003) observe, still more empirical, conceptual, and methodological research needs to be done.

Pessar and Mahler (2003), for example, call for bringing gender in. The state and the social imaginary, they argue, are relevant in gendering transnational processes and experiences. *See also*: **Documentation; Migration processes; Social networks.**

References

Appadurai, Arjun. 1996. *Modernity at Large: Cultural Dimensions of Globalization*. Minneapolis: University of Minnesota Press.

Basch, Linda, Nina Glick Schiller, and Cristina Szanton Blanc. 1994. *Nations Unbound: Transnational Projects, Postcolonial Predicaments, and Deterritorialized Nation-States*. Amsterdam: Gordon and Breach.

Bourne, Randolph. 1916. Trans-national America. *Atlantic Monthly* 118:778–786.

Chaney, Elsa. 1979. The World Economy and Contemporary Migration. *International Migration Review* 13:204–212.

Chinchilla, Norma, and Nora Hamilton. 1999. Changing Networks and Alliances in a Transnational Context: Salvadoran and Guatemalan Immigrants in Southern California. *Social Justice* 26(3–4):1–22.

Cinel, Dino. 1991. *National Integration of Italian Return Migration, 1870–1929*. Cambridge: Cambridge University Press.

Clifford, James. 1997. *Routes*. Cambridge, MA: Harvard University Press.

Foner, Nancy. 1997. What's New About Transnationalism? New York Immigrants Today and at the Turn of the Century. *Diaspora* 6(3):366–375.

———. 2002. Response. *Journal of American Ethnic History* 21(4):102–119.

Georges, Eugenia. 1990. *Making of a Transnational Community: Migration, Development, and Cultural Change in the Dominican Republic*. New York: Columbia University Press.

Glick Schiller, Nina, Linda Basch, and Cristina Blanc-Szanton, eds. 1992. *Towards a Transnational Perspective on Migration: Race, Class, Ethnicity, and Nationalism Reconsidered*. New York: New York Academy of Sciences.

Goldberg, Barry. 1992. Historical Reflections on Transnationalism, Race, and the American Immigrant Saga. In *Towards a Transnational Perspective on Migration: Race, Class, Ethnicity, and Nationalism Reconsidered*. Nina Glick Schiller, Linda Basch, and Cristina Blanc-Szanton, eds. Pp. 201–216. New York: New York Academy of Sciences.

Gupta, Akhil, and James Ferguson. 1992. Beyond "Culture": Space, Identity, and the Politics of Difference. *Cultural Anthropology* 7(1):6–23.

International Migration Review. 2001. Special Issue: Transnational Migration: International Perspectives. Edited by Peggy Levitt, Josh DeWind, and Steven Vertovec, 37(3).

Kearney, Michael. 1995. The Local and the Global: The Anthropology of Globalization and Transnationalism. *Annual Review Anthropology* 24:547–565.

Mintz, Sidney. 1998. Localization of Anthropology Practice: From Area Studies to Transnationalism. *Critique of Anthropology* 18(2):117–133.

Moran-Taylor, Michelle. 2004. Crafting Connections: Maya Linkages between Guatemala's *Altiplano* and *el Norte*. *Estudios Fronterizos* 5(10):91–115.

Pessar, Patricia, and Sarah Mahler. 2003. Transnational Migration: Bringing Gender In. *International Migration Review* 37(3):812–846.

Popkin, Eric. 1995. *Guatemalan Hometown Associations in Los Angeles*. Pp. 35–40. Los Angeles: The Center for Multiethnic and Transnational Studies.

Portes, Alejandro, Jaime Guarnizo, and Patricia Landolt. 1999. Introduction: Pitfalls and Promise of an Emergent Research Field. *Ethnic and Racial Studies* 22(2):217–237.

Rouse, Roger. 1991. Mexican Migration and the Social Space of Postmodernism. *Diaspora* 1:8–23.

Wyman, Mark. 1993. *Round-Trip to America: The Immigrants Return to Europe, 1880–1930*. Ithaca, NY: Cornell University Press.

MICHELLE J. MORAN-TAYLOR

U

UNAUTHORIZED IMMIGRATION. An undocumented immigrant is a foreign national who has entered the United States, a sovereign territory, without legal authorization or without legal documentation permitting entry or permanent or temporary residency (LeMay 2004). The majority of undocumented immigrants are either: (1) those who entered the country without valid documents; or (2) those who entered with valid visas but overstayed their visas or otherwise violated the terms of their original admission to the United States (Chiswick 1988).

"Undocumented immigrant" is a term equivalent to unauthorized migrants, undocumented aliens, undocumented entrants, unauthorized immigrants, and "indocumentados" (Chavez 1992). The term "undocumented" became synonymous with the term "illegal" on or around the passing of the 1986 Immigration Reform and Control Act (IRCA), which granted amnesty to undocumented immigrants who met specific requirements. The terms "illegal alien" and "undocumented immigrant" both refer to a "non-U.S. citizen who has entered the United States illegally (i.e., without proper documentation and without complying with legally required U.S. immigration procedures). The term "undocumented immigrant" is used by those who presume this individual to be "innocent" of violating U.S. laws whereas "illegal alien" is used when the individual is assumed to have deliberately tried to evade the law (Adversity.Net 2004).

Based on the March 2002 Current Population Survey, an estimated 9.3 million undocumented immigrants reside in the United States plus 3 million children with U.S. citizenship who belong to at least one undocumented parent. The total number of undocumented immigrants was estimated at 4.5 million men, 3.2 million women, and 1.6 million children (Urban Institute 2004). A twofold method is used to estimate the undocumented population. Visa overstayers are estimated with data based on the I-94 form. One part of the form is collected at entry and the second part is collected when the visitor departs. Thus incoming forms without departure forms at the end of the year may include: those not required to depart; aliens who have acquired another status; aliens who departed but lost the second part of the form; and aliens who should have departed but remained in the United States. The number of aliens in the fourth category is calculated by estimating the number of those in the first three categories (Passel 1999).

Estimates for immigrants entering illegally, referred to as "entries without inspection" or EWIs, are based on 2000 census statistics for the foreign-born population, compared with government statistics on immigrants admitted, deportations, and numbers of non-immigrant residents, such as temporary workers. The Immigration and Naturalization Service (INS) was responsible for admitting immigrants, issuing visas, and monitoring the undocumented problem until March 1, 2003, when the Homeland Security Act of 2002 (H.R. 5005) went into effect. This act effected a major reorganization of several government agencies (Transportation Security Administration, Coast Guard, Customs Service, Federal Emergency Management Agency, Secret Service, and most of the INS) into the Department of Homeland Security (DHS). Within the DHS, U.S. Citizenship and Immigration Services now has oversight for all aspects of immigration, non-immigrant residents, and citizenship matters.

Undocumented immigrants come to the United States from all countries in the world. The annual growth of the undocumented population can be grouped into four categories: (1) Mexico, with more than half of the annual growth, adds just over 150,000 undocumented residents each year; (2) six countries—El Salvador, Guatemala, Canada, Haiti, Honduras, and the Bahamas—each add between 6,000 and 12,000 annually; (3) 13 countries each add about 2,000 to 4,000 annually; and (4) the remaining approximately 200 other countries add a total of about 30,000 undocumented residents each year. More than 80 percent of all undocumented immigrants are from countries in the Western Hemisphere (USCIS 2004a). There are approximately 1 million undocumented immigrants from Asia living in the United States. California has the highest number of undocumented immigrants at 26 percent followed by Texas at 12 percent, then Florida (10 percent) and New York (8 percent), where the majority of the Chinese immigrants settle (Chin 1999; Urban Institute 2004). Since the mid-1990s, the most rapid population increase of undocumented immigrants has occurred in the Rocky Mountain, midwest, and southeast regions of the United States.

Immigration has played an important role in American history, and the United States continues to have one of the most open immigration policies in the world. The concept of the "American Dream" combined with that of Manifest Destiny, and soon America was attracting thousands of new migrants each year and filling the continent with settlements and industries. In 1942, during World War II, the need for agricultural labor in California and elsewhere in the United States led to the creation of the Bracero program. Under this program, needed agricultural laborers would migrate to the United States with the seasons, work during the spring and summer months, and return to their home countries during winter (Chavez 1992). Others would stay several years, send money home, and return to live in their country of origin once enough had been accumulated. For two decades, approximately 100,000 people per year—and up to 400,000 per year in the peak years of the late 1950s—came as "temporary [agricultural] workers" (USCIS 2004a). This pattern of migration became an integral part of the lives of a generation of migrants, often becoming their only means for earning a living and an essential and reliable source of labor for agricultural employers.

Due to the objections of American labor unions, the United States ended the Bracero program in 1964, but the demand for labor did not diminish, and the number of undocumented immigrants rose dramatically (Heer 1990). Some of the workers employed under the Bracero program remained in the United States as undocumented immigrants while others continued the tradition of crossing the border to work, although this migration became illegal when the United States created new laws to restrict border movement.

Undocumented immigrants view the United States as the "land of opportunity ... where hard work and sacrifice can earn them upward mobility" (Chavez 1992). The standard of living is higher in the United States in comparison to most sending countries. For example, a typical Mexican worker earns one-tenth as much as his American counterpart, and numerous American businesses are willing to hire cheap, compliant labor from abroad. These businesses are seldom punished for hiring undocumented immigrants because our country lacks a viable system to verify the eligibility of new workers.

Chain migration is another factor influencing immigration (Papastergiadis 2000). Communities of settled legal immigrants help create immigration networks used by undocumented immigrants and serve as incubators, providing jobs, housing, and financial assistance (Center for Immigration Studies 2004). In addition, economic and social factors in the sending countries contribute heavily in the decision to migrate. Many immigrants face limited economic opportunity in their homeland due to their lack of social connections or education. Factors for migration vary between men and women. While men migrate mainly due to economic reasons, some women may combine this with relationship issues, whether to accompany a man or to escape or avoid a troubled relationship. Some undocumented women believe that U.S. society exhibits less social judgment toward abandoned women or mothers with children out of wedlock (Chavez 1992). While undocumented immigrants from El Salvador, Nicaragua, Guatemala, and Honduras come for many of the same reasons as those from Mexico, there is often an additional factor of wanting to escape an environment that is fraught with the personal risks and economic instability that result from ongoing political conflicts in their countries (Chavez 1992).

While the majority of the factors surrounding undocumented immigrants seem to be based on the push rather than the pull theory, there are important pull factors to consider. Some economic factors within the United States have led to encouragement of undocumented immigrants, thus creating a diversified demand for Mexican labor (Cornelius and Bustamante 1989). While the agricultural sector remains a strong pull, the service industry sector increasingly appreciates the undocumented immigrants' flexibility and willingness to accept low job security combined with high variability in working hours and working days per week. In addition, the fact that these workers have no legal avenue and no state or federal protection and are unlikely to organize into unions also makes undocumented immigrants attractive to employers (Andreas 2000).

Another pull factor is the decline and aging of the United States labor force due to low birth rates since the mid-1960s and the decrease in unskilled legal immigrant workers (Cornelius and Bustamante 1989). There is an inadequate supply of U.S. labor willing to work under some of the conditions that undocumented immigrants will accept. Although the economic factor is not the only reason leading to the decision to migrate, it does provide the undocumented immigrant workforce with a 96 percent employment rate (Urban Institute 2004). The decision to migrate as an undocumented immigrant usually must meet three criteria: the desire to migrate, an inability to obtain legal documentation, and a willingness to violate U.S. law in order to migrate (Chiswick 1988).

Human trafficking of undocumented immigrants into the United States is a business worth approximately $3 billion a year (Papastergiadis 2000). Undocumented immigrants must also believe that the rewards of immigration are greater than the risk of being exploited (Papastergiadis 2000). For example, undocumented immigrants from Latin America encounter high risks in order to cross *la frontera*, or the border. Approximately 75 percent of these undocumented immigrants use a *coyote*, a professional human trafficker that charges anywhere from $250 to $1,500 per immigrant for guiding the immigrant across the border (Andreas 2000). While the fee charged to immigrants from Latin America seems high, Chinese immigrants must pay approximately US $30,000 to be smuggled into the United States by people known as "snakeheads" (Chin 1999). Fees for any immigrant smuggled into the United States are usually paid by a relative or contact in the United States upon delivery of the immigrant. Smuggled Chinese arrive in the United States by various routes, often illegally crossing borders from Mexico or Canada or arriving in container ships, though this method is less frequent since the Golden Venture incident when 10 people died. For immigrants from Latin America, scouts may be used to run interference with the U.S. Border Patrol to make the actual crossing safer and quicker (Rotella 1998). Other coyotes resort to tunneling under the border defenses and yet others have resorted to filling 18-wheelers with immigrants and take advantage of the high volume of cross-border trucking brought on by the North American Free Trade Agreement (NAFTA) (Andreas 2000).

While some coyotes are concerned with the welfare of their clients, others may commit theft and physical abuse, demand an increase in fees upon delivery to a safe house, rape the women, punish those who cannot pay by shaving off their hair and eyebrows, or even abandon them (Rotella 1998; Andreas 2000). Many Chinese immigrants who cannot pay the entire fee are forced to work off their debt in restaurants or garment factories or as drug couriers or prostitutes (Chin 1999).

Other immigrants take the chance of a solo journey without experienced help and run the risk of becoming lost in the desolate areas outside U.S. border cities, being victims of vigilantism by U.S. ranchers, or even dying (Nevins 2002). While migrating to and from the United States, there is a risk of being attacked by thieves and gangs, who wait on traditional migration routes knowing that the immigrant may be carrying items such as money, jewelry, or other valuables. The stress of migration is coupled with the fact that undocumented immigrants are forced to live in fear and are vulnerable to criminals and unscrupulous employers because they have no legal recourse.

Enforcement of laws against unauthorized immigration is the responsibility of the U.S. Citizenship and Immigration Services (USCIS), but Congress has ultimate control over all U.S. immigration issues. The Illegal Immigration Reform and Immigrant Responsibility Act of 1996 attempted to restrict immigration by eliminating federal benefits for illegal aliens and legal non-immigrants such as travelers and students. While the USCIS attempts to enforce the U.S. immigration policies, a major problem is that these policies are linked to other U.S. foreign policies and domestic economic conditions and may have a widespread effect within the United States (Chin 1999). Border enforcement personnel can only cover approximately 10 percent of the 2,000-mile U.S.-Mexico border (Andreas 2000). For Latin American immigrants the main point of entry is the U.S.-Mexico border while the points of entry for Chinese and Asian immigrants are varied. These immigrants attempt to enter the United States via sea (12 percent) or air (40 percent) or through the U.S.-Mexico or U.S.-Canadian border (40 percent) (Chin 1999). The majority of undocumented immigrants who are apprehended are immediately deported back to their homeland without much, if any, detention. A study on the long-term impact of the mass legalization for undocumented immigrants permitted by the 1986 Immigration Reform and Control Act concluded that this amnesty program reduced apprehensions of persons attempting to cross the border in the short term but "did not change long-term patterns of undocumented immigration from Mexico" (Orrenius and Zavodny 2003). *See also*: **Demography; Effects of unauthorized immigration; Human smuggling; Migration processes; U.S.-Mexico border.**

References

Adversity.Net. 2004. Definitions: Illegal Alien vs. Undocumented Immigrant. Adversity .Net for Victims of Reverse Discrimination. April 12. http://www.adversity.net/ Terms_Definitions/TERMS/Illegal-Undocumented.htm.

Andreas, Peter. 2000. *Border Games: Policing the U.S.-Mexico Divide*. Ithaca, NY: Cornell University Press.

Asian Law Caucus. 2004. Asian Law Caucus Supports New Comprehensive Immigration Reform Legislation. May 27. http://www.asianlawcaucus.org.

Center for Immigration Studies. 2004. Illegal Immigration. May 25. http://www.cis.org/ topics/illegalimmigration.html.

Chan, Sucheng. 1991. *Asian Americans: An Interpretive History*. New York: Twayne Publishers.

Chavez, Leo R. 1992. *Shadowed Lives: Undocumented Immigrants in American Society*. Ft. Worth, TX: Harcourt Brace College Publishers.

Chin, Ko-Lin. 1999. *Smuggled Chinese: Clandestine Immigration to the United States*. Philadelphia: Temple University Press.

Chiswick, Barry R. 1988. *Illegal Aliens: Their Employment and Employers*. Kalamazoo, MI: W.E. Upjohn Institute for Employment Research.

Cornelius, Wayne A., and Jorge A. Bustamante, eds. 1989. *Mexican Migration to the United States: Dimensions of United States–Mexican Relations*. Vol. 3. San Diego: University of California.

Foner, Nancy, Ruben G. Rumbaut, and Steven J. Gold, eds. 2000. *Immigration Research for a New Century: Multidisciplinary Perspectives*. New York: Russell Sage Foundation.

Heer, David M. 1990. *Undocumented Mexicans in the United States*. New York: Cambridge University Press.

LeMay, Michael C. 2004. *U.S. Immigration: A Reference Handbook*. Santa Barbara, CA: ABC-CLIO.

Nevins, Joseph. 2002. *Operation Gatekeeper: The Rise of the "Illegal Alien" and the Making of the U.S.-Mexico Boundary*. New York: Routledge.

Newsbatch. 2004. Immigration Policy Issues. May 27. http://www.newsbatch.com/immi gration.htm.

Orrenius, Pia, and Madeline Zavodny. 2003. Do Amnesty Programs Reduce Undocumented Immigration? Evidence from IRCA. *Demography* 40(3):437–450.

Papastergiadis, Nikos. 2000. *The Turbulence of Migration*. Malden, MA: Blackwell.

Passel, Jeffrey S. 1999. *Undocumented Immigration to the United States: Numbers, Trends, and Characteristics in Illegal Immigration in America: A Reference Handbook*. David W. Haines and Karen Rosenblum, eds. Pp. 27–111. Westport, CT: Greenwood Press.

Rotella, Sebastian. 1998. *Twilight on the Line: Underworlds and Politics at the U.S.-Mexico Border*. New York: W.W. Norton.

U.S. Census Bureau. 2004. Immigration. April 12. http://www.census.gov/population/ www/socdemo/immigration.html.

U.S. Citizenship and Immigration Services (USCIS). 2004a. Executive Summary: Estimates of the Unauthorized Immigrant Population Residing in the United States: 1990 to 2000. April 18. http://www.uscis.gov.

———. 2004b. US and Mexico: Immigration Policy and the Bilateral Relationship. April 16. http://www.uscis.gov.

Urban Institute. 2004. Undocumented Immigrants: Facts and Figures. Jeffrey S. Passel, Randolph Capps, and Michael E. Fix, Urban Institute. April 21. http://www.urban .org/url.cfm?ID=1000587.

HEIDI WILSON AND JEANNE ARMSTRONG

U.S.-CANADA BORDER. The 5,525-mile border between the United States and Canada has been heralded as not only the longest international boundary in the world but also the most economically significant and one of the most peaceful. Apart from the 11 crossings on the isolated 1,538 miles of border that Canada shares with Alaska, there are 143 ports of entry along the 3,977 miles from the Pacific to the Atlantic. In 2003, $441.5 billion worth of goods crossed from one country to another, the highest cross-border volume and economic value in the world (Department of Foreign Affairs and International Trade 2004). In the same year, nearly 12 million people crossed the border into the United States (BTS 2003). Apart from the distinctiveness of Quebec, similarities of culture, language, history, and living standards have facilitated the cross-border flow of both people and commerce.

While emerging out of dispute along much of its length, today the U.S.-Canada border is punctiliously regulated and seems to run tangentially to two national identities (Fraser 1989; New 1998). Smuggling of goods and undocumented crossings became more the source of legend than of sustained political attention in either country. Until recently, in fact, the northern U.S. border has seemed almost inconsequential when compared to the contentious debate and public concern about immigration that have characterized the U.S. border with Mexico.

Canada, with an immigration rate second only to Australia (as measured by proportion of population that is foreign-born), is one of the world's largest immigrant societies. In 2004, Canada admitted about 235,000 people, of which 10 percent were refugees from around the world. Like most industrial societies today, immigration is critical to Canada's population replacement. Immigrants presently account for about one-half of Canada's population growth and nearly

70 percent of the growth in the nation's labor force (Citizenship and Immigration Canada 2005). The source countries for Canada's immigrants have changed drastically since the 1960s. Prior to that time, most immigrants came from European countries and the United States, but today the leading source countries are in Asia, the Middle East, and Africa. One result of the changing immigration pattern is increased ethnic diversity, with the proportion of visible minorities in Canada greater than ever before. The prevailing settlement pattern has been one of high urban concentration, with the vast majority of immigrants locating in Canada's three largest cities, Toronto, Montreal, and Vancouver.

While most immigrants to Canada come through legal channels, including relatively open movement between British Commonwealth countries, unauthorized entry—long regarded as principally a U.S. problem—has increasingly become a Canadian concern as well. In 1999, a ship with 599 people aboard, most from the Fujian province of China, was intercepted off the coast of British Columbia, and others have been detected since.

For many immigrants who settle in Canada, the United States is the ultimate destination. Over the last century, thousands of European immigrants settled on the Canadian prairies with the goal of eventually making their way to the United States. In recent years, the step-migration to Canada and then into the United States has been noteworthy in the case of Chinese immigrants to Canada. The real and feared "spillover" has raised the profile of the U.S.-Canada border since September 2001, although increased U.S. security controls and expansion of binational coordination of practice and enforcement along the border appear to be bringing greater control over international crossings.

With respect to cross-border migration, historically Canadian immigration to the United States has been much greater than American immigration to Canada. A notable example, chronicled in *Evangeline* by Henry Wadsworth Longfellow, involved French-speaking people in the Maritime Provinces in the mid-eighteenth century. Doubts about their loyalty resulted in mass expulsion, and the ensuing Acadian immigration to what was then the Louisiana Territory led to the eventual emergence of what is today known as the Cajun culture. During the twentieth century, large numbers of Canadians moved south in search of employment opportunities. In recent years, the term "brain drain" has been used to describe the movement of educated professionals to the United States in search of higher salaries and lower taxes. Although the brain drain was first noted in the 1920s when the Canadian Parliament expressed concern about the outflow of Canadians, it has accelerated following the implementation of the North American Free Trade Agreement (NAFTA) due to the relative ease of movement by professionals with renewable visas.

Although the flow of immigrants is mostly north to south, this pattern has at times reversed, particularly during times of political strife in the United States. Reminiscent of the migration of large numbers of "Loyalists" to Canada during the Revolutionary War, anywhere from 30,000 to 90,000 Americans relocated to Canada during the Vietnam War to avoid the draft (Struck 2004). Following a 2004 U.S. presidential election that portended a continuation of U.S. military involvement in Iraq and elsewhere overseas, Canadian immigration authorities reported a significant increase—from 20,000 per day to over 150,000—in the number of inquiries made about immigrating to Canada (Lyman 2005). The election inspired such creative Web sites as MarryAnAmerican.ca, on which Canadians can take a pledge to marry American liberals seeking refuge from four more years of an unpopular administration.

Canada's reputation for benevolent refugee admissions reflects the significant role of immigrant societies in Canadian politics, which has had its own impact on the immigration climate of the United States. The distinctive Canadian refugee policy, regarded as "soft" by some U.S. policymakers, has prompted calls for greater "harmonization" of policies of the two countries to bolster security in North America against terrorism. Canada has exercised caution in the push toward harmonization on both humanitarian and sovereignty grounds. However, immigration officials in both countries increasingly share information and cooperate more effectively in dealing with criminals and other undesirable individuals attempting to enter either country.

U.S.-Canada border security was not an overriding concern for either country until recent years. As security has come to dominate thinking about the role and function of the border, both countries have stepped up efforts to intercept the flow of illegal drugs and undocumented migrants. Today the U.S.-Canada border has taken on many of the characteristics of the U.S.-Mexico border, with increased surveillance and more careful inspections and documents required. New security measures that impede the flow of people and products represent problems for business activity between the two countries. Goods held up at the border signify losses of income and sometimes even of cargo, if perishable.

To address border slowdowns caused by new security measures, a number of actions have been taken. Many of these were spelled out in the Smart Border Declaration, approved by both governments in 2001. Under a program called NEXUS, frequent travelers whose backgrounds have been run against crime and terrorism indices are issued a special card allowing them to be waived expeditiously through the port of entry. NEXUS is currently operating at 11 crossings: Blaine/Point Roberts, Washington (3 crossings); Buffalo; Detroit (2 crossings); Niagara Falls (2 crossings); Port Huron, Michigan; Highgate, Vermont; and Champlain, New York. The NEXUS program had enrolled approximately 80,000 participants as of January 2006 and new NEXUS lanes have been scheduled to open at other locations.

Since most commerce crosses the land border in trucks, there has been a strong focus on initiatives that expedite truck traffic while ensuring the security of drivers and cargo. One program, called Free and Secure Trade (FAST), allows low-risk and carefully screened carriers and drivers to be pre-approved and thus allowed relatively unimpeded movement across the border. FAST is currently operating at 19 of the highest volume land border crossings. Pre-clearance systems for land and rail containers are also in place using detection equipment known as Vehicle and Cargo Inspection System (VACIS). Containers are screened for radioactive and other substances at the point of entry, rather than at the international border.

Canada and the United States have established joint border facilities at six locations, with the number due to expand in future years. Other cooperative strategies include establishment of joint U.S.-Canada container targeting teams that scrutinize containers entering North America at the first point of arrival at selected marine ports (Department of Foreign Affairs and International Trade 2004). The human intricacies of immigration, on the other hand, go beyond the technological sophistication that can be applied to trade. Differing and developing national perspectives regarding the value and level of immigration will continue to complicate the separation and integration that converge along this long line. *See also*: **Expedited entry and removal; International accords; National security; U.S.-Mexico border.**

References

Adelman, Howard. 2002. Canadian Borders and Imigration Post 9/11. *International Migration Review* 36(1):14–28.

Bureau of Transportation Statistics (BTS). 2003. Border Crossing Data: U.S.-Canada. http://www.bts.gov/programs/international/border_crossing_entry_data/us_canada/index.html. Accessed February 10, 2005.

Citizenship and Immigration Canada. 2005. *Facts and Figures 2004: Immigration Overview—Permanent and Temporary Residents*. http://www.cic.gc.ca/english/pdf/pub/facts2004.pdf. Accessed March 8, 2006.

Fraser, Marian. 1989. *Walking the Line: Travels along the Canadian/American Border*. San Francisco: Sierra Club.

Department of Foreign Affairs and International Trade, Government of Canada. 2004. United States–Canada: The World's Largest Trading Relationship. http://www.canadianembassy.org/trade/wltr-en.asp. Accessed February 10, 2005.

Hagan, John. 2001. *Northern Passage: American Vietnam War Resisters in Canada*. Cambridge, MA: Harvard University Press.

Kusch, Frank. 2001. *All American Boys: Draft Dodgers in Canada from the Vietnam War*. Westport, CT: Praeger.

Lyman, Rick. 2005. Some Bush Foes Vote Yet Again, with Their Feet: Canada or Bust. *New York Times*, February 8, A16.

New, W.H. 1998. *Borderlands: How We Talk about Canada*. Vancouver: UBC Press.

Struck, Doug. 2004. For This War, Canada Isn't Embracing U.S. Deserters. *Seattle Times*, October 24, A10.

DON K. ALPER AND JAMES LOUCKY

U.S.-MEXICO BORDER. Borders are generally defined as international boundaries between nation-states. The definition of the U.S.-Mexico border has received a multiplicity of foci that refer to historical epics, geographical regions, zones of political influence, culture, identity, and symbiotic communities transcending governmental demarcations and boundaries. Alvarez (1995) argues that the U.S.-Mexico border "has become the icon and model for research into other borders as well as for the elaboration and refinement of the boundaries of several salient concepts and their referents."

The U.S.-Mexico border region was initially the northern extremity of the Spanish colony of New Spain in the Americas. After 1821 it became a part of the newly independent Republic of Mexico. The landscape of this immense territory was marked by sparse settlements whose economy was largely based on mining and ranching. Effective settlement of this region by Mexico was inhibited due to the long distances between the region and the population centers of central Mexico, numerous Indian uprisings, and internal political disorders that accompanied the turbulent Mexican post-independence period. In 1835 Tejanos and Anglo Texan settlers staged a successful revolt in the Mexican province of Tejas that would ultimately lead to strained relations, hostilities, and war between the United States and Mexico (Meyer et al. 2003).

On February 2, 1848, the Treaty of Guadalupe Hidalgo formally ended the U.S.-Mexican War, the military engagement between Mexico and the United States. Signed in the pueblo of Guadalupe, Hidalgo, which is now incorporated into the northern section of Mexico City, the treaty reformulated the political boundaries between the two nations that are largely in effect to this present day. Aside from the later Gadsden Purchase (1853), the treaty established the current border between the United States and Mexico that stretches from the Gulf of Mexico to the Pacific Ocean, for a payment of $15 million. In return the United States was ceded more than 525,000 square miles of land that now comprise the present states of Arizona, California, Nevada, New Mexico, Texas, and Utah as well as the southern and western parts of Colorado. As part of the treaty's terms, Mexico additionally agreed to settle the more than $3 million in claims made by U.S. citizens against the Republic of Mexico. The annexation of nearly half of Mexico essentially completed the bulk of continental expansion by the United States and provided much-coveted ports on the Pacific Ocean that would link the United States with trade routes to Asia and the Far East (Meyer et al. 2003).

The U.S.-Mexico border region links the populations of the two countries in a complex and vibrant network of trade and commerce as well as cultural, social, and institutional relationships. The border represents one of the most dynamic boundaries in the world that is witness to high population growth, economic expansion, mobile labor forces, linguistic hybridization, high crime rates, and an artistic renaissance that impacts the social and psycho-cultural character of each country (Martinez 1994). It is estimated that 12 million Mexican and U.S. citizens now live in the counties and municipios that stretch from the Pacific Ocean to the Gulf of Mexico, and that some 350 million people legally cross each year from one country to the other (Ruiz 1998). A large portion of border populations are concentrated in the metropolitan areas of two sets of sister cities: San Diego, California–Tijuana, Baja California, and El Paso, Texas–Ciudad Juarez, Chihuahua. Within those four cities nearly a third of the border population reside. The San Diego population alone nearly encompasses one-half of the total U.S. border population (Ham-Chande and Weeks 1992).

Large populations along the border were not always present. In 1900, cities such as Tijuana had a population base of fewer than 250 people, while San Diego's population did not exceed 18,000. Many of the border communities were and still are dependent upon economic boom-and-bust cycles that in turn are predicated upon the market value of agricultural commodities, mineral prices, and raw materials as well as the industrial and commercial trade relations that occur between the two nations. In many ways Mexican border towns, spurred largely by American entrepreneurs and organized crime, have traditionally capitalized on restricted and illegal commodities and activities within the United States. During the era of Prohibition, border cities such as Tijuana, Ciudad Juarez, and San Luis featured illegal alcohol, night clubs, bars, resorts, racetracks, and gambling halls. The Agua Caliente sector of Tijuana featured dog racing, horse racing, theatrical performances, night clubs, and bordellos that catered to the Hollywood entertainment community in addition to the naval and marine corps personnel situated in San Diego. Ciudad Juarez and Tijuana continue to serve as a rite of passage for many military personnel, college students, and others who seek exotic and illicit entertainment (Ruiz 1998). Border communities have also been a destination and central locale for the trafficking and distribution of illegal drugs and undocumented workers.

Migratory flows across the fixed U.S.-Mexico border of both legal and un-documented workers over a 150-year period have been a result of political tur-moil, economic growth cycles and downturns, dependency, and immigration regulations chiefly imposed by the U.S. government. The flow of migration has always been couched within the political and economic interests of the United States while in some respects providing a safety valve for Mexico's unemployed and poor masses. Since 1924 with the inception of the Immigration and Natu-ralization Service and the Border Patrol, undocumented labor and passage into the United States have been restricted and border policy has been enforced in line with U.S. national policy and needs. Cheap labor has continued to be an indis-pensable commodity in the development of industry, agro-production, and ser-vice industry sectors not only in the West but throughout the entire United States. The flow of Mexican labor across the border supports many of the economic development objectives of the Southwest and a large part of U.S. entrepreneurial activity (Martinez 1994).

The U.S.-Mexico border has been a stimulus to the development and com-modification of mobile labor forces intended to fuel economic synergy within the United States and Mexico. The initiation of the Bracero program (1942–1964), a guestworker program that was originally intended to bolster the labor shortage of U.S. workers during World War II, is indicative of the political and economic arrangements that have been mutually negotiated between both nations to spur employment and economic activity along the U.S.-Mexico border. The later in-ception of the Border Industrialization Program (BIP) was the primogenitor for the creation of greater numbers of assembly plants, called *maquiladoras*, in Mexican border cities such as Tijuana, Ciudad Juarez, and Matamoros (Ganster et al. 1997). BIP represented the increased globalization of world economic trade and the marked shift toward export processing zones where duty-free compo-nents could be shipped across the border into Mexico, where they were assem-bled with low-cost labor and then exported back into the United States. In 1965 the number of maquiladoras along the U.S.-Mexico border numbered 12; by January of 2000, there were well over 4,000 (Crosthwaite et al. 2003).

The industrialization of Northern Mexico through BIP and other economic mechanisms has led to increasing concerns about the environmental and eco-logical integrity of the U.S.-Mexico border. Industrial waste by large corpora-tions and pharmaceutical companies has added a great deal of pollutants and spurred chemical dumping all along the border and more specifically within the Rio Grande river basin (Ganster et al. 1997). These conditions have contributed to high rates of cancer, skin diseases, premature births, and other maladies at-tributed to PCBs and polluted ground water.

Since the initiation of the North American Free Trade Agreement (NAFTA) in 1994, economic interdependence between the two countries has grown extensively. Currently, the United States is Mexico's largest trading partner and the principal source of capital for Mexican investments, while Mexico is the second most im-portant trading partner for the United States. Commerce and trade across the U.S.-Mexico border have increased exponentially along with NAFTA and promises to eclipse the present trade volume within the next decade (Ganster et al. 1997).

An ancillary but increasingly critical by-product of expanded trade agreements, globalization, Mexican high unemployment rates, the growth of the U.S. service sector, and the continued need for cheap labor has been the large influx across the border of Mexican undocumented workers during the 1980s and 1990s and well into the beginning of the present century. Border control policies effectuated by the United States in the 1990s point to increasing militarization of the U.S.-Mexico border. Demands by nativist groups and U.S. politicians along with a fear that foreign workers will displace the U.S. workforce have spawned several U.S.-Mexico border initiatives by the U.S. government designed to apprehend and deport Mexican undocumented workers. Initiatives such as Operation Blockade (later named Operation Hold the Line) in El Paso, Operation Gatekeeper in San Diego, and Operation Safeguard in Arizona were intended to curb the tide of undocumented workers but to date have shown little overall success (Nevins 2002). Spending related to these initiatives has been in the billions of dollars and has resulted in the construction of massive bulwarks on the border and increased border personnel throughout the region.

The enhancement of border enforcement, vigilantism, and the crackdown by U.S. customs and border officials have led to many reports of physical abuses, rapes, and deaths along the U.S.-Mexico border (Palafox 2000). Falcon (2001) believes that rape has now become an instrument of choice employed by the Immigration and Naturalization (INS) and other border enforcement agencies along the U.S.-Mexico border in much the same manner that rape was utilized in Yugoslavia and other conflicts where abuse of power and violation of women were seen as elements of control and power. As undocumented workers continue to seek opportunities, they will meet with increased hazards, opposition, and regrettably at times with loss of life.

Border culture has been and will continue to be a vibrant entity. The presence of Mexican and Latino populations on both sides of the international boundary, stimulated by strong social and cultural linkages, will dramatically assist in redefining the character of American society in this century. Oscar Martinez (1994) discusses the emergence of groups of borderlanders who will be able to function in an interdependent society that brings together distinct traditions, cultural mores, music, food, language, literature, and belief systems. Joel Garreau (1981) defines the border as "a place . . . that appears on no map. It's where the gumbo of Dixie gives way to the refried beans of Mexico." The binational cross-cultural activities, pageants, sports events, telenovelas, and musical corridos are all part of the crucible of mestiza-o culture that Anzaldúa (1999) writes about in her epic book *Borderlands/La Frontera: The New Mestiza*: "To live in the Borderlands means to put chile in the borscht, eat whole wheat tortillas, speak Tex-Mex with a Brooklyn accent; be stopped by la migra at the border checkpoints."

Guillermo Gomez Peña, in his border narrative "Warrior for Gringostroika," speaks of a displaced identity wedged in between two fault lines: "I live smack in the fissure between two worlds, in the infected wound; half a block from the end of Western civilization and four miles from the beginning of the Mexican/ American border, the northernmost point of Latin America. In my fractured reality, but a reality nonetheless, they cohabit two histories, languages, cosmologies, artistic traditions, and political traditions which are drastically counterposed" (1996:101).

For over 150 years the U.S.-Mexico border has been an economic giant, an enigma, a field of contention and a spur to reconfiguring our cultural consciousness. It poses both challenges and remarkable solutions for the continued existence of two intertwined and interdependent nation-states. *See also*: **Border control; Borderlands; Unauthorized immigration.**

References

Alvarez, Robert R., Jr. 1995. The Mexican-U.S. Border: The Making of an Anthropology of Borderlands. *Annual Review of Anthropology* 24:447–470.

Anzaldúa, Gloria. 1999. *Borderlands/La Frontera: The New Mestiza*, 2nd ed. San Francisco: Aunt Lute.

Crosthwaite, Luis Humerto, John William Byrd, and Bobby Byrd. 2003. *Puro Border*. El Paso, TX: Cinco Puntos Press.

Dunn, Timothy J. 1996. *The Militarization of the U.S.-Mexico Border, 1978–1992.* Austin, TX: CMAS Books.

Falcon, Sylvanna. 2001. Rape as a Weapon of War: Advancing Human Rights for Women at the U.S.-Mexico Border. *Social Justice* (San Francisco) 28:31–51.

Ganster, Paul, Alan Sweedler, James Scott, and Wolf Dieter-Eberwein. 1997. *Borders and Border Regions in Europe and North America.* San Diego, CA: San Diego State University Press.

Garreau, Joel. 1981. *The Nine Nations of North America.* Boston: Houghton Mifflin.

Gomez-Peña, Guillermo. 1996. Warrior for Gingostroika. In *The Late Great Mexican Border: Reports from a Disappearing Line.* Bobby Byrd and Susannah Mississippi Byrd, eds. Pp. 101–107. El Paso, TX: Cinco Puntos Press.

Ham-Chande, Roberto, and John Robert Weeks. 1992. *Demographic Dynamics of the U.S.-Mexico Border.* El Paso: Texas Western Press.

Hart, John Mason. 1998. *Border Crossings: Mexican and Mexican-American Workers.* Wilmington, DE: Scholarly Resources.

Martinez, Oscar J. 1994. *Border People: Life and Society in the U.S.-Mexico Borderlands.* Tucson: University of Arizona Press.

Meyer, Michael, William Sherman, and Susan M. Deeds. 2003. *The Course of Mexican History*, 7th ed. New York: Oxford University Press.

Nevins, Joseph. 2002. *Operation Gatekeeper: The Rise of the "Illegal Alien" and the Making of the U.S.-Mexico Boundary.* New York: Routledge.

Palafox, Jose. 2000. Opening Up Borderland Studies: A Review of U.S.-Mexico Border Militarization Discourse. *Social Justice* 27:56–68.

Ruiz, Ramon Eduardo. 1998. *On the Rim of Mexico: Encounters of the Rich and Poor.* Boulder, CO: Westview Press.

LARRY J. ESTRADA

W

WOMEN. Almost every immigration flow has an imbalance of men and women (Chant 1992). Women worldwide take active part in the decision to migrate and many women immigrate autonomously, while others follow family or spouses. Documented immigration from Central and South America, the Caribbean, Southeast Asia, and Europe to the United States is clearly female dominated.

Feminist migration research first drew attention to the importance of women in the migration process and how female migration might be related to factors associated with class, race, and socioeconomics while embracing macroanalytic reasons as well (Castro et al. 1984; Morokvaic 1984; Crummett 1987:247). Feminist research focused on the meaning of being female in the migration process and included sex roles, sexual division of labor, ideological constructions, and self-perceptions of women in the study of migration. Feminist migration researchers demonstrated that female migration processes differed from male processes and women could take the initiative to migrate (Morokvaic 1984; Boyd 1986; Caspari and Giles 1986). Feminist immigration theory proposes three causes for female migration: socioeconomic reasons, familial reasons, and gender role constraints (Morokvaic 1984; Crummett 1987; Safa 1987). Hamilton and Chinchilla (1991) demonstrated how socioeconomic and political reasons for immigration are intrinsically inseparable for Central Americans. Therefore, for the immigrants and refugees from countries with high rates of political violence, political causes for immigration need to be considered as well.

Traditionally, immigration researchers assumed that numerous gender role and economic restrictions exclude women from immigration, even if there is a substantial demand for female labor. Childcare and sociocultural restrictions, such as gender roles, are often considered barriers for women in internal and transnational migration (Chant and Radcliffe 1992:16). In patriarchal extended families, women are usually not free to migrate even if they traditionally generate part of the income for household expenditures (Hugo 1992). Marriage and childrearing restrain women from participating freely in the migratory process (Radcliffe 1992). Frequently, women immigrants are confined to low-paying jobs and earn less than men at the destination of migration. Therefore, it might be economically more beneficial for a family to have their son migrate than their daughter (Chant 1992:204).

However, migration is an extremely dynamic process and gender ratios can change over time, and despite the gender role and economic restrictions, women participate in immigration. Among the many factors that facilitate women's participation in transnational migration, research has also focused on conditions in the host country. Demands for low-wage female labor in industrialized countries (Sassen-Koob 1983, 1984; Hondagneu-Sotelo 2000) and government policies of immigrant-receiving countries have been held responsible for perpetuating female immigration (Caspari and Giles 1986). Female migration has been interpreted as the result of unequal development in the worldwide capitalist system. For example, women from poorer nations are incorporated into United States manufacturing industries, such as the garment industry, an industry that would not exist in the industrialized countries if it did not use a supply of underpaid immigrant women to compete with low-cost producers in other countries (Sassen-Koob 1983, 1984).

Another area of employment is domestic work (Hondagneu-Sotelo 2000). Similarly, young women have been migrating to "Free Trade Zones" in Mexico, Puerto Rico, and Southeast Asia to provide cheap labor for manufacturing industries. The historical-structural approach (Sassen-Koob 1983, 1984) has been criticized for emphasizing women's role in production and neglecting women's reproductive roles. Productive roles consist of women's participation in wage labor. Reproductive roles include childbearing, childcare, and domestic chores (Brydon and Chant 1989:10–11; Chant and Radcliffe 1992:22). Among the different theoretical approaches, the theory of household economics appealed to researchers who are concerned with female migration such as Patricia Pessar (1982, 1988), Sarah Radcliffe (1992), and Sylvia Chant (1992). Household economy brought attention to how power relations in the household shape decision-making processes and division of labor in the household. Those gender role expectations might, for instance, make women solely responsible for raising children and absolve men from involvement in household activities. Therefore, those men might be more likely to participate in migration than women.

Although household economics presents a breakthrough in the study of female migration it has some major drawbacks. As with many theoretical models, it tends to homogenize women's situations within a nationality and not to consider the variety of cases. It ignores the fact that women, besides pursuing collective group interests, might have individual, non-economic reasons for migration, like the desire to escape from oppressive or violent situations. In addition, household economics heavily emphasizes economic motivations as a counter-reaction to traditional immigration research that postulated that women do not have any economic reasons for migration.

However, there are three major limitations in the new feminist literature on migration. Feminist migration researchers were so concerned in proving that women have their own economic reasons to migrate that they placed a heavy emphasis on how economic reasons specific to women facilitated their migration. Political causes and economic causes for migration are regarded as separate categories. Additionally, feminist migration researchers only superficially investigated social power structures that inhibit or facilitate women's migration. Immigrant women's own voices are very rarely heard (Foner 1986; Gonzalez 1986). Feminist research failed to document women's macro and microeconomic reasons in their home communities and home countries that perpetuated their participation in the migration process (Momsen 1992:81). Instead, it examined which economic conditions in the host country favored women's immigration (Momsen 1992), how immigrant women were incorporated in the host country's economy (Sassen-Koob 1983, 1984), and how immigration affected their gender roles (Castro 1982; Pessar 1982, 1988).

Single women or married women without spouses comprise a considerable percentage of all immigrants (Morokvaic 1984). Among an increasing number of countries, women outrank men among transnational migrants during the early 1990s (Donato 1992:159). Women predominate among documented immigrants to the United States (Tyree and Donato 1986). As previously stated, marriage and childcare are usually factors that restrict women from participating independently in transnational migration (Kohpahl 1998). Although childcare is often regarded as a barrier for women to migrate, some women leave their children with relatives in their home countries and participate independently abroad. Caribbean female heads of households might leave their children behind with relatives because they do not have any other option (Chant and Radcliffe 1992:16; Ho 1993; Hondagneu-Sotelo 2000). In these cases, women were the only ones who could migrate because the spouse was absent or was an unreliable economic provider. Therefore, in countries with high marital instability women are more likely to cross transnational borders (Jasso and Rosenzweig 1990).

Another illustration of how marital instability expedites women's migration is Ho's (1993) research on the immigration of Caribbean women to the United States. She found that the majority of female Caribbean immigrant women in Los Angeles were heads of households who were fully responsible for the economic survival of their families. Kohpahl (1998) documented cases of Guatemalan single heads of households who migrated independently from spouses. Guatemalan and Trinidadian female heads of households were not able to fulfill the role of economic providers because of limited economic opportunities for women in the Caribbean and Central America. Immigration to the United States is an option for Caribbean and Central American women to secure the economic survival of their families. However, Ho's analysis did not explain why Caribbean men could not immigrate separately from women to the United States. Patricia Pessar's work (1982, 1988) on Dominican immigrant women in the United States demonstrated how lack of income possibilities for women forced Dominican women to migrate to the United States. Pessar focused primarily on the economic aspects of female migration using the theoretical orientation of household economy, but did not fully explain what social conditions in the Dominican Republic allowed Dominican women to leave and if women were able to leave independently or came as dependents of spouses and families.

Another reason why women may be preferred migrants despite gender role restrictions is that daughters might be more reliable in sending home money once they left. Momsen (1992:90) found that in the case of Caribbean migrants, women were more reliable in sending money home because daughters understood themselves as part of their family network at home. Sons were more likely to work for their own personal benefit.

Other authors emphasize this escape from restrictive gender roles (Castro 1982; Yang 1984; Kibria 2000) and abuse (Arguelles 1993) as a cause for women's migration. However, migration does not always liberate women from traditional gender roles. In some cases, immigration strengthens traditional roles and women are under more control of male authorities than in their home country (Morokvaic 1984:892). In the case of Puerto Rican women in New York, women carried the burden of the double day, overburdened by underpaid work, household chores, and childbearing (Foner 1986). In such cases, immigration does not appear to yield a wholly desirable result for women. *See also:* **Domestic work; Gender; Transnationalism.**

References

Arguelles, Lourdes, and Anne M. Rivero. 1993. Gender/Sexual Orientation Violence and Transnational Migration: Conversations with Some Latinas We Think We Know. *Urban Anthropology* 22:259–276.

Boyd, M. 1986. Immigrant Women in Canada. In *International Migration: The Female Experience.* Rita James Simon and Caroline B. Brettell, eds. Totowa, NJ: Rowman and Allanheld.

Brettell, Caroline B., and Rita James Simon. 1986. Immigrant Women: An Introduction. In *International Migration: The Female Experience.* Rita James Simon and Caroline B. Brettell, eds. Pp. 3–20. Totowa, NJ: Rowman and Allanheld.

Brydon, Lynne, and Sylvia Chant. 1989. *Women in the Third World: Gender Issues in Rural and Urban Areas.* New Brunswick, NJ: Rutgers University Press.

Caspari, Andrea, and Wenona Giles. 1986. Immigration Policy and the Employment of Portuguese Migrant Women in the UK and France: A Comparative Analysis. In *International Migration: The Female Experience.* Rita James Simon and Caroline B. Brettell, eds. Pp. 152–177. Totowa, NJ: Rowman and Allanheld.

Castro, Mary García. 1982. *Mary's and Eve's Social Reproduction.* New York: Center of Latin American and Caribbean Research, New York University.

Castro, Mary García, Jean Gearing, and Margaret Gill. 1984. *Women and Migration—Latin America and the Caribbean: A Selected Annotated Bibliography.* Gainesville, FL: Center for Latin American Studies.

Chant, Sylvia, ed. 1992. *Gender and Migration in Developing Countries.* London: Belhaven Press.

Chant, Sylvia, and Sarah A. Radcliffe. 1992. Migration and Development: The Importance of Gender. In *Gender and Migration in Developing Countries.* Sylvia Chant, ed. Pp. 1–29. London: Belhaven Press.

Crummett, María de Los Angeles. 1987. Rural Women and Migration in Latin America. In *Rural Women and State Policy: Feminist Perspectives on Latin American Agricultural Development.* Carmen Diana Deere and Magdalena León, eds. Pp. 239–260. Boulder, CO: Westview Press.

Donato, Katharine M. 1992. Understanding U.S. Immigration: Why Some Countries Send Women and Others Send Men. In *Seeking Common Ground: Multidisciplinary Study of Immigrant Women in the United States.* Donna Gabaccia, ed. Pp. 159–184. Westport, CT: Greenwood Press.

Foner, Nancy. 1986. Sex Roles and Sensibilities: Jamaican Women in New York and London. In *International Migration: The Female Experience.* Rita James Simon and Caroline B. Brettell, eds. Pp. 133–151. Totowa, NJ: Rowman and Allanheld.

Gonzalez, Nancie L. 1986. Giving Birth in America: The Immigrant's Dilemma. In *International Migration: The Female Experience*. Rita James Simon and Caroline B. Brettell, eds. Pp. 241–253. Totowa, NJ: Rowman and Allanheld.

Hamilton, Nora, and Norma Stoltz Chinchilla. 1991. Central American Migration: A Framework for Analysis. *Latin American Research Review* 26(1):75–110.

Ho, Christine. 1993. The Internalization of Kinship and the Feminization of Caribbean Migration: The Case of Afro-Trinidadian Immigrants in Los Angeles. *Human Organization* 52(1):32–40.

Hondagneu-Sotelo, Pierrette. 1994. *Gendered Transitions: Mexican Experience of Immigration*. Berkeley: University of California Press.

———. 2000. Feminism and Migration. *Annals of the American Academy of Political and Social Science* 57:107–120.

———. 2001. *Doméstica: Immigrant Workers Cleaning and Caring in the Shadows of Affluence*. Berkeley: University of California Press.

Hugo, Graeme. 1992. Women on the Move: Changing Patterns of Population Movements of Women in Indonesia. In *Gender and Migration in Developing Countries*. Sylvia Chant, ed. Pp. 174–196. London: Belhaven Press.

Jasso, Guillerma, and Mark R. Rosenzweig. 1990. *The New Chosen People: Immigrants in the United States*. New York: Russell Sage.

Kibria, Nazli. 2000. Power, Patriarchy, and Gender Conflict in the Vietnamese Immigrant Community. In *Contemporary Asian America: A Multidisciplinary Reader*. Min Zhou and J.V. Gatewood, eds. Pp. 431–442. New York: New York University Press.

Kohpahl, Gabriele. 1998. *Voices of Guatemalan Women in Los Angeles: Understanding Their Immigration*. New York: Garland.

Momsen, Janet Henshall. 1992. Gender Selectivity in Caribbean Migration. In *Gender and Migration in Developing Countries*. Sylvia Chant, ed. Pp. 73–90. London: Belhaven Press.

Morokvaic, Mirjana. 1984. Birds of Passage Are Also Women. *International Migration Review* 18:886–907.

Pessar, Patricia R. 1982. The Role of Households in International Migration. *International Migration Review* 16:324–364.

———. 1988. The Constraints on and Release of Female Labor Power: Dominican Migration to the United States. In *A Home Divided: Women and Income in the Third World*. Daisy Dwyer and Judith Bruce, eds. Pp. 195–215. Stanford, CA: Stanford University Press.

Radcliffe, Sarah A. 1992. Mountains, Maidens and Migration: Gender and Marginality in Peru. In *Gender and Migration in Developing Countries*. Sylvia Chant, ed. Pp. 30–48. London: Belhaven Press.

Safa, H.I. 1987. Urbanization, the Informal Economy and State Policy in Latin America. In *The Capitalist City: Global Restructuring and Community Policies*. Michael Peter Smith and Joe R. Feagin, eds. Pp. 272–274. London: Basil Blackwell.

Sassen-Koob, Saskia. 1983. Labor Migrations and the New International Division of Labor. In *Women, Men, and the International Division of Labor*. June Nash and Maria Patricia Fernandez-Kelly, eds. Pp. 175–204. Albany: State University of New York Press.

———. 1984. Notes on the Incorporation of Third World Women into Wage-Labor Through Immigration and Off-Shore Production. *International Migration Review* 18:1144–1167.

Tyree, Andrea, and Katherine Donato. 1986. A Demographic Overview of the International Migration of Women. In *International Migration: The Female Experience*. Rita James Simon and Caroline B. Brettell, eds. Totowa, NJ: Rowman and Allanheld.

GABRIELE KOHPAHL

WORK. So much of what is supposed to be the essence of America—land of opportunity, where anybody can succeed by pulling themselves up by their bootstraps, and even become president—relates to work. So the story of immigrant America is fundamentally also one of work—hard work.

Immigration in the last decade of the twentieth century reached levels not seen since the turn of the last century, with over 9 million legal and 3.5 million unauthorized immigrants arriving in the United States. By 2000, the foreign-born population had grown to more than 30 million, representing 11 percent of the U.S. population, up from less than 8 percent in 1990. Of these immigrants, half originated in Latin America, a quarter in Asia, and 14 percent in Europe, marking a dramatic demographic shift in the U.S. foreign-born population (Hagan 2004).

The wave of immigrants also represented a large economic workforce. Most immigrants arriving in the United States during this period were young people of working age, particularly males, who maintained strong ties to the labor market. Because of the dip in population growth among U.S. citizens over the last few decades, the under-35 immigrant population accounted for all the labor force growth within that age group. However, even in the 35–44 age groups, immigrants accounted for more than a third of growth in the labor force (Sum et al. 2002). The net result was an increase in the share of foreign-born workers in the U.S. labor force, from 1 in 17 in 1960 to 1 in 8 by the year 2000 (Bean and Stevens 2003).

Clearly, economic motives are one of the primary determinants of immigration to the United States, and economic opportunities and obstacles acutely affect further decisions as well as relative assimilation into or exclusion from U.S. society and economy. Long hours, low pay, and difficulty of occupational advancement are typical characteristics of the sectors where immigrants work. However, it is a common stereotype of immigrant labor that puts such immigration in the context of foreign labor fleeing repressive homelands for the freedom of the United States. A closer look at immigration patterns and their relation to U.S. economics points to the economic situation of the United States itself as a draw for foreign labor.

U.S. immigration policy is closely tied to its domestic economic situation, with relative inclusion and exclusion reflecting upturns and downturns in the economy and their related labor requirements. Such political and economic context strongly determines the likelihood of immigrants arriving and their success in finding work. Until 1875, no federal limitations were imposed on immigrants. Growing fears of cheap labor from Asian countries, however, lead to tightening of immigration policies, including the implementation of the Chinese Exclusion Act of 1882 and the Gentlemen's Agreement in 1907. Throughout the 1920s, as the Great Depression loomed over the country, the first quota system was imposed on the number of immigrants based on national origin. The policy reduced the total number of immigrants and favored those coming from Northern and Western Europe, barring or deporting those from Asia and Mexico.

Policy can be a major draw as well as a moderator for immigrant labor. This is clearly evident in the rise and fall of the Bracero program, when a growing need for agricultural labor in the United States led to the recruitment of Mexican and Mexican American farm workers for temporary employment. The program was ended in 1964, amid concerns that migrant labor had driven down wages for native-born workers, and by the mid-1970s, another quota system had been implemented, this time allowing large numbers of legal immigrants from Latin America along with smaller flows from Asia.

More recently, the economic restructuring of the urban United States in the late 1970s and early 1980s has given rise to a labor market enticing to immigrants from peripheral countries. Since the 1990s, privately owned corporations have realized an increase in profits as they downsize operations, shift to flexible production, employ fewer workers, and move to other countries (especially those in Southeast Asia) that claim cheap labor. Service jobs (now the largest sector of employment in the United States and a major source of new jobs) are replacing many of the disappearing industrial jobs. In contrast, the rise of a high-wage-earning professionalized class created another market for a low-paid service sector (often including the informal economy) with workers in boutiques, housekeepers, nannies, dog-walkers, and specialty food preparers, all of which are known to offer no occupational mobility or job security. The restructuring resulted in labor polarization and a concurrent rise in the demand for "dead-end, low-wage" labor. While many immigrants are highly skilled and able to find U.S. jobs that reflect those skills, foreign-born workers disproportionately make up the latter type of labor force (Rodriguez 2004).

Today, immigrants face an increasingly saturated labor market, reflected in an "hour-glass" employment profile in which there is a widening split between low-wage jobs and high-wage jobs, a more stagnant economy, and further effects of a de-industrializing economy. In 2000, for example, almost half of the immigrants from Latin America (the majority of whom were from Mexico) were employed in either service jobs (22.7 percent) or low-skilled labor (25.1 percent), with less than 12 percent involved in managerial or specialty professional positions. By contrast, over one-third of foreign-born workers from Europe and Asia found work in managerial and professional jobs (Smith and Edmonston 1997; Bean and Stevens 2003). Thus, one can see the bimodal structure of employment as immigrants are increasingly focused in either high-paying highly skilled jobs or low-paying low-skilled jobs. These trends can be seen clearly in the healthcare industry, where Asian immigrants make up 23.9 percent of the physicians and surgeons, more than any other foreign-born category and far more than the 8.2 percent of Latin American immigrants. Latin Americans find their greatest numbers in the lower-paying healthcare jobs, especially nursing (37.2 percent) (Lowell and Gerova 2004).

This bimodal structure of employment is reflected in and affected by the education levels of incoming immigrants. According to U.S. census data for 2003, immigrants are less likely than the native-born population to have completed high school, but equally or more likely to have completed an advanced degree. This points to a bifurcated educational distribution of immigration, in which growing gaps in education arise between various immigrant populations, leading to their involvement in disparate economic niches. Immigrants from Latin America, for example, have a high school completion rate of 49.1 percent, far lower than the 86.9 percent rate of native-born. Immigrants from Asia, with a high school completion rate of 84.0 percent, arrive in the United States much more on par with the native population (U.S. Bureau of the Census 2003).

As we can see, although new immigrants tend to fill the low-income jobs, immigrant distribution in employment sectors varies immensely depending on an immigrant's country of origin. While Europeans and Asians collectively represent only 30 percent of foreign-born workers, nearly 40 percent of both immigrant groups hold management or professional positions as compared to only 12 percent of Latin American immigrants. Similarly, 24 percent and 27 percent of Europeans and Asians, respectively, hold technical, sales, or administrative positions, while only 16 percent of Latin American immigrants hold the same positions. Conversely, Latin Americans are heavily overrepresented in the service industry, craft production, and the agricultural industry; the percentage of Latin American workers in most of these fields is higher than the native-born and in some instances higher than the percentage of native-born, European, and Asian workers combined (Hagan 2004).

One exception is sports, which employs a high percentage of immigrants, many Latin American (Maguire 1999). In baseball, for example, a quarter of all major-league players are from Latin America, and almost half of all minor leaguers. In the 2005 All-Star Game, a record 24 of 60 players were Latin American, half from the Dominican Republic alone. Baseball players from Japan, basketball stars from Nigeria and Balkan countries, and hockey players from Canada and the Czech Republic have become as common as, say, apple pie.

Among other sectors, immigrant labor can play a vital role in the maintenance or even expansion of a workforce. Agriculture remains one of the most immigrant-dependent industries (Rothenberg 1998), but others include the garment industry, cleaning and housekeeping work, gardening, and manual labor jobs such as carpentry and auto repair. By hiring immigrants, employers gain not only cheap labor, but also a plentiful and self-organized source of workers. Foreign work crews often take over the responsibilities of recruiting and training new members, freeing employers from the cost of recruitment. Immigrant workers are also much more easily controlled. The isolated nature of agricultural and garment work, as well as the lack of language skills and education among the immigrant populations, curtails workers' opportunities for legal advising, alternative job openings, or organizing unions. The seasonal nature of farm work also keeps workers moving frequently, another obstacle for organization.

Undocumented workers and unauthorized immigrants are often the most easily exploited labor pools available. Because undocumented workers and unauthorized immigrants have no legal recourse and no regulations, employers are free to decide on work conditions, wages, and work schedules, which workers must accept or go without work. Sweatshops, first used as a term in the 1850s, initially described work that was contracted out of the factory to be performed and completed at home. Historically and today, sweatshops are known for their unsanitary conditions, long hours, and low pay. Immigrants fleeing political persecution, especially, are left to work in low-wage factories, requiring little skill because of their vulnerability as illegal immigrants and because few income-generating alternatives are available to them. Immigrants often obtain sweatshop jobs similar to farmwork through step migration. If a familial connection is not possible, immigrants often rely on ethnic community ties or informal communications networks to set them up with jobs.

Undocumented workers face many unique threats when coming to the United States seeking work. Thousands of workers are recruited by trafficking brokers who demand fees as high as $12,000 to smuggle laborers into the country, where they may be introduced to a factory manager or even funnelled into indentured servitude. The fees demanded by the brokers are generally covered by the employers who recover the money plus interest, fees, and other expenses from the workers' wages. Often these workers receive very low wages, placing them in a situation where they have little chance of ever making enough to pay off their smuggling debts, which can expose them to intimidation, harassment, threats of violence and deportation, and, in some cases, outright physical confinement. Employers commonly confiscate workers' passports and other papers as added insurance on their investment. Of workers smuggled into the United States, up to 30 percent may be forced into prostitution, while others are placed in agricultural, domestic, or factory jobs (Finley 2005).

Even for those unauthorized workers who come into the United States of their own accord, exploitation is a real fear. Contractors often hire workers for a day's or week's work and then refuse to pay them for their labor, fully aware that undocumented workers have no legal recourse to seek compensation. Even when undocumented workers receive pay, their wages are often considerably less than documented and native workers; while legal immigrants average $7.50 per hour in wages, undocumented workers average only $5.70 per hour in wages (Martinez and Martinez 2005).

As immigrants arrive in the United States, they rely on a variety of strategies to find work, just as employers use a number of methods to attract immigrant labor. Workers may seek work through day-labor pools or through social networks, while employers also use networks (which may include labor recruiters or smugglers) to find immigrant workers. Various methods of employment and labor mobility also change based on ethnic and gender roles. Hiring of immigrant women for household work is often done through social networks among both female employees and workers, while indentured employment is more characteristic of Chinese immigrants, who pay large fees to smugglers. Throughout the country, groups of immigrant men seeking day-labor can be seen, waiting for employees to drive by and pick them up (Rodriguez 2004).

One survival technique of immigrants that has proven to be very successful is running one's own business. In order to find economic or occupational advancement, while asserting ethnic pride and the value of time with family and community, immigrants have turned to self-employment. The reasons immigrant entrepreneurship exceeds that of the general population are much debated by scholars today. Some see this as a response to a hostile economic atmosphere, others as an avenue of social and economic mobility. Whether it means starting a family-run Mexican restaurant or a supermarket featuring products from Southeast Asia, individually owned businesses often serve primarily immigrants of the same ethnicity or locality and economic situation.

Entrepreneurial efforts provide benefits to the entire immigrant community, including increased job prospects and social benefits. Foreign-born employers are likely to employ members of the same immigrant community, often because of social ties, shared language, and cultural knowledge and skills. Ethnic succession is perhaps the primary vehicle by which immigrant economies become incorporated into the larger economy (Waldinger 1990). With time, aging immigrant workers vacate an occupational niche (such as being an entreprenuer), especially when their children follow other opportunities that may be more accessible for the native-born, leaving an incoming immigrant group to fill the opening job (Mahler 1995).

A central issue in the U.S. debate around immigration is the effect of immigrant employment on the economy. Research has shown that immigration is not only beneficial to the economy, but also vital to the growth and maintenance of the job market. In 2002, the Center for Labor Market Studies at Northeastern University prepared a statement on immigrant employment for the National Business Roundtable in Washington, D.C., highlighting the positive effects of immigrant labor on the U.S. economy. Without the large wave of immigration in the 1990s, the job market would have grown by only 5 percent over the entire decade, resulting in serious constraints in both job and economic growth. The male job force in particular was sustained by immigration throughout the 1990s, with immigrants making nearly 80 percent of the male labor force growth (Sum et al. 2002).

Another contentious facet of the debate is whether immigrants, particularly the unauthorized, are a blessing or burden to the economic system, an issue that takes on new urgency in light of current U.S. economic and policy debates, such as about social security. The Immigration Reform and Control Act (IRCA) of 1986 penalized employers for hiring workers without valid identification, thus prompting unauthorized immigrants to seek false documentation of their right to work in the United States. When hired, these workers are put on the payroll and pay taxes on their income, leading to a relatively reliable, albeit indirect, way to monitor the contribution of unauthorized immigrants to the U.S. economic system. Social security officials estimate that nearly three-quarters of unauthorized immigrant workers pay payroll taxes, which amounted to nearly $56 billion paid into social security in 2002 and almost $200 billion during the 1990s (Porter 2005).

All told, foreign-born workers play a huge economic role in terms of purchasing power and economic activity. In 2004, America's Latino population (including both foreign-born and native-born) is estimated to spend approximately $1.33 million per minute, the equivalent of $700 billion annually. This is more than the 2002 GDP of Mexico, estimated by the World Bank as $637 billion (Montemayor and Mendoza 2004). The economic effects of foreign-born workers in the United States spread far beyond the country as well. As workers earn a living in the United States, remittances become an increasingly important source of revenue and investment in their countries of origin. Research by the Inter-American Development Bank (IADB) showed that Latin American immigrants to the United States send upward of $30 billion annually to their families abroad. Remittances range from 50 to 80 percent of household income in the countries of origin (Montemayor and Mendoza 2004).

Increasing numbers of immigrants paired with declining wages and fewer opportunities suggest that increased immigration has put new immigrants in competition for declining resources. Bean and Stevens (2003) cite a number of sources and studies that point to few adverse effects of immigrant labor on native workers, except quite notably already disadvantaged African Americans concentrated in poor urban areas. Immigrants today, as throughout the history of the United States, continue to rely on hard work, strong cultural ties, and informal communications networks. *See also*: **Agricultural workers; Food processing;**

Guestworkers; Human smuggling; Informal economy; Labor organization and activism; Migration processes.

References

Bean, Frank D., and Gillian Stevens. 2003. *America's Newcomers and the Dynamics of Diversity*. New York: Russell Sage Foundation.

Finley, Bruce. 2005. Indentured Servitude. *Denver Post*, March 27, A1.

Hagan, Jacqueline Maria. 2004. Contextualizing Immigrant Labor Market Incorporation: Legal, Demographic and Economic Dimensions. *Work and Occupations* 31(4):407–423.

Lowell, B. Lindsay, and Stefka Georgieva Gerova. 2004. Immigrants and the Healthcare Workforce. *Work and Occupations* 31:474–498.

Maguire, Joseph. 1999. *Global Sports: Identities, Societies and Civilizations*. Cambridge: Polity Press.

Mahler, Sarah J. 1995. *American Dreaming: Immigrant Life on the Margins*. Princeton, NJ: Princeton University Press.

Martinez, Tony P., and Alison P. Martinez. 2005. Mexican Migration Project Sheds Light on Workers in the Shadows. *Hispanic Outlook on Higher Education* 15(10):23.

Montemayor, Robert, and Henry Mendoza. 2004. *Right Before Our Eyes: Latinos Past, Present and Future*. Tempe, AZ: The Tomas Rivera Policy Institute.

Porter, Eduardo. 2005. Illegal Immigrants Are Bolstering Social Security with Billions. *New York Times*, April 5, A1, C6.

Rodriguez, Nestor. 2004. "Workers Wanted": Employer Recruitment of Immigrant Labor. *Work and Occupations* 31(4):453–473.

Rothenberg, Daniel. 1998. *With These Hands: The Hidden World of Migrant Farm Workers Today*. New York: Harcourt, Brace, Jovanovich.

Sassen, Saskia. 1988. *The Mobility of Labor and Capital: A Study in International Investment and Labor Flow*. New York: Cambridge University Press.

Smith, James P., and Barry Edmonston. 1997. *The New Americans: Economic, Demographic, and Fiscal Effects of Immigration*. Washington, DC: National Academy Press.

Sum, Andrew, Nita Fogg, and Paul Harrington, with Ishwar Katiwada, Mykhaylo Trubskyy, and Sheila Palma. 2002. Immigrant Workers and the Great American Job Machine: The Contributions of New Foreign Immigration to National and Regional Labor Force Growth in the 1990s. Prepared for the National Business Roundtable, Washington, DC, August. http://www.businessroundtable.org/pdf/781.pdf, accessed April 20, 2005.

U.S. Bureau of the Census. 2003. Foreign-Born Population of the United States Current Population Survey—March 2000. http://www.census.gov/population/www/socdemo/foreign/ppl-160.html.

Waldinger, Roger. 1990. *Ethnic Entrepreneurs: Immigrant Business in Industrial Society*. Newbury Park, CA: Sage Publications.

JAMES LOUCKY AND JAIME LOUCKY

Appendix: Chronology of U.S. Immigration Legislation

1790   **Naturalization Act enacted.** Federal government establishes a two-year residency requirement for "free white persons" wishing to become U.S. citizens.

1819   **Reporting rule adopted.** Data begins to be collected on immigration into the United States. Ships' captains and others are required to keep and submit manifests of immigrants entering the United States.

1875   **Page Law enacted.** This first exclusionary act denied entry to women brought for prostitution and Chinese, Japanese, and other Asian laborers forcibly brought to the United States.

1882   **Chinese Exclusion Act passed.** The federal government moves to firmly establish its authority over immigration. Chinese immigration is curtailed. Additional legislation excluded ex-convicts, lunatics, idiots, and those persons likely to become public charges. In addition, a tax is levied on newly arriving immigrants.

1885   **Foran Act/Alien Contract Labor Act barred entry of contract laborers.** This new legislation reverses an earlier federal law legalizing the trade in contract labor.

1891   **Bureau of Immigration created.** Established as part of the U.S. Treasury Department, this new office is later given authority over naturalization and moved to the U.S. Justice Department. (Today it is known as the U.S. Citizenship and Immigration Services.) In the same year, paupers, polygamists, the insane, and persons with contagious diseases are excluded from entry into the United States.

1892   **Ellis Island opened.** Between 1892 and 1953, more than 12 million immigrants will be processed at this one facility.

1903   **Additional categories of persons excluded.** Epileptics, professional beggars, and anarchists are now excluded.

1907	**Exclusions further broadened.** Imbeciles, the feeble-minded, tuberculars, persons with physical or mental defects, and persons under age 16 without parents are excluded.
	"Gentleman's Agreement" between United States and Japan signed. An informal agreement curtails Japanese immigration to the United States. Also, the tax on new immigrants is increased.
1917	**Literacy test introduced.** All immigrants 16 years of age or older must demonstrate the ability to read a 40-word passage in their native language. Also, virtually all Asian immigrants are banned from entry into the United States under a provision called the "Asiatic Barred Zone" that excluded immigrants from India, Burma, Siam, Malaysia, Arabia, Afghanistan, part of Russia, and most of Polynesia.
1921	**Quota Act enacted.** An annual immigration ceiling is set at 350,000. Moreover, a new nationality quota is instituted, limiting admissions to 3 percent of each nationality group's representation in the 1910 census. The law is designed primarily to restrict the flow of immigrants coming from Eastern and Southern Europe.
1924	**National Origins Act enacted.** The act reduces the annual immigration ceiling to 165,000. A revised quota reduces admissions to 2 percent of each nationality group's representation in the 1890 census and denies entry to those who are ineligible for naturalization, applying the racial criteria of the 1790 act to exclude Asians. The **Labor Appropriation Act** of 1924 officially established the Border Patrol. Paul Brigham and others design immigrations quotas around preferred populations to be admitted into the United States. Nativist interests collide with those of corporate agricultural entrepreneurs.
1927	**Immigration Ceiling further reduced.** The annual immigration ceiling is further reduced to 150,000; the quota is revised to 2 percent of each nationality's representation in the 1920 census. This basic law remains in effect through 1965.
1929	**National Origins Act revised.** The annual immigration ceiling of 150,000 is made permanent, with 70 percent of admissions slated for those coming from Northern and Western Europe, while the other 30 percent are reserved for those coming from Southern and Eastern Europe.
1940s and 1950s	**Bracero programs initiated.** Reaction to shortage of labor during the war years and the booming postwar economy of the United States. There was a relaxed immigration posture to Mexicans and Latin Americans entering the country. Recruitment of Mexican and Latin American labor coincided with both wartime and later agricultural production interests.
1945 and 1947	**War Brides Acts enacted.** The acts allowed wives of U.S. servicemen to enter the United States.
1948	**Displaced Persons Act enacted.** Entry is allowed for 400,000 persons displaced by World War II. However, such refugees must pass a security check and have proof of employment and housing that does not threaten U.S. citizens' jobs and homes.

1952   **McCarran-Walter Act passed.** The act consolidates earlier immigration laws, continues to limit Asian immigration, and maintains national origins quotas. In addition, the act introduces an ideological criterion for admission: immigrants and visitors to the United States can now be denied entry on the basis of their political ideology if they are suspected "subversives." The act created a preference system based on job skills or having relatives who are U.S. citizens. At the same time it abolished the policy of denying entry into the United States based solely on race.

1965   **Immigration and Naturalization Act of 1965 (79 Stat. 911) passed.** Nationality quotas are abolished. However, the act establishes an overall ceiling of 170,000 on immigration from the Eastern Hemisphere and another ceiling of 120,000 on immigration from the Western Hemisphere.

1966   **Immigration Act of November 2, 1966, to Adjust the Status of Cuban Refugees (80 Stat. 1161) passed.** Natives or citizens of Cuba who have been admitted to the United States after January 1, 1959 and have lived in the United States for a minimum of two years are eligible to have their status adjusted by the Attorney General to an "alien lawfully admitted for permanent residence."

1978   **Worldwide immigration ceiling introduced.** A new annual immigration ceiling of 290,000 replaces the separate ceilings for the Eastern and Western Hemispheres.

1980   **Refugee Act of 1980 (94 Stat. 102) passed.** A system is developed to handle refugees as a class separate from other immigrants. Under the new law, refugees are defined as those who flee a country because of persecution "on account of race, religion, nationality, or political opinion." The president, in consultation with Congress, is authorized to establish an annual ceiling on the number of refugees who may enter the United States. The president also is allowed to admit any group of refugees in an emergency. At the same time, the annual ceiling on conventional immigrants is lowered to 270,000.

1980s   **Rise in legal and illegal immigration.** During the 1980s, Latin Americans and Asians accounted for 84 percent of all immigrants, but this does not count the large number of undocumented immigration. Nativist sentiment and the Select Commission on Immigration Policy gave rise to the 1982 Simpson-Mazzoli Immigration Reform Bill, which featured employer penalties as well as amnesty for undocumented immigrants. The Simpson-Mazzoli Bill eventually is contained within the Immigration Reform and Control Act.

1986   **Immigration Reform and Control Act of 1986 (100 Stat. 3360) passed.** The annual immigration ceiling is raised to 540,000. Amnesty is offered to those illegal aliens able to prove continuous residence in the United States since January 1, 1982. Stiff sanctions are introduced for employers of illegal aliens. As part of its legalization aims, IRCA also included significant legislative provisions: the Seasonal Agricultural Worker program (SAW), the Replenishment Agricultural Worker program (RAW), and the H-2A (guest-worker) program. SAW permitted legal residence, followed by possibility for citizenship, for those who could prove they had worked in the agricultural sector for at least 90 days between 1980 and 1985. RAW was established to replace workers legalized under SAW who subsequently left farm work. H-2A allowed agricultural employers to hire undocumented workers to meet impending labor shortages in the absence of suitable U.S. employees, provided that minimum wage, housing, and work conditions were met.

1990   **Immigration Act of 1990 (104 Stat. 4981) passed.** The annual immigration ceiling is further raised to 700,000 for 1992, 1993, and 1994; thereafter, the ceiling will drop to 675,000 a year. Ten thousand permanent resident visas are offered to those immigrants agreeing to invest at least $1 million in U.S. urban areas or $500,000 in U.S. rural areas. The McCarran-Walter Act of 1952 is amended so that people can no longer be denied admittance to the United States on the basis of their beliefs, statements, or associations.

1990s   **Operations Gatekeeper in San Diego, Hold the Line in El Paso, and Safeguard in Tucson and other federal initiatives.** These represent the beginning of intensive militarization of the U.S.-Mexico border with increased use of U.S. and Mexican military personnel, coupled with the construction of extensive physical barriers and high-technology detection of illegal immigrants. Stricter border control under these policies has resulted in vigilantism toward illegal immigrants and increased deaths of immigrants who cross through desolate areas attempting to enter the United States through Mexico.

1996   **Illegal Immigration Reform and Immigrant Responsibility Act of 1996 (Public Law 104-208) enacted.** In an effort to curb illegal immigration, Congress votes to double the U.S. Border Patrol to 10,000 agents over five years and mandates the construction of fences at the most heavily trafficked areas of the U.S.-Mexico border. Congress also approves a pilot program to check the immigration status of job applicants.

     Personal Responsibility and Work Opportunity Reconciliation Act of 1996 (Public Law 104-193) passed. President Clinton signs this welfare reform bill, which cuts many social programs for immigrants. Legal immigrants lose their right to food stamps and Supplemental Security Income (a program for older, blind, and disabled people). Illegal immigrants become ineligible for virtually all federal and state benefits except emergency medical care, immunization programs, and disaster relief.

1997   **NACARA (Nicaraguan Adjustment and Central American Relief Act) passed.** Provided for adjustment of status of all Nicaraguans and Cubans continuously present in the United States since December 1, 1995, including spouses and children. In response to *American Baptist Churches v. Thomburgh*, 760 F. Supp. 796 (N.D. Cal. 1991), the legal decision which found INS had inappropriately applied refugee policy, NACARA provided legal remedies for Central Americans who had applied for asylum prior to April 1, 1990.

2000   **Legal Immigration and Family Equity Act passed.** Temporarily reinstated Section 245 (i) of the Immigration and Nationality Act of 1952 (Public

Law 82-414), which allowed undocumented immigrants to apply for visas without requiring them to leave the United States. This section permitted approximately 640,000 undocumented aliens to apply for visas if they were sponsored by a legally resident relative or an employer and applied prior to April 30, 2001.

2001   **Child Citizenship Act (Public Law 106-395) passed.** This act allowed approximately 150,000 children to become U.S. citizens on February 27, 2001 if they had one U.S. citizen parent and were under 18 years of age.

USA Patriot Act (H.R. 3162) passed. This act affirms patriotism and espouses protection of civil rights of all Americans. It also provides for ensuring adequate personnel on both borders, establishes a fingerprint identification system for ports of entry, and strengthens immigration provisions. It mandates detention of suspected terrorists and suspends habeas corpus under certain circumstances. This act also requires monitoring entry and exit of foreign students, travelers, and others on temporary visas and requires machine-readable passports.

2002   **Homeland Security Act (H.R. 5005) passed.** This act transfers functions of the INS, including the Border Patrol, to the Department of Homeland Security, with responsibility for securing "borders, territorial waters, ports, terminals, waterways and air, land and sea transportation systems of the United States." The INS was abolished as of March 1, 2003, and a Bureau of Citizenship and Immigration within the DHS as well as a Bureau of Customs and Border Protection were established to carry out enforcement of immigration policy.

2005   **Border Protection, Antiterrorism, and Illegal Immigration Control Act (H.R. 4437).** This bill would provide additional military support and increased surveillance along the U.S.-Mexico border. It also would provide for the construction of major physical barriers and detention of all illegal immigrants who are apprehended crossing the border, as well as heavy sanctions placed upon employers utilizing undocumented workers. Under this provision, knowingly giving refuge to or harboring undocumented workers could result in a felony violation.

2006   By mid-2006, the U.S. Senate, the House of Representatives, and the president were pushing different versions of "immigration reform." Any compromise bill between the two houses of Congress was almost certain to have elements that would remain contentious after passage and ratification, including tighter immigration controls (such as border walls, high-tech surveillance and identification, and deployment of National Guard troops along the U.S.-Mexico border), strategies for regularizing the status of those in the country without authorization, temporary worker provisions, size of quotas for new entries and family members, and sanctions on employers.

Annotated Bibliography

BOOKS

Alba, Richard, and Victor Nee. 2003. *Remaking the American Mainstream: Assimilation and Contemporary Immigration.* Cambridge MA: Harvard University Press. This book addresses the widely accepted yet controversial concept of assimilation by surveying patterns of social mobility and language. Despite new origins, immigrants continue to profoundly change U.S. society even as they are incorporated into the mainstream and as ethnic boundaries blur.

Bean, Frank D., and Gillian Stevens. 2003. *America's Newcomers and the Dynamics of Diversity.* New York: Russell Sage. Drawing largely on census reports and law, this in-depth treatment provides a good overview of the characteristics, levels of integration, and impacts of new immigrants.

Borjas, George J. 1999. *Heaven's Door: Immigration Policy and the American Economy.* Princeton, NJ: Princeton University Press. On the question of how many immigrants are "good" for America, this controversial book argues that economic benefits are minor and that numbers should be reduced. While somewhat alarmist, it also recognizes that political and humanitarian concerns determine who finds an open door.

Castles, Stephen, and Mark J. Miller. 2003. *The Age of Migration.* New York: Guilford. This accessible and comprehensive book on processes, patterns, and policies associated with contemporary population movements provides an invaluable global perspective for understanding complex issues facing the United States, such as ethnic group formation, the role of the state, and political involvement of immigrants.

Chavez, Leo R. 2001. *Covering Immigration: Popular Images and the Politics of the Nation.* Berkeley: University of California Press. This creative examination of media coverage of immigration reveals how images and opinions reflect public ambivalence and shifts, ranging from exaggeration and alarm to reasoned acknowledgment of the economic and cultural contributions as well as the inevitability of immigration.

Cohen, Robin, ed. 1995. *Cambridge Survey of World Migration.* New York: Cambridge University Press. This comprehensive collection is organized by broad topics ranging from early European colonization and cross-Atlantic migrations to recent trends, notably the dramatic exodus of refugees from Southeast Asia as well as diverse flows from across Asia, the Caribbean, and Latin America.

Cornelius, Wayne A., Takeyuki Tsuda, Philip L. Martin, and James F. Hollifield, eds. 2004. *Controlling Immigration: A Global Perspective*. Stanford, CA: Stanford University Press. This ambitious set of essays addresses how industrialized countries confront fundamental questions of how many immigrants to accept, how to control unwanted flows, and whether to extend rights and services. The relative success of measures chosen elsewhere informs debate concerning legalization, enforcement, and refugee policy in the United States.

Daniels, Roger. 2002. *Coming to America: A History of Immigration and Ethnicity in American Life*. 2nd ed. New York: HarperCollins. Covering immigration patterns and policies since colonial times, this text reveals why and how people immigrate to the United States. Rich accounts of the varied experiences of ethnic groups reveal the multicultural and demographic benefits associated with both historical and contemporary immigration.

DeLaet, Debra L. 2000. *U.S. Immigration Policy in an Age of Rights*. Westport, CT: Praeger. Drawing on human rights and international law, this book concisely reviews recent changes in U.S. immigration policy. Civil rights concerns are shown to positively affect immigrant status, while unintended implications of family reunification and employer sanctions policies are also highlighted.

Dinnerstein, Leonard, and David Reimers. 1999. *Ethnic Americans: A History of Immigration*. New York: Columbia University Press. This classic study of U.S. immigration knowledgeably encompasses post-colonial and 1890s–1920s waves, contemporary refugee crises, prevalence of women, diversification of source countries, and debates relating to ethnic mobility and assimilation.

Foner, Nancy. 2000. *From Ellis Island to JFK: New York's Two Great Waves of Immigration*. New Haven, CT: Yale University Press. This engaging account traces lives and livelihoods within the diverse immigrant communities of America's preeminent port of entry. Comparing the peaks at the start and end of the twentieth century illuminates what shifting ethnic identities and socioeconomic mobility may lie ahead.

Foner, Nancy, Ruben G. Rumbaut, and Steven J. Gold. 2003. *Immigration Research for a New Century*. New York: Russell Sage. The complex implications of immigration are addressed in these probing essays by both established and emerging scholars from a range of disciplines. From high-tech engineers to uprooted small farmers, intriguing portrayals of the newest Americans are posed alongside proposals for needed research.

Gozdziak, Elzbieta M., and Susan F. Martin, eds. 2005. *Beyond the Gateway: Immigrants in a Changing America*. Lanham, MD: Lexington. This unique book addresses competing theories and measures of integration and presents insightful case studies by social scientists in rural and suburban communities, which are rapidly becoming the newest destinations for immigrants to the United States.

Gutierrez, David, ed. 2004. *The Columbia History of Latinos in the United States since 1960*. New York: Columbia University Press. This interdisciplinary volume contains essays on the six major Latino immigrant groups: Mexicans, Cubans, Puerto Ricans, Dominicans, Central Americans, and South Americans. Contributing authors consider how growing Latino immigration affects cultural and political developments, gender issues, and transnationalism.

Haines, David W., and Karen E. Rosenblum, eds. 1999. *Illegal Immigration in America: A Reference Handbook*. Westport, CT: Greenwood Press. Addressing undocumented immigration, this volume reveals how "illegal" is an arbitrary concept that depends on prevailing conditions at time of arrival. Essays are organized into broad categories of official policy, work opportunities, responses to illegal immigration, and global perspectives.

Hamamoto, Darrell, and Rodolfo Torres, eds. 1997. *New American Destinies: A Reader in Contemporary Asian and Latino Immigration*. New York: Routledge. Current trends, where a majority of immigrants come from Asia and Latin America, are examined through gender, ethnicity, and labor markets, and in the context of the global dominance of the United States.

Hirschman, Charles, and Philip Kasinitz, eds. 1999. *The Handbook of International Migration: The American Experience*. New York: Russell Sage. This edited collection of essays by notable immigration scholars is organized into three main categories: theories of international migration, adaptation and incorporation, and societal responses to immigration.

Hondagneu-Sotelo, Pierrette, ed. 2003. *Gender and U.S. Immigration: Contemporary Trends*. Berkeley: University of California Press. Featuring key researchers and case studies from Latin American, Asian, and European immigrant communities, this book highlights how gender both affects and is affected by networks, work, political participation, values associated with children, and intergenerational relations.

Jacoby, Tamar, ed. 2004. *Reinventing the Melting Pot: The New Immigrants and What It Means to Be American*. New York: Basic Books. The eminent social scientists, journalists, and authors included in this volume provide illuminating views on the ethnic, political, and economic aspects of both historical and contemporary U.S. immigration.

LeMay, Michael. 1999. *U.S. Immigration and Naturalization Laws and Issues: A Documentary History*. Westport, CT: Greenwood Press. This comprehensive volume documents U.S. immigration chronologically, with organization by colonial period (1700–1880), era of limited restrictions (1880–1920), period of quotas (1920–1965), and the era of globalization (1965–1996).

Ng, Franklin, ed. 1998. *The History and Immigration of Asian Americans*. New York: Garland. This collection of previously published articles on the history and trends of Asian immigration includes Chinese, East Indian, and Filipino immigrants, as well as overviews on globalization and immigration of highly educated Asians.

Portes, Alejandro, and Ruben Rumbaut. 1994. *Immigrant America: A Portrait*. Berkeley: University of California Press. This readable and informative book provides qualitative and quantitative evidence of the social incorporation of new immigrants, the critical arenas of language learning and schooling, and the integration and identity challenges faced by children and subsequent generations.

Rumbaut, Ruben, and Alejandro Portes. 2001. *Ethnicities: Children of Immigrants in America*. Berkeley: University of California Press; New York: Russell Sage. In a major collaborative effort documenting the varied paths and prospects of children of immigrants from diverse groups, incisive empirical evidence from leading scholars is blended with rich descriptive accounts. Along with a companion volume (*Legacies*), this key reference reveals the new face of America and how the second generation is faring.

Smith, James, and Barry Edmonston, eds. 1997. *The New Americans: Economic, Demographic, and Fiscal Effects of Immigration*. Washington, DC: National Academy Press. This report summarizes the conclusions of a panel of experts called by the National Research Council to investigate the impact of immigration on the future composition of the United States. It considers how immigration affects wages and jobs, and fiscal effects at different levels of government.

Suárez-Orozco, Carola, and Marcelo M. Suárez-Orozco. 2001. *Children of Immigration*. Cambridge, MA: Harvard University Press. With children from immigrant families in schools in every state, knowledge of family roles and intergenerational dynamics is essential. This study draws on interdisciplinary longitudinal research to affirm the powerful influence of both parents and schools in shaping competencies and new hybrid identities.

Thernstrom, Stephan, ed. 1980. *Harvard Encyclopedia of American Ethnic Groups.* Cambridge, MA: Belknap Press of Harvard University. Published a quarter-century ago, this encyclopedia remains relevant as the first comprehensive guide to the history and distinctive cultural characteristics of the major ethnic groups in the United States. In addition to entries on over 100 groups, thematic entries deal with significant topics such as ethnicity, assimilation, prejudice, and pluralism.

Waldinger, Roger, ed. 2001. *Strangers at the Gates: New Immigrants in Urban America.* Berkeley: University of California Press. The current situation of immigrants and implications for poverty and employment levels are examined in major urban centers that include New York, Los Angeles, Miami, San Francisco, and Chicago.

ORGANIZATIONS AND ELECTRONIC RESOURCES

Center for Comparative Immigration Studies, at the University of California, San Diego (http://www.ccis-ucsd.org), makes available working papers by researchers who investigate significant contemporary migration issues affecting the United States as well as other countries.

Center for Immigration Studies (http://www.cis.org) provides a wealth of news, commentary, and events in daily or digest format. Dedicated to expanding knowledge about the need for immigration policy that gives first concern to broad national interest, CIS generally supports a restrictionist agenda.

Center for Migration Studies (http://www.cmsny.org) in New York publishes the influential *International Migration Review*, provides a searchable catalog and links to other immigration institutes, and promotes research on social, economic, and political aspects of migration and refugee movements.

Executive Office for Immigration Review (http://www.usdoj.gov/eoir), within the U.S. Department of Justice, provides government statistics and publications as well as links to the Virtual Law Library, which in turn includes links to the Attorney General, Board of Immigration Appeals, and other notifications.

Immigration History Research Center (http://www.ihrc.umn.edu), at the University of Minnesota, maintains archives on American immigration and ethnic history (primarily of groups originating in Europe and the Middle East), in addition to sponsoring research and public education on the immigrant experience in the United States.

International Organization for Migration (http://www.iom.int) offers a variety of publications, including *Migration*, a quarterly review on current migration issues. It encourages broad social and economic development and defense of human rights, with many policy implications for the United States.

Migration Dialogue/Migration News (http://www.migration.ucdavis.edu) gives timely information and analysis through online newsletters that focus on international developments (organized by region, including North America), rural migration in the United States, and research and seminars.

Migration Policy Institute (http://www.migrationpolicy.org) publishes a wealth of research data and statistics, primarily through Migration Information Source (migrationinformation.org). A main focus is immigrants and refugees in the United States and North America, as well as Europe and Australia.

National Network for Immigrant and Refugee Rights (http://www.nnirr.org) serves as a forum for information and analyses on key immigration issues and government initiatives. It promotes immigrant rights, public education, and coalitions in its advocacy of a relatively open U.S. immigration policy.

U.S. Citizenship and Immigration Services reports activities of the government agency that oversees immigration and citizenship policies, and publishes the *Yearbook of Immigration Statistics* (http://www.uscis.gov/graphics/shared/aboutus/statistics).

OTHER NOTABLE RESOURCES

A variety of relatively objective sources of immigration information and assessments include the Urban Institute (http://www.urban.org; under "People"); PEW Hispanic Center (http://pewhispanic.org); Asian-Nation (http://www.asian-nation.org); the search engines of the Governmental Accountability Office (http://www.gao.gov) and the Congressional Research Service (http://www.opencrs.com); academic centers, such as the Institute for the Study of International Migration at Georgetown University; and special series like the "New Immigrant Series" by Allyn and Bacon. Immigration liberalization sources include the National Immigration Forum (http://www.immigrationforum.org), American Friends Service Committee (http://www.afsc.org/immigrants-rights), Migration and Refugees Services of the U.S. Conference of Catholic Bishops (http://www.usccb.org/mrs/mrp), and the AFL-CIO (http://www.aflcio.org/issues/civilrights/immigration). Immigration control advocates include the Federation for American Immigration Reform (http://www.fairus.org/site).

FILMS

Documentaries

Abandoned: The Betrayal of America's Immigrants. 2000. Bullfrog Films. This film shows the effects of 1996 immigration law on detention and deportation of legal residents and asylum seekers as well as undocumented immigrants.

American Stories: The American Dream. 1998. Films for the Humanities. This five-part series tells the stories of 10 families over three generations that range from post–World War I to the early 1990s.

Facing Up to Illegal Immigration. 2004. Films for the Humanities. Originally an ABC news program, this film looks at various concerns about undocumented immigrants, including their impact on jobs and the role of "porous borders in a time of terrorism."

Well-Founded Fear. 2000. Epidavros Project. This film examines the asylum-granting process in the United States under the (then) Immigration and Naturalization Service. Guidelines for granting asylum have become even more restrictive since the film was made.

Feature Films

In America. 2003. Fox Searchlight Pictures. A modern-day Irish family crosses the Canadian border, headed for New York in an effort to achieve the American dream.

The Joy Luck Club. 1993. Hollywood Pictures. Based on the novel by Amy Tan, this film relates the experiences of four Chinese women who emigrated to the United States and their first-generation daughters.

Mi Familia. 1995. New Line Cinema. Following a Mexican immigrant from his arrival in Los Angeles and marriage to another immigrant, this film traces challenges and adjustments across three generations.

Mississippi Masala. 1992. Columbia TriStar Home Video. The daughter of an Indian immigrant family, which came to the United States via Uganda, falls in love with an African American man.

Spanglish. 2004. Columbia Pictures. A Mexican mother enters the United States with her young daughter and accepts a position as a domestic.

The Wedding Banquet. 1994. Fox Video. A gay Taiwanese man in New York under pressure to marry plans a fake marriage to a young Chinese woman who needs a green card.

Index

Note: Page numbers in **bold** indicate main entries.